STANLEY

STANLEY

The Impossible Life of
Africa's Greatest Explorer

TIM JEAL

Yale University Press
New Haven and London

First published in 2007 in the United Kingdom by
Faber and Faber Limited and in the United States by Yale University Press.

Typeset by Alex Lazarou, Surbiton, Surrey, England

Printed in the United States of America

Library of Congress Control Number: 2007923548
ISBN 978-0-300-12625-9 (cloth: alk. paper)

A catalogue record for this book is available from the British Library.

The paper in this book meets the guidelines for permanence and durability of the
Committee on Production Guidelines for Book Longevity of the
Council on Library Resources.

10 9 8 7 6 5 4 3 2 1

To my sister, Thomasina

... away from people who had already made up their minds about me, I could be different. I could introduce myself as ... a boy of dignity and consequence, and without any reason to doubt me people would believe I was that boy. I recognized no obstacle to miraculous change but the incredulity of others ...

Tobias Wolff, This Boy's Life

CONTENTS

vii

LIST OF ILLUSTRATIONS

LIST OF PLATES

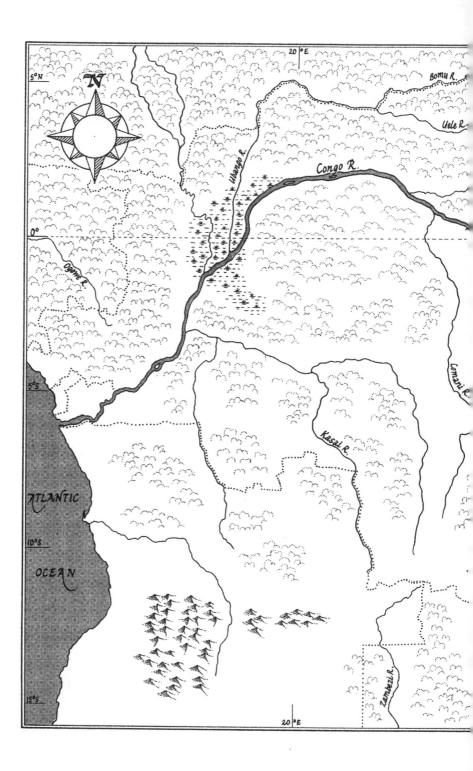

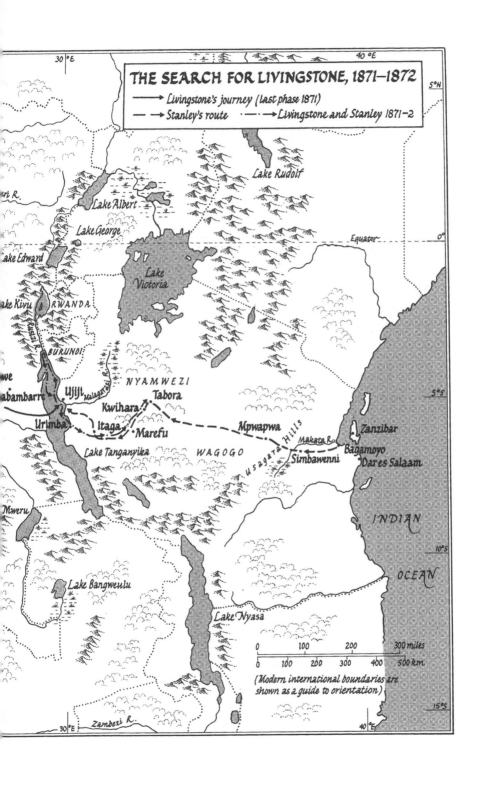

THE SEARCH FOR LIVINGSTONE, 1871–1872
→ Livingstone's journey (last phase 1871)
- - → Stanley's route   ·—·→ Livingstone and Stanley 1871–2

30 °E

40 °E

5°N

Lake Rudolf

Lake Albert

Lake George

Equator   0°

Lake Edward

Lake
Victoria

Lake Kivu   RWANDA

Ruzizi R.

BURUNDI

Malagarasi R.

NYAMWEZI

abambarre   Ujiji   Tabora

Kwihara

Urimba   Itaga   Marefu   Mpwapwa

Lake Tanganyika   WAGOGO

Usagara Hills

Makata R.

Simbawenni

Zanzibar

Bagamoyo
Dar es Salaam

Mweru

5°S

INDIAN

10°S

OCEAN

Lake Bangweulu

Lake Nyasa

0   100   200   300 miles
0   100   200   300   400   500 km

(Modern international boundaries are
shown as a guide to orientation)

30 °E   Zambezi R.

40 °E

15°S

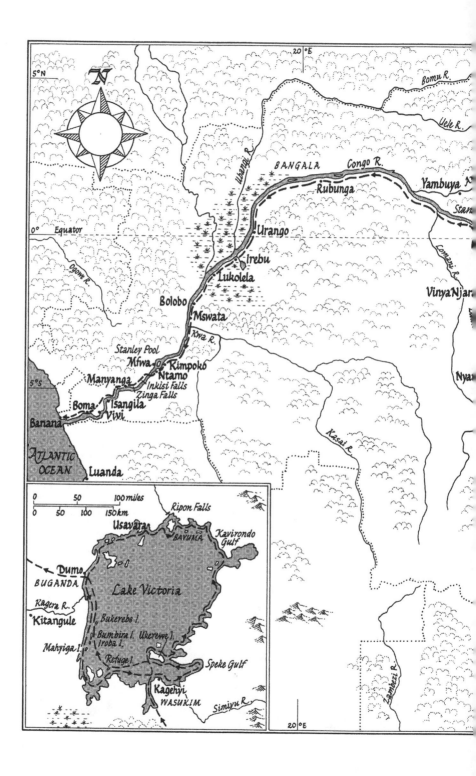

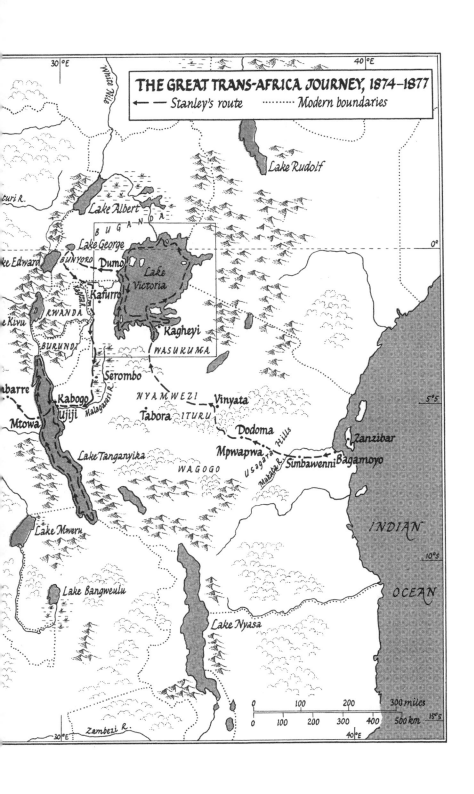

THE GREAT TRANS-AFRICA JOURNEY, 1874–1877

←— Stanley's route ·········· Modern boundaries

White Nile

30°E   40°E

Lake Rudolf

turi R.

Lake Albert

B U G A N D A

0°

Lake George

BUNYORO   Dumo

ke Edward

Lake Victoria

RWANDA   Kafurro

e Kivu

BURUNDI   Kagheyi

WASUKUMA

Serombo

5°S

NYAMWEZI   Vinyata

Kabogo   Tabora ITURU

Ujiji   Dodoma

Mtowa   Mpwapwa   Zanzibar

Malagarazi R.   Bagamoyo

Lake Tanganyika   WAGOGO   Simbawenni

Usagara Hills

Makata R.

INDIAN

Lake Mweru

10°S

OCEAN

Lake Bangweulu

Lake Nyasa

0   100   200   300 miles

0   100   200   300   400   500 km

15°S

30°E   40°E

Zambezi R.

barre

Mtowa

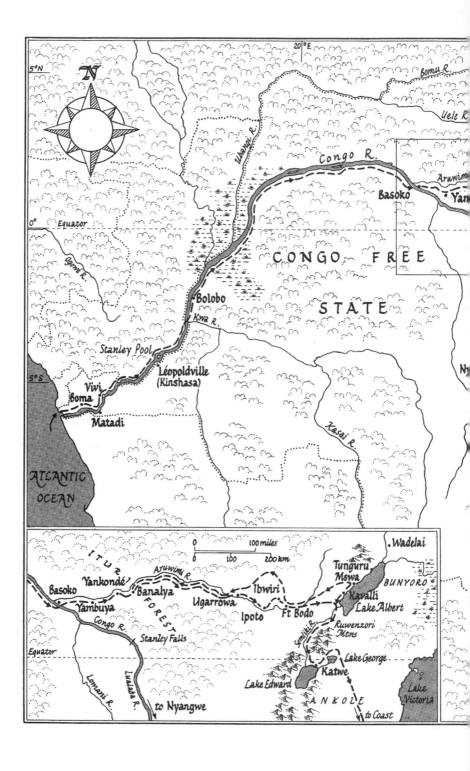

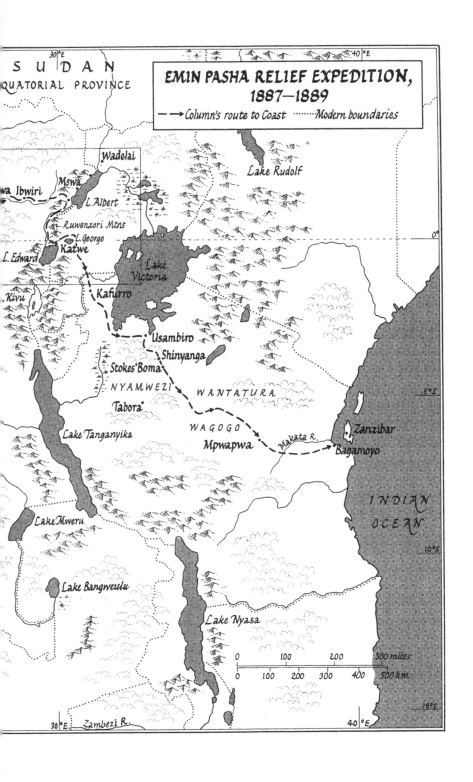

EMIN PASHA RELIEF EXPEDITION,
1887–1889

- - → Column's route to Coast ········ Modern boundaries

S U D A N
QUATORIAL PROVINCE

Wadelai

Mswa

Ibwiri

L. Albert

Ruwenzori Mtns

L. George

Katwe

L. Edward

Kivu

Kafurro

Lake Rudolf

Lake Victoria

Usambiro

Shinyanga

Stokes' Boma

NYAMWEZI

WANTATURA

Tabora

Lake Tanganyika

WAGOGO

Mpwapwa

Makata R.

Zanzibar

Bagamoyo

Lake Mweru

INDIAN OCEAN

Lake Bangweulu

Lake Nyasa

0   100   200   300 miles

0   100   200   300   400   500 km

Zambezi R.

INTRODUCTION

How I came to write the life
of Africa's least understood explorer

> When I contrast what I have achieved in my measurably brief life with
> what Stanley has achieved in his possibly briefer one, the effect is to
> sweep utterly away the ten-storey edifice of my own self-appreciation
> and to leave nothing behind but the cellar.
> *Mark Twain writing in 1886*

In January 1963, when I was a few days short of my eighteenth birthday and waiting to go to university the following October, I set out
overland from Cairo to Johannesburg on a zigzagging journey which I
expected to last about four months. I made my way south, at first by
Nile steamer and then in a succession of decrepit buses and trucks that
juddered along roads at times resembling riverbeds, or sped along
rust-coloured laterite tracks from which their tyres flung up clouds of
choking dust. In small out-of-the-way places, a few care-worn travellers seemed always to be waiting anxiously at dusk, hoping to persuade our exhausted driver to take them on with him next day for
whatever money they could afford to pay.

Such roadside staging posts would typically boast a single shop or
duka, stocking cigarettes, matches, Coca-Cola and canned fish, with
perhaps a bicycle repair shed nearby, and a single fuel pump, and
someone selling steamed green bananas or cornmeal porridge under a
tree. For a while those waiting would scan the road eagerly for a distant plume of dust, but would sink into a fatalistic reverie after a day
or so. Until a vehicle appeared they could go no further, and with the
nearest village perhaps a hundred or more miles away, there was absolutely nothing they could do about it.

Away from the 'main' road, a maze of faint single-file paths, which
only locals knew, fanned into the bush. A guideless stranger would

soon be lost and in real peril when his water ran out. In fact if anyone became separated from his fellows far from a village, he or she was likely to die in the bush, if not from thirst or exhaustion then in the jaws of a wild beast. In regions where the tsetse fly killed horses and oxen, riding and travelling by cart were impossible, leaving walking or cycling as the only remaining options. But who would try to walk hundreds of miles across uncharted country, when the rains could turn a road into a muddy morass within hours, and in high summer the heat could kill anyone without water and a shady place to rest? So the next truck, with its drums of extra fuel, spare tyres and life-saving food and water, offered the only chance.

Night comes rapidly in Africa, with twilight hardly existing, and the blackness seeming darker on account of its sudden arrival. For a while lamps and candles glow in huts and shacks, and adults talk and children play, but rarely till late in small wayside places. After that, on starless nights, the darkness is almost tangible, and when the crickets fall silent, the barking of a dog or the distant growl of some unidentified beast merely serves to emphasize the eerie silence that blankets the endless bush for miles around. At such moments, when I was not fretting over whether there was a snake or scorpion on the earth floor somewhere near my sleeping place, or whether my paludrine tablets, my insect-repelling creams and rarely used mosquito net would save me from malaria, I reminded myself that the Victorian explorers had possessed none of these things and yet had crossed the entire continent, not on known roads and tracks but through virgin bush and jungle, and along those dangerously illusive, vanishing paths that I would never consider using unless riding in a sturdy vehicle with someone who knew the area well.

During my trip, it first dawned on me why nineteenth-century explorers had needed a hundred or more African porters to accompany them into the interior. How else, lacking wheeled transport and draught animals because of the tsetse, could they have carried with them enough food and water, and sufficient beads, cloth and brass wire to buy fresh food supplies? And since their highly visible trade goods would have been a constant incitement to theft (a bit like carrying a bank around everywhere), I understood why expeditions had routinely been protected by armed Africans. As I passed slowly through recently independent Uganda, and soon to be independent Tanganyika, I was well aware that the great explorers were considered anachronistic embarrassments in this era when Africa's future, rather than its colonial past, rightly claimed our attention. Even so, from that time onwards the realities of earlier exploration fascinated me, and in the early 1970s, a few years after I left Oxford, I wrote a life of David Livingstone that is still in print today.

Thirty-five years on, it is still hard for us to appreciate the immensely powerful hold that exploration exerted on the public imagination in nineteenth-century Europe and America. Then, the world had not yet been shrunk by the automobile and the aeroplane, and the planet's remotest places seemed as inaccessible as the stars. From mid century, successful explorers were revered in much the same way as the Apollo astronauts would be just over a hundred years later. Very few achieved fame after 1871 – the year in which Stanley 'found' Livingstone – since by then, apart from apparently inaccessible central and sub-Saharan Africa, the only significant parts of the planet left unexplored were the equally daunting polar regions, along with northern Greenland and the north-east and north-west passages. But for the rapidly increasing populations of Europe's and America's factory towns, the romantic appeal of the world's wilder outposts grew stronger. Stanley wrote in the 1870s that, in Africa, he felt freed from 'that shallow life which thousands lead in England where a man is not permitted to be real and natural, but is held in the stocks of conventionalism'.

In an untamed land, a man was imagined to be free to cut down trees at will, kill game and navigate rivers, and to assume total responsibility for his own life. And *that* was what the explorers were imagined to be doing in Africa, with little account being taken of the appalling problems that overwhelmed most of them. In the novels of Fenimore Cooper, and those by Stanley's friend Mark Twain – especially his two great novels of boyhood – the values of the frontier were exalted above those of the city. American adulation of frontiersmen like Boone and Crockett, and the heroes of the Wild West, was paralleled in Britain by a passion for African explorers, and a revival of interest in the Elizabethan seafarers. Then came Rider Haggard's *King Solomon's Mines* and *She*, and novels by Ballantine, Mayne Reid and Stevenson, which together completed the romantic (as opposed to the economic) underpinnings of the imperial impulse.

As an adventure-loving boy, Joseph Conrad had been entranced by 'the blank spaces [on the map] then representing the unsolved mystery of that continent'. Yet romantic longings were so far removed from the realities of African travel that it is hard to imagine why so many men entertained them for so long. Really there was no mystery about why

Conrad's 'blank spaces' persisted, and why none of the great lakes had been 'discovered' by 1850, and why the continent's two longest rivers, the Nile and the Congo, were still uncharted twenty years later. The awesome problems besetting Africa's explorers began at the coast. Most rivers were harbourless and obstructed by surf-beaten sand bars, and blocked upstream by impassable rapids. In 1805 Mungo Park, a Scottish surgeon, and forty of the forty-four Europeans he had engaged to find the source of the river Niger, perished in the attempt. Park himself was murdered, while most of his men died of malaria. In 1816, the British naval officer James Tuckey was one of fourteen men to die on the Congo out of thirty who had volunteered to go on with him beyond the first cataracts. They travelled only 170 miles from the sea. Thirty-eight men died of fever out of forty-seven Britons on the Niger Expedition of 1833 to 1834, and Richard Lander, their leader, was murdered.

By crossing Africa between 1853 and 1856 and living to tell the tale, David Livingstone demonstrated that quinine aided resistance to malaria. But all Stanley's white companions died during his search for Dr Livingstone, and the same thing happened during his trans-Africa journey. In fact, throughout the century, malaria remained a serious threat to life (as it still is), as did yellow fever and sleeping sickness. The health of survivors was often undermined, and very few saw old age. Lady Burton described her husband after an African journey as being 'partially paralysed, partially blind ... a mere skeleton, with brown yellow skin hanging in bags, his eyes protruding, his lips drawn away from his teeth'.[1] And this degree of ill-health was not unusual.

Since the late Victorians were fixated by the need for manliness, the astonishing bravery of explorers earned them universal admiration. During my journey I had sometimes wondered how scared I would be if I ever found myself marooned in a truck that had broken down beyond repair in a rarely visited region. I imagined it would be like being shipwrecked on an inhospitable atoll and left to starve unless rescued. And this had been the fate of Victorian explorers deserted by their carriers, who had taken away with them the bales of cloth and sacks of beads with which their employers had hoped to pay for food. A traveller left with only a handful of porters had been utterly helpless with his human ship and lifeline gone.

While researching my life of Livingstone, I was shown by a collector of African manuscripts a most evocative sheet of paper. It turned out to be an important moment for me. On it was written in Henry Stanley's hand the desperate appeal he made on 4 August 1877, when struggling towards the trading post of Boma on the Lower Congo, just seventy miles from the Atlantic. He had just become the first man in history to have followed that great river 1,800 miles from the heart of the continent, and was now close to completing one of the most dangerous and sublime journeys of all time.

To any gentleman who speaks English at Emboma

Dr Sir

I have arrived at this place from Zanzibar with 115 souls, men, women & children. We are now in a state of imminent starvation. We can purchase nothing from the natives for they laugh at our kinds of cloth.... [he then explained that unless supplies could be sent to him within two days...] I may have a fearful time of it among the dying...' [Stanley ended with a brief postscript]

P.S. You may not know me by name – I therefore add that I am the person who discovered Livingstone in 1871. H.M.S.[2]

Given that during his extraordinary trans-Africa expedition he had circumnavigated two of Africa's three great lakes for the first time, and had solved the mystery of the central African watershed by separating the Congo's source from the Nile's – not one word of which was mentioned in his letter – I found it immensely poignant that Stanley, the illegitimate workhouse boy, had still needed to attach his name to Livingstone's in order to make himself seem worthy of assistance. It reminded me of just how far he had come from a childhood world of parental rejection and poverty, and how, if he had not emigrated to America aged eighteen, he would never (in class-stratified Britain) have been taken on by one of the world's great newspapers, and so would probably have lacked the self-belief to attempt his unparalleled journey. During it, 132 of his original 228 expedition members had died, including all three of his white companions, and by the end of it he had lost almost a third of his body weight and looked fifteen years older than his thirty-six years. But at least he had survived, unlike Park, Lander, Clapperton, Tuckey, and Livingstone, to name but a few earlier explorers.

And now, at last, the huge blank in the centre of the map of Africa, which for a century had exercised a Grail-like fascination throughout Europe, had been filled in, largely thanks to this one stupendous journey. As I read this stained and faded letter, I felt strongly drawn to write Stanley's life. It seemed an incredible irony that he was remembered more for his misjudged attempt at *sangfroid* – 'Dr Livingstone, I presume?' – than for the wondrous journey that had been almost beyond imagining, let alone completing.

Then, several months before I finished my *Livingstone* in 1972, the journalist and author Richard Hall wrote to me, explaining that *he* was writing Stanley's life and suggesting that we meet and talk. We did, and got on well; and I acknowledged to myself that my hopes of writing about Stanley were realistically at an end. Hall had partial access to the Stanley family's immense, uncatalogued collection of journals and letters and, just as significantly, permission to quote from an unpublished 283-page typescript written by Gerald Sanger, a retired film and newspaperman man, friendly with Stanley's adopted son, Denzil, who had shown him many new letters and diaries.[3]

Hall's book came out in 1974, a year after my *Livingstone*, and marked a significant advance on all previous biographies of Stanley, despite the family's decision to deny him the letters of the earliest love of Stanley's life, Katie Gough Roberts, and his letters to his wife after their marriage. Hall therefore had no means of knowing whether Stanley's marriage had been successful, or a sham, concealing homosexual preferences, as would later be claimed. The great journeys were dealt with rather briskly by him, as was the pioneering of the Congo Free State, and Stanley's relations with King Leopold II. But Hall subjected Stanley's so-called *Autobiography* to its first sceptical examination.

When I had been working in the National Library of Scotland, researching *Livingstone*, I had come across Stanley's letters to his close friend and confidant Alexander Bruce – David Livingstone's son-in-law. I brought back copies to London for Richard Hall, and for myself. They showed a man remarkably different both from the ruthless and obsessively driven explorer – who had nevertheless existed – and from the insecure and bombastic Welshman who had pretended to have been born to American parents, and had antagonized key figures in the British establishment. These letters dated from the period of Stanley's life ten years after he became famous, and they revealed to me an unexpectedly self-effacing man, who was generous and loyal to friends, and seemed to accept that, mainly through his own faults, he was doomed never to attract the type of woman with whom he was prone to fall in love. Stanley possessed a touching, almost childlike faith in Bruce's advice. It seemed as if – lacking a family of his own – he had made Livingstone's son-in-law a kind of revered elder brother. This dependence was so far removed from Stanley's public image that, excellent though Hall's book was, I felt later that the man's complexities had eluded him.

Seventeen years passed. In 1990 I reviewed John Bierman's well-written short biography, *Dark Safari*, and found it followed Hall closely, without staking out new ground for itself. In 1990 I also read a more ambitious life of Stanley, which had appeared a year earlier and would become the most influential book on the explorer yet written. This was the first volume of Frank McLynn's biography, *Stanley: The Making of an African Explorer* (1989); volume two, *Stanley: Sorcerer's Apprentice*, would appear in 1991. McLynn's judgements were largely negative, though not entirely. He certainly acknowledged that his subject was a great explorer, but because he focused primarily on the aggressive side of Stanley's nature, McLynn saw his principal motivation as being 'a volcanic rage against the world' as a result of his wretched childhood. According to McLynn, Stanley was 'neuter-like' and impotent, and his eventual marriage a sham because he was allegedly a repressed homosexual. The major influence on the second half of Stanley's life, McLynn argued, was King Leopold II, whose 'sorcerer's apprentice' he became – the implication being that Stanley was putty in the king's hands, enabling Leopold to carry out his later brutal exploitation of the Congo.

This, in conjunction with John Bierman's statement that Stanley had 'duped' more than 300 chiefs out of their land, and had thus handed to Leopold 'the legal basis for his so-called Congo Free State',[4] would destroy Stanley's reputation in the 1990s, when interest in the atrocities in the Congo became intense. McLynn's suggestion that Africa had been essential to Stanley as somewhere 'permitting the exercise of homicidal impulses without incurring lethal social consequences' would contribute to the widespread belief that Stanley had been a violent and paranoid man.[5] Bierman's belief that Stanley had used Africa as 'an escape ... and a quest for self-esteem' struck me as altogether more convincing.[6] I was puzzled by how different Frank McLynn's picture of Stanley was from the gentler, sadder person, with a longing to marry and have children, whom I had glimpsed years ago when reading Stanley's letters to Alexander Bruce.

From McLynn's and Bierman's notes on sources, I learned that a massive amount of new material might one day become available to future biographers. Both men had complained bitterly (and who could blame them?) that they had been denied access to the enormous collection of papers that the Stanley family had sold in 1982 for £400,000 to a third party acting for the Musée Royal de l'Afrique Centrale in Brussels. In the mid-1990s I contacted the museum and was told that nobody would see the papers until they had been catalogued, and this process was not in prospect. Microfilm of some of the papers had been placed in the British Library, but there was no knowing what had *not* been microfilmed, since the papers that had gone to Belgium had filled six large crates.

In September 2002 I was invited, as David Livingstone's biographer, to give a lecture at Christie's, London, on the famous meeting between Stanley and Livingstone. The occasion was the auctioning of the Stanley family's immense collection of books, maps, spears, presentation caskets, photograph albums, lantern slides, guns, medicine chests, chronometers and sextants – in fact all that remained of the great explorer's possessions after the family's earlier sale of his letters, journals, and exploration notebooks. So my pleasure can be imagined when, before my lecture, I was introduced to Maurits Wynants of the Musée Royal in Brussels, who had come over to bid for items in the sale. I was astonished to hear that Maurits and his colleague, Peter Daerden, were cataloguing not only the 1982 collection, but a slightly smaller archive of intimate family papers that had been sold privately to the museum in 2000 for a similar sum to that paid to the family in 1982, without any microfilm or photocopies being demanded by the Board of Trade, despite their historical importance.

Mr Wynants said that, although the catalogue was not yet complete, I would be welcome to come to Brussels, if I wished, and that he and Peter Daerden would do whatever they could for me. I was told that the museum possessed all Stanley's letters to his wife and hers to him, from the time of their meeting until his death, and also her private diaries, and approximately 5,000 letters written to Stanley from an extraordinarily wide range of correspondents – from members of his own family, from prime ministers such as Gladstone and Salisbury, from cabinet ministers, and from many of Stanley's closest friends, including the first woman he had wished to marry (whose letters had been thought to have been destroyed), as well as from his closest male friend, Edward King, and his valet, William Hoffman. There were also many letters from the one woman whom he would have been ideally suited to wed, if only she had been single. This was the American author and journalist May Sheldon. Other correspondents of immense interest ranged from the members of Leopold's cabinet, to Stanley's publisher, to his close friend and mentor, Sir William Mackinnon, and his sponsors, James Gordon Bennett Jr of the *New York Herald* and Edwin Arnold of the *Daily Telegraph*. The inventory, when it was finally completed, was 427 pages long, and listed over 7,000 items, some of which are letter books and journals containing scores of pages.[7]

I learned that, apart from an American geographer, James Newman, who was focusing on Stanley's journeys and was not attempting a definitive biography, nobody was writing anything substantial about Stanley. (James Newman's *Imperial Footprints* was published by an American specialist publisher in 2004 and has not appeared in Britain. While he paints a more benign and fairer picture of Stanley as a traveller, the man's personal life, and his political and colonial ambitions and relationships, are not examined in detail. The authors of two other recent books did not visit Belgium. These were Daniel Liebowitz and Charles Pearson, whose brisk and often patronizing account of Stanley's Emin Pasha Expedition, *The Last Expedition*, relied solely on printed sources. Martin Dugard's *Into Africa: The Epic Adventures of Stanley and Livingstone*, 2003, was written as a straightforward adventure story and contains many inaccuracies.)

Several months after meeting Maurits Wynants, I went to Brussels for a preliminary visit of three weeks to see whether, if I wrote Stanley's biography, I would be able to add new dimensions, not only to the story of his life but also to the record of his work and its morality, and to the vexed subject of his colonial influence. During this brief period, I did indeed find a mass of material striking me as both historically important and new. From reading Stanley's letters to his wife and hers to him, it seemed that their marriage, though unhappy at times, had been a sexual one and not a sham. Also, on reading letters to Stanley from some of the young men – to whom it had been suggested he might have been homosexually attracted – I realized how inadequate past surmises had been. I was excited to find that many new insights into his early life were contained in his letters to the first woman he had wished to marry, which had not been destroyed, as had been thought. Many new papers covering his American years led me to wonder whether Stanley had ever met the man whom he claimed had adopted him in America. Other correspondence strongly suggested that Stanley himself, rather than James Gordon Bennett Jr, had come up with the idea of 'finding' Livingstone. Lastly, I was surprised to find not hundreds of treaties made by Stanley with Congolese chiefs, but only one – and this solitary treaty in Stanley's hand had not required the chiefs in question to surrender their land. Was it possible that the widespread supposition that Stanley had stolen the Congo for Leopold was wrong? I knew this key subject would require a great deal of research.

I returned to London feeling that my trip had given me what I had needed. A month later, I signed a contract with Faber & Faber. I felt very lucky, and not a little dazed, that after so many years I had unexpectedly been given a chance (which I had long ago despaired of) to make a major reassessment of a giant in the history of exploration, and in the story of Europe's encounter with Africa. But I had misgivings, too. In 1996, when I was writing the introductory chapter to the catalogue of the National Portrait Gallery's Livingstone exhibition, it had occurred to me that no similar event was ever likely to be mounted for Stanley – a man who had been refused burial in Westminster Abbey, and whose birthplace had been allowed to be pulled down. Since the appearance of Frank McLynn's biography, it had been treated almost as an established fact that Stanley had been the most brutal explorer of the nineteenth century, and remarks to this effect are still dropped into newspaper articles and general books of African history, as if there can be no dispute about them. Stanley's name is more and more often linked with that of King Leopold II, as if he had been responsible, with the king, not only for founding the Congo Free State but also for creating the moral atmosphere in which crimes against humanity were likely to be committed in that country.

I knew already, from my reading of published sources and microfilm in the British Library, that Stanley was not a racist like Sir Richard Burton or Sir Samuel Baker, so I was puzzled by the confidence with which some authors had characterized him as such. Right from the beginning of his first African trip, Stanley was, he wrote: 'prepared to admit any black man possessing the attributes of true manhood, or any good qualities, to my friendship, even to a brotherhood with myself'.[8] Between 1879 and 1884, he repeatedly described Dualla, a

Somali, as his most important member of staff – his virtual prime minister – who by 1883 was receiving the same pay as white officers. Two other Africans, Wadi Rehani and Mabruki Ndogo, were also as close to Stanley as were his two favourite whites, Anthony Swinburne and Albert Christophersen. He hated it when any black man was called 'nigger' by a white – 'that ugly derisive word', he called it.[9]

Stanley always found Africans pleasing to look at: 'Each age has a beauty of its own ... the skin may be more velvety than velvet, smoother than satin, or coarse as canvas ... but its warm brown colour seems to suit the African atmosphere – the contour of the body is always graceful.'[10] By contrast, white people struck him as awkward. To get on with Africans, he told his young white officers 'to relax those stiff pallid features; let there enter into those chill icy eyes, the light of light and joy, of humour, friendship, pleasure; and the communication of man and man is electric in its suddenness.'[11] He adored African children. 'The sight of these tender naked little beings following my camp into the wilderness, and laughing in my face, and hugging my knees, just thrilled me.'[12] And if Stanley had really been brutal to the Wangwana – the Swahili-speaking blacks of Zanzibar, engaged as his carriers on all his major journeys – I could not understand why large numbers had elected to serve with him again and again.

So how was I going to reconcile the discrepancy between Stanley's many positive and even loving statements about Africans, and his statement that he had been obliged to fight with tribesmen many times – something that other European explorers either had not done, or had chosen to conceal? Since he had been a journalist, and his two most successful journeys had been financed by newspapers, it crossed my mind, even before I began my archival research, that he might have exaggerated the number and intensity of his conflicts with Africans in order to make his copy more exciting. I hoped, by comparing the number of Africans whom Stanley recorded as having been killed (in encounters with his expeditions) with the numbers of fatalities quoted in the diaries of his travelling companions, that I might be able to establish whether apparently damning material should be treated as literal truth or journalistic hyperbole.[13]

Stanley was hated and envied by the Portuguese, the Dutch and the French for having successfully planted trading stations in the best positions on the Congo, for the benefit of King Leopold's so-called International Association. He himself believed that jealousy accounted for stories of his brutality spread during the 1880s, and repeated again and again over the years. So perhaps I would find evidence one way or the other? As early as 1970, Professor Norman R. Bennett of the University of Boston – an outstanding historian of East Africa – wrote at the start of the introduction to his magnificent edition of *Stanley's Despatches to the New York Herald,* 'There is no apparent reason why, more than three-quarters of a century after his last venture, Stanley should continue to be singled out for his supposed excesses in Africa, while other Europeans often responsible for far more loss of African life than Stanley, receive sympathetic treatment.' Some years ago I noted, in a biography of Pierre Savorgnan de Brazza – an explorer usually acclaimed for his peaceful travels – that the Frenchman had shot Africans (in self-defence, he claimed), even while protesting that he 'never was in the habit of travelling round Africa as a warrior, like Mr Stanley'.[14] From earlier reading, I was aware that General Gordon, though seen as a martyr, had killed many members of the Bari tribe in southern Sudan, and had believed that there were times when Africans had to be shot in self-defence: 'These things may be done, but not advertised,' he remarked to Richard Burton, with Stanley in mind.[15] Frederick Lugard would be ennobled and become a British colonial governor, despite, as his biographer conceded, shedding far more blood on the shores of Lake Victoria than Stanley ever had. Even Livingstone, as I recorded in my life of him, shot dead several tribesmen, and burned their huts. This had been in 1861, south of Lake Nyasa (Malawi), when these African (Yao) slave traders had attacked the mission village of Magomero.[16]

Stanley, according to most of his biographers, had been highly volatile as a young man, and at times ruthless – and I knew for a fact that his treatment of his two white travelling companions on the Livingstone search expedition had been harsh. But I also knew what malaria could do to more long-suffering temperaments than Stanley's. Dr Livingstone, at the sober age of forty-six, had once had a fistfight with his clergyman brother in south central Africa, in which both men had drawn blood. Burton and Speke had fallen out, forever, during their expedition to Lake Tanganyika. Yet though many white men behaved badly in Africa, Stanley alone stood condemned, principally by the things he himself had written about his actions at a later time and by the tone he employed. An excellent example is the much-quoted passage about how, by beating his carriers, he restored 'the physical energy of the lazily inclined' and encouraged them often 'to an extravagant activity'. I had quoted this myself in my *Livingstone*.[17] But I realized, as I began work on Stanley, that sardonic humour would not have been encouraged or taught in the St Asaph work-house, where he lived and was educated as a boy.

However, as a young and insecure 'special' correspondent in East Africa in 1868, Stanley had been immensely impressed by the insouciance of upper-class Englishmen in the military. I wondered whether he had been tempted to emulate, in despatches to the *New York Herald* and in *How I Found Livingstone*, the cheerful heartlessness of army officers' casual conversations and the off-hand way in which they wrote of death and disaster in their memoirs. I certainly suspected that rejection by his parents had left him needing to describe himself as hard and powerful in order to survive. Yet whatever I might find out, it would make no difference to the fact that he had left himself permanently vulnerable to hostile selective quotation. In recent years such quotes have very rarely been counterbalanced, in print, with any of his far more numerous positive statements about Africans.

Unwisely, given the lip-service paid to religion by his contemporaries, Stanley made influential enemies as a young man by poking fun at churchmen and pious evangelicals. His famous offer to them of 'seven tons of Bibles, four tons of Prayer Books, any number of surplices, and a church organ into the bargain' if they could reach longitude 23° 'without chucking some of those Bibles at some of those negroes' heads' would be quoted against him time and again, as would his surmise that 'the selfish and wooden-headed world requires mastering as well as loving charity'.[18] But by his forties he would number missionaries among his friends. Such were W. Holman Bentley and Alexander Mackay, who by the late 1880s had lived many years in Africa and, like Stanley himself, sometimes beat their carriers, as did virtually all European travellers. With trade goods dwindling and little food to be bought, expedition leaders argued that they had to drive their men on for the sake of their own survival.

There were three occasions during Stanley's sixteen years in Africa when I knew he had taken the extreme step of hanging a man. He claimed in mitigation that his whole expedition would have fallen apart, and most of its members have starved to death or been killed, if he had not ended a spate of violent thefts and mass desertions by a single draconian act. But would his justifications on these three occasions carry conviction when subjected to close examination?

I was well aware how hard travel had been for Livingstone as he entered regions where Africans (already victims of slave raids) refused to sell food to his people. His dilemma had been whether to take food by force, or to risk marching on in the hope of obtaining food at the next village. On many occasions, he was obliged by destitution to throw himself on the mercy of the Arab-Swahili slave traders and ask them to feed him and his followers. During my first visit to Belgium I read a very significant passage in one of Stanley's diaries, which I had never seen quoted in any book. In this entry, Stanley showed that he had recognized the fundamental moral problem facing all European travellers. 'We went into the heart of Africa self-invited,' he wrote; 'therein lies our fault. But it was not so grave that our lives [when threatened] should be forfeited.'[19]

This was the conundrum facing explorers of Africa – especially in the 1870s and 1880s, when attacks on them were much more numerous than had been the case in the relatively peaceful 1850s. As they had indeed come 'self-invited', could their efforts to make geographical discoveries be morally justified, given that they would almost certainly be obliged to shoot in self-defence an unknown number of Africans (who had only been trying to defend their land)? Stanley himself argued – as Livingstone had done before him – that, by the 1870s, the terrible and worsening humanitarian situation in Africa had made exploration, and opening the continent to European influence, imperative on humanitarian grounds.

I had learned when writing my *Livingstone* that the East African Arab-Swahili slave trade was far older than the Atlantic trade, and increased in volume from the 1860s, just when the Royal Navy had at last managed to strangle the seaborne trade from West Africa to the Americas. During the nineteenth century, some 2,000,000 slaves were estimated to have sailed from Africa's eastern shores or been taken overland to Egypt, Arabia and the Gulf by trans-Saharan routes. In 2002, Ronald Segal, in his masterly history of that neglected trade, confirmed these figures and argued that African chiefs had also been deeply implicated.[20] I recorded in my life of Livingstone that – shortly before his meeting with Stanley – the doctor spent many days explaining to chiefs that 'if they sell their fellows, they are like the man who holds the victim while the Arab performs the murder'.[21] He asked them repeatedly why they found it necessary to sell their people to a handful of intruders, and was told: 'If so and so gives up selling so will we. He is the greatest offender in the country.' 'It is the fault of the Arabs who tempt us with fine clothes, powder and guns.' 'I would fain keep all my people to cultivate more land, but my next neighbour allows his people to kidnap mine and I must have ammunition to defend them.'[22] I also quoted Dr Livingstone saying that 'this perpetual capturing and sale of children' from subject tribes (by Africans) was a crime that made the Arab and Portuguese slave trades 'appear a small evil by comparison'.[23]

The old fabric of tribal custom, such as hospitality to strangers, had broken down largely because of the violence spread by the Atlantic and the East African slave trades. Yet African tribal migrations like those of the Ngoni, Kamba and Yao also contributed to the spreading frontier of violence. Stanley narrowly escaped death at the hands of Mirambo of the Nyamwezi, when that brutal ruler was fighting the Arab-Swahili for control of the eastern slave routes. Later, Stanley wrote that he and his men felt that they were 'considered as game to be trapped, shot or bagged at sight'. Both he and Livingstone witnessed horrific massacres.[24]

It appears to be widely imagined today that Africa was a paradise before Stanley and other explorers entered it – indeed, Liebowitz and Pearson end their book with a statement to that effect. 'He [Stanley] and his ilk broke Africa wide open, and no one has yet found a way to put it back together again.'[25] In reality, Stanley was a latecomer. The Arabs had arrived on the East African coast in the ninth century. Livingstone had found African middlemen of Portuguese slave traders at the heart of south-central Africa on the Zambesi in 1851 and, twenty years later, he met Arab slavers at Nyangwe on the Congo, in the very centre of the continent. By the 1880s estimates were appearing in Europe that put the figure for depopulation at half a million a year in central Africa alone. Earlier, Livingstone had argued that the situation would only improve if Europe tried to develop Africa economically through colonization. Stanley has been attacked for holding similar beliefs about the desirability of colonies. So the nineteenth-century context for such beliefs was clearly going to be another key subject for me to address. Would Stanley number among the genuine idealists, or the exploitative money makers who urged on the earliest Empire builders in Africa?

Thirty years ago, I wrote about one of the greatest of the many ironies affecting Stanley's reputation. This was the fact that he had done more than any living man to create the myth of saintly Dr Livingstone, only to suffer for it ever afterwards by being adversely compared with the good doctor. Yet no irony affecting Stanley's reputation seems as great as the one that was revealed to me as I started my research. He had stated that he longed to do something wonderful for the African tribes along the Congo, and instead, as would become all too apparent, had set them up for a terrible fate. In 1877 he came down the great river as the first European ever to do so, declaring his hope that the Congo should become like 'a torch to those who sought to do good'.[26] Instead, it became the torch that attracted the arch-exploiter King Leopold II of Belgium.

The shadow of Leopold, the misdeeds of the officers of the Rear Column during Stanley's last expedition and his pre-emptive attack on the natives of a small island have dogged Stanley down the years, and have combined to prevent his being remembered in any positive way. Now, with the poverty of Africa still being blamed on colonialism as much as on natural disasters, or the Cold War, or the unfairness of twentieth-century Western trade policies, or the corruptness of African governments – it is inevitable that many sceptics will be unconvinced that a man with Stanley's beliefs about the benefits of 'European civilization' deserves a fresh hearing, even in the light of copious new evidence of what he really did and thought. Yet to shirk looking again at Stanley's life simply because many minds are made up already would be to deny another post-colonial generation the chance of gaining new insights into a unique phase of world history and the story of an astonishing man, who has scarcely been acknowledged as British, let alone as Africa's greatest explorer.

Tim Jeal
London
October 2006

ONE

Dreams of Love and Freedom

John Rowlands – who would one day be known to the world as Henry Morton Stanley – was five and a half when a great disaster befell him. His grandfather, Moses Parry – once a prosperous butcher, but now living in reduced circumstances – dropped dead in a potato field on the outskirts of the Welsh market town where John had lived all his life. The place was Denbigh, the date 22 June 1846, and the old man was seventy-five years old.[1]

John was born illegitimate, and his eighteen-year-old mother, Elizabeth Parry, had abandoned him as a very young baby and had then cut off all communication. She would go on to have five more children – by two, or possibly three other men – only the last child being born in wedlock. Yet all these children would be granted some attention by her, unlike her rejected firstborn, John, who would be doubly disadvantaged, since he would never meet the man named as his father in the parish registers.[2] It is not known why John alone should have been abandoned by her. From his earliest months, he was cared for by Moses Parry, his maternal grand-father, which was why Moses' sudden death was such a shattering blow. Twenty years after the event, John – by then calling himself Henry Stanley – was moved to write a tribute to his grandfather on a scroll of special blue paper. In his best calligraphy, he described Moses' cry, as he raised both hands to his chest and fell, taking just three more breaths before dying. Every detail recorded by a local journalist was precious to the grown-up John, who ended by listing the virtues of the only relation who had ever cared for him: 'Let us emulate his goodness, his kindness, his good deeds, for they were worthy of EMULATION.'[3]

The old man had taken a liking to John from the beginning, and shortly after the boy's birth had thrust a gold sovereign into his mouth so he could bite on it and guarantee himself a prosperous future. His grandson would remember him as 'a stout old gentleman, clad in corduroy breeches, dark stockings, and long Melton coat, with a clean-shaven face, rather round, and lit up by humorous grey eyes'. The little boy accompanied Moses everywhere, including to the town's Wesleyan chapel, where he would struggle not to fall asleep among the lavender-scented pews. At home, sitting on the old man's knee, John was taught to write his letters on a slate.[4]

Stanley's grandfather's cottage, where he was born

After his grandfather's death, John's uncles, Thomas and Moses junior, decided – though they were prosperous butchers – that John would have to leave his late grandfather's cottage in the shadow of ruinous Denbigh Castle. At first they arranged for him to be boarded out in an overcrowded cottage close to his old home and placed in the care of its owners, Richard and Jenny Price, a couple in their fifties, four of whose children still lived with them. Richard maintained the castle bowling green and was known as 'the green-keeper'. He also dug the graves at nearby St Hilary's Church, where John had been baptized. The Prices were very poor and refused to look after John for less than half a crown a week, perhaps £60 in today's money. In the day, John briefly attended the Free School in the crypt of St Hilary's Church. After a few months the place was closed down because 'the floor and seats were broken, and damp from the church-yard penetrated into the crypt'. No arithmetic had been taught there and few children could even read words of one syllable. John took away with him the memory of 'a terrible old lady with spectacles and a birch rod'.[5]

At the Price's cottage, John played on the grassy slopes beside the Castle, just as he had done when living with his grandfather. He also continued to witness the arrival of the well-dressed members of the bowling club, whose refreshments were sent up to the castle by vari-ous purveyors, in baskets with the names of their businesses on the sides. The boy studied these names carefully. '"Well, John, what do they mean?" asked a member of the Price family. He answered in Welsh, "Byddigion," which is the infantile word for "gentlefolk".'[6] His precocious awareness of his own low social status would make the next development in his life all the harder to bear.

About six months after his arrival at the Prices, when the little boy had settled in well, his uncles decided to stop paying for his keep.[7] Richard and Jenny Price suspected that John's relatives were gambling on their being too fond of the boy to part with him. The Prices were having none of this and told their twenty-seven-year-old son, also called Richard Price, to get John Rowlands ready for a journey.

Richard's own account of what happened was given to a journalist forty years later, at which date he still lived in the cottage where John had once been cared for. 'So I requested my mother to dress him ... Then I put him to stand on that chair there, and taking his little hands over my shoulders, I carried him down through the town passing the houses of his well-to-do relatives ...' For part of the journey, Richard let the boy walk. The six-year-old John was very anxious and often asked in Welsh: 'Ble rydan ni'n mynd, Dick?': 'Where are we going, Dick?' John had been told that he would soon be seeing his aunt Mary, who lived in a hamlet to the north of Denbigh. When their eight-mile journey ended at the doors of the St Asaph Workhouse, and Richard Price turned to leave, having rung a bell that clanged deep within the building, the child asked him where he was going. 'To buy cakes for you,' replied the shamefaced Price, before hurrying away. The 'false cajolings and treacherous endearments' lavished upon him during that journey on 20 February 1847 would live forever in Henry Stanley's memory.[8] 'Since that dreadful evening,' Stanley would write in his fifties, 'my resentment has not a whit abated ... It would have been far better for me if Dick, being stronger than I, had employed compulsion, instead of shattering my confidence and planting the first seeds of distrust in a child's heart.'[9]

There has been a lively debate among scholars about how humane, or inhumane, the St Asaph workhouse really was – with one historian arguing that a child in this newly built institution was better housed, better fed, better clothed and better educated than many a boy or girl reared with his or her parents in a rural cottage.[10] Yet emotional deprivation is immensely more damaging than ignorance or poverty. Nor should the main social objective of workhouses be forgotten. Apart from preventing the poor from starving in the streets, they were meant to deter people who had failed to provide for themselves from ever failing again, and to persuade anyone who might be thinking of relying on the state, rather than on his or her own labour, to reconsider.

The new arrivals, whether adult paupers or deserted children, were subjected to a humiliating ritual. First they were washed in cold water, then their hair was cropped short and, to complete the removal of their individuality, they were clad in identical drab fustian suits if male, or striped cotton dresses if female. If, for any reason, they ever left the workhouse, which required permission, they would at once be recognized as inmates. It was as if, wrote Stanley, they had committed a crime, and yet their only offence was to have 'become old, or so enfeebled by toil or sickness that they could no longer sustain themselves', or, if young, their sin was to have been deserted.[11] Workhouse inmates were at the bottom of the social heap, in a cruelly snobbish society, and were made to know their place every day of their lives. They rose at six, and were penned into their dormitories at eight in the evening. Their bread and gruel was unappetizing, and meant to be. Husbands and wives were separated, parents and children too, and even brothers and sisters were kept apart. 'It is a fearful fate that of a British outcast,' wrote Stanley, 'because the punishment afflicts the mind and breaks the heart.'[12]

Stanley exaggerated and lied about the level of brutality at St Asaph – his most notorious false claim being that a boy had been beaten to death by James Francis, the schoolteacher. The workhouse records were kept with bureaucratic thoroughness, and they show that nothing of the kind took place when Stanley was there; as they do again, on the day on which Stanley claimed to have left for good, after having beaten his teacher insensible, following a brutal assault by the man. The only diary record of his early years is a brief and fragmentary affair, written by him four decades later in Swahili – as if, even then, he had still needed to distance himself as far as possible from the pain of those days. The entry for 5 January 1854 reads in translation: 'He [Francis] hit me a lot today for no reason. I will never forget,'[13] and this perhaps explains his need to console himself with fantasies about overcoming the man who had symbolized his captivity. There was no adult at St Asaph willing, or able, to comfort him. 'It took me some time to learn the unimportance of tears in a workhouse. Hitherto tears had brought me relief in one shape or another ...'[14] His inability to convey in words the extent of his mental suffering accounts in part for his exaggeration of the physical violence in the workhouse.

The inspector's report on St Asaph in the year of Stanley's admission was very bad. The girls – there were nineteen of them – were said to have been corrupted by prostitutes and from them 'had learnt the tricks of the trade'; the men had taken part in every possible vice, and the boys slept two in a bed, an older with a younger, 'so that from the very start ... [they] were beginning to understand and practise things they should not'. The master, as distinct from the teacher, was censured for being drunk and 'taking indecent liberties with the nurses'. In the words of the report, the teacher, James Francis, aged thirty-two, had 'received no training, and speaks very broken English and appears to understand the language imperfectly'. Out of thirty boys, ten were learning to write but 'only one copy-book was well-written'.[15] Yet Stanley would state a dozen years after leaving: 'I had a pretty fair education during my ten years in St Asaph workhouse.'[16] And he was being serious – vice, brutality and low academic standards had also been prevalent in the country's most famous schools, such as Eton and Winchester. Nor was it disastrous that a teacher should speak poor English in a school where the first language of most children was Welsh. In fact the inspector's reports improved so much as the years passed, that a satisfactory situation was recorded by 1856, the year in which Stanley left. Francis even received an efficiency award and a rise in salary.[17]

Stanley learned to read and write, and even to love books – though the only novels given him to read were pious morality tales.[18] He was good at arithmetic and geography and could write remarkably neatly at an early age. From time to time he was even called in to help with the workhouse accounts.[19] His teacher, James Francis, who had left the mines after losing his hand in a pit accident, asked Stanley, as head boy, to deputize for him when he was away, and rewarded him with small gifts. Stanley did not, however, escape all punishment, and he would never forget being beaten after an illicit blackberrying expedition.[20] On several occasions, Francis called on Stanley's uncle Moses and 'urged him to do something for little John, since he was an excellent scholar and endowed with extraordinary talents'. But Moses always refused to help.[21]

Why Stanley chose to represent Francis as a sadistic monster will never be known with certainty. Francis was a bachelor, and his many gifts to chosen boys would undoubtedly raise eyebrows in any school today.[22] The fact that homosexual practices among the boys were remarked upon by the inspectors suggests a possible reason for Stanley's hatred. An unwanted sexual advance by his bachelor teacher may account for his violent antipathy. His mother's promiscuity meant that, as a young man, Stanley was disgusted by overt sexuality, and especially by prostitutes. In his letters to his first serious girlfriend, he insisted that he had remained 'pure' in the workhouse.[23] A sexual advance by his teacher would therefore have been an especially shocking betrayal. A simple withdrawal of favour hardly seems adequate motivation for Stanley's vilification of someone who had once rewarded and praised him.

A momentous event occurred in December 1850. The boy was a month short of his tenth birthday. Without warning, during the dinner-hour, Francis took John aside and 'pointing to a tall woman with an oval face, and a great coil of dark hair behind her head', asked him if he knew her.

'No, sir,' I replied.
'What, do you not know your own mother?'
I started with a burning face, and directed a shy glance at her and perceived she was regarding me with a look of cool, critical scrutiny. I had expected to feel a gush of tenderness towards her, but her expression was so chilling that the valves of my heart closed as with a snap.[24]

In reality, the boy's longing to be loved by his mother had not been turned off as if by some convenient tap. Elizabeth Parry had never before come to see John during his four years in the workhouse, and

now she only came because she and two of her other children had been
admitted as destitute paupers. But this did not stop him dreaming of
winning this aloof woman's love. Despite his rage at being thrown
away by a mother who kept her younger children with her, he would
for many years persist with attempts to please her, even after humiliating setbacks. No photograph of Elizabeth Parry as a young woman
survives, though Stanley once carried one with him everywhere. A
photograph of her aged about fifty – the only one known to exist – is
published for the first time as this book's Plate 3. The square shape of
her head is very similar to her famous son's, as is her resolute and
determined expression.[25]

People who are shut up in institutions often have fantasies of escape
and freedom, of climbing over walls, living in woods, and walking for
days towards far horizons. It is easy to see why Stanley's years in the
workhouse would predispose him towards travel in a limitless continent. Stanley felt imprisoned and cut off. It was as if he and the others
'were in another planet ... Year after year we noted the passing of the
seasons, by the budding blossoms, the flight of bees, the corn which
changed from green to gold.' Meanwhile, in his own words, he 'vege-
tated within the high walls surrounding our home of lowliness'.[26] On
rare occasions, when permitted to visit the small town of St Asaph,
John, with his pale face and fustian garments, was amazed at the good
fortune of the local boys who could eat raisins and sugar, and wear
colourful neckties. The desire to escape was in him early. When he was
ten, he ran away to Denbigh. But the outcome of this trip was so
painful that he never wrote about it.

Once over the wall, John had nowhere to go except to his neglectful
relatives. So he headed for the house of his uncle Moses Parry, whose
successful butchery business enabled him to live in Vale Street, the
most desirable address in town. In 1851, Moses and his wife, Kitty –
who had played the leading role in forcing little John out of the house
where he had been born – had two sons: a baby and a boy of three.
They also had two servants.[27] In the 1880s Kitty told a journalist how
she had woken one morning to find John at her door. She asked him
in Welsh where he had come from.

'With twinkling eyes, he replied: "Dw'i wedi dengid." ("I have escaped.") Since
daybreak, he had walked eight miles ... I washed his face and hands and then gave
him a good breakfast. During the rest of the day he played about the place with
his cousins. That night I put him to bed with one of my boys. Late that night,' con-

tinued Mrs Parry, 'his uncle Moses came home and I told him that his sister, Betsy's little boy was in bed upstairs. Moses was on bad terms with his sister, and he ordered me to send him back to St Asaph in the morning.'[28]

Moses was a respectable tradesman, and the feckless Elizabeth with her four illegitimate children was not the kind of sister who would help anyone's business, but his mother's promiscuity was not John's fault. He had spent a happy day and night in an ordinary home and witnessed the natural affection between a mother and her sons. Yet his prosperous uncle sent him back to the workhouse in the name of respectability. Years later, a tugboat skipper who had been at St Asaph with Stanley wrote to him saying that he well recalled the morning when he came back from his cousins' house in a state of collapse. John Rowlands's prostration had been due to his forcible return to a loveless institution, after having been part, albeit briefly, of an ordinary family.[29]

So how did John finally get free of the workhouse? In the discharge book, it is stated that he left St Asaph on 13 May 1856, and the entry reads: 'Gone to his uncle at the National School, Holywell.'[30] Although this was wrong – since he went to his cousin, who was the schoolmaster at nearby Brynford – the entry suggests that before he left the workhouse a plan had been made for him to become a trainee teacher. In his fantasy of escape from the workhouse after administering a beating to his master, Stanley claimed to have run away with a boy called Mose. In due course, Mose and John, in the fictitious account published in the *Autobiography*, arrive at the house of Mose's mother. Stanley's account of their welcome reveals his own keenest desire at the age of fifteen.

When Mose crossed the threshold, he was received with a resounding kiss, and became the object of copious endearments. He was hugged convulsively in the maternal bosom, patted on the back, his hair was frizzled by maternal fingers, and I knew not whether the mother was weeping or laughing, for tears poured over smiles in streams. The exhibition of fond love was not without its effect on me, for I learned how a mother should behave to her boy.[31]

At the time of this imagined homecoming, John's own mother was giving birth to her fifth illegitimate child, James – the second son fathered by Robert Jones, the local plasterer who would become her husband in 1860.[32]

Given his mother's promiscuity, there is no certainty about the identity of Stanley's father. He himself believed him to have been John

Rowlands, junior, of Llys (son of John Rowlands, senior, of Llys, who owned a farm outside Denbigh). Indeed John, junior, is named in church records as the father of John, who is described as the bastard son of himself and Elizabeth Parry.[33] In 1886, Stanley's mother, Elizabeth, would tell the Welsh journalist Owen 'Morien' Morgan that John Rowlands, junior, had died at about the time of Stanley's birth – whereas in fact, as Elizabeth had known well, he survived for a further thirteen years.[34] Despite this, she had also told her son John that his father had died in 1841.[35] So why did Elizabeth Parry lie to her son? Plainly, she must have wanted to stop him seeing, or even contacting, his supposed father, as he would have done at once had he known that he was alive. But considering her desperate financial difficulties, and the fact that John Rowlands, senior, was prosperous, it is surely very surprising that Elizabeth did nothing to secure his financial help – if only to keep her firstborn out of the workhouse.

Of course, if John Rowlands was *not* Stanley's father, it is at once apparent why Elizabeth should have told her son that his 'father' had died years ago. Elizabeth's puzzling reticence about John Rowlands, junior, lends significant weight to a well-attested local belief that Stanley's father had really been a Denbigh solicitor, James Vaughan Horne. The Horne theory gains strength from the fact that it was, and is, believed in by the descendants of a tight-knit group of professional people – mainly fellow lawyers – ideally placed to have known the personal habits of the man. Logic suggests that Elizabeth's most potent reason for telling that lie to Stanley – about his father being dead when he was very much alive – would have been her fear that the drunken John Rowlands, junior, would have told her son John the truth about James Horne (who has been said to have paid John Rowlands, junior, to accept paternity). In my opinion the balance of probability favours James Horne as Stanley's father[36] [see this note for further evidence]. Unfortunately, Horne and his wife had no children within wedlock, and his only relation was a childless sister. So the paternity conundrum cannot be discussed with any descendants, and no daguerreotypes, miniatures, or even amateur drawings of the elusive Mr Horne have survived to show a possible resemblance to the adult Stanley.[37]

To young John's immense relief, one member of his family was prepared to help him when he left the workhouse. Fortunately, this particular relation offered a better chance of self-improvement than John would have gained from living with any of the others. In 1856, Moses Owen, the second son of Elizabeth Parry's widowed sister, Mary, stood out as a remarkable twenty-year-old.[38] After taking an honours degree at University College, Bangor, he had at once been appointed headmaster of the National School at Brynford, near Holywell. A house went with the job, as did a housekeeper. Although Moses was a prim and didactic young man, he was generous too, and the fifteen-year-old John learned a great deal from him, particularly in mathematics and literature. Every day, Moses tutored his cousin for several hours after school.[39] Thanks to Moses' small library, John learned how to use books for research purposes.[40] Without these skills acquired at Brynford, he might never have possessed the confidence needed to seize his chances in journalism ten years later.

Moses' ambitious mother, Mary Owen, believed he would spoil his marriage prospects by harbouring his feckless aunt's bastard son. Her nagging soon started to affect the young head teacher's treatment of his teenage cousin. Often young John went to bed in tears after being accused of being 'good for nothing but to cobble pauper's boots'.[41] Then the pupils at the school mocked him for his 'ignoble origins'. As Stanley recalled: 'The effect of it was to drive me within my own shell,' to feel 'forever banned by having been an inmate of the workhouse'.[42] It is difficult to grasp today exactly how disgraceful illegitimacy and living in a workhouse were thought to be in the nineteenth century.

One day, a teacher called Hughes found John reading Dr Johnson's short novel *Rasselas*.[43] There is something terribly poignant about the workhouse boy reading this book with its theme of the vanity of all human wishes. Rasselas, mythical Prince of Abyssinia, has been reared in the 'Happy Valley' where his every wish has been granted. So he becomes desperate to escape his boredom and find new pleasures in the outside world. Instead of happiness, he finds disappointment. Johnson suggests that it is our ability to imagine a richer, happier life that causes our unhappiness by making us long for what we have not got. Rasselas returns chastened to the 'Happy Valley' to learn to be satisfied with his old life. Stanley could not have enjoyed this ending. If anywhere was going to offer *him* happiness, it was going to be the outside world rather than where he had come from.

At the end of nine months, John's cousin Moses sent his young pupil teacher for a break to Fynnon Beuno, the small farmhouse six miles north-east of Denbigh that was run by his mother, Mary Owen, who had some cows, sheep and pigs, and brewed beer for her own tavern. Stanley believed that Moses would never invite him to return, and he was right. But he knew and liked the farm, having worked there for a month on leaving the workhouse. This earlier stay had enabled him to earn enough money to pay for some new clothes to replace his workhouse uniform. His aunt Mary had arranged for him to be photographed in his new suit, and this picture – the first ever taken of him – is remarkable. The future Henry Stanley's expression is one that would remain characteristic for the rest of his life and combines extraordinary determination, with vulnerability and unhappiness – the mouth turned down, the lips compressed, the eyes unusually piercing, especially the left, and his whole posture awkward and yet at the same time somehow defiant in his ill-fitting Eton collar and tight waistcoat. In fact Stanley was a little podgy, a problem that would afflict him on and off over the years. The chairman of the workhouse board, Captain Leigh Thomas, had upset him once by suggesting, tongue in cheek, that 'it would be of vast benefit' to him if he 'were put under a garden roller'.[44] A sense of humour was not yet among Stanley's attributes. But to date his life had given him little to laugh about.

He had not been long at Fynnon Beuno (St Beuno's Well), in the hamlet of Tremeirchion, when he realized that his recently widowed aunt Mary meant to get rid of him after a few months. If she had ever shown him any affection, he wrote later: 'I should have become too home-loving ever to leave ... I would have served my aunt for years, for a mere smile, but she had not interest enough in me to study my disposition, or to suspect that the silent boy with a somewhat dogged look could be so touched by emotion.'[45] John did not want to leave. He was content to mow, plough, shear sheep and mix pigswill, and he also became fond of the bleak surrounding hills and enjoyed driving out the cows to 'Craig Fawr', a rocky outcrop affording views of Denbigh.

While at Brynford, John had read Robert Browning's recently published poem 'Childe Roland to the Dark Tower Came' and had been overwhelmed by it. Out on 'Craig Fawr', or wandering among the windswept hills, he imagined being Childe Roland, the legendary knight of Charlemagne, as he set out on an impossible quest. The Roland of the poem is, like John himself, depressed and fearful of the future. His old companions have let him down, and now everything is up to him, though his chances of success on his military mission are poor. He cannot go back, so he must let go of his past and press on into the unknown. He is a man whose great destiny may also be his doom. The poem's mix of pathos, self-dramatizing whistling in the wind and genuine nobility held great appeal for the troubled adolescent. It ends with Roland raising his famous horn to his lips and preparing to charge, though death looks sure to follow. A decade later, Stanley would write about the importance of this poem to his developing psyche in a series of letters to his first significant girlfriend. The fact that Roland was so close to his own surname, Rowlands, would have added to the mystique of the poem.[46]

To get rid of the unwanted boy, Aunt Mary now enlisted the help of her older sister, Maria Morris, who lived in Liverpool. Maria delighted Mary by announcing that her husband, Tom, knew the manager of a Liverpool insurance office, who would definitely be able to offer work to John. Mary now instructed her nephew to write a grovelling letter to his uncle in case he failed to come up with a firm invitation to Liverpool. John began by apologizing in case he had displeased Tom Morris in any way (though it is hard to imagine how he could have done) and told him about his aunt's and his anxiety. 'Dearest Uncle, I sue to you for kindness. I have nowhere to go unless I procure a place ... Hoping sincerely you will return me an answer by return of post. I shall feel extremely obliged to you, so I remain, Your very humble nephew, John Rowlands.'[47] His uncle Tom, a soft-hearted man, wrote back swiftly, summoning him to Liverpool. The plan was that he should arrive there in a month's time, in August 1858.

Though John was relieved that the uncertainty was over, when the moment to leave finally came he felt nostalgic and emotional. He had spent his entire life at one end or other of the beautiful Vale of Clwyd, and it was his attachment to the landscape, rather than to his aunt and cousins, that made the leaving difficult. Years later, he quoted Wordsworth to explain:

'... The hills,
Which were his living being, even more
Than his own blood ... had laid
Strong hold upon his affections ...'[48]

But like Childe Roland, the seventeen-year-old knew that he had to be bold and leave. From his first sight of Liverpool, as he stood on the deck of the packet steamer, John was dazed by 'the masses of houses, immensely tall chimneys, towers, lengths of walls, and groves of ships' masts'. The press of drays, carts and carriages in the streets, and the grinding sound of their metal wheels, were all new to him. His aunt Mary escorted the future explorer through the teeming city, and before parting gave him a guinea, with the words: 'Be a good boy and make haste to get rich.'[49]

Initially, John found greater kindness in the back streets of Liverpool, living with the Morris family, than he had at Fynnon Bueno.[50] He liked his bluff and hearty uncle and, to start with, had few problems with his younger cousins. But his genial uncle was overextended. He had been a railway official, but for some reason never explained had lost his job and now earned a pound a week checking cotton bales. When Uncle Tom's insurance contact failed to produce the hoped-for job, Aunt Maria asked her nephew for his suit and his overcoat so they could be pawned. She also took the guinea he had been given by his aunt Mary. John was left with no illusions about the straitened circumstances of his hosts.

After tramping the streets for days, he found a job as a shop boy in a haberdasher's, trimming lamps, sweeping floors and polishing windows from seven in the morning till nine at night. A week of illness cost him this job. And now he could contribute nothing to the family's expenses. As hungry for affection as ever, Stanley was disillusioned to find that even bluff Uncle Tom was cooling towards him. After more weeks of tramping, Stanley found work as a butcher's boy in a street close to Brambley Moor Dock. 'It was then,' he recalled later, 'that I came across the bold sailor-boys, young middies, gorgeous in brass buttons, whose jaunty air of hardihood took my admiration captive.' Delivering meat to ships in the docks, he 'marvelled at their lines and size and read with feelings verging on awe the names *Blue Jacket ... Pocohontas, Sovereign of the Seas*. The perfume of strange products hung about them. Out of their vast holds came coloured grain, bales of silks ... hogsheads, barrels, boxes, sacks.'

One day John delivered meat to an American packet ship, the *Windermere*, 1,107 tons, registered at the port of Boston. The captain, David Harding, invited him into his cabin and showed him its fine furnishings and gilded mirrors. Harding promised John five dollars a month and a new outfit if he joined the ship's company as a cabin boy. Numerous other boys before him had been lured by the same bait, only to endure such terrible treatment on their passage that they deserted at the first American port, enabling the captain to pocket their wages. Knowing nothing of this, the butcher's boy accepted the offer.[51]

Although John felt again the terror of impending change, he was on the verge of making one of the bravest and most crucial decisions of his life. Even when his aunt and uncle tried to dissuade him, he refused to change his mind. He could not bear to continue his 'slavish dependence on relatives who could scarcely support themselves'.[52]

A few days before Christmas 1858, a month before his eighteenth birthday, John gazed back at Liverpool from the foredeck of the *Windermere* as she was towed out from the docks into the river Mersey through flurries of snow.

TWO

In the Name of the Father

Two days after the *Windermere* docked in New Orleans in February 1859, after a passage of seven weeks, John Rowlands 'jumped ship', having been outraged to be treated not as the cabin boy he had signed on to be, but as the lowest deckhand. When the ship was tied up alongside the famous levee (the principal flat-topped embankment that extended along the river acting as a dike and quay), John strode ashore and was filled with the 'blissful feeling that rises from emancipation ... at last the boy was free!'[1] In the workhouse, and then at Fynnon Beuno, he had known 'scarcely an hour free from the supervision of someone'. But America was different. 'For the first time I was addressed as a reasonable being ... We seemed to stand in the relation of youth to age, not as pupil or servant ... The only difference between us was of years.' In New Orleans, he wrote later, 'I felt that my person was sacred & inviolable.'[2]

This democratic sense of the value of everyone (at this date, provided their skin was white) was America's great gift to him, easing the humiliation of having occupied, as a workhouse bastard, the lowest conceivable position in a society worshipping rank and class. Between 1820 and 1860 more than half a million people came from Europe as immigrants to New Orleans. Many continued on up the Mississippi to the interior, but enough settled in the city to ensure that the majority of its citizens were foreign born. Because very few claimed their social standing by right of birth or length of residence, newcomers were accepted without many questions asked.

After spending his first night ashore in the open air on some bales of cotton, John walked along the waterfront past immense warehouses smelling of fermenting molasses, green coffee and Stockholm tar.

What happened next is debatable, and I will give what I believe is a true version of events, after repeating Stanley's account, given in Chapter Four of his *Autobiography*. This starts with him suddenly spotting a man in a dark alpaca suit and a tall hat, sitting outside a wholesale store and warehouse, near the Custom House. This genial-looking man was reading a newspaper, and his name, John claimed later, was Henry Stanley. Needing work to feed and house himself, John came to the point with Oliver Twist-like succinctness: 'Do you want a boy, sir?' The man in the tall hat asked him to read a few lines from his newspaper, and then to mark some letters on a sack with a paintbrush. Having passed this simple literacy test, John was introduced by Mr Stanley to his friend James Speake, in front of whose business premises he (Henry Stanley) had just been sitting. On Mr Stanley's recommendation, Mr Speake offered Rowlands a job as a clerk at five dollars a week.[3] Soon afterwards, the *Autobiography* account has Henry Stanley leaving New Orleans on a month's business trip up the Mississippi. In the meantime, John spent his days taking groceries on trolleys from the depths of the store to the sidewalk, or rolling barrels of flour or liquor to the quayside where he marked them for shipment to sundry Mississippi ports. At the end of his week's trial, he was engaged at twenty-five dollars a month, and would prove himself a model employee – never arguing or contradicting, and on one occasion exposing the petty thefts of two slaves. His salary would soon be raised by another five dollars.[4]

According to the *Autobiography*, Henry Stanley had 'a desk in the store, which he made use of when in town, and did a good deal of business in produce both with Mr Speake and other wholesale merchants'.[5] The next time John saw him, Mr Stanley invited him to call at St Charles Street, where he lived with his beautiful young wife in a highly respectable boarding house with pillared porticoes and cool verandas. It was evident to John Rowlands that Mr Stanley was a rich and successful businessman. But the real revelation was Mrs Stanley. Her refinement captivated John – in fact, he wrote, 'kindled as much reverence as I ever felt in my life'. In Mr and Mrs Stanley's rooms, the *Autobiography* has John hearing, for the first time, well-informed conversation on politics, literature and other subjects.[6]

Just when John's new life in America seemed to be progressing so well, an epidemic of yellow fever and dysentery visited New Orleans. One of the victims was James Speake (John Rowlands's employer) who died in October 1859, eight months after John had started working for him. According to the *Autobiography*, Mrs Stanley also succumbed while Mr Stanley was said to have been absent on business in St Louis. The beautiful woman's last words to John were just what he might have wished an ideal surrogate mother to breathe to him at the end: 'Be a good boy. God bless you!'[7]

After James Speake's death, his widow sold the business, and left for Louisville with her two daughters, never to be seen again – at least by Rowlands, who was now out of a job. He acted as paid carer to an ailing sea captain for a few weeks, and later, failing to find any work beyond odd jobs, decided to ask Mr Stanley's aid. Although the rich businessman had made no effort to find his young protégé, he seemed deeply moved to see John when he turned up in St Charles Street. Not many days later – or so it is stated in the *Autobiography* – Mr Stanley declared that he wanted to make himself responsible for John's future. This was the moment John had dreamt of in the workhouse – a rich and cultivated man declares himself ready to be his father, and embraces him. Yet that was not the end of it; Henry Stanley, having once been a religious minister, enacted a quasi-Christian ritual of adoption, re-baptizing John Rowlands with water and the sign of the cross, and telling him: 'in future you are to bear my name, "Henry Stanley".'[8]

After this life-changing event, young Henry claimed that he travelled for two years with his father on riverboats between New Orleans, St Louis and Louisville, and more frequently on the lower Mississippi tributaries. Henry Stanley is described in the *Autobiography* as 'a kind of [cotton] broker who dealt between planters up-river and merchants in New Orleans'.[9] But, strangely, Mr Stanley's plans for his new son's future career did not involve cotton or its transport. Instead, unaccountably, all this voyaging was said to be preparing the former John Rowlands for a life among these up-river planters as the owner of a country store at Pine Bluff on the Arkansas River – a place 400 miles away from New Orleans by river.

In September 1860, it is claimed that Mr Stanley left young Henry to serve a kind of apprenticeship with a landowner friend in Saline County, Arkansas. Then Mr Stanley left for Havana where his brother was said to be dangerously ill. About eight months later – say, June 1861 – young Henry, by now living and clerking in a store at Cypress Bend, learned that his 'father' had died suddenly in Cuba. Later still, he heard that no provision had been made for him, and that he was once more on his own.[10]

If only because of his long-standing desire to find a new family, John's adoption by Mr Stanley can only set alarm bells ringing. As late as the 1890s, the fifty-year-old Stanley would write of how often he had thought, during childhood, 'What ecstasy it would be if my parent came to me, to offer a parent's love, as I had enviously seen it bestowed on other children.'[11] Indeed, the 'adoption narrative' has the quality of a fairy tale in real life – a heart-warming sense that even lives afflicted by the worst privations and unhappiness can change for the better by a happy chance, dealing out rewards commensurate with the deserts of those who have hitherto been unfairly disadvantaged. So what really happened to John Rowlands in New Orleans? Of Stanley's recent biographers, John Bierman gives the most realistic assessment of the 'adoption'. He rules it out and concludes: 'Mr Stanley did, indeed, take an interest in the young Rowlands, but it was not nearly so intense an interest as the lad had hoped for.'[12] But even this, in my opinion, misses the mark. Because what truly happened in New Orleans is essential for forming an understanding of the man who emerged as Henry Morton Stanley, I mean to lay out some of the evidence.

I first suspected that John Rowlands had never met anyone called Mr Stanley because there are so many discrepancies between the accounts of his adoption given by him verbally to his relatives in late December 1866, and the marvellously detailed draft chapters he wrote in the mid-1890s for his *Autobiography*, not long before he finally abandoned the whole project. In 1866, when aged twenty-five, John Rowlands would describe the man he had met at the grocery store on that first morning after he had 'jumped ship' as having been encountered *inside*, rather than *outside*, and not wearing a tall hat and alpaca suit. In reality nobody had been sitting outside the store. So John, who had in fact seen a sign on the door bearing the words 'Boy Wanted', had entered and asked a bespectacled man, whom he found deep in the store, whether he might have a job. 'The shopkeeper', John Rowlands told his mother in 1866, gave him a literacy test and then employed him. After that, 'he was treated always by that shopkeeper with every kindness, and he adopted his name as his own. The shopkeeper was elderly, childless, and his relatives became fiercely jealous of the little Welsh boy.' John did not tell his family that the real name of this man was James Speake. Instead, he told them he was a Mr Henry Stanley. John claimed that after he had spent several years with him, Mr Stanley dropped down dead, without having made a will.

This story was told to the Welsh journalist Owen 'Morien' Morgan, in 1886, by Stanley's mother, Elizabeth Jones (née Parry), shortly before her death.[13] She had relayed it almost verbatim in 1872 to the author and publisher John Camden Hotten, who quoted her at length in that same year in his *Henry M. Stanley: the Story of his Life*, issued under the insinuating pseudonym of Cadwalader Rowlands.[14] These almost identical versions of the adoption story would be lifted, in later years, from Owen Morgan's newspaper accounts, and from John Hotten's book, by the authors of many different lives of Stanley that began to appear from 1890 onwards.[15]

So, instead of feeling that he could abandon the untruths that he had told his family as a young man, Stanley in his maturity would feel compelled to repeat them in his *Autobiography* manuscript and to iron out their many inconsistencies. He therefore changed his earlier claim that there had been one man responsible for both employing *and* adopting him. Even in the 1890s there had been too many people still alive in New Orleans who knew that James Speake, of Speake & McCreary's store, had been John Rowlands's first employer for it to have been safe for the great explorer to claim that he had worked for Mr Henry Stanley.[16] To get round this problem, Stanley in his 1890s manuscript claimed that Speake had been his employer, and Mr Stanley had been Speake's close friend, with an office desk in the shop. In this clever scenario, Speake maintained a role in John's life, but Mr Stanley became his original benefactor. It was a most attractive solution to the problem of how to give Speake – his real benefactor – some credit for helping him too.

But was there any truth in it? Did Mr Stanley often come to Speake's store and do business there? It seems very unlikely. There was only one Henry Stanley in the cotton trade in New Orleans at this date: Henry Hope Stanley, who had the controlling interest in the largest company in town compressing and baling raw cotton mechanically, and who was also the lessee of six shipping wharves with offices in Exchange Place. For two reasons this made him a most improbable candidate for having a desk in a grocer's store. In the first place, his extraordinarily lucrative business, and Speake's more mundane one, were very different; and in the second, Mr Stanley's offices at 24, Exchange Place were only three blocks away from Speake's store at 3, Tchoupitoulas Street – so why should he have needed a desk there?[17] That Speake was only a wholesale grocer is recorded in Charles Gardner's *New Orleans City Directory*. So, even if he sold produce for other suppliers on commission, this would not have made him a credible business partner for a real entrepreneur like Mr Stanley. In reality, James Speake had been the *only* person who treated Rowlands well – employing him, giving him promotion and agreeing two raises in salary, and suggesting to him that, if he wanted to get on in life, he should aim to open a store on the Arkansas River.[18]

Before John Rowlands chose to claim as his adoptive father the richer and much more influential Henry Hope Stanley, whom he had heard about only by repute, he had been thinking of casting the humbler Speake in that role. Very revealingly, Henry Morton Stanley wrote in his large diary for 15 October 1895, when visiting New Orleans for the last time: 'Father's house is between Common [Street] and Canal St – No. 3 ...' But this was not where Henry Hope Stanley, his supposed adoptive father, had lived. On the same day, he wrote truthfully in a small notebook: 'Speake's house was between Common & Canal St – No. 3 ...' James Speake's store and dwelling were indeed at 3, Tchoupitoulas Street, which is in the block 'between Canal Street and Common Street'.

Among Henry M. Stanley's earlier drafts of the *Autobiography* is a touching passage entitled 'Death of father', in which he stares at the dead man's face – he never names him – and asks himself whether he had behaved to him as well as he ought to have done. Then, 'a craving wish to hear him speak but one word of consolation, to utter one word of blessing made me address him as if he might hear, but no answer ever came and I experienced a shiver of sadness, & then wished that I could join him.'[19] Nothing identifies this effecting piece with Mr Stanley – though it has been said to be a description of his invented death, proving that the writer suffered from serious neurosis.[20] But it seems to me much more likely to be a description from life of an actual corpse, and John's intense feelings towards a real man who had just died. Indeed, James Speake had done exactly that while John Rowlands was still working for him. That was in late October 1859. One indication that John's relationship with Speake had been close enough for him to have written a moving piece about his death is the fact that Speake's widow, Cornelia, asked John Rowlands to watch over her husband's body for the whole night prior to his funeral – surely a most unusual privilege for any ordinary employee.

While Henry Morton Stanley never knew where Henry Hope Stanley's grave was, he knew exactly where Speake was interred, having been present at the burial. In fact, he revisited the grave in October 1895 as a matter of personal sentiment. James Speake seems to have been the only man, from that period of his life, whom he truly mourned.[21] This contrasts with his attitude towards the alleged death of the rich cotton broker. In the *Autobiography*, H. M. Stanley claimed to have been overwhelmed with grief at parting from his new 'father' but, unaccountably, he did not describe his emotions on hearing about the man's death – an event that his early versions of the adoption story had all included. In his first and original manuscript of the *Autobiography* he had not mentioned the death either, but his widow, Dorothy, added in her own hand, writing as if she were her late husband: 'He died quite suddenly in 1861 – I only heard of his death long after.'[22] In fairness to her, this may have been what Stanley had always told her had happened in 1861 – although the real Mr Stanley would not die until 1878. If John Rowlands had only been satisfied to have been highly regarded, and even loved by the humble James Speake, and had not surrendered to his tormenting insecurity and substituted a more impressive man, his true account of this period of his life would have moved everyone who read about it.

The fact that James Speake was John Rowlands's only benefactor is proved beyond doubt partly by the contents of the earliest discarded drafts of the *Autobiography*[23] [see this note for examples], and partly by H. M. Stanley's extraordinary mistakes and omissions in describing his 'adoptive' family. Mr Stanley's second forename, Hope, is never mentioned by him, nor did he ever record that the unforgettable Mrs Stanley was called Frances, and was Henry Hope Stanley's second wife, and had been a Miss Miller from Cheshire, in England, and had been only fifteen when she met and married Mr Stanley in 1847.[24] Nor is it stated anywhere that Mr Stanley also came from Cheshire – surely a noteworthy fact, being so close to north Wales – and had remained a British subject. When describing Mr Stanley as childless – which was strictly true, since he had no natural children – it was strange not to mention that living with Mr and Mrs Stanley in 1859 was an adopted daughter, Annie, then aged thirteen[25] [see this note for further striking omissions]. If John Rowlands had really lived with Mr and Mrs Stanley, he would have known many of the above details and would have felt bound to include them in the draft manuscript of his *Autobiography* to give it verisimilitude. Furthermore, even if he had parted from the Stanleys after a bitter quarrel, as has been claimed by three of his most recent biographers,[26] some friend or relation of Henry Hope or Frances Stanley would have been bound to contact him – there being no difficulty about locating such a famous man – to tell him when they had died and where they were buried.

Both Frances and Henry Hope Stanley died in 1878, and not in 1859 and 1861 respectively, as was claimed in the *Autobiography*. So why did he tell this particular lie?[27] He killed off Mr and Mrs Stanley suddenly and prematurely, first to explain why he had not kept in touch with his adoptive parents after he left New Orleans; second, to explain why neither parent, both of whom had supposedly loved him, had found time to change their wills in his favour; and third, and most importantly, because these incorrect dates of death would prevent subsequent researchers from identifying *his* Henry Stanley with Henry *Hope* Stanley. Indeed, all the omissions of correct facts about Henry Hope Stanley must have been deliberate, enabling him, if relatives of Henry Hope Stanley should ever have challenged his claims to have lived with the cotton magnate, to say that he had lived with another Mr Stanley. This desire not to identify himself in any precise way with Henry Hope Stanley also explains why he claimed that *his* Henry Stanley had lived in a St Charles Street boarding house – although any street directory would have told him that Henry H. Stanley had lived at 904, Orange Street, opposite Annunciation Square.[28]

So how was it ever supposed that Stanley once lived in Orange Street, New Orleans, with his 'father' – something stated as fact in the most recent biography with any pretensions to being definitive? The idea derives from an anonymous article in the principal New Orleans newspaper, the *Daily Picayune* (28 December 1890), in which it was stated that Rowlands passed 'many days in play in hall and balcony and in the square', and that 'men who were children of the neighbourhood then, remembered him ...'. The author also stated that Rowlands and the Stanleys' adopted daughter, Annie, had played together as children at 904, Orange Street. This was repeated in an influential article in the *Roosevelt Review* in June 1944, and thereafter crept into most subsequent biographies.[29] But this must be wrong, since there is documentary census evidence to show that Rowlands could only have lived in Orange Street for six weeks in 1860, when he was nineteen years old – hardly the right age to be playing with 'children of the neighbourhood'.[30] Strangely, no author, or journalist, would remark, until the 1940s upon the very puzzling differences between the Henry Hope Stanley of the *Daily Picayune* and the Henry Stanley of the *Autobiography*.[31] Even when, in 1990, John Bierman expressed his scepticism about the extent and intensity of the relationship between Rowlands and Henry Hope Stanley, he did not question that there had been a genuine link between the two. I can only assume that this link has not been challenged until now because it seemed impossibly audacious for Rowlands to have appropriated another man's name and claimed a close relationship, not simply without his knowledge or consent, but without ever having known him.

Yet no one was harmed by the story. James Speake died before knowing that Rowlands had assumed the name of a stranger, rather than his own. Henry Hope Stanley had himself been dead a dozen years before any connection was made between him and Henry Morton Stanley and, as already noted, ten years before he died Stanley abandoned any idea of completing or publishing his *Autobiography*. If the first third of the book (which was all that he ever managed to complete) had remained unpublished – as he had imagined it would – the manuscript would have constituted private therapy, rather than public record. Yet his 'lies' have led his critics to treat him with disdain and condescension ever since. His private lies to his mother were made public by her without his knowledge, thus making it all but impossible for him to be honest later. Young people who lie usually do so because they feel bad about themselves and need to enhance their self-esteem. That Stanley should have been trapped for the whole of his life by what he had said to his mother during his twenties was a personal tragedy for him, and for his subsequent reputation.

The death of James Speake, in October 1859, was not only a great personal loss, but threw John out of work, without any means of support. Yet the reassurance he had gained from being praised by the good-natured storekeeper was not all lost.[32] Nor were his orderliness, and the phenomenal memory that had made him 'a walking inventory' of the store's contents, going to be anything but assets in the future.[33] However, the first work he found was not in a store but as assistant to the cook on a Mississippi riverboat. This job did not last long. According to the New Orleans census taken on 1 June 1860, a seventeen-year-old clerk called J. Rolling (a variant of Rowlands, and similar to John Rollins, the name by which several friends knew him) was living in a boarding house in St Thomas Street with various sailors and clerks. But he left again not long afterwards by riverboat for the Arkansas River, 400 miles to the north.[34] In St Louis, he had found nothing after ten days of constant tramping.

So he travelled on to Cypress Bend, fifty miles south of Little Rock. Here, he came to a decision, comparable in significance with the one he had made in Liverpool docks eighteen months earlier, at another low point in his life. In the *Autobiography*, he writes only a single sentence about arriving at Isaac Altschul's store for the first time: 'I had no sooner introduced myself than I was accepted by the family with all cordiality.'

It is a great shame that his commitment to his tale of a spurious adoption prevented him from writing an accurate account of this turning point in his life. In all probability this was the moment when he introduced himself as Stanley for the very first time. How do I know? Because he left New Orleans sometime in June or July calling himself Rowlands or Rollins, and arrived at Altschul's store about a month later. He was sleeping there on 22 August when a census taker called. Apart from listing the names of all the Altschuls, this official added the name of a seventeen-year-old clerk called William Henry Stanley. (In fact, Rowlands was nineteen but did not then know the date of his birth.)[35] William would be gone within a year, but Henry would survive – though Stanley would not add the 'M', as in Henry M. Stanley, until 1868 and would not finally settle on Morton until 1872, after trying, and abandoning, other names: Morelake, Morley, Moreland, etc., etc.[36]

What can have been John's feelings when he knocked on the storekeeper's door and gave, as his own surname, a name he had chosen for himself? He could hardly have guessed that, just ten years later, it would be famous throughout the world. By leaving Britain he had distanced himself from his illegitimacy and the grim world of his childhood. Now, by giving himself a new name, he felt that he was completing the process. If he hated the baggage of his past, why should he be condemned to carry it always? It had long been his desire to 'wash out the stains ugly poverty had impressed upon [his] person since infancy', and to rid himself 'of the odium attached to the old name and its dolorous history'.[37] To associate himself with the name of New Orleans's best-known cotton broker clearly appealed to him, as may have done the word's decisive sound. Yet not for half a dozen years would he fix on a story to tell people to account for his name-change. Many years later, a local female friend who had known John well in New Orleans was quoted in a local newspaper as saying that up to the time when he 'suddenly disappeared' from the city in mid-1860, he had been called John Rollins. This woman later moved to New York, and Stanley saw her there on several occasions during 1864, at which time he was calling himself Henry Stanley. She discovered this because the friend who came with him called him Henry. What she then told the journalist destroys any notion that the Stanley name was 'given' to Rowlands.

I asked him (Rollins) whether he had two names. He said no; but that his mother had recently married again, and that the name of her second husband was Henry Stanley, and that he had taken this name.

So in 1864, it is clear that Stanley was still experimenting with the details of the adoption story. The quality of the information this unnamed woman gave in a long article, entitled 'Stanley's Early Life', published in the New Orleans *Daily States* in mid-April 1891, proves beyond a shadow of a doubt that she had known John well.[38] As with many of Stanley's fictions, there was a grain of truth in what he said. His mother had indeed recently been married (in 1860), but for the first time, and not to a man called Stanley, but to one called Jones.

From the summer of 1860, while living in America, Rowlands would call himself Stanley, although when he paid brief visits to Wales in 1862 and 1866, he would revert to the Rowlands name. But at the very end of December 1866, when he was staying near St Asaph, at the public house kept by his mother, letters arrived addressed to him as Henry Stanley, and so he was rushed into telling the adoption lie that would entrap him forever – not just as an American (when that worked against him in England), but as a man who always feared any scrutiny of his past.

Because Henry was not his baptismal name, biographers after the name change have called him plain Stanley, without exception, all the time. I mean to call him Henry, as well as Stanley, from now on.

THREE

A Terrible Freedom

The country store where Henry worked from August 1860 was a riverside log cabin containing a combination of those things sold by gunsmiths, drapers, stationers and ironmongers. Mr Cronin, the Irish salesman, could talk the women from the back-country into buying almost anything, and his charm dazzled the envious Henry. However, Stanley learned from Cronin all there was to know about Ballard, Sharp and Jocelyn rifles, and the comparative merits of Colt and Smith & Wesson revolvers.

The local planters lived like princes, with power of life and limb over hundreds of slaves, and did not tolerate being checked by anyone. It shocked Henry, after the civilities of the city, to witness gunfights and to hear about murders and disappearances. With so many vain and violent men around him, possessing natures 'as sensitive as hair-triggers', he was careful not to argue with any backwoodsman or planter who might draw a gun on the least provocation. 'However amiable they might originally have been, their isolation had promoted the growth of egotism.' These southern 'gentlemen' talked endlessly about their 'honour' and often acted to avenge it. In this environment it was every man for himself. So, in case of trouble, Henry bought a Smith & Wesson revolver, and practised with it until he could 'sever a pack thread at twenty paces.'[1]

So what sort of a man was the nineteen-year-old Stanley when he arrived at Cypress Bend? In New Orleans, one female friend had described him as 'burly ... undersized, and yet well proportioned, and one of the smartest and biggest talkers I ever met'. Yet he became tongue-tied if ever asked about his family, typically muttering: 'There is a mystery about my birth.'[2] A Swiss clerk, Anton Schumacher, who worked at a doctor's surgery near Speake's store, had found Stanley friendly and sympathetic. Both young men were lonely, and together looked after a bulldog for an absent vet. They also shared their cigarettes and sweets. Schumacher recalled Stanley's 'melancholy look', his cleanliness, and his neat straw hat and check neckerchief.[3]

Unlike most young men living in boarding houses frequented by sailors, Stanley had avoided brothels. However, on one occasion only, he had been taken to 'a gilded parlour', where he saw 'four young ladies, in such scant clothing' that he was, he wrote, 'speechless with amazement ... When they proceeded to take liberties with my person, they seemed to me to be so appallingly wicked that I shook them off and fled ... My disgust was so great that I never, in after years, could overcome my repugnance to females of that character.'[4] Abandoned by a promiscuous mother, Henry's mistrust of prostitutes was not hypocritical. Another incident confirmed his sexual naivety. In his overcrowded boarding house, bed-sharing was not unusual. Once, Stanley slept in a four-poster with a youth called Dick Heaton, who had also jumped ship. Although Dick was 'so modest he would not retire by candle-light', and walked in a suspiciously female manner, Stanley only twigged 'his' true sex at the end of three days.[5] Dick was no fantasy figure, indicative of sexual ambiguity, but was real enough to be mentioned in a letter written to Stanley by a friend from his New Orleans days.[6]

Although Stanley would say that his trusting nature had inclined him to obey authority, he also had a rebellious streak. So this sexual innocent and teetotaller, who had brought to America a Bible he had been awarded by the Bishop of St Asaph as a prize for good conduct, was hard to fathom. 'Self-willed, uncompromising, deep', he had been called by a teacher at Brynford in Wales.[7] And he was all those things, as well as innocent and sensitive.

At Cypress Bend, Henry first suffered from malaria – about three attacks a month – and despite taking quinine, his weight was soon a puny ninety-five pounds. This did not stop Mr Altschul sending him out to collect bad debts – a dangerous duty. But greater danger was looming, as he learned from Dan Goree, the son of the store's most important customer. According to Dan, 'the election of Abe Lincoln, in November previous, had created a hostile feeling in the South, because this man had declared himself opposed to slavery; and as soon as he became President in March, he would do all in his power to free the slaves. Of course, said he, in that event all slave-holders would be ruined.' Dan predicted that the South would fight to stop men like his father being robbed. Dr James L. Goree was a medical doctor, who, besides his practice, also owned a plantation, and 120 slaves worth from $500 to $1,200 a head. In May 1861, Arkansas seceded from the Union, joining other Southern states.[8] The North's seizure of the forts at the mouth of the Mississippi persuaded Henry that a blockade would ruin a riverside shop boy like himself, just as it would a plantation owner. Though Henry expressed no revulsion towards slavery in the Deep South – which was legal and accepted by everyone he knew – he was not prejudiced against black people. Indeed, he had lived in a New Orleans boarding house that was owned by a freed black woman and had been recommended to him by two of James Speake's slaves.[9]

A frenzied desire to fight the 'Yankees' inflamed most of the young men Stanley knew – and most of the young women urged them on. Many customers of the store joined up after Captain Samuel G. Smith raised a local company called the 'Dixie Grays'. Because Henry felt the quarrel was not really his, and was puzzled that whites meant to fight one another over the rights of blacks, he did not enlist. But on receiving, in a parcel, 'a chemise and petticoat, such as a negro lady's-maid might wear', he felt compelled to act, not least because suspecting that the sender was one of Dr Goree's beautiful daughters. Later, he would think his standing on his 'honour' a ludicrous mistake. But in 1861 'it was far from being a laughing matter' to be called a coward.[10] Overwhelmed by his old insecurity, on 1 June 1861 Henry enlisted as a private soldier under the name of William H. Stanley. Confederate records state that he was a member of Captain Smith's company, the Dixie Grays, when it was mustered into the 6th Arkansas Infantry at Pocahontas, near Little Rock, on 26 July. Stanley's account of the war, when tested against contemporary accounts and the records of individual soldiers mentioned by him, proves to be remarkably accurate.[11]

Henry's military career started in Little Rock in early August with bands playing and crowds cheering. 'We raised the song, "We'll live and die for Dixie," and the emotional girls waved their handkerchiefs and wept … The facets of light on our shining muskets and bayonets were blinding … We strode down to the levee with "eyes front," after the manner of Romans when reviewed by their tribunes!' Only days later, the straps of Henry's kit bit into his flesh, and his feet became so sore and blistered that he was compelled to rest at the roadside before limping after the column. A diet of fried, or raw, bacon and horse-beans made men ill, as did the heat and lack of shelter on the 600-mile march to Columbus. It was not long before 'the poetry of the military profession had departed under the stress of … squalid camp life'. Yet though regretting his folly in devoting himself 'to be food for powder', Stanley was determined to do his duty because he loved his 'Southern friends'.[12]

The 6th Arkansas Infantry arrived at Corinth, Tennessee, on 25 March 1862. Private William H. Stanley was about to fight in the most significant engagement of the war to date – the Battle of Shiloh. General Ulysses S. Grant and almost 50,000 Federal troops were held up at Pittsburgh Landing, on the Tennessee River, awaiting the arrival of reinforcements before they marched on Corinth. General Albert S. Johnston decided to attack Grant before he was reinforced, and marched his 40,000 men out of Corinth on 4 April.

Shortly before dawn on the 6th, the Confederate army prepared to hurl the Federals into the Tennessee River. The 6th Arkansas Infantry were deployed at the centre of a three-mile line, advancing through thin woods. Alongside Stanley, his seventeen-year-old friend Henry Parker put some violets in his cap, hoping that the enemy would take this for a sign of peace and not kill him. Stanley placed flowers in his own cap too. The Dixie Grays were armed with obsolete muzzle-loading flintlocks, much inferior to the Union soldiers' Minié and Enfield rifles. In the grey morning light, the Dixies blundered into the enemy line.

I tried hard to see some living thing to shoot at, for it seemed absurd to be blazing away at shadows … at last I saw a row of little globes of pearly smoke streaked with crimson, breaking out … from a long line of bluey [sic] figures in front … After a steady exchange of musketry, which lasted some time, we heard the order: 'Fix bayonets! On the double-quick!' … The Federals appeared inclined to await us; but, at this juncture, our men raised a yell … It drove all sanity and order from among us.

The Dixie Grays charged through the tented camp of their adversaries, killing men who had just woken and were still half-dressed.

As the light grew brighter, Henry saw more tents ahead. Bullets hummed past him, and men began to drop. An officer yelled at them to get down. As Stanley heard 'the patter, snip, thud and hum of the bullets', it amazed him that anyone could live 'under this raining death'. He turned to the man beside him 'and saw that a bullet had gored his whole face, and penetrated into his chest. Another ball struck another man a deadly rap on the head, and he turned on his back and showed his ghastly white face to the sky.' Stanley heard

a boy's voice cry out: 'Oh, stop, *please* stop a bit, I have been hurt, and can't move.' Henry Parker, with the violets in his cap, was staring at his smashed and bleeding foot. Newton Story, a regular at the store, strode forward waving the Dixies' banner, and called out, 'Why don't you come on boys? You see there is no danger!' His smile and words acted on us like magic.

A quarter of the men in the Confederate army were under twenty years old.

Although the Dixie Grays, and their neighbouring regiments, captured the second Federal line, they could not drive their enemies into the river. The sun was up by now, and Stanley would never forget what he saw. One dead face had upon it 'a look similar to the fixed wondering gaze of an infant'. It shocked Stanley 'that the [human] form we made so much of should now be mutilated, hacked and outraged; and that life, hitherto guarded as a sacred thing ... should be given up to death'. Everywhere he could smell blood. 'I cannot forget that half-mile square of woodland.' The thousand or so dead were buried in long trenches, side by side, 'all their individual hopes, pride, honour, names, buried under oblivious earth'. Among the dead was General Albert S. Johnston, commander-in-chief of the Confederate army.[13]

Next day, as the fighting was starting, Henry's pride was stung when Captain Smith called out: 'Now, Mr Stanley, if you please, step briskly forward!' This made Henry rush forward 'like a rocket'. He was not alone. Colonel Thomas C. Hindman's brigade, which included the Dixie Grays, and a brigade to their left, advanced too far and were outflanked before being broken up in hand-to-hand fighting. During this brutal process, Henry became cut off from his companions and was captured.[14]

First he was taken to St Louis, and then by railroad car to Camp Douglas on the outskirts of Chicago, and confined in a huge cattle shed where he slept on a wooden plank bed. The battle's outcome would filter through to him in time. The Federals had been pushed back three miles but not as far as the river. Of General Grant's five divisions, one no longer existed, and four had received a mauling, but he had been reinforced by 20,000 fresh troops. So Grant gave no ground on the second day. Consequently, General P. G. T. Beauregard (Johnston's successor) had to withdraw to Corinth. The Union had

13,047 casualties and the Confederates 11,694 in two days' fighting. The dead were shared equally and amounted to more than 3,500. Brought up on the Ten Commandments, Stanley was shaken to hear killing loudly applauded. But this was war, and there was nothing to be done. The Battle of Shiloh gave warning that the Confederacy in the West would soon be defeated – though three years of fighting lay ahead in the East. One letter survives from a soldier who fought alongside Stanley. He was Private James Slate, and after the battle he regretted seeing 'our boyish-looking Stanley no more'. 'We all loved you,' he wrote, explaining that his personal gratitude was because 'you have wrote many letters for me'.[15]

In Henry's first week at Camp Douglas almost 220 of the 8,000 prisoners in the camp, died of dysentery and typhoid.[16] Each day Stanley watched the dead rolled in their blankets and 'piled one upon another, as the New Zealand frozen-mutton carcases are carted from the docks'. The vermin, the stench of the latrines and the constant fear of falling sick filled Henry with a sense that 'we were simply doomed'.

A contemporary drawing of Camp Douglas

He did not blame the camp commandant, Colonel James A. Mulligan, or the civil commissioner of the camp, Mr Shipman, for the deaths, and later admitted that he and other Confederate prisoners were better fed than Union prisoners were in Southern camps.[17] After Stanley had been at Camp Douglas a few days, the apparently kindly Mr Shipman told him, and a few other prisoners, that they would be released if they agreed to become Union soldiers. Why stay, and risk dying of disease, when the South's cause was morally rotten? Despite the continuing deaths, Henry held out for six weeks before changing sides. He had been through hell with his fellow Southerners and felt disloyal. But as a foreigner embroiled in the war by chance, and having little understanding of the conflict's true significance, Stanley's behaviour was not unforgivable. To save his life, as he saw it, he enrolled in the Union's Artillery service on 4 June 1862.[18]

There has been some dispute about whether Stanley was ever at Camp Douglas, or ever joined the Union army.[19] However, the records of the Adjutant General's Office in the National Archives in Washington confirm his capture at Shiloh, his imprisonment at Camp Douglas, Illinois, and his enlistment for three years in the 1st Illinois Light Artillery, 'L' Battery. Federal records also show that he dropped the forename William while a prisoner in Camp Douglas, since he enlisted in the artillery as Private H. Stanley. Henry gave his age as twenty-two, his height five foot six, his eyes light blue, his hair auburn, his place of birth New York, and his place of enlistment Chicago.[20] Apart from the place of birth, which moved him closer to claiming to be an American, the other details were not far out. His regiment left almost at once by railroad car for Harper's Ferry, West Virginia. Soon after arriving there, Stanley collapsed, suffering from the same dysentery and fever that had been carrying men off by the score in the prison camp. He was admitted to the local hospital, and was left there on 22 June when the regiment moved on.[21]

In his *Autobiography* manuscript, Stanley claims that he was discharged by the Federal army at this point. In fact, he was ordered to report for duty when in better health. For over a year, Battery 'L' remained in West Virginia, at New Creek, so his rejoining would have been perfectly straightforward. His failure to do so led to his being listed a deserter on 31 August 1862.[22] Soon after the 22nd he discharged himself from hospital, having decided that he would not fight for the North. Having been coerced into joining up, he probably felt that desertion was not dishonourable. Yet he did feel he had been cor-rupted by the fighting: 'Only thirty minutes sufficed to drive out all that we had ever heard of goodness, love, charity, all memories of church, God, heaven';[23] every day in the army, 'a host of influences was at work sapping moral scruples', and 'all that was weak, vain, and unfixed in my own nature conspired to make me as indifferent as any of my fellows to all sacred duties.'[24]

Free of the army at last, he headed for the east coast, hoping to work his passage to Liverpool. Undoubtedly, he had failed to prosper during his two and a half years in America. But he hoped his relations would accept that this had not been his own fault. Surely they would rejoice with him for his having survived a great battle, though he owned no more than the clothes on his back? It took a week to walk a dozen miles eastwards along the Hagerstown road. Weak and ema-ciated, Henry had to rest every few hundred yards. Four miles from Sharpsburg, he collapsed. A farmer, called Baker, rescued him and spread some straw as a bed in an outhouse. For a month this good Samaritan fed him on milk and light food, until he was well enough to help with the last days of the harvest. In mid-August, Mr Baker drove Henry into Hagerstown and paid his railroad fare to Baltimore.[25] Stanley worked for a few weeks on an oyster schooner in Chesapeake Bay, and then, in late September, sailed from Baltimore to Liverpool.

The *E. Sherman* entered the river Mersey early in November with H. Stanley among her complement of deckhands. On landing at the once familiar Liverpool docks, Henry went to see his uncle Tom and his aunt Maria Morris, and spent his first night in Britain with them. His plan was to travel the following day to Bodelwyddan village, near St Asaph, where his mother and her husband, Robert Jones (they had married two years earlier), kept the Cross Foxes public house. Jones had been a plasterer, and had only recently become a publican under his wife's influence.[26] Tom Morris told his nephew that his new step-father was 'a scamp' for having deserted Elizabeth Parry after she had given birth to his son, Robert, in 1848. What kind of man would let the mother of his children spend three months in the workhouse, and then wait another four years before marrying her? Tom said that Jones was the type of man who only married a woman 'better able to look after herself, than he was'.[27] And Elizabeth was indeed capable – being the landlady of a second pub in Denbigh. Uncle Tom warned Stanley (who resumed his Rowlands name for this trip) that his mother's youngest son had died in the summer from meningitis, at the age of six, leaving her grief-stricken.

Exactly how high Stanley pitched his hopes of succeeding with his mother is unknown. With the income from two pubs, she was prosperous; and with a settled domestic life, perhaps she was at last in a position to help her firstborn. Yet nothing should detract from the immense courage it must have taken to seek her out after being ignored for twenty-one years. Many adults rejected in childhood prefer the pain of loneliness to risking a new experience of annihilation. And Henry knew little about his mother. Suffering can harden people as often as it can make them more sympathetic, and he had no idea which effect it had had on her. Years later, he wrote: 'With what pride I knocked at the door, buoyed up by a hope of being able to show what manliness I had acquired, not unwilling perhaps to magnify what I meant to *become* ...'[28]

In a recently discovered letter, Stanley gave a graphic account of what happened when he arrived, ill and exhausted, at his mother's pub near St Asaph, having walked the last fifteen miles of his journey. He knocked at the side door as night was closing in.

My mother opened it, starting back, aghast at seeing me. The couple were at supper when I had thus appeared. My mother said very little – but what she did say will never be forgotten. Her husband merely looked up but uttered no word ... I was very hungry – and as it was a matter of necessity I took a plateful of rice pudding and slept that night – but at 5.30 a.m. next morning I was off again, not having exchanged a word with R. Jones.[29]

What Stanley's mother had said to her sick and penniless son was: 'Never come back to me again unless you are in far better circumstances than you seem to be in now.'[30] And to make sure that there could be no misunderstanding, this mother of five illegitimate children added with breathtaking hypocrisy and cruelty that he was 'a disgrace to them in the eyes of their neighbours' and that he ought to leave 'as speedily as possible'. No one who has not been gripped as a young adult by an unsatisfied hunger for parental love will find it easy to imagine how Stanley could have endured such treatment and still have longed to be accepted by this mother who had wronged him all his life. But, despite his humiliation, Stanley was far from finished with his family, and he knew, even then, that he would be impelled by his neediness to try again, as soon as he had made some money. For him, an utterly indifferent mother was still better than no mother at all. But his awful experience at the Cross Foxes had the effect of driving the tenderness in his nature further below the surface.[31]

As Stanley started the long walk to Liverpool, his misery was intense. Unloved and deeply sensitive, but angry too, and understandably self-pitying, he knew that, for the present, there was nothing to keep him in Britain. But what could he possibly do that might one day gain him the position and money that might soften her heart towards him? Riches could never be achieved by mundane clerking, or work as a glorified shop boy.

On leaving north Wales, he stayed briefly with Tom and Maria Morris, the kindliest of all his relations,[32] and sailed from Liverpool docks in December 1862. Between then and July 1864, little can be said of his movements. He returned to seafaring for at least six months, on one occasion deserting his ship in Barcelona and begging his way through Catalonia to the French border, before sailing from Marseilles as a deckhand in another vessel. Most of the ships he sailed on plied between Liverpool and the ports on North America's eastern seaboard. Sometimes he was hired as a deckhand, sometimes as an assistant cook.[33]

A shipmate, Thomas Nisbet, sailed with him on a Nova Scotia vessel, the *Burmah,* taking a cargo of gas, coal and machinery to New Orleans, and then on to the Caribbean islands. Nisbet wrote to Stanley later:

We were off Jamaica with the Blue Mountains in sight, do you remember going out on the studding sail boom in the dusk ... and catching an eagle, bringing it down and giving it to the captain on the quarter deck? You used to go from one mast to another on the stays, hand over hand, instead of coming down the rigging ... You had the same quiet pluck and daring on that ship that you have displayed since ...[34]

Whatever Henry's inner feelings, the impression he gave was of a tough and resourceful young man. By late October 1863, Stanley was in Brooklyn, clerking for and lodging with a hard-drinking notary public whom he called 'Judge' Thomas Hughes. One night Hughes attacked his wife with a hatchet, and Henry separated them. In the summer of 1864, he came to an astonishing decision: he resolved to join the Federal armed forces for the second time. This may have been partly because Hughes's business partner, Lewis Stegman, had just joined up to escape their drunken employer. Stanley chose the Federal navy, rather than the army. He was familiar with ships, and knew very well that if he had rejoined the army his earlier desertion might have come to light. At this time he was living immediately opposite the Brooklyn Navy Yard.[35]

On 19 July 1864, Henry enlisted for three years. His age, he said, was twenty, when really he was twenty-three.[36] Two years earlier in Chicago he had claimed to be twenty-two – but creating this age difference was deliberate. He needed to differentiate naval Henry Stanley from Henry Stanley the army deserter. To achieve this, he also changed the colour of his eyes from blue to hazel and made his hair dark. His place of birth now became England. He seems to have felt, after all his sufferings, that he had a right to sprinkle official forms with untruths. Henry made no mention of having been a seaman, only that he had been a clerk. This meant that he was listed as a 'landsman' – making him more eligible, he hoped, for the post of ship's clerk or writer. He would not be disappointed. Soon after joining the 3,300-ton screw steamer USS *Minnesota* at Hampton Roads, Virginia, he was given that position.

The ship's writer rated as a petty officer, and his duties included keeping the ship's log and other records, and working closely with the first lieutenant. Stanley would now do civilized work, and have time for reading travel books – a new passion. The *Minnesota* saw no action after being involved, peripherally, in the bombardment of Fort Fisher in December 1864. Apart from writing an official account, Henry wrote a more highly coloured version of the bombardment and managed to sell it to several newspapers. These descriptive paragraphs marked his debut as a journalist – a significant moment in his life.[37]

In January 1865, a synchronized Federal land and sea attack on Port Wilmington's defences was at last successful, effectively ending Stanley's hopes of further active service. For six months, he had been getting to know members of the *Minnesota*'s 600-strong crew, among them Commodore Joseph Lanman's fifteen-year-old messenger boy, Lewis Noe. Stanley always envied people with relaxed personalities and a graceful way of moving – traits that his self-consciousness denied him. He described Lewis as having 'regular classical features, and a pair of laughing, mischievous black eyes'. Tall for his age, and slight, Lewis Noe seemed to Henry 'a thorough specimen of an American boy'. Lewis could, in addition, 'whistle every known song … catch balls like a juggler, imitate a cat to perfection and excellently perform difficult acrobatic feats'.[38] Such circus tricks might have been expected to wear thin, but they did not. Lewis's boyish admiration soothed the insecure, though outwardly blasé Stanley.

The dynamics between the twenty-three-year-old ship's writer and the much younger Noe were not homosexual as has been suggested.[39] Stanley's day-to-day family, in so far as he had ever had one, had consisted of his young friends at the workhouse, rather than his relations. At St Asaph, as head boy, he had enjoyed power and kudos among the boys, which had helped him believe in himself. Without support from parents or relatives, this desire to be admired by boys and young men would continue into his adult life as essential underpinning for his self-esteem. There would also be an imaginative and creative component in his attachment to youth and youthful interests.

Like many boys his age, Lewis was a natural escapist who enjoyed stories of the Wild West and far-flung colonial outposts. Stanley loved these stories too, and ever since his confinement in the workhouse had entertained fantasies of escape into exotic regions. Lewis Noe would often see Henry reading 'adventures and foreign travels'. One of his favourite authors was Thomas Mayne Reid, the prolific writer of boys' adventures that were set in every part of the globe. And Stanley could communicate his excitement. 'He was full of aspirations for adventure,' wrote Noe, 'and told marvellous tales of foreign countries, and he urged that when we should leave the service, I should accompany him on a proposed tour in southern Europe. Being of a romantic turn of mind, I was pleased at the suggestion.'[40] Lewis's grasp of world geography is probably to blame for his supposing that the region Stanley wanted to travel through was southern Europe, when he (Stanley) always referred to it as Asia Minor, and sometimes as the Levant. But poor geographer though Noe was, Stanley's friendship with the young American enabled him to make the imaginative leap required to place him on the road to becoming an African explorer.

It is scarcely conceivable that Stanley's omnivorous reading would not have included the three most famous travel books of the period, all set in the general region he wished to visit: Alexander W. Kinglake's classic *Eothen or Traces of Travel brought back from the East* (1844), W. G. Palgrave's *A Year's Journey through Central and Eastern Arabia in 1862–1863*, and Richard F. Burton's *Personal Narrative of a Pilgrimage to Al-Madinah and Meccah* (1853). In these books about Middle Eastern travel, their authors had recorded adventures of varying degrees of danger. Inevitably, it occurred to Henry that if *he* could complete a comparable journey, he too might manage to write a best-seller about it. As a famous travel author, he would surely be able to win his mother's heart by giving her rare foreign carpets and silverwork. In most well-known travel books, the author was a romantic hero, often dressing like the local people in order to understand them better, or disguising himself, as Burton had done, for a secret objective. Stanley had himself photographed in Arab dress a few years later, plainly influenced by such books. With Livingstone, Burton and Speke all writing about their travels, African exploration was in a league of its own for generating admiration; but the Levant had the advantage of being cheaper and easier to reach, and a lot less dangerous.

In February 1865, in order to expedite his travels with Lewis, Stanley suggested that they should both desert from the navy. This was another of those extraordinary, spontaneous decisions that would change the direction of Henry's life. Incredibly, he and Lewis were undeterred by the fear of a possible death sentence or a term of imprisonment. Stanley was a skilful copyist, so he had little trouble creating bogus passes for the two of them, complete with Commodore Lanman's faultlessly forged signature. They would desert, he decided, when the *Minnesota* had her next re-fit at Portsmouth Navy Yard, New Hampshire. Henry bought civilian clothes from some carpenters working on the ship. These garments he and Noe put on under their naval uniforms, which they meant to discard as soon as they had safely left the dockyard. Everything went to plan on Henry's chosen day, 10 February 1865. Their passes were not challenged by the sentries at the dockyard gate, and this unlikely duo mingled unnoticed with the local citizens on their way out of town.[41]

There followed a chaotic year during which Henry turned his back on safe employment and, despite acts of dishonesty and violence and numerous failures of judgement, launched himself on the uncertain path that within four years would bring him within sight of the greatest adventures the age had to offer. By wielding a Svengali-like influence over the admiring younger man, and persuading him to do things he would never have dreamed of doing if left to himself, Stanley could feel powerful. For the next year and a half, as if he was addicted, Henry's passion for adventure overwhelmed almost every practical and moral consideration.

On arriving in New York, although he was a recent deserter and ought to have feared being traced, Stanley accepted employment once again from Mr Hughes, whose drinking was no better than it had been in 1863. When Noe failed to find work, Stanley suggested another way to earn the money they needed for their life-changing Middle Eastern travels. The Union's military authorities were offering a bounty to anyone recruiting a volunteer. So, if Lewis were to enlist in the army, Henry could collect the bounty; and if he later deserted, and then re-enlisted in another unit, there would be another bounty to be collected. And of course the brilliant planner and penman would assist with passes, civilian clothes and anything else required. Unfortunately, without warning, Lewis told his father that he had deserted from the navy. His horrified parents begged him to join the army at once under an assumed name so he would not be caught and hanged. The boy did as they asked. He had no problem choosing a false surname, since Stanley had already suggested Lewis Morton as the name under which he should make his first attempt at 'bounty-jumping'. (Morton was not yet settled as Stanley's middle name.)

Henry was enraged when told that Lewis had joined the army. How could they go travelling now? He ordered him to desert at once, but Lewis refused; so their Levantine journey would clearly have to wait. Fortunately, at this frustrating moment, Henry heard about major finds in the Colorado goldfields. Out West, he might make enough money to pay for Noe's travel expenses as well as his own. So Henry gave up his clerical job and left for the Rocky Mountains. Stanley left 'Judge' Hughes at just the right time. Days later, the lawyer jumped from a fifth-floor office window, and broke his neck on the sidewalk.[42]

On the eve of his departure for a life dedicated to risk-taking, Stanley, at twenty-four, was a changed man from the eighteen-year-old who had arrived in America six years earlier. The biddable and obedient workhouse boy had survived the Battle of Shiloh in the physical sense, but the absence of all morality during those years of conflict had left its mark on him. Henry's changing sides at Camp Douglas had been a matter of self-preservation, but his enlistment in the Federal navy had been entirely different: almost a demonstration of thinking himself above, or at least outside, the framework of rules by which ordinary people lived their lives. Yet Stanley would probably have been shocked if anyone had accused him of undermining Noe's sense of right and wrong. In all his letters to Lewis he called him his 'friend and brother', and was plainly eager to ingratiate himself with the boy's sister and his father, and to correspond with both. His old longing to be part of a close-knit family – and the Noes appeared to be just that – persisted. And though, in Henry's eyes, Lewis had disappointed by failing to be guided by him, 'brother Henry' still needed Lewis's unquestioning loyalty.

As a mark of especial 'brotherly' favour, Stanley had shown Lewis a photograph of his mother, declaring that 'he was the only person he had ever shown it to'.[43] That he had a mother who had rejected him at birth was the most intimate revelation Stanley could make. Although Henry would soon meet a new protégé, he still thought of Noe as his special confidant and ideal brother, and would not forget him when the time came to mount his full-scale dress rehearsal as an explorer.

FOUR

An Accident-prone Apprenticeship

In early May 1865, Stanley travelled to St Louis and managed to get himself taken on by the editor of the *Missouri Democrat* as an 'attaché' (an occasional correspondent) reporting from the Colorado diggings.[1] But part-time journalism was never going to earn him enough money for his foreign travels, so he also worked as a book-keeper and a printer in Central City – once described as 'the richest square mile on earth' – and then tried his hand at prospecting in the goldfields, without any success. After moving to Black Hawk City, Henry secured a well-paid job in a smelting works, where he made friends with another young journalist, William Harlow Cook – like himself supplementing his income by labouring.[2] In Lewis Noe's absence, Cook became the essential admiring youth. Ideal for this role because so naive, Cook was enraptured when his new friend challenged a bullying engineer to a fight to the death after being insulted by him. The engineer took one look at Stanley's hand on his revolver, and begged forgiveness on his knees.

Henry's experience of gun-law conditions in Arkansas was definitely useful in this new environment. His inscrutable expression also made people think twice before tangling with him.[3] Henry was already Cook's hero when he suggested, out of the blue, that they navigate the Platte River together in a flat-bottomed boat. Cook agreed without hesitation. While nailing together the planks of their simple craft, Stanley mentioned his temporarily postponed trip to Asia Minor, and suggested that Cook come along. Little imagining where this might lead, he accepted.

By the time they launched their home-made craft at Denver, Stanley had confided that after Turkey they would travel on east through

Armenia, Georgia, Bokhara and Kashmir. Then they would 'write a great book of adventure'. At this point, Henry dropped in the fact that they would be travelling with his 'half-brother', Lewis Noe. Having to share Stanley was not something Cook had anticipated, but though disliking the idea, he kept his reservations to himself.[4]

The Platte River was not the Congo – even so, it was full of snags, eddies and shallows, and Indians lurked along its banks. Their plan to float down the river for 600 miles in a home-made boat was downright foolhardy, and the acolyte's faith in his charismatic leader was about to be severely tested. Even so, Cook – though he had no means of knowing it – was sharing the very first geographical adventure of a man destined to be the greatest explorer of the century.

The Platte was a fast-flowing river, and on their sixth night afloat they hit a submerged log and capsized. By swimming to the shore and then running along the bank, Henry managed to grab the boat in some shallows and drag it ashore; but the guns and ammunition, which they had intended to take to Turkey, were flung into the water and lost. Soon afterwards, they were stopped by an officer with orders to track down deserters from nearby Fort Laramie. On the point of being arrested on suspicion of desertion, Stanley drew his revolver. Having few men with him, the officer backed down and the two desperadoes continued their journey unmolested. Near the end of their trip they capsized again. Henry, who was asleep at the time, was thrown from the boat, while Cook clung to the hull and managed to right the vessel. Cook then floated on, as Stanley hurried overland, hoping to intercept the boat downstream. But he kept arriving just too late at various hoped-for points of rendezvous. In the end, with no sign of his hero, Cook left their battered craft at Omaha, Nebraska, and Henry only caught up with him at his parents' house in St Louis.[5]

Undaunted by this fiasco, Stanley lost no time in leaving for New York, with Cook in tow. Arriving at Sayville, Long Island, where Noe's parents lived, Henry feared they might still be angry enough with him over his role in Lewis's desertion to stop their son going to Turkey. But Henry's 'winning manners, and gentlemanly bearing' charmed the Noes into treating that incident as an isolated aberration. Now Stanley promised to give Lewis 'the polish that could best be obtained by intercourse with the world', and declared that 'diamonds, rubies ... and rich India shawls' could all be bought cheaply in 'Central Asia'.[6] As a schoolmistress, Lewis's sister might have been expected to challenge these absurdly optimistic predictions. But she raised no objections – perhaps finding Henry attractive. (*He* noted in his diary that she had 'voluptuous lips, and dark glittering eyes'.)[7]

Stanley's trip to 'Asia Minor', as he usually described it, is of interest because it would be the only land expedition he attempted, as leader of his own party, before finding fame as Livingstone's discoverer. Being badly planned and starved of money, the expedition got off to a terrible start. Henry alienated Lewis Noe by forcing him to work his passage in the fruit ship that took the three of them from Boston to Smyrna (now Izmir), the main port of western Turkey. Stanley and Cook did not, for they had saved money from their wages at the smelting works. But the guns and clothes lost on the Platte River could not adequately be replaced, and in Turkey, Stanley could only afford to buy two horses. Thus Noe found himself walking, and deeply resenting Cook for usurping him as Henry's principal companion.

Really, Stanley was fonder of Noe, but, as Cook rightly observed, Henry brooded on slights, and Lewis rarely stopped irritating him. Lewis had started with a massive black mark earned by having refused to desert from the army at Henry's bidding. This explains why Stanley favoured Cook from the outset. Consumed by rage and jealousy, when two days inland, Noe set fire to some bushes to scare the sleeping Cook. He succeeded beyond his expectations. The fire spread, out of control, and the enraged peasants persuaded the local police to take Stanley and Cook into custody. By the time Henry had talked his way to freedom, Lewis had fled to Smyrna under no illusions about how angry his 'brother' was going to be when he caught him. Indeed, Henry treated the youth to what Lewis called a sadistic flogging, but which Stanley himself described as no more than 'a few strokes of a switch'.[8]

Three hundred miles inland, at a village called Chihissar, a controversial incident occurred. According to Noe (who came to hate Henry before the trip was over), Stanley tried to murder a Turk in order to steal his horses. Henry would claim that the Turk had made obscene overtures to Noe, and he (Stanley) had then slashed at him with his sword to defend his young friend. Stanley's diary confirms that the Turk had been sexually drawn to Noe when they were riding together in a group. But Henry may have used his disgust as a pretext to attack and attempt to rob the man. If he had really been contemplating murder, he would surreptitiously have loaded a gun in advance to be able to shoot the Turk without risking a hand-to-hand tussle with a man used to fighting with swords and daggers. But Henry had made no such preparation. (After his hands had been badly cut in the fight, and he was desperate to end it, he failed to lay hands on a single loaded gun among the weapons he had brought with him.) When the Turk ran off, Stanley undoubtedly took his horses, but this was dictated by the need to escape, since the man seemed certain to return with a gang of his friends – as indeed he did.

Within hours, Stanley, Noe and Cook were surrounded on a hilltop, and though possessing 'the best Sharp's fliers and Colt's revolvers', decided not to offer resistance to ten well-armed Turks.[9] The three were then robbed of everything they possessed, before being dragged to the nearest village where Stanley and Cook were beaten, trussed up like chickens, and left in the open overnight. Lewis, meanwhile, was raped at knifepoint by several men. Luckily for the American trio, the local Cadi, or magistrate, heard of their plight and arranged for them to be conveyed to the nearest prison to await trial before him.

At this point Stanley acted like a born leader, as even Lewis acknowledged.[10] With a fine show of injured innocence, he pulled the rug out from under his accusers by persuading the Cadi that they had been the robbers, and that he had only acted in self-defence. The Cadi believed this when items belonging to the Americans were found under the Turks' clothing. Released from prison on 27 September, Stanley's remaining weeks in Turkey were occupied with giving evidence during the trial of the Turks, and claiming compensation from the Turkish government. His claim was for $2,000, and he eventually settled for $1,200, although he and the others had spent nowhere near that amount on their horses, guns, cooking pots and other impedimenta that had been stolen.[11] Noe would claim in 1872 that Stanley had refused to give him any part of a £150 loan handed over by Edward J.Morris, the American Ambassador in Constantinople, after the robbery. In fact, Noe signed a receipt stating that he had received from Stanley £27 and 93 piastres (about four dollars), say £28 in all. Henry noted in his diary that he paid Cook £59 and himself a few pounds more, so Noe had good reason (especially since he had suffered most at the hands of the Turks) to feel angry about the distribution, though not to deny that it took place.[12]

While Cook stayed on in Turkey for the later stages of the trial, Stanley and Noe sailed from Constantinople for Marseilles, en route to Liverpool via Paris and London. The date was 9 November, and they were not on speaking terms. Watching the city's domes and minarets falling astern, Henry knew that his first attempt at a land expedition had been an unmitigated disaster. Nothing had been achieved, and he had fallen out with the member of his expedition to whom he had once been closest. Yet despite failing so badly, one promising omen had been noted: the man whose name would soon be a byword for decisive action had not let down his companions at the most dangerous moment of the whole misbegotten enterprise. At one stage he and Cook had been hoisted into a tree with lariats round their necks, as if about to be hanged. But, instead of collapsing under pressure, Stanley had turned the tables on the Turks with ice-cool nerve by convincing the Cadi that he and his companions were victims, not aggressors. Years of imprisonment in a verminous Turkish jail had been avoided, and Henry's ability to retrieve a situation when absolute disaster seemed certain had been exercised for the first time.

FIVE

War Correspondent

Long before Stanley reached Liverpool, he knew that his stay in Britain would be brief. America still offered him, he believed, a better chance of making a living, but this did not make his imminent journey to Wales any less important to him. To guarantee success there, he had taken the precaution of visiting a tailor in Constantinople and had spent part of Ambassador Morris's loan in purchasing a made-to-measure naval officer's uniform. In this spurious outfit, Henry intended to present himself to his mother and to pretend that after various acts of heroism he had been made an American naval officer. As the sharp-eyed US ambassador had noticed when Stanley had worn the coat in his presence, the buttons were Turkish rather than American.[1] But Henry was confident that no one in Wales would know the difference. All that mattered was that his mother should be impressed. Before sailing, he had himself photographed in this uniform and meant to give all his relations *carte de visite* prints before he left Wales.[2] But should he write his new name or his real one on the back?

Before Henry left Turkey, he had led Ambassador Morris to believe that his 'father' was a lawyer at 20, Liberty Street, New York. So, plainly, at this date the best-known cotton magnate in New Orleans had not finally been selected as his adoptive father.[3] Stanley knew that his mother would be sure to ask numerous questions if he claimed to have been adopted by anyone, and he still doubted whether he was ready to be grilled. The way in which he signed the visitors' book of the Denbigh Castle Bowling Club on 14 December 1866 tells us exactly what he told his relatives to explain his turning up in Wales dressed as a naval officer.

John Rowlands formerly of this Castle now ensign in the United States Navy in North America belonging to the US ship 'Ticonderogo' [sic] now at Constantinople, Turkey, absent on furlough.[4]

While in Constantinople, Henry had spotted the USS *Ticonderoga* – a larger warship than the *Minnesota* – and had decided that, once in Wales, he would say he was on leave from this vessel. In this way he could talk of having been in Turkey without mentioning his failed expedition. En route to Denbigh he stayed overnight at the Black Lion in Mold, where he hired a carriage and pair, donned his bogus uniform and, in due course, entered the town of his birth in triumph.[5] Since all he possessed in the world was the remains of the ambassador's loan, he could ill afford to hire carriages and buy presents, but he felt an overwhelming need to be treated respectfully by the people who had once thought so little of him that they had allowed him to rot in the workhouse. His mother might be incapable of love, but if the smallest scintilla of affection remained buried deep within her, he reckoned it would only emerge if lured out by greed for his new-found wealth. As his coach clattered into Denbigh at the start of this tragicomic charade, Stanley knew that he was about to deceive his relations, but his longing to see them humbled by his achievements overruled every other thought.

No description of any of his meetings with his mother exists, but since Stanley was in Denbigh for at least three and a half weeks, clearly he got on far better with Elizabeth Jones than on his last disastrous visit. She was shuttling to and fro between the Castle Arms, Denbigh, and the Cross Foxes at Bodelwyddan, and Henry saw her in both establishments. Richard Price, who had taken young John to the workhouse, saw him at the Castle Arms with his mother, and in the churchyard visiting his grandfather's grave. Price remarked upon Stanley's naval uniform, which he confused with the blue coat of the Federal army.[6]

For a few days before Christmas, Stanley stayed in Vale Street with his uncle Moses and his aunt Kitty – magnanimously forgiving them for having sent him back to St Asaph. While under their roof, he developed a crush on his cousin, Catherine, aged fifteen, whom he later described as attractive and a talented harpist, but 'giddy-headed, ignorant' and a gossip.[7] His greatest triumph was to spend Christmas Day 1866 at the Cross Foxes with his mother, his stepfather, his two half-brothers, Robert and James William Jones, and with his half-sister,

Emma. Although no account of this extraordinary day exists, it can only have been an unforgettable one for him – the very first Christmas he had ever spent with his family. It is known that Stanley was at the Cross Foxes then, because on the 25th, he wrote to Lewis Noe (who had been left with the Morris family in Liverpool) giving his address as Bodelwyddan.[8] Noe then wrote back to 'Henry Stanley' at the Cross Foxes. Years later, Elizabeth Jones told the Welsh journalist Owen 'Morien' Morgan about the arrival of these 'Henry Stanley' letters.

'I told the postman,' said Mrs Jones, 'that there was no one of that name here. John overheard me and cried out, "They are for me mother." I went to him with the letters, and asked him seriously, "What have you done, John, that you have been obliged to change your name?" He laughed, and assured me he had done nothing wrong, and it was then he told me about the shopkeeper of New Orleans.'[9]

So Stanley had been surprised into telling his mother the adoption story before he was ready[10] [see this note for evidence of the date]. At least it must have been a relief for Henry to be able to reduce her irritation with him for dropping his Welsh name by saying that he had been 'given' it, rather than having chosen it simply because he wanted to. Stanley also told his stepfather that he might only go on calling himself Stanley while he was establishing himself in the world. Jones seemed puzzled, so Henry explained 'that he wanted to do his marketing [of himself] before he admitted who he really was'.[11] He then told his mother a fantastic story about being made an officer after swimming 500 yards under fire to get a hawser aboard a Confederate ship and capture her.[12] Later, a close friend would say that Stanley's most truly American quality was his 'showman's determination to put all his best wares in his window'. Naturally enough, being an illegitimate Welshman was not something he categorized as 'best wares'.[13] From now on, Stanley's relations knew that, despite his need to be close to them, he believed his career would be best served by denying his Welsh connections, until he had achieved something. Given the snobberies and prejudices of the age, and his treatment as a child, his point of view is easy to understand.

Of course, Henry realized that there might be problems ahead. John Hotten confirmed in his book that 'at this date [1866–67] and long afterwards ... John Rowlands and Henry M. Stanley were one and the same person to the good folks of Denbigh',[14] so clearly when the 'good folks' realized he meant to deny being Welsh entirely, they would resent it. But for now, while Stanley was not yet famous, the double name caused no real difficulty. Who cared if he wanted to call himself Stanley in America, while he remained true to his 'real' identity at home in Denbigh? While staying with his mother, he went to the St Asaph workhouse as John Rowlands, wearing his naval uniform. Being such a 'successful' former inmate, he applied to the Guardians for permission to entertain the children to a slap-up tea, and gave a pep talk about the excellent education he had received, and how pleased he was that they too were enjoying the same opportunities that had enabled him to become a naval officer. Then, the self-declared ensign was thanked by Captain Leigh Thomas, chairman of the Guardians, and praised for not being 'ashamed to acknowledge having been reared in the workhouse after raising himself to the position he now held'. To be esteemed in a place where he had once scarcely existed meant a lot to him, as did fooling the workhouse authorities.[15]

Before returning to Liverpool, Henry decided to replace Lewis Noe as his travelling companion. Still needing an admiring youth to bolster him, he urged his workhouse contemporary Thomas Mumford to come to America. When Mumford declined, Stanley tried to persuade the St Asaph Guardians to let him take a senior boy from the workhouse. In the end, the chosen boy's mother refused her permission.[16]

On 7 January, Stanley booked into a hotel in Liverpool rather than stay with Lewis and the Morris family. Lewis had caused Henry great embarrassment by convincing Tom and Maria Morris that he had treated him cruelly.[17] Nevertheless, Henry and Lewis met up the following day and made a temporary truce while visiting a library and a museum.

According to Lewis, Stanley now told him something of immense significance:

It was while I was at Liverpool [December 1866 to January 1867] that Stanley spoke to me of Dr Livingstone's explorations in Africa. They seemed to be an object of great interest to him. He expressed a desire to go into Africa himself and said he should aim to do so as a correspondent of the *Herald*, and thereby make a story and a sensation, and gain both fame and money.[18]

Stanley himself would later attribute the brilliant idea of finding Livingstone to James Gordon Bennett Jr, owner of the *New York Herald*. But since Stanley's entire career then depended upon his employer's continuing patronage, it seems likely that he 'gave' the idea to Bennett to please him. (Nor would he ever wish to admit that the inspiration for finding Livingstone had been due to a desire to make his name rather than to bring succour to the missing man.) Lewis later told various local people in his home village of Sayville that Stanley had 'continually talked about Livingstone' in 1866. Certainly, Stanley himself stated that soon after leaving St Asaph workhouse he had read Livingstone's best-seller, *Missionary Travels*, and been captivated by it.[19]

It might be objected that Stanley would not have talked about 'finding' Livingstone in December 1866, because the explorer had only returned to Africa ten months earlier and was not considered 'lost'. But, in fact, just when Stanley and Noe were in Liverpool, articles were published in the British press speculating anxiously about Livingstone's whereabouts.[20] And further evidence supports Noe's claim that Stanley originated the century's greatest newspaper coup. Of the two elements in Noe's account of his conversations with Stanley, his mention of the *New York Herald* would seem far more likely to have been untrue than the references to Stanley's interest in Livingstone. In fact, after leaving Wales and before returning to Liverpool, Stanley went to London for a meeting with the *New York Herald*'s representative in the capital, Colonel Finley Anderson. There could never have been any chance that such an inexperienced young man would be sent to central Africa, but the meeting was positive enough to enable Stanley to re-approach the *Herald* later, with momentous consequences. So as Henry trudged along the grey streets of Liverpool, with the disenchanted Lewis in tow, it seems all but certain that they discussed the dazzling idea that would make Henry a world celebrity six years later.[21] Although Stanley tried hard to patch up his friendship with Noe, he failed, and the two of them returned to America on different ships, never to meet again.

Early in February 1867, Stanley arrived in St Louis and visited the offices of the *Missouri Democrat* – the newspaper he had worked for as an occasional correspondent during 1865. After an initial rebuff, he kept calling in and his persistence finally paid off. In late March he was offered a full-time job on the paper at $15 per week and expenses – this was the first regular employment he had had in his life. Never again would he feel the need to resort to fraudulent ways of acquiring money, as in Turkey. The security of a regular income transformed his life. Yet Henry's desire to take risks to achieve fame did not go away, and it seems that his successful charade in Denbigh had boosted his self-confidence. For the present, he sensibly postponed planning ambitious projects until he had honed his skills as a journalist. And now fortune smiled. A day after being taken on, he landed the plum assignment of covering General Winfield Scott Hancock's Indian campaign against the Kiowas and the Comanches. Henry caught up with the general on the Saline River a few days later, on 1 April.[22]

As well as learning the art of writing and filing his copy on time, and finding stories, Stanley would discover much about the origins of racial conflict. White settlers and American Indians were murdering each other, and at first, like many observers, he was disgusted by the Indians' atrocities and sympathized with the settlers. 'Are our countrymen to be murdered and scalped without retaliating?' he thundered.[23] But even at this early stage, Henry favoured the creation of Indian reservations rather than driving the tribes from the Plains.[24] On 21 August, he wrote to the *Democrat* from Sioux City, placing the blame for conflict squarely on the whites:

Now the great cause of all these troubles – these blazing farms, these mutilated corpses, these scalped and wounded men – will be found in this: that the Indian was an outlaw ranked with the wild beasts. If a white man shot an Indian, what law touched him ...? It was as if he had shot a buffalo ... And the red man, to make matters straight, killed the first white man he came across ... Immediately a cry went up to heaven ... extermination. Thank heaven for radicalism [whose policy is] to draw within the mighty circle of our civilization men of every colour ... all men are free; if the red man will come to us let him come.[25]

While Stanley argued that the Indians ought not to be allowed to interfere with the building of railroads and the development of the West, he demanded that the government provide agricultural help for 'these wronged children of the soil', enabling them to lead a settled existence, tending flocks and herds.[26] On one occasion, Stanley dissuaded General Hancock from burning an Indian village. He quoted the words of Chief Santanta: 'I love the land and the buffalo and will not part with any. But I want you to understand also that Kiowas do not want to fight.'[27] Henry had come a long way since fighting for the slave-owning South.

As well as writing about the moral issues, he gave graphic descriptions of events such as the fate of a telegraph repairer after an Indian attack on a train. Blood and horror were expected by his readers.

People came from all parts to view the gory baldness that had come upon him so suddenly. The man was evidently suffering tortures. He showed a gaping wound in the neck and a bullet hole in the muscle of his right arm. In a pail of water by his side, was his scalp, about nine inches in length and four in width, somewhat resembling a drowned rat, as it floated curled upon the water.[28]

Henry conducted some remarkably modern-sounding interviews. His approach to 'Wild Bill' Hickok, the famous scout, was characteristically direct: '"I say, Mr Hickok, how many white men have you killed to your certain knowledge?" After a little deliberation, he replied, "I suppose I have killed considerably over a hundred."' From March through to 21 November 1867, when he wrote his last letter to the *Democrat*, his stories appeared every few days under the name 'Stanley', or simply 'S'.

But though Henry was a more mature and self-controlled person than the gun-toting young man who had threatened to shoot an army officer near Fort Laramie, he could still lose his temper if insulted. In Omaha, during July and August 1867, Henry fell in love with Annie Ward, a singer and actress. The editor of the *Omaha Herald*, F. M. MacDonough, known as 'Little Mac', published an article making fun of Stanley's romance, because Annie had secretly married someone else, and was also being pursued by another journalist. Annie, it was said, preferred this other journalist to Stanley, who was making a fool of himself by attending all her performances. MacDonough claimed that Annie had kicked from the stage a bouquet given her by Stanley. Annie's few surviving letters to Henry are too pleasant to make this anecdote seem very likely. When 'Little Mac' wrote a second article, in which he described Stanley as 'a lying, loafing scamp', the insulted man went to the newspaper's office and kicked MacDonough into the street. The editor sued for assault, but though Stanley landed in jail for a few days, he was acquitted by a jury on the grounds that he had delivered 'a justifiable chastisement'.[29]

The year 1867 was a crucial one for Stanley. During it, he not only came of age as a journalist, but the American frontier introduced him to a key concept of imperialism: that the populations of industrialized countries had a right to expand into undeveloped parts of the world. The American West was widely thought of as 'a vast body of wealth without proprietors', presenting extraordinary opportunities to the federal government and to adventurous individuals.[30] Large parts of Africa would soon be thought of in the same way. While Stanley disapproved of land theft, he sensed that he was witnessing an inevitable process that was operating worldwide. He felt 'deep sympathy' for the Indian chiefs, but also believed: 'it is useless to blame the white race for moving across the continent ... If we proceed in that manner we shall presently find ourselves blaming the Pilgrim Fathers for landing on Plymouth Rock.'[31]

For Stanley, a formative period was ending. Since 1864, a passionate desire to travel had never left him. In 1867 he gave to a journalist friend a collection of explorers' writings called *The Footprints of Travellers*.[32] His fascination with Dr Livingstone (which he had confessed to Lewis Noe) persisted. And since no Midwestern newspaper was going to send him on an African assignment, Stanley made up his mind to see whether a New York paper might be willing to oblige. With a scrapbook full of his articles for the *Missouri Democrat*, and several pieces from the *St Louis Republican* and the *Chicago Tribune*, he now fancied his chances in the big league.[33]

On 16 December 1867, showing extraordinary self-belief, Henry entered the offices of America's most famous newspaper. At this time, the *New York Herald* had the largest daily sale of any American newspaper, and its owner, James Gordon Bennett Jr, had one of the highest incomes in the land, placing him alongside Commodore Vanderbilt and William B. Astor. When Stanley stood face to face with this 'fierce-eyed and imperious-looking young man', they were both twenty-six years old. Their starts in life could hardly have been more different, yet Stanley was not cowed by this man with a million dollars a year, and a terrifying reputation. Bennett had a rich man's scorn for ordinary mortals, boasting: 'all the brains I want can be picked up any day for twenty-five dollars per week.' Renowned for his brawling and whoring, he would shortly disgrace himself by urinating, when intoxicated, into a drawing room fireplace in his fiancée's New York residence. Far worse were his deliberate campaigns against his own staff. 'I want you to remember,' he told an executive, 'that I am the only reader of this paper. I am the only one to be pleased.' Men were sent scampering about the earth only to find themselves sacked on their return. Although this was known to Henry, so too was the fact that if a journalist succeeded at the *Herald*, a well-paid career was guaranteed – elsewhere, if not on the *Herald*.[34]

Stanley had taken a great risk in resigning from the *Missouri Democrat* with $3,000 of savings, and coming to New York. Since an article had recently been published in *The Times* establishing that Dr Living-stone was not lost, but travelling purposefully to the west of Lake Tanganyika, Henry could not try to interest Gordon Bennett in his most brilliant idea. Fortunately, he could pitch another African news story. This was the punitive expedition that the British were about to mount against Theodore, Emperor of Ethiopia.

Bennett had read and admired Stanley's despatches from the Plains, but he still had no intention of offering him a staff position, or even paying his expenses for a perfectly good story like the Ethiopian one. So when Henry asked the mogul to pay him to cover the expedition 'as a special or at a moderate salary', Bennett slapped him down. Americans, he said, had very little interest in Africa. Stanley asked whether, if Bennett paid him instead by the letter, he could write for other papers too. The young proprietor replied regally: 'We do not like to share our news that way; but we would be willing to pay well for exclusive intelligence.' Only when Stanley had agreed to pay his own expenses and to write for the *Herald* alone was he at last told what he had hoped to hear, namely that if he made a success of his assignment and got his copy in promptly, he would be placed on 'the permanent list'. So by putting up with wholly unreasonable terms, Henry had got himself a trial for a permanent post on America's most profitable newspaper. Now all he had to do was deliver the goods, and who could say what other great stories he might not soon be covering? Holding in his hand James Gordon Bennett Jr's letter of authority to his London agent, Stanley left the room feeling that from now on anything was possible.[35]

The campaign destined to make or mar Stanley's fortunes was a tragicomic affair. Theodore, Emperor of Ethiopia, was a Christian convert who until recently had enjoyed diplomatic relations with Britain and France, and had been presented with a pair of engraved duelling pistols by Queen Victoria. His great ambition was for his envoys to be received by the Queen in London. Unfortunately, the Emperor's letter requesting this royal reception was docketed by Foreign Office clerks and then unintentionally mislaid. After nine months of silence, the enraged Theodore imprisoned the British consul, Captain Charles Cameron, along with the French consul and twenty white missionaries. From time to time he manacled them, and let them hear the screams of Ethiopian prisoners being murdered in nearby cells. After protracted efforts to get him to free the envoys, the British government sent an ultimatum, and when it was not complied with, declared war. To be sent to report on this peculiar 'little war' could hardly have been a better task for a man eager to re-invent himself.

On 20 January 1868, he arrived at Suez, where he promptly bribed the senior telegraph clerk to send his telegrams in advance of all the others. This was undoubtedly 'sharp practice' but, in his defence, Stanley was on trial for his future career and was paying all his own expenses. Failure would leave him jobless and penniless. At Annesley Bay, on the Horn of Africa, Henry found thirty steamers at anchor and 30,000 men (including 13,600 fighting troops, and their supports and servants) encamped behind the baking sand dunes. Also present were 2,500 horses, 44 elephants and 16,000 mules. Given that the opposition was an African ruler with an untrained army, primitive firearms, and artillery pieces that were as likely to kill their operators as the enemy, this was a case of taking a very large sledgehammer to crack a very small nut. From the beginning Stanley noted with derision 'the silver helmets' of the cavalry officers, and 'young lordlings wearing kid gloves and green veils'. Initially, he felt mistrustful of the officer class.

I am under the impression that they consider me to be an unsophisticated kind of a Yankee, for I am sensible that I am the object of a good deal of chaff. They tell me all manner of incredible stories and sometimes so seriously that I do not know what to believe ... They have servants, even to fan them and keep them cool.[36]

It was a strange experience to be passing himself off as an American while living among fellow Britons, but Henry did not become churlish, even when referred to by some young officers as 'Jefferson Brick' – the name of the pushy young American journalist in Charles Dickens's *Martin Chuzzlewit*. In fact, the senior officers were very pleasant to him, especially the commander-in-chief, General Sir Robert Napier. When invited to dine with the general and his staff, Stanley enjoyed their erudite conversation even more than the food.[37] Incredibly, only a year earlier, the man who dined so cordially with General Napier had dressed up in a bogus uniform to impress his neglectful mother. Stanley's American impersonation was advantageous. As a foreigner, he was not labelled as belonging to any class. He therefore got on well with most members of the press corps. From the *Daily Telegraph*'s correspondent, Lord Adare, he bought an Arab stallion for £60. By the end of the campaign he was almost penniless, but he had enjoyed riding a horse better bred than many of those owned by the aristocratic officers. Later, he sold this stallion to James Gordon Bennett Jr.[38]

The march inland to Theodore's mountain fortress at Magdala was a mere 250 miles as the crow flies, but given its 10,000-foot altitude and the formidable ravines and escarpments en route, the actual distance was twice that far. Despite storms and flash floods, the military outcome of the campaign was never in doubt. Theodore's army was routed with heavy casualties, while the British suffered only forty killed in action. Before Magdala fell, 300 Ethiopian prisoners were butchered on Theodore's orders, but the European hostages were spared. The Emperor himself committed suicide with one of the ornamental pistol's given him by Queen Victoria.

After outpacing all the other correspondents to the coast, Stanley managed to embark on the same steamer as Colonel Millward, the official courier, who had in his bag General Napier's despatches and some of the British journalists' reports. At Suez, their ship was quarantined for five days but, unlike the unsuspecting Millward, Stanley smuggled his letters ashore and got them to his friend in the Telegraph Office. His reports reached London many days ahead of the official despatches and those of his rivals. By an extraordinary coincidence, a fault developed on the line between Alexandria and Malta only minutes after the clerk had telegraphed Stanley's reports. This served to extend his lead over his rivals by several more days. So when news of Napier's victory appeared only in the *New York Herald*, there was general incredulity. Mr Bennett greatly enjoyed the discomfiture of the entire British press corps, and praised *his* man, not only for his speed, but for 'his vast superiority in style of writing, minuteness of detail and graphic portrayal'. As might have been expected, Henry Stanley was offered a permanent post on America's best-selling newspaper.[39] If, in the whole of his life, he had achieved nothing more remarkable than this scoop, Henry would still have progressed an astonishing distance from his workhouse origins. Yet he considered this to be no more than a modest first step. The time to make the Livingstone story happen was surely approaching.

SIX

How are we to be Married?

By the time Stanley was ready to find Dr Livingstone in the summer of 1868 – and James Gordon Bennett Jr was prepared to send him – they had learned that letters had arrived in Zanzibar from the great explorer, removing the element of mystery required to make locating him a great news story.[1] In the absence of this stupendous challenge, Henry was at a loss. The two opposing poles of his nature were about to collide: his need for love and security, and his need to escape his old persona through work, adventure and fame. In the summer of 1868, with his big story denied him, his need for love would be given the greater scope. After Stanley had spent a dull month in Alexandria recuperating from African fever, Finley Anderson, the *New York Herald*'s London agent, ordered him to Crete to report on the islanders' independence struggle against Turkish rule.

Henry stopped off, en route, at the island of Siros (Sira), where a number of Cretan refugees were living. On this island he would be powerfully drawn to the idea of marriage, with its promise of love coupled with stability. A shipboard acquaintance had given him an introduction to a local businessman, Christos Evangelides, who turned out to be a keen amateur matchmaker. Stanley was captivated by this white-bearded 'cicerone of youth' from the moment he introduced him to a beautiful young woman from a respectable Greek family. This was the sort of girl, said Christos to the smitten Stanley, who would do as her parents wished if they blessed the union. Sixteen-year-old Virginia Ambella lived on the square in Hermopolis (Ermoupolis), and in Henry's eyes 'came as near as possible to the realisation of the ideal which [his] fancy had portrayed'.[2] But Henry's reverie was cut short when Virginia's mother disconcerted him by asking what he felt about a rapid marriage.

Henry could not decide whether he was involved in 'a farcical adventure' or something 'serious'. 'No doubt ... as beauty goes, Virginia is sufficient,' he decided, but she spoke no English and only a little French. Languages could easily be learned, however, and maybe he should simply go ahead and discover whether marriage could end his sense of being unloved. Though his basic salary of £400 per annum was hardly enough, the thought of marriage thrilled him:

A wife! My wife! ... To be loved with heart and soul above all else, for ever united in thought and sympathy with a fair and virtuous being, whose very touch gave strength and courage and confidence! Oh dear! how my warm imagination glows at the strange idea![3]

The following day, Christos confided to Henry that if he proposed, Virginia would say yes. Though powerfully attracted to Virginia, Stanley realized he did not know her at all. Nevertheless, when Evangelides suggested he write 'a formal declaration by letter', Henry did so eagerly enough. At this critical moment he had to leave for Greece to report on the baptism of the young Prince Constantine.

Just over two weeks later, on 10 September, Henry returned and learned to his joy that he had been accepted. Would he therefore name the day? asked Christos. In a fever of excitement, Stanley suggested the very next Sunday for their marriage. That evening, he was allowed to see Virginia, 'and, in a short time, whatever misgivings I may have had as to the wisdom of my act were banished by the touch of her hand, and the trust visible in her eyes'. Ironically, just when Stanley felt that he was ready to marry Virginia, her parents were becoming less sure about him. Could they be certain that he was the well-paid and successful man he appeared to be? When they explained their worries, Henry was full of understanding and offered to send references. The following day Virginia played the piano and sang French and Greek songs. 'She is in every way worthy,' he decided.

The day after Stanley sailed from Siros – en route to Alexandria, where he was to await Bennett's instructions – he wrote to a retired Egyptian official, Joseph Hekekyan Bey, whom he had met in Cairo two months earlier, asking him to write commending him to the Ambellas. The Egyptian was now working in the field of antiquities, preparing *A Treatise on the Chronology of Siriadic Monuments* in twenty-four volumes.[4] Just the man to pen a solid reference.

Dear Sir,

I want you to do me a favour – I am in love. The object is a Greek girl steeped in poverty, but famous for her beauty ... The parents refuse to give sanction unless something is known of me ... I know you will do it well ... I have offered to settle on the poor girl $50 per month as long as she lives ... upon receipt of this will you be kind enough to write at once and state to them that by refusing me they have lost a most eligible offer.[5]

Less than two weeks later Stanley wrote again: 'I hope you gave me a good character to my *inamorata*.'[6] Before replying to the Ambellas, Hekekyan Bey had contacted Charles Hale, the American consul in Alexandria, who confirmed that Stanley was with the *New York Herald* but advised Hekekyan to write a less than enthusiastic reference, since Stanley's long absences on roving assignments would make any future wife unhappy. Henry also wrote to the *Missouri Democrat* for a reference, but it seems that nothing was sent to the Ambellas.[7]

Virginia's parents took three months to reach a final decision, which owed less to references than to their fear that once Virginia was married they would see little of her. They therefore vetoed a marriage unless Henry confined his newspaper work to the Mediterranean. Stanley sent several temporizing replies, although knowing he could never accept their terms.[8]

So how important to Stanley was the Ambella incident? The language barrier, and the extremely artificial circumstances in which they had met, meant that Henry had been much more in love with the idea of marriage than with Virginia herself; but that did not stop him feeling the pain of rejection.[9] With his loveless background, any kind of dismissal was painful – and the ending of this chimerical romance was no exception. For a while, he became despondent about life in general.

As for me, I know not what I lack to make me happy. I have health, youth and a free spirit; but ... the fluctuations to which the spirit is subject, hour by hour, forever remind me that happiness is not to be secured in this world, except for brief periods.

Though work was his usual panacea for unhappiness, at times escape seemed preferable. He was growing older with little to show for it – or not enough, he felt, to make people respect him. But even if his self-imposed treadmill of work brought him fame through travel, he still might not be happy. 'If I could find an island in mid-ocean, remote from the presence or reach of man, with a few necessaries sufficient to sustain life, I might be happy yet; for then I could forget what reminds me of unhappiness.'[10] Of course, an explorer would be in that very situation – isolated and remote from people of his own society.

In October 1868, Stanley was sent to Spain to cover a convulsion already being compared in the world's press with the French Revolution. However, he was not destined to stay long, for on the day he landed in Barcelona, 8 October, a letter from Sir Roderick Murchison, one of David Livingstone's closest friends, was published in *The Times*. In it, Murchison, the President of the Royal Geographical Society, claimed to have received 'telegraphic news' to the effect that Livingstone was heading east to the coast, and was within a few weeks' march of Zanzibar.[11] On the 13th, Stanley received a telegram ordering him to come to London, where on the 16th he saw Finley Anderson, the *Herald*'s London bureau chief, in his office near Trafalgar Square. According to Stanley's diary, Anderson 'was rather mysterious, and proposed to defer the subject [of his next assignment] until tomorrow, but I was to remain assured it was no mean mission'. Since Anderson knew very well what had been in *The Times* on the 8th, and had been aware of Stanley's interest in Livingstone since first meeting him in January 1867, it has to be assumed that he delayed telling him anything definite until a telegram arrived from Bennett giving final approval to an attempt to interview the explorer. Until then, Anderson would not have wanted to enthuse about Livingstone, only to have to disappoint Stanley if Bennett's answer was no[12] [see note for additional reasons why Stanley was the originator of the Livingstone mission].

The following day, the 17th, when Stanley returned to Anderson's office, a reply had been received from the great proprietor. Mr Bennett, Henry noted briskly in his diary, 'having a high idea of my intelligence and enterprise', had agreed to send 'a correspondent to intercept and interview Dr Livingstone, who was reported to be advancing towards the Zanzibar coast'.[13] On 20 October, Anderson handed Stanley his written instructions: 'The *New York Herald* desires you to proceed to Suez, or if practicable to Zanzibar to meet him ... You may assure him that the people of the United States not less than the people of Great Britain have anxiously looked for his safe return.' And then came an instruction to use the costly Bombay telegraph in the event of success, 'regardless of expense'. This was eloquent proof of the extent to which Mr Bennett had been persuaded by Anderson (himself earlier persuaded by Stanley) of the extraordinary public interest that would be aroused by the first sighting of Dr Livingstone by a fellow white man in two and a half years.[14]

Before Stanley left on what he believed would be his most dangerous and important mission to date, he moved to the Queen's Hotel in St Martin's Le Grand, where Finley Anderson also had rooms. From there he sent a telegram to his mother, Mrs Jones, asking her to come to London at once, bringing with her, if possible, her niece, the attractive but ignorant Catherine Parry, to whom he had taken a fancy on his last visit to Wales. Clearly, he was rallying after the loss of Virginia – but Catherine's mother refused to let her daughter come. So Mrs Jones brought Stanley's half-sister, Emma, then working as a servant near Denbigh. Mrs Jones and Emma were not invited to stay at the Queen's, but between the 18th and 22nd were booked in by Henry at a nearby pub, the Castle & Falcon. There he explained to his mother and half-sister that treats like this one would depend in future on their discretion.

Mother is amazed at what she calls the grandeur of her rooms ... She affects to be now proud of me, but my fear is that her vanity may make public what the public are not likely to regard as creditable either to her or to me. Personally I wish I could sponge out of my memory what makes the past so hideous to me, and persuade mother to keep silence out of regard to my pride and her interests. However indifferent she may be to what her neighbours may say of her, I cannot as yet pretend to be indifferent to what the world may say of me. I want none of its false pity or mock sympathy. But living in a small hamlet in Wales, she cannot understand why I object to publish wherever I go the story of my origin and boyhood ... On the evening of the 22nd, she departed with a purse of £100, while Emma was made happy with one that contained £25. I hope the money will not spoil them. On Emma, who is sensible, I can rely, but mother is of a different fibre.'[15]

Elsewhere, Stanley wrote that his gift to his mother was £50, and to Emma £20. Even the smaller sums would have been astonishing presents to their recipients, since many working-class people did not earn as much in a year. Since Stanley's salary was £400 per annum, his generosity was remarkable.

So what should we make of this family visit? That Stanley wanted to see his mother before going on a mission that might cost him his life? Maybe – but there is a distinct possibility that by enabling her to be in London for five days and by giving her money, Henry may have experienced a welcome sense of taking charge and wiping out his childhood powerlessness. Since secrecy was essential to the success of his mission, it seems most unlikely that he risked telling his mother or half-sister that he was about to try to find Dr Livingstone. He would certainly never have written to them about it, since both were illiterate and his letters had to be read aloud by a friend of his mother's.[16]

Between mid-November 1868 and the following February, Henry made enquiries in flyblown Alexandria, and in Aden, and boarded every homeward-bound ship, but he could find out nothing about the doctor.[17] He wrote to Captain Francis Webb, the US consul in Zanzibar, enquiring in strictest confidence whether the rumours about Livingstone's imminent arrival at the coast were true.[18] Webb's reply did not reach him until 1 February, and it merely confirmed what Stanley had sensed by then, 'that there was not the slightest chance of Livingstone coming via Zanzibar'. The unpalatable truth was that the missionary explorer might be almost anywhere in the interior, and impossible to find.[19]

In Aden, Alexandria and Cairo, Henry ploughed his way through the Bombay and English papers, and started to convert his Abyssinian diary into a book.[20] He tried and failed to give up cigarettes and cigars, and struggled to banish 'vile thoughts that stained the mind'. These lustful desires might have been satisfied with perfect propriety if he had only married Virginia. Meanwhile, to make things worse, the English community in Alexandria gossiped incessantly about love and sex.[21] Henry's depression deepened when he overheard two upper-class Englishmen mocking him cruelly – thinking themselves safely out of hearing. He was suffering from fever at the time and knew he was about to be recalled, having learned not a single thing about Livingstone.[22]

In London, Stanley was shocked to learn that Finley Anderson had been replaced by Douglas A. Levien, who now informed Stanley that he was to be sent to Spain at the same salary as before. Bennett's sacking of Anderson made Stanley fear for his own future. If the Livingstone adventure remained a non-starter, what then? This new source of insecurity made the still-wounded Henry surprisingly receptive when a new matrimonial proposition was put to him out of the blue.

When staying in Denbigh in January 1867, Stanley had been introduced by his mother to a young woman called Katie Gough Roberts. The next day, at the father's invitation, Stanley and his mother had called at the Roberts' respectable residence in Vale Street.[23] Stanley recalled, two years later, that after this first meeting he had remembered Katie as 'good-looking ... with long fair hair down her back'.[24] On 3 March 1869, Henry was staying at the Queen's Hotel near Trafalgar Square waiting to return to Spain for the *New York Herald*, when Katie and her father, Thomas Gough Roberts, turned up uninvited at the hotel. Thinking that Mr Roberts was 'a well-to-do solicitor', Henry was flattered to find him 'so frank & good-natured as to be oblivious of St Asaph [the workhouse]'. Yet Roberts's behaviour was exceedingly strange. It would have been unheard of at this date for a gentleman to bring his daughter to see a young man to whom she had never been remotely close, and had not seen for over a year, and then to 'hint' – as Stanley recorded that Roberts did: 'if I center [*sic*] my affection on the young lady, he would dower her with a thousand pounds'. Stanley noticed that Roberts was red-faced and 'not strong on teetotalism'. This was a considerable understatement, since Roberts would drink himself to death within less than a year.[25] At the time of this trip to London with Katie, his wife was mortally ill; and with his own health as precarious as his finances, he was desperate to find a husband for his oldest daughter.

Ironically, although Henry felt honoured to be pursued by this member of Denbigh's elite, Roberts's background was less 'well-to-do' than he imagined. Though Stanley thought him a retired solicitor, Thomas Gough Roberts's name does not appear in any Law Lists of the period, or in any local trade directories of the 1850s and 1860s. Nor was he listed as a barrister in the admission registers of any of the four Inns of Court.[26] Roberts was the son of a small landowner from Llanrhaeadr near Denbigh, and had left Wadham College, Oxford, without taking a degree.[27] A subsequent falling-out with his father may explain why, aged twenty-five, he was a publican in Denbigh, living in a poor part of town. In 1859 he moved to Vale Street and began describing himself as a gentleman, thanks to a legacy from his grandmother rather than to professional earnings.[28] Given this background, Mr Roberts's interest in a clever workhouse boy, with a regular income, is easier to understand. (He would leave £5,000 in his will when he died in 1870 – not a large sum to be divided among seven children.) So Stanley seemed a more than satisfactory catch for a girl who would not have been considered by a prosperous solicitor from, say, Shrewsbury or Chester.

Since backgrounds came no humbler than his own, Henry never suspected Roberts's motives; and soon he was in the same state of rapture he had experienced when imagining himself married to Virginia Ambella. 'One of my secret aspirations has been to wed some fair-haired girl of discreet and amiable disposition whose affection for me would enable me to forget the ills of life & live up to that ideal [of] ... blessedness.' Yet at this point it did finally strike him that Roberts should not have pushed his daughter at him. Nevertheless, he decided, 'it may be that fate has chosen this singular way of conquering my reserve, for I know no man less forward than I in the presence of a woman'.[29]

Three days later, Stanley took his mother and half-sister, Emma, to Paris for a brief holiday. While walking in the Bois de Boulogne, Mrs Jones told her son that she wanted him to marry a Welsh girl and not 'a vile foreigner'. Henry now suspected that she had encouraged Mr Roberts to bring his daughter to the Queen's Hotel. With Emma at present working as the Roberts's house maid, her involvement, and her mother's, seemed all but certain.

Back in England – although he did not record it in his diary – Stanley followed his relatives back to Wales, and stayed with his mother at the cramped Castle Arms tavern. From this improbable headquarters he conducted a whirlwind romance with Katie. The fact that his mother approved of Katie would probably have increased her appeal to him. In a letter to Katie's father, written a month later, Henry gave a thumbnail description of the week's momentous events.

During the middle of March, I revisited Denbigh ... Your daughter, Miss Katie M. Roberts, paid a visit to my mother, who keeps a little tavern. I was struck very much with Miss Roberts' appearance, her very ladylike deportment and her excessive amiability. I conversed with her and found her well educated ... I began to admire her but that admiration was quickly succeeded by love. I proposed to her, in a letter, and was accepted. From what Miss Katie has informed me, I find that Mrs Roberts does not object to me as a son-in-law.

He ended his letter by asking Mr Roberts whether he too consented to a future marriage.[30]

Stanley's proposal of marriage is contained, rather obliquely, in a long autobiographical letter, which was written at the Queen's Hotel on 22 March, the day he returned to London from Wales. In it, he told Katie: 'I am an illegitimate child of Elizabeth Parry and John Rowlands ... I was a waif cast into the world ... Neither of my parents ever deigned to take the slightest notice of me ... it was decided that the waif should go to the workhouse – the Almshouse, the Poor House.'

Along with these painful truths, Stanley included – as if to compensate – his invented acts of heroism in the American Civil War, and an exaggerated account of his wealth and income. But this bluster does not devalue the immense personal achievement of telling another human being the unvarnished truth about his origins and about his rejection by his entire family. 'For nine years the waif lived within the workhouse, uncared for by all relations.' Given the gossip in Denbigh, he would have had no choice but to tell Katie some of these facts, but by no means all of them. Describing himself as the 'workhouse brat', as well as 'the waif', he wrote much of the letter in the third person, only able to describe the misery of his youth by distancing himself from it. After saying that 'the waif' was 'very ambitious', Stanley added: 'He could do even better with a wife, not a pretty doll-faced wife, but a woman educated, possessed of energy.' Then suddenly he switched to the first person: 'Along with her aid ... I would defy the world; I write to you, having seen such a one as I desire; I request you write to me as quickly as possible, as I am going to Spain next Wednesday. Couch it in plain terms, discard all ambiguity, as I have done ...' He signed off 'as one who loves you', and asked to be addressed as Henry.[31]

None of Katie's replies have survived, but in an undated and incomplete letter from Stanley (written in March or April), he implored her: 'Write to me fully, declare once more your promise or withdraw it. Tell your love for me as often as your heart's dearest impulse will prompt you ... Send me also a lock of your hair, and I shall encase it in richest gold, I shall blush to tell you how often I should kiss it.'[32] In mid-May Katie had apparently begged Stanley not to 'forsake' her now that her mother had recently died. He replied: 'Over the grave of your dead mother ... I repeat my vow to make you my wife.'[33] So this was serious indeed.

Shortly before his wife's death, Thomas Gough Roberts gave his consent to the marriage – Stanley merely being asked to confirm whether or not he was a member of the Church of England.[34] For a young man in a delicate position, he replied with commendable honesty: 'Very little veneration do I have for any church ... People are too muffled up in the infallibility of their own sects ... Katie may profess what she pleases'.[35] Roberts seemed content with this reply.

Between the spring and autumn of 1869, Stanley was sent back to Spain by Levien to report on the spasmodic fighting between the Monarchists and the Republicans. Although he went on writing lovingly to Katie, the man of action in his make-up was tugging him away from his yearning for marital security into an increasing fascination with danger. In September 1869, Stanley was ordered to Valencia to report on the stiffest street fighting in the war to date. Before leaving Madrid, he had met a young journalist of twenty-one working for the *Boston Morning Journal*. His name was Edward King, and he too was bound for Valencia where he soon described the fearless war correspondent at work.

When Stanley first breezed into the hotel where King was staying, the younger man was immediately struck by the extraordinary energy emanating from this 'short, swart young man ... He accosted me in Castilian whereupon I shook my head. Then he burst into a gratified laugh and seized my hands.' Then, since their train did not leave for an hour, Henry jumped into a carriage to get a clean shirt from his hotel, returning in fifteen minutes. King thought him 'the very perfection of activity'. He noticed that, though Henry often smiled, 'his eyes seemed always to be looking far away at something to be reached and won'.

They arrived at Valencia, thanks to Stanley's decision to abandon the train and travel on from Alicante by ship. Outside the war-torn town, fleeing people were fighting for carts and horses. Henry scrambled onto a mound of luggage and appealed to anyone in the crowd who might be prepared to help them get into town. Nobody responded to this dangerous request, until at last a sixteen-year-old boy agreed to lead them through the back streets. In the central square 400 soldiers were drawn up with loaded rifles. An officer told Stanley and King that they could not reach their hotel because the *insurrectos* had barricaded the very street it was in, and were shooting anyone who stepped into the thoroughfare. Stanley smiled at King, and said that the royalist rebels were rotten shots. Then, with King's valise under his arm, he sprinted across the street as bullets whizzed past him. King and the boy followed suit. All three reached the hotel unscathed, and ate a huge breakfast on arrival. When Henry stepped onto the balcony outside their room, a bullet literally parted his hair. White with shock, 'he sat down upon the sofa very quietly for a few minutes'. Although he blocked the windows with furniture, another bullet smashed through the glass and pinged into the room. That afternoon the barricade outside the hotel was stormed, costing the Republicans many lives. Afterwards Stanley interviewed generals and rebels 'with the most careful fidelity and compared their statements'.

King learned a lot from Henry and remained a close friend until the late 1880s – 'friend of my soul', Stanley called him.[36] Henry had warmed to him at once because, like himself, Edward King had suffered in childhood – his father having killed himself by jumping from a steamship on a voyage of recuperation. King had then left home at sixteen to become a reporter. His first book, a personal appreciation of Paris, had been published a year before he met Stanley.[37]

But his love of dangerous work did not stop Henry longing for Katie. 'My usual thoughts, ambitions, hopes, aspirations have utterly left me,' he confessed to her, 'eclipsed by constant unrepressed thoughts of you ... The love I feel for you absorbs all – it is ardent, whole-souled.'[38] Though he dreaded her abandoning him because of his origins, he loved her enough to write: 'It would shock me greatly to receive a letter withdrawing your promise, but it would shock me still more to think you were suffering for my sake.' He explained that his time in America had enabled him to see Denbigh as it really was: 'a small place with petty jealousies'. He hated to think of her exposed 'from morning to night to scandalous gossip fouling everybody's character'. Stanley's mother, and his sister, Emma, were scandalmongers, and Emma even hinted to Katie that her half-brother was already married. Being jealous of Katie, she threw several of Henry's letters into a water butt to harm his chances. She knew that if Henry marred Katie there would be no more lavish gifts for her, or trips to Paris.[39] Yet Stanley forgave his sister, asking Katie to 'think of both of us how we were brought up, and have mercy'. Henry was confused by his fiancée's closeness to members of his family. He vacillated between wishing Katie to cultivate his mother, and wanting her to condemn the woman.

'I do not believe she ever loved me. I do not believe she <u>can</u> love now ... When she tells me she loves me, I listen and appear gratified but I know better ...'

So what a change had been effected! Mrs Jones had actually told her 'waif' that she loved him. Katie was an expert peacemaker, who persuaded Stanley to make up with his mother by writing 'a penitent letter', having arranged for Mrs Jones to send Stanley a photograph of his youngest half-brother, James, with a loving note.[40] But discord followed, and Stanley asked Katie to keep his mother at a distance. 'When you marry me, you marry myself only, for I am isolated as I have been from the age of five.'

Even when Katie's involvement with his family upset him, Henry told her tenderly that he read her letters several times, 'until I hear a sweet voice that seems to knock at the gate of my heart ... thrilling in its deliciousness and sweetness, and I listen and listen until a dreamy exquisite feeling of domesticity begins to creep over me such as I never experienced before'.[41] At times, seeking to impress, he was unintentionally comical.

Today I wear underclothes of silk ... and a white linen suit ... The pantaloons are what are called 'peg tops' ... The coat is loose, braided around with silk cord. Hat is of white silk with black riband & black binding; shoes brown French gaiters, gloves fawn color [sic] ... There you have a perfect picture of me. Am I not dainty?[42]

Only the final, rhetorical question saves him from absurdity. He could seem frighteningly certain of his destiny. Yet given what Stanley would achieve in Africa, at immense cost to his health, his self-dramatizing bravado seems eerily prescient.

So long as my health lasts I feel myself so much a master of my own fortunes that I can well understand Caesar's saying to the sailors, 'Nay be not afraid for you carry Caesar and his fortunes.' I could say the same, 'My body carries Stanley and his fortunes.'[43]

But Henry's glorious future meant little to Katie when her present worries became pressing. Her father was a drunkard, and was not expected to live long. So, after her mother's unexpected death in May, she knew that unless she married soon she would become, as the eldest daughter, responsible for the care of her younger brothers and sisters. She begged Henry, for her sake, to avoid the fighting and come home soon and marry her. His reply was not reassuring.

You know that I am not master of my own actions, I am at the beck and call of a Chief whose will is imperious law ... The slightest forgetfulness of duty, the slightest laggardness is punished severely ... I do not mean to be discharged from my splendid position ... My great love for you cannot blind me, it cannot lead me astray from the path I have chalked out ... And yet my whole future is risked each time you ask me to name the day I come to England. Know once for all, I cannot come to England without permission unless I throw up my position.

The best she could hope for, he explained, would be to see him after he had reported on the opening of the Suez Canal early in November.

How are we to be married you ask? If you cannot come to London with your father to be married to me by licence, you don't deserve to be married. My dear girl, can you not understand ... it is only by railway celerity that I can live. Even when I come to Denbigh I feel out of the world, my conscience accuses me of forgetting duty, of wasting time ... I cannot help that feeling. It makes me feel as if the world was sliding from under my feet.[44]

In this remarkable letter, Henry confessed to Katie that work, above all else, was his essential way of blotting out unhappiness. 'It is only by railway celerity that I can live' is a most revealing statement. And now at last he acknowledged that his need to live at a hectic pace could pose a problem in relation to marriage. With all this travelling, how could a shared life be possible? But perhaps they could travel together, like Samuel Baker and his wife, Florence? This, however, would be expensive, so Stanley reminded Katie that her father had once offered a dowry of £1,000. Even £500 would cover her accommodation and trousseau for the foreseeable future. Yet given the true state of Mr Roberts's finances, Henry's request alarmed father and daughter enough to damage his chances of marrying her. Katie knew only too well that her father had dangled a generous dowry as a lure, but had hoped to slip out of paying once Henry was properly infatuated. Stanley seemed completely unaware that Thomas Gough Roberts's aim in marrying off his daughters had always been to spare himself expense rather than to incur it.[45]

By the autumn of 1869 Katie's letters were starting to dry up, but at this critical time Stanley was summoned from Spain by James Gordon Bennett Jr to meet him in Paris. He now also arranged to meet Katie and her father on a lightning visit to London. As Henry's private life reached its defining moment, so too, unfortunately, did the great news story that had tantalized him for years. In Paris, at the Grand Hotel, on 28 October, Bennett announced that the moment had finally arrived to resume the search for Dr Livingstone. This would not have been a complete surprise to Stanley, since, back in June Douglas Levien, the *Herald*'s London agent, had written hinting that he was actively trying to revive Bennett's interest in the great explorer.[46] Bennett now told Stanley what he planned for him. First, he was to travel for a few months in Egypt, Palestine, Syria, Iraq, the Crimea, Persia, and finally India; and only after that should he sail from Bombay to Zanzibar to start his long-deferred attempt to find Livingstone. Some sixth sense was apparently telling Bennett that this lengthy prelude to the task in Africa would make ultimate success more likely, though Henry feared the delay would give Livingstone time to reach the coast, or even die, before he could reach him.[47]

But James Gordon Bennett Jr's decision to delay the search would turn out to be spot on. Less than a month after the proprietor's meeting with Stanley, the *Bombay Gazette* (20 November) published a letter written by Livingstone six months earlier, on 30 May 1869, from Ujiji on the shores of Lake Tanganyika. Bennett's new hope was that by the time Stanley had travelled to all the places he had listed a year would have passed and, with luck, nothing more would have been heard from Dr Livingstone. In Stanley's famous published account of the Paris interview, he quotes Bennett as saying: 'Draw a thousand pounds now, and when you have gone through that, draw another thousand, and when that is spent draw another ... and so on; but, FIND LIVINGSTONE.' Proof that he said no such thing is contained in a letter that Stanley sent to Bennett from Zanzibar on 17 January 1871, a year and two and a half months after the Paris meeting. As might have been expected, given the on–off nature of the Livingstone search project, there had in reality been no dramatic injunction to FIND LIVINGSTONE at whatever cost, as Stanley would state in his best-seller, *How I Found Livingstone*. Instead, in his letter Stanley recalled for James Gordon Bennett Jr's benefit that he (Bennett) had decided to send him on a year's course of travel through the Middle East ending at Zanzibar.

James Gordon Bennett Jr

'How much do you allow for this?' I asked.

'Oh! As much as it will cost. Draw £500 now and when that is over, draw another – and another etc.,' you replied.

'Well I have drawn but £600 that has lasted me a year … .'

So clearly the '£500 … etc.' had only referred to the Middle Eastern journey. The vexed question of how much the African journey would cost had not been touched upon at the meeting on 28 October – which was why in this same letter (17 January 1870) Stanley, by now at Zanzibar and expecting a large remittance, pointed out anxiously that $4,000 or $5,000 would be needed fast, in order to find Livingstone in the interior.[48]

When Stanley met Katie and Thomas Gough Roberts in London two days after his vital meeting with Bennett, it could not have been easy for him to break the news to them that he was about to be sent abroad again, for even longer this time. Here then was a crucial moment of choice for Stanley, which his earlier rejection by the Ambella family should have prepared him for. If he told Roberts he was going to Africa, or even around the world, the man would be horrified. White men often died in Africa, and journeys round the world could take years. Naively, Stanley hoped that if he merely told Roberts that he would be in the Middle East for a year, and if he suggested an immediate marriage in London followed by a period travelling together, Roberts would agree to his daughter marrying. But Mr Roberts would only allow him to marry Katie if he abandoned all lengthy foreign assignments. It should have been clear to Stanley at this point that he could have either marital security *or* distant fame and glory, but not both – or at any rate, not with Katie.

This all-important meeting with his fiancée and Mr Roberts took place in a house in the Euston Road and lasted about an hour. Stanley thought his fiancée looked at him rather coolly – as indeed she might, given the unwelcome news about his new assignment. She seems to have felt the same about his behaviour, for later she said that he had merely been 'business-like'.[49] Roberts refused to let Katie travel, and after rejecting an early marriage told Stanley he would have to wait to wed until he was able to stay in Britain long enough to show commitment to a settled way of life.[50] Stanley must have realized that this postponement would probably be fatal. But while he did not give up, he never for a moment thought of abandoning his African quest. *That*, in the last resort, mattered most of all to him. Yet Stanley still longed for the security of marriage, and hoped he could find Livingstone *and* marry Katie. He wrote to her from the steamer *Europe,* on 8 November, while in the Grand Harbour at Malta:

Those few minutes I have passed with you [in London] have done me infinite good. My love for you is now rich and deep, it is also respectful. I find it impossible to express it all ... there is no being on earth I love as much as my own dear, dear girl.[51]

Two letters from Katie reached Stanley in Constantinople in April 1870 and he replied by offering to marry her if she came out to Turkey at once, the alternative being for her to wait two years until he came home.[52] By the time this letter reached Katie, her father had died. She wrote several grief-stricken letters, none of which reached Henry. Her father had left her only a few hundred pounds in his will and she wanted help now, not in two years' time. With her bereaved family needing her so much, how could she possibly join Henry in some remote place? It was the end for her.

It is unknown whether Henry wrote to Katie between mid-April and early October 1870. But on 7 October he wrote from Bombay, having learned at last, from an old letter of hers that had been awaiting his arrival since July, that Thomas Roberts had been dead for months. Stanley expressed sympathy, but felt unable to tell her more about his coming expedition than: 'I shall be absent from 6 months to 1 year in Africa.' Katie was not to worry about the money she had expected to inherit. 'Your poverty will make no difference with me ... I shall hurry up with my business, and marry you. I swear it by all I hold sacred.'[53] But could he really have believed that a girl who had lost both her parents in a short space of time, and had money worries, would be prepared to wait for him, knowing nothing of his mission? The choice had really been between her, or James Gordon Bennett Jr and Africa, as Henry must have known since their meeting in the Euston Road almost a year before. The romantic side of his nature told him that their story *ought* to end in marriage: the workhouse boy, having distinguished himself beyond all expectations, weds the daughter of the respectable local gentleman, and they live happily ever afterwards in a big house just outside the town where they had spent their youth. But Katie had never understood his inner conviction of being chosen for a great task. *Her* ambition was to have a husband with her to help raise their children.

It is not known when she met the architectural student whom she married in September 1870. Despite Urban Rufus Bradshaw's magnif-

icent names, he was not from a privileged family, his father being a
Manchester policeman. But if he lacked Stanley's self-made glamour,
at least he was able to be with Katie when she needed him. By the time
Stanley wrote his last surviving letter to Katie from Bombay's Byculla
Hotel, she was already living as Mrs Urban Bradshaw in Pendleton,
outside Manchester, and taking in piano pupils.[54]

In late October 1869, after his key meeting with Bennett, Stanley had
stayed with Edward King in Paris, but refused to tell him about his
assignment. On the day of Henry's departure, the two friends set out
together for the Gare de Lyon. Before boarding the train, Stanley said
very solemnly: 'I may not be back for many years, but I *shall* come
back. Goodbye!'[55] King did not doubt him for a moment. Whenever
attacks were made on Stanley in the press in the years to come, King
would always believe in him.

Oddly, the only person Stanley told about his Livingstone search in
advance of leaving appears to have been a precocious thirteen-year-old
American boy, Edwin Balch, whose wealthy parents lived in Paris.
Henry visited them when he came to see Edward King, or Mr Bennett,
who preferred Paris to New York. Edwin wanted Henry to take him
travelling and wrote many wheedling letters, which received kind but
discouraging replies.[56] Yet Stanley still relished boyish admiration. In
fact, when he had first met Edwin in February 1869, the boy's enthusiasm for exploration had impressed him so much that he had given
him a copy of Livingstone's *Missionary Travels*. Though not permitted
to come travelling, Edwin was told the Livingstone secret. He wrote to
Henry on 21 May, informing him that he had seen reports in a French
newspaper stating that Sir Roderick Murchison believed Livingstone
was 'crossing the [African] continent on the Equator'.[57] In Murchison's most recent statement, it had merely been said that Livingstone
was not approaching Zanzibar, as had been rumoured.[58] So Henry
was desperate to see this French article, which Edwin eventually ran to
earth. Its author suggested that Livingstone would eventually emerge
on the west coast, rather than on the east, and this – though untrue –
had come as welcome news to Stanley, whose greatest fear had been
that Livingstone might emerge any day at Zanzibar.[59]

During the year that followed Stanley's meeting in Paris with James
Gordon Bennett Jr and his farewell to Edward King at the Gare de

Lyon, he reported on the opening of the Suez Canal, peered into the excavations at Jerusalem, visited Odessa and the battlefields of the Crimea, interviewed the governor of the Caucasus at Tiflis and journeyed to the Persian Gulf via Persepolis.[60] And at the end of all this, in Bombay, where Stanley was waiting to sail for Africa, what news did he hear about Livingstone's whereabouts? Incredibly, in October 1870, no more was known about the great explorer than had been known a year earlier. And no other letter had been received at Zanzibar, or anywhere else.

Challenging though this uncertainty was, it remained the ideal situation that Mr Bennett had dreamed of when postponing the search. When Dr Livingstone had written his last letter to Kirk on 30 May 1869, the explorer had been at Ujiji on Lake Tanganyika, and had been proposing to cross the lake and head west into Manyema, where the people were said to be cannibals. But whether he was still there, or had gone elsewhere, or been killed and eaten, was a mystery. Stanley was about to take an immense gamble – the kind that other gambling men would have thought far likelier to end with his death than with his success.

SEVEN

The Long-imagined Quest

Stanley sighted the island of Zanzibar on the morning of 6 January 1871 from the deck of an American brigantine, the *Falcon*. In the hazy distance he could see, beyond the masts and rigging of the ships at anchor, a jumble of white, flat-roofed houses, and the blood-red banner of the Sultan streaming out over his unfinished palace. Wafting into Henry's nostrils, on a scarcely discernible breeze, was an odour that in years to come would summon up in an instant this gateway to Africa: a heady mix of spices, tar, rotting vegetables, excrement and drying hides. The sun had not yet burned off the early morning mist, and across the strait 'the high lands of the continent loomed like a lengthening shadow'.[1]

Here, at last, was the 'Dark Continent' – that double-edged designation Stanley would one day use in two best-selling books. But despite his later commercialization of the phrase, it had not been coined by him but by the early nineteenth-century missionaries. To them, Africa's 'darkness' had not been principally due to its geographical mystery, or even to the colour of its inhabitants. For men like Moffat and Livingstone, Africa's 'darkness' was a spiritual and intellectual one, requiring the Gospel's light. For settlers and explorers, the continent's darkness had more to do with the unknown extent of it. But the darkness that troubled them most of all was the shadow of death. The death rate on the four expeditions sent from Britain to the rivers Congo, Zambezi and Niger between 1816 and 1841 had been over 60 per cent. Since then, although the principal explorers in east and central Africa (Speke, Burton, Baker and Grant) had survived, they had all come close to death, surviving only through liberal dosing with quinine – prescribed with the laxative resin of jalap by the greatest survivor of them all, David Livingstone.

For a man like Stanley, who needed to prove himself after his child-hood rejection, mastering Africa was a test that could scarcely be bet-tered. The task would have an epic dimension, involving power, pride and, above all, endurance as he battled with the African environment and with his own human limitations. At the heart of the non-con-formist Christian education of the workhouse had been the idea of redemption through suffering – becoming a new man. In the vastness of Africa, as ruler of his small party – away from the social distinctions of north Wales, from the greed and materialism of the slave-owning Deep South, from the helpless boy he had once been – there might emerge the new, perfected Stanley. He could so easily have spoken the words that Patrick White gave to Voss, the eponymous explorer hero of his masterpiece: 'To make yourself, it is also necessary to destroy yourself.'

In 1841, the year of Stanley's birth, when the twenty-eight-year-old Livingstone stepped ashore at Cape Town for the first time, the geog-raphy of central Africa was as much a mystery to Europeans as it had been to the Greeks and Romans 2,000 years earlier. The existence of the great lakes was not suspected, and the position of the sources of the Nile and Congo were matters only for fruitless conjecture. Then, between 1853 and 1856, Livingstone, in a majestic journey, crossed Africa along the line of the Zambezi. He suffered twenty-seven attacks of malaria and almost died at the half-way stage. Two years later, Richard Burton and John Speke reached Lake Tanganyika, and that same year Speke gained his first sight of an immense lake, which with typical Victorian cultural arrogance he called Lake Victoria. He returned in 1862 and found the vast lake's narrow northern outflow, which he would claim as the source of the Nile. In 1864 Samuel Baker reached a large lake north-west of Speke's Victoria Nyanza, the Luta Nzige, which he renamed Lake Albert. But none of these men had proved whether these nyanzas were single bodies of water, or groups of lakes. Nor did anyone know whether Lake Tanganyika – lying to the south-west of Lake Albert – fed it by a connecting river. If it did, Tanganyika (being so far to the south) would be the primary source of the Nile, rather than Speke's Victoria. This link was something Stanley wished to investigate, should he reach the Tanganyika in his search for Livingstone.

As Henry wandered through the crooked lanes of Zanzibar, seeking out the red-turbaned Banian, or Indian traders, from whom he would buy his supplies, nervousness vied with justifiable pride. He had taken many risks to secure his present opportunity – first offering to go to Abyssinia for Bennett at his own expense, then to travel through the Middle East with no guarantees of how much money would be available for the African part of his journey. But he had let none of this discourage him. The concept was so perfect that fear of insufficient commitment from Bennett and the *New York Herald* had never for a moment deterred him. Newspaper despatches made a journalist's name better known with every column inch that was published. So Stanley expected that the letters he would soon be writing to the *Herald* from Africa would build him an immense readership long before his enterprise was over and he wrote his travel book, which would surely outsell Livingstone's best-selling *Missionary Travels*, which Henry had read in his teens. To have put together a newspaper and book package, centred on a stunt, was an advanced idea to have had in the late 1860s, when most newspapers (notable exceptions being the *New York Herald* and *New York Sun*) simply reported the news in a frankly pedestrian manner.

It was a terrible shock to Stanley, on arriving at Zanzibar, to find that Bennett had let him down by not sending any money. However, because Henry had been left penniless by Bennett at the end of the Abyssinian expedition, even being reduced to selling his watch to buy food, he had taken care to bring Levien's letters proving that he was on a *bona fide* assignment for the *Herald*. He took these to the American consul, Francis Webb, to whom he had written two years previously, enquiring confidentially about Livingstone's whereabouts. This letter, along with those from Levien, gave Consul Webb enough confidence in Stanley to agree to pledge his own credit. Reassured by the US consul's guarantee, the merchants of Zanzibar accepted two drafts that Stanley now drew on the *New York Herald,* for $3,750 and $1,250, respectively.[2]

Because Stanley found Gordon Bennett's behaviour so personally insulting, he would never in print admit to what had happened. Hypersensitive to slights, Henry exaggerated the cost of his journey because he needed to give the world the impression that the *New York Herald* was 100 per cent behind him. In his first despatch to the *Herald*,[3] he claimed that he had just spent $8,000 on cloth, beads and wire alone – an immense exaggeration. Since his journey is still thought – even by scholars – to have been lavishly funded, it is worth quoting the sum Stanley told Mr Bennett was essential for his mission – a mere $4,000 to $5,000, with a basic figure of $3,842 given at the end of a detailed list. That this really was the modest sum he thought adequate can be verified by comparing it with the calculations he made on the endpapers of his copy of Richard Burton's two volume work, *The Lake Regions of Central Africa*, amounting to $3,280 for all men and supplies.[4] Stanley would later say that Mr Bennett had paid £4,000 for his expedition, equivalent to about $20,000 – an even larger exaggeration. In order to make such an over-estimate seem credible, Stanley destroyed his contemporary accounts and wrote out a new version, substantiating the $8,000 figure for supplies alone. Getting in on the act, Mr Bennett stated that the expedition cost him between £8,000 and £9,000.[5] Because Henry willingly connived in these exaggerations, his critics would one day say that whereas rival explorers were under-funded, he had had everything he needed and more, and had therefore had an easier time. Incredibly, Stanley's funding was inferior to Burton's and Speke's, and even to the £2,000 raised by Livingstone in 1866, which the doctor condemned as wretchedly inadequate.[6]

Stanley's need to feel important after his workhouse years led him into another unfortunate exaggeration: that his expedition was larger than all recent ones. In his first African despatch to his newspaper, he gave the total number of his *pagazi* or porters as 82 men, rather than the 157 he would claim in his book to have hired. In this same despatch, his total for the expedition was 111 men. The figure he gave Bennett was 100 *pagazi*, with a total for the whole caravan of just over 120, as opposed to the 192 claimed in his book and accepted by recent biographers.[7] His diary puts it beyond doubt that the lower estimates are reliable. Plainly, Stanley's achievement (unrecognized till now) was the greater for having been won with far slenderer resources than those stated by all his previous biographers.

Zanzibar's European residents had seen other expeditions in preparation, and swiftly realized that Stanley meant business. So how did he manage to purchase as much as he did with such a modest budget? Having worked as a clerk in a store, he knew about the fixing of prices and easily acquainted himself with *all* the varieties of cloth and beads his expedition would need to carry. As he made his purchases, nothing was too small to merit his attention: the screws needed to hold together his portable boats (ten pounds of two-inch and one-inch), his dozen bottles of Dr Collis Browne's Chlorodyne stomach medicine, his hand vice, two gimlets, hinges for a boat's rudder, and four ring bolts to secure it.[8]

Athough Stanley claimed to have been 'totally ignorant of the interior' before setting out, he did his research carefully.[9] He read Speke's *What led to the Discovery of the Source of the Nile* (1864) and Baker's *The Albert N'yanza* (1866), and his copious notes inside the covers of Burton's book show how useful he found that author's work.[10] Stanley would owe Burton and Speke a further debt when he hired Bombay and Mabruki, *their* principal 'captains', as *his* principal captains, and four other 'faithfuls' from their expeditions as the core of his own enterprise.

Zanzibar's residents – European, Indian, African and Arab – knew perfectly well that Stanley was mounting a significant expedition. But he told no one except Consul Webb that he meant to find Livingstone. Instead, Henry pretended that he meant to explore the upper reaches of an unimportant river, the Rufiji. This was what he told Dr John Kirk, the British political agent and acting consul, when Francis Webb took him to meet him at the British Residency on 9 January. Dr Kirk, a highly intelligent Scot, was a medical doctor and had been Livingstone's botanist and MO during the Zambezi Expedition. When Stanley trotted out his Rufiji story, Kirk did not laugh in his face but did the next best thing: 'he lifted his eyelids perceptibly, disclosing the full circle of the eyes ... I would call it a broad stare'. Stanley had been rumbled, and knew it.[11]

Kirk was invariably described as 'the companion of Dr Livingstone', and the two men regularly corresponded. The acting consul was also responsible for sending him supplies. In return, Livingstone confided his geographical plans. Henry knew that he would be mad not to pick this perceptive man's brains before he left the island, and so he went back to see Kirk ten days later. Henry claimed to have introduced Livingstone into the conversation with such subtlety that the acting consul did not realize he was being pumped.[12] In reality, Stanley came clean with Kirk, who responded well to this new openness, and the journalist in turn found himself 'attracted by the apparent [*sic*] frank manner & bonhomie of Kirk ... Who could resist it?' In reply to a direct question from Stanley about where Livingstone was, Kirk replied with admirable straightforwardness:

Dr Livingstone is on the western side of Lake Tanganyika. He expects shortly to come to Ujiji [on Lake Tanganyika], which is about four months travel from here. I have sent him some fresh supplies & boatmen, and they are on the other side – that is on the coast at Bagamoyo, about 25 miles from here preparing to start for Ujiji.

Then the acting consul horrified his visitor with a warning:

Dr Livingstone is pretty well known to me, and I know that with all his modesty, he ... appreciates more than any other man what he has done. If he hears of Baker in the neighbourhood he will go further away ... If Burton & Speke were at Ujiji he would take himself to the west side of the Lake. He hates Burton like poison. He is a man of strong likings & dislikes. He is vain, and easily annoyed. Any slights – no one would take them so much to heart as he himself.

This was an indiscreet but truthful portrait of Livingstone, and Kirk could have said far worse. At the end of the disastrous Zambezi Expedition, Kirk had described his boss as 'about as ungrateful and slippery a mortal as I ever came in contact with', and 'one of those sanguine enthusiasts wrapped up in their own schemes whose reason and better judgment is blinded by headstrong passion'.[13] Kirk would have recalled Livingstone's fury with various journalists over their

Dr John Kirk

coverage of the Zambezi Expedition. So why would he want to have anything to do with an American newspaperman? Kirk's off-putting words had been the truth as he saw it. And since he believed that two of his three caravans sent to Livingstone between the end of 1869 and early November 1870 had arrived (though only one of them actually had), he felt no misgivings about discouraging Stanley from trying to find the man.[14] In any case, he knew that Stanley would try to find Livingstone anyway, and therefore, before the journalist left, handed him a packet of letters for the great explorer.[15]

Stanley was badly shaken by the diplomat's words. What if Livingstone really did dash away into the bush the moment he heard that a white man was approaching? If there was no interview, Bennett might sack him and refuse to honour the drafts, secured through Consul Webb's pledges. If so, Henry would feel obliged to repay Webb at least part of his losses from his own modest savings of just over £550.[16] From the start, then, Stanley was under immense pressure to succeed.

One way to have lightened the load on his own shoulders would have been to take an experienced second in command – such as a European elephant hunter. But before Stanley had even reached Zanzibar, he had engaged a Scottish sailor who had been first mate on the vessel in which he had made the crossing from Bombay. William L. Farquhar had had no African experience, but was employed because he could navigate and was a fair mathematician. When it became apparent in Zanzibar that he was a heavy drinker, Stanley did not pay him off. His own days as a merchant seaman had

John Shaw and William Farquhar

left him sympathetic towards all mariners. The essential quality he looked for in white expedition members was obedience. Originality and initiative, he did not desire. In fact, any gentleman or military officer likely to question his authority would have been anathema. The other white man chosen was a Cockney called John W. Shaw, the third mate of an American merchantman, who had recently been unjustly accused of mutinous conduct. Stanley hired him because he was skilful at sewing canvas, and would be able to make tents as well as bales and sacks for trade goods. Yet Shaw, like Farquhar, was a drinker with a liking for African prostitutes, without regard for the risk of contracting venereal disease.[17]

The employee whom Stanley would describe as 'the most important member of the expedition apart from myself' was Selim Heshmy. Stanley had taken on this clever teenage Syrian Christian as his personal servant and translator when passing through Jerusalem in January 1870, and he had been with him ever since in Palestine, Iraq, Russia, Persia and India. He now expected Selim, a Swahili speaker, to communicate with the Arabs in the interior.[18] Maintaining discipline would become a priority for Henry for psychological and practical reasons. Bombay, the captain of Stanley's twenty-strong escort of armed *askari* or soldiers, had been punched in the mouth by Captain Speke and had broken teeth to prove it. Henry predicted that Bombay would not have 'the audacity to stand up for a boxing match' with him because he would learn respect from the outset.[19] Yet Henry was genuinely prepared 'to admit any black man ... to [his] friendship'.[20] He thought the Swahili-speaking Zanzibari blacks, the Wangwana – most of them free men and a few the slaves of local merchants – 'far more intelligent than I could ever have believed ...'.[21] Stanley spent a month on Zanzibar before sailing for Bagamoyo on the mainland, the starting point for his journey.

While at Bagamoyo hiring porters, Stanley discovered a state of affairs that would lay the foundations for a disastrous feud with Dr Kirk. Henry found that the supplies bought with £500 – half the sum voted to Livingstone by Parliament in May 1870 – were still sitting in a hut in the town in February 1871, three months after being despatched from Zanzibar, simply because the seven-man escort engaged by the British diplomat had not troubled to leave for the interior. Five of these seven porters were slaves, a strange choice of carriers for the arch anti-slavery propagandist Dr Livingstone.[22] Stanley was amazed that Kirk had not himself crossed to Bagamoyo with the porters to see them on their way. In fact, Kirk only came a week after Stanley's arrival, and not primarily to see whether Livingstone's supplies were by now en route, but to shoot big game with the officers of a British warship. By the time Kirk returned to Bagamoyo from his shooting party, he found that the caravan had left two days earlier, its leaders having got wind of the fact that he was coming.[23] Stanley was appalled that supplies for Dr Livingstone should be treated by Dr Kirk as such a low priority.

Stanley led the vanguard of his caravan out of Bagamoyo on 21 March 1871.[24] Four other columns had already gone ahead, one commanded by William Farquhar. In his book Henry said he himself had twenty-eight *pagazi* or carriers with him, but the true figure was ten, with nine *askari* or soldiers under Mbarak Bombay, who was also in charge of seventeen donkeys. The *pagazi* were carrying, along with trade goods, his portable boat for use on Lake Tanganyika.[25] Selim, the translator, and John Shaw, the sailor, were in charge of the donkey and cart, and brought up the rear. Stanley rode ahead of his column on a magnificent Arab stallion – the gift of an American living in Zanzibar. Behind Henry's horse trotted his dog, Omar, bought as a black-and-tan puppy in Bombay, to guard his tent.[26]

Stanley felt wildly exhilarated. Just five years after the shambles of his Turkish expedition, here he was in Africa on his way to death or glory. Like a monarch, he referred to his followers as 'my people'. They called him 'Bwana Mkuba' or 'big master', and defined his various roles as 'the vanguard, the reporter, the thinker, and leader of the Expedition'.[27] Stanley listed what he described as the expedition's 'defence weapons': 'one double-barrel breech-loading gun; one American Winchester rifle, or "sixteen-shooter"; one Henry rifle, or "sixteen shooter"; two Starr's breech-loaders; one Jocelyn breech loader, one elephant rifle ... two breech-loading revolvers, twenty-four muskets (flint-locks), six single-barrelled pistols, one battle-axe, two swords, two daggers ... one boar-spear, two American axes 4 lbs each, twenty-four hatchets, and twenty-four butcher-knives'.[28] Probably this fire power was overstated, like so much else about his retinue. However, four modern repeating rifles between three white men was not unusual or excessive: hunters like Selous and Gordon Cumming invariably carried more.

After several blasts on a kudu horn, Henry's caravan started on the road into the interior, 'a mere footpath, leading over a sandy soil of surprising fertility'. Out in front, the American flag sewn by Mrs Webb, the US consul's wife, was held aloft.[29] At this moment of departure, Stanley must have wondered, and not for the first time after Kirk's warning, what manner of man he was gambling his life upon finding in the heart of Africa.

EIGHT

'I Cannot Die!'

In 1871, David Livingstone was fifty-eight but looked ten years older, as he told his favourite daughter, Agnes: 'with cheeks fallen in ... the mouth almost toothless ... my smile is that of a hippopotamus ... a dreadful old fogy'.[1] The missionary explorer had always had a mordant sense of humour, which on the Zambezi he had frequently vented on his white travelling companions. Kirk had been right about his high opinion of his own merits as an explorer, and about his caustic criticism of other people, particularly travellers. Indeed, Livingstone detested Burton and Baker, partly as rivals but partly because he thought them unsympathetic towards Africans. He himself, by contrast, was usually patient and considerate to blacks, and had a passionate hatred of the slave trade. A sincerely religious man, he was indifferent to worldly wealth; and although it gratified him to have been awarded a gold medal by the Royal Geographical Society, the actual achievement of a great object delighted him more than any plaudits.

As Stanley set out to 'find' him, David Livingstone was almost a forgotten man to the public at large. The fame he had achieved as a result of his epoch-making trans-Africa journey of 1853–6 had been eroded by the costly failure of his government-sponsored expedition to the Zambezi. In 1867, when he had briefly been supposed dead, the coverage in the British press had been derisorily brief. During his last visit to England Livingstone had felt insulted by the coolness of the foreign secretary, Lord John Russell, and he had thought his lordship's offer of £500 towards his next trip outrageously mean. Although he had been given the honorary rank of consul, he had been told by Russell, with a bluntness he deeply resented, that this post carried no salary and that he could expect no pension.[2] Only when Sir Roderick Murchison threatened to shame the government by appealing to the public for money did the Cabinet authorize a grant of £1,000.[3] Had Stanley known how low Livingstone's reputation stood among Britain's rulers, he might have felt less sanguine about his own journalistic aim. Yet perhaps even in that case he would have predicted that to pluck a neglected and needy man from the wilds of Africa, and make him famous all over again, would actually make a far better story than finding a popular and well-supplied explorer who needed nothing and was not bothered by having seen no white face for five years.

Livingstone had been a child factory worker in a cotton mill near Glasgow, and had lived with his family of six in a single room in a factory tenement. Yet in 1841, this amazing ex-factory boy sailed for South Africa, having been ordained as a Congregationalist minister, and having put himself through medical school on his earnings as a cotton spinner and qualified as a doctor. Thereafter, Livingstone spent ten frustrating years in Botswana as a medical missionary, making but one convert, who lapsed – a fact unknown to the public at large until the publication of my biography in 1973. His missionary father-in-law had spent a lifetime converting twenty or so people, but Livingstone saw no point in doing likewise. Since tribal and Christian institutions were irreconcilably different, he decided that no large-scale Christian progress would be possible until tribalism had been weakened by widespread European trade and settlement. Livingstone understood Africans and admired many aspects of their communal existence, and yet he felt obliged to try to change their entire way of life, and their societies, in order, as he saw it, to save their souls.

Opening up Africa to 'trade and the Gospel' and ending the slave trade through exposing it became his twin objectives. 'The slave trade must be suppressed as the first great step to any mission – that baffles every good effort.'[4] But Livingstone had actually gone back to Africa in March 1866 because urged by Murchison of the RGS to settle the dispute raging between Speke and Burton about the true location of the source of the Nile. Livingstone hoped that if he found the Nile's source his outstanding achievement would lend weight to his attempts to convince politicians and businessmen that 'legitimate' European trade with African chiefs would give them a lucrative market for their goods, removing the need for the chiefs to make money to buy western goods by selling their own people.

So, in 1871, did Livingstone need to be found and aided by anyone? By July 1868 – after two years of travelling – Livingstone's original fifty-nine followers had dwindled to just four, through desertions, dismissals and deaths. The popular image of Livingstone's followers as being a Sunday school on the move could not be further from the truth. Sixteen-year-old Chuma, one of his 'faithfuls' (who had been liberated from a slave column by Livingstone), smoked marijuana whenever he could get it, and had sex with prostitutes or with absent men's wives. On one occasion Livingstone fired his pistol at Chuma because he would not march with the rest. Fortunately for Chuma, and for his master's reputation, the bullet missed. Gardner (another so-called faithful), like Chuma, regularly captured women and held them against their will. Simon (also a 'faithful') actually murdered two people in Manyema and sold others to slave traders. All Livingstone's followers stole from him; and Susi, whom he trusted more than the rest, never reported these thefts.[5] His deserters had left Livingstone with so few trade goods and supplies that from as early as May 1867 he had been obliged to travel with Arab-Swahili ivory and slave caravans far more often than he had been able to travel alone.

Livingstone could endure his humiliating dependence on men he considered evil-doers largely because he made a distinction between Arab slavery as an institution – the treatment and possession of domestic slaves – and the cruel process by which Africans were torn from their homes. The slaves' journey by land and sea was appallingly cruel, but upon arrival in Arabia they were usually treated better than were many British factory workers.

Being reduced to four followers by the middle of 1868, Livingstone knew he had no hope of carrying enough trade goods to pay chiefs for the right of passage through their territory. Yet for two months, with just these four followers, he did briefly leave the sustaining caravan of his friend Muhammad Bogharib, and on 18 July 1868 arrived at Lake Bangweulu, in what is now north-eastern Zambia. This lake, with its surrounding marshes, he would soon establish was the source of the mighty, northward-flowing Lualaba River, which he now strongly suspected flowed on to become the Nile. A year later, in July 1869, once more travelling with Bogharib, Livingstone left Ujiji and crossed Lake Tanganyika to Manyema, intending to trace the Lualaba northwards from the town of Nyangwe, and thereby solve the Nile mystery once and for all. As Stanley began his journey into the interior, in late

March 1871, he was ignorant of Livingstone's plan, which made a meeting between them extremely unlikely. Nothing more had been heard of Livingstone since he left Ujiji.

As Stanley, resplendent in solar topee and white flannels, rode out of Bagamoyo on his thoroughbred stallion, between hedges of mimosa, his men shared his buoyant mood.

We were all in the highest spirits [he recalled]. The soldiers sang, the kirangozi [guide] lifted his voice into a loud bellowing note, and fluttered the American flag, which told all on-lookers, 'Lo, a Musungu's [white man's] caravan!' and my heart, I thought, palpitated much too quickly for the sober face of a leader. But I could not check it; the enthusiasm of youth still clung to me despite my travels ... Loveliness glowed around me. I saw fertile fields ... strange trees – I heard the cry of cricket and pee-wit, and sibilant sound of many insects ... What could I do but lift my face toward the pure-glowing sky, and cry, 'God be thanked!'[6]

As Stanley saw for the first time giraffe, hippopotami, and antelope, he compared himself with 'an English nobleman' in his immense park. 'I felt momentarily proud that I owned such a vast domain, inhabited with such noble beasts ... the pride of the African forests.'[7] This was the workhouse boy in paradise. In travelling with his young servants – especially with Selim, his translator, and, in a month or two, with young Kalulu, the slave-boy whom he would free by purchase to be his butler and valet – Henry would be reminded of the boys at the workhouse, who had been his *de facto* family during his adolescence. Not that his affection for them would stop him beating both Selim and Kalulu for 'crimes' such as stealing food and breaking things. But with his bearskin rug covering the ground inside his tent, and his cream pots, candlestick and bottle of Worcestershire sauce on his folding table, Stanley – when in good health – would feel as much at home on safari as he ever did.[8] For this was a young man who had had no home of his own, anywhere in the world, since his grandfather's death when he was five.

For a few more days, fortune smiled on Henry. But the Victorian African explorer was always wise to be wary. Within days, Stanley's two Arab horses were killed by the tsetse fly – as if to teach him early that transport of goods, within much of Africa, could only be upon the heads or backs of men. Some of Stanley's donkeys – a species that showed greater resistance to the fly than other draught animals – were also sickening. Henry's caravan had travelled 125 miles, and was near the town of Simbawenni, when he felt obliged to flog his cook 'for incorrigible dishonesty and waste'. Stanley was never going to let *his* expedition be destroyed by the pilfering and carelessness that had destroyed so many others. He therefore pretended to expel the cook from the expedition, imagining that the threat alone would make him beg to be taken back, since expulsion might be a death sentence. But Stanley's stratagem misfired, and just when the caravan was about to leave the dry, lightly wooded tableland to cross the Makata swamp, the cook deserted.

Many explorers would have let the matter rest there – glad to see the back of any man who had proved impossible to discipline – but Stanley demonstrated at this early stage the steely determination that distinguished him from other explorers. *He* was not going to allow desertion, and sent three soldiers after the cook. These hapless soldiers were then arrested under suspicion of murder by the female chief of Simbamwenni town, who had just heard that the cook's donkey had been found by some of her people, but no cook. Henry therefore had to send out Shaw and another two men to look for the missing soldiers. The soldiers were eventually released, and the cook returned to Zanzibar, where he made a claim against his late employer for $100 for his lost beast and clothes![9]

The failure of his first attempt to compel the return of an absconder left Stanley no less determined to compel all future deserters to return and honour their contracts. A few days later, a carrier decamped after enduring many hours of misery getting the expedition's property across the swollen Makata river. Henry sent in pursuit his 'two detectives', as he called Uledi (James Grant's former valet) and Sarmian, both of them armed with American breech-loaders. They very soon recaptured the missing *pagazi*, who was beaten, and chained for a few days. His re-capture inevitably caused other carriers to think hard about the advisability of running away.

Yet, despite some successes of this kind, this was the first of Stanley's major journeys and he still had much to learn. He had split his expedition into five caravans or columns, in order to discourage attacks by African rulers who might have thought a single large caravan too threatening. But Henry's separation from his other columns reduced his influence over most of his expedition. With one white man, John Shaw, also in his own column, as well as Bombay, Uledi and Mabruki, his principal lieutenants, there were sure to be desertions from the other columns, especially since the only other white man, Farquhar, was a poor leader of the second largest column.

The five days it took the expedition to march through the 'cataclysm' of 'knee deep water and black mire' that was the Makata swamp resulted in Stanley, Shaw and Selim all contracting malaria, along with many of the *pagazi*. They had no idea, at this date, that the numerous mosquitoes they saw in clouds over the marshland were responsible for their misfortune. Dysentery and smallpox also afflicted the travellers, and in a few weeks Stanley's weight plummeted from 170 to 130 pounds. One of the *pagazi* very soon died of dysentery, as did Omar, Stanley's young dog, of whom he had already grown fond.[10] Stanley narrowly escaped death when the sick and shaky Selim rested his double-barrelled smooth bore on something jagged, accidentally firing it. By now, Stanley was suffering from fever 'with its insane visions, its frenetic brain-throbs & dire sickness'.[11] Ten days later he and Shaw were still sick, and Henry wondered whether he would ever have the strength to reach Ujiji.

On African expeditions, relationships between Europeans often became hostile and even paranoid. The dangers, the discomforts, and above all the pain and misery brought on by African fevers all undermined sociable impulses. Almost everything annoys the malaria sufferer: he is intensely sensitive to light and to the loud voices and vigorous movements of healthy human beings. The sufferer must be covered with heavy blankets until the malarial convulsions and the interior freezing coldness subside, leaving him weak, exhausted and querulous. Only men respecting one another when fit have any chance of remaining on good terms.

Even before malaria had afflicted them, Stanley, Shaw and Farquhar had fallen out. Farquhar's objection to sewing together some rubberized cloth to make a mackintosh for Selim had struck Henry as mutinous.[12] After drinking and whoring on Zanzibar, Farquhar had quarrelled with Shaw, and Stanley had become disgusted with him. Drink had been the ruin of Henry's father – or the man he *thought* was his father – and sexual promiscuity had led to his own illegitimacy and wretched childhood. Shaw also sought out whores, and despite this close contact angered Henry with his racism.[13] Nor could he control the donkey pulling the baggage cart, and this delayed the whole column.[14]

When Stanley and Farquhar fell ill, relations between them worsened beyond repair. This happened after the swamps had given way to the Usagara hills, and they were struggling up and down steep slopes, in and out of vegetation-choked valleys, under a blazing sun. When Henry overtook Farquhar's column, he found him 'sick a-bed with swollen legs (Bright's disease, engendered by general debauchery), unable and perhaps not a little unwilling to move'.[15] In fact the Scotsman was probably suffering from elephantiasis. He had used up an excessive amount of cloth, not just to buy food for his carriers, but to purchase chickens and other delicacies for himself. Worse still, all nine of the donkeys entrusted to him were dead or dying. The overweight Farquhar had regularly been riding the same donkey day after day until the wretched creature collapsed, and similar behaviour had led to the deaths of many of the nine.

On 20 May, after ten days' travelling together, the Scotsman was too ill to walk even a few yards, and had to ride all day and every day, with fatal consequences for whichever donkey he was riding. Stanley came to a decision for which he would later be upbraided. This was to leave the sick man with a village chief and with enough cloth to keep him alive till the expedition should pass by again. The alternative, if the caravan was to be kept moving, would have been for him to die in the saddle, after killing more donkeys. And if more donkeys were lost, Henry would find himself scouring the countryside for additional porters, wasting many days.[16] Farquhar died five days after the expedition's departure – and though Stanley would not have been able to save him if he had stayed, he must have regretted not remaining with him for a few more days.[17]

Relations with Shaw did not improve when Farquhar had been left behind. On one occasion Stanley knocked him down for insolence, and later Shaw – half-crazed with fever – put a bullet through Stanley's tent when the journalist was sleeping within.[18] Such recklessness was not uncommon among African explorers.[19] At the age of thirty, Henry could be ruthless. He was obsessed with the success of his mission, and knew he would be ruined by failure. He therefore tended to equate any weakness that delayed him with a treacherous lack of will power. His own periods of helplessness, he pardoned – but, in fairness, he was not incapable for weeks at a time, as was Shaw. Yet Henry never would acknowledge that his magnificent constitution was a great rarity.

Though impatient with white colleagues, he showed commendable restraint with Africans. The Wagogo, whose territory lay midway between the coast and Lake Tanganyika, were 'clannish and full of fight', and their young warriors repeatedly rushed up to within a few feet of him and shouted in his face before moving closer to inspect his clothes.[20] The traveller in Wagogo territory, wrote Henry, 'was tempted, a score of times each day to draw a bead with his rifle ... but such an outburst of anger would be bitterly regretted afterwards'.[21] Stanley was ill with fever at the time, and on two occasions lashed out with a whip. But he paid these people generously for the right of passage through their territory – the equivalent of $170 in gold.[22]

Henry arrived in the district of Unyanyembe – over two-thirds of the way to Ujiji – on 23 June, having marched 525 miles from the coast in 84 days, much faster than Burton and Speke's time of 134 days.[23] Two weeks before reaching the town of Tabora in Unyanyembe desertions became uncontrollable, and on arrival he had a mere twenty-five men. Arab settlements always proved powerful magnets for his Wangwana followers.[24] At this time, Henry learned that an Arab-Swahili caravan, which had just arrived from Manyema on the far side of Lake Tanganyika, had brought news that Livingstone was dead. This conflicted with earlier rumours that he had shot himself in the thigh while hunting buffalo and planned to return to Ujiji as soon as he had recovered.[25] These reports were alarming. Slightly earlier intelligence given him by an Arab caravan leader was that 'Dochter Fellusteen' was in Manyema where he had been deserted by all but three of his people. This too was far from reassuring. If the doctor really had only three followers, how would he ever be able to return to Lake Tanganyika?[26]

Stanley was now in the land of the Nyamwezi, who were the greatest African traders and travellers of central east Africa – they also provided a high proportion of the *pagazi* to be hired at Bagamoyo. European purchases of ivory increased dramatically from 1850 onwards, with demand for ivory combs, billiard balls, ornaments and piano keys seemingly insatiable. When Sultan Said Barghash of Zanzibar found that this new market could not be satisfied with the erratic supplies brought to the coast by the Nyamwezi, he sent his own Arab and Swahili-speaking African subjects inland to procure more ivory. These new caravans were financed by the capital of the Banians, the Indian traders of Bombay and Zanzibar. Along with this ever-expanding market for ivory came an increasing demand for slaves. By the time Stanley reached Unyanyembe for the first time, the Arab-Swahili traders in ivory and slaves – a slave would carry a tusk, until himself becoming saleable at Bagamoyo or Zanzibar – had journeyed as far west as Uganda, Rwanda, Burundi and the banks of the Lualaba and Lomani rivers over a thousand miles from the coast. A few Arabs had even crossed the continent from Kilwa to Luanda. Among the Arabs' defended trading settlements and staging posts were Ujiji, and Unyanyembe at the heart of the Nyamwezi chiefdom.

Initially the Nyamwezi derived great advantage from being hosts to a large Arab-Swahili community, since the traders brought the commodities of the industrial world, but as these guests, in time, achieved a near monopoly of the ivory and slave trades between Unyanyembe and Zanzibar, the Nyamwezi faced being squeezed out. However, in 1871 their chief, the magnificently named Mirambo, who possessed personal magnetism and considerable military skill, decided to take control of the main trade route to the ivory regions of central Africa. To achieve this, he meant to fight the Arabs of Unyanyembe. To win, he was prepared to employ Ngoni mercenaries – who for several decades had been moving up from southern Africa, spreading destruction as they went. Mirambo, like the Arabs, was also buying slaves and ivory on his own account. Unfortunately for the *New York Herald*'s special correspondent, this remarkable man would make his first concerted move against the Arabs just as Henry was planning to leave Unyanyembe for Ujiji.[27]

He brought with him letters of introduction written by the Sultan of Zanzibar Barghash to Said bin Salim, the Governor of Unyanyembe, and his henchman Shaykh bin Nasibu.[28] Now, Henry was given a feast by these grandees, and was allocated a *tembe* – or stockaded house – for himself and his followers. The Arabs confided that war with Mirambo was imminent and suggested he fight on their side. Their force numbered roughly 2,200, so Stanley's few men would hardly sway the balance. He tried to attract 'volunteer refugees', as he called them, but only managed to engage another twenty men, bringing his numbers to about fifty.[29] Then he dithered for a month or so – worried about fighting again in someone else's war. It seems he only committed himself after the Arabs had convinced him that Mirambo was a bandit, who had usurped the Nyamwezi chiefship and was only holding onto it with the help of mercenaries – 'ruga-ruga' – from neighbouring tribes.[30] Stanley was comforted to have this justification for fighting. Mirambo and his force were blocking the route to Ujiji, 250 miles to the west, and seemed unlikely to move until attacked. Unless

Henry could soon resume his march, he would be compelled to return to the coast for more supplies – and in that case, Mr Bennett would abandon him. So clearing the road to Ujiji was a necessity.

A fortnight before the fighting began, Henry was unconscious for several days with fever, and delirious for a week after that. So when the march against Mirambo began on 29 July,[31] he was still very weak, though strong enough to give Bombay, his chief soldier, a few cuts with his cane when he kept the whole party waiting for several hours while he had intercourse with his favourite whore. Three days west of Unyanyembe, John Shaw, Henry's only remaining white colleague, lay on the path and said that he was dying. Then, somehow, he clambered onto his donkey and kept moving for a few days more.

On 6 August, the Arab-Swahili army, and Stanley's small group with it, was approaching Mirambo's stronghold at Wilyankuru. Too sick to take part, Henry was a bystander when 500 men, under the son of a local Arab merchant, captured the central stockade. Mirambo only briefly defended it, before withdrawing with 400 of his men, leaving behind twenty dead warriors. Flushed with their 'victory', the Arabs left, loaded with a large amount of abandoned ivory and grain. But Mirambo's withdrawal had been a ruse. The unsuspecting Arabs were ambushed in nearby woodland by the Nyamwezi, and massacred to a man. Stanley had waited a few miles away with the bulk of the Arab force, which fled when news of the massacre broke. Scarcely able to stand, Henry would have been left behind in the general flight if his young translator, Selim, had not saddled his donkey and lifted his master onto the beast's back.[32]

When Mirambo sacked Tabora several days later, burning a quarter of the town, Henry remained holed up in his *tembe* in the nearby suburb of Kwihara. Here he heard the grim news that his closest acquaintance among the Arabs, Khamis bin Abdulla, with his son, and the son of Shaykh Nasibu, had been killed in a doomed effort to defend Tabora. In line with his usual tendency to exaggerate his own numbers, Stanley later claimed to have had 150 men in his *tembe,* prepared to resist Mirambo's anticipated attack on Kwihara. In fact, according to his diary, he had a mere thirty men with him on 22 August. Ironically, this made his decision to resist far braver. The following day Henry's followers were joined by the twenty or so *pagazi* who had reached Unyanyembe, out of the thirty-three hired by Kirk to carry Livingstone's stores to Ujiji. These men had been enjoying themselves in Tabora since

May. Stanley now took over Livingstone's stores, which included seventeen bales of cloth and twenty-two boxes of wire and beads, as well as a packet of letters.[33] As Henry ran up the Stars and Stripes and waited for Mirambo's army, he hoped his fifty followers' muskets would discourage a frontal assault on the *tembe*. He seemed unaware that Mirambo's tactics would be to set fire to his *tembe*'s thatch in order to force him into the open. His body would then be mutilated, as had been those of his Arab acquaintances, whose faces, genitals and stomachs were all boiled and eaten by Mirambo's men, mixed with a little rice and goat meat.[34] Fortunately for Henry, Mirambo chose to back off just when his enemies were at his mercy. Why, is a mystery. Perhaps he feared his men would be vulnerable to counter-attack when weighed down with their plunder. But Stanley remained deeply anxious, and decided it could be suicidal to try to reach Ujiji by the direct westerly route. He therefore planned to avoid the war entirely, by marching south and south-west for ten days and only then starting to head north to Ujiji.

By 7 September Henry's numbers had dwindled from fifty to thirty-three – a small party indeed to travel in such dangerous territory. The same day, he bought the freedom of an eleven-year-old slave boy, whose name was Ndugu M'hali, which meant 'my brother's wealth'. Stanley wanted this boy to act as his personal servant and gun-carrier. Disliking the boy's name, Henry renamed him Kalulu, which in Swahili meant a young male antelope.[35] As Stanley prepared to leave the *tembe* in Kwihara, Shaw became too sick to move, even in a travelling cot.[36] Six days later he was no better, and Selim was also dangerously ill. Henry did his best to nurse them both, while railing at the delay. 'The Apostle of Africa, Livingstone, is always in my mind, and as day after day passes without trying to find him, I find myself subject to fits of despression ... Shaw is sick, stubbornly so.' Incredibly, Stanley had not yet told the Cockney that they were in search of Livingstone.[37] At last, on 19 September, Henry believed he would be able to leave Kwihara next day. That night his fever left him, and though depressed by Arab warnings that he would die before reaching Ujiji, he wrote by candlelight:

I have taken a solemn, enduring oath, an oath to be kept while the least hope of life remains in me, not to be tempted to break the resolution I have formed, never to give up the search, until I find Livingstone alive, or find his dead body ... No living man, or living men, shall stop me, only death can prevent me. But death – not even this; I shall not die, I will not die, I cannot die![38]

So how had Dr Livingstone fared in the meantime? From July 1870 to February 1871 – the month in which Stanley had left Zanzibar for the African mainland – Livingstone had been totally immobilized by dysentery and anal bleeding, and by terrible flesh-eating ulcers on his feet. During this time of illness and depression at Bambarre (Kabambare), in Manyema, he fell victim to various delusions. He read the Bible through four times and persuaded himself that Moses had travelled from Ethiopia to Manyema in search of the Nile's source. Livingstone also read Herodotus' *History,* and found references that he thought supported his theory that the source of the Nile lay far to the south. Isolation and illness were loosening Livingstone's hold on reality and leading him to grasp at any straws that seemed to undermine the belief of Speke and Baker that the Nile's source lay in the northern lakes.

By February 1871 Livingstone was well enough to travel towards the river Lualaba with thirteen followers – ten of whom had been engaged by Dr Kirk at the coast early in 1870, and had arrived in Manyema a year later, against all odds. In March, Livingstone passed through a region devastated by Arab-Swahili slave raids, and arrived by the month's end at the town of Nyangwe on the great river. In order to trace the Lualaba northwards he needed canoes, but the local slave traders refused to sell him any in case he planned to spy on their activities. Meanwhile, his own followers were scared by the prospect of a long river trip, and did their best to stop him acquiring boats. Livingstone offered the immense sum of £400 to Dugumbe, the leading Arab in the town, if he would merely ferry him across the river, but on 15 July – the very day he made this offer – a massacre took place that shocked Livingstone more than any event he had ever witnessed. It was sparked by a trivial argument in Nyangwe's market but ended with the Arabs shooting into a crowd of fleeing people, many of whom dashed into the river and were drowned. The Arab estimate of 400 dead was probably 200 too few. Livingstone's outrage was too great for him to stay on any longer trying to buy Dugumbe's canoes. Two years of effort had come to nothing. There was now only one course open to him: to return to Ujiji, although he had not learned where the Lualaba went.[39]

On 8 August, Livingstone was ambushed not long after leaving Nyangwe, and was fortunate that two spears thrown from bushes only feet away both missed him.[40] He was passing through cannibal country, but was not alarmed. Failure weighed upon him more heavily than fear of death. The traders had got their ivory and slaves, but: 'I alone had failed and experienced worry, thwarting, baffling, when almost in sight of the end towards which I strained.'[41] The prospect of returning to Ujiji after having made so little progress in two years was intolerable. In his worst dreams he had not expected to be returning like this.

Stanley left Kwihara on 20 September 1871 with a group of men that he had, as he put it, 'selected to be crowned as Immortals'. He listed these, in his book *How I Found Livingstone,* as numbering fifty-four – twenty more than the true figure.[42] That same evening Stanley had another severe bout of fever, and many of his men took the opportunity to hurry back to Kwihara for 'one last debauch'.[43] The men drifted back next day, and as the column headed south its leader was too ill to inflict any punishments. Three days later, Asmani, the man in charge of Livingstone's supply caravan, deserted, taking his gun with him. Stanley sent Bombay, with three 'soldiers', in pursuit. He then gave the order to the rest of his men to march. Seven *pagazi* refused to lift their loads, saying they were sick. Stanley put several in chains and beat the rest. Naively, he would describe this punishment later in his book – as if unaware that other travellers kept quiet about such matters. But, having survived in the workhouse by concealing his vulnerability, Henry still needed, as a young man, to be thought harder and more formidable than other explorers.

John Shaw's illness grew critical in the first few days of the march, and on 26 September Stanley decided that if he were ever to leave in pursuit of Livingstone, the man would have to be taken back to Kwihara. The sailor had been ill for so long that any more marching would have killed him. Being close to Arab supplies, he was not going to starve. Shaw himself was eager to be left behind, and his last evening with his leader was amicable.

The night before we parted, Shaw played some tunes on an accordion ... though it was only a miserable ten-dollar affair ... The last tune played before retiring was 'Home Sweet Home'; and I fancy that before it ended we had mutually softened towards each other.[44]

Two days later, Shaw was in Kwihara, and Henry and his men were travelling through a dense forest. Malaria was tormenting Henry again. Apart from the violent shakings and sweats and Arctic coldness, he experienced 'strange fancies which sometimes assume most hideous shapes'. Between bouts of delirium, he felt 'insanely furious'. On recovery, he would feel 'ludicrously amiable'.[45] The Arabs had warned him that the southerly route to Ujiji would force him into the territory of the Ha people, who were notorious for making exorbitant demands on travellers. Stanley had no objection to paying 'hongo' – a levy for right of passage – but the Ha tried his patience to the limit. During two days spent crossing their land, he wrote, they 'mulcted me of half the available property of the expedition'.[46] But in late October, at the Malagarazi river, Henry was electrified to hear that a white man with grey whiskers had just arrived at Ujiji from Manyema. To avoid more time-wasting negotiations with Ha chiefs, he led his men on a lengthy detour along a reedy river bank and then through a bamboo jungle.

During the early stages of his march from Unyanyembe, Stanley and his men passed through forest and marshland, and then clambered over hills and rocky ridges. Nearing Lake Tanganyika, as he and his men swung northwards, the countryside became gentler, 'the green hills crowned by clusters of straw-thatched cones'. And then a notable announcement: 'We cross the Mkuti, a glorious little river'[47] – 'glorious' because, at last, they were just hours from Ujiji, though they could scarcely believe it. In camp that evening, Stanley ordered Selim: 'Lay out my new flannel suit ... oil my boots ... chalk my helmet, and fold a new puggaree around it, that I may make as presentable an appearance as possible before the white man with the grey beard, and before the Arabs of Ujiji; for the clothes I have worn through jungle and forest are in tatters.'[48] Stanley was in no doubt from the information he had that Livingstone was indeed at Ujiji, and yet he was still fearful that this man, whom Dr Kirk had represented as a reclusive misanthrope, would resent being 'found'.

Livingstone's return journey from Nyangwe to Ujiji was one of the most agonizing he ever undertook. He could not dismiss from his mind 'the sad scenes of man's inhumanity to man'. He was emaciated from dysentery, and his ulcerated feet caused him misery. 'I ... arrived, a mere ruckle of bones ... I felt as if dying on my feet.'[49] Then, at Ujiji, a savage blow: Sherif Bashakyh bin Ahmed – the man whom Kirk had placed in charge of the supply caravan despatched early in 1870, which had arrived at Ujiji a year later – had systematically pillaged his supplies and sold them off. Thus Livingstone found on arrival that all he had left was 'a little coffee and sugar and some few unsaleable beads'. Livingstone wrote: 'I was like the man who went from Jerusalem to Jericho, but no good Samaritan would come the Ujijian way.'[50]

Five days after David Livingstone had arrived at Ujiji, the man who had once been John Rowlands was camped on a hill less than ten miles away, looking down 'as in a painted picture, at a vast lake in the distance ... set in a frame of dimly-blue mountains'. Several hours later, after 'tearing through the cane-breaks of the valleys', Henry Stanley and his men were close enough to the lake to 'hear the sounding surge on the pebbled shore and to see ... by the lake, embowered in palms, on this hot noon, the village of Ujiji'. Ahead of them, the path 'curved under the trees into the town'.[51] Henry was ecstatic.

At this grand moment we do not think of the hundreds of miles we have marched, of the hundreds of hills we have ascended and descended, of the many forests we have traversed, of the jungles and thickets that annoyed us ... of the hot suns that scorched us ... At last the sublime hour has arrived! – our dreams, our hopes and anticipations are now about to be realized!

Then, as his men fired repeated volleys – the immemorial custom when a caravan entered a town – Stanley ordered the Stars and Stripes to be unfurled and borne at the head of the column by the gigantic Asmani. Crowds surged around the newcomers, among them 'a man dressed in a long white shirt, with a turban of American sheeting around his woolly head'. This man shouted in English: 'How do you do, sir.' To which Stanley, replied:

'Hello! Who the deuce are you?'
'I am Susi, the servant of Dr Livingstone.'
'Now, you, Susi, run and tell the Doctor I am coming.'[52]

Crowds were also forming outside Livingstone's house by the time Susi dashed back, shouting: 'An Englishman coming.' The caravan was not far behind Susi, and from beside his flag bearer, Stanley, who was riding a donkey, saw a grey-bearded white man, in a navy cap with a faded gold band round it. As David Livingstone came towards him, Stanley noticed the explorer's old red waistcoat and grey tweed trousers. Seeing the American flag, Livingstone fancied he knew the stranger's nationality. He imagined that he was 'no poor Lazarus' like himself, since the newcomer was dressed in a freshly pressed flannel

"DR. LIVINGSTONE, I PRESUME."

The meeting in the famous engraving in Stanley's book
How I Found Livingstone

suit, and wore glistening boots and a dazzling white helmet. This man now clambered down from his donkey's back.[53] The evidence (as I will show) suggests that he did not then say 'Dr Livingstone, I presume', but something less memorable and more human than the famous words, which he thought up later as fitting for this unprecedented occasion.

NINE

Canonizing Dr Livingstone

'Dr Livingstone, I presume?' is probably the most famous phrase in the history of journalism; and that Stanley is supposed to have said it is the most widely known 'fact' about him. Yet if my doubts about its authenticity become widely accepted, I hope this will not affect Stanley's public fame. It seems to me that his invention of an adoptive father, and his setting himself the task of finding Dr Livingstone long before he had interested a newspaper in the idea, were remarkable enough in their own right to merit remembrance. To go on from there to invent a greeting so memorable that it would be recognized by millions over a century and a quarter later places him in a class of his own. The fact that Stanley would be ridiculed and patronized as a direct result of this greeting, which he almost certainly never uttered, is painfully ironic. He invented it because of his old insecurity about his background. Ill at ease among the British officers in Abyssinia, he had admired their laconic, understated style and had hoped to emulate it. He had been struck especially by an anecdote in Kinglake's *Eothen* concerning two English gentlemen whose paths had crossed in the wilds of Palestine, and who had uttered no words of greeting but merely lifted their caps and walked by. Henry had thought this the height of gentlemanly insouciance.[1] Of course, many English gentlemen would have thought it unfriendly and absurd. But how could the insecure outsider have known this?

Later, when people were laughing at him for coming up with a parody of drawing room gentility at this highly emotional moment, instead of a joyful exclamation, Stanley knew he had made a fool of himself, but by then it was too late to retract. The phrase had appeared in too many newspapers to be denied. Instead, in his draft

Autobiography, he would try to explain away the phrase, most unconvincingly, with the claim that he had panicked because not knowing what to say, and because he had not been entirely sure whether it really was Dr Livingstone standing before him.[2] In *How I Found Livingstone*, he would combat the scoffers by describing his need to do what was 'dignified' in front of a large crowd of Arabs and Africans. 'My heart beats fast, but I must not let my face betray my emotions, lest it shall detract from the dignity of a white man appearing under such extraordinary circumstances.'[3] But, in reality, he thought hard for many months after the meeting, before deciding what memorable words to give himself.

Whatever incident one studies in Stanley's life, his earliest description invariably proves to be the most reliable version, and the only one that can be authenticated by reference to other sources. 'Dr Livingstone, I presume?' has no credibility because Stanley destroyed his earliest description of the famous meeting. His original diary entry for the day of the meeting ends at the bottom of a page: 'I saw a pale looking white man in a faded blue cap with an arc peak, tarnished gold lace, joke red jacket, sheeting shirt, tweed pants, as I saw him I dismounted ...' – and there the entry stops, in mid-sentence, the description plainly having been continued on the next page, which is torn out along with the one after it.[4]

David Livingstone, in *his* journal, does not record any words spoken by Stanley, or by himself, at the moment of their meeting. But in many contemporary letters Livingstone quoted the words shouted to him by his servant, Susi, on rushing back to their *tembe* after spotting Stanley: 'An Englishman coming! I see him!' Livingstone also described, in most of his letters written that November, the American flag being borne aloft at the head of the caravan. In his letter to James Gordon Bennett Jr, merely dated November 1871, Livingstone again quoted Susi's remark and mentioned the flag, before adding: 'I am as cold and non-demonstrative as we islanders are generally reputed to be; but ... I said in my soul, "Let the richest blessings descend from the Highest on you and yours!"' In a letter to his daughter Agnes (18 November), Susi and the flag appeared as usual, as did a wealth of other detail, such as the 'baths, tents, saddles, big kettles ... and abundance of goods' carried by Stanley's men. But as always, there was nothing about what Stanley said. It was the same story in a letter to Lord Granville, the foreign secretary.[5] In fact, in no letter written by

Livingstone after the meeting have I been able to find a single mention of those most unusual words, which Livingstone would surely have quoted had they really been addressed to him. After all, in letter after letter he took the trouble to record Susi's much less memorable exclamation.

It is impossible to say when Stanley wrote 'Dr Livingstone, I presume?' for the first time. His carefully written large journal, which starts with the meeting, has hitherto been assumed to have been written in Africa, but was actually composed in London with the help of his earlier diary and various notebooks, *after* the publication of *How I Found Livingstone*, in November 1872 – a year after the meeting.[6] The date on which the world would first read the phrase would be 2 July 1872, when the *New York Herald* published its first triumphant account of the meeting, which included the greeting. But despite its nominal date of 23 November 1871 (thirteen days after the date on which Henry thought he had met Livingstone), it is impossible to say exactly when Stanley wrote this despatch. (No handwritten original has survived.) To have made publication possible on 2 July, he need not have finalized his despatch until 29 May 1872, when he left Zanzibar – seven months after the meeting. From Zanzibar, his despatch was carried by ship to the recently opened telegraph station in Suez.

It is more than possible that Stanley, to seem dignified, did indeed say *something* stilted but unmemorable. In his original diary he wrote: 'What would I have given for a bit of friendly wilderness wherein I might vent my joy in some mad freaks, such as idiotically biting my hand, turning a somersault, slashing at trees, or something in order to purge these exciting feelings before appearing in the presence of Livingstone,' but added that he had needed 'to keep control over [his] emotions' – supporting the idea of a contrived remark.[7] But what motive could he have had for destroying those next crucial pages, unless to change his account of the words actually spoken? The late Richard Stanley – the adopted son of Stanley's adopted son, Denzil – was quoted in the *Radio Times* (6 January 1972) as saying that his grandfather probably never said the famous words. This was not followed up by Stanley's biographers because Mr Stanley later got cold feet (perhaps at the enormity of what he had said), and retracted his statement, claiming, in a letter to me,[8] that he had been misquoted. Since then he has died, but his widow, Jane, has told me that he and his father before him had indeed had doubts.[9]

The date of the meeting is disputed, since both Livingstone and Stanley had lost track of the precise passage of time during repeated bouts of fever. A date in late October or early November is nevertheless all but certain[10] [see note for full details of the controversy]. Stanley had feared that, on seeing him, the explorer might leave Ujiji. 'That he was specially disagreeable and brusque in his manner, which would make me quarrel with him immediately, was firmly fixed in my mind. Besides, he was an Englishman [sic] – perhaps a man who used an eye-glass, through which he would glare at me ferociously or icily.'[11] Only when Livingstone ushered him into his *tembe*, and the local Arabs and other onlookers withdrew, was it evident to the younger man that the doctor viewed his arrival as the answer to a prayer. Livingstone repeated several times, 'You have brought me new life,' and tears sprang into his eyes.[12] At first Henry was too mesmerized by the man to make any written notes. 'The interest I take in him is too overpowering ... my eyes rove over his face to speculate on every line & facial movement.'[13]

Livingstone explained, sadly, that he had been robbed by 'Sherif, the half-caste drunken tailor ... sent by the British Consul', and admitted he was all but destitute.[14] He then described being forced back from Nyangwe by the slaves Dr Kirk had sent him, and by the resident Arabs. This information fanned the anger Stanley already felt towards Kirk for failing to make sure that Livingstone's caravan had set off promptly from Bagamoyo.[15] Henry was immensely impressed when Livingstone asked him to bring him up to date with world events, before as much as glancing at his letters. 'He had acquired the art of being patient long ago, he said, and he had waited so long for letters that he could well afford to wait a few hours more.'[16] So Stanley told him about the Franco-Prussian War, the opening of the Suez Canal, the Spanish Revolution, the completion of the Pacific railroad, and the election of General Grant as president.

What pleased Stanley most about Livingstone was that he was so ordinary-looking, like a book 'with a most unpretending binding' that 'gave no token of what element of power or talent lay within'.[17] It was this deceptive ordinariness – his man-of-the-people quality – that made Livingstone unique among Victorian heroes, and very different from men like Wellington and Palmerston. Stanley soon realized that he was Scottish, not English as he had at first thought, and that they shared a Celtic background – not that Henry was going to represent himself as anything but an American – but he sensed at once that Livingstone was not the misanthropic solitary that, thanks to Kirk, he had feared he might be. In his late fifties, Livingstone had softened somewhat from the domineering, self-obsessed man who had shown little compassion to those who had died in Africa as a result of his over-optimistic estimates of the suitability of the Shire region for missionary settlement. His own wife had died during the Zambezi Expedition, and his eldest son had perished in the American Civil War – these two devastating blows falling almost in successive years.

When Livingstone declared that he had no intention of going home until he had finished his work, even though he longed to see his daughters, the younger man was overwhelmed by such dedication.[18] But Henry sensed that there was more to Livingstone than 'Spartan heroism', since along with religious faith there seemed to be 'something seer-like in him'.[19] Livingstone's belief that he had been called to serve Africa made a lifelong impression on Stanley, influencing his own behaviour and attitudes. When Livingstone told him, 'I have lost a great deal of happiness I know by these wanderings. It is as if I had been born to exile,' Henry felt a bond of fellow feeling. He too believed he had been born to labour and achieve rather than to enjoy his life. In January 1870, Stanley had discussed the purpose of human life with the rich and sybaritic American consul in Cairo, Mr G.C. Taylor. Taylor had argued that, since man was fated to be 'dust like the beasts', a life of idealism and self-sacrifice made less sense than a life of pleasure-seeking. Stanley had disagreed. Even if life could be proved to be purposeless, he told Taylor, it would still matter to him personally: 'for my own spirit's satisfaction ... It is in my nature to toil, as it is in the other's nature to enjoy.'[20]

The day after his arrival Stanley plucked up the courage to tell Livingstone that he was a special correspondent of the *New York Herald*. 'That despicable paper,' snorted the doctor, but changed his tune when told that James Gordon Bennett Jr had sent Stanley specifically to get whatever news of his discoveries he would like to give – and to assist him, if he could.[21] Still smarting from the meanness of the British government, Livingstone found it moving that an American newspaper editor had found him sufficiently newsworthy to pay for a reporter to travel to the far side of the globe to assist him.

Although Livingstone at nearly sixty seemed old to Stanley, who was then thirty, he recognized 'much endurance and vigour within his frame'. Livingstone's hazel eyes struck him as 'remarkably bright, not dimmed in the least', and his hair merely 'streaked here and there with grey over the temples'. His teeth, however, 'showed indications of being worn out'.[22] Livingstone's clothes were patched, but clean, and he did not smoke. He drank only occasionally, making an exception when Henry opened a bottle of Sillery champagne to celebrate their meeting. Henry also drank little, but smoked heavily, cigars and cigarettes. The two of them were keen tea drinkers, downing as many as nine cups a day. Sitting with Livingstone on his veranda, Stanley was overwhelmed with pleasure. He had little dialogues with himself: 'What was I sent for? – To find Livingstone – Have you found him? – Yes, of course; am I not in his house? What compass is that hanging on a peg there? Whose clothes, whose boots are those? Who reads those newspapers?'[23]

From the beginning, Stanley found Livingstone easy to get on with, like 'an old friend'. 'There was a friendly or good-natured abandon about Livingstone ... He had not much to offer ... but what he had was mine and his.'[24] Livingstone often 'relapsed into his own inner world'; but this did not worry Stanley, who could be self-absorbed himself. Stanley admired his understated faith: 'It is of the true, practical kind, never losing a chance to manifest itself in a quiet, practical way ... It governs his conduct towards his servants, and towards the natives ...' Religious sentiments, it seemed to Stanley, had muted Livingstone's more masterful characteristics.[25] When it is recalled that in New Orleans Stanley had attributed to the rich cotton broker, Mr Henry Stanley, many holy traits – even insisting that his make-believe 'father' had been a part-time clergyman – it should come as no surprise to find him seeing Livingstone's character in a rose-tinted light. And since Livingstone seemed sure to be his open sesame to a life of celebrity and acceptance, no wonder the young journalist felt warmly towards him. 'His manner,' enthused Stanley, 'suits my nature better than that of any man I can remember ... I should best describe it as benevolently paternal ... it steals its influence on me without any effort on his part ... [he] is sincerely natural and converses with me as if I were of his own age or of equal experience. The consequence is that I have come to entertain an immense respect for myself, and begin to think myself somebody, though I never suspected it before ...'[26]

When Stanley had arrived at Ujiji, he had been suffering from intermittent fever, and soon took to his bed. 'In an instant his [Livingstone's] tone changed and had he been my own father, he could not have been kinder.'[27] The father and son aspect of their relationship did not exist solely in Stanley's imaginings. Livingstone came to think of Stanley in precisely that role. 'That good brave fellow has acted as a son to me,' he would tell his daughter Agnes, after Stanley had left for the coast.[28] And by asking Stanley to find the grave of his son Robert, who had died in the battle of Gettysburg, and to erect a memorial stone over his body, Livingstone was entrusting to him a filial task. Stanley, like Robert Livingstone, had fought in the Civil War, and this was an emotional link. Livingstone was unbuttoned enough to describe his wife's death: 'For some time I felt that I should never get over it.'[29] For this deeply private man, such self-revelation had been non-existent until now.

Livingstone was extremely secretive about his theories concerning the Nile's source, and warned his daughter Agnes to tell no one his theories – not even his old friend Sir Roderick Murchison.[30] So it was a remarkable compliment to Stanley that the doctor kept back from him nothing about the central African watershed, as he believed it to be. More remarkable still, a mere four days after the meeting, Livingstone proposed to Henry that they should travel together and finish his geographical work. Henry agonized over this flattering and life-changing offer, but eventually refused, knowing what Mr Bennett's attitude was likely to be towards a project that might keep him in Africa for another two or three years. 'It is an honour, but I must do my duty which is to hurry to the coast & London to give the news to the Herald.'[31] Given Livingstone's dislike of travelling with Europeans, it was clear that he had done Henry a very great honour.

Livingstone's longing to expose the slave trade persuaded him to write three long letters to the New York Herald.[32] 'He is truly pathetic,' observed Stanley, 'when he describes the poor enchained slaves & the unhappy beings whose necks he has seen galled by the tree forks ... I am becoming steeped in Livingstone's ideas.'[33] Indeed, few men wrote as movingly on the subject. 'The strangest disease I have seen in this country [Manyema],' wrote the doctor, 'seems really to be broken-heartedness, and it attacks free men who have been captured and made slaves.'[34]

Henry would spend four months with Livingstone, and his decision to represent him to the world as someone 'as near an angel as the nature of a living man will allow' had more to do with his own emotional needs than any desire to be objective.[35] In his despatches, his speeches, and then in *How I Found Livingstone*, Stanley described the explorer as a near saint, and gave birth, almost single-handedly, to the Livingstone myth of the noble, self-sacrificing missionary. When the Zambezi Expedition had been recalled, *The Times* had launched a scathing attack on the promises Livingstone had made:

We were promised cotton, sugar and indigo ... and of course we got none. We were promised trade; and there is no trade ... We were promised converts and not one has been made. In a word the thousands subscribed by the Universities and contributed by the Government have been productive only of the most fatal results.[36]

Then there had been reports of the many pointless deaths. It is a measure of Stanley's talent as a journalist that he would manage to persuade the public to forget five years of failure, during which 'saintly' and 'angelic' had not been adjectives ever applied to Dr Livingstone. But what did Stanley really think of his father-figure?

The first indication that he realized there was another side to the doctor's character came after they had been together for six weeks. One day, Livingstone 'expressed a strong contempt for the weak dawdling creatures who called themselves missionaries and who, when confronted with their fields ... wanted to go away'. He then attacked the Universities' Mission, six of whose missionaries had gone to Africa at his behest and died. Livingstone blamed them, rather than himself. 'The more you do for people, the more ungrateful they are,' he insisted.[37] A month later, the doctor was complaining about the Royal Geographical Society, saying that the RGS had caused a large map of central Africa to be printed, which, though based on his scientific observations, did not carry his name. 'If some of them came to Africa they would know what it costs to get a little accurate information about a river.'[38] Since Stanley shared Livingstone's tendency to suspect that people were in league against him, he accepted his complaints without question.

On 3 March 1872, Stanley made an important admission in his diary:

Livingstone reverted again to his grudges against the missionaries on the Zambezi and one of his officers (naval) on the Expedition. I have had some intrusive suspicions & thoughts that he was not of such an angelic temper as I believed him to be during my first month with him, but for the last month I have been driving them steadily from my mind ... when however he reiterated his complaints against this man and the other – I felt the faintest fear that his strong nature was opposed to forgiveness & that he was not so perfect as at the first blush of friendship I thought him.

Casting around for excuses for ignoring the great man's vindictiveness, Stanley argued that it was not really 'a weakness to dwell on these bitter memories' because he (Stanley) had 'pestered him with questions'.[39] Although Stanley's doubts persisted, this did not stop him representing Livingstone as faultless.

One reason for this deliberate whitewashing was Stanley's desire to tell his family and friends that he had been cherished, as a son, by a truly good man. (Another was his longing to find a man possessing the goodness he had never found in any adult during his childhood.) But his journalistic instincts probably influenced him more. And they told him that to have 'found' a forgotten saint made a better story than to have found an embittered recluse. Stanley was being less disingenuous than might be supposed. He shared Livingstone's inability to forgive slights and mistakes, and would not have seen this character defect as a grave failing.

The two men disagreed over politics. Interestingly, Livingstone was a Tory whereas Stanley was a staunch supporter of the Liberal leader, Gladstone.[40] Yet Livingstone did not dwell on serious topics. He even favoured Henry with the occasional risqué joke, such as one about John Speke and the Duchess of Sutherland, who had asked the explorer whether African women really walked around naked. They do indeed, he assured her.

'Oh, but surely they wear something,' the Duchess insisted. Whereat Speke replied: 'Maybe a string or so down here,' and suited the action to the word in a way that caused several ladies to cry, 'Oh! Captain Speke!' and the Duchess to hide her face with her fan.[41]

Stanley was never starry-eyed about Livingstone's prowess as a missionary. Indeed, he realized rapidly that preaching to Africans, as one travelled along, was pointless. 'For at intervals of ten or twelve days' journey – Livingstone would enter on a new country which had a new language; and, of course, he would never stay long enough anywhere to learn it.'[42] When they discussed the problem, Stanley was blunt. 'I cannot see how one or two men can hope to make an impression on the minds of so many millions.' Livingstone countered: 'Someone must begin the work. Christ was the beginner of the Christianity that is now spread over a large part of the world. I feel sometimes as if I was the beginner for attacking central Africa.'[43]

During November and December 1871 they went travelling to the northern end of Lake Tanganyika, on what was to be their only shared exploration – a round trip of about 300 miles. Before setting out, Stanley divided all his supplies and trade goods into two piles and asked Livingstone to choose for himself whichever pile he liked best. Stanley told his men that Livingstone, not he, was the leader of the expedition; this was the only time Henry would make such a gesture. Not that he had any desire to travel as the doctor had often done: Livingstone told him that when he had been near Lake Nyasa, the Arab caravan leader, Muhammad bin Salih – on whom he had then depended for protection – had persuaded all but two of his (Livingstone's) men to desert 'by selling the favour of his concubines to them'. This had left him helpless – in his own words, 'like a slave to every village chief [he] came across', unable to leave until these local potentates permitted it.[44] Livingstone eventually agreed with Stanley that small expeditions of fewer than forty men were simply not viable, and so desertions would have to be prevented by corporal punishment if need be.[45]

Nevertheless, on their journey by canoe to the head of the lake, Stanley was often influenced by Livingstone's gentler ways. He wanted to fire shots to scare some screaming, stone-throwing Africans and admitted:

If Livingstone had not been in the boat, I would certainly have tried to teach them a lesson – for I have already begun to learn that the meeker [one is], the more natives of this temper encroach upon forbearance ... The doctor said from his experience elsewhere the Arab slave traders must have been here & angered these people by their conduct. His explanations were so wise that I was glad we had not been driven to retaliate.[46]

Stanley was also impressed when two drunken chiefs threatened violence, and Livingstone merely rolled up a sleeve, showed them the whiteness of his arm, and asked whether either of them had ever been hurt by a man of that colour.

The two men got on well during their journey, and this was despite the intermittent malaria that plagued Stanley for most of the four weeks, and despite the older man's ulcerated feet. A minor irritation irked Henry briefly when they travelled overland, rather than by water. Livingstone's habit of walking all the time was unwelcome to

Stanley who liked to ride a donkey for part of every day's march. It made him uncomfortable to ride while the doctor was 'tramping it on foot like a hero'. 'Sometimes,' Stanley admitted, 'an unworthy thought comes into my head that he does it to vex me ... it is an odd taste to prefer walking to riding.'[47]

On reaching the northern end of Lake Tanganyika on 28 November, they found that the river there – the Rusizé – flowed into the lake and not out of it. This was an important discovery, finally establishing that lakes Tanganyika and Albert could not be connected by a river. Until then Livingstone had thought that Tanganyika might be a more important source of the Nile than lakes Albert and Victoria. Had Livingstone known when he had arrived at Nyangwe in March 1870 that the Lualaba was the only alternative, as a Nile source, to Victoria and Albert, he would have taken immense risks to cross the two-mile-wide river, perhaps even building a raft when canoes had been unobtainable. Now there could be no solution until someone returned to the Lualaba at Nyangwe and traced the great river northwards.

The two men returned to Ujiji on 13 December and spent the next fortnight getting their men and stores sorted out for the march to Unyanyembe, where Stanley had been obliged to leave most of the supplies sent by Kirk for Livingstone in November 1870. Livingstone's plan was to take possession of these trade goods, and then to wait at Unyanyembe while Stanley returned to the coast and sent on to him the additional stores and carriers he would need for the next phase of his journey. At this point, Stanley made a determined effort to persuade Livingstone to return to Britain with him, before returning later to the Lualaba. He needed to have an operation on the haemorrhoids that were already causing regular blood loss. Unfortunately, at about this time Stanley let slip that John Kirk thought the doctor should abandon his work on the Nile sources in favour of a younger man. Livingstone at once suspected that Kirk himself wanted to 'finish up the sources' and therefore wanted him to go home.[48] Another reason Livingstone gave for staying on in Africa was that he had recently lost £2,300 – a fortune at the time – in the collapse of a Bombay bank. 'To return [home] unsuccessful,' he feared, would mean 'going abroad to an unhealthy consulate to which no public sympathy would ever be drawn.'[49] His determination never to give up, but instead to risk his life without complaint or self-pity, formed an important bond between these remarkable men. Stanley had already shown that he possessed the same courage.

That two awkward and shyly defensive men should have grown so fond of one another was due to Livingstone's intuitive sympathy for Stanley's insecurity. He shared the journalist's introversion and, like him, was often brusque and rude. This could have led to misunderstandings had they not recognized that they shared the same traits. Both men were neat and methodical too, and Stanley greatly admired Livingstone's tin boxes and their contents, which were, he observed, 'in a better condition than my own though this is his seventh year of travel ... His compasses & sextant are in first rate order, his journals are clean & almost blotless, as if a copyist had lately been writing it up.'

The two men left Ujiji for Unyanyembe on 27 December with five of Livingstone's followers and about forty of Stanley's men. For a week they travelled south by water, and then overland for forty-seven days, following the same route Stanley had taken to avoid Mirambo on the way to Ujiji. On setting out, Henry felt a heavy sense of responsibility to be choosing a safe route for the world's most famous explorer. Then, during the second half of February, Stanley fell ill again, and their roles reversed – with him being carried in a cot. Soon after Stanley's recovery, Livingstone was stung by a swarm of bees. Despite suffering terribly, that same evening he dined with Stanley, who gave his cook, Ferajji, stern instructions to produce for dinner the best meatballs and custard dessert in his repertoire.[50] Unyanyembe was reached on 18 February and the pair settled down in the *tembe* in Kwihara, which Stanley had occupied before leaving for Ujiji.

The first letter Stanley opened on arrival was from the US consul, Francis Webb, informing him that James Gordon Bennett Jr had repudiated his (Stanley's) draft for $3,750. 'The amount will ruin me,' a distraught Webb told Henry, 'unless you can certify me that you will be able with private means to meet all these obligations.' Clearly, Henry could not do that. He said nothing to Livingstone, who was happily reading some letters from his grown-up children. Despite his extraordinary achievement, it occurred to Henry that Bennett was about to treat him as he had treated others. Near the bottom of the pile, he came across a later communication from Webb enclosing a letter from a man called Hosmer – apparently Levien's replacement in London. Hosmer announced that the *Herald* was now prepared to cash all drafts drawn by Stanley.[51] He breathed again.

At Kwihara, Livingstone and Stanley were once more among Arab-Swahili traders. Although the doctor was 'driven almost into a passion' when the subject of Arab atrocities came up in conversation, he tenderly nursed Mwini Mokay, a dying slave trader, who had left a trail of blood and havoc in Manyema.[52] Yet while caring for others, however undeserving, the doctor neglected his own health. Stanley feared that he would jettison the shallow-draught boat he meant to leave for him, and prefer to wade through swamps. Henry wrote prophetically: 'His weakest point is dysenteric attacks.' And these, Stanley had noted, had been worse when Livingstone had got wet. So what would happen in the rainy season, as Livingstone rounded the southern sources of the Lualaba through endless marshes?[53] Because of the war still raging between Mirambo and the Arabs, Livingstone said he would not risk heading due west to Nyangwe to trace the Lualaba north from there. Instead, he meant to make for the southern foot of Lake Tanganyika, and only after sorting out all the sources of the Lualaba would he head north for Nyangwe where he had last seen the great river.

As their time together moved to its melancholy close, Stanley became increasingly worried. Although Livingstone had put on weight during the four months they had spent together, and looked much younger, Stanley was alarmed by his frequent bouts of bowel trouble, which he would never let stop him.[54] 'I shall see Livingstone no more,' Henry confided to his diary, 'unless he finishes his task.'[55] 'At his age, drawing near his 60th year it appears to be a big task – from the cannibals on the Lualaba's banks, & the multitude of rivers he has mentioned.' Stanley doubted he could have endured such a journey: 'My shrunken muscles & whimpering stomach urge me to leave the black man's land before another bout of fever lays me low under the sable soil.'[56] The doctor filled the time by writing helpful letters of introduction for Stanley to make use of in Britain.[57]

On the evening of 11 March, Stanley's men began to sing 'a slow and mournful refrain about the white man going home – oh, oh, oh ...' The 13th was planned to be the last full day Stanley would spend with 'dear old Livingstone'. That evening, the dividing door between their rooms was closed by the doctor:

and we both think our own thoughts. What his are I know not. Mine are sad. My days seem to have been spent far too happily – for now that the last day is almost gone, I bitterly regret the approach of the parting hour. I now forget the successive fevers, and their agonies, and the semi-madness to which they often plagued me. The regret I feel is greater than any pains I have endured ... the Farewell, I fear may be forever. Forever? And For Ever ...[58]

Stanley had turned down Livingstone's invitation to travel with him, partly in order to fulfil James Gordon Bennett Jr's brief, but also because fearing that he had never been 'made for an African explorer', for: 'I detest the land most heartily.'[59] Yet feeling closer to Livingstone than to anyone he had ever known, Stanley was racked with nostalgia, both for the man and for the extraordinary continent he had made his own. That night, for the first time, Livingstone gave Stanley proper thanks

uttered with no mincing phrases, but poured out as it were at the last moment until I was so affected that I sobbed as one only can in uncommon grief ... that kind of praise that steals into one & touches the softer parts of the ever veiled nature ... for a time I was as a sensitive child of eight or so and yielded to such a burst of tears that only such a scene as this one could have forced.

Livingstone told him that when he had marched for the coast 'this house will look as if a death has taken place'. It worried the doctor that Stanley was still weak, and he advised the journalist to delay his departure till after the rains. But Stanley knew that until he reached the coast and despatched to Livingstone the fifty *pagazi* he needed, the explorer would not be able to leave on his epic journey.[60]

On the following day, the 14th, both men were up at dawn and sat down to 'a sad breakfast', which Henry could not eat. He offered to leave two men with Livingstone in case it was found that he had forgotten something, and they could then bring it on. In fact, Livingstone was not ready to part with Stanley quite yet, and said he wanted to accompany him for a few hours. 'I must see you fairly off on the road.' While they walked side by side, Stanley 'took long looks at Livingstone to impress his features thoroughly on the memory'. But at last the moment for parting came.

We wrung each other's hands & I tore myself away before I unmanned myself again before others; but Susi & Chumah, & Hamydah – the doctor's faithful followers, then came to shake & kiss my hands before I could turn away.

'Goodbye, Doctor, dear friend.'

'Goodbye.'

'March! Why do you stop? Go on! Are you not going home?'

We came to a ridge, and I looked back & watched his grey figure, fading dimmer in the distance ... I gulped down my great grief and turned away to follow the receding caravan.[61]

Later, Stanley wrote in his diary: 'I felt very lonely all afternoon – as if I had but just parted with my family ... I cried at parting with the good doctor ...'[62] Then Stanley penned a letter, which he never sent.

My dear Doctor, I have parted from you too soon. I feel it too deeply ... The utter loneliness of myself, the void that has been created, the pang at parting, the bleak aspect of the future ... Why should people be subjected to these partings ... I shall think of you constantly, until your last wish has been attended to. In this way the chain of remembrance will not be severed. 'Not yet,' I say to myself, 'are we apart' ....[63]

David Livingstone died thirteen months later near Lake Bangweulu, so they never met again. This friendship between the nineteenth century's two greatest explorers was the relationship in Stanley's life that came closest to giving him the father and son bond he had dreamed about since his workhouse days. Unlike his make-believe love for the cotton broker Henry Hope Stanley in New Orleans, his devotion to Livingstone was real, and was to some extent reciprocated. Whenever Livingstone encountered any criticism of Stanley, he defended him. He had heard from his son William that John Kirk had told him that Stanley would 'make his fortune out of Dr Livingstone'. 'If he does,' Livingstone told his eldest brother, John, 'he is heartily welcome, for he saved me a wearisome tramp ... and probably saved my life.' In many letters home, Livingstone described Stanley as being like an ideal son. He also wrote to friends asking them to entertain Stanley and treat him 'just as you would me'.[64] Livingstone's reward would be the picture of himself as a near saint, which Stanley painted in his great bestseller, *How I Found Livingstone*, and which would remain largely unchallenged until my biography a century later.

Yet how much had the future direction of Stanley's life been changed by the famous meeting? Had he 'found' himself by 'finding' Livingstone – at least in the sense of finding his vocation as an African explorer? Indeed he had, although he would not understand this fully for another six months. Now, as he marched towards the coast, protecting his scoop was what mattered most of all to him.

A week after their parting, Henry sent a letter to Livingstone by Susi and Hamoydah, who had brought some mail from the doctor. After making a touching but rather awkward admission to Livingstone – 'very few amongst men have I found I so much got to love as yourself' – Stanley made a request that mirrored his immediate concerns: 'Do not forget the Herald. The Herald will be gratified to me for securing you as a Correspondent.'[65] Clearly, at this moment, Stanley expected to continue his career as a journalist.

From the coast Henry wrote to Gordon Bennett, briefly complaining about his dishonoured bank drafts, but ending with the kind of flattery the mogul expected: 'Congratulating you upon the successful termination of this arduous enterprise – because the glory is due to the "Herald".'[66] It is easy to see why it was advantageous for Stanley to continue to attribute the story's invention to his employer. But he did so not just so that Bennett would send him on high-profile missions in future. In truth, Henry feared that if it ever became known that for many years he had viewed finding Livingstone as a way to become famous, people would find it distasteful that he had rescued a great explorer as a career move, rather than solely for altruistic reasons. (Of course, since then, the mission had come to mean a great deal more to Stanley than fame and money.)

At Stanley's urgent suggestion, Livingstone had penned two letters to Bennett for publication in the *New York Herald*, as a token of his gratitude for being re-supplied. The doctor had written these letters willingly enough, seeing them as an opportunity to put his views on the slave trade before a vast audience, and to give publicity to the massacre he had witnessed at Nyangwe.[67] Mr Bennett was prepared to pay $8,000, or £1,600 – more than the original cost of the expedition – to have the two letters telegraphed to New York in their entirety, and thus protect one of the greatest news stories of the century.[68]

Nothing that Stanley wrote in 1871 or early 1872 shows that he had any idea that his meeting with Livingstone would turn out to have been a key event both in the history of African exploration and in the future colonization of Africa. But how could he have known this – not yet having written the book that would turn cantankerous Dr Livingstone into a secular saint? Nor could Stanley, or anyone else, guess that, after dying in south-central Africa, his friend would become a mythical and iconic figure, attracting hosts of missionaries, settlers and explorers to Africa. Yet one passage in Stanley's diary – written a day before he parted from Livingstone – shows that at a deeper level he realized that his new vocation was already forming. 'I think it only needed this softening [Livingstone's admission of how grateful he was] to secure me as his obedient and devoted servitor in the future, should there ever be an occasion where I could prove my zeal.'[69]

TEN

'Fame is Useless to Me'

I detest & shrink from it [fame]. What a contrast this world [fashionable London] is to the sinless, peaceful life that I enjoyed in Africa. One brings me an inordinate amount of secret pain, the other sapped my physical strength and left my mind expanded and was purifying ...
Stanley's Diary, 11 August 1872

As Stanley approached Bagamoyo on the coast – after completing, in an astonishing thirty-five days, a journey that had taken him three months in the reverse direction – he knew that his success in 'finding' Livingstone was about to make him famous – just as he had wanted. Inevitably, he had no idea what fame might actually be like. James Gordon Bennett Jr cabled: YOU ARE NOW [AS] FAMOUS AS LIVINGSTONE HAVING DISCOVERED THE DISCOVERER. ACCEPT MY THANKS, AND WHOLE WORLD['S].[1] It was sad that Livingstone had not thought to warn his young friend that fame excited resentment and envy, unless its possessor were modest and conciliatory. Though self-aware enough to know he could be over-sensitive and hot-headed, Stanley was ill-equipped to deal with the events and personalities he would shortly encounter.[2] Though returning to a country where he had once been rejected, he was not going to be able to act the wronged and now vindicated hero – without seeming touchy and arrogant. In fact, he meant to conceal his past entirely, which removed that problem, but meant that people would see him as a successful American and, inevitably, this would make them underestimate his real achievement. But he would pay any price to avoid being publicly branded a workhouse bastard.

Stanley's party entered the dusty little town of Bagamoyo at sunset on 6 May 1872, firing guns and blowing horns. To Stanley's surprise he saw a young, red-headed white man standing in front of a white-painted wooden house set among huts and palm trees. This was Lieutenant William Henn, RN, of the Livingstone Search and Relief Expedition sent out to Africa by the Royal Geographical Society, after the Mirambo war had made the Society's governing council fear that Kirk's supplies would never reach Livingstone. Another of the expedition's members, Lieutenant L. S. Dawson, RN, shocked Stanley deeply: 'The truth is,' said Dawson, 'they [the RGS council] didn't want you to find him [Livingstone]. You cannot imagine how jealous they are at home about this expedition of yours.'³ Without considering how bitterly disappointed *he* would have felt if the Royal Geographical Society's expedition had forestalled *him*, rather than vice versa, Henry jumped to the conclusion that RGS officials had taken against him personally. So he behaved coolly to Dawson, Henn and twenty-one-year-old Oswell Livingstone, who had come out hoping to aid his father. This meant they would all speak ill of him to Sir Henry Rawlinson, the RGS's new president.

Stanley's most important task on Zanzibar was to recruit and send *pagazi* to Livingstone at Unyanyembe. Henry devoted infinite care to the selection of these men and sent them off in person, along with twenty who had served with him. These fifty-seven carriers arrived at Unyanyembe in mid-August 1872; the doctor wrote rapturously to friends and family about their good qualities, and never changed his mind. The vast majority would be with him when he died nine months later, and would help carry his body to the coast. After watching them sail for Bagamoyo, Stanley wrote in his diary: 'I felt strange and lonely, somehow. My dark friends who had travelled over so many hundreds of miles, and shared so many dangers with me, were gone and I was left alone. How many of their friendly faces shall I see again?' His servant, Selim, he sent back to his native Jerusalem, but Kalulu, the eleven-year-old former slave boy, would return with Stanley to be educated in London.

At Marseilles, on 24 July, en route to England, Stanley gave his first major press interview as a celebrity to the *Daily Telegraph*'s John Le Sage, who described Stanley as an American with 'a very broad chest and powerful-looking frame and a most intelligent expression of countenance; his hair, naturally curling, once light in colour, has turned quite grey during his expedition'.⁴ In fact, Stanley's hair was only flecked with grey, but he still looked considerably older than his actual age of thirty-one. He had been so emaciated after twenty-three attacks of fever that several acquaintances in Zanzibar had failed to recognize him.[5] After describing the far-from-perfect Dr Livingstone as 'the bravest and noblest gentleman and truest Christian living', Stanley launched into the first of his ill-judged public attacks on Dr Kirk for betraying Livingstone. Le Sage was clearly disconcerted, adding, 'Mr Stanley is far from well' and Dr Kirk will 'probably explain himself'.[6]

In Paris, a few days later, at a banquet presided over by the US ambassador, Mr E. B. Washburne, much was made of Stanley's American nationality. The hero of the hour then spoke of Livingstone's saintly character before launching into another fierce onslaught on Dr Kirk. But this time, he knew he had gone too far: 'I was led by the warmth of the occasion to speak more hot-headedly about Kirk than I intended ... it does not do to run atilt at anybody in a mixed assembly of this kind.'[7] Stanley's continuing antagonism arose because Kirk was claiming in public that Livingstone was angry with him solely because of what he had been told by Stanley. This was untrue. In two letters to Kirk written by Livingstone several weeks before his meeting with Stanley,[8] the doctor rebuked the consul for employing a dishonest and incompetent man, Sherif Basha, to bring essential supplies and carriers to him in the interior in 1870. The carriers had then plotted with local Arabs to stop him crossing the Lualaba – in order to avoid risking their lives on a long exploring trip. These men had mostly been slaves, costing Livingstone $60 per annum each, rather than the $25 he would have been charged for free men. Sherif went on to steal all Livingstone's stores.

The explorer therefore declared that all his plans had been destroyed by Kirk's choice of Sherif and his caravan of slaves. Undeniably, Stanley had added to Livingstone's fury with Kirk by telling him that a year later the consul had allowed his goods to rot for months at Bagamoyo without going near them, and had only arrived on the mainland after a shooting holiday, when the carriers had already left. Kirk would claim in letters to friends and to the foreign secretary, Lord Granville, that he had himself sent off, and even travelled for several days with part of the supply caravan. Incensed by this lie, Henry wrote to *The Times* saying that if Kirk had really seen the carriers, he would certainly have written a letter to Livingstone for them to take into the interior. But no such letter existed.[9] Stanley had also been upset that

US Consul Webb had sent to him, while he was with Livingstone, eleven packages by various Arab-Swahili caravans. But Dr Kirk, in the same period, had sent Livingstone nothing. The doctor referred sadly to this fact in correspondence.[10] Yet though Kirk had been a lot less energetic than he should have been, Stanley's filial devotion to Livingstone seems to have made him hate the British consul as intensely as he might have done had Livingstone *really* been an adored and maltreated father. While Kirk only attacked Stanley in public, he railed in private about 'the insult' of Livingstone's letters.[11]

In the French capital, Stanley saw his old friend Edward King, who called him 'my dear celebrity' with affectionate irony.[12] But Stanley's fame had a less pleasing effect on another American journalist, Edward Virnard, whom he had known in Egypt in 1868, and who had saved his life in a sea-bathing incident. Virnard was not prepared to wait outside his hotel room while Henry was seeing someone else, and left muttering that Stanley was 'too full of conceit now to think of early friends'. Stanley noted: 'This remark hurts me very much.'[13] Worse difficulties lay ahead.

There is no evidence in his diary that Stanley was thinking at this time about the female adulation that would very likely be in store for him in Britain as the rescuer of Dr Livingstone. He had known before setting foot on the African continent that he would never marry Katie Gough Roberts – and so he was not about to receive a painful shock. Yet his memory of sending her a long and revealing autobiographical letter preyed on his mind, especially when he thought of the sizeable sum a London newspaper might offer her, should she decide to sell. That letter could end his pretence to be an American. The press had been full of his 'finding' of Livingstone since the early summer, and Stanley suspected that Katie and his Welsh relations would certainly be considering how best to cash in on his fame.

Already, an enterprising London publisher, John Camden Hotten, was preparing for the press a book about Stanley's Welsh childhood and his years in America. His research had included interviews with Elizabeth Jones, who, despite Stanley's pleas to her to keep silent, had been massively indiscreet. Stanley knew it would now be harder to suppress the story of his Welsh connections, which were being referred to in local papers like the *Rhyl Journal*. He lost no time in writing to *The Times* to repudiate 'anything and everything he [Hotten] may relate concerning me and mine ...'.[14] The book came out a few months after Stanley's arrival in England and contained an account of his reception at Dover – an event that Stanley himself found too upsetting ever to describe in print.

Mr Stanley's appearance in this country was anxiously awaited, and although he knew quite well that he would be the hero of the hour, it is pleasant to record the satisfaction he manifested at meeting his half-brother, Mr Robert Jones, and his cousin, Mr [Moses] Parry on the pier at Dover, when he landed. They then travelled in company to London, and before their departure to Denbigh, they spent a considerable time in his company.[15]

Stanley's twenty-four-year-old half-brother, Robert, and his twenty-five-year-old first cousin, Moses Parry, were indeed on the pier to greet him. But far from being pleased to see the enterprising duo, who had travelled all the way from Wales to congratulate him, Stanley was aghast. Both young men were drunk. 'I was utterly unprepared for the scene that met me,' he recalled. 'All the railway porters were there, not merely to see the Finder of Livingstone, but also to see the brother of the loud-spoken & intoxicated young men who had revealed so much family history to them.' Robert had been born in 1848, but Stanley had not seen him until his own brief and humiliating overnight stay with his mother early in 1862, when Robert had been thirteen and he twenty. In 1869 he had seen his half-brother again, this time for three weeks. His meetings with his cousin Moses had been just as infrequent. Hotten's claim that they all travelled to London together is fanciful. Stanley wrote of being 'utterly disgusted' and having travelled in a compartment where 'I could be free from them ... At the station I had an opportunity to say a few words to the effect that they had taken an unwarrantable liberty with me in public etc., etc. ... Robert Jones Jnr & his cousin returned home.'[16] 'I never felt so ashamed and would have given all I was worth to have been back in central Africa.'[17]

A few days later, Robert senior – whom Henry suspected had sent his young relations to Dover – appeared at his hotel, the Langham, in Portland Place, London. Stanley treated his step-father to an angry tirade.

You remember in 1862 when I was poor ... weak & needy, you refused to speak to me, because as your wife said, 'I was a disgrace to her & to you in the eyes of your neighbours.' Six years later, when I had gold and I freely parted with it, you were glad to see me. Now that my name is boomed in the press, you come to seek me. I was sick & poor & I disgraced you. Your son was drunk – beastly drunk and he disgraced me. Now I want to know by what right you seek me at all? Have you, or any connection of yours ever done anything for me that you can claim a right to send your son reeling drunk on a public platform at Dover, and there proclaim that I am related to you? Have you or your wife any right to follow me to a hotel of this kind, and to draw me out of my privacy in order that I may acknowledge you as my step-father? ... You may have arrived at that age that you can bid defiance to public opinion – but I have not. It is only now that I have begun life, and as there are no favours in the past, no protection, no kindness, no paternal or maternal love ... I shall be obliged to you if you would not pursue me in this fashion ...[18]

Jones had come to London to ask for money, and accepted his stepson's verbal lashing philosophically. He knew that Henry wanted to keep him quiet, and would pay. A few days later, Stanley sent £100 to his mother – Jones's wife.[19] Most of the family had far worse money problems than Elizabeth Jones. Moses Parry, Henry's young cousin who had come to Dover, was on the verge of bankruptcy.[20] 'I discover a disposition among all the members of mother's family to indicate to me very plainly that having acquired this wearying newspaper fame, I must pay in cash handsomely to all & every member.'[21] And if he would not satisfy them, the thinly veiled threat was always there: maybe some obliging newspaper might.

Yet on his arrival in London, Stanley became aware that his family might not be the worst of his problems. Far from being treated to a civic reception for saving a British national hero, nobody from any official quarter came near him. This was partly because his Kirk-bashing speech in Paris had appeared in the press. But a significant section of the press were against him for other reasons. The *Standard*'s leader writer first gave credence to an idea that was gaining ground: that Stanley had forged Livingstone's letters. This owed something to the fact that Livingstone, for the benefit of the *New York Herald*'s readers, had rhapsodized about the beauty of Manyema women and had shown an improbable knowledge of American politics and poetry. It was rumoured that Stanley had not been within a thousand miles of Livingstone but had simply acquired his diary and letters by robbing an African messenger and carrying them to the coast. The story of the meeting – so went this canard – had then been invented to explain his possession of the letters. 'The general opinion,' wrote an anguished Stanley in his diary, 'is that I am a fraud.'[22] A communication from the foreign secretary stating that there was 'not the slightest doubt as to the authenticity of Dr Livingstone's despatches' put an end to the charges of forgery, at least in England.[23] Nevertheless, the whole idea of a newspaperman's turning explorer was anathema to many journalists. *The Spectator*'s editor found it ludicrous for a reporter to risk his life 'in the regular exercise of his profession, moved neither by pity, nor love of knowledge, nor by desire of adventure, but by an order from Mr Bennett'.[24]

But derision hurt Stanley less than the frosty silence of the RGS, which, within a week of his arrival, issued a public statement signed by its president, Sir Henry Rawlinson, to the effect that the Society did not hold functions in the summer and so could not entertain Mr Stanley. However, the journalist would be invited to address the geographical section of the British Association at its annual conference in Brighton later in the month.[25] Sir Henry had sent the Livingstone Search and Relief Expedition to Africa, and had been shaken to the core by Stanley's success, even suggesting in the press that 'if there has been any discovery and relief it is Dr Livingstone who has discovered and relieved Mr Stanley ....'.[26] Though the publication of Livingstone's letters scotched this self-deluding idea, Rawlinson kept Stanley waiting six days before sending an insultingly brief letter of thanks on behalf of the country's geographers.[27]

One leading RGS council member was the Revd Horace Waller, who had got to know Livingstone in Africa during the Zambezi Expedition in the 1860s, when he himself had been a missionary. Now a leading light in the campaign against the East African slave trade, Waller had somehow stayed on good terms both with Livingstone and with Dr Kirk. His friendship with the latter had led to the marriage of Kirk's brother to Waller's sister. This connection caused Waller to call on Stanley at his hotel and reproach him for his attacks on Kirk. Waller also wrote to Sir Henry Rawlinson denouncing Stanley's attempts to ruin his brother-in-law. The result was an English upper-class closing of ranks against 'the American'.[28]

Punch had some splendid fun with the president of the RGS as the man 'who discovered that Livingstone had discovered Stanley ... and [who] has at last discovered that Stanley is in England',[29] but Rawlinson continued to deny Henry the official praise he deserved. This created an impression that there was indeed something questionable about Stanley's achievement. He himself felt hurt and bewildered:

All the actions of my life, and I may say all my thoughts since 1872, have been strongly coloured by the storm of abuse and the wholly unjustifiable reports circulated about me then. So numerous were my enemies that ... I had to resort to silence as a protection against outrage.[30]

As Stanley's hopes of praise and acceptance faded, his remaining optimism was crushed. He had at least expected sympathy from his fellow journalists, but most laughed at the absurdly formal words of greeting he claimed to have addressed to Livingstone. Dressmaker's dummies asked one another, 'Dr Livingstone, I presume?' in the pages of *Tailor & Cutter*, and strangers called out to Stanley the fatal words that insecurity had led him to invent. Then there were jokes about the good doctor himself. Even the loyal Edward King said it was a shame Stanley had not brought home 'the d—d old missionary ... and chained him to a Scottish crag with strict instructions never to hide himself again, not even though he may sometimes madly recall the dusky beauties'.[31]

On 16 August, in Brighton, when Stanley spoke to the geography section of the British Association, he was asked to confine himself to the only original geographical achievement of his trip, namely his and Livingstone's 'Discoveries at the North End of Lake Tanganyika'. But arriving at the concert room in Middle Street to find nearly 3,000 people packed into the 200-foot-long hall and its gallery, Stanley rebelled against shrinking the most important emotional experience of his whole life into a series of scientific facts about Lake Tanganyika. There were not many geographers there, among numerous local ladies and a sprinkling of celebrities – such as the exiled Emperor Louis Napoleon and his Empress, and the philanthropist Baroness Burdett-Coutts.

'When I rose,' recalled Henry, 'my head was in a whirl and ... I was speechless. I directed my eyes around & saw only a sea of faces, darkened by bonnets & heads. A dead silence prevailed. I managed to say, Mr President, your Imperial Majesties, my Lord, ladies and gentlemen, I ... I ... I and then stopped ...' Then jettisoning his prepared script, Henry blurted out: 'I consider myself in the light of a troubadour, to relate the tale of an old man who is tramping onward to discover the source of the Nile.' Pure adventure was what most of his audience wanted, and they applauded loudly when they got it. But the meeting's chairman, Francis Galton, FRS, traveller, anthropologist and secretary of the Livingstone Relief Expedition, rebuked those who cheered. 'I must beg to remind you that this is a serious society constituted for the purpose of dealing with geographical facts and not sensational stories.'

After this rude rebuff, Stanley heard speaker after speaker assert that Livingstone's Lualaba was the Congo, and not the Nile. Henry had his own doubts about the river because of its altitude, but his admiration for Livingstone made it very painful for him when Colonel Grant, Sir Henry Rawlinson, Francis Galton and many others all dismissed Livingstone's conclusions. Enraged by their complacent upper-class voices, Stanley disparaged them as 'easy chair geographers'. In his opinion, he declared to the hall, a great explorer, 'who after thirty years of African travel' locates a mighty river, and follows it for 500 miles due north, should be taken seriously when he says he thinks it is the Nile.

When Galton asked Stanley whether he had found the waters of Lake Tanganyika sweet or brackish, Stanley decided he was being mocked, and replied that there could be no sweeter water for making a cup of tea. This earned him laughter and applause, as did his attack on the chairman: 'Our most worthy President, Mr Francis Galton, FRGS, FRSXYZ and I do not know how many other letters, with an elongated smile, and exceedingly bland accents, has said that you have not met to listen to sensational stories but to serious facts.'[32] Well, he had some 'serious facts' about Mr Galton. As an explorer, he had turned back before reaching Lake Ngami and had then been awarded the Society's gold medal for his failure. Galton counter-attacked by raising the subject Stanley most dreaded: 'The public would be very grateful to Mr Stanley if he would be so good as to say ... whether ... Mr Stanley was a Welshman?' Stanley dashed this aside as 'idle curiosity', though shaking with indignation. Stanley had already sent denials that he was Welsh to national newspapers; and the *Illustrated London News* had just published a description of him as 'a Missourian, 28 years of age', as had *Harper's Bazaar* and the *New York Herald*.[33] Yet though, incredibly, he was winning the battle to be thought of as an American, he felt anything but safe.

I am constantly apprehensive as though some great calamity impended over me, for I really do not know to what length my greedy stepfather will drive his wife ... I offered to settle on her £50 as long as she lived but she laughed at it ... I have smacked my lips over the flavour of fame – but the substance is useless to me – as it may be taken away at any time.[34]

Before leaving Brighton, an overwrought Stanley walked out of a banquet at the Royal Pavilion given in his honour by the Brighton and Sussex Medical Society. He thought his speech had been mocked by several guests. J. C. Parkinson of the *Daily News*, who interviewed Henry next day after riding with him on the Downs, recalled that most of the diners had been enjoying his talk when the incident occurred, and that Stanley had been much too thin-skinned.[35] Stanley would forgive and forget these doctors, but not the British establishment. Instead, he threw down his gauntlet at the feet of the well-heeled luminaries of the RGS.

> If the *Saturday Review* wishes to know what I do resent, let it be understood that I resent all manner of impertinence, brutal horse-laughs at the mention of Livingstone's name, or of his sufferings; all statements that Livingstone is either insane or irritable ... all statements that I am not what I claim to be – an American; all gratuitous remarks such as 'sensationalism', as directed to me by that suave gentleman, Mr Francis Galton ... and all such nonsense ...[36]

Stanley next became embroiled in an acrimonious correspondence with Clements Markham, the secretary of the RGS, who had taken Galton's part at Brighton and was now determined to deny 'the American' the Society's gold medal on a technicality. Markham did not question the importance of the journey to the north end of Lake Tanganyika, but disqualified Stanley because he had not taken scientific observations for longitude and latitude in the time-honoured scientific manner with a sextant and chronometer watch. Recording the number of hours he had marched on particular compass bearings was just not good enough. Henry, however, got the better of Markham by leaking the text of his patronizing letter. In the end, public opinion swung in Stanley's favour, and he learned in October that he would, after all, receive the gold medal. This was after the Queen had expressed her own view of the matter by giving Stanley an audience, and presenting him with a gold and lapis lazuli snuff box embellished with her VR cipher in rubies and diamonds.[37]

During this unhappy period, Stanley made several good friends who helped him for many years to come. The first was Edwin Arnold, the forty-year-old editor of the *Daily Telegraph*, who was also a poet and distinguished Orientalist. Unlike the exclusively educated Markham and Rawlinson, Arnold was a grammar school boy, who was disgusted by how Stanley had been treated. From now on, while Arnold was in the editor's chair, Henry could depend upon the *Daily Telegraph*'s support. Another important friendship was with Edward Marston, a partner in the London publisher Sampson Low – the firm that, for an advance of £1,000 and a generous royalty, had bought the

British rights to his book about the Livingstone quest. Stanley began writing in mid-August, having moved from the Langham Hotel to a flat in nearby Duchess Street, off Portland Place. Amazingly, he delivered a 700-page manuscript in late September – thanks to his outstanding capacity for hard work. Marston sensibly advised him to tone down his preface, cutting phrases such as 'I was hooted at, reviled and calumniated', and any other passages that would be seen as 'a general challenge to all creation'.[38] Against his publisher's advice, Stanley included some niggling criticisms of Kirk and a reprise of his grievances against the RGS.

The book was published in November 1872, under a title invented by Marston, *How I Found Livingstone*, which Stanley's critics would say was typical of his conceit. It received mixed reviews, *The Times* describing it, a little unfairly, as 'not so much a book as a series of letters from a special correspondent', and accusing Stanley of 'displeasing egotism ... and still more displeasing sensitiveness and acrimony'.[39] Despite the book's hasty composition, Stanley's lasting achievement was to have written a portrait of the Scottish missionary and explorer that would form the basis of the myth of saintly Dr Livingstone, transforming the way future generations saw him. In many episodes, including the fight against Mirambo, and almost every scene with Livingstone, Stanley showed that he was a master of narrative and could depict character with ease and economy.

His book was an extraordinary feat for someone of his background, yet was marred because his editor did not prevent him foolishly including episodes of corporal punishment, some of which seem to have been invented. As a result, Stanley misrepresented his real attitude towards the men he called his 'dark companions', most of whom served with him again in Africa. Such passages enabled his enemies to describe his dealings with Africans as the very opposite of Livingstone's gentle proceedings. Because Livingstone's journals were heavily edited, it was imagined that *he* never resorted to the whip or cane. This was not so, although he disliked using corporal punishment. By writing about beatings in a jocular fashion – something commonplace in soldiers' memoirs – Stanley shocked humanitarians in Britain, and earned Florence Nightingale's famous criticism of *How I Found Livingstone* as 'The very worst book on the very best subject'.[40]

A famous example of this jocose tendency occurs when Stanley describes his attempt to slip past a hostile tribe by night. Unable to bear the tension, the wife of one of his carriers suddenly becomes hysterical and starts screaming. Her distraught husband suggests cutting her throat, but Stanley resorts to the whip. 'I asked her to desist after the first blow. "No!" She continued her insane cries with increased force and volume. Again my whip descended on her shoulders ... Louder and louder she cried, and faster and faster I showered the blows for the taming of this shrew.'[41] This was improbable behaviour for a man anxious to restore silence, since it could only have resulted in more, rather than less noise. It therefore seems unlikely that the incident ever occurred. Equally damaging was a full page illustration (facing page 642 of the book) showing a man up to his neck in a river, with a box on his head. This was said to contain Livingstone's diaries, and Stanley was depicted pointing a revolver at his head. The caption reads: 'Look out, you drop that box – I'll shoot you.' This was equally unconvincing since the threat would only have terrified the man and made him more likely to stumble – and, if carried out, would have led to the certain loss of the diaries. In his desperation to appear masterful, and impossible to thwart, Stanley was responsible for sowing the seeds of his reputation for brutality.

In this same book, Henry advised every white traveller

to learn the necessity of admitting that negroes are men, like himself, though of a different colour; that they have passions and prejudices, likes and dislikes ... in common with all human nature ... Though I had once lived among the negroes of the Southern States, my education was Northern, and I had met in the United States black men, whom I was proud to call friends.'[42]

Since tribal Africans were commonly called savages and niggers by Stanley's contemporaries, and were written about as such in popular books, his general reflections about Africans seem unusually enlightened, while his heartless passages are no worse than examples to be found in many other books.[43] Nor should it be forgotten that corporal punishment was commonplace in British society at large.

Shortly after his book became a runaway best-seller, Sir Henry Rawlinson and the secretary of the RGS, Clements Markham, gave Stanley a large banquet in Willis's Supper Rooms in St James's Square, at which Rawlinson delivered an apparently heartfelt apology for causing Stanley so much distress. Mark Twain, who was present, described it as 'the most manly and magnificent apology ... that I ever listened to'.[44] But Stanley was not so easily mollified. 'I could forgive the English geographers for their unkind remarks, made when I was absent – if I was not aware that the same principle of hostility still lives, and is busy.'[45] His problem with English gentlemen was that he could not believe that when they shook hands and apologized, they really meant it, and so he never gave his former critics a chance to get to know him and change their minds. In the workhouse, enemies had remained enemies.

But Henry showed his gentler side to two of Livingstone's closest friends, William and Emilia Webb, and to their children, when he went to stay with them in October at Newstead Abbey, near Nottingham, their historic country house (formerly Lord Byron's ancestral home). Livingstone had been the Webbs' guest for eight months during 1864 and 1865, while writing his book about his ill-starred Zambezi Expedition. Despite being rich, the Webbs were open-minded and well-travelled. Emilia and her daughter Augusta described Stanley as 'a typical American journalist, almost aggressively so', and 'very rough in all his ways, and as unlike the Stanley of his later years as a prickly chestnut burr is to the smooth brown chestnut within'. Augusta and her mother realized that he was defensive because still 'smarting and bruised' from his maltreatment by the press and the geographers.

Emilia noticed how awkward Stanley was with strangers, becoming like 'a perfect porcupine', yet being 'so very nice' when alone with her family. Stanley was 'abstemious in his habits, and rather silent', yet as the days passed, he became much less like 'a perfect Ishmaelite with his hand raised against every man and feeling every man's hand raised against him'. Augusta saw him grow steadily 'gentler, and happier, whilst the hard lines on his face became less visible'. Emilia took Henry for rides in her pony phaeton and found that he had 'a great loneliness of heart', and 'under all his roughness one of the most affectionate natures' she had ever encountered. Stanley even confided to Emilia 'all his sad early story'. Livingstone had been Stanley's idea of an ideal father and, at Newstead, Emilia seems to have become something approaching his ideal mother.

Augusta thought Stanley's appearance striking. 'He had at this time the most extraordinary and wonderful eyes I had ever seen. They were like small pools of grey fire, but the least provocation turned them into grey lightning ... his whole personality gave out the impression of overwhelming and concentrated force ...' Augusta reckoned that this scared people and made them dislike him without quite knowing why.[46] His stay with the Webbs was a brief period of peace before an exhausting series of book lectures. While speaking in Scotland, he met Livingstone's elder daughter, Agnes, who a few days after his arrival in England had sent him a letter of heartfelt thanks, which had comforted him while the RGS was being so insultingly silent.[47]

The most stressful lecture of his English tour took place in the Free Trade Hall in Manchester, early in November. Many of his Denbigh relatives occupied the best seats, and sent up notes, which he refused to answer. 'The truth is: between myself and my countrymen is a great gulf now ... They cannot understand why I should not be proud of the little parish world of northern Wales and I cannot understand what they see to admire in it.' He was staying that night with the president of the local Chamber of Commerce – and to this man's front door came Katie Gough-Roberts, now Mrs Urban Bradshaw, with her husband. She must have realized that Stanley would have been enraged to discover that she had allowed Hotten to reproduce, in his book, a photograph of a page of his long autobiographical letter to her. Katie gave the servant a note to take to Stanley. In it, she offered to return his long letter if he would come down for it in person. But Stanley knew she was with her husband, who would have read all his love letters, so, out of pride, he refused to see her.[48]

This incident confirmed his growing conviction that fame was useless to him. It not only made his relatives more grasping, but brought threatening letters, and numerous invitations from strangers. Most days Henry would get thirty or more letters from people he had never heard of. Since he hated being stared at in the street, he felt obliged to take expensive hackney cabs everywhere. He also had to spend money on new clothes in order to dine with important people, and on stamps and stationery to reply to all his mail. And although the £2,000 paid him in advance by British and American publishers, along with large lecture fees, substantially exceeded his £400 per annum basic income from journalism, his poverty-stricken childhood still made him eager to save money rather than spend it.[49]

All the time, he felt he was viewed with 'an immense amount of envy': 'I can count my friends on my fingers but my enemies are a host.' Certainly he *did* have friends, such as Marston and Arnold, but neither belonged to his generation. If Edward King, who was working as the *Boston Morning Journal*'s Paris correspondent, had only been living in London in 1872, Henry would have had someone with whom to talk through his problems. As things were, he only saw him in Paris en route to somewhere else. At their last meeting Henry had given him a gold watch, as a token of their 'unwavering' friendship.[50] Meanwhile, Madame Tussaud's made a waxwork likeness of the lonely young man.

The celebrity who interested Henry more than any other while he was in London was Richard Burton, the scholar, author and explorer, whom he met twice. Stanley was fascinated that Burton chose to 'present himself to the public as aggressively as possible'. It seemed that Burton actually 'wished to be thought wicked & hard ... No wonder society is shocked by his open defiance and his sneers at what he calls "goody-goodiness".' Stanley's own sensitivity to criticism made him wonder whether Burton could really be indifferent to public opinion, or whether he felt 'secret pain' at being shunned. Perhaps Burton's determination to present himself 'aggressively' helped the younger man decide that the best way to deal with his own vulnerable feelings would be to hide them behind a stern façade.[51]

On the eve of sailing for America, for more lecturing to sell the Scribner's edition of his book, Stanley was in a strange position – he hated 'the scavenger-beetles of the press', and detested 'the vulgar, even hideous nonsense [and] untruths published' by them.[52] Yet here he was, about to go to New York in part so that he could beg James Gordon Bennett Jr to send him on some journalistic assignment (which in his heart he knew could only be an anti-climax after his finding of Livingstone). His situation was all the more ironic since by early October 1872, his mind was already turning to Africa again. In this month, the press was agitating for the RGS to spend on the good doctor all the £3,750 still remaining of the £5,000 subscribed by the public for the ill-starred Livingstone Search and Relief Expedition.

By early October, Henry had decided that his true vocation was as an explorer. On the 5th he wrote telling Clements Markham that all the remaining geographical problems of the central watershed could be solved if the Society sent out an experienced traveller – hinting that he would be the right man. Markham ignored his hint, and in his reply failed to mention that the RGS was about to send a young naval officer, Verney Lovett Cameron, to contact Livingstone and assist him from the east, while a second naval officer would be sent to reach him from the Atlantic coast via the Congo.[53] (Markham had himself once held a commission in the navy.)

When he imagined these young officers completing Livingstone's geographical work, it seemed to Henry that he had been offered the chance of a lifetime and had tossed it away. All the time Africa had been his destiny, without his realizing it. The memory of his happiness with Livingstone also haunted him. 'I seem to see through the dim, misty, warm, hazy atmosphere of Africa, always the aged face of Livingstone, urging me on in his kind, fatherly way.'[54] It is clear from a letter Lieutenant Cameron sent to Stanley on 25 October that Henry had written to him humbly, a few days earlier, suggesting that they pool their resources to help Livingstone. Cameron replied coolly: 'I regret exceedingly that circumstances have arisen which render me unable to join my expedition to yours. I am very sorry indeed to be unable to avail myself of your experience ...'[55] Those unspecified 'circumstances' would have included a direct prohibition from Markham and Rawlinson to co-operate with 'the American'. Cameron was 'the Protégé of the RGS', chosen to eclipse the 'damned penny a liner' and avenge the defeat of the RGS Livingstone Search and Relief Expedition.[56] Henry's unnecessary quarrel with the RGS now looked likely to deny him all future exploring opportunities under their control.

Nothing in Stanley's papers suggests that he ever asked Bennett to pay for him to return to Africa to trace the Lualaba with Livingstone. The mogul would certainly have argued that a great scoop could never be repeated. However, it *is* likely that during October 1872 Henry suggested to Edwin Arnold of the *Daily Telegraph* that solving the Nile and Congo mystery with Livingstone could be made into a story as popular as 'finding' him. But if Arnold was asked, he must have refused the bait. The unpalatable fact was that another man looked set to solve the age-old mystery of the central African watershed in partnership with Stanley's ideal father, and there was absolutely nothing that he could do about it – except, of course, pray that Cameron would fail. A despondent Stanley sailed for New York, and his well-paid American lecture tour, on 9 November, three weeks before Verney Lovett Cameron sailed for Zanzibar.

ELEVEN

A Destiny Resumed

On 20 November 1872, Stanley's Cunarder, the *Cuba*, steamed into the Hudson River and was met by a tug dressed overall with flags and flying from her masthead a gigantic banner bearing the words: WELCOME TO STANLEY. She had been hired by the *New York Herald* to take the returning hero ashore, and was filled with journalists and notabilities. Yet when Stanley arrived at the *Herald*'s offices, James Gordon Bennett Jr granted him a mere ten minutes of his time. It was said that the egotistical proprietor had become insanely jealous because Stanley, rather than himself, had become world famous as a result of the Livingstone mission.[1]

Whatever the truth of this, Bennett allowed to be published in the *Herald* an unnecessarily cruel account of Stanley's first lecture in the Steinway Hall. One of his journalists, George O. Seilhamer, condemned the subject matter as 'intolerably dull', the speaker's delivery as fast and hesitant, and his voice as being 'pitched in a sing-song and doleful monotone'.[2] It seemed that Stanley had made the disastrous decision to give in New York the kind of academic talk that would have delighted the Brighton geographers – whereas 'the sensational stories' that Mr Galton had hated would have been far better suited to the Steinway Hall. Stanley's second lecture was more entertaining, but the hall was only one-third full. The next talk had to be cancelled when a mere scattering of people turned up. Effectively, Henry's tour had been destroyed by the *Herald*. Small wonder that this incident fed his suspicion that even people with good reason to be grateful turned against him eventually. Meanwhile, the songs and humorous vignettes of two Broadway extravaganzas, 'King Carrot' and 'Africa', puzzled and upset him, because they burlesqued Livingstone and

149

himself, and not just the slave traders and the stuffed shirts of the RGS.³

Although Henry had imagined he needed a period of rest and tranquillity, he felt lonely and neglected now that he had it. He moved from the Fifth Avenue Hotel to rooms on East 20th Street and lived quietly. In the summer, Lewis Noe had sold to the *New York Sun* his story about his sufferings in Turkey, with details about the joint desertion from the US navy. He also claimed that Stanley was a Welshman called Rowlands and that he had forged Livingstone's letters. This would be repeated across America. For a month or so, Bennett had used these revelations to sell yet more newspapers, before squashing the *Sun*'s story with overwhelming evidence.⁴ But with many aspects of his rackety past now in the public domain, Stanley's old sense of security in America was gone. Not that he would ever lose his gratitude for what the country had done for him. At least he still had friends to chat with. From time to time, Edward King – working briefly in Boston – visited his old friend in New York.⁵ Finley Anderson also called in regularly. And since both men were bachelors, they talked about women and love. Henry wrote to Anderson about two particular females. Could he put in a good word with one? 'I cannot make love for you,' replied the former London bureau chief. 'If I should make the attempt, possibly *you* might not get her.'⁶

Even after Bennett's monstrous behaviour, Stanley did not resign from the *Herald* – though he did investigate whether another paper might send him back to Africa. He certainly tried his utmost to persuade Louis Jennings, the editor of the *New York Times*, to send him to the Lualaba. But it was Jennings who, early in 1873, effectively delivered the *coup de grâce* to his hopes of aiding Livingstone again: 'We think on careful reflection, that another African expedition would be like threshing out the beaten straw. A second enterprise of that sort could not possibly equal the success of the first, and the *Herald* has rather used up the general subject.'⁷ It was a deeply depressing moment for a man who had so recently achieved the century's most enduring scoop.

While in America, Stanley wrote a curious book, *My Kalulu, Prince, King and Slave*, which he called a romance for boys, but which was really a strange combination of fantasy and adventure novel. Its heroes were Kalulu and Selim, modelled very loosely on his two youngest servants in Africa. The background is the Mirambo war;

many sickening acts of violence are committed, similar to acts that Stanley had witnessed or heard about. Henry implored Edward Marston not to allow 'anything vulgar to creep in', but though a reference to slaves being 'compelled to attend to a call of nature' was cut, bucketfuls of blood remained.[8] Not that bloody scenes were anything but commonplace in Victorian adventure fiction. And sentimental relationships, such as that between Kalulu and Selim, were routine in novels of public school life. But Stanley was no novelist, and the book lacked focus and momentum – the very qualities his travel writing always had. When *My Kalulu*'s sales were poor, he vowed never to attempt another work of fiction for readers of any age.[9]

In April 1873, Mr Bennett sent a telegram from Paris summoning Stanley back to work. Though Henry had no idea what assignments he might be offered, he was relieved to be on the verge of resuming his former profession. But first he wanted to place Kalulu in an English school. The young African – now nearly twelve – had lived in London and New York with him, and in both cities had obligingly sung Swahili songs for any visiting journalist, and agreed to be photographed in tribal attire beside Stanley in his exploring outfit of thigh-length boots and pith helmet.[10] Back in England, before leaving the boy at a church school in Wandsworth, Henry took him as a treat to stay with the Webbs for a few days.[11] Despite such acts of kindness, Stanley exploited the boy to publicize his book and his lectures. Yet Kalulu's lot, had he remained a slave in Africa, would hardly have been preferable to his peripatetic existence with Stanley.[12]

On 2 May 1873, Stanley met James Gordon Bennett Jr in the Hotel des Deux Mondes in Paris and was told that he must resume his old job in Spain. Faced with the prospect of returning to the very work he had been doing in the Madrid bureau before he became famous, Henry must have been saddened. But his posting was brief, and in October Bennett sent him to cover a British military campaign in West Africa. At least he would be in Africa again, though nowhere near the central watershed. Unless he had asked for a rise before leaving, Bennett would not have raised his salary to £1,000 per annum from the miserly £400 it had been since 1869.[13]

This West African story was not a new one to Britain's colonial authorities. In fact the invasion of the Gold Coast protectorate by the neighbouring Ashanti (Asante) that had just occurred was the seventh of the century. The British government had therefore decided to send a talented general, Sir Garnet Wolseley (later Field Marshal Lord Wolseley), to punish the invaders. Sir Garnet's briskly efficient campaign ended with the sacking of the Ashanti capital, Kumasi, the levying of a fine of 50,000 ounces of gold on the defeated ruler, and the extraction of a promise that he would abandon human sacrifices, keep open the road to Kumasi, and never again attack the Fanti (Fante) tribe on the coast. Stanley chronicled this 'little war' with his usual efficiency, from its start to the predictable overkill at its conclusion. British casualties on the fifth and final day of the advance were four killed and 194 wounded. Ashanti casualties may have been as high as 2,000. After the burning of Kumasi, Stanley was disturbed to be shown, just outside the town, a grove where Ashanti kings had, for at least a century, ritually decapitated slaves, criminals, and enemies at a rate of about a thousand a year. Their blood was kept in a huge bowl and used for fetish purposes. Countless skulls lay in heaps, alongside putrefying bodies. Yet Stanley still praised the cultural achievements of the Ashanti: their extraordinary skill at carving and metalwork, and the artistry of their designs.[14]

One aspect of Stanley's Gold Coast assignment is of particular biographical interest. On this trip, he reverted to travelling with a hero-worshipping teenage servant. Before the campaign proper began, Stanley and the well-known writer of boys' adventures, G. A. Henty, reporting for the *Standard*, ventured along the coast in a small steamship. The hero of Henty's next boys' novel, *By Sheer Pluck*, was a teenage boy, resembling Stanley's clerk and valet, Anthony Swinburne, who travelled with them. Stanley did not mention Anthony in any of his writings, until he employed him six years later.[15]

Stanley had first met Anthony Bannister Swinburne in London in September 1873, when the boy was fifteen and had just left Christ's Hospital School to become an apprentice tea broker in the City.[16] His clergyman father had died suddenly in 1866, leaving his widow, Frances, with very little money. She and Anthony had then been constantly on the move from one lodging house to another.[17] Mrs Swinburne's struggle to help her boy get on in life moved Stanley, precisely because his own mother had *not* struggled for him. Fatherless boys aroused Stanley's deepest feelings of compassion, because he himself had never known a father. With Anthony, the older-brother dimension of Henry's relations with young males was replaced by something paternal – a feeling that would ultimately become a longing for fatherhood.

Frances Swinburne had felt, intuitively, that she could trust Stanley to look after Anthony, and she was right. In late December, when the campaign was effectively over, she wrote telling Stanley: 'I can scarcely say what he [Anthony] does not feel you are ... I almost believe you are his idol – certainly his beau ideal of all that is good and true.'[18] Henry had never allowed young Swinburne to come near the fighting; but he could not save him from contracting fever. Anthony did not complain, but wrote from his sick bed at Cape Coast Castle: 'You have behaved like a father to me and I am sure I cannot express my thanks ... If you are ever in want of anyone ... and you cannot get better than myself, I am at your service.'[19]

Compared with the way in which Stanley had treated Noe and Selim, his kindness to Anthony shows a perceptible softening in his character. Although it would be naive to suppose that his time with Livingstone had fundamentally transformed him, there can be no doubt that it had had a maturing effect. His concern for Anthony would not end with their return to England. Fanny Swinburne sent him pictures of her son as he grew older, and Stanley placed these in his *carte de visite* album, with those of friends and famous acquaintances.[20]

During his voyage to England, Stanley reached the island of St Vincent on 25 February 1874 to learn that Livingstone was dead.[21] Arriving in London on 17 March, he wrote next day to Agnes Livingstone telling her that he was 'stricken dumb' by the news. 'I cannot give you a description of the misery I felt.' Then he assured her that 'no daughter was ever beloved so deeply as you were ... How I envy you such a father. The richest inheritance a father can give his children is an honoured name.'[22] Given Henry's earlier fears about Livingstone's ill health, and the immensity of the task he had set himself, Stanley could not claim to have been surprised. Now, in the *Herald*'s London office, as he read about Livingstone's death near Lake Bangweulu, though grieving, Stanley knew that the doctor and his unfinished work was hot news again.[23] The story of how, after his death, his body had been eviscerated, dried and preserved by his followers before being carried a thousand miles to the coast inside a bale of tarred sailcloth was a remarkable one. Indeed, Livingstone's dogged refusal to give in when facing overwhelming odds, his uncomplaining acceptance of agonizing pain and his lonely death still conjure up powerful images. Coupled with Stanley's picture of saintly Dr Livingstone, his martyr-like death made him an instant myth.

Stanley sensed this, not just as a journalist, but as a devoted disciple. To finish the dead man's work now became a sacred trust. As he wrote again to Agnes, 'the completion of your father's discoveries ... [is] like a legacy left me by Livingstone'.[24] This idea of being bequeathed the task of unravelling the world's greatest remaining geographical mysteries was an inspiring one for Stanley, legitimizing *him*, rather than Kirk, Waller or even Livingstone's sons, as the great man's true heir.

"THE MAIN STREAM CAME UP TO SUSI'S MOUTH."

Livingstone travelling through marshes weeks before his death,
from his published *Last Journals*

In his diary for 25 February 1874 – the day on which he had first heard that Livingstone was dead – there can be found the kind of devotional entry that would have been sure to appeal to pious contemporaries, and has suggested to all Stanley's previous biographers that it was only after hearing about Livingstone's death that he decided to give up journalism and devote himself to exploration. This was what he wanted them to believe – it seemed to him that his story would gain in drama if it were thought he had decided to return to Africa only after Livingstone's passing. But in fact this diary entry was written when Henry was working on his autobiography in the 1890s, and inserted in his old journal at the appropriate point. It reads: 'Dear Livingstone! another sacrifice to Africa! His mission, however, must not be allowed to cease. Others must go forward and fill the gap. Close up boys! Close up Death will find us everywhere. May I be selected to succeed him in opening up Africa to the shining light of Christianity!'[25] (His debts to Henry Newbolt and his famous poem *Vitaï Lampada* (1897), with its refrain of 'Play up! play up! and play the game', are clear.) To this entry Stanley added – in the late 1890s – some sentences that would often be quoted against him in the future: 'My methods, however, will not be Livingstone's. Each man has his own way. His, I think had its defects, though the old man, personally, has been almost Christ-like ... The selfish and wooden-headed world requires mastering, as well as loving charity ...'[26] The obituary of Livingstone that Stanley wrote for the *Graphic* (published 24 April) better reflects his feelings at the time.

Though the heart of Livingstone ... has ceased to beat, his voice rings out loud ... He has bequeathed a rich legacy to fight the evil horror of the slave trade ... and left an obligation on the civilized nations of Europe and America, as the shepherds of the world, to extend their care and protection over the oppressed races of Africa.

At this time Henry received the final letter Livingstone had written to him – it was one of the very last he ever wrote, since, although undated, it was headed 'Lake Bangweolo'. Livingstone deeply regretted that, in the chaos of assembling his caravan at Unyanyembe, he had not 'expressed half the gratitude that welled up in [his] heart for all the kind and able services [Stanley] rendered [him] at the coast'.[27]

While Livingstone's death and burial did not determine the future course of Stanley's life, they certainly strengthened his existing determination to solve the Nile problem. Stanley was one of that select body of officials, friends and family who went to Southampton to see the body brought ashore on a wet and windy mid-April morning.[28] The Royal Horse Artillery's twenty-one-gun salute, at minute intervals, and the military band playing the 'Dead March from Saul', gave notice of a great national event in which fate had given the former boy from St Asaph a leading role. As befitted a national hero, Livingstone's coffin lay for two days in the Map Room of the headquarters of the RGS in Savile Row, Burlington Gardens. The prime minister, Benjamin Disraeli, and the Prince of Wales were mourners at the funeral itself, and emotional crowds lined Pall Mall and Whitehall. As a pall bearer, Stanley was conveyed to Westminster Abbey in the third of twelve mourning carriages, along with several fellow pall bearers, the detested Horace Waller and two of Livingstone's friends,

William Cotton Oswell, the hunter and explorer, and E. D. Young, leader of the first Livingstone Search Expedition.[29] Kalulu, in a new grey suit, travelled in the second carriage with William Webb of Newstead, Dr John Kirk and Jacob Wainwright, one of the doctor's African followers. Agnes Livingstone had implored Stanley to forgive John Kirk 'over the grave of my dearest & best'. [30] If he had only obliged her, he would have saved himself much anguish.

The funeral made a lasting impression on Henry, as it did on many others in the Abbey – among them missionaries who would start new missions in Africa, and two businessmen who would found a great African trading company, along with two shipping magnates who would between them donate a million pounds to African projects.[31] But it was the influence Livingstone had already exerted on Stanley that would have by far the greatest effect on subsequent African colonial history.

On 7 April 1874, Stanley had learned that Lieutenant W. J. Grandy's RGS-sponsored Congo expedition had been recalled, having achieved nothing.[32] How Cameron was faring, he had no idea, and so had to live with the possibility that the naval officer might succeed in his mission and thus write him out of history. But this uncertainty did not stop Stanley trying to get a new African expedition off the ground. Nor, fortunately, did it stop newspaper editors seeing that Livingstone's death changed everything. Finishing his uncompleted work would now be a great story. Henry's friend, Edwin Arnold, the idiosyncratic editor of the *Daily Telegraph*, wrote to him saying: 'this great question [the identification of the Nile's source] is a subject in which my heart & soul are engaged'.[33] Arnold set up a meeting on 14 June with the paper's proprietor, Edward Levy-Lawson, who was understandably sceptical when Stanley said he meant to find the answer to all the great geographical questions of the central watershed left unsolved by Speke, Burton, Grant, Baker and Livingstone. Yet, in the end, Henry persuaded Lawson to offer a magnificent £6,000, conditional upon James Gordon Bennett Jr contributing the same. Rather than allow himself to be left out of an enterprise promising substantial newspaper sales, Bennett telegraphed a grudging one word reply: 'Yes'. But that single word spelled the difference between a viable mission, and no mission at all.[34]

To say that at the age of thirty-three Stanley stood on the brink of greatness would be true. But in the summer of 1874, the most likely possibility was that he would die long before finding out central Africa's remaining secrets.

TWELVE

Love and the Longest Journey

Before his crucial meeting with Edward Levy-Lawson and Edwin Arnold, Stanley had gone to stay at Newstead Abbey to finish his book, *Coomasie and Magdala*, which combined in a single volume his accounts of the campaigns he had reported on in West Africa and in Abyssinia.[1] Though suspecting that the book would not sell well, he did not brood on this. He had all the preparations for his next great journey to attend to, and out of the blue he fell in love for the first time since his relationship with Katie Roberts. On 13 May 1874, shortly after returning from Newstead, Henry wrote in his diary: 'This day I first got acquainted with a young lady called Alice Pike, daughter of Mrs S. N. Pike of 613, Fifth Avenue.' Three densely written pages followed, describing this meeting with Alice and her family at a dinner table at the luxurious Langham – Henry's favourite London hotel.

On that momentous evening, Alice – the youngest of three daughters – was the only one to whom he felt drawn. The eldest daughter, Nettie, who was also there, he dismissed as 'rather fast', and also because she wore her hair in fashionable 'frizzles', and talked too loud. But as for Alice, he was at once struck by her 'soft girlish profile' and 'self-contained way'. He liked her blue-grey eyes and soft, large mouth, and thought 'the carriage of her head indicated that she was cool and self-possessed'. His only criticism – a serious one in his eyes – was that she wore too many diamonds, which made him fear 'inordinate vanity with over-much wealth to gratify it'. She was also, he said, 'very ignorant of African geography, & I fear of everything else'.[2]

Three days later, Stanley went driving in the park with the girls. Though he was twice Alice's seventeen years, and knew all her foibles, he sensed that he was on the brink. 'I fear if Miss Alice gives me as much encouragement as she has been giving me lately, I shall fall in love with her, which may not perhaps be very conducive to my happiness, for she is the very opposite of my ideal wife.'[3] When Henry called the following morning, the 17th, Alice read him a love letter she had just received from a French count, laughing at his flowery sentiments. Stanley resolved never to write affectionately until *she* 'had first made a declaration ... However pretty, elegant etc. she may be, she is heartless, and a confirmed flirt.'[4] Yet this did not save him from himself.

Now, almost every day, the distinguished, cigar-smoking, moustachioed thirty-three-year-old explorer, with his dark wavy hair, greying at the temples, and the pert, self-confident daughter of Samuel N. Pike, the recently deceased owner of the Cincinnati and New York Opera houses, met each other. Alice's father had also owned numerous hotels and several of America's largest whisky distilleries, and had had an annual income of $3,000,000. It seems most unlikely – despite Stanley's apparent disdain for ostentation – that Alice's staggering wealth was not fascinating to him. Perhaps this compensated for her ignorance and immaturity, which would normally have repelled a serious-minded man who had worked so hard to educate himself.

On 13 June, Alice sailed home to New York, and Stanley went to see her off at Liverpool docks, where he had once delivered meat to the ships. 'This day,' he wrote, 'I saw my fiancée, Alice, for so I must call her, depart from Liverpool.'[5] Two months later, Henry himself sailed for New York, ostensibly to see Gordon Bennett but really to be with Alice. At his two meetings with Bennett, the proprietor's arrogance and hypocrisy were as bad as before. At their first appointment, he simply dismissed Stanley, saying he was too busy to see him. 'This is rather an unkind way to receive one whom he is about to send to Africa,' noted Stanley with amazing restraint.

Given what he had already done for the *New York Herald*'s sales, and what his new journey promised to do, Bennett's ingratitude was staggering. On 11 July Bennett, who had shamelessly exaggerated the amount he had spent on the Livingstone search, now refused to sign a contract committing himself to spend the full £6,000 he had promised for the new trans-Africa expedition. Instead, he said he would deposit a smaller sum at a bank – to be topped up 'as the necessity of the case demanded it'.[6]

Henry's meeting with Alice next day, at 613, Fifth Avenue, was far more pleasing. During it, they both pledged themselves in writing to get married when Henry returned from Africa.[7] On his last night in New York, Alice again promised to marry him 'whether her mother were willing or not', he wrote, for 'in deference to her mother she had postponed our marriage for two years'. Before they parted, Alice 'raised her lips in tempting proximity to mine and I kissed her on her lips, on her eyes, her cheeks, and her neck, and she kissed me in return'. But, as Stanley reflected anxiously, 'two years is such a long time to wait, & I have so much to do, such a weary, weary journey to make before I can ever return. No man had ever to work harder for a wife.' And what if he should fail to get back in two years, which Alice declared was the longest she would wait? [8]

Their farewell took place on the 18th on pier 52, with all three Pike sisters coming to wave their handkerchiefs from the dock. Stanley could not bear to prolong the scene and gestured to them not to stay any longer: 'Alice kissed her hand to me and resolutely turned away ...'[9] When Alice's letters started to arrive, her failure to ask questions about his expedition, or to express anxiety about his very real chances of dying, must have disturbed him. She had told him to sign himself Morton in his letters to her, since she preferred that name to Henry. He did not demur.

When it became public knowledge that he was about to mount an expedition, Stanley received scores of applications to accompany him – 1,200 in all, from America and Europe as well as from Britain. Those volunteering included several high-ranking army officers and many junior ones[10] but, as with the Livingstone expedition, Henry chose young men from his own social background. *They* would be less likely to challenge his leadership than self-confident officers. But this was not his only rationale. Stanley enjoyed giving a helping hand to men like himself, born with few if any advantages. Whatever his reasoning, there is something impressively daring about his choosing, as his first recruit, a clerk working at the Langham Hotel. According to Henry, young Frederick Barker had badgered him for weeks to be taken, and had remained adamant despite repeated warnings about the dangers of Africa. His job would be to keep an up-to-date record of the expedition's stores. Francis and Edward Pocock, also in their early twenties, were the fishermen sons of the skipper of Edwin Arnold's yacht, which the *Daily Telegraph*'s editor kept on the river Medway in Kent.[11] To circumnavigate vast lakes, Stanley would need experienced boatmen. However, no member of this trio had ever been abroad, let alone to Africa. Henry would describe his white companions as servants, rather than colleagues. Kalulu was taken out of school so he could return to his homeland as his master's page and butler.

Henry arrived on Zanzibar on 21 September 1874, twenty-eight months after he had last been there. An Anglican cathedral was in the early stages of construction on the site of the closed-down slave market, formerly East Africa's largest. That slavery had been abolished on Zanzibar in June 1873 (with immense consequences for the sea-borne slave trade) had owed much to the publication of six of Stanley's despatches – in several of which he had described Livingstone's account of the massacre at Nyangwe – a week before the House of Commons debated the report of the Select Committee on the East African Slave Trade.[12] The credit for the treaty would generally be given to Sir Bartle Frere (a former Governor of Bombay) and to John Kirk, who signed for the British government, as consul in Zanzibar. But every bit as influential had been Stanley's public promotion of Livingstone's despatches at exactly the right time. Nevertheless, on land the trade was expanding. The decline in slave prices, as export markets shrank and disappeared, made the ownership of slaves more attractive to African purchasers. On the Mombassa coast between 1875 and 1884, almost 50,000 slaves worked in the clove plantations and also in producing grain, oils seeds and gum copra. In Zanzibar itself, by 1870, Indian merchants owned 8,000 slaves, and the Sultan 4,000 slaves for work on his clove plantations alone. Leading citizens routinely owned between 500 and 2,000 slaves. These numbers increased in the 1880s.[13] Many slaves employed on the East Coast had come from as far away as Lake Nyasa (Malawi), Buganda, and even from Manyema and the Upper Congo. Within Africa, warlord rulers like Mirambo and Msiri employed thousands of slaves as soldiers, making the continent an even more dangerous place.

Henry Stanley did not look as though he possessed an iron constitution. He had put on weight while in Europe, had smoked too many cigars, and was not only rather red-faced but suffered occasionally from a racing heart and from indigestion. He was broad-shouldered and powerfully built in his upper body, but his short legs were not ideal for walking immense distances. Yet in the flesh at this date he made a powerful impression – his face, particularly his blue-grey eyes, had an almost mesmerizing quality, which many people remarked upon.

His picture was not taken immediately before his greatest journey, but a small and indistinct photograph has survived of his fellow explorers, Frank and Edward Pocock, Frederick Barker and Kalulu. They are lined up on a flat roof, overlooking Zanzibar harbour, and sit cross-legged on the ground, looking diffident and ill at ease – a totally improbable group of adventurers about to begin one of the greatest journeys of all time. Yet the unseen photographer was their leader, whose burning determination to succeed without dying in the process promised to make up for their inexperience. They appeared to have no sense of occasion on this day of preparation as they stared stolidly ahead at a spot midway between the camera and the ground. Their lives had not yet rearranged themselves as history. For the engraving based on this badly faded photograph, Stanley included the expedition's dogs: a bull-terrier, Jack; two mastiffs, Castor and Captain; a bulldog, Bull; and a black retriever, Nero.[14] The rate of survival for canines would prove even worse than that for humans, with all these

Improbable heroes on a flat roof in Zanzibar (from left to right) Frank Pocock, Frederick Barker, an unknown local boy, Edward Pocock and Kalulu, from the engraving in Stanley's *Through the Dark Continent*

animals dying during the journey. Henry loved dogs and had chosen three of his five from the Battersea Dogs' Home.

While working hard at the recruitment of his carriers, Stanley unpacked the components of his exploring boat, named the *Lady Alice* in honour of his fiancée, whom Kalulu referred to, a little condescendingly, as 'your girrl' [sic].[15] The boat was constructed in sections that proved to be too broad to be carried along narrow African paths, so she was now re-built in smaller portable parts by a skilful ship's carpenter, whose steamship happened by a lucky chance to be in the harbour just then.

Stanley was thankful to be able to employ for this trip some of his most loyal and competent followers from his Livingstone expedition. These included Manwa Sera, Mabruki Speke, Chowpereh, Uledi, Ferajji and several of Livingstone's servants, including the ultra-loyal Gardner and Majwara, the boy who had fallen asleep in the explorer's hut shortly before he died. Originally, these men had been enticed or coerced from their tribal environments by slave and ivory traders operating deep into the interior. From the ranks of displaced Yao hunters and Swahili trading agents, freed slaves and mission 'boys', came many remarkable career servants of white travellers. Their courage and endurance would be essential to the success of the explorers who opened up East and Central Africa in the last third of the nineteenth century. On numerous occasions, Stanley would acknowledge his immense indebtedness to the Wangwana – the black freemen of Zanzibar, who were his rank and file. Even before the start of his greatest journey, he had already declared them to be 'clever, honest, industrious, docile, enterprising, brave and moral'.[16] His white followers also pleased him – the young Pocock brothers surprising everyone by giving a concert for local merchants and diplomats. Frank played the concertina and Edward the bugle, while both also sang.[17] Yet these outwardly cheerful young men knew what had happened to Farquhar and Shaw, and had just learned that two of Cameron's white companions had recently suffered the same fate.

In articles booming Stanley's forthcoming journey, the *New York Herald*'s editor had stated that their special correspondent would be 'in command of an expedition more numerous and better equipped than any that has ever entered Africa',[18] and in his published accounts of the journey Henry supported this idea, claiming that he had left the coast with 356 people: carriers, women and children. The idea that

Stanley always travelled with vast, well-provided expeditions is so widespread that it is necessary to emphasise once more that, as on his search for Livingstone, his insecurity led him to exaggerate, and again to diminish his real achievement.[19] In letters to several friends, he gave the total figure as 347, which would also feature in several places in his diary.[20] But in the most credible diary entry, for 12 November, the day on which his expedition embarked from Zanzibar in dhows, Stanley states that '224 answered to their names' before sailing. With himself and his three white companions added, this figure rose to 228. The only surviving muster list for the expedition – which, though undated, was plainly written at the outset – contains 227 names.[21] So, in reality, soon after the start of his epic journey Stanley had been leading about as many men as Speke and Burton had led in 1857, and Speke and Grant in 1861. His expedition was by no means the overlarge, invulnerable outfit it has been described as in all previous accounts.

While Stanley was on Zanzibar and still able to communicate with the outside world, the letters he received from his fiancée dismayed as well as delighted him. Because the mails were irregular, Alice decided that Henry was a poor correspondent, accusing him of being 'real mean about writing', and saying that she was 'real angry with Africa'.[22] She added a description of her sister's wedding: 'I wish you could have been there to see me, I had the greatest crowd of men around me all the time young & old.' Having complained about tedious gentlemen callers who stayed with her late into the evening, Alice had the gall to rebuke him for having written to an acquaintance of hers called Mamie Anderson. In a letter dated 2 December, which would have worried him acutely if it had reached him before he left, she responded to one he had sent her from Zanzibar, in which he had finally admitted that his journey would probably take three years. After pointing out that this was a whole year longer than she had expected, Alice demanded: 'And suppose you are not home then, where will you be? Dead or still seeking the Nile?'

This was a reasonable worry. If he were to be away for three years, why not four or five, and how could she ever be sure he had not died in the meantime?[23] Henry had hoped that if he could get her to accept a wait of two years (rather than scare her off with three years straightaway), he could then more safely try to extend the permitted time limit to the three years he actually needed. This subterfuge backfired badly, making her wonder whether he would stick to any agreed schedule.

Stanley caused additional grief by accusing her of encouraging men – an understandable allegation, given her references to swarms of admirers. 'That is wrong,' she insisted; '… it is natural that they should like me … it is really no fault of mine if they are conceited enough to think I will accept them if they only ask me.' But even if the infatuated Henry had read this arrogant letter before the start of his journey, he would still, in all likelihood, have travelled across Africa with her photograph wrapped in an oilcloth packet next to his heart.[24] Perhaps this frivolous girl, who was utterly unimpressed with his bravery and commitment, was the type of lover best suited to spur on a man of his temperament to achieve the impossible.

His first objective on his epic journey was to march just over 700 miles to Lake Victoria, and then circumnavigate and map the lake in order to establish whether Speke had been right to suppose that Victoria was a single lake with one outlet on its northern shore – his much-vaunted Nile source. Henry also aimed to show whether Burton was right to suggest that another, more southerly outlet, perhaps connecting Victoria with Lake Albert, could claim primacy as the Nile's source. If there really were (as Burton believed) two or three lakes, rather than one, then the most southerly would surely possess an outlet with a better claim to be the source than Speke's. After solving this major geographical conundrum, Stanley planned to travel 500 miles to the southwest and circumnavigate Lake Tanganyika. He meant to find its outlet and see whether it connected with Lake Albert to the north (as Samuel Baker believed was possible) or with Livingstone's Lualaba to the west. Finally, the Lualaba itself would have to be followed wherever it went to establish whether it was, as Livingstone thought, the Nile – or, as many geographers asserted, the Congo.

The first leg of this unprecedented 7,000-mile journey began at Bagamoyo on 17 November under 'an intensely bright and fervid sun'.[25] Soon his men were crossing open savannah, after travelling for miles in single file on a narrow path barely a foot wide. As a rule, they started their march soon after dawn, hoping to achieve most of the day's mileage (usually six to nine miles, though sometimes more) before the heat of the sun was too great. The stronger and generally younger men carried sixty-pound bales of cloth, which would be reduced in weight as the journey proceeded and they grew frailer. Older men carried the precious barometers, watches, sextants, mercury bottles, compasses and photographic equipment, packed in boxes of forty pounds. The all-important chronometers, vital for fixing the expedition's position, were stowed in balls of cotton in boxes of twenty-five pounds, and carried by the most responsible men.[26] Marching with the men (and included in the 228 people who answered their names) were thirty-six women – most of them the wives of his Wangwana 'captains' and senior *pagazi* or carriers.[27] As the path dipped and rose, the long line of porters, with the occasional brightly dressed woman among them, stretched out for several hundred yards, curving and twisting as they crossed a wooded hill, then straightening as they passed fields of manioc, maize and millet.

In these first few weeks, though two dogs died, there would be few problems with carriers. Yet this honeymoon period would be brief; and as backs and feet became sore, and discipline began to irk them, men started to desert. In the next three and a half months, Henry was appalled to lose fifty of his 228 followers – some dying of diseases, some in fights with tribesmen, but over half through desertion – and this was despite his using a group of skilled and trusted men – his 'detectives' – to track down absconders.[28] To stem the tide Stanley even resorted to chaining recaptured men for a few days, preferring this punishment – despite its unfortunate slave trade connotations – to beating offenders and causing life-threatening ulcers. Being fluent in Swahili, Henry was able to inspire his men and understand their complaints, which he felt should have enabled him to prevent serious losses. So his failure to do so, despite his best efforts, made the experience all the more frightening at the start of an unprecedented 7,000-mile journey.

When at last Stanley managed to stop the desertions, new problems afflicted him. Two of his white companions contracted malaria, and the rains began in earnest.

I am in a centre-pole tent, seven by eight. As it rained all yesterday, the tent was set over wet ground, which ... was soon trampled into a thick pasty mud, bearing the traces of toes, heels, shoe nails and dogs' paws. The tent walls are disfigured by large splashes of mud ... and there is an air of forlornness and misery ... I sit on a bed about a foot above the sludge.[29]

On the march, the clayey path was slippery, causing men to slip and fall under their heavy sixty-pound loads. Then in the constant rain the mud became thick and adhesive, making every step an effort. There was a food shortage in the surrounding country, and in these awful conditions the wretched carriers had to be put on half-rations. Two weeks later the rains ended, but Henry's difficulties did not.

In January 1875, after a gradual ascent, he and his followers reached an endless tableland covered with dense low bush. In this scrubland there was not one large tree from which the shape of the forest could be discerned; instead, as far as the eye could see, dwarf varieties of acacia, mimosa and rank-smelling gum trees and euphorbia were tangled densely together. 'The lower branches,' observed Stanley, 'were so interwoven one with another that it sickens me almost to write of.'[30] Sharp thorns cut through clothing, and at head height shoots and stubby branches threatened eyes and faces. Three days passed without a single sighting of game or any signs of cultivation. Occasionally they came across granite boulders the size of cottages, and massive tree roots erupting from the earth. Their guides deserted them on the fourth day, so Henry led them on north-west by compass. Not a single hopeful thing was sighted, but on the fifth day they found a small pond and drank its nitrous water. By the eighth day, hope for their survival was fading since no food had been obtained and people were starting to starve. In fact on that day, five men fell down in the bush and died before they could be found, and four other sick carriers lagged behind and were lost.

Henry had to decide whether, in this uninhabited waste, where no birds or wild animals could be found to shoot, he would simply lose more lives if he were to send out a rescue party. He decided he would. So instead, on the ninth day, he sent ahead forty of the fittest men with instructions to find the nearest village and bring back grain. This proved to be the right decision. Within twenty-four hours the forty returned with food, which saved their companions' lives. The effect of this period of deprivation was felt for several weeks. Four more men died, and over a score remained on the sick list. On 12 January, Stanley wrote: 'I must now wait until my people are strengthened, refreshed & perfectly rested. I propose to deal very liberally with all to repay them for their sufferings ...'[31] Looked back on from the vantage point of a year ahead, this ten-day ordeal would not stand out as one of the expedition's most frightening episodes, even though everyone in the party had faced the real possibility of collapsing and dying in the bush without hope of rescue. A graver danger soon confronted them.

Beyond the forest, though passing through a land of cultivated fields and plentiful cattle, Henry noticed 'a strange and peculiar air of discontent' among the local Africans. 'They were seen hurrying their women and children away, and deserting their villages while others hovered round our camp menacingly, carrying in their hands a prodigious quantity of arms – spears, bows and arrows and knob-sticks.'[32] So Stanley was obliged to resume the march much sooner than he wished. Many of his men were still emaciated when the column entered southern Ituru – the land of the Warimi: a people he described as 'remarkable for their manly beauty, noble proportions and nakedness ... Only the women bearing children boasted of goat skins.'[33] These people were very suspicious and only grudgingly sold food. They had no paramount chief, authority being shared between the headmen of individual villages.

At this point one of Stanley's three young English companions, Edward Pocock, fell seriously ill. Edward had roused the expedition each morning with some notes on his bugle. Like his brother, Frank, Edward had formerly been a fisherman on the river Medway. Henry at first suspected typhoid fever and, despite the local people's hostility, decided that Edward would have to rest whether the local chief's consent were given or not. But after a few days the chief's threats forced them to move on again, with Edward being carried in a hammock. By 15 January a rash of red pimples with white tops had broken out on his chest, suggesting smallpox. Stanley halted at once for Edward's sake, but he died early the following morning. Henry read the burial service in a shaking voice, while Frank Pocock wept over his brother's freshly dug grave. There would be no opportunity for Stanley to send a letter of condolence to Edward's parents for several months.[34] By now, he himself was suffering from intermittent fever, as was Frederick Barker, his young clerk and storekeeper.

When the march was resumed, Henry allowed a carrier suffering from asthma to follow the caravan at a slower pace, hoping he would catch up when they next halted. But with all members of the rearguard currently employed as carriers rather than as 'soldiers' because of the number of men sick, the hapless Kaif Halleck was waylaid and hacked limb from limb by warriors of the local tribe, the Wanyaturu. This happened on 21 January, as the caravan was approaching the village of Vinyata. Stanley had been gripped by 'a presentiment of evil' ever since entering the region of Ituru, and had been doing his utmost to propitiate the locals by handing over liberal presents. Even after Halleck's murder, he warned his men against trying to avenge the killing.[35] Two days later, while still camped at Vinyata, about a hundred natives assembled near the camp. They were wearing war-paint and made threatening gestures with their spears and bows.

I sent a message to ask them if they came to fight with us, and if so for what cause; if there was cause, I was quite willing to remove it. They replied that one of my men had stolen milk and I must pay cloth. The cloth was paid & they said they were satisfied. Five minutes later, two of my men [Sulieman and Soudi], who had gone to cut wood were attacked. One was killed by a spear in the back, the other narrowly escaped with a few flesh wounds of spear & knobstick. After this, all simultaneously came forward towards our camp discharging arrows.[36]

As these projectiles fell on the camp, Stanley ordered his men to fire back. The ensuing fight was not as one-sided as might have been expected with many of Stanley's men being armed with modern rifles. As he explained to a friend:

They attack in such numbers and so sudden [sic] that our repeating rifles and Snyders [sic] have to be handled with such nervous rapidity as will force them back before we are forced to death; for if we allow them to come within forty yards, their spears are as fatal as bullets ... while their contemptible looking arrows are deadly weapons.[37]

Six of the Wanyaturu were killed in this initial skirmish, Stanley himself 'dropping' one of the tribesmen with a long shot. He commented, 'God knows there was no cause for war & I cannot presume any other cause for their wanton attack on us than a desire for plunder & savage thirst for blood'[38] – though a desire to defend their land seems no less likely. On the following day, the Wanyaturu came again 'with shouts of derision & invited us out'. Henry sent forty men with Snider rifles to drive them away and snatch food from their villages. The result was not what he expected. His men disobeyed his instruction to keep their formation and chased on wildly after initial success, allowing themselves to become separated and picked off in small groups. In this way, he lost three men speared at once, and fifteen others driven away and presumed hunted down and killed. In his face-saving despatch to the *New York Herald*, dated 1 March, Stanley estimated the Wanyaturus' casualties at thirty-five, but the true number was probably fewer.[39]

After losing twenty-two of his followers over some stolen milk, Stanley was in no mood to fight again unless he had to. 'As God is my judge, I would prefer paying tribute and making these savages my friends rather than enemies.'[40] His losses meant that once again personal baggage, books, extra tents and even some beads had to be abandoned, so that essential impedimenta, such as the parts of the boat that he meant to launch on Lake Victoria in order to circumnavigate this vast 'nyanza', could still be carried. The number of carriers had to be stabilized at all costs, and from now on Henry worked his small party of trackers hard. On 5 and 6 February, the men he called his 'dusky detectives' tracked down and arrested four miscreants. One had deserted with a box of ammunition – an offence endangering the whole column. Many of his followers thought the man should be shot, but Stanley chose to beat him and put him in irons for a few days.[41]

On 19 February, as they came closer to the lake, they found themselves crossing a green, rolling plain, dotted with feeding cattle and broken here and there by rocky outcrops. They were now able to purchase a chicken for a necklace of beads, 'an ox for six yards of sheeting material, a sheep for two yards'. Yet despite receiving nourishing food, Frederick Barker, the clerk, did not recover from the fever that had been afflicting him for weeks. On 27 February he was too weak to walk when Frank Pocock raced down from the brow of a hill, 'his face beaming with joy', shouting: 'I have seen the lake, sir, and it is grand!'[42] Below was 'a gulf edged by a line of green wavy groves of trees scattered along the shore ... the lake stretching like a silvery plain far to the eastward'.[43] They had travelled 720 miles in 103 days, averaging, despite many delays, seven miles per day. Given all their problems and the days lost while resting, it was a magnificent rate of progress.[44] Yet Henry had lost sixty-two men either through desertion, fatal illness, or being killed or missing in fights with Africans.[45] Out of the original 228 men and women, only 166 were left.[46] It was sobering to reflect on these grave losses, after only 720 miles marched, and with more than three-quarters of the journey still ahead.

For Henry personally, an even more testing part of the journey was about to begin. But on the margins of the great lake, where violent events would soon change his life forever, he felt an overwhelming sense of peace.

I was as gratified as though I possessed the wand of an enchanter ... Only my gun-bearer was near me ... and the voices of the Wangwana came to me now and again faint by distance, and but for this, I might, as I sat there, have lost myself in the delusion that all the hideous past and beautiful present was a dream.[47]

On 8 March 1875, Stanley set sail on Victoria Nyanza, Africa's largest lake, in his twenty-four-foot boat, the *Lady Alice*, accompanied by ten of the expedition's fittest Wangwana. If Henry had been able to take twice that number, he would still have been vulnerable to a determined attack by tribesmen in their large canoes. A young man called Zaidi Mganda was his steersman at first, while Safeni, one of his most trusted captains, came as his adviser and translator. Stanley's aim was to map and circumnavigate the lake, establishing whether it was one body of water or several, and whether its northern outlet really was, as John Speke had claimed, the source of the Nile. Local people predicted that Stanley and his men would 'all drown in the lake, or die at the hands of the ferocious people living on the shores'.[48] The risks in venturing into this unknown region with so few men in a small boat were clearly enormous; and Henry knew very well, when he parted with Frank Pocock and Frederick Barker, that he might never see them again.

Before embarking for Africa, he had written to a fellow journalist about living with extreme risk, and had admitted that he had only a small chance of returning to England.

At the same time I cannot say that I feel any melancholy at the hopeless prospect, but rather a careless indifference as to what Fate may have in store for me. I say truly that I don't care whether I return or not. I have disciplined myself to look at my long journey in this light ...[49]

This fatalism – and the sense that his deprived childhood had left him with precious little to lose – helped him endure misfortune, since it could never surprise him as it did more fortunate men. His pessimism was probably also rooted in his fear that Alice would not wait for his return.[50] Yet the puzzle of why he was prepared to take death-defying risks and to inflict terrible harm on his body is not easily unravelled. Certainly he was hazarding his life not simply on account of his hunger for discovery, or his longing for fame – great though both were. For Henry, the quest of unlocking Africa's greatest secrets and completing Livingstone's work had always been more than a purely physical search.

THIRTEEN

The Island of Death

The eight months during 1875 that Stanley spent sailing on Lake Victoria and investigating the surrounding shores would have a major impact on African history. They would also change Henry's life through two linked incidents that would damage his moral reputation so seriously that his subsequent achievements would never properly be recognized.

Sailing north from a broad bay, which he named Speke Gulf in memory of the first white man to have seen the lake thirteen years earlier, Henry and his eleven crew members were soon battling with a ferocious gale. With the wind behind them and their single sail reefed to the smallest possible size, they surged along, in the twenty-four-foot *Lady Alice*, towards the mouth of the Simiyu river.[1] From there, they sailed eastwards along the southern side of the lake, until heading north along the lake's 200-mile eastern shore. Several days later, passing the island of Ukerewe, Stanley made a grim discovery – the slave trade had already reached the lake, causing warfare between tribes, and tempting chiefs to sell members of their own vassal tribes to the slavers for guns, cloth and other trade goods. Stanley found that the Arab-Swahili slave trader Mse Saba kept an immense thirty-ton dhow on Ukerewe. He and another Arab, Tarib Sungoro, with the help of the island's chief, were capturing men and women from the Gaya tribe and enslaving them. 'If ever a pirate deserved death for inhuman crimes, Sungoro deserves death,' wrote Stanley.[2] The slave trade bred suspicion of strangers, and made life far more dangerous for travellers.

On 28 March, while passing between two islands on Lake Victoria's eastern shores, the *Lady Alice* was surrounded by thirteen canoes crewed by about a hundred warriors of the Wavuma tribe, whose mariners habitually attacked vessels belonging to the Ganda. These Wavuma were fearless people, and Stanley's encounter with them ended badly. He called them 'pirates', and indeed they came close enough to snatch trade goods from the *Lady Alice*, and then blocked her escape route into open water, after threatening her crew with their spears. For a boat containing only eleven men, this was a life-threatening moment. Stanley responded by shooting one man dead, and killing maybe three others when he fired into the hull of a canoe and sank it.[3] Stanley believed that, if captured, he and his crew would have been enslaved, or put to death.[4] His experience with the Wanyaturu had convinced him that once Africans had made overt threats of violence, they would treat as weakness any subsequent attempts to placate them.[5]

On 4 April 1875, Stanley landed on the northern shore of the lake not many miles west of Victoria's main outflow, which had been named the Ripon Falls by the British explorer John Hanning Speke. Mutesa, the Kabaka or King of Buganda, sent his prime minister, or Katekiro, to welcome Stanley at the royal lakeside hunting resort of Usavara, where 2,000 Ganda warriors loosed off their guns in salute and beat tribal drums. After receiving a gift of ten oxen, sixteen sheep, and three dozen chickens, Henry walked to Mutesa's residence along 'a broad street, eighty feet wide and half a mile long', lined by 3,000 royal attendants. The Kabaka rose from a chair on Stanley's arrival – 'a tall and slender figure, dressed in Arab costume'. As soon as Mutesa began to speak, Henry 'became captivated by his manner, for there was much of the polish of a true gentleman about it'.[6]

In 1862 Speke had dismissed Mutesa as a bloodthirsty despot, who even allowed his favourite pages to shoot and kill passers-by at random.[7] Stanley attributed the subsequent improvement in Mutesa's behaviour, to the civilizing influence of the Unyanyembe ivory trader, Khamis bin Abdullah al Barwani, who had lived at court for a year. Stanley liked the embroidered Arab jackets and curved daggers worn by courtiers, and he was not offended when Mutesa declared himself 'a follower of Islam'.[8] But it horrified him that the Kabaka had allowed his country to become 'the northern source of the [East African] slave trade'.[9]

Near the start of his 1875 diary, Henry sounded uncannily like Livingstone when stating that he 'often entertained lofty ideas concerning regenerative civilization, and the redemption of Africa'.[10] Having

1 Bowling Green Cottage, Denbigh. John Rowlands lodged here with the Price family between July 1846 and February 1847
2 St Asaph Workhouse where Stanley lived and was educated between the ages of six and fifteen

3/4

5/6

3 Stanley's mother, Elizabeth Jones (née Parry) in middle age in a previously unpublished photograph and the only one that is known to exist
4 Stanley's first love, his first cousin, Catherine (Katie) Parry, who is said to have resembled his mother in her youth
5 John Rowlands aged fifteen, shortly after leaving the workhouse
6 The first photograph of Stanley in America, when he was nineteen

7 Stanley aged twenty-three, when serving in the US Federal Navy
8 Lewis Noe
9 Stanley in the bogus American naval officer's uniform he had made for himself in 1866,
with the wrong buttons
10 Stanley photographed in Alexandria in June 1868 on his return from Abyssinia

11 David Livingstone in England in 1864 before his final return to Africa
12 Stanley wearing Arab dress on a brief visit to Berbera, on the Somali coast, in January 1869. He had been influenced by Richard Burton and other authors of adventurous travel books

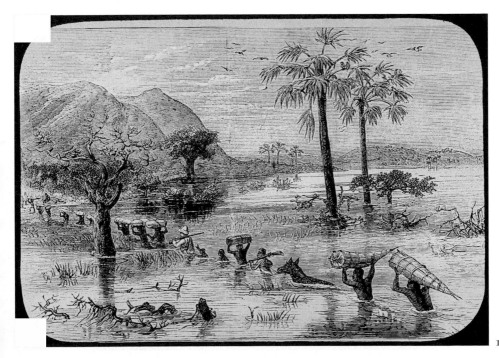

13 Stanley's hat (left) and Livingstone's cap (right) worn by them on the day of their meeting

14 Stanley's carriers crossing the Makata swamp

15

16

15 A bearded Stanley photographed on Zanzibar with Selim and Kalulu on reaching the coast after the Livingstone meeting
16 Stanley aged 31, a London studio portrait after his return from finding Livingstone and being insulted by the RGS – his expression sad, withdrawn and vulnerable despite his recent success

17 'Look out, you drop that box – I'll shoot you.' A lantern slide version of the probably invented incident in which Stanley threatened to shoot the man carrying Livingstone's journals if he dropped them. The original for the slide is the engraving facing page 642 of Stanley's *How I Found Livingstone*

18/19

18 The jewel-encrusted snuff box given to Stanley by Queen Victorian in 1872
19 Emilia Webb of Newstead Abbey, in whom Stanley confided when feeling persecuted in 1872

20/21

22

20 Alice Pike aged seventeen, at the time of her engagement to Stanley in 1874
21 A romantically dressed Stanley at the time of his ill-attended American lectures in 1873
22 Stanley on the South Downs near Brighton in 1872 with the journalist J.C.Parkinson, who interviewed him for the *Daily News* after his upsetting British Association lecture

arrived in this country corrupted by Arabs, he decided that the Kabaka was in urgent need of new moral advisers: Christian missionaries. Livingstone, Henry knew, would have seen the establishment of missions as the only remedy. Of course, nothing could be done unless Mutesa agreed to receive missionaries. But believing the Kabaka was more sophisticated than the chiefs with whom Livingstone had been friendly and yet had failed to convert, Stanley imagined the Bugandan ruler would be more receptive to the Gospel.[11] Henry meant to use the press to reach out to thousands of potential missionaries. But, first, he needed to be sure that Mutesa would welcome them. If he could be persuaded, he 'would do more for Central Africa and civilization [than] fifty years of gospel teaching'.[12]

At the perfect psychological moment, Henry scored a timely success by shooting dead, at Mutesa's request (and in front of his 300 wives), a baby crocodile basking on a rock a hundred yards away.[13] Whether he realized that this proof of the superiority of his guns over the Arabs' muskets accounted for Mutesa's sudden keenness to meet more Europeans (from whom he hoped to buy modern weapons) is uncertain. The Kabaka also hoped that his new white friends might help him halt the encroachments of Colonel Gordon – at this time Governor-General of the Khedive of Egypt's southernmost province of Equatoria.[14] So when Mutesa gave orders for the Ten Commandments to be translated into Kiganda, from a Kiswahili version provided by one of Stanley's missionary-school-educated followers, it seemed natural for him to agree a few days later 'to observe the Christian Sabbath as well as the Moslem Sabbath'. In future, 'Stamlee' – as Mutesa called him – would disclaim having converted Mutesa, except in a purely 'nominal' way. Indeed, a man who retained hundreds of wives would have been a most unusual convert.[15] The moment Mutesa had made his decision, Stanley wrote a letter to the *New York Herald* and to the *Daily Telegraph* that would have an immense impact in Europe, and later in Africa. Stanley wrote:

It is not the mere preacher that is wanted here ... It is the practical Christian tutor, who can teach people how to become Christians, cure their diseases, construct dwellings, understands agriculture and can turn his hand to anything ... He must be tied to no Church or sect, but ... be inspired by liberal principles, charity to all men, and devout faith in God ... Such a man or men Mtesa, King of Uganda ... invites to come to him.[16]

Mutesa had pretended, for his own political reasons, to be a more humane ruler than he really was, but although he may have hoodwinked the explorer, it would be Stanley's hopes for the future of Buganda, rather than Mutesa's, that would be realized – the kingdom eventually becoming a British colony, and Christianity thriving there. Because Stanley omitted from his appeal the fact that Mutesa was guilty of selling captives to the Arab-Swahili, he misled the future missionaries about the situation they would face. Henry left behind with Mutesa one of his brightest young men, a mission-educated sixteen-year-old called Dallington, who knew the Bible well and was a clever linguist, in the hope that he would instruct Mutesa as well as enable him to communicate with the English-speaking missionaries when they came. Henry took away with him, on the Kabaka's insistence, Kadu, one of his teenage pages, with the intention of sending him back to Buganda once he had seen England and could report back favourably.[17]

Stanley's letter of appeal was delivered safely and swiftly to Britain by an amazing coincidence. A few days after Stanley first set foot in Buganda, Colonel Ernest Linant de Bellefonds, one of Colonel Gordon's officers, arrived at Mutesa's court with forty Sudanese soldiers, on a diplomatic mission. Despite being rivals for Mutesa's favour, both men got on well, and Bellefonds, on leaving, took Stanley's appeal north with him along the Nile.[18]

Before Stanley left Mutesa's capital, with its impressive palisades and circular courtyards, Mutesa promised that his grand admiral – a man called Magassa – would provide thirty canoes, so that on Stanley's return to his base at Kagehyi in the *Lady Alice* he would be able to transport all his men back to Buganda by water. On his return to Mutesa's kingdom Henry intended to travel overland to Lake Albert, which he meant to map before going south to Lake Tanganyika. Magassa, after endless procrastination, at last admitted he could only lay hands on ten canoes; he promised to do better soon. But Henry gave up waiting on 21 April, and sailed south towards the first act of a two-part tragedy that would dog him for the rest of his life.

Half-way down the western side of the lake – which he mapped as he went – Henry had an unnerving experience at a place called Makongo near the mouth of the Kagera River, where he and the *Lady Alice*'s eleven-man crew had camped for the night with the sanction of the local chief. In the middle of the night, they were awakened by furi-

ous drumming and found themselves surrounded by hundreds of warriors, armed with bows, shields and spears.

There was something very curious in their demeanour. For there was no shouting,
yelling or frantic behaviour, as we had several times witnessed on the part of savages when about to commit themselves to some desperate deed. They all wore a
composed though stern and determined aspect. It was a terrible moment to us ...
We feared to make a movement lest it might precipitate a catastrophe ... so we
remained a few moments silently surveying each other.

At this moment of immense danger, Stanley and his men were saved
by the unexpected intervention of the chief. 'He had a long stick in his
hand, which he flourished before the faces of the savages, and by this
means drove them several paces backward. He then came forward,
and, striking the boat, ordered us to get off, and he himself lent a hand
to shove the boat into the lake.' He explained that the *Lady Alice* had
been pulled up too high on the beach. 'We replied that we had done it
to protect the boat from the surf, and were about to add more reasons,
when the chief cut the matter short by ordering us to shove off.'[19] The
whole episode amazed Stanley, since he was still in Mutesa's territory
and being escorted by two Ganda canoes as proof of royal approval.
The Africans ran down to the water's edge in large numbers, shaking
their spears as his men started to row away. Henry reflected that if the
Ganda had not also managed to get away, he would have been obliged
to fire into the mass of men on the beach in order to save his escorts'
lives. In every way, he had had a narrow escape, and left this place feeling deeply apprehensive.

The *Lady Alice*'s course being into the wind, her single sail was useless and her crew worked hard at the oars all day, thudding into steep
waves whipped up by the headwind. Stanley and his crewmen were
ravenously hungry by the time they reached nearby Musira Island. Here,
they ate some bananas before sailing on to an island thirty-five miles to
the south-east – named Alice Island by Henry. They managed to buy a
few fish from local fishermen,[20] but for eleven people, after a hard day's
rowing, this amount of food was wholly inadequate. The following day,
Stanley tried to barter for food but was curtly refused. Leaving his
Ganda escort at Alice Island, he headed south-west for a large island
called Bumbireh, which he had heard was twenty-five miles away. 'With
every prospect of starvation' facing him and his men, Henry knew how
vital it would be to win over these islanders.[21] Happily, the wind was
now blowing from the north-east so he and his men could rely on their

sail for much of their journey, though 'rain, thunder, lightning and a sounding surf on all sides' meant they spent many hours baling to stay afloat. They passed a wet and exhausting night under the lee of a small uninhabited island, before sailing on to Bumbireh itself, arriving at about 9 a.m. on 28 April. 'As we entered the cove we saw the plateau's summit lined with men, and heard shouts like war cries, yet imminent starvation compelled us to ground our boat and endeavour to entice the people to part with some food for us for cloth or beads.'

Hunger had forced Stanley to take an immense risk, within sight of an overwhelming number of armed men. But he ordered his men to re-launch the boat at once the moment he saw forty or fifty men rushing down the beach. His crew, however

did not stir a hand to obey, but began to make friendly speeches to the natives who now numbered several score, to say that they were Wangwana, friends of Mutesa come to purchase food. The natives at this lowered their spears, and advanced towards the boat with friendly gestures, but as soon as they touched the boat, they dragged her with their united forces far on dry land ... While they were doing this my revolvers were twice aimed at them, but I was each time entreated by my men to be patient, and finding my people so deluded with the idea that we were among friends, I contented myself with sitting in the boat until they were taught by experience that friends never act so outrageously.[22]

Stanley's reception on Bumbireh

Whenever Stanley believed the moment for shooting had arrived, his men restrained him. 'Violent language and more violent action we received without comment or word … Spears were held in their hands as if on the launch, arrows were drawn to the head and pointed at each of us … I never saw mad rage or wild fury painted so truly before on human features.'

At one point Wadi Safeni, Henry's coxswain and interpreter, received a push that knocked him down, Saramba, the guide, was hit with a club, and Kirango, the youngest crewman, was struck with the staff of a spear. Henry, whose sense of his own dignity had been vital to him ever since his workhouse days, had to endure having his hair tugged to see if it was a wig.[23] At this dreadful time, Safeni, Saramba and Baraka, Henry's interpreters, 'employed to the utmost whatever gifts of persuasion nature had endowed them with and fear created in them'. To Stanley's surprise, 'the imminence of death brought with it a strange composure. We did not fear it as I imagined we should'.[24] For three hours, Stanley listened to the heroic efforts of his interpreters, occasionally making suggestions. Eventually, to his great relief, Shekka, the chief of this island offshoot of the Haya tribe, agreed to accept 'four cloths and ten necklaces of large beads as his price for permitting us to depart in peace'. Soon after these goods had been handed over, 'Shekka ordered his people to seize our oars, which was done before we understood what they were about. This was the second time that Shekka had acted cunningly and treacherously, and a loud jeering laugh from his people showed how much they appreciated his wit.' The Wangwanas' drum was also taken.

After Chief Shekka and his warriors had gone to their village to eat their midday meal, evidently believing that Stanley would not be able to leave without his oars, a woman came and warned Henry: the chief 'had determined to kill us and take everything we had'. Yet when Stanley sent his coxswain to proffer terms of brotherhood to Shekka, the chief pretended that friendship would be restored the following day.[25] By three in the afternoon this illusion was no longer tenable. Shekka appeared on the hillside, and waved his men down the beach with spears poised for the kill. Stanley screamed to his men to launch the *Lady Alice*.

With one desperate effort my crew of eleven men seized the boat as if she had been a mere toy and shot her into the water. The impetus they had given her, caused her to drag them all into deep water. In the meantime the savages, uttering a furious howl of disappointment and baffled rage, came rushing like a whirlwind to the water's edge.[26]

As his men desperately tried to pull themselves out of the water into the boat, tribesmen fired arrows at them and Stanley responded with his elephant gun, killing 'one of the foremost'. Then, as his men continued clambering aboard, he kept off the pursuing men with a shotgun loaded with buckshot. Resourceful as ever, his crew tore up the boat's bottom-boards and used them as paddles to get the *Lady Alice* away from the shore.

These tribesmen on Bumbireh had upset Stanley more than any other Africans ever would. Their pretence of friendship, followed by an attempt to terrify him into parting with all his trade goods, succeeded by a promise of blood brotherhood – itself swiftly followed by the theft of his boat's oars – angered Stanley as much as the fact that he and his eleven men would have been murdered if they had not managed to manhandle their heavy boat into the water.

Just as Stanley would seek to escape the sense of humiliation that had dogged him since boyhood by pretending that he had beaten his cruel schoolmaster and then run away in triumph, he now began to ponder how to represent in a more satisfying light the indignities he had suffered on Bumbireh Island. He wanted to feel less of a victim than he had been in reality. Only by distorting the facts could he make the memory become less painful. He wrote up his diary that evening and, as usual, this first account was to be his most honest description. In it, the only damage he mentioned having inflicted on the islanders was one man killed and another wounded. He mentioned no injuries occurring as a result of firing buckshot. Yet two months later, on 29 July, he wrote a disastrous despatch to the *Daily Telegraph* and *New York Herald*, claiming to have killed nine or ten people – a figure he would later increase to fourteen.[27] But in two personal letters, written on 15 and 19 May – much closer to the event – the figures he gave were one killed and one wounded in the first letter, and nobody killed in the second.[28] In the *Autobiography*, the islanders' casualties would be represented accurately, as one killed and one wounded.[29]

So why did he exaggerate the casualty figures in that disastrous newspaper despatch, which would be so damaging to his future reputation, especially when taken in conjunction with what would happen three months later on his second visit to Bumbireh? He seems to have been influenced by a combination of factors: first, as already stated, a passionate desire to show that he had not really been made a fool of by 'savages'; second, the knowledge he had gained, when reporting from the Indian Wars, that Americans liked to read about 'Red Indians' being killed in retaliation for injuries; and third, his memories of the terrible week he lived through after leaving Bumbireh.

All but helpless in the *Lady Alice*, he and his men became the playthings of gales lashing the lake. Without oars, and with their sail ripped to shreds, they had to endure seven terrifying days being buffeted on the open lake before limping back, with improvised paddles, to Kagehyi, in a state of physical collapse. At any time they might have been driven onto an uninhabited island, their boat wrecked on rocks, and they themselves doomed to die of starvation. Or they might have been stranded on the mainland and murdered by tribesmen; or, if their boat had capsized, crocodiles would have made short work of them.[30] It was small wonder that Henry's feelings towards Bumbireh's inhabitants made him wish he had punished them more severely than he had managed to do in reality. And so he exaggerated the number he had killed. In general, Stanley's critics have tended to believe his accounts of controversial events when they have made him seem brutal, but to disbelieve them whenever showing him in a favourable light.

On 5 May, the *Lady Alice* arrived back at Kagehyi on the southern shores of Victoria, after a fifty-seven-day circumnavigation of the lake. Stanley had gone a long way towards proving that Speke's claim to have located the primary source of the Nile in Lake Victoria was true. The huge task that remained, in order to make Speke's claim unassailable, was for Henry to investigate Samuel Baker's counter-claims for Lake Albert and Livingstone's for the Lualaba River. Yet even if Stanley had decided to return now to the coast, without adding to his exploration of Lake Victoria, his journey would still have been the equal of Speke and Burton's to Lake Tanganyika, and Speke and Grant's to Gondokoro and Lake Victoria.

No man before him had ever mapped the lake, and Stanley's formidable skills as a cartographer are plain to see in his notebooks, where his delineation of the lake closely resembles the outline in modern charts. He used an artificial horizon, a sextant and a chronometer to make thirty-seven separate observations for latitude and longitude. The lake's height he estimated with a boiling-point apparatus – his revised measurement being 4,093 feet above sea level. With his sounding line he established that, in places, the water was 275 feet deep.[31]

Stanley's men welcomed him back to Kagehyi with much cheering and firing of guns. But his elation turned to sadness when Frank Pocock told him that Frederick Barker, the clerk from the Langham Hotel, had died of fever almost two weeks earlier.[32] Half the white men who had left Zanzibar were now dead. Nor had death spared some of Stanley's most dependable Wangwana. The best-known of those who had died while he was away was Mabruki Speke, who had also served Speke, Grant, Burton and Livingstone. Dysentery had killed him.[33] Livingstone's faithful servant Gardner, who had been with him for nine years, had died in mid-February, of typhoid, as had Ulimengo, who had been on the *Herald*'s Livingstone expedition.[34] It was a great relief to Henry that the hugely capable Manwa Sera, the Wangwana captain of all his carriers, was still alive. Frank announced that he had dined in his absence with Sungoro, the slave trader, who had said that the village of Kagehyi 'belonged to the Sultan of Zanzibar' – chilling proof of the rapidly expanding frontiers of the slave trade.[35]

Stanley's immediate problem was how to transport to Buganda the 155 men whom Frank had fed and kept together at Kagehyi while he had been away. Magassa had still not brought the thirty canoes promised by Mutesa, but by now Stanley favoured going by land, along the western side of the lake, as the first stage of a journey through western Buganda to Samuel Baker's Lake Albert, which he intended to explore thoroughly. At this critical moment, Rwoma, ruler of the intervening state of Bukara and an ally of Mirambo, sent a message telling Henry he would fight him if he entered his territory.[36] Immediately to the north of Rwoma's domain was the land of Chief Antari, an equally hostile ruler, who was paramount chief over a lakeside kingdom and several islands, which included hostile Bumbireh. But rather than abandon his proposed visit to Lake Albert – thus leaving it to be explored by Colonel Gordon's officers – Stanley decided he would have to go by water once again. Having been let down by Mutesa and his unreliable admiral, Henry bought from the King of Ukerewe twenty-three very leaky canoes, which arrived at Kagehyi on 13 June.[37] A week later he embarked the majority of his men.

Two days on, a storm hit his fragile fleet, sinking five canoes and costing the expedition five guns, a case of ammunition and a great many stores. Somehow Henry managed to rescue everyone from the wrecked canoes and ferry them in the *Lady Alice* to his new camp on

an island, roughly halfway to Buganda. It took him a month to transport all the stores from Kagehyi to this island base.[38] The unhappy
chance that had prevented him from travelling by land to Buganda
was now threatening to force him to sail through the narrow strait
between Bumbireh and the equally hostile mainland – a perilous position indeed. But to cross the centre of the lake in his frail canoes was
out of the question. In this appalling situation, Henry decided that
nothing less than holding as hostages Shekka, the chief of Bumbireh,
and two of his principal headmen would guarantee him a peaceful
passage and immunity from a combined attack by Antari and his subject people on Bumbireh.[39] To achieve his objective, Stanley managed,
by a subterfuge, to capture the chief of the neighbouring island of
Iroba, and one of Antari's sons. To regain their freedom, Stanley told
his captives, they must send orders to their men to capture Chief
Shekka of Bumbireh and two of his sub-chiefs.

On 24 July, to Stanley's delight, Shekka was brought to him by the
Irobans, though without his sub-chiefs. Henry kept his word and
released the Chief of Iroba, but kept the son of Chief Antari, along
with Shekka. Yet even now, Stanley doubted whether he could expect
good behaviour from Bumbireh when he passed by, or even whether
the islanders would sell him the food he desperately needed for his
men. One reason for his doubts was that he had recently seen, from a
vantage point on Mahyiga Island – the closest to Bumbireh – eighteen
canoes packed with reinforcements heading from the mainland to
Bumbireh.[40]

On 27 July, when Stanley was still on Mahygia Island, forty men
sent by Mutesa made their appearance in a large canoe. Their mission
had been to obtain news of Stanley, whom Mutesa feared was dead.
On the following day, six more Ganda canoes arrived, and a few days
later a further eight, giving Henry a total of thirty-seven vessels.[41]
Although Stanley's position was much stronger now, the problem of
how to feed his enlarged force was worse than ever. The truculent
Antari refused to sell anything, and Henry feared that the reinforced
islanders of Bumbireh would do likewise. To counter the threat of a
combined attack, and to compel the islanders to sell food, Stanley
decided to play his hostage card. He sent a message to Antari,
Shekka's superior chief, asking him to redeem his son and Shekka with
five bullocks, thirty billhooks and forty spears, and thus enable him
(Stanley) 'to proclaim peace'. 'The alternative,' Antari was told, 'is

that I will punish the natives of Bumbireh, and take all my prisoners with [me] to Mutesa King of Uganda to be dealt with by him ... as he only sees fit.'[42]

On 3 August, Stanley noted down Antari's uncompromising reply: 'to the effect that if I did not surrender my prisoners he would attack me'. Deciding this was a bluff, and that the now-leaderless people of Bumbireh might well be cowed by a large party of Ganda coming to Bumbireh to buy food, Stanley agreed with Sabadu, the commander of the Ganda, that the latter should visit Bumbireh with ten canoes crewed by about 150 men – an impressive delegation.[43] But Bumbireh's warriors met these canoes scornfully with a hail of spears and arrows – killing one of the emissaries and wounding eight so seriously that six of them later died.[44] It now seemed certain that there would be a showdown when Stanley's fleet (part of which was unseaworthy) sailed north between Bumbireh and Antari's mainland territory through a strait a few miles wide. Although his Ganda escort numbered about 400 men, Stanley doubted whether the islanders would be deterred. Their treatment of the large Ganda food delegation suggested they would not – especially now that they had been reinforced by Antari.[45] So, the attack that Stanley now planned to launch on Bumbireh appears to have been genuinely defensive in purpose – although he also saw it as punishment for recent murder, and for the attempted murder of himself and his men in April.

On the arrival of the *Lady Alice*, Bumbireh's armed warriors were already assembling in bays and on foreshores, their hilltop look-outs indicating the course of Stanley's boats to the men below. Before Stanley's vessels came near the shore, crowds of islanders had raced down to beaches where they expected the white man and his followers to land. Armed with spears, bows and arrows and rocks, they shouted defiantly and, as Frank Pocock observed, they even 'beckoned for us to go on shore, but that we would not do'. Pocock also heard many Ganda soldiers demanding 'to go on shore', and noted in his diary that 'Master [Stanley] would not let them'.[46] Nobody was allowed closer inshore than fifty yards – from which distance Sniders were deadly weapons, but bows and arrows were useless.

By the time Stanley and his men had finished firing, thirty-three men lay dead or gravely wounded on the shore. If Stanley felt revulsion, he did not say so. Remembering the American Indian Wars, and African violence such as he had witnessed in the Mirambo war and during his unsought fight with the Wanyaturu, which had cost him the lives of twenty-two men, his attack on the islanders did not strike him as extreme. The hope expressed in his diary that evening was that, as a result of their losses, the men of Bumbireh would 'in future behave with some regard to the rights of strangers', since 'it had been common practice with them to seize on all canoes, Waganda or Wakerewe, and hold the crews as slaves'.[47]

The most dubious aspect of Stanley's attack was that he had killed men who had not *at the time* been threatening the lives of himself and his men. His object had been to treat them to a display of power that would dissuade them from attacking his canoes in concert with their ally, Antari, as his expedition's vessels passed through the narrows. Whether an attack would really have been pressed home is unknowable, but Stanley clearly felt he could not take a chance. On this awful day, Henry can be given credit for preventing a general massacre: first by stopping the Ganda landing at the start of the action, and then by preventing them doing so after it was over. 'When our force saw that the savages were defeated, the chiefs begged earnestly that I would permit them to land and destroy the people altogether; but I refused, saying I had not come to destroy the island.'[48]

In Chapter Fifteen, I will describe the furore that broke out in Britain over this bloody incident, and will also give details of the trigger-happy misbehaviour of other European explorers, and the general level of indigenous violence they, and Stanley, encountered in Africa. Against this contemporary backdrop, it will be possible to view more objectively the arguments of those who condemned him. The fact that Stanley's return to Britain was delayed for two more years left his enemies free to blacken his name as they wished, without his having any opportunity to explain why he had made his pre-emptive attack. Stanley felt no guilt, believing that in the long term more lives would be saved than he had taken, and that in future travellers would enjoy right of passage on the lake without fear of attack or capture.

The islanders were not popular with other nearby chiefs (Antari apart), and 'the next day,' Stanley noted with satisfaction, 'we were beset with congratulations and gifts from the Kings Kytawa and Kamiru. Three oxen, three goats, and 50 bunches of bananas, besides milk, chickens, and ripe plantains in abundance.' Since he had come close to starvation on this coast after his earlier escape from Bumbireh, this sudden glut of food was extremely welcome.[49]

Stanley landed at Dumo, Buganda on 12 August, hoping to set out as soon as possible for Lake Albert, with a royal escort furnished by Mutesa. He aimed to establish that lake's precise relationship with the larger Victoria, and then to discover whether Albert was fed from the south by a river, which might itself have a claim to be the Nile's source. He had received a letter from Gordon via de Bellefonds, in which the Governor of Equatoria told him that he was steaming down the Nile constructing stations and would help him with supplies if they should meet. Since Gordon's letter was dated 20 April and had come from Rajef on the Upper Nile, Stanley expected that the Governor would already have beaten him to Lake Albert.[50] But even if Gordon solved all the outstanding geographical puzzles connected with Albert, Stanley felt that he could still open up Mutesa's kingdom to European trade by pioneering a route to Lake Albert and the Upper Nile from Buganda.[51] On leaving Albert, Henry meant to march south to Lake Tanganyika, and then to follow the Lualaba north from where Livingstone had left it in 1871.

Unfortunately, within a week of Stanley's landing in Mutesa's kingdom, the Ganda were at war with the neighbouring Wavuma – the people who had attacked Stanley in canoes on the eastern side of the lake. There was now no question of Stanley being lent the substantial force that Mutesa had promised would escort him to Lake Albert.[52] Without such help, Henry had been warned, the warlike rulers of Bunyoro and Ankole would kill him before he reached the lake. After two months of waiting, Stanley at last met up with the 2,000 men originally promised by Mutesa. He himself had just under 170 men of his own.

By early January 1876, Stanley and his party had travelled 350 miles to the north-west and found a stretch of water, which he thought was an arm of Lake Albert but which was in fact a small lake unknown to Europeans at the time. The Bunyoro chose this moment to make an appearance in full war paint, and to threaten bloodshed unless Stanley and his allies left at once. When his Ganda escort refused to risk offending these warriors, Stanley had no choice but to head south for Lake Tanganyika, leaving Lake Albert's mysteries intact. En route, he spent several weeks exploring the Kagera River, which flowed into the western side of Lake Victoria and which he had first seen before meeting Mutesa. Even at that first sighting, he had suspected, because of its depth, width and rapidity of flow, that it might be 'the real parent of the Victoria Nile'. Now, he sounded it at

Kitangule and found it was 84 feet deep and 120 yards wide. Henry attempted to trace it into Rwanda 'but was driven back to the boat by war cries, which the natives sounded loud and shrill'. On the verge of 'another grand discovery', to quote him, he was thwarted.[53]

The Kagera river's most southerly source has recently been located (March 2006) in western Rwanda's rainforest of Nyungwe by a three-man New Zealand and British expedition, and claimed by them as the Nile's most southerly source – though because scores of feeders drain into Lake Victoria, it seems unlikely that the lake itself is about to be usurped as the Nile's primary source.

Two months later, still heading for Ujiji, Stanley met the African ruler who had come close to killing him when he had been journeying to meet Livingstone in 1871. These two great figures in African history – Stanley and Mirambo – came face to face at the village of Serembo. This was a perilous situation for Henry, since the warlord had with him an army of 15,000 men.[54] Mirambo was in his mid-thirties, and surprised Henry by being 'mild, soft-spoken, and with a meek demeanour ... indicating nothing of the Napoleonic genius which he has for 5 years displayed in the heart of Africa'. That evening, in the warlord's tent, the two men became blood brothers 'by an incision in each other's right leg above the knee until a couple of drops of blood were drawn; which [were] interchanged and rubbed on with butter'. Before the ceremony, Stanley was told by one of Mirambo's chiefs: 'We never take middle aged men, or old men to our wars, always youths not yet troubled with wives or children. They have keener eyes and lither limbs.' 'Boys', the same chief called them.[55] This employment of boy soldiers was not a complete surprise to Stanley, who knew that Mirambo had killed tens of thousands of men, and that 'skulls lined the road to his gates'.[56]

Stanley and his men arrived at Ujiji on 27 May 1876, after travelling roughly 3,500 miles by land and water since leaving Zanzibar in November 1874.[57] Without Livingstone there to greet him, he found Ujiji 'forlorn and uninteresting'.[58] For weeks now, he had been obsessed with finding letters from Alice awaiting him in this Arab settlement. But there were no letters at all. Because he now planned to sail round Lake Tanganyika, and expected this to take two months, he ordered five of his most trustworthy men to travel to Uyanyembe – a round trip of 600 miles – to bring back any mail that might be stuck there, including letters from Alice.[59]

For a week after his arrival Stanley was ill with fever, then, for Alice's benefit, he sat down and wrote a letter, which his chosen men would take with them. He told her that though he had not 'torn his hair and shrieked', he had 'soberly grieved' over his lack of letters. His weight, he informed her, was 118 lb, rather than 178 lb, as it had been when he had last seen her – meaning that he had lost a third of his body weight. 'I am sure that if you saw me now you would deny acquaintance with me ... Yet the same heart throbs with deepest love.' Stanley outlined for Alice his plans.

In about five days I am going to set out in the 'Lady Alice' for a voyage round the Tanganyika, which is 600 geog. miles long by about 30 in width. The task I have to do is to discover the river which flows out of the lake. A great many noble rivers enter the lake, but the question is where is the river which discharges the surplus water ... Lieut. Cameron, who was here two years ago, says he has found it to be the Lukuga on the south-west coast. Perhaps he has found it, but the Arabs and the natives all deny that the river which he saw flows out. They say that it flows in.[60]

This was a matter of considerable geographical significance, since if the Lukuga really did flow out of the lake and then, after 200 miles, entered the Lualaba, which itself then flowed north into Lake Albert, and thence into the Nile, as Livingstone had believed, Lake Tanganyika would qualify as the the most southerly reservoir of the Nile, cutting out Lake Victoria.

By 31 July, Stanley was back at Ujiji after fifty-one days spent mapping the lake. He was the first man to have circumnavigated Tanganyika – proving it to be 450 miles from north to south, and therefore the longest freshwater lake in the world. It is also the second deepest lake in the world – being in places (as Henry found) almost 1,300 feet deep. More significantly, Henry confirmed Cameron's claim that the Lukuga river was the lake's only outflow, apparently draining into the Lualaba.[61] This river also turned out to be an important slave route. While on its banks, Stanley encountered a caravan of 1,200 men, women and children captured in Manyema, bound for Ujiji. Many of the children were close to death. 'The chest jutted out with the protuberance of a skeleton frame ... legs were mere sticks of bone, trembling weak supports to the large head and chest.' These were the very sights that had caused Livingstone such anguish. Near this place, Stanley came across 'many detachments of banditti ... fired by avarice and blood'. These were Africans – Nyamwezi and Ngoni professional fighters, who had settled north-west of Tabora, and were known there as Watuta. Mirambo employed them and they were more generally known by the name *ruga-ruga*. Now they were raiding in Manyema, 'depopulating extensive lands and driving despairing files of slaves to the Arab markets'.[62]

On returning to Ujiji, Henry was dismayed to learn that his messengers had not yet returned from Unyanyembe. But though he longed for news of Alice, there was no question of staying on in Ujiji where fifty people were dying each day from smallpox – indeed, five of his own men had recently perished and six more were very sick. So on 14 August he wrote Alice what he believed would be the last letter he would be able to despatch till triumphing or dying. In it, he said little about his fears, but instead told her he hoped to reach Zanzibar by December 1877, having followed the Lualaba to the Atlantic. Evidently, he had by now dismissed the possibility that the Lualaba might be the Nile. He ended: 'My love towards you is unchanged, you are my dream, my stay, my hope, and my beacon ... I shall cherish you in this light until I meet you, or death meets me. This is the last you will get, I fear for a long time. Then my darling accept this letter with one last and loving farewell.'[63] He signed this letter, as all his others to her, Morton, in deference to her whimsical dislike of Henry. Several days after writing, Henry was shivering with the onset of malaria, though the temperature was 138° Fahrenheit in the sun.

Yet while at Ujiji, Stanley heard one piece of glorious news, which he related to his co-employer, Edward Levy-Lawson.

We have obtained a signal triumph over Cameron, the Protégé of the RGS, whose attainments were said to be vastly superior to those of Burton, Speke, Livingstone & Baker – if [Clements] Markham [Secretary of the RGS] was to be believed ... By crossing the Lualaba and striking off in the wrong direction he [Cameron] has left the question of the Lualaba where Livingstone left it.[64]

So, Cameron, like Livingstone, had failed to cross the Lualaba at Nyangwe and follow it north. Instead, he had headed south-west on a trans-Africa journey of no particular significance. Now Stanley knew that – if he could only stay alive – he could complete Livingstone's work, becoming, in a century of great explorers, the greatest. On 25 August, he finally felt strong enough to leave for Manyema. The hardest of his three labours now lay ahead of him – and for it, he was going to need the unquestioning loyalty of his followers. He was therefore appalled when the roll was called that same day and he found he now had only 132 men. Fifteen had recently died, and more than twenty had deserted, apparently too scared to travel through Manyema with its cannibal tribes.[65] Henry was now down to a mere thirty men who could be trusted with the expedition's Sniders. The prospect of losing any more guns before the most dangerous part of his journey started was a horrifying one.[66]

During the relatively short land journey along the shores of the lake to the crossing point for Manyema, Henry lost another three men through desertion. And on the far side came a worse blow – Kalulu deserted. Given the time they had spent together, Stanley felt personally betrayed. Yet though distressed to lose the boy he had paid to educate, it was a great tribute to the loyalty he commanded that so many of his men did *not* desert him at Ujiji, when all he was offering them, instead of an early return to Zanzibar, was a journey of unimaginable dangers. The loyalty of men like Manwa Sera, Wade Safeni and Uledi would amaze Henry repeatedly. A few deserters were recaptured quickly, with Kalulu being caught on a small island near the Lukuga, negotiating a passage back to Ujiji.[67] So when Stanley began his march to the Lualaba, Kalulu began the fateful journey in chains.

When Stanley met Livingstone in 1871, the great explorer had just returned from two and a half years in Manyema, and he had been full of tales of the region's majestic scenery. Stanley also found beauty, but deplored 'coarse grasses that wound like knives ... tough reeds tall as bamboos, creepers of cable thickness ... and thorns like hooks of steel.'[68] Halfway to the Lualaba was Bambarre, a place where Livingstone had suffered from horrifying flesh-eating ulcers and had been unable to leave between July 1870 and early 1871. While the doctor had been waiting for his feet to heal, James, a teenager and one of his dwindling band of followers, was killed and eaten by cannibals.

Yet Livingstone had not turned against the Manyema. He pitied them for the way they were being enslaved and their ivory stolen. Stanley asked Chief Mwana Ngoy what he recalled of the doctor and was told: 'He was good to me, and he saved me from the Arabs many a time ... often he would step between them and me.'[69] Henry also learned that Manyema chiefs, including Mwana Ngoy, had offered slaves and ivory to various Arabs so that they would agree 'to assist them in destroying their neighbours'. Henry was himself offered bribes by three chiefs to attack nearby villages. He was told by them, when he refused, that 'white men were not as good as the Arabs, because – though it was true we did not rob them of their wives, ravish and steal their daughters, enslave their sons, or despoil them of a single article – the Arabs would have assisted them'.[70] These shortcomings did not blind Henry to the fact that the Manyema were the victims of a terrible crime against humanity. Wade Safeni, his coxswain and translator on Lake Victoria, told him that eight years previously this whole region 'was populated so thickly that we travelled through gardens and fields and villages every quarter of an hour. There were flocks of goats and droves of black pigs round every village.' Today, this same country was very sparsely peopled.[71]

On 17 October 1876, a month after leaving the western shore of Lake Tanganyika, the expedition arrived at Mkwanga, where Stanley saw the Lualaba for the first time. He was at the very heart of the African continent, more than a thousand miles from any coast, and yet in front of him was an immense pale grey river, winding its way slowly northwards into the unknown. Almost a mile across, it contained numerous small islands. Stanley was reminded of the mighty Mississippi 'before the impetuous, full-volumed Missouri pours its rusty brown water into it'.[72] For the sake of this river, Livingstone had sacrificed himself, having traced it for much of its 1,300-mile course from its origins in Lake Bangweulu. How far it had yet to flow before reaching the sea as the Congo, or merging with the Niger or Nile, Stanley had no idea. But however far it might be, he knew he was going to solve the last great problem of African geography, or die in the attempt. Yet it was a daunting fact that Livingstone in 1871, and Cameron in 1874, had stood near this spot, and yet both had failed to follow the Lualaba north.

The following day, at the Arab-Swahili trading post of Mwana-Mamba, Stanley made one of the key decisions of his life. Here he met the most important Arab slave trader in central Africa and, calling to mind Livingstone's and Cameron's failures, decided he had no choice but to do a deal with him. The Zanzibar-born Tippu Tip – whose nickname supposedly mimicked the sound of bullets, and whose real name was Hamid bin Muhammed el Murjebi – was master of the land between Lake Tanganyika and the Lualaba, and to have tried to press on northwards against this man's wishes would have got him no further than Nyangwe. Another consideration made Tippu Tip's support an absolute necessity. In the Arab-Swahili town of Nyangwe, Henry's Wangwana carriers would face the same temptations to desert as at

Ujiji, only this time more acutely, since ahead lay the terrifying Lual-aba and a thousand miles of territory that was a blank on the map. And thanks to the local slave traders, there would be hostile tribes on both banks for more than a hundred miles. But if Tippu Tip were to provide an armed escort through this dangerous country, Stanley's Wangwana would not try to slip back to Nyangwe.[73]

In 1876, Tippu was a handsome, black-bearded man of forty-six and had been in Manyema and its environs for about fifteen years, amassing a huge fortune in ivory.[74] He was attended by a large retinue of Arabs, Wangwana and Nyamwezi. Stanley considered him 'the most remarkable man' he had ever met among Arabs in Africa. One of his grandmothers had been the daughter of a Lomani chief – a fact explaining his dark skin.[75] 'His clothes were of a spotless white, his fez-cap brand new ... his dagger was splendid with silver filigree, and his tout ensemble was that of an Arab gentleman in very comfortable circumstances.'[76]

Tippu Tip

Between 19 and 22 October, Stanley negotiated an agreement, by which he would pay the Arab $5,000 (about £1,000) in exchange for which Tippu would accompany him for sixty marches north of Nyangwe – a march being no more than four hours long. The entire engagement should not exceed three months. Tippu agreed to bring with him 140 armed men, whose food Stanley would pay for.[77] Cameron had attempted to persuade Tippu to accompany him north but had failed, though he had had ample funds.[78] Yet something about Henry's character persuaded Tippu that this particular white man was special.[79] It occurred to the prescient Tippu Tip – despite the many dangers involved – that there might never be a better chance than the one being offered by this self-willed man to pioneer a route along the river. The outcome might be the opening up of a vast new area in which to steal ivory, and capture slaves. After all, who else but this Stanley, with his piercing grey-blue eyes, had ever travelled the 340 miles from Lake Tanganyika to the Lualaba in forty-three days? Most Arab caravans took three months. And who else had discovered as much about central Africa? Only 'Daoud Liviston', and Stanley was only half his age.[80]

So how blameworthy was Stanley to have gone into partnership with this prince of slave traders in order to achieve his geographical objective? Certainly no more culpable than David Livingstone had been for travelling with Tippu Tip for four months in 1867. Livingstone had justified himself by observing that individual Arabs, like Tippu, and Muhammed Bogharib, treated their personal slaves better than British factory owners treated their 'free' workers. Arabs were not thoroughly dominated by the profit motive, as were, for example the plantation owners in the southern states of America.[81] Livingstone, Stanley and Cameron had all been drawn to the man, despite hating slavery. It was some mitigation that because of Britain's naval blockade, few of the slaves captured by Tippu Tip in Manyema were being marched to the coast these days.[82] (Instead, they were used as carriers between places like Nyangwe and Ujiji, or were becoming the armed followers of Arab traders.)

Yet though exonerating Tippu Tip from the worst forms of brutality, Stanley knew that the Arab-Swahili rulers of Nyangwe were cruel and ruthless men, who hunted down Africans rather as rich English gentlemen conducted drives for game.[83] A day after Stanley's arrival in this unhappy town perched on a reddish bank above the Lualaba, the Arab slaver Mtagamoyo launched a night attack on the Wenya fishermen of the left bank of the river, and brought back fifty to sixty women and children in chains. A week earlier 300 slaves had been brought in from the west.[84] Henry's deal with Tippu marked no soft-

ening of his opposition to such deeds. In a passionately indignant letter written to the *Daily Telegraph* and the *New York Herald* from
Nyangwe, Stanley charged the Arab-Swahili traders of Manyema, Rua
and Ujiji 'with being engaged in a traffic specially obnoxious to
humanity – a traffic founded on violence, murder, robbery and fraud'.
'I charge them with being engaged in a business which can be called by
no other name than land piracy, and which should justly be as pun-
ishable as piracy on the high sea.' Stanley ended with a plea that
Britain should act against 'these whole-sale murders of inoffensive
tribes in the interior of the sad continent'.[85]

In Nyangwe, Stanley stayed in a mud house, only thirty feet from
the ruins of Livingstone's residence of five years ago. 'Not a whit of
my admiration and love for him has lessened,' wrote Stanley.[86] On 5
November 1876, Henry left Nyangwe with 146 of his own followers,
only 107 of whom were contracted men on wages, the rest being
women and children – mainly the wives and progeny of his Wangwana
'captains'. Stanley listed forty-eight of his men as having guns of some
sort, and thirty-two of them as being proficient in their use. The
majority of his men he described as 'mere dummies'.[87] These were
inadequate numbers, and the only reason Stanley believed he would
survive the next 200 crucial miles was that Tippu Tip had just arrived
with almost 300 people – about 140 of whom had guns, seventy had
spears, and the rest were a mixture of slaves, women of his harem and
their children.[88] But while these men might shield him and prevent
desertions for a couple of months, Stanley knew he would be on his
own again, in *terra incognita*, for many months after Tippu Tip had
left him. And on the great river, he would face the risk of death by
drowning, by starvation, by disease or by African attacks. Before leaving Nyangwe, he wrote to his close friend Edward King a letter
acknowledging that they might never meet again. Just as Mungo Park
had been killed by Africans on the Niger, Stanley admitted that he
might lose his life on the Lualaba.

I can die, but I will not go back ... The unknown half of Africa lies before me. It
is useless to imagine what it may contain, what I may see, what wonders may be
unfolded ... I cannot tell whether I shall be able to reveal it in person or whether
it will be left to my dark followers. In three or four days we shall begin the great
struggle with this mystery ...[89]

FOURTEEN

'The Great Struggle with this Mystery'

On leaving Nyangwe, the combined expedition headed north along the Lualaba's eastern bank, from which they would be able to investigate any major tributary flowing towards the Nile or Lake Albert. After only a day the pleasant meadowland came to an end, and they plunged into 'the dreaded black and chill forest called Mitamba'. Stanley made the mistake of letting Tippu Tip's 'heterogeneous column of all ages' enter the forest ahead of him, so that he and his men, who were used to rapid marching, were obliged to advance by fits and starts, while 'down the boles and branches, creepers and vegetable cords, moisture trickled ... and the trees kept shedding their dew ... like rain in great round drops'. The undergrowth was twenty feet high, and above it stretched 'wide-spreading branches, in many interlaced strata, each branch heavy with broad thick leaves ... We knew not whether it was a sunshiny day, or a dull, foggy, gloomy one ... The path soon became a stiff clayey paste, and at every step we splashed water over the legs of those in front.' Progress was also hampered by deep streams crossing the path. The Wangwana carrying the dismantled parts of the *Lady Alice* had the hardest time, often lagging behind the others by several hours.[1]

Stanley sent men ahead with axes to cut a path and make life easier for the boat-carriers, but the adhesive clay still slowed their steps. 'Such crawling, scrambling, tearing through the damp, dank jungles' was soon undermining morale. From the branches of a tree, Henry looked ahead 'over the wild woods, which swept in irregular waves of branch and leaf' as far as the eye could see. For weeks or even months, they might have to struggle on in the dark, unhealthy, hothouse air beneath the canopy of this vast tropical forest. Insects bit them constantly, and snakes were commonplace, 'a python ten feet long, a green viper and a monstrous puff adder' being spotted during a single march. Less threatening were the many monkeys and chimpanzees. But 'each night was made hideous' by the harsh cries of lemurs.[2]

After ten days' travelling, his men's faces told Stanley that 'all their courage was oozing out'. Ahead lay 'nothing but the eternal interlaced branches ... and a tangle' through which they 'had to burrow and crawl like wild animals on hands and feet'.[3] On 14 November, Tippu Tip announced that because conditions were so much worse than any he had ever experienced, he would not continue for sixty marches as per his contract. Very reluctantly Henry agreed to reduce the marches from sixty to twenty, if the fee was cut commensurately. But he still hoped to get far enough from Nyangwe in Tippu's protective company to pass through the territory of the tribes made hostile by earlier slave raids.[4]

On 19 November, the combined expedition reached the Lualaba. The local Wenya tribesmen refused to sell them canoes to enable Stanley and Tippu Tip to transport their entire following across to the less thickly forested western bank. So, after bolting together the *Lady Alice* and launching her, Stanley and his men stole five canoes.[5] He now went on by river, with about thirty men in the *Lady Alice* and twenty in his canoes. Frank Pocock led the remainder – about ninety men – by land alongside Tippu Tip's larger party of 300. In the nearest village, almost 200 human skulls lined the main thoroughfare. Nearby, Frank Pocock saw similar sights. 'These people are real cannibals,' he noted. 'They cut the ears off slaves and captives and eat all their flesh.'[6] Yet cannibals or not, Stanley tried to buy vegetables and fowls from the Wenya – only to see the entire population of the village decamp.

Kacheche and several trusted men managed to purchase supplies from a village a few miles away. But then 'the natives surrounded them and one of them threw a spear at Kacheche, who shot him dead'.[7] A sadder incident occurred when an old man approached the stolen canoes – now being used by the expedition to transport men and supplies – and attempted 'to repossess himself of one'. When he advanced, waving a spear – to the cheers of his fellow tribesmen – Billali, one of Stanley's young gun-bearers, panicked and shot him dead. Stanley wrote sadly in his journal: 'I was absent, having gone up the Lualaba ... or I might have saved the foolish but determined old man.'[8]

At about this time, Stanley was enjoying the bustle of a riverside market. 'Then a little child ran up the river bank ... and screamed: "The Wasambye, the Wasambye," in an agony of alarm. At the dread name the market dissolved ... Where but a few seconds before there was joy, gaiety, marketing and peace, at the sound of the words: "The Wasambye," there was emptiness.' The Wasambye was the name the Wenya gave to the slavers of Nyangwe – men like Mtagamoyo. In their white clothing, the Wangwana looked identical to these persecutors.[9]

Eighty miles north of Nyangwe, spears were thrown into Henry's riverside camp, luckily missing everyone. Stanley described this minor skirmish as 'our first fight on the Lualaba'. Later, because he would claim to have had thirty-two fights on the river, this would be taken as proof of his willingness to kill people to please newspaper readers. In fact, many so-called fights – like this first one – did not deserve the name[10] (see this note for fuller details). But a well-planned attack remained a distinct possibility, so Henry was eager, as soon as possible, to unite his land party with his river party.

In early December, several hundred natives fired poisoned arrows at his boat's crew and would not respond to overtures of friendship. They only desisted when three had been killed by rifle-fire from the *Lady Alice*. On the same day, Stanley's men were hemmed in by eight large canoes. These people, as Stanley knew, were attacking in the belief that he had come to steal their property and enslave them. This knowledge made it a distasteful business to have no alternative but to shoot at them, in this instance killing one. It was therefore a relief, on 11 December, to join up with the land party. Henry now had a large enough force to deter minor attacks, and shortly afterwards his diplomatic efforts bore fruit. 'Today I succeeded in checking the demonstrativeness of the Mpika Island people and induced them to refrain from indulging in war. We made peace and brotherhood with them, and the news spread quickly, and we heard shouts of "Go in peace".'[11]

Two days after Christmas, at Vinya-Njara, Stanley finally parted with Tippu Tip. During December the Arab leader had lost his three favourite concubines through smallpox, and another seven of his followers died in a four-day period between the 11th and the 15th. Almost seventy people from both parties were suffering from chest diseases, ulcers and fever, so nothing could persuade Tippu to delay his return to Nyangwe.[12] Henry feared that at the moment of parting his men might mutiny and refuse to embark in the twenty-three canoes he had purchased for them from the Wenya. After all, Nyangwe was still a mere 125 miles to the south, and they would have a better chance of staying alive if they returned there with Tippu Tip than if they risked life and limb on the awesome Lualaba. Six weeks earlier, Stanley had questioned his men and discovered that only thirty-eight of them intended to carry on with him after Tippu Tip had headed south. Even Manwa Sera's loyalty was in doubt.

Stanley told Tippu emphatically that if he turned a blind eye and permitted his (Stanley's) Wangwana to follow him back to Nyangwe, he would denounce him to the Sultan of Zanzibar, who would then force him to pay compensation. Although the Arab was incensed, he did not want to make Stanley his enemy. He therefore advised the explorer to tell his men that the Sultan would punish them severely if they broke their contracts. Tippu then addressed the Wangwana very sternly, saying he would shoot them if they tried to desert Stanley. This threat proved effective, and Henry's men got into their canoes. Stanley gave Tippu Tip a draft for $2,600, a silver cup, a wooden box, a gold chain and large quantities of cloth, beads, shells and brass wire.[13]

On 28 December 1876, as the *Lady Alice* floated by at the head of Stanley's flotilla of twenty-three canoes, Tippu's men on the bank sang an emotional song of farewell. Soon most of them were weeping 'as though they were nearly heartbroken'.[14] Henry shouted in Swahili: 'Sons of Zanzibar, lift up your heads and be men. What is there to fear? ... Strike your paddles deep, cry out Bismillah! and let us forward.'[15] He then urged his men to sing, but not even his normally stoical coxswain, Uledi, could manage more than a croak.

Three days later Stanley gave his numbers as 143 people. He reckoned that only thirty-four of his 107 contracted men (and he included himself and Frank) 'would be able to make a tolerable resistance'. The expedition, at this stage, included eight children and sixteen women – most of them the wives of his captains. One of these, Amina, the wife of Kacheche, died of fever at this time in the bottom of her husband's canoe.[16] Many more deaths lay ahead, but by now the canoes were being swept downstream at a speed that made it futile to think of going back. Many of his men were totally inexperienced on water, and although their incompetence reduced the chances of desertion, it scared Henry, whose voice was soon hoarse with shouting warnings.

The Wangwana smoked a great deal of *banghy* or cannabis, which slowed their reactions and befuddled them. Indeed, some of them did extraordinary things – like the man who, on being told to grab an overhanging bush on the bank to slow down his canoe, jumped from his craft onto dry land and hugged the riverside bush, while his canoe floated away without him.[17]

On 1 January 1877, after a long river passage through uninhabited forest, they came to a settlement where they were called Wajiwa, rather than Wasambye. Stanley hoped that these new people might not automatically suspect his men were slave traders.

We were gliding gently down past the settlement and attempting in mild terms to make pacific overtures, addressed them as Friends, and greeted them with the word *Sen-nen-neh* or 'Peace'. We got no answer, though we saw them plainly enough behind the plantains and trees, crouching with drawn bows. We passed them by. Then our gentle and quiet behaviour was regarded by them as cowardice … and immediately 14 canoes well-manned dashed out from the creeks.

So Stanley found himself facing the usual choice of kill or be killed, and having to choose the former. He hit two men with the same bullet, not knowing whether fatally, and this scared off the canoes. Before this encounter, his interpreter had heard men saying in the canoes: 'We shall eat Wajiwa today.' And indeed the taunting cry, 'Niama, niama' – 'meat, meat' was often heard. For all these Africans, who had seen no white men or guns before, their enlightenment was very painful.[18] But Stanley's position was impossible. The only way he could have avoided bloodshed would have been to anchor his entire fleet – no easy matter – and then have tried to purchase a peaceful passage with lavish gifts of beads, shells and cloth. Yet, on each occasion, this process would have taken several days, and could easily have ended in fighting, with the element of surprise lost.[19]

At the start of this most challenging part of his journey, Henry was enraged by the attempt of one set of villagers to catch him and his boat's crew in a large net. 'They considered us as game to be trapped, shot, or bagged at sight.'[20] He nevertheless regretted his rapid mode of travel: 'One must not run through a country but give the people time to become acquainted with you and let their worst fears subside.' During this stage of his expedition his problem, he claimed, was that 'the river bore [his] heavy canoes downwards', and that in addition these goods would have been rapidly exhausted had he negotiated with every tribe along the banks: 'To save myself and my men from certain starvation, I had to rush through.'²¹ And in all probability, nothing Stanley could have said would have reconciled these tribes to his unprecedented intrusion.²² 'In our waters,' a member of the Soko tribe told him nearly ten years later, 'we never heard of a tribe moving downriver with many canoes, unless it came for war. So when we heard of this tribe [Stanley and the Wangwana] we moved out of our river to fight it.'²³

Stanley could do nothing to allay the suspicions he provoked. One tribe expressed to him a confusion that was general: 'How can he be a good man who comes for no trade, whose feet you never see, who always goes covered with clothes, unlike all other people? No, there is something very mysterious about him, perhaps wicked, perhaps he is a magician.'²⁴ Even the act of writing on paper was described as 'witchcraft, which must be punished with death'. On one occasion Stanley was told: 'The white chief must instantly deliver his notebook (his medicine) to be burned, or there would be war on the instant.' So Stanley handed over his collected Shakespeare, Chandos Edition, which was duly burned. 'For a time it was like another jubilee. The country was saved; their women and little ones would not be visited by calamity.'²⁵

Yet Stanley's problems were as often to do with the geological configuration of the continent as with its people. On 6 January, after travelling 400 miles due north, the expedition came to the first cataract in a chain of seven that extended over sixty miles and would later be called the Stanley Falls. Now all the boats had to be taken out of the water and dragged overland past the first falls, along paths hacked through the jungle with axes. The larger canoes, being immense dugouts, had to be pulled along a track of logs acting as rollers. When possible, these vessels were attached to ropes and thick hawsers made from rattan creepers, and lowered down through the roaring white water. The noise of the river crashing over rocks and funnelling into narrow channels and gorges was so loud that, for hours at a time, Henry and his men could not hear each other speak, though standing side by side.

While getting their boats past these seven cataracts, the smallest of which extended for several miles, Stanley and his men were forced to live on land, and were therefore exposed to attack at close quarters by forest-dwelling tribes. Constantly worried by what he called 'the senseless hate and ferocity of these primitive aborigines' – most notably the Kumu, who had subjugated three neighbouring tribes, and were cannibals – he built thorn *bomas* for his men, and positioned riflemen to protect his pioneers while they were cutting through the dense brushwood. To make sure the Kumu would not imagine that he could easily be defeated, Stanley drove off a group of spear-waving men who had been shouting war cries, and burned their village.[26] Not that this prevented future attacks. One night, the pioneers' camp was attacked by 'a desperate savage with a knife 18 inches long', with which he killed a Wangwana, Muftah Rufigi – the wretched man having his arm almost severed from his shoulder, and the blade then 'buried up to the hilt in his chest'.[27]

On 19 January, Stanley's men captured eight members of the Wané-Mpungu tribe, who told him that the larger Kumu tribe 'ate old men and old women, as well as every stranger captured in the woods'.[28] Near the junction with the Aruwimi River, Stanley noted:

Evidences of cannibalism were numerous in the human and 'soko' (ape) skulls that grinned on many poles, and the bones that were freely scattered in the neighbourhood, near the village garbage heaps and the river banks ... The most positive, and downright evidence in my opinion, was the thin forearm of a person that was picked up near a fire, with certain scorched ribs.[29]

Soon after passing the seventh fall and entering the territory of Bemberri, where the locals responded to cries that they had 'no cause for war' with a fusillade of stones, Henry refused to let himself be provoked, and recorded 'We endeavoured to do our best to avoid a conflict and happily succeeded' – though these people, the Barundu, followed in canoes for a few miles. Henry by now had only fifty-two guns when he would have needed 200 to feel safe.[30] The fear of being overwhelmed during a concerted land and river attack haunted him.

I pen these lines with half a feeling that they would never be read by any other white person ... If we suffer on this journey, we suffer for the injuries done to the tribes above by Mtagamoyo and his confederates ... Day and night we are pained with the dreadful drumming which announces our arrival and their fear of our purposes ... It may truly be said that we are 'Running the gauntlet'.

Stanley's progress along the rapids took twenty-four days, and he found soon after the final falls that the river turned decisively westwards. Then on 7 February – a historic day – he heard the river referred to as 'Ikuta Yacongo', leaving no doubt that the Lualaba was the Upper Congo.[31]

Now they had left the Wenya tribe behind, they had no interpreter and so could not make themselves understood. Worse still, with at least 800 miles to go, their ammunition was running low. 'I began to fear we should find ourselves hemmed [in] by savage enemies without means of resistance.'[32] On 7 February, Stanley knew that unless he could buy food by the end of the day, he and his men would have to take it by force. At the village of Rubunga they were met aggressively by three canoes, but still displayed copper rings, brass wire, red beads and shells in an effort to initiate bartering. They then raised hands to mouths and pointed to their stomachs. Henry was kept waiting so long for a positive reaction that his men said they were being made fools of and ought to shoot and take whatever they wanted. 'I saw the natives so clearly, they presented such easy targets that a blind man might have shot a dozen,' wrote Stanley, but he decided to wait

thinking it a pity to shoot people who took no pains to conceal themselves. Besides their conduct, though somewhat distrustful was not to be compared with the arrogant savages [past whom] we had run the gauntlet lately. I told them in a mixture of Kiswahili, Kukisu and Kibaswa that if they did not bring food, I must take it or we would die. They must sell it for beads ... or brass wire ... I drew significant signs across the throat. It was enough ...

When he threw ashore a copper bracelet and a string of beads, 'they clapped hands, laughed'; the two parties 'hurrahed, and made blood brotherhood'.[33]

For several days, this friendliness persisted among the riverside people they encountered. Stanley and Frank allowed men in canoes to come right up close to them – believing that these villagers of Urangi, like those of Rubunga, were not cannibals – and the two white men 'smiled in the midst of a tattooed group, remarkable for their filed teeth and gashed bodies, and bearing in their hands fearfully dangerous-looking naked knives'.[34] But on the 11th, the *Lady Alice*'s crew were fired at from canoes manned by tribesmen whom they had thought friendly. This was the first time Stanley had 'seen the smoke of gunpowder drifting away from a native canoe'. One of the Wangwana shouted: 'Master, one of our men is killed.' Stanley at once ordered his men to return fire, and the result was that two or three Africans were shot dead, while Rehani, one of the expedition's men, was also killed.[35] While this encounter brought a frightening new danger, it proved that they had arrived at the furthest point on the river to which indirect Portuguese influence had penetrated from their trading stations near the coast.

The following day the Congo increased from two miles across to seven, with many low, reedy islands in the main channel large enough to hide an army of musket-wielding tribesmen, and also to be home to numerous varieties of bird and animal. On one island Stanley saw an elephant, and on another several buffalo. But though he longed to land to shoot for the pot, he did not dare, for fear he might be targeted by concealed Africans. At least the width of the river meant that the flotilla could stay out of range of either bank, and the scenery was exceptionally beautiful as they glided 'between palmy and spicy islands, whose sweet fragrance and vernal colour cause us to forget our dangerous life'. It was the sheer variety of foliage and trees that amazed him: 'Teak and cotton-wood palms ... the tall cane with its drooping feathery leaves, the bushy and many rooted mangrove ... and the low grassy banks from which the crocodile plunges into the brown depths.' But war drums could dispel enjoyment of the scenery in an instant.[36]

In the second volume of Stanley's book *Through the Dark Continent*, he wrote an exciting set piece about an encounter with between fifty and sixty canoes – manned by members of the Bangala (Ngala) tribe – that extended from the morning of the 14th to the late afternoon of 15 February. This was a very testing encounter, but in respect of the number of Bangala canoes mentioned by Stanley, it qualifies as one of his classic exaggerations. A comparison with Frank Pocock's diary establishes that fighting did indeed go on for two days, and that many shots were fired at Stanley's flotilla, but the comparison also shows that the number of African canoes involved never exceeded eight at any one time, and the total of the vessels pursuing them, over the two days, was about twenty. But even eight canoes, with crews of twenty or more men to each, and carrying, along with those paddling, additional men with guns, posed a formidable challenge. So how did Stanley behave when faced with this new danger?

According to Frank, even when his master knew that there were muskets in the canoes, he ordered his men not to fire until they themselves had been fired upon. Frank described the casualties inflicted upon the pursuers rather vaguely as 'some killed and wounded'. So Henry caused totally unnecessary damage to his reputation by inflating the incident into a major battle in his book – suggesting, by implication, that many more Africans would have died than the three or four mentioned in his diary.

Stanley's previous biographers have accepted the highly coloured account in *Through the Dark Continent*. This resort to fiction would appear to be largely due to a journalist's hankering for the best possible story. Despite the fact that his navigation of the Congo was self-evidently one of the greatest journeys of all time, it can only strike one as sad that he had still felt the need to pep it up. In fact the two days in question were extremely dangerous, as Frank Pocock affirmed, with 'five hours hard fighting against guns, [and] the bullets whistling over our heads'. Being subjected to this sniping for hour after hour, with men occasionally suffering flesh wounds, would have been a ghastly experience regardless of the number of canoes involved, especially since when individual canoes dropped out they were often replaced by others.[37] The British missionary William Holman Bentley, who attempted to convert the Bangala in the 1880s, had no doubt that Stanley would have 'had to fight in self-defence, or walk quietly to their cooking pots, and submit to dissection and the processes of digestion'.[38]

Apart from one brief attack on 9 March, this two-day ordeal would turn out to be the last of its kind – from now on, famine and cataracts would threaten the expedition more often than guns and spears. Before the end of February, after a period of great anxiety about food, they were managing to buy goats, fowls and bananas with cloth and brass wire. The people selling to them also had guns, 'old American flintlocks', and 'murderously long knives'. But despite having no interpreter, 'we did very well with signs', recorded Stanley.[39] During the first week of March, the expedition had completed the immense 1,200-mile hoop-like bend of the river and arrived at the junction with the Kwa River. Fifty miles to the south, the Congo widened into a huge lake. Henry claimed that Frank suggested to him that this seventeen by fifteen mile expanse of water be called Stanley Pool, but it seems more likely that he himself gave it this name, which would endure until the independence of the Belgian Congo in 1960. On the northern shore, the capital of the French Congo, Brazzaville, would one day be built, while to the south Leopoldville (modern Kinshasa), capital of the Belgian Congo, would stand. The relative friendliness of the Africans around the pool Stanley attributed to the influence of Portuguese commerce ('trade has tamed their natural ferocity') – although no white person of any nationality had ever penetrated closer to Stanley Pool than 278 miles.[40]

Because two months earlier Stanley had succeeded in descending the Stanley Falls with short detours overland, interspersed with periods on the river, he decided to ignore local warnings and to try to do the same again when passing the formidable cataracts below the pool. He had no idea that there would be thirty-two falls. Stanley later described this final leg of his journey as 'a tragic period, before which our running the gauntlet through the cannibal lands seems child's play'. Of course he knew that the cataracts would bring conditions unimaginably 'different from that soft, glassy flow of the river by the black forests ... where a single tremulous wave was a rarity', when they 'glided day after day'.[41] Yet Stanley had experienced one extraordinary event on the Stanley Falls that should have given him a presentiment of what lay ahead.

A canoe had been smashed on rocks in some rapids, and the man paddling had been flung into the water and swept onwards to the brink of the next vertiginous falls. By an amazing stroke of good fortune, he managed to clutch a rock in midstream right on the very lip above the maelstrom below. Though Zaidi, who had been on the Livingstone expedition, seemed doomed, Stanley risked his best men and canoes in trying to rescue him. He attached an unmanned canoe to a rattan hawser and then inched it closer and closer to the stranded man. But, halfway there, the rattan snapped 'like a pack thread', and the canoe hurtled over the falls. Next, Henry put two volunteers – Uledi, his experienced coxswain, and Marzouk – into a canoe and attached three rattans. With immense bravery, even after two rattans had parted, the two men had continued edging ever closer to the falls, somehow managing, at the last moment, to pull Zaidi into the canoe. Descending these new cataracts, such bravery was likely to be needed again. By now, Stanley's total of men, women and children had fallen from 143 to 129. In reaching Stanley Pool, fourteen had died by drowning, or by disease, or in African attacks. During the same period the number of canoes had dropped from twenty-three to fourteen.[42]

Now, Henry was about to ask the Wangwana for a commitment that might reasonably have been asked of soldiers in war, but not from contracted civilians. Nevertheless, he appreciated their qualities as few earlier explorers had done, and ungrudgingly acknowledged his indebtedness. Without them, Burton's, Speke's and Grant's achievements, like his own, would have been impossible. Stanley accepted that men subjected to an endless physical and mental ordeal could be forgiven for lapsing into despair and depression at times. To help the Wangwana, he meant to lead by example and show them that 'they could endure like Stoics, and fight like heroes'.[43] The ultimate compliment he paid to the best of them can be found in a letter to his close friend, Edward King: 'The execution & fulfilment of all plans, and designs was due to the pluck and intrinsic goodness of 20 men ... take these 20 men out and I could not have proceeded beyond a few days journey.'[44] On the later Emin Pasha Expedition, most of his white colleagues would remark on the very special relationship Stanley enjoyed with his Wangwana carriers.

At especially dangerous moments, Henry would work on the Wangwana by shaming as well as exhorting.[45] 'Will you go back and tell my friends you left me in this wild spot, and cast me adrift to die ... Speak, Wangwana, and show me those who dare follow me!' Some of them, such as his coxswain, Uledi, his detective, Kacheche, his adviser, Wadi Safeni, his storekeeper, Wadi Rehani, and his chief captain, Manwa Sera, were men of extraordinary courage, endurance and fidelity, often placed in situations so dangerous and stressful that only a very exceptional European would have proved equal to coping with them. Just such a man was the only other surviving European member of the party, Frank Pocock, the Kentish boatman. 'An extraordinary man,' Stanley called him, 'respected, beloved ... of cool steadfast courage.' So brave in fact that once, on his master's request, though well aware that three tribesmen's muskets were aimed at him at a distance of a few yards, he lowered his gun so that Henry could 'exhaust all endeavours for peace' before precipitating them into another fight.[46] Though a marvellous seaman and swimmer, Frank had recently been leading land parties, marching more miles than his master and wearing out his last pair of boots in the process. After that, sandals made from portmanteau leather had exposed his feet to attack by parasites. Now, Frank had to be carried or to travel by canoe, since his feet were 'almost in a state of mortification'.[47]

On 15 March 1877, they all started down the river, believing they were about 500 miles from the sea, and never supposing that their worst ordeal was just beginning.[48] The first rapids reminded Stanley of 'a strip of water blown over by a hurricane, with every interval of fifty or a hundred yards marked by wave-towers ... and the mad clash of watery hills ... The roar was tremendous and deafening. I can only compare it to the thunder of an express train through a rock tunnel.'[49]

A few days later, the expedition lost its best seventy-five-foot canoe, which was torn from the hands of fifty men and swept away. Men slipped and injured themselves on wet rocks, and Stanley 'fell down, feet first, into a chasm, 30 feet deep between two enormous boulders, but fortunately escaped with only a few rib bruises'.[50]

On 29 March the steersman of the canoe in which Kalulu was travelling, along with Ferajji, a Livingstone search veteran, and three others, let his vessel drift into the fastest flowing part of the river at a point where Stanley had urged all coxswains to hug the right bank. In the centre the current was so powerful that 'human strength availed nothing and the canoe and its unfortunate people glided over the treacherous calm surface like an arrow to doom'. Approaching the fatal lip of the falls, the canoe was 'whirled round three or four times, and presently we saw the stern pointed upward and knew that only by a miracle could any of the crew be saved'. A miracle was not forthcoming, and all six men were drowned. 'My heart aches sorely for them especially for Rehani, Ferajji, Mauredi and Kalulu.' After Kalulu's desertion at Lake Tanganyika, his unique status had been lost, and Stanley did not mourn him as long as he might have done if he had proved faithful.[51]

Death of Kalulu

The horrors of that day were not over:

Fast upon this catastrophe, before we could begin to wail their loss, another canoe with two men darted by, borne like lightning on the placid but irresistible water to apparent nay, almost certain destruction ... By a strange chance, or his dexterity, he [the steersman] shot his canoe over the Falls, and lower down in calmer water he contrived to secure his canoe to the shore. The two men were presently seen clambering over the rocks towards the point opposite our camp ... Our pity and love gushed strong towards them, but we could utter nothing of it. The roar of the Falls mocked and overpowered the feeble human voice.

Henry now insisted that all canoes must be attached to a tow-line, held by at least two men on the bank. Yet before this instruction could be acted upon, 'a third canoe darted past with only one man [on board]'. This was Soudi, who had been wounded by a spear during the fight in Ituru, on the way to Lake Victoria. Now, he shouted to Stanley: 'I am lost, Master; there is but one God.' The river swept him down over no less than four falls, 'great waves striking madly at him, yet his canoe did not sink, and he and it swept behind the island and we could see nothing more, for darkness fell on us and on the river'.[52] Three days later, to everyone's amazement, Soudi returned to the expedition. He had been kidnapped on landing, and only released when it was realized that he served that great magician, 'the white man with large fiery eyes'. On the same day the other two absentees 'made their appearance in our camp to our general joy', having hidden for two days to avoid being caught and enslaved.[53]

Frank Pocock was not abashed by what had happened, and guided three canoes down some white-water rapids a week later 'in first rate style'. On the same day, Frank, thanks to his prowess as a swimmer, saved a man 'who was half drowned ... after he had sunk once'.[54] On 12 April, Stanley and a skeleton crew on the *Lady Alice* were lucky to survive a botched attempt to lower them down some rapids. The men holding the stern rope failed to stop the vessel swinging out into the stream; so Henry and his crew found themselves descending the rapids, completely out of control. 'As we began to feel that it was useless to contend with the current, a sudden terrible rumbling noise caused us to look below, and we saw the river almost heaved bodily upward, as if a volcano had burst under it.' By some frantic oar strokes, they avoided being sucked under as their bows plunged down the side of this 'watery mound'. 'Once or twice we were flung scornfully aside, and spun around contemptuously, as though we were too insignificant to be wrecked.' At last, they managed to steer the boat to the bank.

In about an hour, a straggling line of anxious souls appeared; and all that love of life ... and full sense of the worth of living, returned to my heart as my faithful followers rushed up one after another with their exuberant welcome to life ... And Frank, my amiable and trusty Frank was neither last nor least in his professions of love.[55]

'Lady Alice' over the falls

In the meantime, just when food was becoming very hard to buy, a bag of Blue Mutoonda beads – among the expedition's most valuable means of exchange – went missing. Even at a moment when lives were in danger daily, Stanley searched remorselessly for these beads until they were found divided among five men's private possessions. These beads were priceless because cloth was almost valueless as currency on this lower stretch of the river, and members of the expedition had been asked to pay as much as a gun for a goat. Despite their hunger, the five thieves were flogged on Stanley's orders. He felt no remorse. What would have been the use of surviving the falls and rapids, only to starve for lack of funds?[56]

In late April, with no path anywhere near the river, and more terrible cataracts downstream, Stanley was obliged to order his long-suffering men to haul six heavy canoes up a 1,900-foot hill. This involved hacking out a path almost a mile long and cutting numerous logs for rollers. But though four of Stanley's men had chronic dysentery, and another eight were suffering from flesh-eating ulcers, the task was managed by the expedition's fit men within a week.[57] The food crisis went on, but Stanley would never condone thefts from local villagers. Henry always paid to release thieves who had been caught, and even took them back to their captors if they escaped, so that proper negotiations could take place. On one occasion, Stanley paid a staggering $150 in cloth for the release of a man who had stolen a chicken. Now that he was on land as often as on water, and therefore frequently face to face with Congolese tribesmen, he was determined to avoid fights.[58]

Most of May was devoted to building two new canoes from massive trees. To speed up the process, Stanley set up a night party under Frank. Since these vessels were made of teak, the work of hollowing them was incredibly arduous, and during it Kacheche had to take the expedition's collection of axes to a local smithy to be honed. When both the new canoes were launched, Stanley redistributed his land and water parties – himself taking command of the land party, hitherto Frank's job, with joint command on the river passing to Manwa Sera, his chief captain, and to Uledi, the expedition's most skilled coxswain. Chowpereh, who had been with Livingstone when he died, was also transferred to the river group. These changes were made because Frank was now too lame to walk. Baraka, a boatman with a ready wit, had coined 'the sobriquet of Goee-Goee, a term quite untranslatable as regards its descriptive humour', though Henry thought that 'despairing, forlorn good-for-nothings' was a fair equivalent. When Baraka called Frank 'a Goee-Goee, he laughingly assented', though really mortified.[59]

On 27 June, Stanley was traumatized to be told by one of his teenagers, Majwara, that he had seen Uledi, of all people, steal some precious Sami Sami beads – an amount sufficient to purchase two days' provisions for the entire expedition. Yet this was the man who had saved thirteen lives at immense risk to himself and had never failed the expedition. When such serious crimes were detected, Stanley asked his captains what punishment they thought appropriate. Despite Uledi's exceptional services, they decided that he should be flogged. But when Uledi's cousin, Saywa, and another man each offered to receive half of Uledi's strokes, Henry was so affected that he merely reprimanded him.[60] In Africa, unaccountable things happened even to the best. Only the day before, Frank had been uncharacteristically careless when piloting the *Lady Alice* through some rapids. The result had been a crunching collision with a rock and a large hole in the hull.[61]

On 3 June, the *Lady Alice*, with Henry aboard, passed perilously close to a massive whirlpool because she was steering badly as a result of 'the growing weight of water' in her hull. From midday, Stanley walked overland. Before leaving the river, he talked to Frank about the difficulties of the next stretch of water, and how he should cling to the bank and use hauling ropes. But with Uledi as his canoe's coxswain, Stanley was not worried about him.[62] That afternoon, Henry was resting on the rocks above Zinga Point, looking upriver through his field-glass. He knew that Frank and Uledi had started later than he and his land party but, even so, was surprised not to have seen them yet. Then to his horror, he saw 'something long and dark, rolling and tumbling about in the fierce waves'. Through his glass he made out eight heads above water, and these same men 'struggling to right her ... and raise themselves on the keel'. Finally, some of them paddled for dear life towards the bank before diving into the water and swimming ashore. Then the empty canoe swept by 'with the speed of an arrow, over the Zinga Falls, into ... the soundless depths of whirlpools'.[63]

'Bad news travels fast. I soon heard the names of the saved and those of the drowned. Among the latter was Frank Pocock, my servant my companion and good friend. Alas, my brave, honest, kindly natured, good Frank, thy many faithful services to me have only found thee a grave in the wild waters of the Congo.' At the head of his diary entry for 3 June, Stanley wrote: 'A BLACK WOEFUL DAY!', but it was infinitely worse than that. 'As I look on his empty tent and dejected servants, and recall to mind ... his extraordinary gentleness, his patient temper, his industry, his cheerfulness and tender love of me ... I feel myself utterly unable to express my feelings or describe the vastness of my loss.'[64] A week later Henry's depression had not lifted. 'Ah Frank! You are happy my friend. Out of this dreadful mess. Out of this pit of misery in which I am plunged neck deep.' Frank's floating corpse was seen by a fisherman several miles downstream, but this man was too scared to retrieve the white man's half-naked body. There would be no other sighting of his corpse. Again, Stanley agonized over why the boat's strongest swimmer had been one of the three to die. He guessed he had hit his head as the boat went over.[65]

Frank's death damaged the Wagwana's morale at a disastrous moment, 'benumbing their faculties of feeling, of hope and of action'. From now on, Stanley noted 'an apathetic sullenness and lack of feeling for themselves and their comrades'. When they fell ill, few requested medicine, or showed solicitude when others were sick. 'Disease, violent and painful deaths ... had finally deadened that lively fear of death which they had formerly shown.'[66] Two days later, eighty of his people 'refused to work, declaring that they would prefer living and hoeing for the heathen than follow this White man longer, for his wages were but the wages of death'. In the past Frank had instilled discipline in men not in Stanley's immediate vicinity, but now Wangwana out of his sight constantly played up. It seemed that the expedition was collapsing after travelling 7,000 miles, and with only a few hundred to go. 'I have publicly expressed a desire to die by a quick sharp death, which I think just now would be a mercy to what I endure daily ... Slavery is abhorrent to my very soul ... but these men make me regard myself every day, as only a grade higher than a miserable slave driver.'[67]

On 20 June they had still not passed Zinga Falls, and though the earlier mutiny had collapsed, a new one replaced it, this time by thirty-one men led by Wadi Safeni, whose courage and common sense on Bumbireh had probably saved the lives of the *Lady Alice*'s crew on their first visit. Because some people were eating rations without working for them, Stanley feared that the expedition might never reach the sea. He implored Safeni to 'hold a palaver with these men [and] work with might and main to clear these Falls and so get away to somewhere where we can get food, or face dying among these savage people from starvation'. Safeni's answer was to lead the thirty-one away into the bush, though they were without trade goods and guns and knew not a word of the local language. Henry sent messengers after them, with warnings that their attempt to reach the sea independently would end in their death. Next day they all returned in the evening and Henry did not reprove them.[68]

He realized that the only reliable way to reach the coast would be to take ten of his best men in a single boat, leaving the remaining 110 members of the expedition behind. But he knew he was not 'capable of it ... far better to die, as we have lived, together, and share fate, even the most fearful. Yet my people anger me, oh so much, and yet I pity and love them ... One man, never remarkable for bravery, fidelity, or anything else save his size, told me flatly today: "That they were tired."'[69] Stanley, with his grey hair and emaciated face was tired too – utterly exhausted. Yet despite the pain and weakness of his physical body, Henry pulsed with almost mystical self-belief: 'For my real self lay darkly encased, & was ever too haughty & soaring for such miserable environments as the body that encumbered it daily.'[70]

And the deaths did not stop. A day after the mutineers returned, the largest of the two new canoes was lost over Zinga Falls, with Salaam Allah, the carpenter who had made her, on board. He was never seen again. At last, in mid-July, Stanley managed to engage 200 'stalwart natives' to carry his six canoes and the *Lady Alice* past the falls, overland.[71] Every day, a few of his men committed thefts in nearby villages, and on 22 July, for the first time, Henry left behind a man who had been apprehended. Had he gone on purchasing the release of every man caught stealing, his men would have felt they could rob the locals with impunity. A few days later another man was caught stealing – just one fowl – but he too was left behind to face possible execution by his captors. Although many of the Wangwana wished to release him by force, Stanley refused, pointing out that the purchase of food would then be impossible. At this time Stanley was only managing to buy a few pounds of ground nuts each day – far too few 'for the preservation of working men's strength'.[72]

On 25 July, Stanley announced to his men that they were 'not far from the sea'. This news had the effect of sending Wadi Safeni out of his mind. The wretched man embraced Henry's feet, crying out:

'We are home! We are home! We shall no more be tormented by empty stomachs and accursed savages! I am about to run all the way to the sea to tell your brothers you are coming!' ... I replied to him soothingly; but he, seizing his parrot and placing it on his shoulder, plunged into the woods. After a few seconds' reflection, it occurred to me that the man was a lunatic and I sent three men to bring him back ... But after four hours' search, they returned unsuccessful, and I never saw the sage Safeni again.[73]

Five days later, Stanley and his men, 'hollow-eyed, sallow and gaunt', arrived at Isangila Cataract, where they learned to their horror that five more cataracts lay ahead. Knowing it would be madness to travel any further by water, Stanley ordered his men to drag the *Lady Alice* and the remaining canoes up onto the rocks above the cataract 'to bleach and rot to dust'. Then he started on the overland march to Boma, where he had just heard that several white men lived, a mere five or six days' march away.[74]

As his enfeebled column filed across the rocky terrace of Isangila, nearly forty men were sick with dysentery, ulcers and scurvy. The path was strewn with splinters of quartz that made crossing them a torment with bare feet. Three mothers in the party were nursing infants under two months old. Henry was deeply concerned, as these women struggled on, like everyone else, across an arid landscape of bleached grass and scattered stones. They kept moving in shorter and shorter marches, until on 3 August they arrived in an utterly exhausted state at Nsanda, 'a miserable little village of about 50 souls'. His people fanned out over the country looking for anything edible: baobab fruits, calabashes, roots. A few pounds of potatoes cost an outrageous four yards of cloth, and the price of ground nuts was as exorbitant. The tribes living nearby all asked for 'dashes', by which they meant rum. But having no rum, and the wrong cloth and beads, Stanley could buy very little, and many of his party remained close to starvation.[75] To end his people's suffering as quickly as possible, he sent ahead four of his most dependable men with an open letter to the Europeans at Boma, begging them to send food. The chosen messengers were the now forgiven Uledi, the ever loyal Kacheche, Muini Pembe, a captain, and Robert Feruzi, who had been educated at the Universities' Mission in Zanzibar and spoke good English.[76]

Village of Nsanda August 4th 1877

To any gentleman who speaks English at Emboma

Dr Sir,

I have arrived at this place from Zanzibar with 115 souls, men women & children. We are now in a state of imminent starvation. We can purchase nothing from the natives, for they laugh at our kinds of cloth, beads and wire. There are no provisions in the country that may be purchased except on market days, and starving people cannot afford to wait for these market days. I therefore have made bold to despatch ... this letter craving relief from you. I do not know you but I am told that there is an Englishman at Emboma, and as you are a Christian, and a gentleman, I beg you not to disregard my request. The boy, Robert will be better able to describe our true condition than I can tell you in this letter. We are in a state of the greatest distress, but if your supplies arrive in time, I may be able to reach Emboma in four days. I want 300 cloths, each 4 yards long of such quality as you trade with, which is very different from that we have, but better than all would be 10 or 15 man loads of rice, or grain to fill their pinched bellies immediately ... The supplies must arrive within two days, or I may have a fearful time of it among the dying. Of course I hold myself responsible for any expense you may incur in this business ... For myself if you have such little luxuries, as tea, coffee, sugar and biscuits by you, such as one man can easily carry, I beg on my own behalf that you will send a small supply, and add to the great debt of gratitude due to you upon the arrival of the supplies for my people. Until that time I beg you to believe me

Yours sincerely
Henry M.Stanley
Cmdg Anglo American Expedition for Exploration of Africa.

P.S. You may not know me by name – I therefore add that I am the person who discovered Livingstone in 1871. H.M.S.

Although Stanley's situation was desperate, this was a remarkably modest letter for a man to have written at the end of perhaps the greatest journey of all time, since it was, in effect, his first announcement to the world that he had traced the Congo from the heart of Africa to within reach of the sea. Yet he made no mention of making history. Instead, he added that final insecure postscript. Henry copied this letter in English, French and Spanish and handed the different versions to his messengers.[77]

For the next two days, he and the rest of his party 'dragged their weary limbs nearer to the expected relief', and on the 7th, soon after setting up camp at the end of their day's march, they were rewarded with the sight of Uledi and Kacheche 'tearing through the grass, holding up a letter to announce to us that they had been successful'. A procession of carriers followed, bearing the goods that Stanley had asked for and, in addition, rum, fish, bread, butter, sardines, jam, peaches, grapes and several bottles of pale ale. Stanley then wrote an emotional letter of thanks to his benefactors, A. da Motta Veiga and J. W. Harrison, of the Liverpool trading firm Hatton & Cookson, in which he told them he would never forget his people's overjoyed expressions at the moment they realized they were saved. Henry admitted in his diary: 'I had to rush to my tent to hide my tears that would flow despite all my attempts at composure.'[78]

When Stanley met two white men and, later, several others at the Portuguese trading post of Boma, he stared at their pale faces, embarrassed to be fascinated by them. This, he realized, was how Africans had viewed his and Frank's 'weird pallor'. In fact the merchants' faces made him shiver.

The pale colour, after so long gazing on rich black and richer bronze, had something of an unaccountable ghastliness. I could not divest myself of the feeling that they must be sick ... Yet there was something very self-possessed about the carriage of these white men ... the calm blue-grey eyes rather awed me, and the immaculate purity of their clothes dazzled me.[79]

It was 9 August 1877, and they had taken four and a half months to struggle past the cataracts from Stanley Pool to Boma. At last journey's end was in sight – the sea was a mere fifty miles away. Stanley's party was taken there by steamer the very next day and put ashore at Kabinda further up the coast, where for ten days they were housed and fed by employees of Hatton & Cookson.[80]

Although overwhelmed with relief that the long ordeal was over, Henry was horrified by the sudden collapse of his followers. The abrupt ending of the daily physical grind 'plunged them into a state of torpid brooding from which it was difficult to arouse them'. Five died, possibly through being properly fed for the first time in years.[81] Although about sixty were suffering from scurvy, fever and dysentery, Henry suspected it was the dread of never again seeing their homes that was killing them.[82]

On 17 August, he wrote to Edward Levy-Lawson and to James Gordon Bennett Jr, telling them: 'You now have a debt of gratitude to pay, in fact you are bound as men of honour ... These poor people must see their homes & relatives again by your means ... If you allow them to work their way across the continent themselves – ignorant of the country ... not one of them will ever see Zanzibar again, and the whole world will condemn you.' Stanley begged Lawson to use his influence with the British government to persuade them

to despatch a small gunboat to take these people to Zanzibar ... If the Govt will not assist you, you will either have to charter a vessel, or abandon them to their own endeavours which would be I fear stamped by civilized people *as a thing you ought not to have done* ... These men's wages must be paid – which will amount altogether to something near £2,500. I have already drawn on the salary you allowed me £1,328 – and I have given a year freely ... You must give me authority to draw on you for £1,250 at once ... I cannot leave my people until the affair is settled, [and] will not ...[83]

In due course the money was paid by Lawson and Bennett, and the British Admiralty sent a gunboat.[84] Stanley's continuing anxiety about his followers contrasts very favourably with Livingstone's cavalier treatment of the 114 Africans, who had made possible *his* great trans-Africa journey between 1853 and 1856.[85]

The fate of his followers was not Henry's only worry, as he told Lawson: 'I have heard that I have been attacked in the press – in fact I have seen three articles condemning me – and none, or nothing in my favour. I suppose I am very unpopular for the style of exploring that I have adopted.' But, as Stanley knew very well, his determination to control the direction in which he had travelled – by limiting desertions and by using force if need be – had enabled him to trace the Congo to the sea, whereas Cameron had followed an Arab-Swahili trade route to the south-west – his failure being due to his inability to shift for himself.[86] Livingstone had failed on the Lualaba for the very same reason.

As early as September 1877 – when Stanley arrived at Loanda in a Portuguese gunboat – he would have been wise to have written for publication a defence of his attack on the islanders of Bumbireh – which he realized, even now, had caused fury among humanitarians. But like his men, he felt drained and utterly listless. 'Frequently, at meals, I found myself subsiding into sleep ... wine had no charm for me; conversation fatigued me.' As always after a journey, he found that with 'nothing to struggle against, the vast resolve, which sustained me through a long and difficult enterprise, died away', leaving behind 'a peculiar melancholy'.[87] Nor had he stopped grieving. 'I doubt whether anybody would believe how much I grieved after Frank's loss. No death ever struck me with grief like this. I wished to die.'[88]

Although Henry managed to write from Kabinda to his publisher, Edward Marston, as well as to Levy-Lawson, and to send from there a long despatch to his two commissioning newspapers, he did not at first send anything to Alice Pike.[89] But en route to Loanda, he had met the explorer Serpa Pinto, and in late August he handed him a letter addressed to Alice. Having explained that the lady was his 'pequena', or girlfriend, he begged Pinto to see that his missive began its journey to New York on the earliest possible mail ship.[90] Stanley suspected that if any letters from Alice existed anywhere, they would be at Zanzibar, and that he would probably have to wait till he got there to read them. Yet however much mail might be waiting for him at Zanzibar, it was agony to have none to read now, having lived for three years without a single message. 'I do not know whether anybody entertains any friendly recollection of me, or how they are disposed towards me ... My hopes of appreciation ought to be great ... but...I am in doubt.'[91]

Having kept his spoilt fiancée waiting for a year longer than had been agreed between them in New York, he had every reason to fear that she might not have waited for him. But despite terrible anxieties, Stanley declined a passage to Lisbon in a Portuguese warship when it was offered. He had decided to accompany the Wangwana to Zanzibar and would never waver. When the British Admiralty at last allocated a warship, HMS *Industry,* to take everyone to East Africa, Stanley admitted to Edward King: 'It surprises me that anybody should do me a kindness for I have heard that ... I have been called "invader", "fighting reporter", civiliser of Africans with explosive shells".'[92]

On 21 October, in Cape Town, Stanley told a journalist on the *Cape Argus* newspaper that he never 'liked to fight for fighting's sake', since it only 'risked unnecessarily the lives of those who were with me'. This was sensible, but did not address the issue of Bumbireh. HMS *Industry* sailed from the Cape for Zanzibar on 6 November and entered Zanzibar harbour twenty days later. Although Stanley did not mention it in his diary, nor anywhere else, there were eight letters from Alice Pike waiting for him at the US Consulate.[93] These had all been written in the year in which Henry had started his great journey, and all had reached Zanzibar after his departure for the mainland. In the last three Alice expressed great indignation that he had been sending long letters to her friend, Mamie Anderson. In a final angry letter of 4 December she said she felt entitled to see other men in future and to write to them too. She signed herself 'Alice Pike', without any endearment, and would write only one more letter to Stanley – this in reply to the one he had sent to her from Loanda at journey's end – but he would not receive it until reaching London in January.[94] For a young woman looking for a way out of an engagement, his innocent correspondence with Mamie had offered an easy exit.

Another letter in the packet at the Consulate was from Henry's publisher, Edward Marston. After congratulating his star author, Marston steeled himself for a less agreeable task:

I now come to a delicate subject which I have long debated with myself whether I should write about or wait for your arrival. I think however I may as well tell you at once that your friend Alice Pike is married! ... Some months ago I received the enclosed letter saying that Miss Alice Pike is now Mrs Barney! ... It will I fear prove another source of trouble to your sensitive nature.

Alice's husband's family owned America's largest manufacturer of railroad rolling stock, and Alice had by now had his first child. Marston ended with information that he mistakenly imagined might be of comfort to the rejected man. The Cretan beauty Virginia Ambella, whose family had rejected Stanley in 1868, had written making it abundantly clear that now Stanley was the most famous explorer in the world, she and her family would be happy to accept him. Stanley glanced at her letter with utter indifference.[95]

Fortunately, Henry had much to do on the island. It would take four days to pay off all his people, and to ensure that relatives of the dead received compensation and the wages due to them. So how many people had died, along with all three of his white colleagues? Stanley had started with 228 people, and brought home 108. He acquired en route two Soko, one Manyema, and one Ugandan, who was cancelled out by Dallington, whom he left with Mutesa. He also added six men, whom he contracted at Nyangwe. In addition three infants had been born on the journey and were included by him in his list of the 108 who returned.[96] His losses through death and desertion therefore amounted to 132 people. He listed 114 deaths in his tables in *Through the Dark Continent*, so the number of desertions and men left behind seems unlikely to have exceeded twenty – an amazing achievement. He himself deliberately compiled no table of desertions to add to his lists of those who died and those who had returned home. Had he added such a table, his exaggerated starting figure could only have been substantiated by admitting to a number of desertions vastly exceeding those that had actually taken place. Since this would have given the impression that he had been a lax and undisciplined leader, he had been unable to fake such a list.

His love of the Wangwana was unfeigned, and the fact that he had brought home only half of those who had set out made the homecoming of the survivors particularly poignant. The last Wangwana death occurred on Zanzibar itself, and was the more distressing because Muscati, the woman in question, was the widow of Wadi Safeni – Stanley's valued counsellor, who had gone insane and vanished into the bush with his parrot on his shoulder. She had recently lived through the pain of losing Safeni's baby in Loanda. Muscati herself lived long enough 'to be embraced by her father, and the next morning died in his arms, surrounded by her relatives and friends': a tragic ending to an extraordinary odyssey. Stanley said that he owed much to the returning women – fourteen of them – since they had lifted spirits by 'transforming stern camps in the depths of the wilds into something resembling a village'. Stanley had also been comforted by the games and chatter of their children.[97]

The women who completed the Trans-Africa journey

On 13 December, as Henry was about to step into the ship's boat that would take him out to the steamer *Pachumba*, bound for Aden, a number of his followers rushed into the water ahead of him 'and shot the boat into the sea, and then lifted me up on their heads and carried me through the surf into the boat'. Another group commandeered a lighter, and rowed out to the steamer.

A deputation of them came on board, headed by the famous Uledi, the coxswain; Kacheche, the chief detective; Robert [Feruzi], my indispensable factotum; Zaidi, the chief, and Wadi Rehani, the storekeeper, to inform me that they still considered me as their master, and that they would not leave Zanzibar until they received a letter from me announcing my safe arrival in my own country ... What wild and varied scenes had we not seen together ... The chiefs were those who had followed me to Ujiji in 1871 ... they were the men to whom I entrusted the safeguard of Livingstone on his last and fatal journey ... In a flood of sudden recollection ... every scene of strife with Man and Nature through which these poor men and women had borne me company, and solaced me by the simple sympathy of shared suffering, came hurrying across my memory; for each face before me was associated with some adventure or some peril.[98]

After this emotional parting, Stanley reflected on what he would miss when back in Britain: the rituals of camp life, his men threading shell and bead necklaces for currency and singing as they worked, and the cheerfulness of his young gun-carriers. He would also miss the fables and cautionary tales told by his followers around the camp fire.[99] Above all, he would miss 'the sweet novel pleasure ... [of] almost total independence ... and indifference to all things earthly outside camp, which is ... one of the most exquisite soul-lulling pleasures a mortal can enjoy'.[100]

As the well-known features of Shangani and Melindi, and the tall square mass of the Sultan's palace, fell further and further astern, Stanley wondered whether he would ever again know such exaltation as he had experienced when solving the planet's last great geographical mysteries.

FIFTEEN

'I Hate Evil and Love Good'

Before Stanley's return to England, Edward Marston, his publisher, had rented for him an apartment at 30, Sackville Street in Piccadilly, doubtless eager for his author to get to work as soon as possible on a colossal bestseller. The returning hero took up residence towards the end of January 1878 after a week of junketing in Paris – unenjoyable except for his reunion with Edward King. Marston had joined him briefly in the French capital and had handed over the only honest communication the jilted man had ever received from his former fiancée.

November 17 1877 New York

Dear Morton,

Amid the many congratulations and praises showered on you receive my humble rejoicing also ...

Poor Stanley! How much you have lost, but your gain has been great indeed. I shed tears when I read of the sad fate of Kalulu and the 'Lady Alice'. I had hoped she would have proven a truer friend than the Alice she was named after, for you must know, by this time, I have done what millions of women have done before me, not been true to my promise. But you are so great, so honoured, so sought after, that you will scarcely miss your <u>once</u> loved friend and <u>always</u> devoted admirer of your heroism. For indeed you are the hero of the day. That alone should console you for my loss. No doubt you will think it a gain, for <u>Stanley</u> can easily find a wife all his heart could desire to grace his high position and deservedly great name ...

If you <u>can</u> forgive me, tell me so; if not, <u>do please</u> be silent ... Adieu, Morton. I will not say farewell, for I hope in some future time we may meet – shall it be as friends?

Alice Barney[1]

Stanley's crushing sense of disappointment reminded him of earlier rejections, and made the immense fame, which he had imagined bringing him love and happiness, seem hollow and absurd. London's *Daily News* was not untypical: 'It is very doubtful whether in all the roll of history's adventurous travellers there is recorded one who did a greater deed.'[2] 'What is the good of all this pomp and show?' Henry asked Edward Marston in Paris, after a celebratory dinner given him by French geographers. 'It only makes me more miserable.'[3] In London, Stanley did his best to escape his unhappiness by writing his 1,092-page two-volume work, *Through the Dark Continent*, in eighty unbelievably frenetic days.

The worst problem Henry faced on his return was how to react to those people whose reading of his newspaper despatches had led them to view his behaviour at Bumbireh as murder. Although his two fiercest critics, Colonel Henry Yule, an RGS gold medallist, and the socialist writer H. M. Hyndman, praised his journey as 'the greatest feat in the history of discovery', they mounted a campaign against him, so skilful and prolonged that his reputation would be permanently damaged.[4] Ironically, Stanley's successful pretence that he was an American denied him the overwhelming public support that would otherwise have insulated him from attack.[5] Starting in the autumn of 1876, soon after the publication of Stanley's despatch about his second visit to Bumbireh, the two men used the columns of the *Pall Mall Gazette* and the *Saturday Review* to mount a formidable case against him. Sadly, because he had been advised by his close friends Edwin Arnold and Edward Marston 'to answer these fools with proud silence', Henry made no immediate response on returning to England.[6] Yule and Hyndman had known better, believing that Stanley would have no choice eventually but to join in a debate that was, in reality, about whether his name was 'to have a place on the honourable roll which bears those of Columbus, Cook and Livingstone, or on another of a different character'.[7] For this reason alone, it is necessary to rehearse again Stanley's reasons for the second attack on Bumbireh, and then to set the incident in a wider context.

What had been so damaging to Stanley's reputation in his disastrous despatch of 15 August 1875 had been the impression given – mainly through condensation of the facts and timescale – that his attack on Bumbireh had been premeditated as an act of personal vengeance ever since his first humiliating encounter with the islanders, and had happened very soon after it. In truth, it had occurred over three months later. And far from wanting to return to Bumbireh, Stanley had done his utmost to avoid going anywhere near the island he detested. If King Rwoma had not prevented him from travelling overland to Buganda, he would never have embarked on water at all. Furthermore, if Mutesa and his admiral, Magassa, had provided thirty promised canoes, or if the King of Ukerewe's canoes had not been in poor condition, Stanley would probably have steered the shorter route across the centre of Lake Victoria, and risked weathering a storm, rather than sailing close to the lake's western shores and gambling on avoiding the hostile islanders and their equally ferocious overlord, Antari, on the mainland opposite.[8]

When Stanley had known he would have to run the gauntlet between the island of Bumbireh and the mainland, his canoes' proven tendency to sink in choppy water had persuaded him he would have to hug the western shore of the island as his fleet sailed north, until it could pass through the strait and sail on to Buganda close to the mainland.[9] Knowing his vulnerability to waterborne attack, he had done his utmost to oblige the islanders to agree in advance to let his expedition pass unmolested. To this end, he cleverly captured their chief as a hostage, guaranteeing their good behaviour, he hoped – and making a pre-emptive attack on them unnecessary. To test the water with Antari, Stanley sent an emissary to ask him to redeem Shekka with a modest payment of spears in reparation for his vassal's earlier aggression. But far from agreeing to pay, Antari declared war on him. Next, by killing the leader of the Ganda delegation to their island and fatally wounding six others, the islanders scotched all Stanley's painstaking efforts to obtain safe-conduct through the strait, and left him – in his own opinion – with no choice but to launch a pre-emptive attack.

The bitterest condemnation of Stanley would arise from his own earlier newspaper admission that he had *already* inflicted a severe punishment on Bumbireh by killing more than a dozen men on his first visit in April. So why, it would be asked, had he needed to punish them a second time in August? In fact Henry had immensely exaggerated the casualties he had inflicted in April. In reality, he had killed only one or possibly two people, rather than the fourteen he had later claimed in print. His psychological need to prove that no one ever got the better of him was a character weakness he felt unable to admit to in public in order to explain his exaggeration. So thanks to this misguided lie, his second visit to the island seemed far more brutal than it would otherwise have done. (He exaggerated again when claiming, in his August despatch, that forty-three men had been killed in his attack, when in his diary the figure given was thirty-three, which tallies with Frank Pocock's total.)

The sensitivity of the early twenty-first-century observer to racial questions makes judging the actions of nineteenth-century explorers with objectivity and fairness extremely difficult. Men coming from a society in which public hangings had only recently been abolished – and where floggings in the armed services, and beatings in workhouses and schools, were ferocious – were bound to have few inhibitions about using a whip on their porters. Nor were Africans themselves strangers to physical punishments in their own societies. Lacking prisons, chiefs often sentenced criminals to death or inflicted mutilations as standard forms of retribution. During the American Indian Wars, most of Henry's readers had regarded the killing of 'Red Indians' as laudable, so it is not surprising that in Africa he described the Bumbireh islanders to his American friend, Edward King, as 'a desperate set of savages rivalling the Apaches in ferocity and determination'.[10] Furthermore, he saw for himself General Napier's army and Sir Garnet Wolseley's expeditionary force kill large numbers of virtually unarmed Africans with the most up-to-date artillery available, and being praised on their return. So Stanley probably did not anticipate that most British humanitarians would view the killing of Africans as barbarous *per se*, except when taking place under the dubious cloak of government campaigns.

In Cape Town, on his way to Zanzibar with the Wangwana, Stanley told a journalist that at Bumbireh he had done nothing worse than was being done daily by the Cape government 'in pursuit of the frontier war in which they were engaged'.[11] This was a good rejoinder, since military responses to border incidents and the suppression of colonial 'insurrections' were not classified as wars by the Colonial Office, and consequently deaths caused during them could be defined as murder under the civil law. Yet, Henry knew that prosecutions of military commanders were incredibly rare, and that there had been little or no outrage over the scores of Indians (many of them entirely innocent) who had been blown from the mouths of cannons in revenge for the Indian Mutiny, without any judicial process. Only ten years before Stanley's attack on Bumbireh, Governor Eyre of Jamaica had been pardoned after hanging almost 450 black 'rebels' and flogging 600 others for their alleged part in a rebellion, on wholly inadequate evidence. Among Eyre's supporters had been Charles Dickens, Charles Kingsley and Thomas Carlyle. So Stanley could have been forgiven for not realizing that it was wise to keep quiet about shooting anyone in Africa. He had simply not understood that Africans had enjoyed special status in the United Kingdom ever since Britain had led the long campaign against the Atlantic slave trade. Aborigines in Tasmania were being brought to the point of extinction by a combination of settlers' bullets, alcohol and white men's diseases, with little notice being taken of their plight – while the same indifference was being shown to similar crimes occurring in Australia and the Islands of the Pacific. But shoot Africans in Africa and admit it, and all hell could be guaranteed to break out.

When Charles 'Chinese' Gordon heard what Stanley had done to Africans in Africa, he was aghast – but not because Stanley might be a murderer. His crime in Gordon's eyes was that he had *written openly* about killing Africans. 'These things may be done but not advertised,' Gordon told Richard Burton. In China, Gordon's 'Ever Victorious Army' had committed a string of atrocities, and in the Sudan he and his subordinates had killed numerous members of the Bari tribe without saying a word.[12] Though Stanley can be accused of being naive about Bumbireh, he was never cynical. Samuel Baker would defend him on the grounds that 'Mr Stanley's publishing of the details of his various encounters with the natives proved that he must have considered them unavoidable – otherwise he would most naturally have concealed them from the public.'[13] Baker had himself killed many more Africans than Stanley, and had also kept quiet – though this had not saved him from a mauling in the British press in 1873 for 'cold blooded murder' and 'massacres', as a result of allegations by men who had served under him.[14] Like Burton, Baker was a racist with extreme views that disgusted Stanley.[15]

It is extraordinary that Stanley should have been singled out as virtually the only explorer who maltreated Africans when other famous travellers had behaved worse. Frederick Lugard, thanks to his biographer, Dame Margery Perham, is considered a humane man, though his actions in Uganda precipitated a civil war, and he was personally responsible for about a hundred deaths on the island of Bulingagwe.[16] Carl Peters, a national hero in Germany, had been unashamedly sadistic and had cut off the heads of Masai warriors.[17] Even the successful missionary Alexander Mackay, who went out to Uganda as a result of Stanley's appeal, shot two porters for desertion, while Verney Lovett Cameron, who was also reputed to be a morally impeccable traveller, shot a man for stealing his goat. He also travelled for months with a slave trader responsible for killing 1,500 people at this very time. Brooding on acts of brutality by Europeans in Africa, Stanley recalled that the Scottish missionaries on Lake Nyasa had sentenced a man to death, and flogged another so severely that he had died.[18] He also listed murders by two British consuls, and reflected that none of these misdeeds could hold a candle to the mass killings by famous chiefs like Mutesa, Mzilikazi and Sebetwane nor compare with the bloody trail left by tribal migrations such as those of the Ngoni during three decades.

Yet Stanley also put his finger on the central weakness of his own position. 'We went into the heart of Africa self-invited – therein lies our fault.'[19] Several years later he would even concede that Africans were entitled to 'assert their undeniable right to exclude strangers from their country'.[20] Indeed the position of all explorers was fraught with flaws and inconsistencies. From whom could they claim to have acquired the authority to kill, even in self-defence? Lacking this, were they not simply buccaneers? The editor of the *Saturday Review* was aghast at the thought of 'a private American citizen, travelling with negro allies, at the expense of two newspapers' causing the deaths of indigenous people 'with no sanction, no authority, no jurisdiction – nothing but explosive bullets and a copy of the *Daily Telegraph* – into a country where he and his black allies are intruders and natural enemies'.[21] Although Stanley brought back evidence of thousands of deaths being caused by Arab-Swahili slave raids, these did not cause the same indignation.

In the end, Henry was rescued by his former enemies at the Royal Geographical Society. Clements Markham began supporting him thanks to his long delayed explanation of why he had attacked the islanders. In the *Geographical Magazine*, Markham now accepted that Stanley had used force only 'under circumstances of absolute necessity'. He also pointed out that Henry's newspaper employers had made the decision that the expedition should go out to Africa bearing arms.[22] Yet even those who conceded that killing in self-defence was legitimate in certain circumstances asked whether expeditions were 'necessary' if they were likely to lead to deaths of any sort. 'Perhaps,' suggested the editor of the *Saturday Review* sardonically, 'the Geographical Society cannot exist without rivers, and it may be so noble an institution that all the horrors of war must be perpetrated rather than it should perish.'[23] This point was met head on by Stanley's old enemy, Francis Galton. 'Stanley,' he wrote, 'has dissected and laid bare the very heart of the great continent of Africa', and beside this astonishing achievement 'the death of a few hundred barbarians, ever ready to fight and kill ... will perhaps be regarded as a small matter'.[24]

In fact, Henry never resorted to such arguments, insisting that he had killed at Bumbireh in self-defence. It had been his inescapable duty to his people to protect them. 'As long as they are in my charge I will not look calmly on a parcel of savages resolved on murder and massacre. Unless they consent to reason, they must accept the consequences.'[25] And Stanley felt he had given 'reason' a very fair chance before his attack. But the murder of the leader of the Ganda delegation – himself a chief – had been an act of war justifying immediate punishment.

At first, Stanley had thought it futile to try 'to refute calumny, based upon cant and malice', because anti-Americanism and hatred of the *Daily Telegraph* would guarantee him enemies whatever he wrote or said. So, after his return to Britain it would be two whole weeks before he spoke in his defence at an RGS banquet in Willis's Supper Rooms.[26] Although Henry's defence – on lines very like mine above – failed to end the sniping, it did at least lead the editor of the *Saturday Review* to concede that 'Mr Stanley must be taken to be the best judge of the necessities of his position.'[27] What particularly annoyed Henry was the way in which editors loved

to point to Livingstone as having been able to travel long distances in Africa without quarrelling with the natives. Well, I have also travelled thousands of miles in Africa without a quarrel, but I well know that though the caravan route to Ujiji has been travelled over numerous times without a breach of amity, a day's march to the North or South could bring me face to face with a difficulty which no tact could remove.[28]

Stanley sometimes spoke of well-known travellers – even as famous as Speke, Burton and Cameron – having travelled for miles by 'Arab parcel post', protected from the violence that they would otherwise have had to face alone and unaided. And a few years later he would point to the many white travellers murdered in supposedly safe East

Africa, just off the beaten track. Yet they had never faced tribes nearly as ferocious as those on the Upper Congo. Nevertheless, Captain Frederick Carter and Lieutenant Thomas Cadenhead were murdered by Mirambo's men at Mpimbwe in 1880, along with more than a hundred of their followers. Yet little fuss would be made in Britain. Later, Stanley also reminded his readers that 'the murder of Bishop Hannington and sixty of his men may be read in his biography', and that 'six French Fathers of Urundi were set upon while celebrating mass, and murdered at the altar with their converts and young pupils'.[29] Mungo Park and Richard Lander had died, a generation earlier, from wounds received in different attacks by tribesmen on the Niger – Henry's point being that Africans could be violent and dangerous too.

But some people were never going to allow that any mitigating circumstance existed. Dr John Kirk was one of them, and in late February 1878, to his great joy, he was asked to mount an official inquiry into the behaviour of Stanley and his men on their epic journey. The ubiquitous Horace Waller – who was related to Kirk by marriage – combined with his other philanthropic duties membership of the executive committee of the Universities' Mission to Central Africa. One of this mission's clerics, the Revd J. P. Farler, was stationed near Bagamoyo, and had recently interrogated a number of Stanley's Wangwana (very likely on Waller's prompting). Farler now claimed to have been told by these carriers that Stanley had stolen ivory from Africans and had sold into slavery people whom he had captured. Since Stanley's diary contains many accounts of forcing his people to return stolen goods, it is hard to escape the conclusion that the Wangwana had been pulling Farler's leg.[30] Improbable though his notes were, Farler sent them to the Anti-Slavery Society, whose secretary passed them on to the Foreign Office on Waller's suggestion.[31]

A couple of months earlier Kirk had written to Stanley's friend, the shipping-line owner William Mackinnon, describing the explorer as 'pugnacious, conceited and small-minded' – confirming (if this were needed) that he was the worst possible person to carry out an impartial inquiry. On his arrival at Zanzibar, in December 1877, Stanley had suggested to Kirk, in an attempt to bury the hatchet, that Kirk, rather than himself, would be the most suitable person to present medals to the men who had brought Livingstone's body home to the coast.[32] Kirk's response was to send a letter to Lord Derby, the foreign secretary, alleging that Stanley had told the Sultan about 'the many collisions he had had with the native tribes who seem everywhere to have given way before Snider rifles and repeaters'.[33]

When Kirk began his investigation into Stanley's 'atrocities', he invited the explorer's captains to his house, and gave them money to tell him what he wanted to hear. The American merchant Augustus Sparhawk had observed their furtive visits to the British Consulate and accused Manwa Sera of being 'a big rascal and too fond of money'.[34] As might have been expected, the report that Kirk sent to Lord Derby on 1 May 1878 was pure character assassination. Stanley was said to have accepted from Mutesa a slave girl as his mistress – a claim that Stanley's unfeigned disgust with Shaw's and Farquhar's promiscuity makes extremely implausible (as does his later advice to expedition colleagues to avoid having sex with Africans).[35] Stanley was accused of gross cruelty to the Wangwana, kicking one to death and keeping many chained for months. Though he sometimes whipped carriers – as all explorers did when faced with thefts or desertion, the rest was simply untrue. Kirk repeated the accusation that Stanley had sold carriers into slavery – an extraordinary claim given the disgust expressed by both Stanley and Frank Pocock at the suffering caused by slave traders.[36]

Since Kirk's principal informants were Manwa Sera and Kacheche – who were described by Stanley and by Pocock as loyal followers and friends – bribery seems the likeliest explanation. Furthermore, since both men had been members of Stanley's expedition to find Livingstone, and both had been happy to re-enlist with him in 1874 and had accompanied him loyally for the next three years without deserting, they could hardly have found him brutal or cruel. (Many would enlist with him again between 1879 and 1884.) Kirk's report would be confidential, and so Stanley never had an opportunity to defend himself against the accusation that his expedition had been 'a disgrace to humanity'.[37] Six weeks later Queen Victoria was writing in her diary that Stanley was cruel to Africans and had kept female slaves – making it clear just how widely Kirk's lies were circulated within the British establishment. The consul's report would ensure that Stanley was received by no government minister or senior civil servant, and that the nearest he came to court was when the Prince of Wales attended two of his lectures and spoke to him at a banquet.[38]

It is therefore intensely ironic that during the opening months of 1878, when Stanley was being pilloried as a monster – angrily in liberal periodicals, and sotto voce in official circles – his greatest ambition was to obtain British government help in making David Livingstone's grand plan for Africa come true. After his betrayal by Alice, it kept Stanley sane to dream of transforming Africa and destroying the slave trade along the lines David Livingstone had described to him in 1872. European trade and colonization, the doctor had explained, were the essential precursors to Christian conversions and 'civilization' in Africa. Henry had been impressed by Livingstone's account of his attempt to open up the Zambezi River as a 'highway' along which settlers, traders and missionaries could embark in steamers and travel rapidly through the fever-ridden deltas into the healthier interior. There they could sell to African chiefs – in exchange for local products such as palm oil, ivory and copal – the beads, guns and European cloth the chiefs coveted. Hitherto, their only way to obtain these things had been by selling their own people to Portuguese and Arab slave traders.[39] Livingstone's secret hope had been that the arrival of traders and missionaries would one day 'result in an English [sic] colony in the heart of central Africa'.[40]

In conscious emulation of Livingstone, Stanley, in his first newspaper despatch from Kabinda on the coast, had urged traders and missionaries to come to West Central Africa and expressed his hope that 'the English [sic] especially' would grasp the commercial opportunity which the Congo, 'that great highway of commerce to broad Africa', now held out.[41] Weeks later, he was more explicit:

I feel convinced that the Congo question will become a political question in time. As yet, however, no European power seems to have the right of control. Portugal claims it because she discovered its mouth; but the great powers – England [sic], America and France – refuse to recognize her right ... The question is: What Power shall be deputed in the name of humanity to protect the youth of commerce in this little known world? ... [unless] England arranges at once with Portugal to proclaim sovereignty over the Congo River.[42]

Yet despite such insistence on the need for 'English' involvement, it was Livingstone's longing to help Africa and Africans that had inspired Stanley, rather than the jingoistic potential of the doctor's colonial ideas. It delighted him to learn that within weeks of his appeal for missionaries appearing in the Daily Telegraph in 1875, £24,000 had been raised, and within a year of his putting pen to paper the first British missionaries had been on their way to Uganda. Henry had written in his final Congo diary in 1877 'I hate evil and love good', and a few pages later had expressed his fervent hope that the Congo would become 'a torch to those who sought to do good': 'I wish I could give utterance to a hundredth part of the noble thoughts I had in Africa.' Just as Livingstone had enjoyed imagining Glaswegian paupers prospering as farmers in Africa, Henry thought that Britain's 'outcast children' (such as he had once been) should be trained in colonial schools as future African settlers.[43]

In mid-January 1878, on his way back to London, Stanley had broken his journey at Marseilles to address the local geographical society. He had been surprised to be greeted on the railway platform by two men sent by King Leopold II of Belgium to secure his services for an African project, apparently close to the heart of the forty-three-year-old monarch. These two diplomats were Baron Jules Greindl, the Belgian ambassador in Madrid, and Henry Shelton Sanford, a Florida landowner and former US consul in Brussels, who now collaborated with the king on various business ventures. Keenly aware of Belgium's size and lack of influence, for almost twenty years Leopold had longed to acquire a colony. Aged twenty-seven he had visited Madrid, not for pleasure, but with the intention of 'going through the Indies archives and calculating the profit which Spain made then and makes now out of her colonies'.[44] Since then he had scanned the world for possible colonial openings in countries as distant as Formosa, Fiji and Sarawak. In January 1876, Leopold had been electrified to read in the London *Times* that a British explorer, Lieutenant V. L. Cameron, RN, had crossed central Africa and had declared it to be 'a country of unspeakable richness', containing an abundance of coal, iron, gold and silver.[45] Overjoyed to believe that in the Congo he had found the perfect money-making colony, Leopold lost no time in visiting the Foreign Office in London, and was vastly relieved to find that Britain had no interest in the Congo basin.[46]

In September 1876, when Stanley had still been marching towards the Lualaba, Leopold hosted and supervised an international Geographical Conference in Brussels, at which he launched what he himself described as 'a crusade' to 'open to civilization the only part of our globe where it has yet to penetrate.'[47] His ostensible plan was to orchestrate a wide-ranging international project with operational bases at Zanzibar and at the mouth of the Congo, and medical and scientific stations in the interior, from which the slave trade could be observed and ultimately destroyed.[48] The International African Association (the AIA, from its initials in French) was formed at the conference. After Leopold had been voted its president and an international committee and a number of national committees had been set up, it seemed destined to be an impressively broad-based body. In reality, Leopold planned to use this innocuous-seeming international structure as a smokescreen behind which he could pursue his own commercial plans. Much faster even than Leopold had dared hope, the international components of the AIA fell away, leaving behind a four-man executive and the Belgian national committee, both controlled by the king himself.[49] Leopold expressed his real purpose in a letter to his ambassador in London, with astonishing frankness and cynicism: 'I do not want to miss the opportunity of our obtaining a share in this magnificent African cake.'[50]

As the king was penning this letter, Stanley was taking the Wangwana home, having focused the world's attention on the Congo. To Baron Solvyns, his minister in London, Leopold explained exactly what he wanted from 'this able and enterprising American'.

I believe [wrote Leopold] that if I commission Stanley to take possession in my name of any given place in Africa, the English would stop me ... I am therefore thinking in terms of entrusting Stanley with a purely exploratory mission which will offend no one and will provide us with some posts down in that region, staffed and equipped, and with a high command for them which we can develop when Europe and Africa have got used to our 'pretensions' on the Congo.[51]

Of course, Greindl let slip none of this to Stanley. Nor did Henry Sanford. Though Stanley later pretended that he had dismissed the king's emissaries almost at once – telling them that for months to come he would be too 'sick and weary' to consider returning to Africa – in fact he had met Henry Sanford the very next day, and spent six hours with him.[52] During this meeting, Stanley learned that the king wanted him to return to the Congo, under the auspices of the AIA, to set up posts, build roads, and pave the way for later commercial developments.[53] At this date, Stanley had had no idea that the king wanted a colony, let alone one that would be his personal fief. Since Henry planned to ask the British government to send him back to the Congo in the interest of international trade, Leopold's project had sounded like a perfectly acceptable *faute de mieux* alternative. So, in case he were to fail in London, Stanley had hinted strongly to the two men that it was just possible that 'six months hence' he might 'view things differently'.[54]

Within days of arriving in England, Stanley had begun a series of meetings with establishment figures, hoping to gain a hearing from government ministers. Earl Granville, the former foreign secretary, currently without a seat in the cabinet, was sympathetic but held out little hope. At three receptions Stanley talked with the Prince of Wales; he also dined with General Sir Garnet Wolseley, the future commander-in-chief, had meetings with Baroness Burdett-Coutts, the patron of numerous missionary societies, and discussed his plans with William MacKinnon, the owner of the Imperial British India Steamship Navigation Company, who wanted to invest in Africa for altruistic, as well as commercial reasons.[55] But none of this talking led to an invitation to brief ministers. After his epic journey, it seemed a personal slight that he was not invited to meet the foreign secretary.

Meanwhile the prime minister, Benjamin Disraeli (recently ennobled as Lord Beaconsfield), was facing a grave foreign crisis. In the wake of the massacre of Bulgarian Christians, Russian forces had reached Constantinople after eight months of fighting, threatening to bring an imminent Turkish collapse, and with it an abrupt end to the European balance of power. So in the very month of Stanley's return to England, Lord Beaconsfield sent the British Fleet to the Dardanelles and was on the point of declaring war. And sadly for Henry, there were other pressing reasons why the cabinet was in no mood for colonial advances in Africa. In Egypt, the Khedive's government was bankrupt, and Britain and France had been obliged to assume control in order to protect the Suez Canal. In the Transvaal, too, the cabinet expected imminent difficulties. The timing of Stanley's pleas for the Congo basin could scarcely have been worse. In any case, just at this crucial time John Kirk's vitriolic report damaged him in official quarters. After reading it, Queen Victoria wrote to warn her cousin Leopold that he should be very careful about employing a brutal man like Stanley. Lord Beaconsfield gave him a similar warning.[56] But the King of the Belgians was not going to be put off, now that he believed he had found the perfect man to create for him his long desired African colony.

SIXTEEN

A Colony for a King

To have solved almost all the greatest geographical questions connected with central Africa in a single journey posed an insoluble problem for the thirty-six-year-old Stanley. Unless he were to transfer his future operations to the arctic and polar regions, the planet had no comparable challenges left to offer. Yet he genuinely felt that doing something beneficial for the areas he had discovered was a perfectly worthwhile way to spend the rest of his life. Bearing in mind his extraordinary talent for exploration, there is, even so, something rather sad about the world's greatest explorer, with his transatlantic dislike of English snobbery and formality (mocked by him as 'full dress, sword and knickerbockers'), donning evening dress every night and telling audiences in the town halls, theatres and winter gardens of thirty towns and cities to urge the British government to recognize the Congo's potential and get involved.[1]

For the first time, Britain's manufacturers were feeling the heat of international competition, so what they needed (as these audiences were surprised to be told by a man with an American accent) was 'a second India' to absorb the cloth of Lancashire's mills and the hardware of Sheffield's and Birmingham's factories. And thanks to his discoveries along the Congo, this diminutive 'American' told them, British traders could steam right up this great river and make contact with a population of 43,000,000 people ready and eager to pay for manufactured goods with Africa's fabulous raw materials.[2] Though unaware that his population figure was massively exaggerated, Henry's audiences knew very well from his recently published *Through the Dark Continent* that the Congo contained not just useful raw materials but impassable cataracts, tropical diseases and cannibals.

Wherever Stanley spoke, Kadu, Mutesa's page, sat beside him. A manager at an electro-plating works in Birmingham recalled the explorer's kindly way of explaining everything to the boy in Swahili, and was surprised to find Stanley 'a much less bouncing person than is generally thought – rather quiet and reserved in fact, & his regard for Livingstone is pathetically filial'.[3] Indeed, at this time Livingstone was frequently in Stanley's thoughts – most often in connection with the expedition he had taken to the Zambezi in 1858, equipped with steamers, a prefabricated trading station, and scientists to assess the Zambezi basin's mineral and agricultural potential. It was now Stanley's dream that the British government might send him on a similar venture to the Congo. But – as he must have known – Britain would never back 'an American' against a native-born Briton. So why could he still not bring himself to admit that he was British?

The perfect chance for doing this had presented itself shortly after his return, when he had been berated for carrying the Union Jack on his travels.[4] Yet instead of claiming it as his own, he had resorted to fiction, saying that the conveniently dead Pococks had persuaded him to let them carry their nation's flag. Yet despite feeling in his heart 'as much British as my Lord Mayor of London', he believed that by taking the American oath of allegiance during the Civil War, he had given up his British nationality, and now feared exposing himself to the risks and disclosures involved in the bureaucratic process of naturalization.[5] So many problems could embarrass him: his assumption of another man's name, with no evidence to support an adoption; his illegitimacy and real name of Rowlands; his mother's unscrupulous use of an admission of British birth to elbow her family's way into his life again; and to cap it all, his desertion from both the US army and navy. Since Home Office inquiries might reveal all of this, he imagined he had no choice but to remain American, to the great detriment of his attempts to sell Africa to his true fellow countrymen. It was like a terrifying cautionary tale about the dangers of lying – and no less tragic for all that.

In October 1878, four months after first meeting King Leopold II, Stanley reluctantly accepted that the Belgian monarch was the only person likely to send him back to Africa. Yet even after agreeing on 3 October to serve Leopold for five years, the explorer went on trying, throughout November and December, to persuade 'Englishmen ... that some day they would regret not taking action [over the Congo]'. And Stanley made these efforts despite being warned by the king's contact man, Baron Greindl, 'to say nothing to incite [British] people to under-take something on the Congo'. So the picture of Stanley, the work-house boy, being easily and rapidly seduced by the wiles and wealth of the sinister Belgian monarch has no basis in fact.[6]

Nor in 1878 did Henry have any means of knowing what the king's real intentions were. Certainly, no royal servant was going to be rash enough to tell him that Leopold wanted to own the Congo basin as his private possession. Instead, Henry had every reason to admire the king. At this date even the secretary of the Aborigines' Protection Soci-ety thought well of Leopold's 'crusade' to open Africa to commerce and to extinguish the slave trade, which he had announced at the Brus-sels Geographical Conference. The fact that Leopold seemed ready to spend his own money on what Ferdinand de Lesseps – the builder of the Suez Canal – called 'the most humanitarian work of this century' gave the king chivalric status throughout Europe.[7] Even Auguste Lam-bermont, secretary-general of the Belgian Ministry of Foreign Affairs, believed that Leopold was 'not thinking about procuring a colony ...'.[8] So Stanley, the outsider, could hardly have known better. Nor did it worry him when he received letters from Baron Greindl advising him

King Leopold II of Belgium

to keep quiet about going to Africa as the king's employee.[9] After all, France and Portugal might imagine their own African interests threatened by the king's philanthropic plans.

Stanley first met the king in Brussels on 10 June 1878, having been brought from the railway station in central Brussels to his palace at Laeken, outside the city, in a royal carriage.[10] Henry was not overwhelmed by the king's grandeur, despite finding Leopold a 'charming' and impressive figure with his 'fine brown beard' and enviable height of six feet five inches.[11] He was dismayed to find that the king did not believe, as he did, that building a railway from Matadi to Stanley Pool should be given priority.[12] When Leopold spoke of wanting to establish a series of posts linking East Africa with the Upper Congo, Stanley countered that it was much more important to build trading stations on the Congo and a railway by-passing the cataracts. To date, three AIA expeditions to East Africa, all inspired by the king, had resulted in the foundation of a single small station on Lake Tanganyika at the cost of many lives.[13]

Far from being overawed, Stanley fought his corner, and by mid-November 1878 had managed to persuade Leopold to concentrate on the Congo.[14] In this month Henry finally signed a five-year contract with the Belgian king, having at last accepted that the British government would never back him. His salary would be £1,000 per annum – by no means large – with £20,000 available for the expedition itself for the first year, and £8,000 annually thereafter. Henry was not to be allowed to lecture or to publish anything without the king's permission, so his annual income was going to be less than when he had been a journalist and author. It has been claimed that Stanley was in fact paid £2,000 per year and received two years' pay in advance, but the evidence for this is flimsy.[15]

To finance Stanley's expedition and associated developments, Leopold set up a syndicate with a capital of 1,000,000 francs, and a committee to run it – the Comité d'Etudes du Haut Congo. Its objective was defined by Leopold as the establishment of stations for scientific, philanthropic and commercial purposes on the Congo. A sum of 40,000 francs was voted for the expedition's first steam launch, with further vessels being promised for a later date.[16] Apart from the king, subscribers included James Hutton, the head of a Manchester firm trading in West Africa, William MacKinnon, Stanley's shipping millionaire friend, and, a little later, Baroness Burdett-Coutts. Stanley had encouraged these British subscribers to invest, hoping that they might ultimately build up a majority shareholding and win control of the syndicate. Although the king and a Dutch company, the Africaansche Handelsvereeniging, held most of the shares, the religious MacKinnon and the philanthropic Burdett-Coutts were confident that Leopold's scheme would benefit the Congolese by giving them 'legitimate' commerce. None of these investors seemed alarmed that a philanthropic body had now acquired the powers of a commercial undertaking. After all, why shouldn't philanthropy on such an epic scale reduce its costs to some extent?

On 10 December Henry signed a three-year contract with the Comité, independent of his five-year contract with the king.[17] At this point the Dutch company – the largest investor, apart from Leopold – went bankrupt. This did not worry the king, who promptly proposed a new scheme to his fellow subscribers. They would not be asked for more money since he would provide the new capital, but he would only do this on condition that the Comité was dissolved and he took control of the entire enterprise. The other subscribers accepted their reduced role with a good grace, because Leopold had taken on all the risk of the venture.[18] Nobody told Stanley that the Comité had ceased to exist – quite the contrary, since the compliant Colonel Maximilien Strauch, the new secretary-general of the AIA, usually wrote to Henry as if from the defunct Comité. The king soon named its successor organization as the International Association of the Congo, the AIC – a name deliberately chosen so people would confuse it with the AIA, the original, genuinely multi-national league of philanthropists and geographers created at the Brussels Conference.[19] In the meantime, Stanley was told by Henry Sanford – the king's American friend and occasional business partner – that Leopold meant to 'bring back the expedition to the purely philanthropic character [Stanley] had suggested at the outset'.[20]

When these devious corporate developments took place, Stanley was at the mouth of the Congo, about to start his expedition and in no position to find out whether the Comité, the AIC and the AIA were fictions concealing Leopold's control of everything. Yet busy though he was, he had noticed *something* suspicious. As he steamed through the muddy green water of the great river's estuary and gazed at the reddish cliffs of the continent where he might shortly die, he wrote in his diary:

The King is a clever statesman – he is supremely clever but I have not had thirty opportunities of conversing with him without penetrating his motives. I am supposed to be an American, and he has been more open than he would have been had I appeared as a British subject. Still he has not been as frank as to tell me outright what we are to strive for. Nevertheless it has become pretty evident that under the guise of an International Association he hopes to make a Belgian dependency of the Congo basin.[21]

The idea that Leopold might hope to own the Congo as his own private possession had not entered Henry's head. A few months later he would remind Colonel Strauch, the king's mouthpiece, 'we are here charged to perform a task which I believe is a sacred one'.[22] That Stanley was returning to Africa with an almost Livingstonian sense of mission is clear from a letter he wrote to Henry Sanford: 'I propose to do my best to open up the valley of the mighty African river to the world's commerce or die in the attempt.' If anyone had told him at that moment that, far from wanting the Congo to be open to the competition of 'the world's commerce', the king meant to (and actually one day *would*) close it to free trade and set up a royal monopoly over the entire basin, Stanley would have resigned rather than risk his life in such a cause.[23]

Henry was inclined to think that even if Leopold did have colonial ambitions, they were unlikely to be realized. In Strauch's office he had seen a map of the Congo on the wall with the proposed stations marked in red. Any visitor could see this. 'The Belgians strike me as being a peculiarly innocent people,' Stanley commented. The Dutch and the Portuguese would not stand idly by if they thought Leopold's real purpose was to take away their trade.[24] The cruel fact was that Belgium was a small country, which was likely, in the end, to be forced out by other nations. So, whatever plans Leopold might have in mind, Stanley believed that he himself could still succeed in his personal 'mission of sowing along the Congo's banks civilized settlements'. If the king were to be elbowed out by more powerful nations, Henry's great hope was that Britain might still pick up the pieces. But for the present, he was happy to serve his royal master. Meanwhile, Henry was indispensable to Leopold. 'We must equip Stanley from top to toe,' the king told Colonel Strauch, 'and give him staff and supplies in abundance, otherwise we are lost.'[25]

To be returning to a camp-fire existence, far from civilization, did not dismay Stanley, despite its dangers. In England, his loveless social life had mainly consisted of meetings with geographers, journalists, businessmen and politicians. And even in Paris, where his admiring friend Edward King and other Americans had founded the Stanley Club, to give their hero a banquet every time he visited, Henry had been moody and lethargic. So in August 1879, steaming up the Congo with his small flotilla of boats, he felt no nostalgia for what he called 'the vanities of life *à la mode*'. Instead, he wrote: 'I am devoured with a wish to set foot upon terra-firma once more and begin my duties.'[26]

His sense of purpose was buttressed by the presence of his recently arrived Wangwana followers – his African family. In March he had visited Zanzibar and shipped sixty-one of them to West Africa, with eight more to follow. These men included Uledi – 'my own dear, brave & faithful Uledi', and Susi, Livingstone's longest-serving companion, who had led the party to the coast bearing the doctor's body in 1873. Wadi Rehani, Stanley's incomparable storekeeper, had volunteered, as well as Soudi – a miraculous survivor of the cataracts and of the battle against the Wanyaturu. The young Mabruki Ndogo, a favourite gun-bearer, was another volunteer. About three-quarters of the others had served in one or other of his expeditions, and a significant number had served in both – a fact eloquently rebutting Kirk's charge that Stanley had been brutal to them.[27] Stanley made signing his contract with Leopold dependent on the king's promise to set aside £2,800 for shipping the Wangwana home at the end of their period of service.[28]

They sailed for the Congo in the steamship *Albion*, under the eye of Anthony Bannister Swinburne, the Christ's Hospital boy whom Stanley had taken to the Gold Coast in 1874, and who was twenty-one now.[29] Swinburne had engineered his employment on the Congo by writing a fan letter to Stanley after his trans-Africa triumph and Henry had been unable to resist the youth's humble admiration.[30] At first as his secretary, and later as a station chief, Anthony would be one of the very few whites to be close to Stanley on this station-building expedition.

Another highly valued assistant was a remarkable Somali youth, Qualla Idris, who had boarded Stanley's ship at Aden in search of a job, when Stanley had been en route to Zanzibar. Qualla – more often known as Dualla – was the son of Aden's chief of police and had recently been a cabin boy on an American ship, and then coachman to a Brooklyn businessman. He spoke English, Swahili and two other East African dialects, and Stanley had sensed on meeting him that he possessed extraordinary charm and would prove 'a valuable acquisition to me in my dealings with chiefs'.[31] Two robust Danish seamen in their twenties – not unlike the Pococks – also found favour. They were Albert Christophersen, a particular favourite, and Martin Martinsen.

From the start Stanley needed, as well as his few favourites, a dozen more whites to man and maintain his launches and occupy his trading stations when built. These included three Belgian ships' engineers, who complained constantly about their wages and resigned within a couple of months.[32] An English replacement engineer died of fever, but an Italian, Francesco Flamini, survived to win everyone's admiration. Engineers were vital for the maintenance of the expedition's four steam launches.[33]

The expedition's dependable chief of stores, the American Augustus Sparhawk, had first met Stanley in 1871 on Zanzibar, where he had worked for a Boston trading firm. His juniors, two Englishmen – J. Kirkbright and A. H. Moore – failed to acclimatize, one dying and the other resigning. From the beginning Stanley warned the elegantly moustachioed Colonel Strauch that his present workforce of 124 (69 Wangwana and the rest West Africans engaged at the coast) was only half of what he needed for his road and station-building.

On 21 August 1879, Stanley's steamers began the 110-mile journey up the wide, brown river, between 'dark walls of mangrove intermixed with palm fronds'. This first phase would take them almost to the Yellala Falls, and the start of the chain of rapids that stretched to Stanley Pool. At Boma the following day, Stanley described its history as 'two centuries of pitiless persecution of black men by sordid whites'. Henry developed a keen dislike of Portuguese traders, and wanted his first station 'to be as far as possible from the wretched rum drinkers & rum sellers of the Lower Congo'.[34] To do anything else would be 'to invite debauchery & vile orgies which I cannot calmly contemplate as possible in any place under my command'.[35]

Stanley aimed to find a place on the river just below the start of the falls, where he would build his first station and start his road to the Pool. On 26 September, not far from Yellala, Stanley was delighted to encounter Chief Dedede of Nsanda, who had befriended him in 1877 on his way to Boma. Dedede now recommended a place called Vivi, and persuaded local chiefs to let Stanley build there. Though this site had the advantage of being at the highest point of navigation on the Lower Congo, its landing place was only 300 yards long, and the elevated plateau, on which the settlement would have to be built, was narrower than Stanley would have liked.

Now some sort of treaty, or lease, would have to be agreed with the chiefs. In his book about the expedition, Stanley would exaggerate the number and scope of treaties he signed between 1879 and 1884, leaving himself open to claims by historians that he had bought from uncomprehending African rulers all their land for a few trifling bits of cloth, effectively stealing their country for Leopold's benefit.[36] This is a travesty of the truth. [For the full facts, see Chapter Nineteen.]

In late September 1879, when Stanley made his agreement with the five chiefs of Vivi, he acted as he thought morally right, and asked no more than that they 'cede to us the right of locating ourselves in any part of their country, making roads etc. for the sum of about £15 a year'. As a one-off payment, he handed over fifty pieces of cloth, three boxes of gin, five military coats, five knives, five cloth waist belts and five ample loincloths of superior quality. He also threw in with the annual £15 rent, 'a monthly royalty of £2 worth of cloth', which he described as purchasing 'the privilege of residence', plainly believing he was the chiefs' tenant, and that they had retained ownership of their land, even in places where he meant to build. Elsewhere he would refer to this payment as 'a rental'.[37] Nor did Stanley suddenly change his good practice. From the beginning of his time on the Congo to the end, he tried to look after the interests of the indigenous inhabitants. Even before his arrival, he had told Strauch that treaties had to be made 'with tact & generosity & by exercising large forbearance ... Such privileges as they grant must be paid for.' Everything would depend upon the chiefs' feeling 'that it is for their own interests to conform to what we wish'.[38]

On Vivi plateau, as the hard-working Wangwana 'saluted the dawn of a new era with the inspiring sound of striking picks, ringing hoes ... and dull thudding of sledgehammers', Stanley believed that, by making it possible for missionaries and traders to come, he was working for the benefit of the local Africans and ultimately the whole region.[39] He sometimes joined the Wangwana and worked with a sledgehammer, breaking up large rocks that could then be beaten into the earth as part of the foundations of the road leading out of the settlement towards Stanley Pool.

The image of Stanley as a hard and unrelenting man would owe something to a light-hearted incident at this time. Nsakala, a local sub-chief, who had been watching him work, cried out, 'Oh that is the way to break rocks,' using the native term Bula Matari, a striker or breaker of rocks. 'Aye fellows, that is a good name ...' Nsakala had a reputation as a humorist, but the name he had coined spontaneously spread from market to market and was soon 'in general use' over a wide region. Stanley reported this fact, not without pride, in his book about the Congo, and his critics saw it as further evidence that he was not just a breaker of rocks but of men too – the ideal conquistador. His self-designed, and unintentionally comical 'Stanley Cap' dates from this period, and with its tall crown, numerous ventilation holes, cloth 'havelock' to shield the neck, and its military peak and leather band, it seems almost to have been intended to make its unsmiling, moustachioed wearer appear worthy of the name Bula Matari – in short, the ideal disguise for a sensitive and wounded man who wished to seem invulnerable.[40]

Wearing his 'Stanley Cap' in 1885

One senses a frustrated homemaker in the attention the thirty-nine-year-old Stanley gave to every detail of Vivi's construction. Determined that the place should not remain bleak, he supervised the moving of 2,000 tons of alluvial soil up onto the rocky plateau to make gardens. He then planted them with mangos and orange trees and numerous vegetables. The first house he built at Vivi was a two-storey chalet with a veranda. This was for the station chief, Augustus Sparhawk. Other houses for European and African workers followed, as did storehouses and poultry sheds. Because it loomed high above the river, Stanley described Vivi as 'our Acropolis'; this hyperbole does not conceal the delight he took when it was completed four months later.[41] He reported to Colonel Strauch that all the houses were 'ornamented sufficiently to suit a modern taste'. The paths were raked, the 'flower mounds, vegetable beds and grass plots' weeded, and all the trade goods for selling to the local Africans safely stored. These included muskets, cutlery, tableware, tin plates, tin trays, fish hooks, hoes, hatchets, fancy boxes, second-hand military caps and uniforms, lackey coats, straw hats, jack-in-the-box and monkey-trick toys, Tyrolese hats, velvet smoking caps, brassware, and umbrellas – all of which were soon on sale to those able to pay with ground nuts, palm oil, ivory, kola nuts and so forth.

But if laying out and stocking Vivi had been pleasurable, the job ahead was not.

It is going to be a tedious task ... and a protracted one to make a road fifty-two miles long [this was to Isangila, the next station, rather than to his final destination, Stanley Pool, 235 miles away] then to come back and transport a boat, which may be moved only a mile a day perhaps, then to come back, hauling the heavy waggon with us to transport another heavy launch and move on a mile a day again, then back for another heavy launch, and repeat the same operation for three boilers three times ... total 936 miles before we can embark for our second station.

To carry out this back-breaking work, Stanley only had '130 efficient working men', many of whom were needed for road-making; those dragging the 3.5-ton *Royal* scarcely weighed as much all together as the vessel.[42] This nightmare of getting steamships onto the Upper Congo above the cataracts, and taking up all the materials for his next station too, was a crushing physical ordeal, made harder by the heat, the rains, and the prevalence of fatal diseases.

Though Henry cherished his labourers, he was said to be harsh to his white colleagues by some of them. His favourite Dane, Albert Christophersen, wrote home saying that Stanley sometimes refused to let gravely sick whites go home; and there was some truth in this. As

A steamer on the Upper Congo

officers in the Great War would one day have to do, Stanley had to decide in each case whether a man was genuinely sick, or simply afraid of dying. If truly sick:

I should not hesitate a moment to let them go ... Personally I do not think I am severe, that is a term which stands for mere firmness with some people. But it requires some firmness to manage such a motley following as I have ... When employer and employee are down with fever, someone must be more magnanimous ... The Zanzibaris are extremely contented, but I know they could be fired into desperate revolt if there was any severity.[43]

By October 1880, a year after work had started on Vivi, four Europeans had died, the same number had gone home, one Wangwana had died, and a shocking twenty-five of the coastal Liberian Krumen were dead. These deaths and illnesses grieved Stanley, though he still tried to get the 'funky Europeans' to be brave. The English storekeeper, John Kirkbright, was often ill and begged to go home. Henry implored him not to 'blame Africa – she is cruel and wild and demands the best of man's parts to enjoy her, but once a man has conquered himself – Africa has as much loveliness as another continent. The fault lies in the man ...' Kirkbright stayed, but six months later he was dead.[44] Even Martin Martinsen, one of the two hardworking Danes, succumbed that summer. Stanley abandoned all work for a day to nurse him. But he still died, 'to the undoubted grief of everyone in camp'. Despite his sorrow, Stanley's general attitude remained stoical. 'Death will over-take the strongest of us all some day, but in the meantime ... be firm and manly and leave Death to strike us when Fate ordains.'[45]

Meanwhile, the struggle to blast away rocks and lay down a decent road surface went on at a rate of a hundred yards a day. Swinburne, who was part of the tight-knit group that Stanley always kept close to him, cut his leg badly with an adze while 'encouraging our West Coast Natives into a little bit more life and animation'. The wound was soon oozing with tropical ulcers, and Anthony had to be sent to recuperate on Madeira. Another European was lucky to escape being crushed to death when one of the ship's three-ton boilers broke free from a wag-gon.[46] The others whom, along with Swinburne, Stanley liked to keep near him were the Danish seaman, Albert, the Somali teenager, Dualla, the middle-aged Yao, Susi, whom Stanley had liked ever since meeting him with Livingstone, and two trans-Africa veterans, Wadi Rehani and Mabruki Ndogo.

The fact that Stanley preferred the company of his 'Dark Compan-ions' to that of most Europeans was deeply resented by the Belgian officers who came out to the Congo in the summer of 1880.[47] Of these first four arrivals, Lieutenant Louis Valcke proved hard-working and capable, but Lieutenant Carlos Branconnier typified for Stanley unde-sirable traits common to many Belgian officers: a tendency to be bru-tal to Africans, and to feel above dirtying their hands and doing the exhausting, practical pioneering work required.[48] This same disincli-nation to work in the torrid heat would lead Stanley to criticize many other Belgians sent out to him in future – most of them possessing 'a fastidious stomach' and each requiring 'a servant to wait on him, a boy to carry his rifle, his haversack, water-bottle & ammunition, three men to carry his portmanteau & trunks, two men to carry his tent, one to carry his cooking utensils, one man to carry his provisions, & one to carry his ammunition and utensils'.[49] What Stanley really needed, he told Strauch, were more 'black men and mechaniciens [engineers]', not officers with 'their never ceasing demands for luxuries and medicine'.[50]

Stanley and his men began to build their second station at Isangila on 18 March 1880, nine days after the arrival of an infuriating letter from Colonel Strauch, warning Stanley most urgently that the Italian-born French naval officer Pierre Savorgnan de Brazza might be about to open a viable route from the coast to Stanley Pool and the Upper Congo, avoiding the cataracts. In 1875, de Brazza had traced the Ogowé river to within 150 miles of Stanley Pool, and was now on the Ogowé once again, possibly with French government backing, hoping to claim Stanley Pool for France and thus establish control over the Upper Congo before Stanley could do so. All that was needed, Strauch told Henry, was for de Brazza to reach the Pool ahead of him, and all would be lost. Since it was three years since he had first reached this Pool that bore his name, Stanley was appalled to be told that de Brazza was acting as if some kind of 'race' were in progress. He wrote testily in his diary: 'Unless there is some other object in view, it would be ridiculous in me to arrest the work here for the purpose of racing to Stanley Pool & saying I was there twice before de Brazza.' Stanley's belief that he ought to keep on with his road-building was unshaken, even when Strauch told him flatly: 'We hope that in the event of his coming down the Almina, he will already find you settled at its junction with the Congo, and in the most favourable site for the establishment of a great station.'

It was horribly frustrating for Henry to find how little understanding Strauch and Leopold had of the distances involved and the logistical problems he faced already. And supposing he were to deplete his force, abandon the road, and the half-built Isangila Station, and rush to the Upper Congo in the hope of reaching the mouth of the Almina first – what good would it do? 'I might secure a hundred sites on the north bank of the Congo but de Brazza, if he had any gumption could easily intrude himself between many of these sites ... The moment we retreated from a post for want of supplies it would be snapped up.' Stanley therefore saw no alternative, unless he received a direct order to the contrary, but to go on building the road and bringing up his steam launches after him.[51] An order came, early in October, 'to proceed to Stanley Pool and obtain concessions from the natives', but Stanley still continued his existing work.

On 7 November, he was in camp close to the new station already under construction at Isangila, having built three bridges, filled numerous gorges with rocks and earth, and completed about forty miles of road. One of his young servants, Lutete Kuna, burst into his tent as he sat reading after his Sunday breakfast. The excited youth handed him a page torn from a notebook, on which were written in pencil the words 'Le Comte Savorgnan de Brazza, Enseigne de Vaisseau'. Unlike Livingstone, who hated the competition of other explorers, Stanley at once welcomed de Brazza as 'a gallant fellow' who 'deserves every credit for a brave feat of exploration'. He had been equally friendly and generous spirited on meeting Linant de Bellefonds in Buganda. De Brazza had emerged on the Congo opposite the mouth of the Kwa, and on descending to Stanley Pool had spent three weeks on the lake's northern shore. He travelled with a small escort of Gabonese, and Senegalese blacks from Dakar, who had been trained as sailors there by the French navy. All twenty-four were armed with Winchester repeaters. One of them, Sergeant Malamine, had been left at the Pool by de Brazza, in command of eight other sailors, with orders to set up a small post at Mfwa.[52] What instructions he had given to his Senegalese sergeant, de Brazza kept to himself.

Pierre Savorgnan de Brazza

As the olive-skinned Italian-turned-Frenchman, in his tattered naval coat, described what he had done, Stanley was struck by 'a kind of rapture that came and went [across his face] with wonderful rapidity'.

Stanley's French was poor, as was de Brazza's English, yet enough came across to make Henry admire his rival. Two days later, after his vivacious visitor had left, he wrote: 'Genius is often distinguished by some eccentricity. De Brazza's is for ragged clothes, & going about the country without working boots.' They parted in a friendly manner, with Stanley handing de Brazza a letter of commendation to the chief of Vivi Station, and lending him his riding ass, and the services of two Wangwana guides.[53]

For Stanley, the next five months were taken up completing the station at Isangila and building another at Manyanga closer to the Pool, while simultaneously carrying on with the road and dragging the steamers *Royal* and *En Avant* ever closer to the point where they could be relaunched on the Congo. But on 27 February 1881, travelling between Isangila and Manyanga, Henry met two Baptist missionaries, W. Holman Bentley and a Mr Crudington, and heard some disturbing news from them. In early October 1880, only a month before meeting Stanley, de Brazza had signed a treaty with the paramount chief, Makoko, on the northern shores of the Pool, and was now claiming that territory for France. Since de Brazza had told Henry that he had been sent to West Africa by the French branch of the AIA, not as 'an agent of the French government', Stanley felt thoroughly disillusioned. Clearly Sergeant Malamine and his men, with their 'magazine Winchester 15 shooters', had been left behind to support a territorial claim.

But what the two missionaries told Henry was not all bad. They had been ferried by the Senegalese sergeant to the south side of the Pool, where they had been met at Kinshasa by a man claiming to be chief over the whole region. His name was Ngaliema, Chief of Kintamo, and he had made sure that the Baptists and their French escort were met 'by a furious multitude', making them fear for their lives until they all escaped in their canoes.[54] Although Stanley knew it would be very hard to win over Ngaliema and other chiefs living to the south of the Pool, he at least knew that de Brazza had made no headway there. Stanley had one advantage – or thought he did. He had become Ngaliema's blood brother on his journey down the Congo in 1877. But before he could seek out his 'brother', Stanley had a close encounter with a more formidable adversary.

During the first few days of May 1881, Henry fell ill. What at first seemed to be a mild fever forced him to bed on the 6th. By the 8th, he was suffering from an acute 'haematuric' attack, his urine being the colour of port wine. This steady loss of blood made him progressively weaker, and though he took doses of quinine as large as thirty grains, the fever did not abate. As he shivered and sweated alternately, a terrible ache started in the very centre of his head. Between the 13th and the 19th he was unaware of his surroundings. On the 20th he regained consciousness, and asked for sixty grains of quinine in a glass of Madeira. This was brought by Dualla, who with Mabruki Ndogo was nursing him round the clock. Shortly afterwards he had a strong premonition that he was going to die and asked Mabruki 'to call everybody up that I might bid them farewell. They lifted the tent walls and I saw my dear followers around. The whites nearest to me. What a joy it was to see Albert tall & straight before me.' Stanley asked him 'to come near & look at me & keep his eyes fixed until I could finish what I had to say'. In a barely audible voice he gasped, 'Farewell Zanzibaris, goodbye boys,' and then added a few words to favoured individuals. Afterwards, he sank back and just before losing consciousness again cried: 'I am saved.' A week later, he had the strength to sit up in bed.

On 1 June, after remarking that he had been 'at the very edge of the grave', he recalled a classic near-death experience: 'I am at the entrance of a very lengthy tunnel, and a light as of a twinkling star is seen an immeasurable length away. There is a sensible increase in the glow – the twinkling ceases, it has become an incandescent globe. It grows larger & it advances ... the light grows blinding.' He had come that close. At the start of his recovery he asked Dualla and Mabruki to carry him out of his tent in a hammock. He looked up 'at the great uplifted sky, so placid, starless, indifferently serene ... and from sheer weakness ... silently wept'. Only Dualla's and Mabruki's nursing, and their provision of beef tea, well-beaten eggs and an occasional thimbleful of fortified wine, had seen him through.[55]

Five days later, when he was still resting for most of the day, he received one of Colonel Strauch's most maddening letters. Leopold had received news of de Brazza's progress, and wanted Stanley to claim the entire Upper Congo for 'the Association'. He asked him to build four new stations above the Pool, and then more between Stanley Falls and Nyangwe. As Stanley noted dryly, 'Nyangwe is 1,300 miles above Stanley Pool. Not a few days journey.' Strauch was promising seventy more men, raising the total to 202, sixty-six of whom would be returning to Zanzibar within a year. Stanley calculated that the four stations up to Stanley Falls would take 260 men three years to create. Yet Strauch was asking for a date by which he would be 'sending goods via Vivi to Nyangwe'. But the *coup de grâce* for Stanley was that Leopold had heard de Brazza was purchasing tusks: 'I am therefore asked to collect as much ivory as I can.'[56]

This communication depressed Henry for weeks. He knew that de Brazza had been given sufficient means by the French government to engage 500 local men and buy fifty canoes, enabling him to purchase and transport his ivory. Stanley wrote back telling Strauch that he would buy ivory at the Pool at once if provided with goods for purchasing tusks and enough men to carry them. When Stanley told Strauch of his fear that Leopold's whole enterprise might become commercial and monopolistic, the king's factotum replied soothingly, emphasizing 'the philanthropic & international character of this enterprise', and that it was 'not for anyone's exclusive profit'. The purpose was 'to bring by degrees the savages of central Africa into the current of progress for the amelioration of their material and moral condition'.[57]

But in Strauch's very next letter, the king's monopolistic ambitions were blatantly expressed. He suggested that all Europeans using Stanley's road to the Upper Congo should pay a hefty toll. In order to be able to implement this, Stanley was told to gain from all chiefs 'a right of controlling the jurisdiction and a deliberative voice in all questions affecting the country'.[58] Henry rejected the protectionist tolls proposal angrily, as deserving 'universal condemnation and odium. You cannot fight Europeans by such a manner ... success is worthless without honour ... Our influence is steadily progressing in the country. No war has taken place since our arrival owing to my efforts.' The only guarantee of safe passage for 'our caravans' between Manyanga and the Pool was by being 'on good terms with the chiefs along the route'.

Stanley did not bother to respond to talk of chiefs granting to him 'a right of controlling their jurisdiction'.[59] Nevertheless, under all this pressure, and fearing that the French really might steal more territory around the Pool, Stanley formulated a new type of treaty giving 'Henry M. Stanley or his representative [not it, should be noted, the Comité or AIC] for an indefinite period ... the sole privilege of occupying, improving, or building upon any part of the river frontage extending along the River Congo' between two stated points. The only surviving example of this form of treaty was signed at Kintamba (Kintamo) on 31 December 1881 and secured a crucial half-mile stretch of the bank between the lower entrance of Stanley Pool and 'the first great cataract'. No claim to sovereignty was made, nor did it need to be, since what he wanted was a site for a trading station and an agreement denying the French the right to build at this strategically vital location. Stanley undertook 'not to disturb or molest any occupant of any portion of this land who may be residing on it at the date of this paper'.[60]

To exclude the French from building posts higher upriver, Henry knew he would have to do as Leopold wished and create new stations 'on the Upper Congo ... to prevent a repetition of the Stanley Pool affair'. Nor was he averse to Leopold's request to have the AIA's flag of gold star on a blue background float above all his stations. He believed that 'old Africa would benefit by this international competition, & civilization will come all the sooner through this rivalry'.[61] But though Leopold wrote to him at the end of 1881, asking him to 'place successively under the suzerainty of the Comité, as soon as possible, and without losing one minute, all the chiefs from the mouth of the Congo to the Stanley Falls', Stanley did not make suzerainty any part of the treaties he subsequently agreed on the Upper Congo.[62]

The reality Stanley faced on the ground was that if he failed to reach agreement with the chiefs south of the Pool — and above all with Ngaliema, the most important ivory middleman on the river — the Upper Congo would be lost to him, even before he started to build stations upriver. Thanks to the diplomatic skills of de Brazza's remarkable Sergeant Malamine, the French presence on the Pool's northern shores had been accepted not only by the paramount chief, Makoko of Mbe, but also by his many sub-chiefs. And Malamine had spread scare stories about Stanley and his men that led to rejection of all his overtures of friendship. Malamine had put it about everywhere that Stanley and his men were evil, and that unless a European arriving at the Jué river — the gateway to the northern shores of the Pool — was carrying a small tricolour, or a cockade of cock's feathers, he was not a friend and should be sent away. Henry met the fine-featured Malamine at this time and was impressed by how 'tactfully and subtly he acted on his master's instructions' when dealing with Africans. With two Gabonese sailors in French uniform following him everywhere, carrying the French flag, he seemed 'a host in himself'. But admiration did not stop Stanley deploring the lies Malamine had told local Africans about the intentions of 'Bula Matari', which had included killing and eating them.[63]

When Henry opened what he believed would be the most important negotiations of his life, he was relieved that Ngaliema remembered him from 1877 and still called him 'Tandley'. Despite possessing a fortune of £3,000 in ivory, Ngaliema, with his dandified coloured silks and polished brass arm-rings, demanded Lieutenant Branconnier's black Newfoundland dog, Flora, as well as Stanley's two best riding donkeys. In exchange, Stanley received a wand of office bound with brass wire. Henry hurried to give the chief jewellery, fancy clasps, brass neck chains, a crimson table cloth, fifteen patterned cloths and a japanned tin trunk. Most reluctantly, he allowed Dualla, at the chief's request, 'to go with him to see the town'. 'Dualla was loath to go, but we had no option ... Unless we smothered him with our gifts ... we could never get a foothold at Stanley Pool.' So Henry accepted the chief's promise that he would return with Dualla in three days.[64]

In early August, Stanley lavished more and more gifts on Ngaliema, but by mid-month he was still not sure of him, and so decided to send Lieutenant Valcke to Loanda to purchase £500 worth of high-quality goods.[65] In the meantime, Henry returned to the essential job of completing the road between Manyanga and the Pool, postponing his final attempt to overwhelm Ngaliema until after the Belgian officer returned with his purchases. But early in November, before Valcke could get back, Ngaliema expelled Susi and the small party of Wangwana, who, in Stanley's absence, had been living in his town at the chief's invitation. Susi was also ordered to take away 'Tandley's' gifts, since no white man was to be permitted to live in the town after all.

It might be supposed that the man who had chastised the islanders of Bumbireh would have lacked the patience to fathom the labyrinthine politics of Stanley Pool. But the circumstances were entirely different. Stanley did not feel that the lives of his followers were threatened, and therefore had no intention of shedding blood in a place that he hoped would one day be a peaceful centre for international trade. Within days he made a very significant discovery, which was that the Bazombo and Bakongo ivory traders – who came up the Congo from the coast to buy Ngaliema's ivory for resale to European trading houses at the mouth – had threatened to fight Ngaliema if he allowed the white man to build at his town. Stanley also learned that these traders had allies among Ngaliema's sub-chiefs. The great fear of all these people was that if white men came to live permanently at the Pool, they would promptly buy up all the ivory amassed by big middlemen such as Ngaliema, cutting out the poorer African traders like themselves.[66] So Ngaliema had turned against Stanley because he feared these adversaries.[67]

On 7 November, Stanley was lucky enough to meet Ngaliema's father-in-law, Chief Makoko of Lema (not to be confused with Makoko of Mbe, with whom de Brazza had signed his treaty), a diminutive and modest man, who nevertheless turned out to be the senior chief of the whole region. Makoko of Lema amazed Stanley with the news that Ngaliema was not a chief by birth, being a member of the Teké tribe from far upriver, whence he had fled as a youth after his family had been killed in a tribal war. Though he had made a great fortune as an ivory trader through cunning and determination, he had only built at Kintamo having gained the consent of the land's three owners – chiefs Makoko of Lema, Ngamberengy and Kimpallam-bala.[68] After telling Henry this very surprising history, Makoko declared that he and his fellow chiefs – who, it now appeared, owned the very river frontage Stanley was so desperate to occupy – would be happy for him to live with them. Overjoyed, Stanley asked Makoko 'to beat his *iwanda* or drum to announce to every man around that he had made friends with the white man and no man was to molest him'.[69] A few weeks later, Stanley leased from Makoko and the two other chiefs the vital stretch of waterfront, which had been his objective all along. It stretched for almost two miles along the southern shores of the Pool, from close to Kinshasa at its eastern limit to the first cataract at its western end. It also extended a couple of miles inland. Stanley negotiated the right to build and to occupy the ground for as long as he wished. The town of Leopoldville (modern Kinshasa) would one day spread around the trading station that he now began to construct.[70]

When news of Stanley's friendship with Makoko of Lema reached Ngaliema, he was horrified. If Stanley came to live with Makoko and was friendly with other local chiefs, Ngaliema realized, he himself would be isolated and would therefore gain nothing from the white man's presence. Henry described what happened next for Colonel Strauch – and it must be admitted that this amusing story sounds almost too good to be true.

'Next morning, prompt as tinder, Ngaliema mustered a hundred men and armed them and came towards me in hot haste, trying every chief by rewards and persuasions to assist him in driving the white man back that very day.' When Makoko refused to help him, all others followed suit, so Ngaliema arrived the following morning at Stanley's camp with only his own men. Luckily for Stanley, he heard in advance that Ngaliema's party was armed and 'ordered all his men to buckle on accoutrements, put guns in their huts under their beds – but all to spring into rank at the sound of the gong with guns in their hands'. Having explained the charade they were expected to act out, Stanley sat down in a chair with the collected plays of Shakespeare in his hands and the aforementioned gong beside him. His only visible attendants were Dualla and Mabruki Ndogo, who feigned great surprise when Ngaliema arrived with a sword in his hand. Ignoring this weapon and the guns of his followers, Henry welcomed his blood brother with broad smiles. Taken aback by Stanley's friendliness, Ngaliema hesitated, and then spotted the gong. Could Stanley beat the thing, asked the great ivory trader. He wished to hear its sound. Stanley refused, explaining that 'the sound of this gong will bring trouble; it is a bad thing'. But Ngaliema insisted, so Henry beat it, with the result that Wangwana leapt up from behind bushes and burst from their tents with guns in their hands, as if magically created by the sound. Ngaliema was scared out of his wits, and his men scurried away in terror.[71] Later, this story would be taken as proof that Stanley had forced treaties on chiefs by using pseudo-magical tricks.

It had taken Henry almost six months to gain his essential foothold on the Pool. The Baptist missionary T. J. Comber wrote that 'by dint of constant, daily exercise of his tact & influence over the people ... Mr Stanley has succeeded in planting his station at Stanley Pool without a fight', despite provocations from 'warlike savages who are very fond of fighting and can muster 3,000 guns'.[72] Yet in England stories were appearing in the press about Stanley's brutality to the Wangwana, based on canards published in the Portuguese *Journal of Loanda*, whose editor was forever looking for stories to discredit the expedition.[73] Ironically, at that very time, Henry wrote this tribute to the beauty of the Congolese:

Every age has a beauty of its own; infancy excites the parental interest ... youth is still more attractive for its elastic & easy motions ... The adults call up ideas of fleetness, vigour, strength ... The skin may be more velvety than velvet, smoother than satin, or coarse as canvas ... but its warm brown colour seems to suit the African atmosphere – the contour of the body is always graceful.

He was endlessly reproving the latest young Belgian military arrivals for their failure to appreciate the merits of either the locals or the Wangwana, all of whom Stanley thought 'superior in proportion to his wages to ten Europeans'.[74] Lieutenants Harou and Orban exasperated him for being unable to communicate with Africans and for their failure to appreciate 'the extraordinary gifts for commerce which these natives possess'.[75] But his greatest anger was reserved for Lieutenant Branconnier, who beat Mabruki Ndogo, and later 'punished him again unmercifully', obliging Stanley 'to notify him [Branconnier] that cruelty was not permissible'. Stanley would eventually get rid of Branconnier for his racism. Anthony Swinburne, on the other hand, kept Stanley's favour, despite occasional laziness, largely because, as chief of Kinshasa Station, he was loved by the local Africans.[76]

With Wadi Rehani and Susi in charge of building, Leopoldville Station was completed by early March, freeing Henry to build new stations on the Upper Congo before the French could do the same. On 19 April 1882, he headed upriver from Leopoldville in the *En Avant* paddle steamer with his favourites, Dualla and Albert Christophersen, and a recently arrived Belgian, Eugene Janssens. He also had forty-eight Wangwana with him – eighteen in the *En Avant*, and the rest being towed by the paddle steamer in a whaleboat and two canoes. As never before, Stanley was aware of the beauty of 'the great brown flood ... and dark green foliage, contrasting with the silver grey stems ... amid the verdure'. He loved 'the crimson glories of the travellers' tree', and found something haunting about 'the steady bright sunshine on the lonely untenanted woods', which stretched for scores of miles along both banks of the Congo. After a week of steady steaming they reached Mswata, sixty miles upstream from the Pool. Here Stanley negotiated with the local chief for a site that would be the expedition's fifth station.[77] In late May Henry was exploring the left, or Mfini, branch of the Kwa, a tributary of the Congo, when he knew from the 'deathly languor' oppressing him that he was about to suffer another attack of fever.[78]

By 2 June 1882 he was enduring the agonies of his third attack of haematuric fever. Realizing he would be lucky to survive without a period of recuperation in Europe, he ordered an immediate return to Vivi, where he arrived five weeks later, still dangerously ill. His passage downstream was incredibly rapid. On 19 July he was on the west coast at Loanda, from where, accompanied by Dualla, he sailed for Lisbon in mid-August, and by the end of the month he was in Brussels.

Dualla, the Somali youth who was Stanley's special envoy
to chiefs and his most indispensable colleague

Thinking back over the building of a 200-mile road and the establishment of five stations without blood being shed, he knew that he
had accomplished much more than had ever been asked of him. Yet
though he had got the better of de Brazza, Stanley did not expect to be
praised when next he passed under the austere classical portico of
Laeken Palace. In his old life as an explorer, success or failure had been
clear, regardless of the level of public applause, but in opening up a
vast new country, who could tell what might be permanent and
deserving of royal approval?

SEVENTEEN

A Banquet in Paris

When Stanley's carriage brought him from the railway station along the Boulevard de Waterloo towards the king's palace in the centre of Brussels, the coachman did not take him to the regal front gates, but before reaching them swung left into rue Bréderode, a narrow and nondescript side street at the back. Here, in a terraced house, the returning expedition leader had an appointment with the dapper Colonel Maximilien Strauch, with his gold pince-nez and neatly combed moustache. Strauch's orders were to pump Stanley politely before he left the city for his royal audience at Laeken the following day.[1]

For the sake of his health, Stanley knew he should delay returning to the Congo for many months. Indeed, he told Strauch that a 'a medical man of great authority' had said he was 'acting a suicide's part in leading this rackety, exciting life'. Yet Henry was keenly aware that this was a critical time for Leopold's entire African operation. De Brazza had been in Paris since June, doing his utmost to persuade the press and public to put pressure on the French government to ratify the Makoko Treaty and claim the whole area north of the Congo between the Gabon coast and Stanley Pool. It also galled Stanley personally to learn in Brussels that his French rival, who had killed Africans in self-defence, was encouraging friends to leak to the press outrageously misleading passages from his private letters: typically, 'Mr Stanley has adopted the practice of making himself respected by dint of gunfire.'[2] Given how hard Stanley had worked to soothe away the anger that de Brazza's Machiavellian Sergeant Malamine had stirred up among the tribes to the south of the Pool, he was all the more distressed to have been betrayed by a man he had welcomed as a friend. Clearly, if de Brazza's personalized campaign brought French ratification, then everything Stanley had achieved on the Congo, and especially at the Pool, would be in danger. In that kind of emergency, who else but he himself would have the knowledge and clout to combat French acquisitiveness in the Congo itself? And he had another important reason for returning: he did not trust the king's plans for the Congo's future and felt he could only counter them on the spot.

Six months earlier Strauch had sent Stanley a deeply disturbing letter marking a seismic shift in the king's ambitions, away from a monopolistic company controlling all the Congo's ivory, minerals, palm oil and rubber – which had been bad enough – towards something Stanley thought even less desirable. Henry had received this letter when too ill to reply to it, but since his recovery its contents had not stopped worrying him. The trouble had started when the king had read an article in the London *Times* – a newspaper delivered to him each day, by steam ferry to Ostend and then by the Brussels express. The piece the king had found so enlightening was about an Englishman, Alfred Dent, who as 'a private individual' had been granted a valuable concession by the sultans of Brunei and Sulu 'in consideration of a certain annual charge'. This concession conferred virtual ownership 'over a vast tract of territory: larger than the half of France, with all the privileges of sovereignty, such as the rights of life and death, to coin money, raise an army, organize a public force etc., etc.'. One senses Leopold's excitement bubbling beneath the surface of Strauch's turgid prose. Although the North Borneo Company 'had obtained from the Queen of England a charter of incorporation', this, claimed Strauch, had 'added nothing to the legal character of the concession itself'. Apparently, Lord Granville and Mr Gladstone (now British foreign secretary and prime minister respectively) had pronounced Dent's legal title 'already perfect before the grant of the charter'.

The Dent concession, Leopold insisted, should be Stanley's template for all new treaties. Anyone drafting these treaties – himself included – should aim at 'avoiding as much as possible to acknowledge the chiefs as having a right of suzerainty on the territories which they abandon to us'. Knowing that Stanley would detest this provision, Colonel Strauch gave many reasons why there was no alternative to acquiring sovereignty for the AIC. Apart from being essential for resisting French land-grabbing, the acquisition of sovereignty was vital if capitalists were to feel secure enough to invest funds in long-term projects like a railway. Stanley was told he would not be 'dispossessing the natives', but rather 'protecting their autonomy' from rapacious European nation states lacking the king's civilizing aims. This self-delusion increased Stanley's anxieties.

The beauty of Alfred Dent's concession, in Leopold's eyes, was that it gave to an individual (if he were rich enough) the right to mimic a nation and take upon himself all powers and reward himself exactly as he wished. But unlike the lucky Mr Dent, who had only had two sultans to deal with, the AIC would have to sign treaties with hundreds of chiefs. This was work Henry dreaded being pressed to carry out as a matter of urgency.[3] The previous December, he had written to Colonel Strauch describing how – after Ngaliema had been ostracized by 'neighbouring chiefs who had accused him of selling the country' – he (Stanley) had calmed local emotions in this key location by telling the chiefs and their people 'that the country had not [Stanley's emphasis] been sold to the white man; but that he had been permitted to build as much as he wished and was a brother with all the chiefs'. This statement, Henry told Strauch, had caused '200 people to shout aloud their joy'. Strauch and his royal master later rebuked Stanley for having given such an assurance just when French plans were making sovereignty a vital issue.[4] Stanley's only consolation was his realization that the king would never gain legal recognition from Britain and the USA for any AIC, so-called free state, or 'confederacy', unless he convinced them that he believed in free trade and meant to keep the river open to all nations.

Still pale and emaciated, Stanley met the king at Laeken on 1 October 1882. The day before, Strauch had warned the explorer that Leopold expected him to return to Africa within a month. But Henry had already chosen not to excuse himself on medical grounds, as he could easily have done.[5] For his own idealistic reasons, he was prepared to risk his life to save what he believed were the fruits of his 'sacred task'.[6] He had just heard two reports of Belgian officers killing Africans. Of one incident, Swinburne had written saying that Valcke and Nilis, two Belgian officers, had fought with 200 men 'over a paltry calabash of palm wine', shooting dead fourteen Africans.[7] Henry therefore began his meeting with Leopold by complaining about his many problems with Belgian officers – especially their lack of sympathy towards Africans – and said that before he could agree to go back to the Congo, he must have the king's permission to send home three or four of the worst of them. He was surprised to have little trouble convincing Leopold that it would be sensible to replace his Belgian incompetents with British officers.[8] In October 1882, out of forty-three European agents of all sorts (clerks, storekeepers, engineers, officers), only three were British, but by the end of 1883, out of 117 agents, forty-one were British.[9] The fact that the king might regard a British ascendancy as a way to warn off France (because the French government feared Britain) was something that Stanley put to the back of his mind.

By now Stanley had lost some of his royalist illusions. 'I think less of the pomp, the ceremony & the glitter surrounding Majesty than I did,' he confided to his diary. But he still managed to persuade himself that Leopold's reassurances about his underlying altruism were genuine. If the king's impressive diplomatic skills ever made his colony a reality, why should it not be run for the benefit of the Congolese while also rewarding the AIC and international traders? On his way down the Congo in 1877, Stanley had 'dreamed of some Rothschild undertaking the civilization of the Congo basin', and he called this to mind as Leopold amazed him with a promise to increase the expedition's annual expenditure from £12,000 to £60,000 and to raise the expedition's force, then standing at about 250 men, to 3,000, if they could be found. Stanley was told that his part of the bargain would have to be sending huge amounts of ivory from the Upper Congo to Vivi. He pointed out that unless a thousand carriers were taken on, he would have to use his entire workforce to carry tusks instead of building the new stations. Henry now made it a condition of his return that he should not be asked to do impossible things.[10]

He also insisted, to the king's face, that he must have a dozen new officers – two to command each of the king's three new stations between the Pool and Stanley Falls, and the rest to be shared out between existing stations. The king consented to this, and in return Stanley conceded the urgency of gaining concessions from chiefs on both banks of the Congo, and on the Kwilu river. If he controlled the Kwilu-Niadi basin, which lay between the Ogowé and the Congo, he knew he could cut off future French expeditions from de Brazza's concessions on the north side of the Pool, making them valueless.[11] Stanley was relieved to be told he would not be expected to make these treaties or any on the lower Congo. In his confidential instructions, dated 1 November 1882 and mailed to him after his last meeting with the king, Strauch stated 'our agents at the Stanley Pool and at Manyanga are to secure the intervening ground with every privilege that may be acquired between Stanley Pool and Mayanga on the left bank – same round Isangla and Vivi on the right bank'. Stanley himself would only have to make treaties connected with his new stations on the Upper Congo.

Though Leopold insisted that the chiefs would have to cede sovereign rights if the Congo was ever to be legally recognized as a 'state', Stanley maintained passionately that the soil itself must remain the property of the chiefs.[12] But with French determination to take over the entire Congo growing almost by the day, Leopold had already made up his mind not to wait for Stanley to come round to his way of thinking. Instead, the king had decided to employ a retired British general and senior Indian civil servant to push ahead with 'confederacy' treaties, by means of which numerous chiefs on the Lower Congo would sign the same form of words, yielding sovereignty through identical agreements in legalese that they could not possibly understand. The obliging Sir Frederick Goldsmid was ordered to explain to the chiefs, through translators, the purpose of the 'confederacy' they would be joining: to encourage mutual defence against intruders, to strengthen their country by raising a 'public force', and to unite them all under the AIC's blue flag with a golden star.[13] Later, Sir Frederick's assistant, Lieutenant Louis Valcke, took over, and an English officer, Major Francis Vetch, would lavish enough cloth, brass wire and beads on roughly 300 chiefs to persuade them to add their names to those already signed up.

The problem Leopold feared most was that, in any confrontation with a European state, a trading company like the AIC would have no right to resist a military attack on its territory. Strauch was soon instructed to send to Stanley a dozen Krupp field guns and four machine guns, but Leopold knew these weapons could do no more than suggest to the Congolese that their possessors were powerful men, to be preferred as allies to de Brazza's people.[14] Certainly, no French expedition could be fired upon without causing an escalation, which would end, inevitably, with France taking everything. Only a state recognized by others could defend itself against another nation, and that was why Leopold was sure he could not wait till Stanley

changed his mind about the morality of 'buying' sovereignty and linking chiefs in illusory political unions.

With Leopold already vexed with Stanley for his attitude to treaty-
making, an event now occurred that greatly increased the king's irritation. From Brussels, Stanley went on to London for a week, and then
to the French capital where he arrived on 19 October 1882, having
accepted an invitation to speak at a banquet mounted by the Stanley
Club. He wrote in his diary: 'As de Brazza will be in Paris, it will be
the best occasion I shall have for explaining what we are doing, & the
truth about de Brazza so far as it may be necessary to disillusionize
[sic] some of our French friends who attribute to him an apostolic
character!'[15] 'What can be done to make Stanley keep quiet?' an anxious Leopold asked Strauch, fearing that incautious criticism of
France's hero would redouble French efforts to secure the Congo. The
king now suspected that Stanley had faked illness and come back to
Europe solely to get even with de Brazza.

Soon after checking in at his favourite rendezvous in Paris, the
Hotel Meurice in the rue de Rivoli, Henry was surprised to be told
that Comte Savorgnan de Brazza was waiting to see him. Far from
refusing to receive the man who had unjustly accused him of brutality,
Stanley welcomed him. 'We had a good deal of talk of an amiable
kind, because personally he is unexceptionable and has lots of good
humour.' Stanley told his fellow explorer about the banquet that was
to be held for him that very evening, and facetiously declared that he
intended to give him 'le coup mortel' in his after-dinner speech. De
Brazza then surprised him by asking if he could come along. As good
natured as ever, Henry said he would ask the organizers' permission.
On arriving at the Hotel Continental, Stanley found that the banquet
was a far larger event than he had imagined. Everyone who was anyone in British and American circles was there, as well as fifty distinguished native Parisians. But Henry was not going to allow the
presence of Frenchmen, or his earlier meeting with de Brazza, to dissuade him from delivering a blistering attack on his rival.[16]

Stanley had always been courteous about de Brazza's claims to be a
great explorer, although he could easily have ridiculed his short journeys on the Ogowé and his brief excursion on the Congo below
Kwamouth. Yet the absurdity of being treated as de Brazza's equal,
when he (not the Frenchman) had first discovered the Upper Congo

and the Pool at great personal cost, finally got the better of him. Stanley also had good reason to resent de Brazza for ordering Malamine to represent him to Africans at the Pool as evil and bloodthirsty, and nor had he liked de Brazza's claim, in a country where fetishism was widespread, that only chiefs who displayed the tricolour emblem would be safe from white men who might otherwise shoot them.[17] But now – whether de Brazza chose to show up or not – Stanley felt that his moment of revenge had come.

He got up at the end of the dinner and launched into a mocking diatribe against the so-called Makoko Treaty. The eulogistic sobriquet, in use by French journalists, that most annoyed Stanley when applied to de Brazza was 'the apostle of liberty' – as if he were a latter-day Livingstone 'who had dealt a death blow to slavery in west Africa'. Could anyone of common sense credit this, Stanley asked his audience, after having described 'the shoeless, poorly dressed person' whom he had first met in 1880 'about forty miles from our lower station'. Then Stanley reached the heart of the matter – de Brazza's deliberate lies about his treaty.

Speaking with heavy irony, Henry asked how anyone could be naive enough to believe that King Makoko of Mbe had been so

struck by the simple ways of the great traveller, and so full of admiration for the tricolour flag ... that he chose a piece of his territory – nine miles long – with its revenues, villages, inhabitants, goats, pigs, all its habitations and presumably its income tax as well, and therewith endowed the traveller, to mark the happy event of his meeting with so marvellous a white man?

Would anyone suppose it possible, when 'all M. de Brazza's presents to Makoko and the chiefs of Mfwa would not pay for the goats they had let him eat'? Stanley said he had learned from talking to 'Makoko's greatest chief, Gobila' that Makoko had never meant to cede an inch of territory to de Brazza. Stanley then poured scorn on the idea that Makoko could have 'known what this document in triplicate meant'. The chief wanted to trade and was happy for de Brazza to have a trading post there, just as the tribes to the south of the Pool had been happy for Stanley to build among them. But they had not given away their land, any more than had Makoko. In any case, de Brazza had been sent out by the French Committee of the AIA and had had no right to make treaties on behalf of France. So he was guilty of a breach of faith with the philanthropic men who had sent him. Having accused de Brazza of introducing 'an immoral diplomacy into a virgin continent', Stanley declared: 'I am an American, therefore free of all political leanings and interested in Africa solely as an unhappy continent.' Much of his speech was perfectly sincere, since he genuinely believed that Leopold's plans for civilizing the Congo were greatly superior to the alternative of its becoming a French colony.[18]

As he sat down to loud applause, Stanley was handed de Brazza's card. Convinced that he had already gained an unassailable advantage, and apprehending no danger from anything de Brazza might say, Henry urged the club secretary to admit him. Resplendent in evening dress, his black beard neatly trimmed, his dark eyes glowing in the gaslight, de Brazza acknowledged the rapturous applause of the French guests. Then, speaking in English, he delivered a well-rehearsed speech, which ended: 'I see in Mr Stanley not an antagonist but simply a labourer in the same field, where our common efforts, although we represent different interests, converge towards the same goal: the advance of civilization in Africa.' He raised his glass: 'Gentlemen, I am a Frenchman and a naval officer, and I drink to the civilization of Africa by the simultaneous efforts of all nations, each under its own flag.'[19] This pretence to amity, although wholly disingenuous, raised a storm of clapping from the French contingent. A number of American guests complained that it was unpardonable for the Frenchman to have 'thrust himself in at a dinner given by a private club of Stanleyites'. They were right that de Brazza had used the Stanley Club event for his own political purposes. He had known about the banquet for several days before he had paid his call on Stanley – time enough to write a speech in English and learn it by heart, working all the while on his English accent.[20]

Next day, when the French newspapers were delivered to his hotel, Stanley realized that he had made a serious tactical error in allowing de Brazza anywhere near his banquet. Although the Frenchman had answered none of Stanley's entirely valid points about the shortcomings of the so-called Makoko Treaty, or denied that he had been sent to Africa to explore for the AIA rather than to annexe for his government, the Parisian press denounced Stanley for mocking the tricolour, for calling their hero a 'va nu-pieds', a barefoot tramp, and worst of all for being 'Albion's Trojan Horse'. At moments of pique, the French press still refers to Britons and Americans indistinguishably as Anglo-Saxons, and on that October morning 'the Anglo-Saxon Stanley' was widely represented as the stalking horse for the British government.

Only a month earlier, because of French dithering, Gladstone's cabinet had felt obliged to abandon Britain's dual control of Egypt with France, and had acted alone against Colonel Arabi to save the Suez Canal from requisition by a military dictatorship. Lord Wolseley's spectacular victory at Tel el-Kebir was seen in France as a defeat for the French nation, since from now on Britain would control Egypt unaided. This wider context shows why Henry had been foolish to give de Brazza the chance to cross swords with him in public. His error of judgement made French ratification of the Makoko Treaty inevitable and ratcheted the Scramble for Africa into a higher gear – exactly what Leopold had hoped to avoid.

Yet Stanley did not allow the unfairness of the newspapers to upset him, as he had done in Brighton a decade earlier. This time, just two days later, he gave a breakfast at the Hotel Meurice for thirty guests, and welcomed everyone cordially. Edward King was there, along with many expatriate friends. But to the surprise of everyone, Stanley had also invited de Brazza, whom he welcomed with a smile. The man had been nothing but trouble to him.[21] So the fact that Henry could behave with civility to someone who had tried hard to thwart his most cherished plans showed what a long way Stanley had travelled, in terms of *savoir faire* and maturity.

Stanley was back in Brussels to see the king on 31 October, when the news broke that the Makoko Treaty would be ratified in Paris later that month. So now Stanley was involved in a more bruising race with de Brazza. Would he be able to found his new stations between the Pool and Stanley Falls before de Brazza could get there? This time he was determined to preserve absolute secrecy about the timing of his return to Africa. The following nine months would determine whether all his efforts since 1878 had just been preparing the ground for another explorer and another nation to take over the river system, which his extraordinary courage and leadership had first revealed to the world.

EIGHTEEN

After the Slave Raids

Stanley was forty-one years old when he paused for a week in Paris in November 1882, on his clandestine way back to Africa via Spain and Cadiz. With his grey cropped hair, pale penetrating eyes, and lean, deeply tanned face, Henry was a more distinguished-looking man than he had been a decade earlier. Not even the guarded detachment with which he faced the camera all his adult life could conceal his greater self-assurance and more reflective cast of mind.[1] His habitual expression of latent sadness, overlaid with masterful determination, spoke eloquently of what he had endured emotionally and physically. After his great trans-Africa journey, the secret ties to his mother and half-sister, which had once been so sustaining, had started to fray and sunder. Now, travelling with Dualla and a recently engaged English valet, Stanley rarely thought of Mrs Jones and Emma. The family that he missed was his African one – Swinburne, Christophersen, Mabruki Ndogo, Susi, Uledi and the rest – with whom he felt at ease, as he never did with well-connected people in London. In Africa, it was always 'a relief to find oneself among unconventional people with whom one can talk without a chance remark being flung & broadcast before readers'.[2] But he still yearned to find a woman to be close to, and perhaps marry.

From Brussels he had written to Edward King, whom he trusted as no one else, and with whom, just before leaving for the Congo, he had holidayed in Switzerland in 1879. To his friend, Henry bemoaned his lack of female companionship, admitting that his rejection by Alice might have been because he was bad at talking to women. 'Fiddlesticks!' King wrote back. 'You can talk to women as well as to African chiefs. Come along over and visit for a fortnight ... Come while the ladies are here ...'[3]

No record survives to identify these ladies, but during his week in the French capital, Stanley met two of King's favourite Americans: Eli Lemon Sheldon, a banker originally from Kansas, and his journalist wife, May French Sheldon, from a well-to-do southern family. The Sheldons divided their time between London, Paris and New York, always staying in the best hotels, or in service flats. When Stanley met Mrs Sheldon, she was a vivacious and broadminded woman of thirty-four. Despite her husband's high income, May often worked as a free-lance journalist. At present, she was translating *Salammbo*, Flaubert's erotic historical epic set in Carthage during its death throes. Mrs Sheldon would later write her own novels and run a publishing house. Her friends, who often stayed with her, were journalists, writers and musicians, like the well-known American soprano and concert promoter Emma Thursby, and the playwright Anna Dickinson.[4]

Stanley had never met a modern woman like May. He was enchanted by her insistence on talking to him frankly, rather than with the feminine wiles of an Alice Pike. 'After the first few minutes of strangeness have gone, she soon lets you know that chaff won't do.'[5] It was a revelation to find that conversations with women did not have to be limited to social trivia. He soon loved talking to the clever but down-to-earth Mrs Sheldon, whose mother had been a doctor and had passed on much medical knowledge to her.[6] May had travelled widely as a child, and her adventurous nature and cosmopolitan opinions appealed to Stanley as the reverse of the smug, stay-at-home insularity he had most detested about the Welsh and the English. Since Edward King was also a great traveller – and, like May, possessed many talents, as journalist, poet, novelist, and expert on all things Parisian – Stanley found his stay with his old friend the most enjoyable for years. All that changed on 12 November.

On that evening, which was scheduled to be his last in Paris, he dined with King and the Sheldons at the Hôtel de Londres. His three friends were all very conscious of his imminent departure, and of the dangers awaiting him in Africa. During the meal, Stanley was wracked by stomach and chest pains so agonizing that he thought he was dying. Smelling salts were brought, and windows thrown open, before the sick man was helped from the room. A doctor was called, who gave him a morphine injection, having debated with May Sheldon whether his patient was suffering from a heart attack, contractions of the pyloric sphincter, or inflammation of the stomach walls. Stanley suspected he had been poisoned by some fanatical admirer of de Brazza, or by a Dutch or Portuguese trader who hated the AIC. A month earlier he had received an anonymous threat of just that. Written in French, this odious note had been mailed from Amsterdam.[7] But recalling the similarity of the pains he had suffered at Manyanga, he accepted his doctor's diagnosis of damage to his stomach's lining by quinine and other medicines. As the morphine took effect, Stanley announced to his friends that he meant to catch the Madrid express at eight that evening, as planned.[8]

His unshakeable determination to return to Africa, whatever the cost, shocked May Sheldon but also thrilled her. She was witnessing true heroism, she was sure. The following day she sent a note to Madrid, expressing her dismay that he had travelled without a doctor, and describing 'the pain it causes your friends to know you suffer away from their tender care'. She also told him that because of his importance to Africa's development, he had 'a solemn duty' to look after his health.[9] Edward King wrote saying he was as worried as Mrs Sheldon, and that they wanted him back in Paris.[10] The public at large never appreciated the great bravery required to return again and again to Africa, especially when enduring the agony of acute gastritis. But Stanley's closest friends, who had just seen what his dedication cost him in terms of suffering, would be his passionate supporters for life. To modern eyes, Henry's insistence on returning when gravely ill seems to emphasize the danger-seeking, masochistic, component in his character. He himself would have argued that deteriorating conditions on the Congo made an early return imperative. His pain continued in the train, only being made tolerable by regular injections of morphine administered by his valet, Walter Illingworth. At sea it comforted him to think that if he lived to see Europe again, he would at least be able to confide in a sympathetic and worldlywise woman.

On 20 December 1882, Stanley's steam launch edged up to the landing-place at Vivi, and he was informed that the two Germans, Otto Lindner and Dr Peschuel-Loesche, who had been chosen by Leopold to run this vitally important station had just quit their posts, leaving the place in chaos. Another royal appointment, Lieutenant Branconnier, the chief of Leopoldville Station, was holidaying at the coast. Meanwhile, the chief of Isangila had returned to Europe without permission; the *En Avant*'s vital steam valve had been stolen by some wreckers and, for no known reason an engineer was working as a clerk at Vivi while two of the expedition's precious steamers were lying in pieces.[11] Though enraged, Stanley concentrated on equipping Captain J. G. Elliott – one of the new intake of British officers – for his expedition to the Kwilu-Niadi basin, and succeeded in getting him on the road by 13 January with seventy Wangwana.[12] He also despatched Lieutenant Hanssens from Manyanga towards the upper Niadi, and sent Lieutenant Van de Velde to take possession of the mouth of the Kwilu. By these three rapid moves, de Brazza would be separated from his 'Makoko concessions' by an immense wedge of land.

Meanwhile, Stanley marched for the Pool en route for the Upper Congo, arriving at Leopoldville on 21 March. He was appalled to see grass and weeds growing on the paths, and not a single paw-paw in the gardens, just the fronds of scattered bananas and several acres of cassava. All the buildings were dilapidated, and when Stanley examined the stores he found only 800 or so brass rods, barely enough to buy food for the station's eleven Europeans and 212 Wangwana for three days. Branconnier had used almost his entire supply to buy ivory, flouting Stanley's cardinal rule to keep at least four months' rods in reserve. Branconnier had recently been obliged to beg food from the Baptist missionaries, who had hitherto owed their survival to Stanley's generosity with his resources. Even the goods Stanley had hoped to take to the Upper Congo for his new stations, including crockery, cutlery, pots and pans and trade goods, had been sold by Branconnier for food and ivory.[13] Almost the last straw for Henry was to be told that a few days ago a young and totally inexperienced Austrian officer had been allowed to go out on the Congo in an overloaded canoe, in full dress uniform and helmet, without a word being said to stop him. Within an hour his canoe had capsized and he had drowned.[14]

Stanley sacked Branconnier, and was promptly warned by him that Colonel Strauch had put a clause in his contract ruling out dismissal. Henry told Strauch exactly what he thought of Branconnier's disgraceful contract, and then wrote demanding of the king: 'Do you not want me to succeed? Then recall me – that is certainly the easiest way – and one that would be readily obeyed at this juncture ... I would rather beg my bread than be a passive spectator of indolence and incapacity and of men coolly sitting down indifferent to this drama on the Congo.'[15] The unfairness of Leopold's support for useless men like Branconnier was underlined for Stanley by the injustice of fate. Two recently arrived Belgians, to whom he had taken an immediate liking,

Lieutenants Grang and Parfoury, had just died, while incompetent officers lived on. His good-natured valet, Walter Illingworth, also succumbed. 'These sad deaths make one pause and ponder over the incertitude of life here. Youth is no protection, a brave and hopeful heart is no shield ... Death levels his dart and the youthful, the brave and the strong are gone from amongst us.'[16] As if this were not enough, another recently arrived officer, called Luksic, shot himself through the heart.[17]

The worst legacy of Branconnier's rule at Leopoldville was a deterioration of relations with surrounding chiefs.[18] Stanley sent Dualla, his chief diplomat, to Kinshasa for five days in early April to try to repair the damage. In the same week, a young Englishman, Harry Hamilton Johnston, reappeared having been travelling on the Congo with Stanley's help since January. Before that, he had been exploring in Angola. Despite Stanley's uncertainties about the sex of this small, effeminately spoken, twenty-seven-year-old, he was charmed by his intelligence – taking on trust, despite his lack of references, that Johnston really was employed by the *Graphic* as a journalist and artist, and had not been sent out by the British Foreign Office to spy on him. Later, Harry would prove that he was no Dick Heaton, as Stanley put it, by catching venereal disease from the whores of Vivi – for which delinquency the normally censorious Stanley forgave him at once, merely remarking that he now knew 'why African travellers are so sternly virtuous'.[19] His high opinion of Harry was not misplaced. The young man would turn out to be a dauntless traveller, and a future high-ranking British administrator in Africa.

In late April 1883, after a spell upriver, Johnston arrived at Kinshasa in time to see Stanley 'seated on his camp chair, his pipe in his mouth', conducting a negotiation with Chief Nchuvila and his heir, Bankwa. Johnston's account of this historic event confirms Stanley's peaceful mode of treaty-making. He described Stanley sitting 'benignly chatting and smoking with native chiefs', and sensed 'the great influence he possesses ... [which] tends towards peace wherever his fame has reached'. Johnston heard Bankwa argue against allowing Stanley to build a station for a young Belgian officer, Lieutenant Alphonse Vangele. 'Today,' said Bankwa, 'they will send one white man here, but next year twenty more will come, and because we have given land to one we must do so to all the others, and so, soon Kinshasa will belong to the white man as Kintamo [Leopoldville] does already.' Johnston conceded that there was a lot of truth in this, although Bankwa had made no allowance for 'the material advantages that would accrue to the people of Kinshasa from the settlement of civilization in its midst'.

In the end Stanley – who throughout had been 'looking at his most chief-like with his resolute face and grey hair and sword of state at his side' – was 'given permission to occupy land and build a station'. If sovereignty and the permanent surrender of land had ever been demanded, Johnston would have mentioned it, but he did not. Stanley's only objective was to plant a station that was accepted by all the local chiefs and villagers as being of advantage to them.[20] In fact, because of Bankwa's powerfully expressed objections, Stanley decided against concluding a treaty, and withdrew Vangele and his men. Kinshasa would not be occupied for the present. When a more propitious moment came to try again, he meant to give the sensitive job to his friend, Swinburne, whose understanding of Africans was unparalleled.

British hostility to the International Association (as Leopold's AIC was generally known) had long distressed Stanley, and he saw Johnston's presence as an opportunity to influence British official opinion, since when the young man returned to England he would inevitably be summoned to the Foreign Office for a grilling. Stanley hated the Portuguese for their covert slave trading, and was dismayed that Britain favoured Portugal as the future custodian of the Congo and denigrated the AIC. Soon after Johnston left the Congo, Stanley wrote warning him that a renewal of the Anglo-Portuguese alliance would 'deliver these people [on the Congo] into the hands of the Portuguese ... soul and body to Hell and slavery. To avoid the imputation of being false and faithless [Johnston should urge Britain] ... to proclaim a Protectorate over the Congo ... You can write, and that well. Set to work.'[21]

Unfortunately for Stanley, Johnston did not represent these views as his own when disseminating them, as Stanley had intended, but made Henry's letter public in Britain in a way that disastrously eroded Leopold's confidence in his Chief Agent. The French would now be more convinced than ever that Stanley's true aim was to create a British colony on the Congo. Stanley's letter to Johnston had, in reality, only been aimed at getting the British government to see that the AIC was a better bulwark against the French than was Portugal. Leopold did not see it that way, and coming after the events in Paris, this letter to Harry Johnston confirmed his suspicion that Stanley was becoming a liability.

Sadly for Stanley, Johnston had arrived on the Congo at the very time when Vivi and Leopoldville had been in chaos, which persuaded the young traveller to tell the Foreign Office that the AIC lacked the ability to administer the Congo, confirming FO officials in their preference for Portugal.[22] Harry Johnston's behaviour saddened Stanley since he felt they might otherwise have become close friends. 'It is about time I stopped in my search for the perfect man,' he confided in a revealing letter, after confessing that almost everyone he had ever trusted 'had ventured to say something unkind the minute I turned my back ... Yet deep down within me lay the sympathy which I would have freely shown had it been solicited.'[23]

Henry was back at Stanley Pool from Bolobo, early in July, when he learned, as he told Strauch on 8 July, that 'Kinshasa [Chief Nchuvila] had finally succumbed & signed the treaty and we are now in possession of the long desired land'.[24] Stanley had been absent when this important treaty was signed, and the negotiation had been conducted by E. Massey Stewart, one of Sir Frederick Goldsmid's negotiators. A copy of it (though not the original) is preserved in the archives of the Belgian Ministry of Foreign Affairs. The chiefs pledged themselves 'to remain under the patronage and protection of the Comité d'Études du Haut Congo, and to adopt the flag of the Comité as a sign to all men that we are allies and friends for ever with the employees and friends of the Comité'; also, 'no stranger, European or African shall obtain any privilege to build, sow, plant, cut timber or grass in our district from us.' Sovereignty was not demanded and no traders were barred, except they could not build or settle on this particular ground, or claim it. This treaty of 'patronage and protection' would have met with Stanley's approval, since it did not remove power from the chiefs or take their land.[25]

On 16 July, Stanley sent Swinburne with seven Haussas (Africans from the Gold Coast) to Kinshasa, convinced that Dualla was right in thinking that the gentle Swinburne would win everyone over because he would 'smile even though he was about to be cut up to little pieces'. Dualla's comical tone should not mislead one into underestimating the risk Swinburne ran of being murdered, when agreeing to go and live at Kinshasa with the volatile Bankwa.[26] But where Branconnier, Valcke and Vangele had failed, Swinburne would not. The importance of the

Kinshasa Treaty lay in the fact that de Brazza had just returned to Africa with twelve fields guns, twenty-seven French sailors from Algeria, and numerous muskets for a native militia. Yet because he first chose to dispute possession of the Kwilu-Niadi basin with Elliott, who had already established an unassailable advantage there, Stanley was given time to win the race on the Upper Congo. Even so, he distributed twelve Krupp guns among his various stations.[27]

In September Stanley transported a new arrival, Edward Glave, to Lukolela on the Upper Congo, where this tall, strong nineteen-year-old was to be station chief. Coming from a large and impoverished Yorkshire family, recently removed to north London, where he had been a warehouseman, Edward was exactly the type Stanley liked best: the determined youth from a disadvantaged background – not unlike Swinburne, or the Danish sailor Christophersen, or himself, of course. Glave had been captivated by the map of Africa in his boyhood classroom, with the estuaries marked boldly, but the rivers 'dribbling away in lines of hesitating dots'. Direct experience of the dots did nothing to lessen his enthusiasm.[28] Stanley was soon declaring: 'I rather like this young fellow. He is very intelligent, speaks well & writes a good letter & gives straightforward manly answers.'[29] Ten years later, only Glave's early death would prevent him from becoming an ideal grown-up son to his former boss. The two men travelled together on the steamer *En Avant* in September 1883, and Glave has left a vivid portrait of their trip. In the evening when they camped on the bank, and the Wangwana were cutting wood for the next day's fuel, Stanley would talk about earlier journeys.

I remember [wrote Glave] – one particular occasion, when the rising moon threw long ripples across the purple waters of the Congo – Stanley, dressed in his campaigning costume of brown jacket and knickerbockers, with his broad-crowned peak cap pushed off his forehead, seated on a log, smoking his briar pipe by the camp-fire whose ruddy flames lighted up the characteristic lines of that manly face ... The top of his little cabin formed his writing table ... and his quarters were so full with bales of cloth, scientific instruments, paper, arms, and ammunition ... that there was only just room to crawl into his bunk ...

The crew slept ashore on mats by the fire where they cooked for themselves. Breakfast for all was baked manioc root and tea, with stewed goat or fowl and rice for lunch and dinner. 'Stanley stood aft and directed the steering ... we were generally under steam about nine hours a day, as we could not carry wood for much more than that time.' At every village, dug-outs would be launched and amazement shown as the paddlers approached the 'buata-meyar', or fire canoe. Drums were beaten, alerting other villages to this unusual event. Yet Stanley's earlier visits and palavers meant there was no hostility. At Glave's village of Lukolela, the medicine man had put it about that the white man who was coming to live with them was 'a hideous form of life, half lion, half buffalo, and was possessed of the blood-thirsty habit of slaughtering and devouring human beings'. A council of head men approached Stanley and asked very seriously whether he had such a creature on board. As a fever-stricken Glave staggered on deck 'the whole crowd broke out into roars of good humoured laughter'. When Stanley returned to Lukolela four months later, Glave had built a house, set up huts for his workers, and planted vegetables. He had also made his own furniture, and become an excellent shot. Best of all, he was on very good terms with the local people.[30] This immensely resourceful man had given Stanley a glimpse of his own adventurous younger self. Sadly, the pleasure of this meeting was succeeded by a nightmare.

Stanley's orders were to head upriver, with three steamers, past Equatorville – his most easterly station, 412 miles above Stanley Pool, and then steam on for a further 600 miles to Stanley Falls. His aim was to make 'verbal treaties with the more populous settlements on either bank' and to found a station at the Falls, as commanded by Leopold.[31] Two hundred miles from Stanley Falls, he decided to explore a major tributary, the Aruwimi, where he learned from the Soko tribe that Sudanese slave traders had come down this river with guns and, after killing a number of people, taken away many women and children.[32]

Having returned to the Congo itself, Stanley heard on 22 November that there were Arab slave traders in the region of Stanley Falls.[33] Three days later he came across two large villages, which he remembered from 1877 as bustling with life, but which were now burned and deserted, with palms cut down, bananas scorched, and many acres levelled to the ground. At a third village, Stanley met dull-eyed people who regarded his men 'with stupid indifference as though they were beyond further harm'. Over half the women and children had been enslaved and two-thirds of the men.[34] By the 27th Stanley was all but certain that the murderers were the Arabs of Nyangwe, who had been emboldened by his epic journey to come thus far on the mighty Lualaba. In the morning, Stanley's flotilla came across the bodies of two women who had been roped together back to back and thrown into the river. A few miles further upstream, Stanley's three steamers came level with a large Arab stockade. He now wished that he had brought a Krupp gun with him. 'I could have annihilated the camp was my first thought.' Yet the Arabs had fifty-four canoes and numbered about 2,000 men – far too many to take on, even supposing that his own eighty Wangwana would fight against their own kith and kin, and in such overwhelming numbers. As his blood cooled, it also dawned on Stanley that he 'represented no government' and therefore had no right to claim 'control over the territory devastated by the Arabs'.[35]

When Stanley went ashore, he found that the Arab-Swahili and their armed slaves from Manyema were commanded by Abed bin Salim, one the founders of Nyangwe, whom he had met in that town in October 1876 and had disliked even then. For eleven months this gang had been ravaging an area somewhat larger than the whole of Ireland for slaves and ivory, killing and enslaving thousands of people. In 1881 and 1882 there had also been raids near here, netting 2,800 slaves. In their present camp they had 2,300 captives, including children, chained together and looking so wretched and despairing that Stanley could hardly believe that 'such awful wickedness was possible'. He guessed that in order to obtain so many slaves the Arabs would have shot the same number of people to prevent resistance. 'They had also cut heads off by the score.'[36] Imagining a peaceful village suddenly visited by these cruel men, Henry felt as if 'in a kind of evil dream'. 'Would to God I could see my way to set them all free, & massacre the fiends who have been the guilty authors of the indescribable inhumanity I have seen today.'[37]

For the first time he was faced with the practical realities with which Leopold had long been grappling. Unless the king could claim that the Congo was a state, bound together by a confederation of chiefs, he would have no legal right to expel the Arabs, the French, or anyone else, and these raiders would soon reach Stanley Pool. If that happened, there would be no chance of bringing trade and Christianity up the Congo. And he himself would earn an infamous role in history as the man who opened the river, not as a Livingstonian 'highway' for civilization, but as an immense conduit for the East African slave trade, which would thenceforth span the continent. If only to stop this happening, it would be essential for a recognized state to stem the Arabs' advance and finally drive them back eastwards. Stanley would never again argue against the idea of a confederacy of chiefs, or even against taking sovereignty. The situation had changed dramatically, and these things might yet be needed to protect the population.

Stanley hoped that by building a station at Stanley Falls he would set a limit to the Arab advances – though since he could only leave behind a diminutive Scottish engineer, Adrian Binnie, with twenty Haussas and ten Wangwana – his hopes of it being a real barrier in the near future were remote. Nor did it reassure him to hear the Arabs express the hope that Binnie would sell goods to them more cheaply than if they were to send for them to Ujiji. Before leaving the area Stanley ransomed eighteen children, intending to give two as linguists to the missionaries of the Livingstone Inland Mission.[38]

Back at Leopoldville – soon to be commanded by an Englishman, Captain Seymour Saulez, of whom Stanley had high hopes – he was delighted to see how many improvements had been made. At nearby Kinshasa, Swinburne had done even better. 'Consistent, patient conduct, and steady forbearance had performed wonders, and the most intractable community on the Upper Congo had been converted to have a perfect faith in our honesty and in the purity of our motives.'[39] Yet at the same time, three Belgian officers on other stations had been responsible for twelve African deaths.[40] Such failures were very painful to Henry, who had just devoted twelve days at Bolobo to making a bloodless peace after the murder of two Wangwana.[41]

Chaos still reigned at Vivi when he returned there, underlining the fact that unless a capable deputy was soon sent out to run the Lower Congo while Stanley himself was upriver, the situation below the Pool would never improve. Horrified by the behaviour of the young officers, which had included assaults on each other as well as brutality to local Africans, Henry told the king that controlling the mayhem might demand 'hanging any person guilty of committing violence upon the body of any of our associates'.[42] Because of the immense distance between the extremities of the Upper and the Lower Congo, Stanley had begged Leopold many times for a suitable second in command, and in February he had received a letter from Strauch, dated 7 January, telling him that General Gordon had entered the service of the International Association. It shocked Stanley when Gordon wrote to him showing no understanding of the realities on the ground, and saying that he looked forward to an all-out war against the slave traders.[43]

Just as decisions regarding treaties had been taken out of Stanley's hands, now he would not, he realized, be consulted about the role Gordon would play on arrival in February. Instead, the man himself was talking about taking on the Arabs as if he had two or three thousand European troops under his command. 'Either the king is mad,' wrote Stanley in his diary, 'or Gordon is about [to enter] on an impossible task through a false conception of affairs.'[44] Because Stanley thought Gordon 'erratic & unstable', he was not sorry when the general dropped Leopold without warning, days before he was due to leave for the Congo. Instead, he returned to the Sudan. 'I expect there will be a big tragedy out at Khartoum,' predicted Henry with remarkable prescience.[45] It was a relief when Leopold chose a down-to-earth general, Sir Francis de Winton – even though de Winton was to be Henry's replacement rather than his deputy.[46]

Sir Francis arrived on 11 May, and Stanley liked him from the beginning. He felt that he needed a break from the Congo and was glad to be leaving. Just two months after Henry had sailed for home, de Winton's position was no better than his had been. He had only six officers upon whom he could rely: Swinburne and three other British officers recommended by Stanley – Saulez, Pollok and Vetch – and the Belgians Valcke and Hannsens. Other Belgians lacked control, he told the king, especially in their dealings with Africans.[47]

In May, a month before Stanley's departure on 10 June 1884, de Brazza made an all-out attempt to acquire the whole of the Congo for France. In doing so he tested to the limits the self-control and courage of Anthony Swinburne, whose patience with the Congolese was legendary, and who was now the only person able to prevent a major disaster for Leopold's whole project. The Pool connected the Lower to the Upper Congo and lay at the head of any future railway, and was therefore indispensable to a future state. Henry had established a chain of stations from Vivi to Stanley Falls, yet if the Frenchman walked into Leopoldville or Kinshasa and gained the local chief's sanction to stay, everything would be lost, regardless of the king's brilliant diplomacy in Europe. Before departing, Stanley explained the situation to Strauch:

Despite the comparatively strong position of the Assn on the Congo, any energetic officers of Portugal or France with 50 men is stronger than we are with a thousand. Why? Because we do not understand whether we have a right to resist any aggressive act of Portugal or France by force of arms. Should we do so what power will uphold us or sympathise with us? ... So long as our status and character are not recognized by European governments, de Brazza with his walking stick and a French flag ... is really stronger than Stanley with his Krupps ...[48]

Just one French gunboat steaming up to Vivi and demanding its surrender could end the whole game.

Several weeks after Stanley wrote the above letter, de Brazza sent presents to the Kinshasa chiefs and persuaded them to visit him – his intention being to tempt them to break their treaties with the Association. However, to determine whether the south side should be French, as well as the north, de Brazza had no choice but to cross to the southern shore in person. And so in late May, recorded Stanley, the Frenchman 'crossed the Pool to our side with 4 canoes and landed on Kinshasa territory, the famous Malamine being with him'. Just outside the settlement, Hassani, one of Swinburne's Wangwana, barred the way. On hearing Malamine say that 'de Brazza was Swinburne's master', Hassani raised his rifle threatening the French party with sudden death, according to Charles de Chavannes, de Brazza's secretary. Stanley claimed Hassani merely 'stoutly resisted the astonishing declaration' (that de Brazza was Swinburne's master).

Swinburne, meanwhile, ran to Chief Nchuvila's compound and persuaded him not to meet de Brazza without him (Swinburne) being present. The young Englishman also armed his Wangwana and ordered them to hide, only showing themselves if the French fired shots. Swinburne then received the three Frenchmen and politely offered them brandy. An argument ensued about who had the right to occupy Kinshasa, with neither side yielding an inch. A palaver with the chief followed, and rapidly became ugly when two of the chief's sons assaulted de Brazza, only being restrained with great difficulty by Swinburne. When asked to punish the duo, Swinburne refused, adding: 'I beg to tell you once for all that we do not recognize any flag but our own, nor do the chiefs ... I have nothing more to say to you, so wish you good morning.' Chavannes claimed that, under his breath, Swinburne had called the French flag a rag.[49]

Believing Swinburne's version, de Winton wrote to him, praising his combination of tact and resolution. De Brazza had been driven off without a shot being fired, with the only aggressive acts coming from the chief's sons. It was the best possible outcome. For saving the king's entire operation, the twenty-six-year-old former apprentice tea broker, who had first come to West Africa with Stanley as a boy of sixteen, was given a 25 per cent increase in salary.[50] Since Swinburne would keep de Brazza out until the Berlin Conference, a Belgian title and a pension would have been more appropriate. But being British, his days in Leopold's employment were already numbered, although he himself had no idea of it.

Because the king had editorial control over Stanley's next book, Swinburne's low-key heroics would be omitted from Henry's *The Congo and the Founding of its Free State*. King Leopold's greatest fear was that if they caused offence to the French, the latter would be goaded into aggressive acts against the AIC. Had not the French ratified the Makoko Treaties precisely because Stanley had insulted de Brazza in Paris? So no reference to any of the confrontations at Kinshasa would ever be made public, on the king's insistence.[51] To compensate his protégé Swinburne for being denied the place in history he deserved, Stanley decided that, apart from King Leopold, Mr A. B. Swinburne would be the only man to merit a full-page picture in his new book.[52] The fact that he thereby caused the king great annoyance is a token of Stanley's capacity for loyalty to his humblest friends.

Before leaving the Congo, Henry begged the king to end 'a disgrace to the Association'. Seven European graves at Vivi were still unmarked. Slate or marble headstones, he insisted, should be shipped without delay: 'I plead for their memories.' Henry's last act as Chief Agent on the Congo was to put up wooden crosses as a temporary measure. This lack of respect for its dead pioneers by those formerly in charge of Vivi Station was not an encouraging augury for the value the Association and its successor state would place upon human life in years to come.[53]

NINETEEN

Who Stole the Congo?

After a brief return to London, Stanley travelled to Ostend, where he arrived on 2 August 1884 for a series of meetings with the king at the Chalet Royal, his seaside summer residence. Although he had laboured hard for five years and checkmated de Brazza and the French on the Pool and Upper Congo, Stanley felt anxious about his reception. In November 1883 his letter to Harry Johnston had been published in *The Times*,[1] and two months later the king had written rebuking him for having told Johnston that a British protectorate at the mouth of the Congo was needed to curb the brutality of the Portuguese. 'You lessen your own work by inciting the English to proclaim an English protectorate,' Leopold told Stanley. 'I earnestly beg you to desist writing in this manner ... it can only produce much harm.'[2]

But in early August, Leopold was no longer worried that Stanley's pro-British indiscretions might upset the Germans and the French enough to stop them recognizing the AIC as an independent state. Stanley had no idea that in April, three months earlier, Leopold had dreamed up a brilliant diplomatic ruse to stop the French seizing the Congo by force. He had offered France first option (the *droit de préférence*) on the AIC's territories – exercisable in the event of his financial collapse. At a stroke this had ended France's fear that the Congo might, as Stanley seemed to wish, one day end up in Britain's portfolio of colonies. Knowing herself heir apparent to the Congo, France no longer wished to do anything to threaten the existence of the AIC. Leopold meant to keep Stanley in the dark about his French agreement for as long as possible, to stop him raising a storm in Britain against the protectionist French.

To retain 'first option' on 1.5 million square miles of central Africa, the French had promised Leopold that they would recognize the AIC as a state the moment they were asked to do so.[3] But Leopold had been obliged to pay a price for his new deal. France's principal demand was that Stanley should never return to the Congo. Six years earlier, the king had assured Stanley that if his work on the Congo was crowned with success, he would be sent back there as Governor-General. But three months ago Leopold had promised Jules Ferry, the French prime minister, that Stanley (the man who had made his future colony possible) would never return to the Congo.[4] It was a betrayal on the grand scale. The French prime minister had also insisted that the king appoint no more Anglo-Saxon personnel, and this too had been conceded without argument. Leopold had decided to keep Stanley sweet by deliberately deceiving him and continuing to hint that he would soon be sent back to Africa.[5]

The king had an immediate reason for wishing to keep his former Chief Agent in a cooperative mood. Leopold knew that an international conference of the great powers would soon determine the Congo's future, and he therefore needed Stanley – as the man who had pioneered the new colony – to mark out its boundaries on a map, so that European governments could approve them at this conference. Knowing nothing of Leopold's cynical intention of one day pillaging the Congo, Stanley (while still at Ostend) obligingly drew a generous outline for the future Congo Free State, extending far to the north and south of the equator, and stretching all the way from the Atlantic to Lake Tanganyika.[6] If he had had the slightest inkling of the horror to come during the 1890s, he would not have picked up his pencil.

It has been suggested by biographers and historians that Stanley was Leopold's eager collaborator in the theft of the Congo from the indigenous chiefs,[7] and since such behaviour – if Stanley were guilty of it – carries an implication of partial responsibility for the atrocities that followed in the Congo in the 1890s, a review of the facts is essential in assessing Stanley's moral character. In the first place, how had Henry reacted in mid-1879 when Leopold had first put to him, via his spokesman, Colonel Strauch, the basic idea that the king believed might one day enable him to own the Congo as his personal possession?[8] Strauch wrote on behalf of Leopold:

It is not a question of Belgian colonies ... It is a question of creating a new state, as large as possible, and of running it ... there is no question of granting the slightest political power to negroes. That would be absurd. The white men, heads of stations, retain all the powers ... [and would be] responsible to the Director-General of Stations, who in turn would be responsible to the President of the Confederation [Leopold].

Then he posed a rhetorical question: 'Should we not try to extend the influence of the stations over the neighbouring chiefs, and then from these stations and their dependencies into a republican confederation ...?'[9] Stanley wrote back describing this idea of a confederation and creating a state as 'madness'. It would be utterly unrealistic to do anything but 'leave the petty tribes as we found them'.

Stanley was unaware that Leopold's interest in 'confederation' was less about creating a new set of tribal relationships on the ground than about being able to produce paper 'evidence' suggesting 'political' linkage between AIC stations and hundreds of tribes, so that Leopold would later be able to claim that the whole Congo basin was a single territory 'justified in claiming the title of nation'. Stanley argued against trying to create a state in which whites became local rulers. 'On the contrary,' wrote Stanley, 'they [the Congolese] will retain their own tribal chiefs ... be as jealous as ever of every tribal right, and resent every foreign interference in their own customs or modes of life ... All that we can hope at present is to win sufferance to live and move about without fear of violence, by patience, good nature and honourable traffic ....'[10] This would remain Stanley's position, although Strauch nagged at him to make 'treaties of alliance' with chiefs that would allow them 'the management of all external affairs and the right to represent them'.[11] But – as indicated in Chapters Sixteen and Eighteen above – Stanley did not try to alienate land from chiefs or claim to exercise jurisdiction on their behalf.

Leopold became exasperated, and wrote testily to Strauch in October 1882: 'The terms of the treaties Stanley has made with native chiefs do not satisfy me. There must at least be an added article to the effect that they delegate to us their sovereign rights over the territories ... the treaties must be as brief as possible, and in a couple of articles must grant us everything.'[12] From this date onwards – without consulting Stanley – the king authorized eight, and then many more, of his subordinate officers to negotiate treaties claiming sovereignty and the right to a monopoly of trade for the AIC. Stanley was not a signatory to a single one of these treaties made in 1882 and 1883[13] [see note for details]. From July 1883, Leopold employed the retired British general Sir Frederick Goldsmid to lead a team of treaty makers specifically to negotiate 'confederacy' agreements. They would be answerable only to the king. In fact Leopold did not discuss his most important plans with Stanley, who many years later would write bitterly to Henry Sanford's widow: 'I was too obscure a personage either for the General or the king to confide in me.'[14]

As late as 11 August 1883, in his fifth year on the Congo, Henry wrote to Leopold telling him that no Belgian officer or any one else was entitled to treat the Congolese 'as though they were conquered subjects ... This is all wrong. They are not subjects – but it is we who are simply tenants.' Or, as Stanley insisted to Strauch a few days later: 'These chiefs own and possess the soil.'[15] Henry not only disapproved of treaties alienating land, but deplored those giving the AIC a monopoly of trade that excluded British and American traders.

Only two original treaties bearing Stanley's signature have survived – the rest appear to have been destroyed, either in the mid-1880s, or in the early years of the twentieth century when so many other early records were destroyed on Leopold's orders. The king did not want it ever to be known that Stanley's original treaties had claimed so little from the chiefs. Forgeries were then substituted by the king in order to prove to the international community that sovereignty had been acquired by his agents on the Congo from the very beginning and therefore gave him a right to have the AIC's territories recognized as a state.[16]

So, what do the only two surviving original treaties bearing Stanley's signature prove? The first was supposedly signed by Henry at Vivi on 13 June 1880. While sovereignty is not demanded, the treaty gave to the AIC a monopoly of trade in Vivi district. Since Stanley had made an earlier treaty with the Vivi chiefs on 28 September 1879 – which no longer exists, but is described fully in his diary and in letters,[17] and which did not contain a clause excluding foreign traders – this later treaty is puzzling,[18] especially since, elsewhere, Henry argued in strong terms against all trade restrictions.[19] This June 1880 treaty is not mentioned in his diary, or in letters, so he may have concocted it later under pressure from Leopold. The only other original Stanley treaty that has survived was signed at Ntamo (on the Pool) on 31 December 1881 and is clearly genuine, being described by Stanley in a letter to Colonel Strauch dated 14 January. In the Ntamo treaty Stanley granted to himself, or to his representative, and *not* to the AIC or the Comité, the 'privilege' of building upon a particular site, where his representatives would be allowed to live and trade with the chief and his people. There was no exclusion of traders of other nations, and sovereignty was not claimed.[20] The second Vivi treaty apart, Stanley's other vanished treaties (as deduced from descriptions in his diaries and from summaries in letters to Colonel Strauch) did not include monopolistic clauses, or clauses involving a change of the ownership of the land.

Yet during 1884, at the very end of his time on the Congo, the bloody Arab-Swahili raids persuaded Henry that, unless the AIC had international authority as a sovereign state to deal with this threat by force of arms, the whole Congo basin would descend into anarchy. So at this eleventh hour, he changed his mind about sovereignty. Whether the Congolese understood the meaning of sovereignty or not, the king would need to claim it (or something like it) in order to argue in Europe that the AIC possessed authority over the country – the essential legal prerequisite for its recognition as a state.[21] This reluctant change of heart does not mean that Stanley suddenly became cynical. He believed that Leopold, unlike the French, would keep the River Congo open for the trade of all nations. After all, the king would have to pledge himself to do so in international treaties in order to get the AIC recognized. Henry did not foresee that Leopold would one day break all his promises to the great powers of the world.

So on 23 April 1884, Stanley reported to the king that on his way downriver from the Pool he had 'made treaties at Kimpoko' and that 'Kimbangu, Mbama, and Mikumga have also accepted our flags and sovereignty'.[22] So, having disapproved of claiming sovereignty up to now, what did Stanley mean precisely when saying that at Kimpoko the chiefs had 'accepted our flags and sovereignty'? Two of these treaties mentioned to the king are among those quoted on pages 195–7 and 205 of Stanley's book *The Congo and the Founding of its Free State,* but in view of the falsification of other treaties by Leopold, these printed versions may well differ from their vanished originals.[23] However, there does seem to be something significant about the only treaty printed in the book that was named by Stanley in his letter to the king of 23 April 1884. This was signed by him at Pallaballa village near Vivi on 19 April 1884. In the first clause – as it stands in the book

– it is stated that at this place he was re-making a treaty that had first been made there by Lieutenant Lieven Van de Velde.

A transcription of Van de Velde's treaty has survived, and in it 'the soil' of the relevant territory was ceded 'in consideration of a present, once and for all': the 'present' had included handkerchiefs, alcohol and items of clothing, such as 'a coat of red cloth with gold facings'. In his re-made treaty, Stanley was at pains to nullify this earlier treaty of 7 January 1883.[24] For Van de Velde, the phrase 'Cession of Territory' had meant 'the purchase of the soil', but Stanley amended this, stating that in his new treaty: 'Cession of Territory does not mean the purchase of the soil, but the purchase of suzerainty by the Association.' So the all-important ownership of the land was returned by Stanley to the chiefs. Purchase of 'suzerainty' is not the same as purchase of 'sovereignty', and implies overlordship rather than the removal of all sovereign rights from the chief.[25]

A typed copy of Stanley's Pallaballa treaty (though not the original) is preserved in the Belgian Ministry of Foreign Affairs library. The most important clause gives to the AIA (rather than the AIC) 'the right of governing, of arranging all matters affecting strangers of any colour or nationality'. Similarly, the chiefs 'declare themselves as accepting the flag of the Association International Africaine as a sign to all men that the Association is their accepted suzerain, and that no other flag shall be hoisted within the limits of the district of Pallaballa'. In return for these concessions the chiefs were to be paid a monthly fee. These provisions were clearly intended to stop the French handing out tricolours (as they had done at Kinshasa), and to prevent them from trying to persuade chiefs to let them settle. Even if Stanley did sign an agreement containing these terms (and because there is no original document, it is uncertain that he did), he could not be accused of having usurped the chiefs' authority over their people in any general way.

Stanley noted in his diary, not long after his August meeting, that he had brought back with him to Belgium 'about 400 treaties', showing that 'we have a comparatively continuous territory from Vivi to Stanley Falls'.[26] The context was once again his recent conversion to the view that Leopold was telling the truth when warning him that the French would close the Congo to world trade unless the AIC could produce at an International Conference treaties made with chiefs across a wide swathe of the country. One of Stanley's recent biographers, John Bierman, has blamed him for having personally 'duped' three hundred chiefs into signing away their land.[27] In fact 320 of the rough total of 400 treaties had been with those chiefs who had signed the 'new confederacy' treaty – supposedly uniting them under the AIC's flag for mutual defence against outsiders.[28] These treaties were almost all the result of the treaty-making of Sir Henry Goldsmid and his team.

Stanley did not mention in his book *The Congo and the Founding of its Free State* (*CFFS*) the fact that he had himself made very few treaties and that he had never alienated tribal land. He had been obliged by his original contract with Leopold to allow the king to prohibit publication, if he wished, and to make editorial changes to any book he might write about his work on the Congo. The king also had the right to approve the final text. The copy of the book's manuscript, which Leopold is known to have cut and altered, has disappeared and was probably destroyed by him.[29]

So why did Stanley allow his book to be heavily edited in a way that gave the impression that he had himself negotiated hundreds of confederacy and sovereignty treaties? He permitted it solely so that Leopold could sustain a legal case for gaining international recognition for the Congo as a state. Unaware of all the underlying facts, many historians – even well-known ones like Adam Hochschild – have accepted, mainly on the basis of *CFFS*, that Stanley took away the sovereignty and the ownership of the land of numerous chiefs for a few bales of cloth and some trinkets.[30] The manuscript pages of *CFFS*, Volume II, pages 195–204 – in which the words of treaties that were allegedly negotiated by him are quoted – are not to be found in the only text of the book that exists in the author's hand, and so could have been added by Leopold. The manuscript has numerous gaps, additions in other hands, and pages of printed material inserted at various points.[31] It is therefore a distressing irony that Stanley's reputation should have been so badly damaged by later generations' reliance upon such a singularly unreliable printed source.

Given the way in which Leopold would later milk the Congo and its people, some historians have assumed that men like Stanley, who had regular dealings with the king in the mid-1880s, must have known what was really in his mind. Yet even razor-sharp Harry Johnston had not been able to work out, on meeting Leopold, whether he was 'marvellously simple or marvellously deep'.[32] The £60,000 a year that Leopold was by now spending in the Congo was a staggering sum; and since the king's returns from ivory sales had been paltry to date, Stanley was irritated on those rare occasions when journalists suggested that Leopold's philanthropy might be fraudulent.[33] In February 1885, William Mackinnon, the shipping tycoon, wrote with absolute conviction of Leopold having undertaken 'the noblest and most self-sacrificing scheme for Africa's development that has ever been attempted'.[34] This was at a time when Mr Dunlop's invention of his inflatable rubber tyre still lay five years in the future, and the value of the Congo's wild rubber was very modest. Nevertheless, given the mutilations and misery to come, it is hard not to gasp at the scale of the king's hypocrisy when reading a fairly typical letter he sent to *The Times* in March 1883: 'The International Congo Association as it does not seek to gain money, and does not beg for aid of any state, resembles in a measure, by its organization, the Society of the Red Cross; it has been formed ... with the noble aim of rendering lasting and disinterested services to the cause of progress.'[35] But at that time, even William Bentley, the often sceptical Baptist missionary, could write 'that this Expedition [the AIC] has been the instrument in God's hand of opening up the country.'[36]

Stanley's respect for the Congolese people adds to the irony that he should still be thought of as their exploiter. This is how he described the ivory traders of Irebu, who lived in 'the Venice of the Congo':

I was very soon impressed by their intelligent appearance ... They had an air of worldly knowledge and travel about them ... For these people were acquainted with many lands and tribes ... they knew all the profits and losses derived from barter; all the diplomatic arts ... They knew the varied lengths of the sina ('long' cloth), the number of matako (brass rods) they were worth, whether of savelist, florentine, unbleached domestic, twill, stripe, ticking, blue and white baft ... No wonder that all this mercantile knowledge had left its traces on their faces; indeed it is the same as in your own cities ... Know you not the lawyer, or the merchant, the banker, the artist or the poet?[37]

Henry even paid tributes to the cannibal Soko tribe for 'their remarkable skill in workmanship ... On a paddle blade may be seen an infinite number of carvings, lizards, crocodiles, canoes and buffalo ... Their spears are as sharp and bright as though they had just left a Sheffield shop ... Physically they are a splendid people.'[38] He suggested that, 'If Europeans will only ... study human nature in the vicinity [of Stanley Pool], they will go home thoughtful men, and may return again to this land to put to good use the wisdom they should have gained, and the kindly social relations created during their peaceful sojourn.'[39]

The king's knowledge that Stanley would never be willing to implement exploitative or protectionist measures on the Congo gave him another reason – in addition to his infamous promise to the French government – not to allow him back to the Congo. Leopold owed everything to his 'enterprising American' who had risked his life so often, yet the prospect of deceiving him for years to come did not worry the unscrupulous monarch. Henry remained trusting, and confident that within a year or so his patron would send him back to run the new colony as its Governor-General. If his private life had only been happier, he would have awaited the king's pleasure with equanimity.

TWENTY

A Pawn in Great Power Politics

On returning from Brussels and Paris at the beginning of September 1884, Stanley had many doubts about the future of the AIC. The 25 per cent mortality of the whites serving under him had been an alarming augury for future traders and colonial servants.[1] He also feared that his public estimate of the Congo's population at about forty million might be a substantial exaggeration (as indeed it was). And fewer Africans living along the river would mean less profit for European traders selling cloth and other goods to them. Then there was the problem of Leopold continuing to spend huge sums year after year and getting no return. How long could that go on? And what might happen if the king were suddenly to die? The *Saturday Review*'s editor asked, very pertinently, what was going to finance the king's efforts when ivory was exhausted? Palm oil, ground nuts, ebony and gum copal were never going to make up for its loss. At this time there was no expectation that rubber might one day be more valuable than ivory.[2] Yet Stanley continued enthusing about the Congo's commercial prospects at large meetings in Manchester, Birmingham and other cities, and urging traders to go there in the footsteps of the hundred or so missionaries who had already done so.[3]

Of course, from a personal point of view, if the AIC failed to achieve recognition and fell into the hands of the Arabs or the French, five unimaginably hard years of his life would have been thrown away for nothing. Three years earlier, Stanley had written in his diary: 'I am devoured with a desire to do something for Africa, and have found in King Leopold one who not only possesses the means but the will to assist.'[4] Stanley's tragedy (though he did not yet know it) was that, after his unparalleled success as an explorer had made future African exploration anticlimactic, his subsequent efforts to improve the lot of Africans were already being subverted by a patron who was about to deceive the world as well as his most famous employee.

For the moment, Henry's negative feelings about Leopold were mainly connected with the unappreciative monarch's failure to consult him about the future of the AIC. After all, he was its architect. In late August 1884, Stanley was sent a renewal of his original contract, but his anxiety about being kept in the dark led him to postpone signing it.[5] A few weeks later, clandestine diplomatic exchanges were used to explain why the king could not yet allow publication of *The Congo and the Founding of its Free State*.[6] Stanley accepted the situation gracefully, though hurt to be told so little.

A few days before Leopold had made his secret agreement with France – again without telling Stanley, the king had engineered the immense triumph of American recognition of the AIC as a state. In November, Henry Sanford, the former American minister in Brussels and now Leopold's emissary extraordinary, had been received by President Arthur at the White House, where Sanford handed over a letter in which Leopold made much of the supposed similarities between his projected 'free state' and Liberia – founded sixty years earlier by American philanthropists as a home for freed slaves. Leopold also stressed the 'fact' that Stanley was an American.[7] Sanford had brought to America copies of various forged treaties, with sovereignty clauses inserted and all monopolistic ones removed. A convinced free trader himself, with plans to start an ivory company on the Congo, Sanford thought these altered treaties genuine.[8] Known as the 'gastronomic diplomat', he had wined and dined numerous members of Congress and Cabinet members, and organized a lavish entertainment for the president at his orange plantation in Florida. His reward, and Leopold's, was that on 22 April 1884 the Senate voted a resolution recommending that the flag of the association should be recognized as the 'flag of a friendly government'.[9]

Recognition by the United States had brought Leopold's dream of his very own African state a lot closer. But to clinch it, the king had to ensure that a treaty Britain had signed with Portugal in February was never accepted internationally. France's ratification of the Makoko Treaty in November 1882 had persuaded Britain that the only way to deny France control of the Lower Congo was to hand that right to Portugal. But after discussions with Leopold, Bismarck rejected the

Anglo-Portuguese treaty in June 1884, effectively killing it. With Germany entering the race for African colonies, the Iron Chancellor had not wanted Britain, the principal power in Africa, to control the Congo through her puppet, Portugal. Nor did Bismarck want Leopold to be forced to hand the Congo to the French. So, the chancellor decided to support the AIC – just as Leopold had calculated he would. In Prince Bismarck's words, the Congo, as a state in Leopold's hands, would be 'useful for diverting troublesome rivalries'.[10]

Therefore when Leopold sent to Bismarck the very map Stanley had drawn for him, the German chancellor accepted its generous dimensions without demur, although he was the one statesman convinced that Leopold's claims to be a philanthropist were bogus. He scrawled the word 'Schwindel' in the margin of one of the documents sent to him by Leopold, just beside some pious anti-slavery rhetoric. Then he wrote 'Fantasies' beside a paragraph asserting that, though ruled by the King of the Belgians, the new state would be administered by a council.[11]

From May 1884, it had been apparent to the great powers and to Portugal that the dispute over which nation should control the Congo and its mouth could be resolved only by diplomacy, or war – though the latter seemed unlikely given the unknown value of the prize. As early as May 1884, the Portuguese had suggested an international conference, and Bismarck had sounded out France as part of his efforts to rebuild Franco-German relations in the aftermath of the Franco-Prussian war. His eagerness to prevent Britain controlling the agenda led him to offer Berlin as the venue. When this location was accepted by France, Bismarck knew that he had his conference.

Still smarting from Britain's assumption of full powers in Egypt in 1882, the French were determined not to let the Anglo-Saxons take over the Congo under the cloak of a Portuguese mandate. Britain, in her turn, would not allow French ambitions in West Africa to threaten British traders on the great oil river, the Niger. Bismarck, meanwhile, was determined to see that Germany did not lose out in Africa. So, before the conference began, Bismarck decided to recognize the AIC as a nation in order to deny the Congo to his real colonial rivals, Britain and France.

It is often said that at the Berlin Conference the European nations carved up Africa. The large map of Africa on the wall behind the horseshoe-shaped table in Bismarck's official residence in the Wilhemstrasse had much to do with this myth. Although *some* carving was undoubtedly done, it was not on a continental scale. The press called it the Congo Conference, or the West African Conference, and these two names broadly defined the area of its remit. However, the conference at Berlin, under whatever name, would turn out to be an important staging post on the road to European control of the greater part of Africa.

Amazingly, though Bismarck sent out invitations to America and to a dozen European nations on 8 October, Stanley would only hear from Leopold's office four days after the press announcement that a conference was to be held in Berlin.[12] The AIC was not yet a nation, and so could not be directly represented, but Stanley still hoped to join the Belgian delegation as an adviser. He would be disappointed. The king's worries about French reactions to his possible presence in Berlin led him to exclude the one man who had a cast-iron right to be there. However, on 16 October, Mr J. A. Kasson, the American minister in Berlin, invited Stanley to join the United States delegation to advise him. When Stanley asked Leopold whether he could accept this invitation, the king said he would first need to know whether the German chancellor wanted him in Berlin. Since Bismarck (unlike Leopold) had no worries about ruffling French feathers, he was delighted to welcome the man who had first navigated the Congo. So, very belatedly, five days before the conference was due to start, Leopold's private secretary informed Stanley that permission to travel to Berlin had been granted by His Majesty.[13]

Since both Germany and Britain were 'free trade' nations and wished to stop the protectionist France occupying the Congo basin, it was inevitable that during the conference both would put pressure on France and Portugal to recognize the AIC as an independent state with adequate access to the sea. Thanks to Leopold's genius as a negotiator, his new state emerged, after protracted horse-trading, as the possessor of both banks of the Congo between Vivi and Manyanga, and the south bank from Manyanga to the Upper Congo. Both north and south banks were awarded to Leopold from Lukolela eastwards to the Lualaba, and beyond that the new state would stretch to faraway lakes Albert and Tanganyika. To cap it all, Leopold would cede the Kwilu-Niadi valley to the French in exchange for a massive southern extension of his borders to Katanga. Since Leopold would turn out to be the very reverse of the benign trustee figure he was universally taken for in 1884–5, the long-term results of the Berlin Conference would be catastrophic. Indeed, even to this day, with chaos and carnage raging in eastern Congo, it can rightly be seen to have been an incalculable disaster for humanity that this vast colony was ever placed in the hands of the King of the Belgians. The role Stanley played at the conference, in supporting the most grandiose definition of the extent of the Congo basin, directly involved him in this terrible misjudgement. But, as with the politicians at the Paris Peace Conference of 1919, where the seeds of the Second World War were sown, the statesmen and their advisers in Berlin in 1884–5 felt that they were placing a large area of Africa safely outside the field of great power competition to the advantage of all peace-loving people.

As Prince Bismarck began his opening address, the ghostly mantle of Dr Livingstone seemed to envelop the proceedings like a benevolent fog, concealing all hints of greed and mutual suspicion.

The Imperial Government has been guided by the conviction that all the governments invited here share the desire to associate the natives of Africa with civilisation, by opening up the interior to commerce, by furnishing the natives with the means of instruction, by encouraging missions and enterprises so that useful knowledge may be disseminated, and by paving the way to the suppression of slavery.

If ever the road to hell can fairly be said to have been paved with good intentions, it was in Berlin in late 1884 and early 1885.[14] Stanley returned to London, genuinely believing that his great work had been saved. He still expected to become the Governor-General of the Congo Free State. And in that supreme position, he would be able to see that all went well for the new state and its inhabitants. Confident of this, he now signed his contract with the king, agreeing to hold himself in readiness to return to the Congo after 1 June 1885, for the consideration of a retainer from Leopold of £1,000 per annum.[15]

Yet as 1885 progressed, Stanley started, bit by bit, to lose faith in the philanthropic monarch. During the Berlin Conference, he was forbidden to lecture in Germany in case he said anything that might upset anyone,[16] causing him to complain that 'the French suggestions against me, with their quotations from my speeches, letters & so forth are only excuses to palliate their evident intention to circumscribe the Congo territory and take a goodly portion of it for themselves'.[17] What rankled with Stanley was that despite his having done so much for Leopold, the king never once saw fit to defend him in public.

A worse betrayal was Leopold's refusal to reappoint Anthony Swin-burne and Seymour Saulez, the two men who more than any others were responsible for saving for the AIC, at risk of their lives, Kinshasa and Stanley Pool – the very core of the new state. And why was the king abandoning them? Because de Brazza had complained about them to the French cabinet, as he had already complained against Stanley for stopping him getting all the territories he wanted. Stanley appealed to de Winton on Swinburne's behalf: 'He is an old friend of mine and he has done his work well and nobly.' De Winton said he could do nothing, and Brussels responded to Stanley's 'urgent appeals ... with studied neglect'. 'I shall remember it to my dying day,' Stanley told de Winton. 'It has cost me continued pain and misery.'[18]

In March 1885, the king and his secretary, Count Borchgrave, at last consented to the publication of *The Congo and the Founding of its Free State*, but insisted on yet more textual changes. Stanley must not criticize any of the Belgian officers who had been brutal or incompe-tent, and, he was told, 'you must not allow a single word to be written so as to hurt the legitimate pride of any power ... His Majesty wishes that your book might be pleasing to all nations.'[19] Stanley explained to Henry Sanford why he nevertheless meant to dedicate the book to Leopold. If the king declined the 'honour' – as threatened in a recent letter from Borchgrave – it would seem 'to the world that we had quarrelled'.[20] One of Leopold's cuts to the book had been Stanley's final words, which I have added in italics to the published final sen-tence. 'I have no reason to believe that His Majesty was displeased with the results of these long years of bitter labour *but I certainly never received any letter or written communication conveying his sen-timents, and I must therefore leave each reader to form his own con-clusions.*'[21] Ingratitude on this scale truly beggars belief.

Just when Stanley's immediate future seemed to be darkening, he was obliged to confront his American past. This arose from the deci-sion of Harper's – his American publisher – not to bring out his new book unless he stopped it being pirated. Because there was no copy-right protection in America for the works of foreigners, Stanley was asked to give proof of nationality, or be naturalized. He had always imagined that by taking the oath of allegiance at Camp Douglas he had become an American, but now he learned that he had not. Unfor-tunately, to qualify for naturalization he would have to visit America and obtain an honourable discharge from the American army, from which he had deserted in the summer of 1862. (He did not intend to mention his later desertion from the US navy.) Since his army desertion had been due in part to a spell in hospital, after which he had become separated from his regiment, Henry decided to claim that he had been given a medical certificate of discharge – now lost. Luckily, the records of Harper's Ferry Hospital had disappeared, so the Adjutant-General was delighted to be fed such a persuasive reason for striking the charge of desertion from the military record of a famous man.[22]

Stanley's humble past surfaced again to upset him on his return. In March 1885, he was described in the very first issue of the Scottish Geographical Society's magazine as 'the Americanized English-speaking Welshman', who had been born in Denbigh, where he had had 'such education as slender means would allow'.[23] Because of his friendship with Alexander Bruce, Livingstone's son-in-law, Henry had come up to Edinburgh four months earlier to give the inaugural address to the members of the Scottish Geographical Society, whose honorary treasurer Bruce was. He therefore felt very bitter that the Society should have published details culled from Hotten's detested book. Henry still could not bring himself to admit the truth about his origins. The account in the magazine made him feel 'belittled', he told Bruce, as if 'his unguarded years' had been 'flung in his face' after all his efforts 'to emerge from the shadow of these unfavourable circumstances'. It made him shudder to think how it would affect his prospects with young gentlewomen.[24] In replying to this tirade, Bruce described himself as naught but 'a common brewer' (he was a director of William Younger's brewery), who comforted himself that 'a man who is diligent in his business shall stand before kings'.[25] Despite the offending magazine, it delighted Stanley to enjoy the friendship of men like Bruce and the Christian shipping magnate, William Mackinnon. These heirs of Livingstone have been described with justice as 'the cream of British humanitarians',[26] and parts of Stanley's Edinburgh speech were music to their ears:

Since David Livingstone has declared that the end of the geographical feat is the beginning of the commercial enterprise, do you wonder that I, the last member of his race who talked with him, should take up his work with the view of redeeming Africa from its poverty by initiating legitimate commercial enterprise?[27]

'Redeeming Africa' was an idea that also inspired Mackinnon, who during this period became as close to Stanley as to Bruce. If the upright, slightly solemn Bruce was like a caring brother, the elegant, white-whiskered Mackinnon was to be, after Livingstone, the last father figure in Henry's life. And to the childless millionaire, Stanley would be the son he had never had, whom he could help, and take pride in as his glamorous partner in the adventure of opening up Africa to Christian influence.

Mackinnon was self-made, having worked in a Scottish grocer's shop before forming an Indian trading and shipping company with a former school friend.[28] His interest in East Africa had first come about through his Imperial British India Steam Navigation Company's traffic between Bombay and Zanzibar. Mackinnon had known Leopold since 1876, when the king had launched the AIA. Since then the Scot had backed several Leopoldian ventures in East Africa, and when the king transferred his attention to the Congo, Mackinnon had followed suit. With his friend James Hutton he had been one of only two British investors invited to participate in the Comité du Haut Congo. After buying them out, Leopold had offered to both men 'a right of preference ... for every commercial or industrial or financial operation issued ... in connection with the Congo', and this had been coupled with a verbal promise of first refusal on the vital railway concession between Vivi and the Pool.[29]

Henry had been fascinated by the railway since 1879, and in the spring of 1885 he was overjoyed to be authorized by Leopold to raise money in London. He came to Mackinnon first. Henry and the shipping magnate believed that if this railway was eventually built by their syndicate, the Congo might yet become a predominantly British sphere of influence. Whenever Henry was dining with Mackinnon in London's exclusive Burlington Hotel, or cruising in the Hebrides on his yacht, the two men talked for hours about their Congo dreams. By the summer of 1885, the railway project seemed to be going well, and Leopold had asked for £200,000 of English capital immediately.[30]

June 1885 was the month when Stanley expected to be sent back to Africa as Governor-General. He therefore purchased a riding donkey, spent £500 on his kit, and wrote to Leopold's secretary, reminding him of their earlier correspondence and detailing why he now expected to return to Africa. Borchgrave replied at the end of the month: 'It is indeed quite impossible for me to determine at present the moment when we will ask you to return to Africa.'[31] A letter from Leopold in late July was just as vague.[32] Although Stanley at last suspected that Leopold might have sacrificed him to French prejudice, he was by no means sure of it and so lived in perpetual hope that the call to depart might suddenly arrive. His life in London seemed eerily empty. Unable to sign a new lease on an apartment, or accept lucrative invitations to lecture, Henry would have found life bleak indeed without his railway dreams. Then, out of the blue, at the end of this disappointing month, a different kind of happiness unexpectedly beckoned.

TWENTY-ONE

'A Kind of Innocence'

In 1882, Stanley had asked his friend Edward King to look out for suitable marriage partners for him, and in Paris, through Edward, he had met not a marriageable woman but a married one whom he had found deeply sympathetic. May Sheldon reciprocated, describing herself as 'his votary', and telling Henry that it gave her 'a rare personal happiness and delight' to know that he would soon be back in Europe. Stanley admitted that women tended to reject him, and asked her humbly: 'Do you think I am a man who deserves fidelity?' In reply, she assured him vehemently that he did.[1] Henry gratified her wish 'to come quickly to Paris' by arriving in the French capital before the end of the month.[2] May had a suite in a Paris hotel, but knowing that Henry would soon be living in London told him she intended to join her husband there.[3] Delighted, Stanley suggested that she and her husband, Eli, come and live in Sackville Street, Piccadilly, in the same building as himself. May pronounced this 'a very charming scheme',[4] and lost no time in taking an apartment in Stanley's building in Sackville Street. So Henry was soon able to see her most days when he was in town. Several amusing photographs from this period have survived. One taken at the Hotel Meurice, when Henry was in Paris in late August 1884, shows Mrs Sheldon (bottom right) with Stanley to the left (see Plate 24).[5]

Shortly before May Sheldon arrived in London, Stanley – greatly daring – asked her how women fell in love. Though normally down to earth, May replied in extremely romantic language.

Love, in its most intense expression comes to two persons simultaneously like a flash of lightning! Two persons meet and their souls recognize kinship without reason, despite circumstances, obeying a law divine above all civil laws. Though

harsh <u>circumstances</u> [May's emphasis] may forever hold them asunder, deep down
... before the altar of their souls forever burns the fire of the one great passion of
their existence.

She then hinted that her marriage was an open one. 'There you see I
do know something about love ... I also know the benediction of a
harmonious union and therefore am <u>safer</u> [May's emphasis] for a
score of experiences!'

It is difficult not to read into 'experiences' romantic and even physical ones. Her 'safety' resided in her not being a young woman whose
marriage prospects could be ruined by scandal. She had a husband
already – an acquiescent one at that – so no harm could come to her.[6]
Eli Sheldon travelled a lot, and was known to chase women. It was
said that he and May had an understanding.[7] When her career as a
journalist obliged her to return to America in October, she wrote at
once on arrival: 'Believe me my dear friend, it cost me much genuine
feeling to leave Europe whilst you were there and we were so housed
beside you.' She added that she had given a public talk about him in
Washington and had reduced people to tears. 'Someone said to me,
"You are a great advocate of Stanley's I see?" "Yes," I responded, "I
glory in the man for every act in his marvellous life ... and quite adore
his royal manliness to say nothing about my estimate of his great
genius.' Then she added, most endearingly: 'Think me not a saphead
for so frankly expressing myself.' May ended by declaring that she was
not ashamed to 'avow <u>my love</u> ... for one of the most intolerant of
blessed tyrants', whom she prayed would soon be coming to America.[8]

Though strongly attracted to Mrs Sheldon, Stanley wanted to have
children, and therefore needed a wife rather than a mistress. So in
May's absence, he continued searching for a suitable bride.[9] Just
before leaving Paris for Brussels, he had written sadly to Edward King,
confessing: 'I am absolutely uncomfortable when speaking to a
woman unless she is such a rare one that she will let me hear some
common sense.' He then told King that only with Mrs Sheldon did he
feel at ease. With others, 'I am just as much a hypocrite as any other
man and it galls me that I must act and be affected and parody myself
... It is such a false position.'[10]

Before she left for America, May introduced Stanley to her rich
friend Henry Wellcome, the pharmaceuticals millionaire, who was
already fascinated by the explorer's career and hoped to supply him
with tropical medicines. Stanley co-opted Wellcome into helping him

with his search for a wife. But when the chemist urged him to take some young ladies boating, the great navigator of the Congo decided he would do better to make his own plans.[11] He accepted an invitation to stay at Newstead Abbey, after his friend Alexander Bruce had predicted that the elder daughters of the Webb family would be interested in him. Once there, Stanley found that they had eyes only for young aristocrats and he 'could scale the moon before making any impression'.[12]

When May Sheldon returned to London from America in June 1885, Stanley had still not found a woman whom he even wanted to get to know. His only involvements had been a brief correspondence with an anonymous Austrian woman, and a period being pursued by a crazed female who seems to have claimed that he was the father of her child.[13] Small wonder that at this juncture Stanley wrote to Mrs Sheldon in her new lodgings in Earl's Court, asking if she could find him a house close to her.[14] 'Bless your heart, my dear friend,' she replied, 'it is no trouble.' She then promised that if they should ever be neighbours again, she would not 'drag [him] out to places or dinners [he did] not care to go to'.[15] Within days she found him a house in Earl's Court – but at this point fate served up to him, at a private dinner party, Dorothy Tennant, an Englishwoman who was single, intelligent, attractive, well-connected, rich and thirty years old – so a potential mother. This introduction had been effected by the editor of the *Daily Telegraph* – Stanley's friend, and former sponsor, Edwin Arnold. 'What a charming lady Miss Dorothy is!' Henry told Edwin the following day, unaware that the venerable editor was himself a former suitor.

On that same day, 25 June, Stanley wrote to May Sheldon telling her that he was in 'a miserable state of uncertainty' and could not make up his mind whether or not to take the Earl's Court house. He gave as his reason the fact that, any day, Leopold might send him back to the Congo. But really he now had another cause for being uncertain what to do.[16] Quite soon he concluded that if he were to have any chance with Dorothy, he ought to see less of Mrs Sheldon. So a few weeks later he moved to another flat, 160, New Bond Street, rather than to Earl's Court.

In most ways, May would have been the perfect wife for Stanley. Unlike Dorothy, she was not interested in 'high society'. Being a journalist, she was never prissy or over-fastidious, and could stand up for herself in any situation. Formal social occasions meant as little to her as they did to Stanley. She enjoyed travelling as he did, and actually became an explorer. But of course she was married, and even if she had decided to divorce her husband, she might not have been able to have children – after all, she was childless after eight years of marriage. So Stanley's best bet seemed to be the younger, unattached Dorothy.

On the evening Stanley had first dined with the Tennants at their house in Richmond Terrace, Whitehall, other guests had included Mr Gladstone, who had resigned as prime minister only days earlier, and Joseph Chamberlain.[17] The hostess was Gertrude Tennant, the widow of Charles Tennant, the former Liberal MP for St Albans and a large landowner. He had died a dozen years earlier, leaving his wife a rich woman. Charles had been fifty-eight when Dorothy – Dolly to the family – had been born, and in childhood she had lived in dread that he might suddenly die.[18] Although he had survived until she was nineteen and he seventy-seven, Dolly was inconsolable after his death. Until the 1890s, she would keep a regular, though not quite daily, diary in which entries would begin, typically, 'Dear Father', or at more highly charged moments, 'My own Darling', and end 'Good night my beloved Father'. The diary itself was not as eccentric as the above might suggest. Though volatile, Dolly was a highly intelligent woman with impressive intuitive and intellectual powers. Most diaries act as their writers' confidants, and Dolly's was no exception, helping her to cope with emotions she could not discuss with her mother, to whom she was oppressively close. Dolly was a more complex woman than the bright, socially adept person she often appeared to be. 'What contradictions we are. Outspoken – and yet never speaking of oneself to anyone – ambitious to succeed and yet caring nothing for oneself. Joyous and pleasure loving and yet so sorrowful in oneself that happiness seems unnatural.'[19]

The ambitions she referred to were for her painting career, and also for an exalted social life, to which she gave as much energy as to her art. The subjects of her paintings included romanticized 'street urchins' and allegorical female nudes. She had been taught at the Slade and had then studied in Paris.[20] (Although verging on sentimental *kitsch*, Dolly's most famous painting, *At Play*, in which four urchins swing on a rail with the Thames in the background, has stood the test of time and can be bought online as a print.) Dolly exhibited fitfully at the Grosvenor and the New Gallery in Regent Street. Watts had painted her portrait with a squirrel in her arms, and Millais had depicted her pondering a letter, in a painting entitled *No!*. In fact the men she fell for tended to be father figures, ten or even twenty years older than herself, and usually married and famous, so she may not have turned down any proposals before she met Stanley.

Edwin Arnold had not been a great passion, though he was the ideal age (twenty years her senior). He was also well known, being the editor of a famous newspaper and the author of a famous poem, 'The Light of Asia', which had sold in over thirty languages, creating an immense interest in Buddhism. In 1885 Dolly was depressed that he rarely came to see her any more. A few years later he would marry, as his third wife, a twenty-year-old Japanese woman.[21] The great Comedie Française actor Constant Benoit Coquelin she had known since her period as an art student in Paris, and she still enjoyed his visits to London, and receiving his letters to 'Ma Chérie'. But though he had visited her quite often in the early 1880s, he too was falling away now. She flirted a bit, these days, with the forty-seven-year-old Sir George Trevelyan, the former Chief Secretary for Ireland, now Secretary of State for Scotland, occasionally giving him paintings, about which he wrote admiringly, but he rarely visited her.[22] As Dolly put it: 'I have mother, my all, and no one else ... I feel desperately lonely.' And this was despite being an acknowledged beauty, with her auburn hair and creamy complexion.[23] So, in the summer of 1885, the auguries looked reasonably good for Stanley who, besides being famous, was mature enough to appeal, being fourteen years older. His only obvious disadvantage was that he was four or five inches shorter than the statuesque Dolly.[24]

She seemed interested from the start. Despite describing him in her diary as: 'A very short ... determined man', she found 'his bearing dignified', and wrote after their first meeting: 'I felt I cared for him. I know he cared back for me.' She also told her diary something very significant: Stanley reminded her of Andrew Carnegie, the steel tycoon, with whom she had been infatuated in 1883.[25] Dorothy wrote to Stanley the very next day, asking him to call on her. So a few days later, Henry returned to 2, Richmond Terrace to take tea. He was admitted by a footman (one of a pair) wearing a yellow coat, knee breeches, pink stockings and powdered wig. Eight servants, including a cook and a butler, looked after Mrs Tennant, Miss Tennant and

Master Charles Tennant in London.[26] The whole house had the air of a Louis Philippe salon with white and gold furniture and marble-topped tables.

As a child and young woman, Gertrude had lived in Paris and taken holidays in Trouville. Her father was said to have been a naval attaché at the British Embassy, but in fact Admiral Collier had been obliged to live in France to escape his creditors. In the 1840s, Gertrude and her sister, Henrietta, had met Gustave Flaubert, who had soon been attracted strongly to each in turn. Even after they returned to Britain, he corresponded with the sisters for the rest of his life.[27] Through Flaubert, Gertrude had also made friends with Alphonse Daudet and developed a lifelong admiration for writers. But her early experience of poverty and exclusion from fashionable society caused her to admire the wealthy and the powerful too. Her daughter, Dorothy, inherited both these traits. Since Henry had no idea that Gertrude had suffered youthful privations, it must have been daunting to be led through these opulent rooms. Certainly, he felt sure that his work-house years ought to be concealed.

The day after Dolly had received him, she offered to paint his portrait. 'I would let you be very comfortable, you shall smoke, and feel just as though you were in your own tent.' She modestly disclaimed any great experience as a portraitist, merely saying that she had 'succeeded before once or twice'.[28] Henry's sittings began in mid-July, and on the first day Dolly wrote a remarkably clear-eyed artist's description of him.

His thick grey hair lies flat and smooth, rather thatch-like ... near silver white; his thick throat supports a splendidly shaped head, broad ... and well-developed ... His forehead is square, his eyes are very remarkable ... they make you sincere, they demand of you your very self ... His mouth is partly concealed by a grizzly moustache ... the nether lip is masterful and determined ... His face is somewhat marked by exposure to the sun, by fever, by responsibility, by anxiety ... His eyes look tender and sorrowful ... He uses his hands very much when talking ... What seized me when I first saw him ... is his powerfulness ... Mother also felt it.

In her small studio, known as the 'Birdcage', Dolly got to know Stanley as he sat for her. He usually came at eleven and stayed till two. 'He speaks so frankly ... so confidingly,' she wrote after a month. 'He tells me about himself, his hopes, his ambitions, his struggles.'[29] He admitted that although he ought to be sent to Africa as Governor-General of the Congo, this might never happen. 'The Belgians murmur at an American, or rather an Englishman, becoming the head of the Congo.' Henry was honest about his job prospects, but not about being Welsh. He spoke of 'simple sights' that gave him pleasure, such as 'seeing children playing on the sands'. On another occasion, he said: 'I am a man of action, a man who must struggle forward to do and to be ... My happiness lies in contending against difficulties.' Yet he conceded that there were 'kinds of happiness unguessed at by [him]'. Dolly then asked if he had ever loved and was rewarded with the story of Alice Pike. 'I felt so sorry for him,' she wrote in her diary; 'there is a loneliness and disappointment about his life, which he will not allow, but which I see ... People touch me very much; more and more I think as I grow older.'[30]

By the end of July, Stanley was dining quite often with the Tennants, having tea, and coming for his sittings. Yet he dared not feel optimistic. He told Alexander Bruce, glumly: 'Further than Platonism I doubt my affair will go ... it is so very innocent ... I am easily rebuffed & very sensitive. If she proposed to me, it might be very different, but if I have to propose to her, do you know I rather think I will not have the courage.'[31]

In the summer of 1885, he also sat to the portrait painter Robert Gibb, best known for his military scenes. While Henry never commented on Dorothy's very competent likeness of him, he showered Gibb's portrait with praise. 'It is my very self,' he told Bruce, showing considerable self-awareness. At first glance, this fine painting merely seems to depict the dour and masterful man of contemporary posed photographs, but a closer look, especially at the eyes, reveals not only a more reflective and sensitive person, but one haunted by a desolating sadness. All the loneliness of his early life seems present in these wary, fearful eyes.[32]

By the time Dorothy went away for a series of summer visits to friends' country houses, including her own family's in south Wales, she had become fascinated by Stanley. And yet a basic incomprehension remained. 'I admire your undaunted courage. The only thing I cannot quite understand is your incentive. What is the fuel which makes the water boil, the steam rises and the paddles move? Why do people do the things they do?'[33] That this puzzlement was mutual became apparent when Dorothy wrote to Henry after she had stayed in Newcastle with the ex-miner Thomas Burt, who had become the first working-class MP in 1874. She described going down a mine and visiting the face, where she saw 'in the darkness, the little twinkling lights ... and the fine strong men hewing away at the walls of coal'. She also described the ships being built along the Tyne and the forest of chimneys and cranes, and explained that she had 'felt intuitively that the future of England depends upon the working classes ...'.[34] Since, over the years, an immense intellectual and emotional gulf had opened between Stanley and his narrow-minded working class relations, Henry could not take seriously Dolly's romantic view of harsh lives. He replied to her letter from Switzerland, saying that the contrast between the 'roar of mechanical Newcastle' and 'the tranquillity and awful calm of the snowy ranges' was too great even to write about, and probably of no interest to her while she was 'surrounded by gaieties'. He was entering a phase in his life when he longed for 'the quiet happiness' of living, he wrote, 'in harmony with my surroundings ... [with] ambitions and dreams laid by'. And yet duty could not be avoided, and he would go on, he told her, 'preparing myself against the contingencies of new labors [sic] in Africa, since as far as I know I am destined for nothing more'.[35]

Hurt by Stanley's supposing her incapable of understanding his love of nature, and also by his apparent determination to return to Africa, Dolly wrote: 'What undiscovered countries we are to each other. And yet you are a great explorer. How is it you have not understood me better?' Yet she was honest enough to admit that her social pleasures were indeed important to her, and that she found 'politics dangerously fascinating'.[36] This exchange of letters marked a new realism, a recognition of real differences, but the continuation of deep affection. Much of October Stanley spent cruising in the Hebrides on William Mackinnon's yacht, but in November he and Dorothy resumed their regular meetings, and at this time Henry gave her a silver map of Africa as a memento.[37]

Much of December was spent by Stanley and his friends, Mackinnon and Hutton, in Brussels, trying to hammer out a definite agreement over the railway concession. But by now, Leopold was furtively raising Belgian capital – his fear being that Stanley's syndicate, besides demanding a substantial share of the railway's profits, would lead to British domination of the Congo. When, just before Christmas, the king declared himself only prepared to sign an agreement 'in principle', Stanley was outraged. He and his friends had received promises of £400,000 of the necessary £1,000,000 from a large number of rich investors; and thanks to Stanley's several visits to North Wales, they had settled on the Ffestiniog slate railway, with its unique twin-boiler locomotive, as being the perfect steam combination for the Congo.[38] On 16 January, Stanley wrote telling Leopold that unless he published a denial of rumours that he (Stanley) had lost the king's favour, it would destroy the British syndicate. This was because major investors, like Mackinnon, would only commit capital if Stanley were placed in charge on the ground.[39] Still unsure of his ability to raise adequate Belgian funds, Leopold was obliged to award Stanley the highest rank in the Order of Leopold and to make a fulsome denial of all rumours that he had fallen out with his former Chief Agent.[40]

While they were in Brussels, Henry told Mackinnon about his desire to marry Dolly. His friend responded by offering to help in any way he could. One problem, Stanley explained, was his lack of family – a problem with which the childless Mackinnon sympathized. On their return to England, Stanley managed to persuade Dolly to come to his New Bond Street flat, with her mother and her sister, Eveleen. 'I have succeeded for a wonder,' he told Mackinnon. '<u>She</u> will come tomorrow ... and therefore you must come, & stand as a kind of amiable friend of established repute to be benignant and good to <u>all</u> of us.' The occasion went so well, with Mackinnon in the role of adoptive father, that two weeks later Stanley was able to tell him: 'I have an invitation for you. Mrs Tennant invites you to dinner & Miss Dorothy seconds ... and they say they will be delighted to lunch on one of your big ships.'[41]

At this time, Dolly gave Stanley a tiny silver token for his watch chain, with her personal emblem, a triangle, and superimposed letter 'T', for Tennant, cut into it and the words 'Bula Matari tala' painted in enamel. Tala means remember in Swahili; so Stanley was being asked to remember Dorothy. He was thrilled by this lover's gift.[42] Soon after making it, Dolly confided to her diary her confused state of mind:

It would be such wonderful happiness to love very much and be loved, if only a little by <u>the hero</u>, whoever that may be. The wise good hardworking, <u>undertaking</u> man ... but perhaps the good man is not the strong man, or the hardworking man is not wise and understanding, and so I care for no one, and invite no one to care for me ... I just cling to men who can be nothing to me, and if they could I should not cling to them, Mr Stanley, Edwin Arnold, Monsieur Coquelin ... I feel a fierce longing to be understood and cared for, and perhaps because I feel safe in the friendship of some few men, I give over much of myself to them. I daresay they are puzzled, possibly flattered, but I do not think they misunderstand me.[43]

Dorothy's most serious reservation about Stanley remained her suspicion that she hardly knew him. The *Belgravia Magazine* had just published a short story called 'Talbot the Traveller', whose eponymous hero was plainly based on Stanley, with similar African achievements and an American past, in which a female friend, like Annie Ward, played a conspicuous part. 'Talbot is a marvellous resemblance to myself,' admitted Stanley.[44] Dolly told him that although she knew a lot about his 'life's work', the Talbot story reminded her that she could 'only guess at what you are'. What she wanted was for him 'to write his biography' [*sic*].[45] Given Stanley's fear of exposing his workhouse background, this was a worrying letter. Yet though she had written coolly about him in her diary, Dolly now penned a meticulous description, showing just how intrigued by him she still was. There is some repetition of her earlier physical delineation, but many details are new and portray the living Stanley as a moving, breathing personality.

When Stanley enters a room full of people, he holds his head rather tilted backwards, in a self-conscious attitude. He is thickly, strongly built, with a deep broad chest and thick short arms ... His look has something intense and penetrating ... giving a sort of earnest grandeur to his expression ... The eye shines out clear, with the observancy of some keen-sighted bird, who is watching you, listening to you rather with the eye than with the ear ... When he is telling us some thrilling adventure in Africa, he conveys his meaning as often by gesture as by word. He raises the imaginary gun to his shoulder, puts his finger to the trigger ... and as he speaks his eyes flicker as though some spirit flame leapt behind the crystaline lens .... When he is very much interested ... he sits on the very verge of his chair ... When he is pleased, he softly rubs his hands together, with invisible soap ... But this is Stanley 'intime'. The better known usual Stanley is cold, silent, rather disdainful, slightly chilling people by his silent observant attitude, making them feel uneasy ... He says 'good day' to you with great solemnity and ceremony, bowing when you offer him a chair. He speaks slowly and most decidedly ... Sometimes with strangers he is rather tense, but his voice is most agreeable, and his slightly American accent ... is interesting ... He has many laughs. The pleased, self-conscious laugh he gives when you flatter him ... and he can laugh vociferously, but he seldom forgets himself enough for that. He has in common with all great men, a great simplicity, shall I call it a kind of innocence? He is proud of himself, but somehow it is partly a not ill-placed consciousness of worth, and partly a kind of simple open vanity, which in Stanley is not offensive.

He has, I should say, a rich vein of tenderness underlying the surface of will and masterfulness, I see it when he talks of little children, of poor unhappy slaves, and of any helpless oppressed beings. His admiration of nature, his keen sense of the dramatic, gives a richness, warmth and depth to his nature, which people would not read in him at first.[46]

In mid-February, Dolly was disappointed to find that Henry did not share her literary tastes. She had sent him two of her favourite books: Henry James's *Daisy Miller* and Mrs Gaskell's *Cranford*. In some ways Daisy, the rich young American girl, with her European hotel life, her naivety and her passion for dating, was not unlike Alice Pike. But, despite this, her fate did not interest Henry, any more than did Mrs Gaskell's small-town lives. Stanley expressed his dislike of both books with withering honesty. In fairness, male admirers of *Cranford* have never been numerous, and Dolly would have been wiser to have tried something by Balzac, or by her mother's beloved Flaubert. (Indeed, Henry loved Flaubert's *Salammbo* when he read it in May Sheldon's translation.) [47]

Now, Stanley fell ill with intermittent fever and was in bed for several weeks. Visiting him in his flat, Dolly 'felt so sorry to see the ebullient, strong, courageous Stanley gentle and helpless as a little child'.[48] Henry's doctors insisted that he spend three months in the south of France recuperating. So at the beginning of March, he set out for Nice, escorted by Mackinnon, who was distraught about him. A relapse on the train forced a return to London and a deferment of departure. Henry did not tell Dorothy how ill he was, but to May Sheldon he confessed he was suffering not only from gastritis, but from 'bad African fever' too. 'Whether sea air, exercise, quinine &c will ever give me another lease of life I don't know.'[49] His recovery came more swiftly than he had expected.

When he reached Nice, Stanley received a telegram from William Hoffman – the young German who had been his manservant for six months – telling him that his mother, Elizabeth Jones, had died the day before, in Bodelwyddan. He had last seen her exactly two years earlier, after a much longer gap. To stop any journalist tracking him down and asking awkward questions, Stanley instructed Hoffman to say nothing to anyone except that his master was somewhere in France, and that he had no idea when he would return. He wrote out the words of a telegram that Hoffman was to send to John Owen, his favourite cousin. 'Am directed to say your friend is exceedingly grieved to hear of the death telegraphed ... Had a slight relapse from fatigue of travel. Hoffman.'[50] At least he would not now need to hide his only living parent from Dolly.

It was early April when Dolly wrote again, and her friend Mr Gladstone was once more in 10, Downing Street, after a General Election victory.[51] She told Stanley that although 'a Liberal to the very core', she was starting to turn against Home Rule for Ireland, and had been discussing matters with Mr Chamberlain. By the time Stanley replied, he was in Rome. Despite Dorothy's reservations about Home Rule, he penned a furious attack on Gladstone for trading on his record as a great reformer in order to sell his 'treacherous' policy to the people. Having battered the Grand Old Man for four pages, he added a dull Roman travelogue. Given Dolly's personal fondness for Gladstone, Henry had been very unwise to mount a personal attack. She replied more in sorrow than in anger.

Gladstone's achievements, his experience, and his age, entitle him to our very great respect; you deny him title to that respect when you venture to say he is only thinking of himself, and thereby imply that he would imperil the country from sentiments of the most abject vanity ... Gladstone I know is possessed with a deep, fervent, religious conviction that what he proposes for Ireland is just and right.'[52]

If ever there was a letter that should not have been argued with, this was it. Yet Stanley replied from Paris with four densely written pages of self-justification. Dorothy must have found his terrier-like desire to win a dispute that should never have started deeply disturbing.[53]

William Mackinnon came over to Paris to talk to Henry about the state of negotiations for the Congo railway concession, and to plan tactics for a projected meeting with Leopold. Stanley mentioned his anxieties about Dolly to his friend, and this was probably why the tycoon decided to ask the Tennants to come on a summer cruise of the Hebrides, which he was planning for sixty guests on one of his ships.[54] On his return to London, Henry's invitations to Richmond Terrace were less frequent than before, but in late July he was going to be with Dolly for ten whole days on board ship. Surely this would be long enough to repair their recent differences?

Neither Henry nor Dolly ever wrote about the cruise, but for Stanley it must have lived up to expectations, since two weeks after it ended, on 16 August 1886, he wrote a letter of proposal. He had arrived, he told Dolly, at a point when almost for his sanity's sake he needed to know her feelings toward him.

You have dropped phrases in my hearing which have induced me to think that possibly I did not love in vain; if I had misconstrued them the punishment is mine ... It is one of the charms of your manner that one departs from your presence with the idea that only he, and he alone, is to be addressed thus ... [For] one like myself, ignorant and unacquainted with these captivating arts, and doubtful of their real meaning, this wonderfully gracious, beaming manner you have, has often sent me home half demented. Nevertheless ... I restrained myself, lest by giving expression to the ardour that possessed me, I should ... give offence to one I had learned to esteem, admire and love with all my heart and soul ... Thus I went to you and came away, visit after visit, always perplexing and doubting ...

One reason for his doubting, he explained, was her wealth and social position.

You are in need of nothing. I cannot advantage you in anything, therein I am poor, helpless, trembling. I am only rich in love of you, filled with admiration for your royal beauty ... Nevertheless bear without offence this declaration of mine, and tell me honestly, candidly, to put an end to this exasperating doubt of mine .... I have no other remedy than to appeal to you for the simple 'yes' or 'no' ...

Henry told her that he might any day be sent by King Leopold to the Upper Congo.

Should he do so, you can imagine my torments while in this state of suspense regarding the wish of my heart. In the ordinary sense of the word I am not rich, but I have sufficient to satisfy moderate tastes, without making further effort. Labour, however, is healthful and pleasant ... If my love is unacceptable to you, merely close this letter in another envelope and return it to me. But if, as I dare scarcely hope, you have penetrated my secret passion before now and have already weighed your answer to me, I pray you delay not the blessed word which will make me the happiest man in all the world ... Yours most devotedly, Henry M. Stanley.[55]

Given his previous disappointments, it would have been strange if Stanley had written a short and self-confident appeal. Though touchingly honest, as when he described returning home 'half demented', and as being 'poor, helpless, trembling', the letter's weakness lay in its author's failure to tackle any of his and Dolly's more obvious differences: in age, artistic taste, social habits, political inclination, and attitudes to nature and urban living. Nor did Stanley make any attempt to say whether he *wanted* to go back to Africa – and if so, for how long. But even if he had done, probably she would have turned him down. Her letter of rejection has not survived, though he would later describe it as being written with 'ruthless cruelty'. His humble background seems to have played a part.

I saw in my imagination you standing indignant, outraged at the "base born churl" etc., daring to approach your queenliness with such preposterous protestations etc. I seemed to hear your storm of reproaches for my audacity and insolence etc. that I shrank into nothingness before you and the devout love was crushed, just as a rose flower too violently clutched would lose its brightness.[56]

Whether Dolly had ever loved Stanley is very hard to say. Maybe the necessary physical attraction was simply not there for her, and this turned out to be more important than whether or not he meant to return to Africa, or what kind of books he liked. Blood-shot eyes, short, thick legs and an awkward physical manner could have been Stanley's undoing, rather than his humble background. And yet she had admired the manliness of his chin and lips, and the powerful shape of his head. At the age of thirty – with other men still interested – she was not yet desperate enough to feel she must marry the best of the men currently available. Clearly she had given Stanley misleading signs – very likely because of her addiction to exceptional men. She confessed to this trait in her diary: 'The fact is many people, gifted, remarkable, original people intoxicate me. I feel a kind of exaltation in their company, and I feel compelled to expand and glow and roar like a furnace when the blast is applied; I forget myself completely and delight to be rid of myself.' In such exaltation, Dolly had treated Stanley with an enthusiasm that had sent him home 'half demented'.[57]

Stanley told her that, if she refused him, her rejection would send him 'away to exile once more'. A month before meeting Dolly in late July 1885, Stanley had written a bitter letter to Henry Sanford lamenting the king's inconsiderate failure to send him back to Africa. If no one but a Belgian could be appointed Governor-General, that was fine by him, he told Sanford. All the king needed to do was tell him the truth and he could resign and do other things. Similarly, there would be no problem over the railway if he and Mackinnon were simply treated with honesty.[58] But during his wooing of Dorothy, his pleas to courtiers like Sanford, and to the king himself, had all but ceased. Now, just days after being rejected, Stanley wrote to 'General' Sanford for the first time in a year.

His letter pulses with his desperation to be sent back to Africa as soon as possible. This time, he said, he did not expect to be Governor-General, but merely 'to supervise and develop the Upper Congo ... assuming command over all river & land routes'. Failing this, he suggested, could not 'His Majesty utilise my services by giving me an exploring mission ... Possibly something advantageous to the state could be found – at least the boundaries north, north east & east could be located.'[59] As if knowing that nothing would come of this approach, a mere five days later Stanley signed up with Major James B. Pond – America's most famous lecture agent, whom he had met earlier that summer – promising to visit the US at the end of November for two months, giving six lectures a week up to a total of fifty.[60] These would begin on 27 November, after he had first delivered thirty-three similar talks in England and Wales. He would cover the Livingstone expedition, the charting of the Congo, and the foundation of the Congo Free State. Thus Stanley began his fightback against misery and humiliation, ending what he called 'my long imprisonment in my London rooms'.[61]

Dorothy's rejection of him made the blow he suffered on 12 September seem even worse. On that day he learned that Leopold had decided to give the railway concession not to his and Mackinnon's syndicate, but to a more recently formed Belgian one. After all the encouragement the king had given him, Henry could hardly believe it.[62] To have been able to take charge of all operations connected with this vital railway would have been some compensation for other disappointments. But now this too would be in other hands. Stanley wrote bitterly to Mackinnon:

I have been living, ever since my book left my hands last year, in a fool's paradise. That woman entrapped me with her gush, & her fulsome adulations, her knick-knacks inscribed with a 'Remember me,' her sweet scented notes written with a certain literary touch ... On leaving her presence, I was buoyed up with some letter or despatch from Brussels which kept me on the stretch of anticipation always. 'We do not know exactly when we shall need you, but we shall let you know, my dear Mr Stanley,' so I lived, constantly happy, hoping ... Nearly 16 months of my life have been lost through these artful people. You can imagine then what cause I have to remember your kindness which looms up through this period more brightly since it is the only brightness in an otherwise gloomy time.[63]

True to form, it would be William Mackinnon, who would put to him, a mere six weeks later, a proposition that would send him back to Africa in a blaze of publicity, ultimately winning him greater fame than any he had known, yet also – through no fault of his honorary father – causing him the greatest distress of his life.

TWENTY-TWO

Why rescue Emin Pasha?

Emin Pasha

In July 1884, six months before General Gordon met his violent end at Khartoum, Stanley had accurately predicted that the British government's decision to send the general back to the Sudan would end in tragedy.[1] It would have amazed him, at the time of his prescient warning, if he had been told that Gordon – whom he had mistrusted in life – would in death provide him with a life-changing challenge. But when

Gordon declined to evacuate the British and Egyptian garrisons from Sudan, as ordered, and was speared to death as a result of defending Khartoum instead, his downfall created a crisis far to the south that did indeed change Henry's life.

On 29 October, Charles Allen, the Secretary of the Anti-Slavery Society, published a letter in *The Times*, which he had received the day before from Emin Pasha, the last of Gordon's provincial governors still alive and at liberty. Emin, it seemed, was maintaining some sort of government in Sudan's southernmost province of Equatoria, despite the steady encroachment of the fundamentalists from the north. The Pasha's letter was dated 31 December 1885 – eleven months after Gordon's death.

Ever since the month of May, 1883 [wrote Emin] we have been cut off from all communication with the world. Forgotten and abandoned by the [Egyptian] government, we have been compelled to make a virtue of necessity ... I do not know how to describe to you the admirable devotion of my black troops throughout a long war .... Deprived of the most necessary things, for a long time without any pay, my men fought valiantly, and when at last hunger weakened them, when, after nineteen days of incredible privation and sufferings, their strength was exhausted, and when the last torn leather of the last boot had been eaten, then they cut a way through the midst of their enemies and succeeded in saving themselves ...[2]

In a similar letter, this time to his friend Dr R.W. Felkin, an Edinburgh doctor and former missionary, and published in *The Scotsman* on 6 November 1886, Emin declared that, although betrayed by the Egyptian and British governments, he intended 'to hold this country as long as possible'.[3]

Leading articles appeared in British newspapers insisting that a relief expedition be sent to save him. Lord Wolseley had arrived too late to relieve Gordon, and now a howl went up lest the same fate should befall brave Emin Pasha – though who Emin was, and whether his administration in Equatoria had ever been effective, were not matters examined in the press.[4]

So who was Emin Pasha? Stanley – like the public at large – had no idea that the Pasha was no dauntless Briton, but had been born Eduard Schnitzer, to Lutheran parents in the Prussian province of Silesia. In 1864, aged twenty-four, this bearded and bespectacled German had qualified as a doctor in Berlin, but having failed on a bureaucratic technicality to be granted a government licence to practise, he settled in Albania – then a Turkish province – where he set up as a doctor. A brilliant linguist, he soon added Albanian and Turkish to the five other languages he already spoke. He was a first-rate pianist and chess player, and also excelled as a botanist and ornithologist. In 1870 Emin joined the staff of Ismail Hakki Pasha, Governor of northern Albania, and served with him till his death three years later. During this time he had an affair with the Pasha's wife, and after she became a widow lived with her as if she were his own spouse. In 1875, he ran out of money and took Madame Hakki, her four children, and six slave girls to stay with his parents in Germany. While there – realizing he could not support ten people indefinitely – he abandoned Madame Hakki, and fled the country. He would not contact his family again for fourteen years.

In December 1875, Emin arrived in Khartoum, where he set up in practice once more. This was how General Gordon – the Governor-General of the Sudan – came to employ him as a provincial medical officer. By this time Emin was using a Turkish name and represented himself as an Arab by birth. All this was part of a conscious effort to distance himself from Germany, the nation he felt had rejected him. In 1878, Gordon appointed Emin his Governor of Equatoria. This, then, was the unknown history of the extraordinary person, whom the British press now demanded should be rescued.

And what was the threat he was thought to be facing in 1886? Five years earlier, Muhammad Ahmad, the son of a boat builder from Dongola in the northern Sudan, had declared himself the Mahdi (the Expected One) and launched a jihad against the Khedive of Egypt and all his Turkish and Egyptian soldiers in the Sudan. When Britain became the *de facto* governing power in Egypt in 1882, her servants also became candidates for holy slaughter by the Mahdi's rapidly growing army. In November 1883, 12,000 Egyptian soldiers were massacred by the Mahdi's force at Kordofan. Darfur and Bahr-al-Ghazal were overrun next. Then, in January 1885, Khartoum itself had followed, leaving Emin as the Khedive's only functioning representative in Sudan. In the deep south of Equatoria, close to Buganda, the Islamic faith was less entrenched, so Emin felt that by moving towards Lake Albert he might yet place himself beyond the Mahdi's reach.[5] In this new region, the main line of communication with the outside world was not up the Nile, but eastwards to Zanzibar. This was the supply line used by missionaries in Buganda. Their inspirational Scottish leader, Alexander Mackay, now became Emin's friend and adviser.[6]

Just as Emin was penning his appeals for help, Mackay was writing home with news of horrifying outbreaks of violence against Buganda's Christian missions and their African converts. Already Bishop Hannington, the first bishop ever to travel to East Equatorial Africa, had been hacked to death with all his followers. Before that, many of Mackay's converts had been impaled on spits and roasted alive on the orders of Mwanga, Mutesa's psychotic successor. Not unnaturally, Mackay believed that Buganda's earthly (as well as its spiritual) salvation depended upon its becoming a British colony.[7]

So when William Mackinnon approached Stanley in London, in early November 1886, to float the possibility of his returning to Africa as leader of an expedition to relieve Emin Pasha, the fate of Buganda's missionaries was of almost equal concern to both men – after all, they had gone out to Buganda at Stanley's urging. Mackinnon's special interest in the region dated back to the late 1870s, when he had hoped to drive out the Arab slave traders by bringing 'legitimate trade goods' from Mombassa on the coast to Lake Victoria by a new railway. When the Sultan of Zanzibar refused to lease any land or commercial rights on the mainland, this had persuaded Mackinnon to invest instead in King Leopold's Comité du Haut Congo. For the next eight years his primary hope, which he had shared with Stanley, had been to create within the Congo a free market dominated by British commerce. That hope had ended in September 1886 with the failure of his and Stanley's attempt to secure the Congo railway concession.

In November 1886, the Emin Pasha crisis caused both men to look once more to East Africa.[8] Perhaps they could rescue Emin Pasha, and simultaneously pre-empt any German move on Buganda and help the British missionaries.[9] So on 15 November, two days before he was due to leave for his American lecture tour, Stanley wrote to Mackinnon accepting unpaid leadership of an expedition to relieve Emin, conditional upon his friend's managing to raise £20,000.

Given the public outcry that had very nearly destroyed Gladstone's administration after Gordon's death, it may be wondered why the Conservative prime minister, Lord Salisbury, had not already despatched a government force to relieve Emin Pasha. In fact, Lord Wolseley, the adjutant-general at the War Office, had ruled this out. 'If Emin Bey, with 4,000 Egyptian troops and his knowledge of the country ... is unable to reach Lake Victoria Nyanza, it is useless to talk of our sending a column to his relief.'[10] Wolseley also feared that if the King of Buganda opposed the column, the missionaries would be murdered as a consequence. Having known since late September that Emin was in danger, the prime minister was greatly relieved to find by December that the more responsible newspapers were recommending a 'pacific' rather than a 'military' expedition.[11] Furthermore, by then it was clear that Emin was not as keen to be 'rescued' as to be given enough ammunition to go on holding out in Equatoria.[12] It was suggested that the required ammunition could best be brought by an unobtrusive private expedition to Wadelai – Emin's Upper Nile headquarters – through Bunyoro, without offending Mwanga of Buganda; and so no large and expensive government force would be needed.

Yet there was plenty of wishful thinking in philanthropic and government circles. No expedition carrying a mass of stores, including guns and ammunition, could go to the heart of Africa without the means to defend itself. The Mahdist uprising, slave raids, and Mwanga's expansion into Bunyoro had made the whole region dangerously unstable. Yet while the government was at pains to tell Mackinnon that they would feel no obligation to rescue Stanley (were he ever to need rescuing), they failed to recognize the dangers involved in backing a well-armed private expedition (and offering it 'all the facilities in their power'), without accepting any responsibility for what it might actually *do*.[13] Even when the Egyptian government, with its dependence on Britain, decided to pay £10,000 towards the cost of Mackinnon's expedition, and when the foreign secretary had formally approved it on behalf of the government, the British cabinet still felt entitled to preserve a detached stance in public.[14]

In America, Stanley had just given his tenth lecture for Major Pond when, on 11 December, Mackinnon's telegram reached him: 'YOUR PLAN AND OFFER ACCEPTED. AUTHORITIES APPROVE. FUNDS PROVIDED. BUSINESS URGENT. COME PROMPTLY. REPLY. MACKINNON.'[15] The next morning, the disappointed Pond saw Stanley and his stenographer hard at work, ordering 'several hundred repeating rifles and a large stock of camp equipment'. The tour had been going well and Stanley would lose about £10,000 by cancelling, so Pond would lose a lot too. But since his client had inserted a clause in his contract permitting him to leave at once if recalled, there was no help for that.[16]

Members of the Emin Pasha Relief Expedition (EPRE) committee included Sir John Kirk and the Revd Horace Waller, old friends of Mackinnon's, with both of whom Stanley now made his peace.[17] Kirk had been impressed enough by Stanley's book about the Congo – especially in respect of his efforts to protect the Congolese from maltreatment by Belgian officers – to recommend him to Mackinnon as the only person who ought to lead the expedition.[18] For the past eighteen months, as Consul-General at Zanzibar, Kirk had lived through the nightmare of believing that either Gladstone's or Salisbury's government would jettison Britain's long-established influence in East Africa and her interest in Buganda and the Upper Nile and allow the Sultan's entire mainland empire to fall into the hands of Germany, simply because German support for British control of Egypt was considered indispensable. But Lord Salisbury had other plans. By the Anglo-German East Africa Agreement of 1 November 1886, the Sultan's mainland possessions were divided into 'two spheres of influence', with Britain acquiring the northern sphere, which extended to Lake Victoria from Mombassa, and Germany the southern sphere, extending from Bagamoyo and Dar-es-Salaam to Lake Tanganyika. As a relieved Kirk told Mackinnon, this left the way open for Britain to make Buganda a protectorate when the time was ripe, and perhaps Equatoria too, if Emin chose to stay on there (though this last would depend upon the relief expedition's succeeding).[19]

For Mackinnon, with his long-term interest in creating a great trading company in East Africa, the Emin Pasha expedition presented a unique opportunity. A memorandum in the tycoon's papers is revealingly headed: 'Syndicate for establishing British commerce and influence in East Africa and for relieving Emin Bey.'[20] Kirk helped Mackinnon by asking his deputy at Zanzibar, Frederick Holmwood, to assist Stanley when he came to negotiate concessions from the Sultan for the new British company. The intention was that Stanley would also establish trading posts between Wadelai on the Upper Nile and Mombassa on the coast. In January 1887, before Stanley left for Africa, he gave an undertaking to Mackinnon that after he had relieved Emin, and persuaded him to represent the company near Lake Victoria, he would himself serve as Chief Administrator, with his headquarters in Mombassa.[21]

The relief committee – of which Mackinnon was chairman, Sir Francis de Winton secretary, and John Kirk and Alexander Bruce members – declared that 'having the fullest confidence in Mr Stanley's experience and abilities', they would 'cease to control the arrangements or interfere with the direction of the expedition' except 'to provide the ways and means considered necessary by Mr Stanley'.[22] So, in deference to Stanley's unparalleled record, the committee abdicated their overall authority from the start.

Stanley sailed into Southampton Water on Christmas Eve 1886, and lost little time in writing to Leopold to ask him to release him from his contract for long enough to lead the expedition. Stanley's resentment of the king for failing to employ him in Africa after June 1885, and for his cynical deception of the British railway consortium, led him to hint strongly that a royal refusal would '[end] my engagement with your Majesty'. He also reproached Leopold for subjecting him to a 'cold disapproving silence' for over a year.[23] This convinced the king that only a personal meeting stood any chance of ensuring that the Congo Free State would benefit from Stanley's impending journey. So, only hours after receiving Stanley's letter, Leopold sent a telegram summoning the disgruntled explorer to his palace at Laeken.

Before crossing to Brussels late on the 29 December, Stanley attended a meeting of the EPRE committee held in his own rooms at 160, New Bond Street. He and Mackinnon, along with de Winton and a few others, discussed the possible routes for the expedition to take, and the explorer argued for approaching along the Congo – because in steamships the expedition would be invulnerable to desertion and to demands from chiefs. Nevertheless, the majority preferred one of several east coast routes, which would enable Stanley to make two pioneering journeys through the East African territory that it was hoped Mackinnon's company would one day administer. Yet Henry did not make an issue of the route at this stage.

As Henry's carriage rattled past the royal stable block at nine the following morning and came to a halt under Laeken's impressive portico, he strongly suspected that Leopold would want him to use the Congo route, as a prelude to securing Emin's services for his Free State. Nine months earlier, Count Borchgrave had alerted Stanley to Leopold's passionate interest in expanding eastwards, so he was not surprised to be told by the king that he would only release him from his contract for the duration of the expedition if he used that river, and then opened a line of communication from the Congo to Lake Albert. Stanley was therefore able, on his return, to compel the committee to abandon their preferred east coast route, without making it a personal matter.[24]

Between visits to Brussels, Henry had very little time to devote to the vitally important task of interviewing men who had applied to be officers on the expedition. This would prove to be a great mistake since the behaviour of two of his officers would bring him more pain and greater public obloquy than anything since the Bumbireh incident. The few men he actually saw were whittled down for him by de Winton and Captain Grant Elliott, who had served under him on the Congo. On a single day, 1 January 1887, eighty applications were received, and there would be hundreds all told.[25] Despite Stanley's personal preference for men from humble backgrounds, he chose to take with him, on this most problematic of all his expeditions, a preponderance of officers and gentlemen – a breed he knew nothing about.

Major Edmund Barttelot of the 7th Royal Fusiliers came highly recommended by General Sir Redvers Buller and by Lord Wolseley. Educated at Rugby and Sandhurst, Barttelot had been promoted brevet-major at the early age of twenty-eight. He had served in Afghanistan and Egypt, where he had been part of the abortive Gordon rescue mission. The second son of a baronet, he was socially self-confident. 'Plenty of physical courage and an aspiring soul,' Henry wrote of him in his notebook, 'but he will have to be treated gingerly.'[26] This was because he seemed rather combative. Stanley had no similar doubts about James Sligo Jameson – a member of the Irish whisky family – who was prepared to contribute £1,000 to the expedition's funds. Stanley's main anxiety about the thirty-one-year-old was that he seemed physically frail. But Jameson reassuringly pointed out that he had survived trips to Borneo and southern Africa, where he had indulged his passion for collecting big game heads, as well as birds, butterflies and beetles.[27]

Arthur J. Mounteney Jephson was twenty-nine and heir, indirectly, to large estates in Ireland. But what probably inclined Henry to choose him was the fact that his clergyman father had died when he was seven, and he had been brought up as one of twelve children in a family of poor cousins to the moneyed line of his family. After leaving Tonbridge School, Mounteney (as he was always called) spent a brief period in the Merchant Navy, and was then taken in by his rich cousin, the Comtesse de Noailles. Mounteney had lived as her companion for several years before applying for a place on the expedition. He came across at interview as such a fashionable young man that Francis de Winton recommended refusal even when the Comtesse offered £1,000. But Henry disagreed. 'I don't think how a man dresses matters a bit. It depends on the nature of the man,' he insisted, before accepting Jephson.[28]

Stanley had high hopes of Lieutenant William Grant Stairs, at twenty-four the youngest of all the officers. Commissioned into the Royal Engineers in 1885, he had been raised in Nova Scotia, and trained at the Royal Military Academy of Canada. He had worked on the New Zealand Trigonometrical Survey, but had no experience of Africa or Africans. He seemed intelligent and disciplined.[29] Captain Robert Henry Nelson was thirty-four, had been educated at Harrow, and was on leave from a famous Indian army cavalry regiment, Methuen's Horse. He had served in the South African War of 1879–80 and was physically strong, and Henry chose him because he liked his good-natured face and modest manner. John Rose Troup, aged thirty-one, was the son of a general, and had served the AIC under Stanley, and then the Congo Free State.[30] Another man who had worked for the State was Herbert Ward, whom Stanley had selected in 1884, and would engage for the expedition on arrival in the Congo. A born adventurer, Ward – whose father was a taxidermist at the London Natural History Museum – had travelled in New Zealand and Borneo, and was a gifted artist and writer. Though a colleague thought him a fantasist who imagined he owned 'Aladdin's Lamp', Stanley considered him 'a young man of great promise'.[31]

Two of the men he brought with him would not be gentlemen. The first of these was Stanley's valet, William Hoffman, who had once been 'the boots' – the boy who cleaned shoes and ran errands – at his apartment block in Sackville Street. Kind-hearted Mrs Sheldon had recommended the seventeen-year-old to Stanley as a servant, while she had been living at the same address. The young man had claimed to have been an apprentice bag maker, but this was untrue. Nor had Stanley taken him to the Berlin Conference because he could speak German, as Hoffman later suggested: his English was so poor that he would have been a hopeless translator.[32] Sergeant William Bonny of the Army Medical Department evaded the screening process by coming unannounced to Stanley's flat, explaining that his lack of skill as a letter writer would otherwise have ruled him out. He had just purchased his discharge from the army, in which he had served as a hospital sergeant. Earlier, he had fought the Zulus in South Africa. But it was his 'pertinacious' refusal to 'take a mild negative', coupled with the fact that he had put on dress uniform and medals for his interview, that somehow touched Stanley.[33] Dr Thomas Parke was taken on by Stanley in Alexandria en route for Zanzibar in late January. Twenty-nine years old, Parke was the son of an Irish small landowner and had trained as a doctor at the Royal College of Surgeons of Ireland before gaining a commission in the army medical service. Like Barttelot, he had served in Egypt.[34]

The expedition's European contingent sailed from England on 20 January 1887, taking with them more goods for barter than any of Stanley's earlier expeditions: an amazing fifteen miles of cloth, two tons of beads, and one ton of wire. In addition – largely for Emin Pasha's benefit – its porters would carry two tons of gunpowder, 350,000 percussion caps, 100,000 rounds of Remington ammunition, 30,000 Gatling machine-gun cartridges, 50,000 rounds of Winchester ammunition, and a Maxim gun with portable stand and shield, donated by its inventor, Sir Hiram Maxim. At Cairo – en route for Zanzibar, whither all this mass of stores and weaponry was headed – Stanley had a significant conversation about firearms with the German explorers Wilhem Junker and Georg Schweinfurth. He noted indignantly in his diary: 'Both have been labouring under the impression that since we take several hundred Remingtons & a Maxim, that we intend to force our way after a military fashion to Emin.' It seemed not to have occurred to them, he complained, that much of this weaponry and ammunition would be handed over to Emin, and what was left would be required 'to defend our charges [carriers, officers, servants, etc.]'; nor, grumbled Stanley, had the two Germans realized that it was ludicrous for the world's press to praise Emin for having 'fought his way through to Uganda', while at the same time getting ready to condemn 'me if necessity compels me to use force to resist attack'.[35]

On his arrival at Zanzibar on 22 February – where he planned to recruit the expedition's Wangwana carriers, and then sail on for the Congo's mouth via the Cape – Stanley was shocked to see six German warships at anchor in a harbour where, on all his earlier visits, the Royal Navy had been predominant. Nevertheless, he realized that this German presence might help him convince Sultan Barghash that his best chance of avoiding losing everything to Germany – including

Zanzibar itself – would be to grant to Mackinnon's British company facilities in the ports of Mombassa and Melindi. The Sultan did not agree at once, but promised Stanley, and the acting British Consul-General, Frederick Holmwood, to sign the relevant papers soon – which he did.[36]

In mid-January, Stanley had discussed with Leopold the necessity of coming to an understanding with Tippu Tip, who controlled the whole region between Lake Tanganyika and the Upper Congo. The Arab was currently in Zanzibar selling ivory and holding discussions with the Sultan of Zanzibar. Six months earlier, Tippu had enraged Leopold by seizing the Congo Free State's post at Stanley Falls, after its English commander, Walter Deane, had refused to surrender a female slave who had sought his protection after a savage beating. The king's financial problems and shortage of manpower continued to make retaking the post an impossibility. As matters stood, Tippu had the power to stop Stanley's expedition getting from the Congo to Lake Albert and the Upper Nile where Emin was. The slave trader could also, if he wished, block Leopold's eager attempts to extend his new State eastwards to the Upper Nile.

The king knew that his colony's very existence would be at risk if Tippu were to capture the guns and ammunition that Stanley meant to transport to Emin. Indeed, if that happened the Arab would be in a position to capture all Leopold's stations before he had the resources to expel the 3,000 Arab-Swahili currently on the Upper Congo. Stanley had therefore suggested to Leopold that, since Tippu was 'in actual possession of the Falls', he might be neutralized if 'recognized as chief or Governor at a nominal salary with a view to using him as a buffer against the hordes above him'. Doing deals with slave traders was certainly undesirable but, for the present, nothing else could be done to stop the new generation of Arab-Swahili slavers pressing down the Congo to Stanley Pool if they wished.

At their first negotiating session, Stanley tried to bluff Tippu into thinking that he would offer his entire arsenal and all his 700 men to the king as soldiers, if he (Tippu) refused to make a peace agreement. If he did refuse, he would have to fight not only Stanley but the king's men too. But, promised Stanley, if Tippu chose peace he would be made Governor of Stanley Falls and paid a salary. Although this offer irritated the Arab (who already controlled the Falls), he did not want to fight all the Europeans on the river. So, after several days of prevarication, he grudgingly agreed to fly the Free State's flag over Stanley Falls, to accept a resident secretary appointed by the State, and, most important of all, to stop his people raiding for slaves below the Falls. One of Stanley's enticements was to offer Tippu himself, with twenty of his wives and eighty-five of his servants, free transport by sea and river to Stanley Falls, via the Cape and the Congo.[37]

Before leaving Zanzibar, Stanley made a second agreement intended to obtain from the Arab the services of 600 porters when the expedition reached the Upper Congo. These men would be expected to accompany Stanley to Wadelai to carry to safety the immense cache of ivory that Emin was said to have accumulated – worth a staggering £60,000, according to Wilhem Junker. Besides a share of the proceeds of the ivory, Tippu Tip was to be paid $1,000 for providing the men.[38]

On 24 February 1887, the entire expedition sailed from Zanzibar for the Congo. It consisted of 805 people – nine Europeans, 623 Wangwana, ninety-six followers of Tippu Tip, sixty Sudanese, thirteen Somalis, two Syrians and two central Africans. One of these last was a teenage boy, Baruti, whom de Winton had brought back to England from the Congo as a servant and had passed on to Stanley to be taken home to his family. Henry was not sorry to be parting with him, since on one occasion he had dangled his housekeeper's baby over the banisters in order to force her to give him some treat from the larder.[39]

The first test for Stanley and his officers occurred only hours from Zanzibar, when a fight broke out below decks between the Sudanese and the Wangwana. Taking Jephson, Jameson and Nelson with him, Stanley ran to the scene. Jameson likened the affray to 'an "Inferno" by Gustave Doré'. Some men had spears, and others sticks and iron bars, and were already inflicting head wounds. Into this melée leapt Stanley, with the Sudanese screaming to him to save them from being murdered by the Wangwana. According to Jephson, Stanley imposed his authority swiftly, promising justice and protection to the Sudanese and forcing back the Wangwana. By then, ten arms had been broken, and numerous cuts and contusions suffered.[40] This shipboard incident was the first indication to Stanley that these Wangwana might not measure up to the standard of the men who had served him so well in the past, and to whose selection he had devoted so much of his time on previous visits. Unfortunately, he had had too many other things to do on Zanzibar. So, this time, his 600 Wangwana were selected for him by Mackinnon's agent, Edmund Mackenzie of Smith Mackenzie &

Co.⁴¹ Most would turn out to be the slaves of various well-known Zanzibar trading houses. An appalled Stanley only discovered when he reached the Pool that no more than 150 of these carriers were free men.⁴² Only one of his former 'captains', the incomparable Uledi, would be with him on his new mission.

But whatever its flaws and failings, when the expedition sailed up the Congo, and disembarked in late March for the 200-mile overland march past the cataracts, the column made a brave show, with the pennant of the New York Yacht Club being carried at its head. (Unaccountably, Stanley had agreed to satisfy what he called the yachting-mad James Gordon Bennett Jr's 'ridiculous whim' to have this flag borne across Africa.) Towards the end of the month, Herbert Ward saw this fluttering emblem coming towards him in the distance, carried by a tall Sudanese soldier.

Behind him, astride of a fine henna-stained mule, whose silver plated trappings shone in the morning sun, was Mr Henry M. Stanley, attired in his famous African costume [Norfolk jacket, matching knickerbockers and his famous flat-topped 'Stanley' hat] ... immediately in his rear were his personal servants, Somalis with their curious braided waistcoats and white robes. Then came Zanzibaris with their blankets, water-bottles, ammunition, belts and guns. Stalwart Sudanese soldiers with dark-hooded coats, their rifles on their backs ... and Zanzibari porters bearing iron-bound boxes of ammunition, to which were fastened axes and shovels ... At one point a steel whale-boat was being carried in sections, suspended from poles ... donkey's heavily laden with sacks of rice were next met with, and a little further on the women of Tippu Tip's harem, their faces partly concealed and their bodies draped in gaudily coloured cloths; then at intervals along the line of march an English officer ... then several large horned African goats ... [next] the renowned Tippu Tip ... in his flowing Arab robes of dazzling whiteness, and carrying over his left shoulder a richly-decorated sabre ... behind him several Arab sheiks ... As the procession filed along the narrow rugged path ... its unbroken line extended over a distance of probably four miles.⁴³

The reality of this picturesque spectacle was that, with few beasts of burden because of the tsetse fly, porters carrying an immense weight of weaponry and trade goods were as inclined as ever to desert and steal, unless stern discipline was maintained. A rifle or a sack of brass wire would be enough 'capital' to start a new life.

Barttelot was given command of the Sudanese, while Stanley's other young officers were made commanders of about 120 Wangwana each. From the moment the officers were landed with their men near Vivi, their ideas about the romance of life in Africa underwent some painful revisions. Jephson felt angry with Stanley for having 'written [in his books] flowery descriptions of King's palaces, court pages ... when the only "king" [Jephson saw] was a dirtily clothed youth seated in the door of a small hut ...'. When Jephson said this, he was reproved as 'a pessimist ... who can see but little to admire either in the country or in the character of the natives'.[44]

However, corporal punishment, rather than Stanley's romanticism, caused most trouble between him and his officers. Barttelot felt that in any conflict between a white man and a black man, Stanley would always side against his fellow whites.[45] The others believed much the same. Ill-feeling arose because the officers felt that Stanley was hypocritical on the issue. Many times he told them to protect the interests of the whole column by not allowing 'confirmed stragglers ... to skulk among the reeds or cool themselves in groves at a distance from the road', leaving the long line of carriers to wait on the stifling path, without a scrap of shade. To make sure 800 people got in to camp each day at a reasonable hour, and to save their food supply by stopping thefts, Stanley recommended that 'a few cuts of the cane' should routinely be given to those lagging in the rear, 'for frequently these dawdlers lag purposely behind for such intentions'.[46] But when his officers followed his advice and chastised malingerers, Stanley invariably rebuked them for brutality, despite the fact that when he himself supervised rearguard duty with his Somali bodyguards, 'he laid his stick about the lazy ones and the Somalis whacked away too'.[47] So when Major Barttelot, whose Sudanese rarely obeyed him, was severely admonished by Stanley for 'striking, punching & throwing men into the river', he felt aggrieved.

Ten days later, Nelson, whom Stanley considered good-natured, hit a man on the legs and cut him badly. Stanley explained as calmly as he could that abrasions on the shins and calves often turned into life-threatening ulcers. If he must hit a man in future, it should be on the back. Nelson took the advice well. Not so Barttelot, who that same day 'punched a man under an eye and opened a big gash'. Stanley told him to get his headmen to use a switch on his men's backs, and not to go for them himself 'with fists, shin strokes, or jabbing at people with a spiked staff'. Barttelot countered that Stanley often lost his temper with individual men and laid into them. Stanley denied this, saying: 'I sometimes affect a great rage, or I taunt them with irony, but I don't pitch into them like a pugilist. Besides, I speak their dialect perfectly.'[48]

But given the terrible arguments that soured expeditions such as Burton and Speke's journey to Lake Tanganyika, and Livingstone's Zambezi Expedition, the rows occurring during the first months of the Emin Pasha expedition do not seem particularly severe. And this was despite the fact that by 20 April, towards the end of the land journey to Leopoldville, most of the party had had fever several times, and they had been travelling in the rains for three weeks, with everyone slipping and falling into the mud. So it was surprising there had been no really serious fallings out. Dr Parke inadvertently allowed nineteen rifles to be stolen and sold under his nose: a horrifying loss, yet Stanley (who thought Parke 'one of the best fellows alive') only raged at him briefly before making up over a drink and cigars.[49] Jameson, though thinking that Stanley was often unfair to his friend Barttelot, considered that 'Mr Stanley, when he throws off his reserve, is one of the most agreeable of men', adding: 'I cannot help admiring him immensely for his great strength of will and power of overcoming difficulties.'[50]

At this time Stanley was facing a grave crisis. In Paris in late January, en route for Zanzibar via Brindisi, he had met his old friend Anthony Swinburne. This meeting is recorded in a series of photographs, showing Swinburne, Stanley, Baruti and Hoffman together at the Hotel Meurice.[51] Swinburne, who was returning to the Congo from furlough in England, told Stanley how he and Henry Sanford (whose ivory trading company he now ran from the Pool) had been let down by Leopold's failure to provide promised river transport for the ivory. Swinburne had warned Stanley about the depleted state of the king's flotilla, and hinted that he himself might lend Stanley his company's steamer, the *Florida*.[52] However, none of this had prepared Stanley for what his former subordinate, Louis Valcke, told him at Boma in late March.[53]

When insisting that Stanley use the Congo route, Leopold had promised that the Congo Free State would 'place at the disposal of the expedition the whole of its naval stock'. Stanley had therefore expected to be able to depend, for the transport of his large expedition, not only on the State's largest steamer, the *Stanley*, but also on the three smaller steamers that had been in service when he had been in charge.[54] Valcke explained that the *Stanley* was damaged, the *En Avant* had no engine, and the *Royal* was 'altogether rotten'. By 1 April Stanley knew that both the missionary steamers were upstream somewhere and likely to be denied him. At this dreadful moment, the loyal Swinburne – although knowing that his boss, Henry Sanford, would be furious if he lent the unfinished *Florida* as a barge – confirmed that he would do so. She could now be towed by the *Stanley* when she had been repaired. Although it was widely known on the river that Swinburne had an African mistress, by whom he had a daughter, Stanley's warm feelings towards his twenty-nine-year-old former secretary remained unaffected. 'Swinburne has behaved nobly all through this business of getting from Stanley Pool,' he wrote after the *Florida* had been handed over for forty-five days.[55]

For six weeks before reaching the Pool, Stanley had lived with the very real possibility that he might be unable to move his 800 people any further east than Leopoldville. 'Help us quickly, or we perish,' the Pasha had implored, and Henry was haunted by his words.[56] The delay that the lack of steamers now seemed certain to cause would increase the likelihood of Emin being cut down like Gordon, after his ammunition ran out.

As Stanley faced probable failure, it was painful for him to recall the praise showered on him before he left. He had stayed at Sandringham with the Prince of Wales, having been presented with the Freedom of the City of London.[57] Never before had he enjoyed the esteem of the British establishment. Nor would he again, it seemed.

TWENTY-THREE

A Fateful Decision

Stanley made a very difficult decision on 22 April 1887, which would come to haunt him for the rest of his life. He was still at Leopoldville when he noted in his diary that since he had too few steamers to take his entire party and its stores eastwards along the Upper Congo in one trip, he might have to split his expedition in two. He reasoned that if he were to set up a staging post at Yambuya, on the Aruwimi river, 1,100 miles to the east, he would be able to leave behind there a Rear Column of several hundred men to look after the bulk of his stores. Meanwhile, a smaller, unencumbered Advance Column would be freed to march eastwards at once from Yambuya to try to find Emin above Lake Albert. Unless this split was adopted, the march from Yambuya to Emin's position would be delayed by two months – which was the time it would take the *Stanley* to make the round trip to Leopoldville to collect the stores and men left behind there, and return to the Aruwimi. If Emin Pasha should be overwhelmed in the meantime, the first question Stanley imagined being asked was why he had not split his expedition.

Stanley improved his prospects by persuading a reluctant William Bentley of the Baptist mission at Leopoldville to lend him his steamer, the *Peace*; and soon afterwards, Lieutenant Liebrichts, the Belgian governor at Stanley Pool, commandeered for him on behalf of the Congo Free State the Livingstone Inland Mission's steamer, the *Henry Reed*. Liebrichts had feared there would be starvation in Leopoldville unless Stanley's 800 people were able to proceed upriver.[1]

At last, on 1 May, Henry assembled his little fleet of three steamers for the 1,100-mile journey upstream from Stanley Pool to the Aruwimi. The *Stanley* towed the *Florida*, both vessels having 168 men on board. The *Henry Reed* towed the *En Avant* and the expedition's steel portable boat, carrying a combined total of 131 people, while the *Peace* also towed two boats containing a further 135 persons.[2] Taking 600 people upstream in a single journey was better than anything Stanley had envisaged a couple of weeks earlier, but he would still need to send the *Stanley* back for 131 men left at Bolobo and for the men guarding the stores at Leopoldville. The steamer's return trip to Yambuya (even carrying fewer men than anticipated) would take two months, so Stanley's rationale held good for leaving part of the expedition at Yambuya, while he led an advance party eastwards.

On 11 May Stanley had a long talk with the capable Lieutenant Stairs about whom to place in command at Yambuya. In Stairs's opinion, Major Barttelot's seniority in the army meant that no one else could lead a detached column. Recalling Barttelot's harshness towards Africans, Stanley asked Stairs whether he would be prepared to stay with the major to steady him. Stairs said he would rather be sent home. Henry therefore suggested Jephson as Barttelot's second-in-command, but Stairs told him that two 'hot-heads' should never be put together. The right men to stay with the major, said Stairs, were Jameson, Ward, Troup and Bonny.[3] Stanley evidently agreed, since these were the men he chose to leave. Barttelot was furious on learning he was to protect stores, rather than have the honour of rescuing Emin Pasha.[4]

Henry remained on edge after his decision, which is probably why he had his worst row yet with his officers as they steamed eastwards. It arose from that most frequent cause of dissension: his officers' treatment of the Wangwana.[5] Early on the morning of May 20, when the flotilla was about a third of the way to Yambuya, two lines of Wangwana came to their leader to complain about 'the way they were being treated by the little masters, especially by Mr Jephson'. If irritated by anything, 'the little masters struck all around as if everyone had done wrong. They clutched people by the throat and half-choked them, or they struck with their fists or sticks ... but yesterday they had behaved worse than ever ...[and] had ended up pitching all their food, bananas, bread, everything – overboard.' Just then, Stanley spotted Stairs and called him over. The young officer explained that the men had been ordered to cut wood, but had looted a local village for food instead. The Wangwana denied all this, and when Henry chose to believe them, Stairs took it as a personal insult. Stanley then chronicled a long list of complaints about earlier beatings that had already been made to him, 'individually and collectively' from the donkey boys right up to the headmen.

At this charged moment, Mounteney Jephson appeared. Stanley was on board ship, and Jephson was ashore, so their conversation had to be conducted with raised voices.

'Mr Jephson, these men have come to complain against you and others for beating them, and throwing all their food overboard. Will you tell me what you know of the matter?'

As Stanley recorded in his diary: 'Jephson calmly looked towards me and said: "You are not to shout at me in that way, sir!"'[6]

At this point Stanley completely lost his temper. To be faced by someone of Jephson's age and class demanding politeness, while failing to answer his reasonable questions, was unendurable.

'You damned son of a sea-cook, God damn you – you come here with a lie in your mouth, you damned puppy. You are tyrants,' he roared at both young men.[7] Jephson's charge that the Wangwana were Stanley's 'dear pets' enraged him even more. 'All are dear to me,' he cried, 'who do their duty, sir, and the Zanzibaris have quite satisfied me on this, and on previous expeditions.' He then told Jephson and Stairs that they were sacked, and shouted: 'You don't even know how to treat native chiefs when they come here with their little presents.'

The last straw for Henry was his suspicion that Jephson, Parke and Stairs were all in cahoots, laughing at him behind his back. He was entirely wrong. Stairs had no time for Jephson, and thought Parke a fool. Nor was Bonny in cahoots with anyone. He despised Barttelot, whom he thought unstable and the worst possible person to be placed in charge of the Sudanese.[8] He thought Ward selfish, greedy and a fantasist. Meanwhile, Ward and Troup detested both Bonny and Barttelot.[9]

Ignorance about his officers was the price Stanley paid for isolating himself. He failed to grasp that any man facing privation needed encouragement, whatever his background. Henry later confessed to an amazed officer: 'I never once suspected that you required occasional doses of pap & sweetness to keep you up to your duty ... No one had ever given pap to me, [so] how could I think that gentlemen of honour required it as a fillip of duty.'[10] A fear of unguarded remarks, in case they were written up in officers' journals, or leaked to the press, led him to dine alone in his own tent, and to avoid praising one man in case it caused jealousy with the others. Nor did he discuss important decisions, in case the expedition became 'a bemuddled debating society'.[11] Insecurity made Henry fear familiarity, lest it undermined respect. The explosion caused by Jephson's aloofness had surprised no one. Though intelligent and amusing, he was thought arrogant by his fellow officers. Nelson called him 'a conceited idiot', and Stairs often parodied his name-dropping.[12] To Stanley's amazement, the one person who behaved well, after his row with Jephson and Stairs, was Major Barttelot. In fact the major persuaded him to reinstate the two men.[13]

The further upriver they steamed, the more important it became to stay on good terms with Tippu Tip, who would be required to collect 600 porters to carry the Rear Column's stores to Lake Albert, and would also be expected to prohibit other slave traders from raiding villages below Stanley Falls and on the Aruwimi. So it appalled Stanley when Dr Parke spoke openly of Tippu's wives as 'filthy dirty, highly smelling women', who ought to be ousted from their steamer cabin, unless they washed. If Tippu wished, he would soon be able to attack Barttelot and steal all his stores. Or he could stop local tribes selling food to the Rear Column. Small wonder Henry forbade all further 'rudeness to our guests'.[14]

The nearer to the Aruwimi they got, the more oppressive the river became. 'It is peculiar what a feeling of hatred the river inspires one with,' wrote Jephson. 'One hates it as if it were a living thing – it is so treacherous & crafty, so overpowering & relentless ... The river God is an evil one I am persuaded.'[15] At Upoto, the last village on the Congo before the Aruwimi confluence, Jameson observed that many people wore necklaces of human teeth, and the captain of the *Peace* confirmed that Soko tribesmen had eaten two west coast soldiers who had fled from Stanley Falls after it had been overwhelmed by the Arabs.[16] The wildness of the riverside tribes made everyone fear an attack while the ships were moored for woodcutting.[17] Meanwhile, Dr Parke noticed that James Jameson was fascinated by the subject of cannibalism.[18]

Three days before reaching Yambuya, the steamers came level with the home village of Baruti, the boy whom Stanley was taking back to his parents. On being reunited with one of his brothers, he seemed eager to rejoin his family, but then changed his mind and decided to stay with Stanley. However, within less than a week he deserted at night, taking a Winchester rifle and two Smith & Wesson revolvers, as well as a silver watch and some money. Some months later, the rifle turned up at Stanley Falls, after Baruti had been ambushed, killed and eaten by cannibals on his way back to his family.[19]

On 15 June the expedition arrived at Yambuya, where Stanley intended to create, close to the village, a camp for his Rear Column. The villagers had other ideas and refused to 'palaver'. Stanley therefore ordered that all the whistles of his steamers be blown loudly, and that Jephson, Nelson and Stairs land with their men, only shooting if attacked. Already scared by Arab raids, the villagers fled. When they did not reappear, Stanley selected the highest point in the village for his camp. The bush was cut back around it and ditches dug. On the 17th a few natives came across the river in canoes to sell food to the newcomers.[20] But they were not followed by others. It was therefore lucky that there were extensive fields of manioc (bitter cassava) close by – large enough to provide food for hundreds of men for months.

Yet though Henry felt there would be no food problem, he had personal misgivings about Barttelot, despite the part the man had played in reconciling him with Stairs and Jephson. When the major arrived at Yambuya after delivering Tippu Tip to Stanley Falls, Stanley was furious to hear that Tippu had been 'disappointed' on learning that the gunpowder he had been promised as part of his agreement had not yet been shipped from Leopoldville. Why had Barttelot not pointed out that Tippu's attitude was totally unreasonable? Stanley had arranged for the powder to be shipped to Yambuya within eight weeks. Now he said vehemently to the major: 'It will be time enough to talk about the powder when he reaches this camp [with the carriers he had promised to collect]. He surely did not expect to get ammunition before he came here for it.' When Henry asked whether Barttelot had seen many carriers at the Falls, the major shook his head and said that Tippu would have 'to send to all the villages around'.[21] This convinced Stanley he had been right to split the expedition, since it would clearly be several months before Tippu Tip brought enough carriers to Yambuya to enable Barttelot to leave with the rest of the stores and follow the Advance Column to Lake Albert.

Stanley handed Major Barttelot his written instructions on 27 June, four days before he (Stanley) left for the east. In them, the major was reminded of the importance of guarding and then bringing eastwards 'the vast store of ammunition and provisions' that would be in the camp after the heavily laden *Stanley* returned from Leopoldville. If these stores were ever lost, Barttelot was warned, the Advance Column would have 'to solicit relief' for itself, rather than provide it for Emin. Sentries were therefore to be posted, day and night, at Yambuya, to guard against any attack on the camp. If Tippu Tip arrived with the full 600 carriers, then the Rear Column would be able to leave with all its stores. If Tippu brought fewer, then some goods would have to be left behind. Stanley therefore listed the indispensable items – ammunition and the most expensive trade goods heading this list. Rather than abandon too many things, it might be necessary to march after the advance party in a series of six-mile marches, doubling back on themselves to bring on more goods each time. Barttelot was given a final choice: he could stay at Yambuya, if marching meant 'throwing too many things away'. Barttelot was to consult his fellow officers when making important decisions. Stanley promised to blaze trees so that Barttelot could easily find the right path when his carriers arrived.[22]

Still angry at being left behind, Barttelot did not comment on his instructions. Jameson thought they 'cleared up ... every point' except 'our relations with Tippu Tip'.[23] This was true. But Stanley knew that if Tippu broke his contract, nothing could be done. Barttelot and his officers would either have to await his (Stanley's) return to Yambuya at the end of the year, or try to move off on their own initiative, having first weeded the stores. The Rear Column's 133 men would by then have been joined by the 131 left behind at Bolobo.[24] Certainly it was Barttelot's fervent hope to leave Yambuya soon after the *Stanley* arrived with Troup and Bonny on board.[25] And Stanley expressed this same desire in his diary on 24 June. Several weeks earlier, he had written to Troup, then still in Leopoldville, telling him that when he (Troup) reached Yambuya, the major 'will no doubt ... push on after me with you all.'[26] It is therefore very surprising that on 19 July Barttelot wrote to his brother-in-law, Major Henry Sclater, claiming that Stanley's last words to him before he left Yambuya were: 'Goodbye, major; [I] shall find you here in October when I return.' Nobody else overheard this, though Jameson was close at hand. Parke claimed that on parting, Barttelot declared he would come after them as soon as he could.[27]

A day before he was due to march, Stanley was in a great quandary over whether to take Lieutenant Stairs with him, since the young officer was very ill with fever. Eventually Dr Parke decided that he could

Yambuya Camp behind its palisade

be carried without danger.[28] Stanley left Yambuya for Lake Albert on 28 June 1887. He had no idea of the full extent of the Ituri Forest, which lay ahead and had never been crossed by an explorer. So Henry was telling the literal truth when stating in his diary that he and his 389 men were pitching themselves 'into the absolutely unknown ... [without] even a ray of light to guide [them]'.[29] Indeed, he was embarking on an ordeal to rival the most dangerous events he had ever lived through.

TWENTY-FOUR

The Enigma of Emin Pasha

When the advance party marched out of the gates of the stockade that they had helped to build at Yambuya camp, they looked a brave and hopeful sight: the 389 men split into four companies of about ninety men, each with their own drummers at the head of a long line of carriers, and, out in front, a party of axe-bearing trail-blazers.[1] During their journey by water, contacts with local people had been very limited, but now they had disembarked and were entering the Ituri Forest, this immunity was over.

Many of the forest dwellers had either suffered an Arab-Swahili slave raid in person, or knew people who had, so it was entirely understandable that they should wish to stop strangers approaching. But for Stanley's men, this attitude was like a death sentence. Local villages offered them their sole opportunity to buy food, and stood on the only track through the jungle. Henry therefore had to visit each settlement, regardless of the feelings of its inhabitants. In happier days, he had acknowledged the right of the Congolese to deny strangers access to their land if they so wished, but not on this occasion when his expedition's survival was at stake. Even so, Jephson thought him 'wonderfully patient & long suffering [with local tribes]'.[2]

As the men of the Advance Column struggled through the steaming jungle, tribesmen fired poisoned arrows at them from behind trees. Stanley was constantly looking out for cleverly disguised pits in the path and small needle-like poisoned sticks stuck in the ground in places where men would jump down from tree trunks placed across the track. The poison was usually fatal, causing men to die in agony within a few days.[3]

On the very first day of their march, the column drew up in front of the village of Yankondé to find their way blocked by 300 warriors, 'gesticulating and shouting, with drawn bows in their hands'. They stood at the end of a section of the path that had been widened. 'We were not long in finding,' wrote Stanley, 'that this apparent highway through the bush bristled with sharpened skewers ... covered with green leaves.' After these poisoned stakes had been gingerly pulled out of the ground, Stanley's men advanced on the bowmen, who released 'a little cloud of arrows', which wounded two men. Rather than retreat – thus sending a signal along the Aruwimi that the expedition could safely be resisted – Stanley ordered twenty men to fire back. The result was a number of warriors killed and others rushing in flight to the river.[4] Henry found the next village empty. Around him were the charred remains of former dwellings. This told him 'that Arabs and Manyema [their African slave-trading allies] must have visited here'. The next village, reached on 5 July 1888, was deserted too, with the fowls and other livestock apparently taken into the jungle. Hunger was soon tormenting every member of the expedition.

Stumbling along in the twilight, beneath the canopy of a tropical jungle, the heavily laden carriers sank into swampy hollows, or slipped in stream beds intersecting the path. 'The unfortunate donkeys floundered about hopelessly,' recorded Jephson, 'and arrived on the other side exhausted and perfectly black. The donkey boys were often up to their waists in thin, unwholesome smelling mud. To add to the unpleasantness a perfect multitude of ants devoured one.' At times the jungle could be beautiful, as when spiders' webs, bejewelled with drops of water, hung like curtains between the trees, with the river sparkling behind them. But such beauty could be the backdrop to shocking violence. After one of Jephson's men shot two tribesmen, all his compassion was aroused. These men had merely been 'taking the liberty of running away from us in their own forest'. Now, one of them had a badly shattered leg bone, and the elder of the two a fatal stomach wound. 'Both looked at me with doglike eyes, like suffering animals. I felt sickeningly sorry for them & awfully choky. It was such a cruel, ruthless, unnecessary thing.'[5]

When Stanley could buy no food, and get no information about the attitude of the people ahead, he captured a few villagers, who were compelled to come along with him for several days until giving all the information they could. Then they were released. A woman captured in this way ran away in the night with her little girl, but leaving behind her baby. Stanley believed that if the infant was left in the same place, its mother would reclaim it when the column marched on. Jephson was less optimistic. 'Poor little thing, it looked so happy as we left it by the fire with its hands full of corn cobs – the natives will certainly eat it.'[6] The marauding Manyema were cannibals, as were the local Soko.

By early August, several men had died of dysentery, and several from wounds inflicted by poisoned arrows. Although Stanley was sending out food parties, with instructions to steal if they could find no game, the results were negligible. 'The people are ravenously hungry ... We have several living skeletons with us already.' The donkeys were also suffering, as grass did not grow in the dark forest. One died and others seemed sure to follow.[7] Above Yambuya cataracts, Henry assembled his metal boat, and with five canoes – bought and stolen – he was able to rest his enfeebled carriers in rotation by carrying some by water while the rest struggled overland.

On 13 August the river party was attacked by a strong force of well-hidden bowmen and five men were hit by poisoned arrows; a sixth, Lieutenant Stairs, received a wound just below the heart that seemed likely to prove mortal. When Stanley came up, he found Stairs's shirt torn open and blood streaming from his chest. Arrows were still being fired from across the river.[8] 'It is a curious sensation,' wrote Jephson,

Lieutenant Stairs hit by an arrow

'being shot at by arrows, one sees & hears nothing but the "pit, pit, pit" of the arrows as they strike the brushwood round.'[9] Dr Parke came upon Stairs soon after failing to save a man with a spear driven into his neck. Stairs was 'very blanched and suffering from shock'. Unfortunately, in falling, he had broken the arrow, turning the tip under a rib where it was inaccessible without intrusive surgery. Parke injected water into the wound and then bravely sucked out the poison with his lips. After administering silver nitrate to the wound, he dressed it, and gave a morphine injection to control the pain. For days the young officer travelled in a tilted chair roped in place in a canoe. Though Stairs was feverish for twenty-four hours, two days later he was getting better, despite a steady discharge. Dr Parke had saved Stairs's life, though he still feared that tetanus might kill him.[10] A week later two other arrow victims expired from lockjaw 'after intolerable agonies'.

Of 373 men in camp, Stanley noted that sixty were now 'fitter for hospital than to continue our wandering life'. It haunted him that he might be leading his men to their deaths in the rain forest. Along with Parke, he took his turn 'giving morphia [sic] injections ... and ministering to their needs'. He confessed that 'a few more days ... listening to the muffled screams' might bring him to despair. On a regular diet of green bananas and plantains, men carrying heavy loads weakened fast. Sixteen had died already.[11] Henry's determination to save men from poisoned arrows meant that while travelling on the river he took no chances. When a man in a canoe drew his bow, he shot him dead – finding beside him a dozen freshly poisoned arrows. The only food in his canoe was a bundle of cooked slugs – a diet proving there was hardly any game in the forest.[12]

During the final week of August and the first two of September, the column lost a further thirty men through death and desertion. By 18 September only 238 out of 340 were fit to march. 'We have had no food for 3 days for the people. These Manyema ruffians have not only driven the people away, but they have destroyed the plantations & there is nothing left on either bank.'[13] The desertions continued, with thefts of rifles, ammunition and preserved food – one man disappeared with nothing but a large box of biscuits, meaning to gorge himself somewhere before dying. Meanwhile, it rained torrentially for part of every day, turning the track into a quagmire. As Dr Parke remarked sadly: 'Zanzibaris can't stand cold and wet. They shiver, develop goose-flesh and turn a greenish yellow.'[14] The doctor noted that Stanley was too depressed to lose his temper. In truth, he was pondering whether it might not be for the best 'to retreat and fall back on our goods [which he hoped were by now moving forward with Barttelot and Jameson] rather than urge on the tired people in this mad fashion.'[15]

In mid-September the desertions went on – the absconders hoping to attach themselves to a Manyema caravan before they starved.[16] At this time, hunger led Stairs and Parke to commit murder. They had hoped to scare the natives of a particular village into flight, so they could steal their livestock. But they failed to get between them and their fowls and goats. So Stairs coolly shot one man dead, and Parke hit another two, who were fleeing with a goat. These desperate and brutal acts did not yield the famished officer and the doctor the fowls and goats they had hoped for, but only some smoked elephant meat and a few bananas.[17] Because they themselves had been starving, it could not have been easy to resist the temptation of stealing food by killing its owners, when easily able to do so. Back home, natives in remote places were routinely called 'savages'. Stairs in addition had nearly died from an arrow wound inflicted by a local assailant, and other men had expired in agony from similar wounds. In this context his aggression can be understood, even if not condoned. Stanley arrived many hours later and probably never heard what had happened.

By 19 September the column had travelled 300 miles from Yambuya, and on that day reached an Arab-Swahili settlement founded by Ugarrowwa, a Zanzibari who had been a tent boy on Speke and Grant's 1864 expedition. He had deserted near Lake Victoria, and in the decades since had made a fortune from slaves and ivory. Ungarrowwa had killed most of the adult males in the land surrounding his settlement, and had enslaved their women for the harems of Arabia. The male children had been 'indoctrinated as menials & foot soldiers'.[18] Stanley was now able to leave behind fifty-six sick men to be fed at the rate of $5 per month. He contracted to pay from the Rear Column's stores, if Ugarrowwa's men delivered a letter to Barttelot. Stanley warned the major of the many difficulties he had experienced and advised him to acquire canoes and use the river as much as possible.[19] Unfortunately, the men taking this letter were attacked by tribesmen and never reached Yambuya. At Ungarrowwa's, Stanley met his first Mbuti pygmy, a 'very prepossessing' young woman thirty-three inches tall.[20] He and his officers were the first Europeans to see these diminutive forest-dwellers.

Now that they were in a region of Arab-Swahili settlements, the danger of the Wangwana deserting *en masse* was acute. When three absconded with rifles and ammunition and were brought by Ugar-rowwa's men to Stanley's camp that evening, after a day's march, he decided that unless he made an example of at least one, his losses would spiral out of control. He recalled that in 1876, before Tippu Tip turned back towards Nyangwe, the Arab had had to threaten to shoot any Wangwana who followed him rather than stayed with the expedition. Without Tippu's timely threat, Stanley would have lost his entire following. His present situation, he believed, was similar, and only a draconian punishment would prevent disaster. He rehearsed a charade with his captains, which was that three thieves would be condemned to death, but after the first had been hanged the captains would beg him to show mercy to the other two. So this was what was done. After one man had been hanged, Stanley's subsequent act of clemency to the remaining two was greeted emotionally with cries of: 'Death to him who leaves Bula Matari! Show the way to the Nyanza!' (words confirmed by Parke in his diary). All the officers supported the punishment, and Jephson, the most sensitive, thought an execution was long overdue, given the frightening rate of desertion.[21] The last public hangings in England had taken place when these young men had been teenagers, and so they were not repelled by capital punishment. In Britain in the 1880s, soldiers could still be hanged or shot for mutiny, or desertion in the face of the enemy. For Africans, the death penalty was commonplace.

As the food crisis deepened, members of the expedition began to starve, and Lieutenant Nelson was among thirty whom Stanley described as 'absolutely incapable'. Though Nelson was white, Stanley was determined he should not be carried and thus deprive the expedition of two fit carriers. So, on 6 October, he announced that Nelson, who could not walk, was to share the fate of 'fifty-two black men to whom we were equally bound by the most solemn obligations', and be left with them in a hastily improvised camp.[22] Jephson was shocked that Nelson would only have food for two days and would have 'to exist on what he can pick up in the shape of fungus & roots'. Stanley later denied having left Nelson so ill-provided. Parke found parting with his sick colleague 'the most sickening, heart-rending goodbye I ever experienced'. Yet he thought Stanley right 'to sacrifice one and save the remainder'.[23]

Jephson, Parke, Stairs and Stanley marched on and experienced the same grim conditions as before, and the same steady trickle of thefts and desertions, interspersed with attacks by tribesmen or bands of Manyema. Feruzi Ali, whom Stanley described as his 'third best man' was wounded in the head by a spear and 'became paralysed and died in agony' four days later.[24] Every day several men died of starvation, as they stumbled on towards Ipoto, the next Arab settlement. Henry sent ahead five reliable men to bring back food from the settlement, but they lost their way and would not be seen for three weeks. By now everyone was eating leathery forest beans, slugs and caterpillars. At a crucial moment, Stanley killed the last of his donkeys and divided it among his men. All this time, Stanley was distraught over what might happen to Nelson and his men; but he knew he would only be able to save them if he could reach the next camp and purchase food there.[25] As Jephson acknowledged, 'Stanley's anxiety has been frightful, for the success of the expedition has been & is indeed hanging in the balance.'[26]

On 18 October they arrived at Ipoto, the creation of another runaway Zanzibari slave, Kilonga-Longa, who had a dozen Arab-Swahili and about 150 Manyema under him. They had assembled a substantial store of ivory, through robbery, and had planted rice, sweet potatoes and beans, and possessed many goats and fowls.[27] Stanley described his men as skeletal, with 'ashy grey skin ...[and] with every sign of wretchedness deep in their eyes'. Even so, he was appalled when his ravenous men 'went mad ... stole freely & slaughtered goats and fowls belonging to the Arabs ... and at last they stole our rifles & cartridges & sold them to the Arabs for just two meals of meat each'. During three disastrous days, thirty rifles and 3,000 rounds of ammunition disappeared, threatening the very existence of the expedition. Stanley knew that he would never leave Ipoto with any kind of column unless he acted decisively. The man he executed, as an example, was called Juma, and he had sold several rifles. Many men had done the same and would be luckier. It is impossible to say whether Stanley could have held his force together without this second execution, but it seems unlikely, since even after the punishment he left Ipoto with a mere 147 men, having arrived with just over 200, and having set out from Yambuya with 389. Life would have been much easier for Stanley if he had only had more cloth to sell, because he would then have been able to build up a reserve of food. But the need to carry ammunition for Emin Pasha had made him skimp on trade goods.[28]

On 26 October, Jephson – the man about town, who had turned out to be a dauntless explorer – was sent back by Stanley with forty men and thirty Manyema to take food to Robert Nelson. Dr Parke accompanied him, with instructions to bring the sick man and other survivors back to Ipoto and to stay with them there. This was hard on the doctor, since it seemed likely to be many months before the Rear Column arrived and took him and Nelson on with them to Lake Albert. On the other hand, it was proof of Stanley's concern for the starving men that he should have left the doctor with Nelson, denying himself Parke's skills. When Jephson reached Nelson on the 29th, he was still alive, but reduced to 'an infirm decrepit-looking skeleton'.[29] Only five men were there out of fifty-two men left with him. Seventeen had died and the rest had fled. At Ipoto, Parke would also look after twenty-nine sick men, left behind by Stanley when he marched for the lake.[30]

Nelson felt very bitter that Stanley had failed to guarantee a better food supply from the Arabs. But having hardly any cloth, it is hard to see what else he could have done – except promise payment when the

Jephson's arrival at Nelson's camp

343

Rear Column arrived.[31] The brutality of the Arab-Swahili at Ipoto and at Ugarrowwa's convinced Henry that an international ban on the import of gunpowder into Africa was essential, along with the confiscation of ivory at the coast. 'It is simply incredible that because ivory is required for ornaments or billiard games, the rich heart of Africa should be laid waste ... [and] populations, tribes and nations should be utterly destroyed.'[32]

On 10 November, Stanley, Stairs, Hoffman and some 150 men reached the village of Ibwiri, about a hundred miles from the lake. Here, the local tribe greeted them in friendship, having had no experience of slave raids. For the first time since entering the Ituri forest four and a half months earlier, they found a substantial clearing – about three miles in diameter – containing fields planted with crops. Here the expedition stayed for two weeks while the men put on weight and strength. Stanley was joined here by Jephson and forty-eight men on the 16th, and the whole Advance Column, now numbering 175 men, left on the 23rd.[33]

Observing his Wangwana as they regained some of their old spirit, Stanley felt humbled by them.

No other body of men in the wide world could have borne such a period of hunger so meekly and resignedly ... their comrades dying at every camp, or falling dead along the track ... Goaded by the protracted hunger and loss of trust in their officers, they might have seized their Remingtons and, by one volley, have slain their white chiefs ... and shaken off their power ... which, so far as they knew, was only dragging them down to certain doom.[34]

Yet even in this hilly grassland, their troubles were not over. Not long after leaving Ibwiri, they encountered a tribe that clearly meant to prevent them reaching Lake Albert.[35]

The crisis came on 8 December, when Stanley and 173 men (his own party plus those brought on by Jephson) entered a broad valley only a few days' journey from the lake. Looking up, they saw 'natives gathered on the hills on either side, shouting & yelling at us'. Given that their adversaries numbered about a thousand, Henry dreaded being rushed from both sides. Hand to hand fighting would be the end of them. And the Africans now descended and began pressing in on them. As they came within 200 yards, Stanley felt his men were in great danger and fired at a man, felling him. At once the tribesmen backed off. In this breathing space Stanley managed to build a thorn *boma* to defend his people. He knew that if the Africans launched a determined night attack, they would be impossible to resist. Even in the day, the cultivated fields of tall-stemmed sorghum gave good cover to spearmen and bowmen. Fortunately for Stanley and his men, the night attack never came.

Next day, he tried to make peace by handing over cloth and brass wire, and offering to become the chief's blood brother. But though these gifts were accepted, the tribe's hostility persisted, and a fight seemed inevitable. To warn them of the consequences, Stanley burned several settlements. 'My idea has been all along to fight as little as possible,' Stanley wrote to a friend, 'but when compelled to do so, to set about the job as efficiently as possible, so that there will remain no doubt in native minds what we propose doing when we tell them.'[36] To his great relief, the chief decided to make peace. For every hundred men who had left Yambuya, only forty-five had reached this point, so he could afford no more losses.[37]

On 13 December, Stanley and his men stood on a hill overlooking the lake. 'Imagine our feelings on seeing the dark blue waters of Albert Nyanza, nearly 2,500 ft below us,' wrote Stairs, who could easily have died from his arrow wound. Henry's observations for longitude and latitude had brought them with perfect accuracy to this point in the district of Kavalli.[38] But gazing through his glass at the lake, it alarmed him to see no canoes or trees large enough to carve into dugouts. In order to bring as much ammunition as possible for Emin, he had been obliged to leave his steel boat at Ipoto. It looked as if he might not be able to reach Emin's base at Wadelai on the Upper Nile without a long overland journey. And since hundreds of natives were even now closing in and firing arrows as they started their descent towards the lake, Stanley knew how dangerous that would be.[39]

On the following day, he tried to convince local villagers that he came in friendship and merely wanted to buy canoes. But the people remained suspicious, refusing to sell them any boats. At last he heard that there was a white man thirty-five miles across the lake at Kibiro. But from the description, this seemed to be the Pasha's friend, the Italian traveller Gaetano Casati, rather than Emin himself.[40] Everyone was deeply disappointed. Efforts to buy canoes continued next day, without success, as did attempts to exchange gifts. 'Look where we might,' wrote Stanley, 'a way to advance was denied to us, except by fighting, killing, destroying, consuming and being consumed.' Ruling out taking canoes by force, Stanley announced to his frustrated officers, Jephson and Stairs, that there was no choice but to return to Ipoto for the metal boat and more rifle rounds. They had only forty-seven cases of ammunition with them, and if they chose to march overland to Wadelai, they might have to use twenty-five of these in defending themselves on the way, leaving a pathetic amount of ammunition to hand over to Emin on arrival.[41]

Both Stairs and Jephson were shocked that a man of Stanley's 'immense experience & marvellous powers of resource' should not have 'hit upon a feasible plan' to find Emin without doubling back to the fringes of the awful forest that they had been so thankful to leave.[42] Yet the expedition was scattered in ill-provided small groups over several hundred miles, and Henry was acutely anxious about the safety of Parke and Nelson. It says a lot for his sense of realism that he was able to accept, after everything they had endured, that finding Emin would be a hollow achievement if the expedition fell apart. Without more supplies, his Advance Column could do little for the Pasha or for itself. The hostility of the lakeside natives ruled out remaining where they were. At Ibwiri the locals were friendly and food abundant, so Stanley now planned to return and build a camp there, to which Parke, Nelson and their men, and the invalids at Ugarrowwa's, could be brought. Only once the united Advance Column had re-provisioned itself from this new depot would he consider a second attempt on Lake Albert.[43]

On beginning the march back to Ibwiri on 16 December 1887, Stanley decided not to climb in daylight up the rocky slope to the tableland from which they had descended to Albert's shores. Instead, he camped at the bottom of the slope without lighting fires or pitching tents. Then just before dawn, he ordered his men to scramble to the summit.[44] At sunrise Jephson looked back and saw a party of Africans trying to get ahead of them to alert the tribesmen on the plateau, who would then have been able to attack the approaching intruders. This was exactly what Stanley had so cleverly avoided.

But, as Jephson recorded, the danger was not over.

Natives began to gather on the hills from all sides & close in on our rear. A large party of them with shouts & waving of spears come on with a rush & made as if to attack the rear. Stanley stepped out and taking a good steady aim with his Winchester Express fired at a native 550 yards distant & shot him through the head. The natives ... were all so utterly thunderstruck at the possibility of our being able to kill a man at such a distance that they took to their heels.[45]

Had Stanley allowed them to come closer, he and his men would have ended up having to kill many more to defend themselves. Yet he had killed – albeit in self-defence – an undoubted owner of the land they were crossing, whose only desire had been to protect it. Stanley was deeply perplexed by the animosity of these tribes to the west of Lake Albert. Later, he would learn that he and his Advance Column had become linked in people's minds with the Warasura – the much-feared bandit allies of Kabarega, the King of Bunyoro.[46]

Back at Ibwiri, on 6 January 1888, Henry supervised the construction of a fort with a sixteen-foot watchtower, and cleared three acres for corn and beans. To protect the log cabins built for his officers and the Wangwana, a ditch and stockade were constructed. Stanley feared attacks by the Manyema, and crop-stealing by pygmies.[47] On 19 January, Stairs was sent with a hundred men to bring back Parke and Nelson from Ipoto, along with the steel boat. Amazingly, he returned in less than thee weeks, having marched 158 miles through difficult terrain. Stanley now pondered whether to return to the lake with his boat and resume his search for Emin, or whether to go back at once through the Ituri Forest to help Major Barttelot's column through the jungle. He finally decided to send Lieutenant Stairs from Fort Bodo to Ugarrowwa's and back – a round trip of 366 miles – with a letter for Major Barttelot, which would be taken on from the Arab settlement by twenty Wangwana volunteers. In the letter, Stanley warned the major that near Arab settlements his column might well break up, and if this process started he should build a strong camp and wait to be relieved by the Advance Column.[48]

At the time of Stairs's departure, Henry was suffering from a huge abscess in his right arm.[49] Then gastritis and haematuric fever laid him low. For a week he drifted in and out of consciousness, while Jephson and the doctor took it in turns to sit with him at night. Parke ordered two Wangwana boys to be with him constantly in the day. One of these teenagers, Saleh bin Osman, became indispensable, and not just because his foot massage helped Henry to sleep. 'Sali' brought Stanley information about what his Wangwana captains and his officers were saying.

Stanley's milk diet was keeping him alive, so Parke lived in fear that his two remaining goats would be stolen. On one occasion, Parke caught Hoffman drinking Stanley's milk, which enraged the sick man so much, when he heard of it, that he tried to hit his valet with a stick, merely jarring his bad arm.[50] Six weeks later, Stanley was better; and at the end of March 1888, having waited for Stairs for as long as he felt able, he departed for the lake, taking 126 men, the steel boat, the invaluable Dr Parke and the reliable Mounteney Jephson. Nelson was left behind with about forty-five men to guard the stores and crops at Fort Bodo. The Maxim would be left for Stairs to bring on to the lake for Emin in due course. The young officer arrived twenty-six days too late, with fifteen survivors from the fifty-six men who had been left with the Arabs at Ugarrowwa's.[51]

A month before Henry reached Lake Albert, Emin Pasha had come down the western side of Lake Albert in his steamer, and had spread the news far and wide that he was looking for a white man who had come from afar. On 14 April, several days from the lake, Stanley heard from members of the Zamboni tribe that '*Malleju*' ('the Bearded One') had recently been at Katonza's 'in a big canoe, all of iron'.[52] On reaching Kavalli's on the 18th, Stanley was handed a packet by Chief Mbiassi, containing a letter from Emin Pasha. Written three weeks earlier, it was, as William Hoffman commented, 'a strange letter to receive from a man whom we had imagined to be in an agony of suspense for relief to arrive'.[53] Not by one word did Emin give the impression that he was pleased by Stanley's arrival. He merely asked him to spread information about his whereabouts so that he could return for him in his steamer. But though cool, the letter showed that Emin was alive – which was a huge relief to Stanley, who promptly sent Jephson and fifteen of his best men up the shore of the lake in the steel boat. A few days later, having heard that Stanley was camped near Kavalli's, Emin steamed south, and having located Jephson, took him on board and continued to Kavalli's, towing the steel boat.[54]

Stanley's valet was chasing butterflies on a cliff above the expedition's camp when he spotted the smoke of a distant steamer. 'I rushed down headlong ... nearly bursting with excitement. "Mr Stanley, Mr Stanley!" I shouted, "Emin Pasha is here."'[55] The date was 29 April 1888. The Wangwana dashed down to the shore, firing their guns in salute. It was eight o'clock and growing dark by the time Emin Pasha, his friend Captain Casati, Jephson and another of Emin's officers walked into the camp above Kavalli's.

I shook hands with all, and asked which was Emin Pasha [recalled Stanley]. Then one rather small, slight figure, wearing glasses, arrested my attention by saying in excellent English, 'I owe you a thousand thanks, Mr Stanley; I really do not know how to

Stanley meets Emin Pasha

express my thanks to you.' ... At the door of the tent we sat, and a wax candle threw light upon the scene. I expected to see a tall thin military figure, in faded Egyptian uniform, but instead of it I saw a small spare figure in a well-kept fez and a clean suit of snowy cotton drilling, well-ironed and of perfect fit. A dark grizzled beard bordered a face of Magyar cast, though a pair of spectacles lent it, somewhat an Italian or Spanish appearance. There was not a trace on it of ill-health or anxiety.'[56]

Emin described this meeting with Stanley as 'a moment I shall never forget'.[57] But before arriving at Stanley's camp, he had written: 'My hopes are not rose-coloured, but my resolution is taken: go I will not!' He was referring to a letter that Stanley had written on 18 April offering to escort him and his officials back to Egypt. By now, Emin knew from Jephson how ill-provided and exhausted Stanley's Advance Column was, and this had dashed his hopes that the newcomer might play an important part in the power politics of the region and thus enable him to stay in Equatoria as he really wished to do. Thirty-one boxes of ammunition and the tattered remnants of Stanley's column were not going to help Emin restore his line of communication to Zanzibar through hostile Bunyoro. Yet Emin had no intention of letting Stanley see, at this early stage, either his disappointment, or what he truly desired. At their first meeting, Stanley invited Emin, Casati and Jephson into his tent and produced five pints of champagne. Soon, despite his lack of 'rose-coloured' hopes, Emin was enthralled by Stanley's account of his misfortunes in the unexplored primeval forest extending from Ibwiri as far as the Congo. 'The hours sped by like a dream till past ten,' Emin confided to his diary.[58]

From the beginning, there was mutual respect between the two men, but this did not stop Emin being secretive and disingenuous from the day of their first meeting. Casati thought Emin's pride prevented him being honest with Stanley. 'To confess his own powerlessness, and censure his own errors, was repugnant to his proud mind.'[59] Stanley appreciated Emin's courtesy, his unconventionality, his interest in science, and the neatness of his journals.[60] Emin's modest height of five feet seven inches and his being only a year older than Stanley were also things they had in common. Henry knew that Emin was a German, and realized that his Turkish name, his marriage to an Abyssinian, and his conversion to Islam made him most unusual; but he had no idea that Emin, like himself, had turned his back on his native land because he had felt rejected by his fellow countrymen.

At their first proper discussion on 30 April, Emin appeared to believe that Stanley's only objective was to persuade him to accompany him to England or Egypt – whereas this was merely one of two options (the other being to move Emin and a number of his men to an area east of Lake Victoria), either of which Stanley would have been happy with. Understandably, Henry and his officers had come to see 'rescuing' Emin, and taking him away from the supposed dangers he had been facing, as justifying all the deaths and suffering the expedition had experienced. So, even when it was found that Emin was not in immediate danger – able, in fact, to supply the expedition with large quantities of grain and meat – this notion of taking him away still held a powerful appeal. Emin was at once aware of this.[61]

On 30 April Stanley told Emin bluntly that if he decided not to return to Egypt, he and his men could expect no more pay from the Egyptian government – in fact no aid of any kind. That same government had paid half the costs of the Emin Pasha Relief Expedition, and since its ministers wanted Emin to evacuate Equatoria, Stanley believed he was morally obliged to put the Egyptian case to the Pasha before suggesting any possible alternatives. So at first, he did his utmost to persuade Emin to leave, emphasizing that it would be impossible to get his people out at some later date through the Ituri

Forest, when he (Stanley) had gone. With Bunyoro closed to him by King Kabarega's hostility, there would be no eastern escape route either. So his Egyptian officials and Sudanese soldiers would never see their homes again unless they took their chance now. Emin agreed that Stanley had a point, but refused to give any decision.[62]

On the evening of the following day, Emin and Henry resumed their conversation. The Pasha predicted that the Egyptians and his irregular soldiers might agree to come too if he left, but many of his regular soldiers, 'who have enjoyed such a free and happy life', would never consent to come away. But if they stayed, would it be right to desert them? 'Would it not be consigning them all to ruin?'[63] Emin Pasha then asked Stanley what would happen 'supposing the men surround me and detain me by force'. It was a great pity both that Stanley brushed aside this possibility, and that Emin did not at once admit that his hold over his men was weakening by the day.

At this same meeting, Stanley abandoned any idea of persuading Emin to leave for Egypt, and instead put forward his two alternative proposals. What would Emin do, he asked, if King Leopold 'found him a sufficient salary, and gave him enough year by year to pay and feed his troops'? The Pasha waved this aside. There was not enough food in Equatoria, he said, regardless of how much money was available. Since Emin had already told Stanley that he needed to take his men to a place in good communication with the coast, where food was plentiful, and where the surrounding rulers were friendly – unlike the kings of Buganda and Bunyoro, and the Mahdists – Stanley was not surprised by this response. He now put his own favourite option. Emin described in his diary his delight on learning that it would be possible for him to 'occupy the north-eastern corner of the Victoria Nyanza, from which communications could be established immediately, and where the country was healthy'. Henry also said this scheme would 'find support in England'. Of course, this was Mackinnon's East African proposal, though Stanley did not name his friend. Emin was euphoric, and, in his own words, 'entered into it heart and soul'.[64]

When they discussed the same subject on 3 May, they agreed, most unaccountably, that the only immediate question that should be put to Emin's troops was whether they would be prepared to return to Egypt. It would take several months to ascertain the wishes of soldiers stationed at posts further north. While this process went on, Stanley offered to leave Jephson and three Sudanese soldiers to represent him, while he retraced his footsteps through the Ituri Forest to find out why the Rear Column had not yet appeared. Recently he had become seriously worried about them. Emin predicted that only his 150 Egyptians would wish to go home. But he and the bulk of his men would stay on in Africa: not in Equatoria, which he agreed was untenable, but somewhere on the Aruwimi, or near Lake Victoria. Stanley knew that resettlement could only succeed if Emin persuaded enough of his men to come with him to the north-eastern corner of that lake to provide – as Stanley told Mackinnon – a disciplined body of men 'by which your territory could be governed & civilized'.[65] Emin was as excited as before, and stayed chatting with Stanley by candlelight until late. Back on his steamship, anchored on the dark lake, he wrote in his diary: 'I think this was perhaps the most memorable day of my life.'[66] Three days later, as keen as ever, Emin asked Stanley to confirm whether it would be possible to recruit most of his soldiers for the new company. Stanley confirmed that it would.[67]

On 10 May, Emin remarked in his diary that the document Stanley had written to be read to his troops (which had been closely based on the Egyptian government's letter) contained two passages that would destroy any chance that the majority might choose to go to Egypt. The first was the insulting 'If you stay here, you are no longer his soldiers'; and the second, 'Your pay continues *until* you arrive in Egypt,' which made Emin suspect that Stanley's intention was 'to discharge all the people here ...'.[68] Indeed Stanley's intention was to make as many men as possible opt to remain in Africa to become employees of Mackinnon's company. He evidently believed he would have plenty of time, after they had rejected a return to Egypt, to sell to them his preferred Lake Victoria scheme. Unfortunately, he had forgotten Emin's anxieties about his men possibly deciding to detain him by force.[69] It is beyond knowing why Emin did not warn Stanley that if his African troops believed that they were going to be dragged off to Egypt, they might mutiny. It is also puzzling that Emin did not tell Stanley that his arrival with such an enfeebled Advance Party, and a mere thirty-one cases of ammunition, had damaged him (Emin) in the eyes of his men, who had expected the greatest explorer in the world to come with enough stores and men to sustain them indefinitely in Equatoria. So when Stanley left for Fort Bodo on 16 June, at the start of his search for Barttelot's column, he was not worried about Emin's safety in his absence. His return journey through the Ituri Forest demanded all his energies.

Travelling with his valet, William Hoffman, 113 Wangwana and 95 local Madi tribesmen, Stanley set a scorching pace. On 17 August, he and Hoffman – paddling on the Aruwimi in a canoe – rounded a bend in the river not far from a village called Banalya and spotted a white man on a landing stage. 'In great excitement,' wrote Hoffman, 'Stanley and I leaped into the water, as soon as it was shallow enough.'[70] Splashing to the bank, they saw that the man was neither Barttelot nor Jameson, but Sergeant Bonny, the medical assistant. What Bonny told them, during the next half-hour, constituted, said Stanley, 'one of the most harrowing chapters of disastrous and fatal incidents that I ever heard attending the movements of an expedition in Africa'.[71] And he was not exaggerating.

TWENTY-FIVE

'Evil Hangs over this Forest...'

Stanley was stupefied to learn from Bonny that out of 271 men left behind with Major Barttelot and his officers in June 1887, only 132 marched from the camp when the Rear Column had finally left just over a year later. They had been heading for Banalya, their present location, ninety-five miles east of Yambuya – their intention being to stay only a short time before continuing their journey to Lake Albert. Accompanying the 132 surviving members of the original Yambuya garrison had been 431 Manyema carriers, who had at last been provided by Tippu Tip, after ten months of desperate pleading by Barttelot.[1] When Stanley arrived at Banalya, the Rear Column had been there a month, but already another forty men had died or were missing, and three-quarters of the Manyema carriers had deserted.[2] Given Stanley's love for the Wangwana, he was outraged to learn from Bonny that seventy-nine of them, and twenty-two Sudanese, had died, and that a further thirty-eight sick men had been left at Yambuya, or abandoned on the road, and could therefore be presumed dead too.[3]

In four weeks, Banalya had become, in Stanley's words, 'a charnel house'. The people there were mostly 'disfigured, bloated, marred and scarred ... Six dead bodies were lying unburied', while living Wangwana were broken men, 'worn to thin skin and staring bone from dysentery and anaemia, with ulcers as large as saucers'.[4] So what could have happened? The answers became painfully clear to him during his interrogation of Bonny, which began on the riverside landing stage.

'Well, Bonny, how are you? Where is the Major? Sick, I suppose?'
'The Major is dead, sir.'
'Dead? Good God! How dead? Fever?'

'No, sir, he was shot.'
'By whom?'
'By the Manyema – Tippu-Tip's people.'

Barttelot had been shot dead a month ago by one of the Manyema carriers eventually sent by Tippu. The shooting had occurred just after
the major had threatened a woman with a revolver. She had irritated
him by beating a drum soon after dawn. Days earlier, Major Barttelot
had flogged a number of Manyema and was extremely unpopular
with them. His killer, Sanga, had thought the major might shoot his
wife, since she had been the one drumming. He was apprehended at
Stanley Falls by Tippu Tip, and was executed after a brief trial conducted by the Belgian resident.[5]

And were the other officers dead too? To Stanley's relief, Troup had
been invalided home, Ward was at Bangala, 600 miles away, and
Jameson had gone to Stanley Falls seeking carriers to replace the mutinous Manyema, most of whom had deserted. Unknown to Bonny,
more recently Jameson had canoed downstream to Bangala, and had
died from fever on the very day Stanley arrived at Banalya. Earlier, at
the Falls, Jameson had tried and failed to get Tippu Tip to agree to
accompany him through the Ituri Forest to find Stanley, offering the
Arab (as only a very rich man could) the colossal fee of £20,000,
which Tippu had not accepted, fearing that any further involvement
with the disaster-prone Rear Column would ruin his relations with the
British at Zanzibar and with Europeans in general.[6]

For now, Stanley's only inside information about events at Yambuya
had to come from the surviving Wangwana and from Bonny.[7] Two
months ago, Stanley had sensed something sinister about the whole
Ituri Forest – a territory where there is slaughter and misery even to
this day. 'Evil hangs over this forest as a pall over the dead ... it is a
region accursed for crimes; whoever enters within its circle becomes
subject to Divine wrath.'[8] And 'crimes' were exactly what he was soon
recording in his diary at Bonny's dictation.

The major caused John Henry, a mission boy, to be flogged 300 lashes. He died
that night. Ward caused a mutineer to be flogged at Bolobo so severely that he also
died within a few hours ... The major kicked his little boy Sudi – a boy of 13 years
old in the shin. I found the boy with an ulcer 2½ by 3½ inches unable to move.
The major caused a Sudanese to be shot by a platoon of his comrades for stealing
a piece of meat. William Bonny relates that the least thing caused the major to
behave like a fiend. He had a steel-pointed cypress walking staff with which he
dealt severe wounds. One man, a Manyema, he stabbed 17 times with the steel

point of his stick ... The major would walk up and down the camp with his large white teeth set firm & exposed ... At such times he would dash at people right & left – as though he were running amuck.[9]

Stanley nursed the boy, Sudi, in his own tent until he died six weeks later.[10] Stanley was unsure whether he could rely on what Bonny told him. After all, this hospital sergeant had flogged two Sudanese soldiers so severely that Stanley noted: 'Never in my life have I seen anything so awful ... two deep hollows [in the buttocks] in which maggots swarmed and a saucer might easily have been put into either hollow.'[11] Bonny's excuse was that he had caught them stealing stores in the chaos that had followed the major's murder. But Henry was not appeased.[12] He warned Bonny that even if these men survived, he might still be charged with murder for not objecting to the execution of the Sudanese who had only stolen some meat.[13]

To take the heat off himself, Bonny told Stanley of a horrifying incident involving the whisky heir, James Jameson. On his way to Kassongo to meet Tippu Tip, Jameson had purchased an eleven-year-old girl and had then given her to cannibals, so he could watch her being stabbed to death, dismembered, cooked and eaten. Bonny said he had seen Jameson's sketches of the whole ghastly process. But Henry remained outwardly sceptical, although informed that Assad Farran, a Swahili-speaking interpreter whom Barttelot had sent home, had seen the murder and had made a statement. Stanley still meant to reserve judgement until he had questioned Jameson, Troup and Ward.[14] Later, Troup confirmed that the major had 'had an intense hatred of anything in the shape of a black man', and that by early May he had been insane.[15] But given the gravity of the allegation and the need to confirm whether the other crimes cited by Bonny had actually taken place, Stanley opened Jameson's box.[16] The whisky heir's journal corroborated everything Bonny had said about Barttelot's and Jameson's behaviour, including the cannibal incident.[17]

In the case of the mission-educated translator, John Henry, who stole Barttelot's revolver and was sentenced to death – though this was a first offence, and he was starving – Stanley learned that Troup had fiercely objected to shooting him. Yet when Barttelot had decreed the far more brutal punishment of 300 lashes, no officer intervened.[18] Men were invariably maimed for life by half as many strokes with the *chicotte* – a whip of twisted hippopotamus hide that drew blood at the first stroke. After fifty blows most men were insensible. It appalled Stanley that one

Sudanese soldier, Burgari Mohammed, who had received a shocking 150 lashes for stealing meat from Ward's house, had then been kept in chains day and night for two months. Somehow, he had escaped from the guard-house, taking his jailor's rifle, knowing he would die in chains unless he got away. But he was recaptured and shot for desertion.[19] Scarcely able to stand after his long period in chains, the man had been forced to dig his own grave. How could the other officers have allowed such a thing to happen, demanded Stanley? Why had they let Barttelot 'kick, strike, & slay human beings whom they were bound to protect'?[20] Because they feared being shot too, replied Bonny, who claimed that Troup had been so scared of the major that he had hidden in his house for several months after an argument.[21]

But, in Stanley's eyes, his officers' greatest crime was their indifference to the daily suffering of all Yambuya camp's 260 Africans – Wangwana, Sudanese and Somalis. Though they had died by twos and threes for months on end, it had not occurred to anyone, as Stanley put it, 'that the simple reason [why their men were dying] was that the major never gave them time to prepare their food properly. He kept them from morning to sunset at work & never paid the least attention to their wants. To satisfy their raging hunger they ate the raw poisonous stuff ...'[22] Before leaving Yambuya in June 1887, he and Parke had explained to the officers and to the Wangwana that the highly nutritive manioc tubers growing close to the camp had to be peeled and softened in water before being dried in the sun for several days. Otherwise the natural cyanide in the tubers would not be eliminated. 'Why should they have permitted themselves to be so blind?' demanded Henry.[23]

Even at this early stage, despite his fury, Stanley had resolved to keep the officers' worst crimes secret if he could. But he felt sick at heart to know that unless he told the truth he would have to treat Barttelot's death sympathetically. Yet it was crystal clear to him that if Barttelot and Jameson were ever exposed for what they had done he would be accused of having left two madmen in charge of the Rear Column. In a letter to Mackinnon, dated 3 September and marked 'Strictly Private', he wrote of the Rear Column's officers being 'utterly incompetent'. The closest he came to outright condemnation was to admit to having heard 'terrible stories of both Jameson and Barttelot'. Yet he added the qualification that: 'It is not right to lay too great stress on them inasmuch as we cannot hear their stories.'[24]

However, unknown to him, James Rose Troup and the interpreter, Assad Farran, who had left Yambuya by steamer on 3 June had already started to talk. Troup accused Barttelot in the British press of 'gross neglect and undue punishments', as well as incompetence. Farran's terrible accusation against Jameson also appeared in print for the first time.[25] The members of the EPRE's committee acted swiftly to snuff out what they called 'unsubstantiated allegations'. Troup was reminded that he had signed a contract that restrained him from publishing anything about the expedition until after the publication of the committee's official report and a book by Mr Stanley. They also scared Assad Farran into retracting.[26]

In one delicate matter Bonny protected Stanley from the truth. All the officers at Yambuya had kidnapped, or bought, Manyema women for sex. The last undated pencil note that Jameson wrote to Bonny included the sentence: 'Two of Major B's slave women have been recaptured.'[27] On 7 March, Ward had 'bought a woman for a pair of long boots ... Troup purchased a slave woman from the Arabs for six pieces of handkerchief [cloth].' Two days later Bonny wrote: 'Our cannibal concubines are quite at home.' Wishful thinking, since on 11 March 'three cannibal concubines broke away from the camp.' Troup caught his and trussed her up to prevent a second escape. Bonny reflected that 'when you kiss your cannibal, she may have blood on her lips'. The cannibalism of surrounding tribes enabled these Victorian officers to feel less guilty about their sexual behaviour.[28] Today, as then, men away from home for long periods often use prostitutes, or find local women to satisfy their needs. Yet when Bonny describes Troup's very young woman 'crying and saying she wants her mama & papa', the callousness of these 'gentlemen' of the Rear Column with their sex slaves becomes starkly apparent.[29]

Ignorant of his officers' cruel debauchery, it saddened Stanley to realize that if people at home knew the truth about Barttelot's brutality and Jameson's crime, they would automatically assume that they had been

originally wicked ... They will not reflect that circumstances changed them ... At home these men had no cause to show their natural savagery ... They were suddenly transplanted to Africa & its miseries. They were deprived of butcher's meat & bread & wine, books, newspapers, the society & influence of their friends. Fever seized them, wrecked minds and bodies. Good nature was banished by anxiety. Pleasantness was eliminated by toil. Cheerfulness yielded to internal anguish ... until they became but shadows, morally & physically of what they had been in

English society ... Home people if they desire to judge fairly must think of all this.[30]

It was a sign of Henry Stanley's innocence that he was so shocked to come across, in Jameson's box, a skilfully drawn caricature burlesquing his African costume of knickerbockers, Norfolk jacket and self-designed hat.[31] While at Banalya, he was also agonizing over a letter written by Stairs to Major Barttelot, in which the capable young lieutenant delivered a blistering attack on his leader (Stanley). Wadi Mabruki, the Wangwana chosen by Stairs as his messenger, had been drowned at a falls on the Aruwimi, and the letter to Barttelot, which had been secreted in a cartridge pouch, had fallen into Stanley's hands. As the explorer pulled out the packet, he saw in Stairs's hand the words 'a former pump of Stanley's'. At first he had thought 'pump' might be 'pimp', but Stairs was referring to the way in which Stanley's tent boys tried to win his favour by 'pumping' people for confidential information that their master might find useful.

Writing in June, Stairs described the Wangwana, Mbaraku, as 'a former pump of Stanley's ... a better specimen of a bum-sucker never existed in this or any other country. The present collectors of information are two: Sali his boy & Faruz Bill Alli [sic] one of Jameson's former chiefs ... Every word [spoken by Jameson] goes to Stanley, magnified 100 fold'. He accused Stanley of meanness and cheating his officers out of their proper share of food, and claimed, justifiably, that William Hoffman was a thief, and divided food unequally. 'You may think I am running down people a good deal, not a bit; the New Bond Street gang [Stanley's London address] are a bad lot.' Stanley scrawled on the lower margin: 'The above letter is singularly untruthful in all particulars relating to me and the language is so shocking that I never could have believed any English officer capable of expressing himself in such a vocabulary.'

Stanley feared that Stairs's view of him might well be shared by Parke and Nelson. But he was wrong to think of them as a united group, since Stairs despised Nelson as a self-pitying grumbler, and thought Parke a ditherer.[32] For months the memory of this letter upset Henry. Given his precarious health, Stanley needed to make sure he had a supply of goat's milk, and felt justified in holding back some Indian corn. So he was deeply hurt to be accused of meanness with food. Stairs, who had reminded him of his younger self, complete with his 'hot and variable temper' and his talent for pioneering, had betrayed him – just as Harry Johnston had done. 'I don't like to confess it to my private page how emotional I felt ... it is so rare, so very rare to find an assistant upon whom one can depend.'[33]

Stanley would never know what a far kinder and better man he was than young Stairs. Unknown to him, soon after he had left Fort Bodo, Stairs and Dr Parke had adopted some horribly cruel measures to stop local pygmies raiding their vegetable gardens – shooting to kill 'thieves', and when catching a woman and her three children in the fort's gardens, cutting off part of their ears as a warning to others to keep out. Both men believed they would not survive until Stanley's return unless they could protect their food, and were quite prepared to shoot women. One was wounded in the leg at first. But rather than accept responsibility and attempt to cure her, Parke ordered that she be shot through the head. By contrast with such utterly ruthless behaviour, Stanley, before leaving Fort Bodo for Yambuya, had asked Parke to treat local people if they fell ill.

After his leader's departure, Parke never attended a single person outside the perimeter fence. Such people, in his eyes, were all potential thieves. He suspected that it would never be safe to release a local woman, whom Stairs had captured for sex. She might betray to her tribe the fact that the camp was thinly defended, so Parke implied that she would have to be killed. In late August, twelve local tribesmen were shot dead among Fort Bodo's tobacco plants. 'The heads of the slain,' wrote Parke, 'we cut off and placed on the paths traversed by the Washenzie.' Surrounding tribes decapitated those killed in battle and displayed their heads as a warning, and this was why Parke and Stairs felt no qualms. Parke reported cheerfully on 19 December – the day before Stanley's return from Yambuya – that there was more food available in the fort 'since the Monbutti [pygmies] have discovered they may never leave'.[34] Stanley was not morally spotless, but he never behaved with the casual brutality displayed by Parke and Stairs, who killed helpless people in cold blood, and mutilated women and children whom they had trapped.

Bonny noted in his diary that Stanley thought Jephson 'the most honourable gentleman of the lot'.[35] And remembering the anger and shock Jephson had felt when his men had needlessly shot two Congolese, one can only applaud Stanley's judgement. Apart from Jephson, only Troup had no obvious stain on his reputation. Indicating how different Stanley was from the young men he commanded, he had decided, before leaving for Yambuya, not to take with him his little terrier Randy (named after Randolph Churchill) in case the thousand-mile journey through the Ituri Forest proved too much for him. But from the moment Stanley left Fort Bodo, Stairs could do nothing with the dog and he died four days later.

I feel certain he died of a broken heart, wrote Stairs. He ate nothing yesterday, and in the evening came up and put his head in my lap several times. At midnight he gave three or four howls, and then turned over and kicked his last. He had been to the Nyanza twice. Stanley will be in an awful way about it and will think I either starved him or beat him to death.[36]

Fred Puleston, a later African traveller, would claim decades later that Roger Casement – then working for Sanford's ivory company – had told him that Stanley, while in the Ituri Forest, had cut off Randy's tail to enrich a thin stew. The story went that when nobody ate the tail itself, Stanley gave it to Randy, who chomped it up greedily. Since Casement had been 1,500 miles away at the time, the story can only have been an invention.[37]

Since smallpox had broken out among the Manyema, Stanley did not stay long in Banalya but three days after his arrival moved the surviving Wangwana, and the Madi carriers who had been engaged in Equatoria, to an island in the Aruwimi fourteen miles upstream. Meanwhile, the 170 Manyema (a figure including their dependents) were ordered to camp on the riverbank opposite. With his usual energy, Henry regrouped the Rear Column, which now numbered 465 people. After ten days' rest and medical care, 283 men were fit to carry loads. Henry had given his word to Emin Pasha that he would be back at Fort Bodo by 22 December and he did not intend to be late.[38] He liked to quote a couplet from Tennyson's 'Ode on the Death of the Duke of Wellington':

Not once or twice in our fair island-story,
The path of duty was the way to glory.[39]

Doing what he had undertaken to do, he saw as his duty; and he would never shirk it. He sensed a difference here between his officers and himself. 'I make my work my fellow. They have lived in society all their lives ... I have been alone 30 out of my 46 years.'[40] Exceptional men are often intolerant of those without their drive, discipline and gift for leadership. For this reason he blamed the officers of the Rear Column for not leaving Yambuya, regardless of whether they had received any carriers or not. Stanley knew that if he had travelled to Stanley Falls and had been promised porters by Tippu Tip for a certain date, and if the Arab had then failed to deliver them, he (Stanley) would not have returned to the Falls even once more to beg for help – let alone six times, like Barttelot and his officers. Stanley wrote: 'I feel that none of these young men ever left the presence of Tippu Tip without feeling a sense of shame at their impotence & a burning indignation at the cause of it.' It amazed him that, after Tippu had first failed to fulfil a promise to them, they had gone on thinking that he meant to bring the porters in a month or two. Clearly, he had broken his word because he had no early plans to assist them.

Stanley was shocked that all their trips to the Falls had involved marching 1,200 miles, a distance greater than that to Lake Albert. If Stanley's men had ever been dying at the same rate, and *he* had had no means of hiring carriers to replace them, he knew he would have marched at once with the men he had. He wrote after reading Jameson's diary: 'When the major decided to remain until Tippu Tip could furnish him with 600 carriers – he embarked on a perilous course for which his inexperience was no guide – for which ... his inherited tastes, his education & his military habits & proclivities entirely unfitted him ... Enduring deadly monotony ... [while] buried in darkest obscurity' could only have been unendurable as 'the graves increased in number ... The cure of their misgivings & doubts would have been found in action.'[41] Thus Stanley blinded himself to the fact that the reason Barttelot had not chosen to march with 200 men was because he had been fearful to abandon more than half his stores and thus have earned his leader's censure.

On 30 August 1888 the expedition struck camp, 239 men setting out overland under Bonny's orders, and 225, under Stanley's command, travelling by water.[42] By mid-September, the foraging parties sent out to find bananas were being attacked, and an average of one a day was killed by the locals. Meanwhile, Stanley, travelling with Bonny, was having to rein him in. 'Leave the Zanzibaris and Sudanese alone,' he advised him. 'Try and reason with these men & you will get on better with them.' He pointed out to Bonny that he could never carry a load as the black people did, and, without them, 'if you took your gun into the next village you would get killed'. Bonny, who had respected no one at Yambuya, was soon writing of Stanley as 'just the man for the work he has undertaken'.

By late October they were still 160 miles from the end of the forest and food was scarcer than ever. Three Wangwana chose this time to steal his goats and slaughter them. Though this could have been a death sentence for him, Henry did not order a flogging but gave each Wangwana twenty-four strokes with a switch.[43] As November started, they had been travelling for two months and the death toll stood at over fifty from all causes: starvation, fever, ulcers, poisoned arrows and smallpox. A very dangerous situation confronted them. On 9 November, a large party of foragers failed to return after a week, and Stanley distributed a final cup of plantain flour to each man. He reckoned that all the 200 men who were with him in camp would be close to death by the end of the week. But a day later the foragers returned, bringing about four days' food.[44]

Life went on this way for a month, foragers going out, the others – many of them sick – waiting for days for food. All the while, William Hoffman was still stealing things to eat. Eventually, Henry forced him to sign a confession of his thefts after a large quantity of biscuits had been found in his box: 'Sitting there, he began to cry & said, (to Bonny), "I have had no food for 3 days."' Stanley had already had to give him a caning, but on this occasion he forgave him on a promise to reform. It would be hard to think of another valet in the world who could have lived a harder year than Hoffman, and Stanley was well aware of this.

On 8 December, Sergeant Bonny reported with grim succinctness: 'Our people are without food.'[45] The success of 300 foragers sent out on the 9th was crucial for the fate of the 130 enfeebled men and women in camp. Around him and his followers 'myriads of trees ... shut out all hope ... burying them out of sight of sky and sunshine.' While the foragers were away, the rest of the people fanned out in the woods to hunt for the red berries of the *phrynia* bush. Saburi, the boy who usually carried Stanley's Winchester, did not return. Stanley sent out men to fire signals after dark, but with no response. Saburi was one of three people who had lost their way that day, or collapsed in the woods. The next day was the sixth since the foragers had gone out. Stanley reckoned that if he allowed all the people in camp to stay in their present position for another three days, they would become too weak to search for food. It was therefore decided that Bonny would stay at the camp with about ninety incapable men and women, while Stanley and Hoffman went off for a week with a party of the fitter men to try to find food. On the day this plan was hatched, little Saburi walked into camp having been lost for forty-eight hours.[46] On leaving next day, Stanley left a note with Bonny:

We set out today with 30 to 40 people able to stagger on to get bananas ... If we meet foragers before 10 tomorrow morning, we shall return on the 3rd day but shall send relief to you right on. It may happen that something has occurred to prevent our return till the eleventh or even twelfth day. Do not begin to despair until then. I commit you and ourselves to that Providence in whose hands we are.

Your friend Henry M. Stanley.[47]

He did not admit to Bonny that he was taking a revolver with him and poison, in case he failed to find the foragers.[48] But the following day, to their great joy, they encountered the foragers, who were driving goats ahead of them, and carried plantains and bananas in their arms.[49] On 20 December 1888, Stanley reached Fort Bodo with 358 people, which was 107 fewer than he had had with him on leaving the island near Banalya. How many of the 107 had died, and how many, mainly Manyema, had joined communities of their own tribe living in the forest, it is impossible to say.

Parke was less than happy to see the state Stanley's party was in, since his leader expected him to give medical attention even to the hopeless cases. The quality of the doctor's compassion can be judged by his tone: 'I never witnessed such a disgusting sight as the unfortunate ulcerated people came dropping in. The stench from the putrid flesh and dirty scraps of bandages was sickening and filled the air round the fort.' But for Stanley, Parke had only warm praise.[50] Indeed, in crossing and re-crossing the immense Ituri Forest again, in order to rescue what was left of the Rear Column, he had risked his own life, and in his determination to save the lives of others had gone beyond what most expedition leaders would have thought necessary, or even possible.

TWENTY-SIX

Keeping Emin Pasha's Secret

Three weeks after his return to Fort Bodo, Stanley was desperately worried about the failure of Jephson and Emin Pasha to communicate with him, either in person or by letter. The arrangement had been that 'in about two months', after finding out what the Pasha's men wanted, they would come to Fort Bodo.[1] However, a few days later, when Henry was starting to imagine that a disaster had befallen them, a messenger arrived at his camp near the lake, bearing three letters from Emin Pasha and two from Jephson all written several months previously. But his relief did not last long. 'As I read them,' confessed Henry, 'a creeping feeling came over me which was a complete mental paralysis for the time.'[2]

Writing on 7 November from Dufile – a station on the Nile 140 miles north of Lake Albert – Jephson explained that a rebellion had broken out there in mid-August and that he and Emin had been taken prisoner by the Pasha's rebel soldiers, who believed that Stanley was 'only an adventurer, and had not come from Egypt'. The rebels also suspected, wrote Jephson, 'that the letters you [Stanley] had brought from the Khedive ... were forgeries ... and that the Pasha and you had made a plot to take them out of the country, and hand them over to be slaves to the English'. Worse still, Jephson informed Henry that Emin had been deposed and his most trusted officers replaced by rebels. 'Plans were also made to entrap you when you returned and strip you of all you had.' Jephson feared that he and the Pasha were unlikely to escape unscathed. Already, loaded rifles had been pointed at their heads. But in two subsequent letters, Jephson reported that the rebels had fallen out over how to respond to the Mahdists' most recent attack, and that in the confusion, he and Emin had been allowed to steam downriver as far as Tunguru on the lake. Jephson's last letter ended: 'I will not disguise the fact ... that you will have a difficult and dangerous task before you in dealing with the Pasha's people.'³

It shattered Stanley that Emin had deliberately concealed from him how precarious his hold over his men had become. Thanks to this incomprehensible reticence, ten months had been wasted and the Pasha's authority had been fatally damaged. Jephson confirmed in his report for Stanley, written on 7 February, that Emin's position with his men had been desperate all along and that he had simply lied. 'Thus we were led to place our trust in people who were utterly unworthy of our confidence and help.'⁴ At a stroke, Stanley's high hopes of settling Emin and a large number of his men north-east of Lake Victoria had ended, as had his hopes of bringing the Pasha to Egypt or England. Now, the relief expedition seemed doomed to end in farcical anti-climax.

Emin Pasha believed, wrote Jephson, that if his men came with Stanley *en masse* and found a place to settle in, they would do so in order to plunder the great explorer on the way, 'taking all his arms and ammunition'.⁵ Of course Stanley now dreaded being overpowered by mutinous soldiers. Any thought of creating a settlement near Lake Victoria was dead and buried, and even Emin accepted this.⁶ With the Mahdists pressing south and the Pasha's men likely to make a deal with them, Stanley felt that Emin now had no choice but to come with him to the coast. What security could he ever know as a solitary wanderer in the interior?

Emin, Jephson, a handful of loyal officers and seven or eight soldiers arrived at Tunguru on Lake Albert in late December, leaving behind a confused situation further north, with some men still loyal to him but the majority not. On 17 January 1889, Stanley wrote to Emin urgently requesting 'a definite answer to the question: if you propose to accept our escort and assistance to reach Zanzibar ... [and] whether there are any officers or men disposed to accept our safe conduct to the sea'.⁷ In a postscript to Jephson, Stanley warned, 'this time there must be no hesitation but positive yea or nay, and home we go'.⁸

Though Stanley could not sympathize with Emin for failing (even after the Mahdist advance) to perform the simple task of getting a thousand men to understand the obvious fact that they would die if they stayed in Equatoria, it is hard not to feel a little sorry for the Pasha. He had survived in the past by confining his operations to his southern stations on Lake Albert, and by making very few demands on anyone. His undoing had been Stanley's request that he recommend a definite plan of action to his men in the north. Now with the Lake Victoria settlement off the agenda, Emin was depressed to realize that *he* had become Stanley's only trophy. 'For him,' wrote the Pasha, 'everything depends on whether he is able to take me along, for only then, when people could actually see me, would his expedition be regarded as totally successful.'[9] Emin himself had no idea what he wanted. One day he said, 'I consider I am absolutely free to think only of my personal safety and welfare'; but the next he declared, 'I know I am not in any way responsible for these people, but I cannot bear to go out myself first and leave anyone behind me.'[10] With the Mahdists pressing southwards, Stanley knew that many of Emin's former fol-

Carrying the possessions of Emin Pasha and his officers up from
Lake Albert to the plateau

lowers would be tempted 'to curry favour with the Khalif of Khartoum by betraying their would-be rescuers and their former Pasha and his white companions into his hands'.[11]

So when Jephson wrote of these Egyptians and Sudanese soldiers as 'depraved villains', and 'brutishly stupid', it enraged Stanley to find Emin still delaying a decision and thus endangering the lives of his own best people, and the expedition's, for the sake of such disloyalty. But at last on 13 February, Emin wrote saying he was coming very soon to Stanley's camp with twelve officers and forty soldiers, who wanted 'some time to bring their brothers' from Wadelai.[12] Since he arrived with 200 large loads as his personal luggage, his friend Casati with eighty loads, Vita, his apothecary, forty, and Marco, the Greek trader, sixty – a total requiring 380 carriers for only four people – Stanley did not like to think what would happen if most of the officers eventually came south from Wadelai. How could he possibly engage enough porters? Emin's old 'Saratoga trunk' on its own required two carriers. 'I tried to lift one end of it ... I should say it contains stones ... What a story that old trunk could tell since it left Cairo. How many poor natives has it killed?' If a hundred officers and scores of dependents came too, Henry wondered how he would ever feed them all without robbing local Africans.[13]

A month later, Emin Pasha asked Stairs and Jephson to help his lieutenant, Shukri Agha, to collect 'slaves' (the Egyptian term was *abid*) for his people – his intention being to force local Africans, at gunpoint, to act as additional carriers and servants. Jephson described these forced labour forays as 'cruel hunts' and complained to Stanley, who told him and Stairs that they need not help the Pasha.[14] When twenty-eight more captives were brought in by Emin's men, a disgusted Stanley ordered their immediate release. 'I am sick of the necessities of these people. I really think they had better die rather than we should unnecessarily inflict misery & commit injustice.' He thought that Emin 'like many scientists was indifferent to the warmer human feelings'.[15]

By late March 1889, Stanley had already been waiting two and a half months for Emin's people to assemble at his camp at Kavalli's, on a plateau above Lake Albert. But when, on 26 March, Emin received a letter from his deputy, Selim Bey, informing him that he would be bringing south from Wadelai a further ten officers and 600 men, Stanley was far from pleased. Not only had many of these officers been rebels, but Selim Bey claimed he could not arrive with them before 10

April – the deadline for departure that Stanley had agreed with Emin and Shukri Agha. Stanley's worries about the loyalty of Selim's men therefore made him still more determined to leave on the 10th.[16] By now Emin Pasha had more than 500 people in Stanley's camp, only 126 of whom were officers or soldiers. Most were petty clerks and officials and their women and children, many of whom were probably going to die on their way to the coast. Add to these people 230 members of the expedition, 130 Manyema carriers and several hundred locally recruited porters, and Stanley's party already numbered almost a thousand souls – a nightmarish number to have to feed. Many were likely to find places to settle en route, but Stanley's responsibility for the safety of the rest weighed heavily on him.

It would have been a great comfort if Emin had even once expressed a firm desire to travel with him, but it was obvious that the Pasha had been overwhelmed by events, and had given up trying to form plans of his own. Yet this passivity was far from supportive. Then on 5 April, Henry's faith in him collapsed completely, when Emin's boy, Serour, told him that the Pasha's entire household, with the exception of two servants, was about to desert, along with all his soldiers. Because during the preceding night a rifle had been stolen from a Wangwana tent, and unsuccessful attempts had been made to steal guns from others, Stanley believed that Emin really was about to be deserted by everyone. To stop this happening, Henry decided he must prove at once to Emin's Egyptians, Sudanese and Africans that he could not be disobeyed.

Acting on instinct, Henry strode across the camp to Emin Pasha's tent and told him that a rebellion would break out unless he mustered all his men and got them to declare in public which of them intended to leave with the expedition. When Emin prevaricated, Henry gave him the alternative of going to a camp two miles away to avoid being kidnapped. The Pasha declined both options, so the explorer insisted he choose one. 'I am resolved, Pasha, I am resolved,' he cried, his patience at an end. When Emin reluctantly ordered his men to leave their tents, they ignored him. So Stanley told Jephson to take thirty Wangwana to force them out. Inevitably, this was done at gunpoint, causing much offence to Emin. But Stanley swept aside his objections, compelling his men to indicate whether they intended to come on the 10th. Not one man said he meant to stay.[17] Once they had assembled in the open, it was apparent that the health of many was precarious.

One Egyptian soldier had been deserted by his wife and was caring for their half-starved baby. Others were in equally desperate plights. But unless they embarked on the dangerous journey being urged on them, they would be massacred by local Africans as soon as their ammunition ran out.[18]

The caravan that eventually left Kavalli's on 10 April 1889 consisted of 1,330 people. Stanley reckoned that 230 of these (mainly Wangwana) were members of his original expedition, 130 were all that remained of Tippu Tip's 431 Manyema carriers handed over to Major Barttelot, 400 were locally recruited carriers, and 570 were Emin's people – about 400 of these being women and children.[19] The extended column stretched for three miles and was 'very gay with flags & the coloured clothes of Zanzibaris & Egyptian women'. Soon Jephson was reporting less picturesque scenes. Two weeks into the journey, one of the Nubians, who was a servant to one of Emin's officers, shot a local African who had been forced to work for the Egyptians. The man's bleeding body was left tied to two other terrified servants. The Nubian was said to have misunderstood an order from his officer and so escaped being hanged, but the ill-treatment of their slaves by the Pasha's people horrified Stanley and Jephson.

When we were by ourselves [wrote Jephson] no such scenes were ever seen in our camp, such few natives as the Zanzibaris caught were kindly treated & looked after ... this was in the camp of Stanley who has been called a pirate & freebooter ... But now that Emin Pasha, who has been represented as one of the champions of Anti-Slavery, has come into our camp, scenes of the most disgraceful cruelty, constant beatings, constant shrieking of women and constant desertions are of daily occurrence.

The expedition had so far cost about 400 lives – a heavy price to pay for saving 'some 50 Egyptian employees, with their wives, concubines, families & slaves, the dregs of Cairo & Alexandria'.[20]

Three days into the journey, Stanley became dangerously ill. There was no question of his travelling, so the expedition was now halted for a month. At the same time Parke and Jephson were prostrated by haematuric fever. It was fortunate that Stairs remained in good health, since on 27 April Emin Pasha confided to him that he had uncovered a plot, involving virtually all his soldiers and carriers, to desert *en masse*. This strongly suggested that the threat Stanley had acted against on 5 April had been entirely real. Stairs and a party of Wangwana disarmed the ringleaders, and Shukri Agha placed them under arrest. Desertions had been going on for days, and next day Emin decided to end the humiliating disloyalty once and for all by trying deserters in future before a mixed court of his officers and Stanley's. On 5 May, Rehan, the ringleader, who had deserted a week earlier taking some men and women with him, was sentenced to be hanged after being found guilty of desertion, of stealing a gun, and of inciting others to desert. With Emin's people still melting away at a disastrous rate, Stanley dragged himself from his bed to see that the sentence was carried out. He felt no unease, and sent a record of the trial to the EPRE's committee. Five witnesses had been called, and among their depositions it was stated that Rehan had been caught with a stolen rifle in his hands. His execution would be the last – although one of Emin's men, who had killed a member of a friendly tribe, was handed over to tribal elders, who had refused to accept compensation in trade goods. No officer objected to the surrender of this murderer, though everyone knew he would be speared to death.[21]

Three days later Stanley was well enough to travel, as was Jephson, who had recently been amazed to be invited to take his meals with his leader and be treated 'like his friend'.[22] As they turned south, bound for Lake Victoria and the coast, they walked at first through 'dewy fields of Indian corn'. Just then, they caught sight of 'the pure snowy peaks [of the Ruwenzoris] seen above the clouds', and were dazed by a feeling 'of mingled wonder & awe'.[23] During the next three months the expedition recorded its most important geographical discoveries. They investigated the seventy-mile-long Ruwenzori range, which Stanley and Parke had first seen a year earlier. (They had thought themselves the first white men to have done so, though in April 1876, when camped near Lake Edward, Stanley's servant, Frank Pocock, had glimpsed a snow-covered peak that could only have been a Ruwenzori.)[24] The expedition marched south, along the western bank of the Semliki river, which Stanley was excited to observe flowed into Lake Albert at its southern end. On the day the expedition crossed the Semliki, Stanley could barely walk a hundred yards. His officers only managed to commandeer three canoes, and so the whole operation took a day and a half, at the end of which just over a thousand men, women and children, and their baggage and goats, had been taken to the eastern bank in hundreds of trips. And although the expedition was then attacked by fifty Warasura, Kabarega's mercenaries, they were driven off with ease at a cost of two of Henry's men killed.[25]

During the month Stanley devoted to exploring the Ruwenzori, he had no trouble feeding his waiting men. The people they encountered made generous gifts of food as soon as they heard that the expedition had driven away their dreaded enemy, the Warasura. The expedition would 'under ordinary circumstances have needed forty bales of cloth and twenty sacks of beads as currency to purchase food. [But] not a bead or yard of cloth was demanded from us.'[26] This friendliness was a great boon to Stanley just when he arrived at the lake that he had very nearly reached in 1876, only to be turned back by Kabarega's warriors. Safe to investigate at leisure, he now named it Lake Edward, after the Prince of Wales.[27] He also established that this lake was the source of the Semliki River, which was a more important reservoir for the Nile than had hitherto been guessed at, since it extended 200 miles to the south of Lake Albert. All the new information Stanley had just gathered about the Nile's western reservoir, and the Ruwenzori mountains that fed it, would have been justification enough for any major expedition. Yet, because it had been incidental to Stanley's main purpose of finding and relieving Emin Pasha, it would always be seen as a footnote.[28]

As Henry travelled on towards the south-western corner of Lake Victoria en route for Bagamoyo and home, he became the blood-brother of Buchunku, son of the King of Ankole – a judicious move since this monarch could muster an army of over 100,000 men. He also took the precaution of demonstrating for the very first time the Maxim gun that had been brought for Emin's defence. Stairs fired a few bursts at a hillside, causing the young man to cry out, either with delight or with terror (opinions were divided which).[29] At this time a small delegation of Bugandan Christians came to Stanley's camp and tried to persuade him to involve himself in their country's politics, which he felt unable to do in his current situation.[30] As Henry continued southwards, he reflected on how sad it was that the missionaries, who had gone to Buganda at his behest, had been obliged to ally themselves with armed factions in order to survive. Alexander Mackay, whose mission station on the southern shores of Lake Victoria was Henry's next objective on his way to the coast, had chosen to flee rather than fight, and had therefore saved the lives of his flock. Three years earlier, about fifty of them had preferred martyrdom to recantation, though knowing that King Mwanga would castrate them, and then roast them alive.[31]

While still in Ankole, Stanley had a furious argument with the Pasha about what duties his armed men should perform. Stanley felt that the Egyptians ought to take their turn at regular rear-guard duty rather than dawdle along as they pleased, but Emin felt unable to ask them. Stanley asked him angrily why he had allowed such useless people to follow him. 'I could not stop them,' he retorted, 'and I am very sorry I came myself.' This was too much for Stanley, who snapped: 'You are simply a most thankless & ungrateful man.' Henry then insisted that in future Shukri Agha alternate with Stairs and Nelson as commander of the rear-guard. 'Do as you like,' Emin told Stanley, 'and you may leave me behind if you please.' To Stanley's surprise, two days later, the Pasha approached him in his tent '& tendered an apology for using such words'.[32] Soon afterwards, they gained their first glimpse of Lake Victoria – a sight confirming that they were well on the way home.

On arrival at Usambiro, the mission on the southern shores of the lake, Stanley took an immediate liking to the bearded missionary Alexander Mackay, who dressed in white linen suits and usually sported a grey Tyrolean hat. 'He is a *little* Scotchman,' he told a friend. 'I am a Hercules by his side, but he is the nattiest, toughest little fellow you could conceive. Young too – probably 32 years of age.' Stanley was impressed by Mackay's refusal to despair after the destruction of his Bugandan mission, and 'the murdering of his Bishop, burning of his pupils, and strangling of his converts'. It was 'the sense of duty' of men like Moffat, Livingstone and Mackay that Stanley found most remarkable – Livingstone refusing to go home though old and ill, Moffat working fifty years in Africa in the same village, Mackay braving every danger for twelve years, and never a thought of leaving his flock for home.[33]

Besides being a man of God, Mackay had once been an engineer, and still taught practical skills, such as boat-building, carpentry and horticulture. More than that, Mackay made Stanley reflect on his own religious feelings – how as a young man he had lost the non-conformist certainties he had known at St Asaph, becoming, in his own words, 'arrogant, self-assertive ... and more obdurate than others'. Ambition and 'absorption in the things of the present' had prevented 'self-communion'. His gradual return to belief was due, he thought, 'to the losses of friends and companions which caused such serious effect on me that often life was almost intolerable ... Countless fevers made me sensible of the fragility of my strength ... As a consequence I fell into a mood more introspective and self-searching ... during which there crept memories of the faith of childhood.' The fact that he had seemed to be 'saved again and again' in Africa forced him 'to recognize the Divine Hand'.[34]

Yet Stanley never found private faith nearly as easy as the idea of a God-given mission of a practical and public kind. The latter had first been made real to him by Livingstone, and would sustain him in the 1890s when 'imperial mission' was taken up by the late Victorian establishment as its central idea. His enemies said that Stanley pretended to be more religious than he was. But in a moralizing age, when the boldest evil-doers feared social disgrace, and Mr Gladstone modelled his style of public speaking on the cadences of sermons, the temptation to sing from an elevated hymn sheet can easily be understood.

At Usambiro, Stanley learned that most of the letters redirected to him and his officers from Zanzibar had been stolen en route to Buganda. But two addressed to Emin had made it from the coast.[35] They plunged him into immediate gloom, for reasons Henry would only discover four months later. Mackay chose this moment to tell Henry and his officers that James Jameson had died of fever on the Congo over a year earlier. Equally depressing was the news that the Germans had moved inland from Bagamoyo, into their East African 'sphere of influence', and had behaved with such heavy-handed arrogance that they had provoked an uprising. That the land in which Stanley had 'found' Livingstone was now in German hands was painful for him.[36] So too was the news that Carl Peters, the German adventurer, had recently fought his way through Masailand, in the more northerly 'British sphere', having set his sights on snatching Buganda for the Kaiser.

More personally hurtful to Stanley than any news about German intentions was the fact that the EPRE's committee had instructed the British traveller Frederick J. Jackson to go to Wadelai to relieve Emin – the assumption being that Stanley must have failed. This made Henry all the more determined to bring Emin and his followers to the coast as rapidly as possible, and show them to the world.[37] But just as Henry's eagerness to exhibit his 'trophy' was intensifying, so too was Emin's desire to wriggle free. The Pasha seized on the arrival of Frederick Jackson to put pressure on Stanley to solicit the Briton's help in settling him and his men at Kavirondo. According to Stanley, when he rejected Emin's plea – on the reasonable grounds that he had far too few followers to make such a settlement viable – the Pasha replied ominously: 'It does not matter ... my life is always at my own disposal and I can end it when I like.'[38] At this time, in a letter to a friend, Emin admitted: 'All my hopes are shattered, and I return home half blind and broken down. I indeed hope that I shall not be judged too harshly.'[39] Another reason why Stanley could feel no pity was that if he had let Emin settle near Lake Victoria, he might have tried to join up with Peters, in order to snatch Buganda for Germany. But above all, Emin could not stay on in Africa because he had too few men for his own safety. 'Out of 10,000 people,' Henry told Mackinnon, 'he has only two servants faithful to him!!!' So, 'Nolens volens, the Pasha had to come home.'[40]

Stanley and his expedition were with the missionaries for nineteen days, and Mackay hated letting him go. 'I shall never forget the pleasure of the alas too few days which your visit afforded me.'[41] It was Mackay's great hope that Stanley would soon return to Africa to run Mackinnon's Imperial British East Africa Company, and secure Buganda for Britain with the help of a rail link from the coast.[42] Stanley tried to persuade Mackay to return home with him for a period of rest and convalescence, but he refused, just as Livingstone had done. To Stanley's grief his new friend would die of fever five months later.[43]

On 12 September, only 559 people marched with Stanley from Mackay's mission – so 60 per cent of those who had left Kavalli's in April were no longer with him. Many of these absentees had been forced to serve as porters and slaves by the Pasha's men, and it seems that Stanley had simply allowed them to return home. The journey from Lake Albert had been peaceful, food had been plentiful, and very few had died.[44] Emin's party had not looked after itself so well. It had been 570 strong at Kavalli's, but numbered 344 men, women and children on leaving Mackay's. Some of Emin's people had been tempted to march back to Equatoria to join up with Selim Bey, but about 200 others had died of sickness, many of them babies and children. Ahead of the seventy-seven surviving Egyptian children stretched 800 dusty miles to the Indian Ocean.

Only two days into their journey, Wakusuma tribesmen started to harass the caravan. According to Jephson: 'Stanley behaved with the utmost patience & forebearance & not a shot was fired. But the very next day the natives became so outrageous that it resulted in a collision.' On 20 September, the Wasukuma ordered Stanley to camp on the spot. He refused '& some men came and struck at Stanley with a spear' upon which they were shot dead by the Wangwana, who then chased after the other Africans who had pressed in on the column and shot a number of them too. The next morning, 'we soon had hundreds of natives following us on either side of the column', their aim being to 'swoop down on the rear-guard & try and get at some of our women & children, but they were always repulsed'.

When these attacks became worse, Stanley sent Nelson and Jephson to burn a village – a process Jephson hated. However, it seemed to bring a change of heart, since on 22 September some Wakusuma appeared saying they wanted peace. Stanley therefore allowed a number of them into his camp, and made no effort to disperse several hundred others who gathered around the camp. But when the 'peace-makers' suddenly killed a man, and wounded two others, the Wangwana fired back killing seventeen. Not even this retribution stopped the attacks, so on the evening of the 24th, when the Wakusuma began to mass again, Stanley authorized using the Maxim – the first time he had ever permitted it to be fired in anger. The result, surprisingly, was just one man killed, largely because the unfamiliar noise of the gun made hundreds flee.[45] Marching on through Ukusuma, Stanley was shocked by the exorbitant amounts of *hongo* demanded. Recently some missionaries had been charged £270 in fees in three days' travel through Ugogo.[46]

On the borders of Masailand, Stanley came to the endless acacia-studded plain he remembered well from his search for Livingstone, when he had been young and in perfect health. To Jephson this country of lions and hyenas was 'a terrible place, burnt up & parched ... a wilderness in which there are great tracts of quivering plains the very sight of which takes one's breath away'. But Stanley felt sentimental, sensing that he would never again see this vast landscape. Leaving Ugogo, he was depressed to be hailed 'with a perfect volley of "Guten Morgens"', on encountering a column of Nyamawezi heading west.[47] At Mpwapwa, on 10 November, Lieutenant Rochus Schmidt greeted the Pasha like a hero, and hinted (as Emin noted with satisfaction) that the German government 'would try to make use' of him 'for East Africa'.[48] Emin observed how anxious this made Stanley. 'When we are alone, he reproaches me for being in sympathy with Germany.'[49] At Mpwapwa they saw the burned-out English mission house and the

Germans' ruined fort. Many people had died in the recent rebellion against the new colonial power.

On 29 November, when the expedition was a few days from the coast, they were met by two American journalists: Edmund Viztelly of the *New York Herald*, and Thomas Stevens (a friend of May Sheldon) of the *New York World*. They were surprised to find that Stanley was 'a quiet-looking, unassuming individual' wearing patched clothes. Expecting him to be taciturn, Stevens found him 'one of the most charming talkers I ever heard', who was even candid about his failures with women.[50] In the last phase of the journey, Henry was more amiable to his officers, but he still could not let them get close to him. 'If I had lifted the lid of my reserve I should have let out that which would harass & worry me more than blackwater fever.'[51] Given the pain he had been caused by those closest to him – his mother, his uncles, and the women he had hoped to marry – his fear of intimacy was understandable. Yet, at the end of the journey he found it in his heart to forgive Stairs for his letter to Barttelot.[52] He also behaved with generosity to his thieving servant, William Hoffman – whom all his officers detested – paying him in full, and then recommending him as a servant to Mr J. Mackenzie of the Imperial British East Africa Company, for whom he would work for a year in Mombassa.[53]

At dusk on 3 December, as they approached the Kingani River, the evening gun on Zanzibar was heard, and the Wangwana 'set up ear-piercing cries of joy'. After their long and terrible journey across the continent, just over a third of the original 623 Zanzibaris were still with him and certain to reach home. At the Kingani, the expedition was met by Major Herman von Wissmann, the German Imperial Commissioner, who escorted them into Bagamoyo, where the familiar streets were decorated with palm branches.[54] The following evening Wissmann threw a banquet in honour of Stanley, Emin Pasha, and the relief expedition. Thirty-four people sat down at a long table in an upper room of the mess-house of the German officers. They included the two guests of honour, as well as Captain Casati, all Stanley's officers, the British vice-consul from Zanzibar, the German consul, the Italian consul, numerous German naval and military officers, and the officers from two British ships. A German ship's band played while a surprisingly varied menu was served, along with some choice wines. Although this was gratifying to Emin, he faced an uncertain future. Further employment with the Khedive was out of the question, so would he be wise, he wondered, to accept employment from his own nationals, or should he wait in case Mackinnon's offer was renewed? And if nothing turned up from his fellow-countrymen, or from Mackinnon, what would happen to him and his six-year-old daughter, Ferida?

As the dinner was ending, Sali, Stanley's head-boy, whispered in his ear that 'the Pasha had fallen down'. At first Henry assumed that Emin had 'stumbled over a chair', until Sali shrieked in Swahili: 'He has fallen over the verandah wall into the street.' When Emin was spirited away to the German hospital, Stanley realized that this strange accident had ended his already remote hopes of taking the Pasha to Egypt or Europe. This fall had not been stage-managed by Emin and the Germans. Stanley saw him in hospital with 'his right eye closed by a great lump formed by swollen tissues'. Most people formed the view that a drunken Emin had gone to watch the Wangwana celebrating in the street, and being so short-sighted had tripped over the balcony wall.[55]

However, in Cairo, Stanley would be told some facts by Georg Schweinfurth, the German explorer, that made attempted suicide seem a possibility. According to Schweinfurth, who knew Emin well, the reason why the Pasha had been determined never to leave Africa had been his fear that in Europe his former mistress, Madame Hakki, would ruin him in a highly-publicized court action. When abandoning the hapless widow in Germany in 1875 (having made out that he was her husband), he had stolen her money and jewels. She had then obtained a judgment from a German court for 10,000 marks in alimony, but could not collect anything from a man hidden away in Africa. The best that Madame Hakki had been able to do was publish a pamphlet in Constantinople naming and shaming Emin.[56] But when she heard that he had been found and would shortly arrive at the East African coast, she had sent letters to him via Zanzibar, demanding justice. Stanley deduced that 'he had received one at Mackay's Mission, which caused that fit of depression wherein he hinted at suicide; a second was handed to him in the mail he opened at Bagamoyo – which contained also the printed story of his desertion of her. To a man who magnified small faults as crimes for which there was no forgiveness, Madame Hakki's terrible denunciations & threats would sound like a sentence of perpetual exile.'[57] At Bagamoyo, Jephson was struck by Emin's 'inexpressible sadness', and pointed it out to Parke.[58]

Believing that Schweinfurth had told the truth, Stanley was placed

in an awkward position. He could, had he wished, have demolished
the idea that Emin was refusing to return to Europe because he had
come to hate his deliverer, but he realized that to give away Emin's
secret 'would be to denounce ourselves as fools'.[59] To have spent so
much money, and to have suffered so many deaths, in order to save a
man who could treat a woman so dishonourably would have been
thought grotesque if known about. Stanley also kept quiet about his
suspicion that Emin might have tried to commit suicide, and he was
wise to do so. With the Pasha's daughter, Ferida, totally dependent on

RESCUED!

'Rescued': a Punch cartoonist jokes about who rescued whom, and discerns the
reluctance of Emin to return but not the reason why

379

him, it seems most unlikely that he would have contemplated ending his life at this particular moment. He had not received any pay since 1883 and was therefore owed at least £5,000 by the Egyptian government. In fact, while in hospital at Bagamoyo, he gave Gaetano Casati 'a general power of attorney', so that his friend could settle his (Emin's) claims against the Khedive's government without him having to visit Egypt in person. When the money was paid, most was placed in a trust for Ferida, but a smaller payment was made to Madame Hakki.[60] The Pasha's private life had certainly given him an exceptionally good reason for wishing to remain in Africa.

Before Emin Pasha left hospital at the end of January, he told Wissmann that he wished to work for Germany.[61] Later Emin disingenuously told Stairs: 'the reason I went over to the Germans was simply because I could not get work with the IBEAC [Mackinnon's company] & could not afford to wait'.[62] Although Stanley knew that his expedition would look ridiculous if the Pasha signed up with Wissmann, this never tempted him to press Mackinnon to make the Pasha a new offer of employment. In fact, out of his genuine concern for Mackinnon's best interests, he did his very best to discourage this, telling him categorically that Emin was unfit to run any large or small enterprise.[63] In March Bismarck approved Emin's 'engagement for foreign service', and in April the Pasha set off from Bagamoyo at the head of a large German expedition. But his hopes of claiming Buganda for Germany were to be dashed by the Anglo-German Agreement of July 1890, by which Buganda was placed inalienably within the British sphere. In less than a year, Emin fell out with his German employers and vanished into the interior on a mysterious mission of his own. In 1892, a hundred miles from the Congo, he was beheaded by Arabs in alliance with a warlord called Kibongo. The Pasha's sixty Sudanese followers were all shot.[64] Stanley's comment was: 'So long as he was in the British camp, he was safe. The very day he was kissed by his countrymen he was doomed.'[65]

Emin had represented himself in his letters to his friends as a man fighting against impossible odds, and had never admitted that his real adversaries were rebels within his own soldiery rather than the Mahdist forces that had swept away Gordon. When, later, Stanley was compared adversely with the 'gentle' Emin, he did not point out that Emin had killed a great many people with his shelling of Kibiro in

Some Characters

1. Chowpereh.   engaged in four of my expeditions 1871-84
2. Zaidi   Saved from the Cataract
3. Sarmini   The Detective of the camp.
4. Wadi Rehani. The Treasurer
5. Manwa Sera. The Headman
6.   A headman
10 Majwara.   He attended Livingstone at his death.
7   Kirango.   First struck at Bumbireh.
8   The guide
9. Wadi Baraka. The humourist at Bumbireh.

23 Some of Stanley's principal Wangwana carriers and their headmen on his great trans-Africa journey. He would write that without twenty of the best of them he could have achieved little

24

25/6

24 Stanley in Paris in August 1884 with friends of Edward King. His own close friend
May Sheldon is in a striped dress bottom right
25 Stanley with Uledi and Manwa Sera in 1877 after their trans-Africa journey
26 Stanley in Paris with old friend and colleague, Anthony Swinburne, late January 1887,
en route to Africa

27a/b

27c/d

27e/f

27 Stanley's Emin Pasha Relief Expedition officers: a) Arthur J. Mounteney Jephson, b) Dr Thomas H. Parke, c) Lieutenant William G. Stairs, d) James S. Jameson, e) Major Edmund M.Barttelot, f) Sergeant William Bonny.

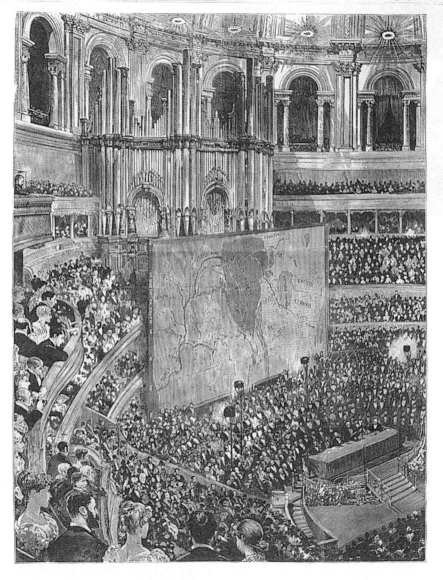

28 Stanley lecturing about the Emin Pasha Expedition at the Albert Hall, from *The Graphic* 10 May 1890

29 Dorothy Tennant in 1890, shortly before her marriage to Stanley
30 Stanley in 1890, the year of his marriage
31 Stanley and Jephson seated, Nelson and Stairs standing, all much aged and reduced by
the Emin Pasha Expedition just ended, December 1889

32

33/4

32 Stanley on a lecture tour in America, with Dorothy in the Henry M.Stanley Pullman Car in 1891
33 William Hoffman, Stanley's former valet, as a lieutenant in the Congo Free State's *force publique*, 1895
34 Stanley and his good friend and ally, the Scottish shipping tycoon, Sir William Mackinnon in 1892

35 Furze Hill, near Pirbright, Surrey, the country house, which Stanley bought in 1899
36 Stanley with his adopted son, Denzil, in 1902
37 Stanley at his desk in 1903, a year before his death

38/9

40

38 Stanley's grave in Pirbright churchyard
39 Stanley's adopted grandson, Richard, in 1954, laying a wreath at his grandfather's statue in Leopoldville, Belgian Congo, now Kinshasa in the Democratic Republic of the Congo
40 Stanley's fallen statue lying forgotten on one of his old steamers in a public works lot in Kinshasa

Bunyoro.[66] Henry's cruel predicament – that he would be damned if he told the truth, and damned if he did not – plunged him into depression, even as he was being bombarded with telegrams of congratulation from monarchs and world leaders. 'I am subject to conflicting emotions of pity for Emin, pity for ourselves, pity for the waste of life, & efforts, & money in a worthless cause, & they often send me to bed sickened in mind.'[67]

Sadly for Stanley, because of Emin's charm, his scholarly habits, his short sight and his capacity for generosity, the popular image of him that has come down is of a peace-loving old man being bullied by a younger and more energetic one. Yet what Jephson would remember most vividly would be the Pasha's Egyptians beating their servants to death and behaving so cruelly that even the cannibal Manyema would not sell slaves to them. 'The Pasha should do something to stop it,' wrote Jephson, 'but he is more incapable and impotent than ever, nor do I think that he greatly cares.'[68] Emin never expressed public gratitude to Stanley, and his letter of thanks to Mackinnon was heavily ironic. But the Pasha's claim that Mackinnon had only sent Stanley to central Africa so that he could take possession of his (Emin's) province and his ivory was unjust. Mackinnon had certainly hoped to combine rescuing Emin with pioneering a permanent route from the Indian Ocean to Lake Victoria to facilitate opening the area to commerce.[69] But this did not mean that his eagerness to rescue Emin was only cosmetic. The Scotsman gave £3,000 personally, and his friends and relatives put up a further £16,000. Stanley had been generous too – interrupting a lecture series in America, costing himself, according to Mackinnon, £10,000; then leading the expedition for nothing, and donating the £2,000 he had been paid for all his reports on the expedition sent to newspapers.[70]

On Zanzibar, Stanley at last reckoned up the human cost of the expedition. He did not, however, enter in his diary a record of the dead, but Jephson in *his* diary stated that out of 708 people who started out from the lower Congo almost three years earlier, only 210 had survived.[71] From Henry's diaries, and from his official report to Colonel C. B. Euan Smith, the British Consul-General on Zanzibar, it is possible to confirm Jephson's figure – although adding to it the two Europeans and twelve Sudanese who had returned home earlier via the Congo, raising the number of survivors to 219[72] [see note for more details]. Since 708 expedition members had sailed from Zanzibar for the Congo's mouth (a total of 805 with the inclusion of Tippu Tip and his 96 followers), it follows that 490 men died of disease, were killed or deserted during almost three years. It is impossible to say how many died and how many deserted, though in a letter written after he had reached the coast Henry stated that the expedition had 'cost us 400 lives', showing that deaths were far more numerous than desertions.[73] But whatever the actual proportion, the loss of 490 men from all causes was a melancholy statistic, which Stanley found it hard to come to terms with or to admit to.

Since the purpose of the expedition had been to relieve Emin Pasha, the fate of Emin's 570 followers, who had left Lake Albert on 10 April 1889, is also highly relevant. By 11 November their number had declined to 294, on which date Stanley made a list: '30 heads of households (Emin Pasha, Signor Marco, Capitano Casati, Osman Effendi, etc.), 71 women, 59 children, 121 servants, 13 carriers'.[74] In his official report he stated that he arrived in Bagamoyo with 290 of Emin's people.[75] So 280 (roughly half) had either died or been abandoned en route.[76] Some chose to stay on Zanzibar, and Stanley eventually repatriated 260 to Egypt. Against this paltry total, he had to set the 400 dead Wangwana, whose lives he thought immeasurably more valuable.

Yet the combined loss of 700 lives (even if raised by say 300 to take account of African deaths) looks modest when placed in a wider African context. Deaths occurring during the Bugandan civil war, the Arab-Swahili uprising against the Germans, the military campaigns of African rulers such as Kabarega and Mirambo, and the continuing slave raids across a wide swathe of the continent, would *each* have dwarfed the loss of a mere thousand lives. Late in 1883, Stanley had learned that over 5,000 slaves had been dragged from their villages in one small area just below Stanley Falls.[77] Such memories increased Stanley's fury with Tippu Tip for his part in the fate of the Rear Column. He reported to Colonel Euan Smith: 'These tragedies and catastrophes, which reduced a completely equipped and well-organized column of 271 men rank and file to 102 meagre, starved, and anaemic souls, were due in the first place to the breach of contract by Tippu Tip.' Undeniably, if Tippu had brought the 400 carriers at the anticipated time – eleven months earlier than he actually did – Barttelot and Jameson would have been able to start in pursuit of the Advance Column long before their men became enfeebled and started dying.[78]

In apportioning blame for the expedition's shortcomings, besides blaming Tippu Tip, Stanley also pointed a finger at King Leopold for misleading him about the number of steamers that would be available at Leopoldville. That unexpected shortage of vessels had plunged him into a crisis that had made splitting the expedition inevitable. Stanley also felt that Emin's letters to friends, in which the Pasha had represented his position as immediately perilous, had put pressure on the members of the expedition to make haste their first priority at whatever cost. Yet though Stanley felt the need to justify himself in his official report, and to blame others – including the late Major Barttelot and his friend James Jameson – the world's press was not yet bothered by the fact that lives had been lost. In fact the sufferings of the expedition's personnel made Stanley's achievements seem all the more remarkable. For in the eyes of the public in Europe and America, his willingness to pay in blood in order to bring the 'noble' Emin and his devoted followers from the heart of Africa to the coast made his feat truly heroic. That he had also united his fractured expedition – nearly starving during an extraordinary feat of inspirational leadership – simply added to his lustre. It would be widely believed, and with good reason, that no other explorer could have kept his expedition in being against such odds, and have brought some of it home after an epic journey of more than 5,000 miles.

Yet when Henry organized payments and bonuses to the widows of the dead Wangwana just before leaving Zanzibar, it appalled him that the people he had tried hardest to protect had suffered most. Saying goodbye to grey-haired Uledi, who had served him loyally on all his major journeys since 1871, Stanley knew that he was also bidding farewell to his own days as an African explorer and pioneer.

TWENTY-SEVEN

The Shape of Things to Come...

On arrival in Zanzibar, early in December, Stanley was photographed with his four officers of the Advance Column, all of them fashionably moustachioed and the three younger men wearing smartly tailored tropical whites while their boss sports a more casual linen jacket with a formal waistcoat. Henry looks like a man of seventy-five: gaunt, hollow-eyed and grim. Stairs and Nelson have aged ten years since they set out – the latter looking sadly reduced and frail. Both have the expressions of haunted victims, rather than aggressors guilty of atrocities, as both men were. The thoroughly decent Jephson (his position next to his leader reflecting Henry's especial regard for him) looks his actual age, although even he stares at the camera with a worried frown. Surgeon Parke was too ill to be photographed, and Bonny had been excluded because of a drunken fistfight with a local doctor in Zanzibar's Grand Hotel. None had any inkling that all were doomed to early deaths – Nelson and Stairs in Africa, thanks to their leader's enthusiastic references, and two at home, Jephson and Parke, through damage already done to their constitutions.[1] On 29 December, Stanley sailed from Zanzibar – after three weeks' recuperation. He and his four officers, and Sergeant Bonny, had all put on weight and seemed in far better health now than three weeks earlier.

Stanley planned to spend several months in Cairo while writing his book about the expedition. He was in no hurry to return home to the loveless life he had escaped by going out again to Africa. The only time he had looked forward to returning had been six years earlier after his pioneering period on the Congo, when Edward King's friend, May Sheldon, had offered to find an apartment for him close to hers in west London. Since his rejection by Dorothy Tennant, he had made no further efforts to seek out marriageable women. But soon after his arrival in Cairo, Stanley wrote to May asking her to tell him honestly what 'our personal friends' thought about the outcome of his expedition. It was for friends like her, he explained, that 'we do our best to please, but sometimes fail despite every effort'. A month later, he invited May to come to Cairo, in the same letter offering her his 'Stanley cap', which he had worn across the continent. Sometime earlier, she had joked about giving him a fancy price for it.[2] Though delighted to be promised his trademark cap, she decided against coming. She was, after all, still married, and, as a journalist, knew how intense press interest was going to be in the great man.

A year later, this intrepid woman sailed to Zanzibar and, without the aid of any white companions, led an expedition of 200 *pagazi* into the East African interior, through Masai country, eventually circumnavigating unexplored Lake Chala near Mount Kilimanjaro. This trip was very much her personal tribute to the man she admired more than any other. On her return to Europe, Stanley poured out his admiration for her to Henry Wellcome, her devoted patron, saying that she had 'distinguished herself in almost everything. Good woman, kind nurse, tender friend, cheery companion, translator, novel writer, sculptress, newspaper correspondent, female physician, & African traveller. She is a paragon & quite deserving of our love and respect.'[3] May would regret her decision not to go to Cairo when, only two years later, her husband died without warning. By then, her 'one great passion' could never be fulfilled. Soon after May Sheldon declined his invitation, Stanley received a brief letter of congratulation from Dorothy Tennant.

On his return to England, before any romantic approaches could be made to him by Dorothy or anyone else, Stanley became totally preoccupied with the power politics that were changing the map of Africa even as he began to write his book. In April 1889, when Stanley had been about to leave Lake Albert for the coast, Sir William Mackinnon (who had just been made a baronet) had written offering him the post of Chief Administrator of the Imperial British East Africa Company, with his headquarters in Mombassa.[4] Given the emotional significance of his chartered company to the childless Mackinnon, it was unfortunate that this important offer should have been handed to Stanley at Zanzibar, just when the prospect of writing his new book was weighing on him like lead, and he had 200 telegrams and almost 400 letters to attend to. Not surprisingly, he temporized over the offer. In Cairo, where he arrived on 14 January, Stanley at last replied to Mackinnon. The ship owner, he insisted, was his 'one good friend', whose interests he had placed above all others during the expedition.[5] But he was sorry that he could not commit himself to any job at this time; and in early February, he repeated this refusal.[6]

For Mackinnon – at sixty-seven – his company seemed to offer the last chance of bringing commerce and Christianity to a large part of Africa (as his compatriot Livingstone would have wished); but Stanley, at forty-nine, suddenly felt that he needed to settle down and lead a more peaceful existence.[7] Perhaps he recoiled from the immense responsibilities that would go with building a railway to Lake Victoria, and installing a more stable king than the butcher Mwanga of Buganda. Yet though Henry had refused a post that would have made him the future ruler of Kenya and Uganda (greater Buganda), he went on supporting Mackinnon's aims – in the first instance by giving his friend the means to enlarge the British East African sphere with territory that would otherwise have become German.

Having seen evidence of German misrule in the shape of burned towns and mission stations, Stanley's 'gift' to his friend's company was intended to prevent similar events in the territory west of Lake Victoria. Henry told Sir William that after crossing the Semliki he had made 'friendly arrangements [in that region] ... verbally but not written'. He then listed the immense territories of 'Ankor [Ankole], Usongora and Unkonju': 'given to me on the same terms treaties are made – and all my rights of course I turn over to you ...'. In reality, though he had arbitrated between a couple of tribes, and had undergone blood-brotherhood ceremonies with several chiefs and with a chief's son, nothing had been ceded to him. But because he had reached the coast at a crucial moment in Anglo-German competition for East African territory, he had decided, on the spur of the moment, that he ought to hand to Britain and Mackinnon some helpful new cards.[8]

In May Mackinnon wrote gratefully to Stanley: 'I have a little note from Lord Salisbury [the prime minister] asking me to send him a map showing as accurately as possible the ground covered by your treaties.'[9] In the negotiations leading to the Anglo-German Agreement of July 1890, Stanley's 'treaties' and maps enabled Sir Percy Anderson, Britain's negotiator, to lay claim to an enlarged Uganda, extending far to the south and south-west of what had previously been thought of as Buganda's borders. Stanley next addressed a large public meeting in the Albert Hall, giving his backing to the Scottish missions, then warning the government against German designs on Nyasaland (Malawi) – the territory Livingstone had tried to make a British protectorate during the 1860s.[10]

For Stanley, too, the prospect of ending the suffering of the slave trade made the colonial development of East Africa urgently necessary. He was one of very few Europeans to have seen with his own eyes the extent of the mass murder in central Africa. In August, Mackinnon said he was determined to build a railway to Lake Victoria 'as the solution of the slave trade question'. Make it, he told Stanley, 'a principal text when you have occasion again to speak about Africa'.[11] With the arrival of traders, chiefs could sell their produce rather than their people (as many did to the Arab-Swahili) in exchange for European goods. As European agricultural methods were employed (so the theory went), Africans would learn to work for wages, which could eventually be taxed and at last make possible the public works – railways, roads, schools, hospitals – on which all more advanced societies depended. As Jephson had put it after talking to Mackay and Stanley:

The ordinary native only grows just enough corn for the use of himself & his family; let him once see that what he grows has a very substantial value & he will cultivate more & be more hardworking & thrifty; he will not then be so ready to go to war with his neighbour ... & the little petty wars which are the curse of Africa, will, with the coming of the railway, & the consequent increase in trade, gradually cease.[12]

Stanley and Mackinnon were paternalists, who believed their own society was superior to tribal ones, but this did not make them hypocrites. For Mackinnon, the prospect of making money during his lifetime from his immense investment in East Africa looked incredibly remote. Despite his own hard beginnings, Stanley believed that industrial societies – in which millions of people could earn more money than they needed for their subsistence – offered to their citizens choices of occupation, and ways of life that could never exist in changeless tribal communities – least of all in those reduced to chaos by slave raids. Even before leaving Zanzibar, he had discussed with the British Consul-General, Colonel C. B. Euan Smith, the feasibility of enforcing an international arms and gunpowder embargo, aimed at crippling the slave trade.[13] That the British government had other more urgent priorities would soon become apparent to Stanley and to Mackinnon, his 'one good friend', with disastrous financial consequences for the latter.

Of course, the argument that the slave trade could only be tackled if Africa were to be colonized offered a convenient justification for the politicians, businessmen and adventurers engaged in the 'Scramble for Africa' for purposes of prestige and financial gain. But Stanley's desire to destroy the slave trade was not a cynical stratagem. While Henry was in Cairo writing his book at the secluded Hotel Villa Victoria, an exhibition was drawing crowds in London's Regent Street. Called the 'Stanley and African Exhibition', the name was a tribute to his unique fame and the fact that a large number of the exhibits came from his collection of African weapons and artefacts. Admission receipts produced a sum that would be called the 'Stanley Fund'. This money, Henry decided, should be spent on building two steamers for the use of missionaries and traders on Lake Victoria. Placing steamers on lakes in order to cut slave routes had been one of Livingstone's big ideas.[14]

While in Cairo, Stanley wrote his book, *In Darkest Africa*, in fifty days – a rate to rival his earlier astonishing feats of book production. Typically, he would rise at six and work till eleven at night, only emerging for meals, and cursing his boy, Sali, for every telegram he brought to his work desk, however exalted the sender.[15] Stanley dedicated his miracle of speed-writing to Sir William Mackinnon. Yet despite the presence of his publisher, Edward Marston, in Cairo, the book went off to the printer containing several passages destined to plunge Stanley into a terrible public row on publication – while nevertheless helping his sales (£24,000 earned in Britain alone in a year).

His book completed, Stanley left Cairo on 7 April 1890, and after a few days with Mackinnon in Cannes, he arrived in Brussels on the 19th for talks with King Leopold, who was still paying him £1,000 per annum as a retainer. The Congo was currently costing Leopold 3,000,000 francs a year – one-fifth of his original fortune *every* year – and he was only getting back one-tenth of this in export duties on ivory and palm oil. (The Berlin Conference had forbidden him to levy any other form of duty.) His courtiers called his expenditure on the Congo 'Congodelirium'.[16] Stanley still resented the way the king had treated him in 1885 and 1886, and did not intend to go back to Africa for him, but he still admired the man's tenacity of purpose and his liberality. He had no clue that Leopold meant to create state monopolies in ivory and rubber and squeeze free trade out of the Congo, in direct contravention of the Berlin decrees.

Sitting at a marble table opposite the king, in a room he knew well, Stanley observed that the king's beard had turned as white as his own shorter hair. Given the king's losses, what more natural than that he should enquire about the trading potential of the enormous tropical forest stretching from the mouth of the Aruwimi to within fifty miles of Lake Albert? 'He listened to what I had said,' noted Stanley, 'with the close attention of one who was receiving an account of a great estate that had just fallen to him.' What was marketable in the forest? Timber, of course, Stanley told him, before adding as an afterthought: 'Almost every branchy tree has a rubber parasite clinging to it ... A well organized company will be able to collect several tons annually.' Since, in 1890, this would have been worth very little to the company harvesting it, Leopold was more interested in the rich variety of hardwoods that could be floated downstream as logs. Stanley made a point of stressing how important 'gentle treatment of the employed natives' would be, if their labour was to be utilized.[17]

Little that Stanley told Leopold gave him any reason to think he would be earning much from the Congo until the railway had been built. Neither he nor Stanley knew that a Scottish veterinary surgeon, living in Belfast, had amused himself in 1887 by fitting an air-filled tyre to his son's tricycle to improve the boy's ride. The ingenious vet had patented his 'pneumatic' tyre a year later, and in 1889 had floated the Dunlop Tyre Company. This would not be established in Europe and America until 1891 – the first consignment of bicycle tyres reaching America on Christmas Day 1890. The great bicycling craze would then begin, lifting the price of rubber to levels that would have seemed unimaginable even a year or two earlier.[18]

When Leopold told Stanley that he wanted him to return to Africa to take Khartoum and join the Sudan to the Congo, Stanley was incredulous. Such a venture would require 5,000 white troops and 10,000 black, and would take several years to prepare. It was, he told Leopold bluntly, 'impossible with your present means'. Frankly, he should not even think of expansion into the Uele and the Bahr el Ghazal regions – there was just one priority, and this was to attack the Arab slave traders between Stanley Falls and the Kasongo and 'stop their awful work' in the Auruwimi valley and on the Lualaba. 'Direct all your strength and means first to extirpate these awful people, and when you have done that then talk about extension of territory.'[19] Before Henry left Brussels for London, he gave an impassioned talk to the Anti-Slavery Conference, then in session in that city, arguing the need for an immediate arms embargo. This should be aimed not only at slave traders but at warlords like Mirambo, and Msiri, who between them had brought terror to a vast area between Lake Victoria and Katanga. The great powers had a moral duty 'to pass stringent laws'. Germany and Britain could together 'prevent the trade altogether [in East Africa]'.[20]

Before Stanley left Brussels, the king presented him with a malachite and ebony casket containing the Grand Cross of his personal order, and the Diamond Star of the Congo. Had Leopold instead persuaded him to take charge of the Congo, a great human catastrophe would have been prevented a few years later.

TWENTY-EIGHT

Dorothy's Other Love

Stanley was greeted by cheering crowds at London's Victoria Station at the beginning of a month of banquets, lectures and celebratory occasions. At Sandringham, where he had been invited to stay, he gave an after-dinner speech on Africa to the Prince of Wales. The Royal Geographical Society, in full retreat from past insults, packed the Albert Hall with royalty, peers, politicians and travellers eager to celebrate his homecoming with the largest reception he had ever been given.[1] Constant exposure to rich food soon brought him to the brink of gastritis. As Henry remarked wryly to Mackinnon: 'When hundreds of feasts are in prospect, the stomach declines to work ... When I had a stomach I had nothing to eat.'[2] Among other honours, Oxford and Cambridge awarded him honorary degrees.

His friend Sir Francis de Winton had taken rooms for him at 34, De Vere Gardens – a desirable street just south of Kensington Gardens – and while he was there, one of Queen Victoria's courtiers came to enquire whether a knighthood 'would be acceptable'. But in 1885 Henry had taken out American nationality in order to protect his American copyrights. And with Scribner's, his US publisher, just about to disgorge £40,000 for his new book, this was hardly the moment to become a British subject again. As de Winton explained to the Queen's private secretary, 'he is involved with publishing transactions that make it impossible [to accept]'. Even so, it was very painful, given Henry's background, to be obliged to sacrifice a knighthood for money – however large the sum.[3] In 1872, Queen Victoria had found Stanley 'not particularly prepossessing' and had disliked his 'strong American twang',[4] but in 1890 she described him as 'the wonderful traveller and explorer'. On 6 May 'the wonderful traveller' came to

Windsor Castle at her invitation, and she discussed with him 'the difficulties with Germany in Africa': 'Then Mr Stanley gave us a most interesting lecture.' The Queen added in her diary that Stanley did not want 'an order to be offered to him'.[5]

Eight days before his stay at Windsor, Henry had been bemused and indignant to receive a letter from Dorothy Tennant asking him to visit her at home. 'I shall be so deeply glad to see you again, not because you have done such great things, but because you have come back safe, because I feared I might never see your face again. Bula Matari, do not be too proud to come, since I am not too proud to tell you how greatly I desire it.'[6] Stanley did not reply. So she wrote again two days later, repeating part of her last letter and adding plaintively: 'Perhaps Bula Matari will never wish to see me again, and yet I shall be so deeply glad to see you again that it is impossible that you should not be just a little glad to see me. If I had my wish you would come tomorrow. Will you?'[7] This letter, in which she failed to mention the pain she had caused him, is scuffed and dirty, exactly as if he had dragged the sole of his shoe across it.

'I regret to say that it is not likely I shall have an early opportunity of paying you a visit,' he replied with cool formality.[8] But before this brush-off could be delivered in the mail, she contrived to meet him at a social function. Dorothy pleaded with him humbly to visit her the following day, and surprised him into agreeing to do so. But when the next day came, he could not bring himself to risk a *tête-à-tête* with the woman who had caused him so much pain. Dolly wrote another note, still trying to lure him into a private meeting,[9] and this time elicited an emotional reply:

I must decline the pleasure of approaching you ... Upon the receipt of your letter in 1886 – only silence could follow ... for this probably I was born ... You will do wisely and well to leave me alone, and some day I have no doubt you shall learn my story ... Meantime ... action cures everything ... No rest, no brooding, but work with zeal and devotion ... Therefore goodbye once again.[10]

Instead of trying for another meeting in this more favourable situation, Dorothy wrote a masterly life-changing letter, which seemed to swell directly from her emotions. In reality it was the result of some very cool calculation.

Before saying goodbye, let me tell you this ... Suppose a wild, uncultivated tract of land, and suppose that one day this land is ploughed up and sown with corn, if the field could speak it might say: 'I have never borne corn, I do not bear corn, I never shall bear corn.' And yet all the while the wheat lies hidden in its bosom.

When you were gone, when you were out of reach, I slowly realized what you had become to me, and then a great anguish filled me. I then made to myself a vow that ... when you came back I would see you, and tell you all quite simply, and say: 'Truly I have never cared for anyone but you. I did not know it when you wrote to me, for till you wrote, the possibility of your caring for me had never even occurred to me. But at that time I was not worthy of your love. Now I believe I am, let me help you and take care of you, and be everything in the world to you.' But there was vanity in this, for it presupposed your still caring for me. Well, dear Mr Stanley, goodbye. God keep and bless you for ever. I shall never again pass across or disturb your life ... If ever you think of me, don't let it be as a poor craven spirit, but as a woman who though she deserved to suffer, has done so bravely, on the whole ...[11]

From the moment she began to read his reply, which was sent from Windsor Castle, Dorothy knew she was making progress.

My dear Miss Tennant,

Your very nice letter was laid on my table yesterday by my black boy, he little knowing from whom it came ... But oh Heavens, had such possibilities approached me in 1886, I would have been delirious with joy ... But instead ... you were absolutely rude in your violent desire to eradicate all love, so that a far different woman from the gracious queenly woman I worshipped rose in front of me. I saw in my imagination you standing indignant, outraged at the 'base born churl' etc., daring to approach your queenliness with such preposterous protestations etc. ... I shrank into nothingness before you and the devout love was crushed ... You permitted me to enter those dark and sorrowful regions [of Africa] with dark sorrowful feelings, and [permitted] the barbed weapon you had flung to enter deeper and deeper into the heart ... I worshipped you as a goddess and the goddess spurned me. If I had not worshipped something else [duty], I had surely been ruined ... Let us meet by all means tonight, calmly and as dear friends ... Your letter has done much to cure an irritating sore ...[12]

When Dolly set out for an evening party – to which she knew Stanley had been invited – her letter had not yet been delivered. As soon as they met, Dolly recorded, '[I] told him quietly that I would be his wife if he still loved me.' Though stunned by her proposal, Henry did not relent, and his next letter must have come as a great disappointment. 'I am grieved, he wrote, ' that I cannot respond as I ought ... From a settled indifference, your words have created in me a profound sympathy ... Let us be good friends.'[13] Most women would have confessed themselves defeated at this stage, but Dorothy, at this point, sat down and wrote another ruthlessly disingenuous appeal. In it she claimed to have 'prayed night and day for three years that you might love me back again'. Representing herself as having been at the time she first met him 'a girl unacquainted with love', she made out that she had not known that her desire to be with him had in fact been love.

I had no former love to compare it with ... I did not understand, and I wrote to you and destroyed all my life's happiness. When you went into that terrible darkness ... I thought of you without ceasing, and then you <u>did</u> come back ... When I saw your dear face, glorified by all you had suffered and endured, I felt my heart leap with joy, but then you looked at me as though you did not know me ... you tell me that I killed your love long ago ... But my love is a flame, never to be extinguished ... I am yours, whether you will or no, till I die ... Goodbye my Beloved. I am yours for ever and for ever.[14]

After reading this letter, Stanley agreed to meet Dorothy at his flat in De Vere Gardens.[15] The only record of the meeting is in her diary, and it strikes a bathetic note after the high drama of her letters: 'On Wednesday 14th I went by invitation to call on him at 34 De Vere Mansions [sic], then we had a short talk and we were engaged.' After that, Dorothy lost no time in going to see George Buckle, the editor of *The Times*, who assured her that he would report the story on Saturday morning. On the 15th Dorothy wrote:

My own beloved Bula Matari,

It is all true – and not a dream, and I am really to be yours. If you did but know how I love you, how intensely I love you ... I long to write to Sir William ...[16]

Mackinnon had been in touch with Dorothy since 1887 and had hoped, for the sake of his close friend, that one day she would change her mind. For this reason, during July 1887, he had invited Dorothy and her mother for a cruise on his line's passenger ship the *Jumna*, and a month later had called on them, admitting that he was worried to have heard nothing from Stanley for several months. In future, he shared all his news of Henry with Dorothy, sending her telegrams in the name Polly Hopkins.[17] Throughout these contacts, which lasted from 1887 to the spring of 1890, Dorothy affected to be relieved and grateful to be kept informed. In May 1889, she even asked Sir William to invite her and Stanley to dinner together when he returned.[18] A year later, after Stanley appeared to have rejected her decisively, she told Sir William how 'dreadfully humbled' she felt. 'Some day I will give you a little token he once gave me – he would perhaps like to have it back. And now goodbye till we meet again.'[19] For the kindly old millionaire, it seemed unbearably sad that these star-crossed lovers should have loved one another so deeply – and yet, tragically, at different times. Sir William was the first person to whom Dorothy wrote after Stanley agreed to marry her. 'I will make him gloriously happy,' she promised.[20] But if the shipping tycoon had known what had really gone on in Dorothy Tennant's life while his dear friend Stanley had been away, he would have been bitterly disillusioned with her.

On 11 March 1888 – a month before Stanley met Emin Pasha on the banks of Lake Albert – Dorothy was rhapsodizing in her diary about another man entirely, whom she had by then met four times, and already loved. The Right Honourable Sir Alfred Comyn Lyall was an old Etonian, a Privy Councillor, and a Member of the Council of the Secretary of State for India. He was also an author, who had lectured in English history at Oxford and was a fellow of King's College, Cambridge. He was six years older than Stanley – the age that the father-fixated Dorothy liked best for her male admirers. Like most of her earlier ones, he too was a married man.

Sir Alfred Lyall

Just when Stanley was approaching the snowy Ruwenzoris, Dorothy was gazing in awe at Sir Alfred, whom she described as being 'like a great mountain, inaccessible – with a top of ice and snow'. Yet, though daunting at times, she found him approachable and modest. Normally when people asked her intimate questions about whether she meant to devote herself to art or to marry, she 'made them regret they had asked'. But this impertinent question seemed enchanting in Sir Alfred's mouth. Her only fear was that this intellectual man might see nothing to interest him in 'a girl who goes out to dinner parties and is fashionable'. Dorothy confessed to her sister, Eveleen (Evie) Myers, how much she loved this fifty-three-year-old luminary of the India Office. In May 1888 Evie took pity on her, promising to invite Sir Alfred to stay with her and her husband in Cambridge later that year. So in July, and in December too, Dorothy and Sir Alfred spent time together under the same roof, enabling Dorothy 'to focus my joys', as she put it.

Frederic Myers, the founder of the Society for Psychical Research, had been a classics fellow at Trinity College, Cambridge, but had resigned ten years earlier to become an Inspector of Schools. He and Sir Alfred read French poetry aloud in the evening, and joined in games of cards with Dorothy and Evie. In the day, Dorothy and her distinguished boyfriend wandered through the courts of the Cambridge colleges deep in conversation. For Christmas 1888, Sir Alfred gave Dorothy a gift of ancient Indian coins, and she confided to her dead father – through the pages of her diary – 'I care for him as much as I care for you, and this you know my dear, dear Father I have never said or thought of anyone – his beautiful gift has swelled my heart with gladness and sorrowfulness.' That Christmas Day of 1888, Sir Alfred called on Dorothy. 'It somehow made Christmas Day *right*,' she felt.[21] (It seems unlikely that Lady Lyall would have shared this opinion.) Whenever Sir Alfred gave lectures, Dorothy was there, as when she went to the South Place Institute in mid-January 1889 to hear him speak about Hinduism. She had brought with her a beautifully embroidered Indian bag, which he had given her. Sometimes Sir Alfred sent her poems, which she usually sent back to him illustrated with her drawings. She went with him to Burlington House art exhibitions, and he lunched with her most Wednesdays and Fridays. And so 1889 passed, with Dorothy longing to see her Alfred more often. 'Just to see him gives the day its worth.'[22]

In mid-May 1889, Dorothy wrote in her diary that Mackinnon 'seems to think I have some lingering tender interest in Stanley; he is quite right in thinking I am interested, but I certainly don't feel in the least tender. I think he is a fine, courageous explorer & pioneer – and I hope he will come back safe, & that is all I feel about him.'[23] So much for her having 'prayed night and day for three years for him to love her back again'.

At this time, she was often at the studio of the young American artist James Shannon, watching him painting a full-length portrait of Sir Alfred. Dorothy loved Lyall's reserve and dignity and found his world-weariness irresistible. Since she suffered from depression, she was paying a great tribute to Sir Alfred when she wrote: 'I can never feel hopelessly, desperately alone as long as he lives.' In June he sent Dorothy a first draft of his life of Warren Hastings for her comments, which she gave him honestly. Yet Sir Alfred could be honest with Dolly too, saying – although he loved her – she ought to find a husband and have children. After one intimate chat, Dorothy recorded: 'He strongly advised me to marry ... I shouldn't of course have any illusions about love but he advised me to marry a man who might be good and honourable without expecting more. He – Sir Alfred – will always be my friend and care for me ... I know he cares for me and I care for him ...'[24]

'I long to see you to prove what I can be,' she wrote, shortly before persuading him to stay with her and her mother in their Welsh country house near Swansea. Before his arrival she had his room redecorated and chose new curtains and new paintings. They worked on Warren Hastings together and went for woodland walks. Dorothy 'felt very happy'.[25] After his visit, she wrote:

Of an evening I sit in your room scented by the fresh magnolias I put there every day ... I am glad and unregretful as to the past ... Don't tell me I have life before me any more. Let us go on without talking of the mileage. So long as you are in the world I can be happy enough.[26]

Yet by the end of the year, although Dorothy still loved Sir Alfred, she knew that his fatalism and detachment would always keep him at arm's length. Yet even a distanced relationship seemed better than nothing. 'Let it be so for ever,' she told him, 'for you are the only being I care to draw near to.'[27]

On 10 December 1889, Dorothy heard that Stanley had arrived safely at Zanzibar, but two weeks later she gave Sir Alfred a little portrait of Warren Hastings as a Christmas present. By February, however, she was seeing less of Lyall, and in that month flirted with a rich Chicago businessman, though nothing came of it. Then on 19 March, she sent a rather late letter of congratulation to Stanley, who was still in Cairo at the time. At this time Henry's name was constantly in the press. By the end of the month, Dorothy had started her campaign to make herself Mrs Henry Morton Stanley. After all, Sir Alfred would not object, since he had said she ought to marry, regardless of whether she fell in love.[28]

To many people Dorothy would pretend that she and Stanley had had an understanding to marry if he came back from Africa. Others, like Mackinnon and Gladstone, were told she had fallen in love when he was away. Because Sir Alfred would never leave his wife, Dolly had decided that the next best thing was to become Mrs Stanley – a role offering her, apart from a marriage in Westminster Abbey, a position in society far more dramatic than she could hope to command in any other way. Famous people and elite occasions banished Dolly's gloom: 'enabling me, she wrote, 'to forget myself completely'.[29]

Her letters to Stanley after their engagement glow with a remarkably fervent quality – as if she really had loved *him* over the past couple of years, rather than Lyall. She resembled a great actress, acting out a theatrical role in real life. But Dorothy genuinely dreaded his returning to Africa. 'Before you say those awful words, "I must go" let me entreat you for my sake – and perhaps our child's sake – dearest, don't go back ...'[30] Many of her letters begin lovingly – My darling, My dear dear Henry, My dear Well-Beloved Bula Matari – just as if the emotions that the occasion required had always been within her. Though she had been 'a great deal in society', Dolly assured her husband-to-be: 'My inner life has been quiet, grave, and much with Mother ... What I dread is dealing with the rough outside world ... But you are beside me now, my rock, my prop, my bulwark against the great breakers of life.'[31] This was the Dorothy who, even aged thirty-five, sometimes described herself as 'a girl' needing protection, when in reality, though sensitive, she was capable of a toughness, at times equal to Stanley's. When he bought her some opulent jewels, which she considered vulgar, she told him very bluntly that she wished him to change them.[32] Frederic Myers – Evie's husband – confided, helpfully:

After she is yours I must not criticize her; so now let me say that she has been somewhat over-indulged in life, and that has left her too impetuous, and not always wise. But you have learnt to rule gently; and you will find, as you already know as well as I, that whatever there may be of over-hasty in her is on the surface only, and that beneath is a power of steady devotion ...[33]

On 17 June Dorothy received from Edward Marston the very first finished copy of *In Darkest Africa*, and declared: 'What a great sensation the book will cause!' She had no idea how right she was. Only three privileged people were allowed to see these pre-publication copies: her mother, her brother Charlie and Sir Alfred Lyall. Few of Stanley's friends and former colleagues were invited to meet Dolly before her wedding: among the chosen ones were Mrs Sheldon, Henry Wellcome, Jephson, Stairs and, rather surprisingly, Sergeant Bonny. But Stanley knew that one day, if he were to have problems with the Barttelot and Jameson families, he would need Bonny to go public with his account of the terrible things that had gone on at Yambuya.[34]

The day before their wedding in Westminster Abbey, Henry was prostrated by his old enemy, gastritis, and was later told by his doctors that he had suffered 'the lightest of strokes'.[35] On that day Mackinnon and Stanley's EPRE officers had planned to give him his 'last bachelor dinner', but the occasion had to be cancelled.[36] Instead, Henry spent the evening at home being given pain-killing injections by Dr Parke. On the eve of his wedding, Stanley wrote to Dorothy: 'I rest in peace now with the thought that you are mine ... There is a world of meaning in that word possession, it ends all anxiety and doubt and the pain of a man's life ... I would not care who knows it ...'[37]

On the morning of her marriage, Dolly told her mother that Henry was 'determined to be married and go [on his honeymoon]. He says if he remains he will die.'[38] Only at breakfast-time did Dolly know that the ceremony would go ahead.[39] Decked out in a dress of white silk and satin, the seams sewn with pearls, Dorothy – for all her horror of vulgarity – flashed with as many diamonds as a Bond Street jeweller's shop. There were diamonds galore in Sir William Mackinnon's tiara (which she wore inverted, as a necklace); there were thirty-eight large stones surrounding the miniature of Victoria given to Stanley by the Queen herself (and now worn by Dorothy as a locket); diamonds galore sparkled in the bracelet bought by her husband-to-be, and even more glittered in the bracelet from King Leopold. As if this were not enough, on her left arm Dorothy wore 'the bracelet given [her] by Sir Alfred Lyall – the gold coins of Chandra Gupta (300 AD) discovered in Oudh and mounted by him in a bracelet'.

Like a royal princess, she drove along Whitehall to Westminster Abbey in a closed carriage, past cheering crowds, and was married to her explorer by the Bishop of Ripon, assisted by the Dean of Westminster, and the Master of Trinity, Cambridge, who gave the address. Present at the signing of the register were Mr Gladstone, the ubiquitous Sir Alfred Lyall, Colonel Grant (Speke's companion) and two of the most famous artists of the day, Sir John Millais and Sir Frederick Leighton. The Lord Chancellor and the Speaker of the House of Commons were present at the ceremony, along with a brace of dukes and numerous peers.

For almost the entire service Stanley was seated, and looked ill enough to die. Close by sat his five Emin Pasha officers, and Sali (Saleh bin Osman) his remarkable Wangwana servant boy. On his way down the nave after the ceremony, Stanley was obliged to lean heavily on a stick. Passing Livingstone's grave, as Stanley had requested, Dorothy paused a moment to lay her bridal bouquet on the polished stone, with its inscription from the *Last Journals,* conferring 'heaven's rich blessing' on any enemy of the slave trade.

The King of Belgium had sent as his representative the Comte d'Assche, with the request that the courtier should be the explorer's best man. Though Stanley must have thought this royal command presumptuous, he may also have felt relieved by it. He would have found it hard to settle on any particular person for the role of best man, if the king had not commanded. William Mackinnon – his honorary father – was too old. Edward Marston, his publisher, and Henry Wellcome, the millionaire chemist, would have been possibilities. But Agnes Livingstone's husband, Alexander Bruce, who had come out to Cairo to be with him and was a regular correspondent, would very likely have been his first choice. Edward King would have been another candidate, as would Anthony Swinburne, if he had not died a few months earlier on the Congo. Not a single member of his own family had been invited.

When Stanley was a young journalist, Katie Roberts had suggested a fashionable London wedding, but his response had been scathing. Why spend money, simply so fools could come and gape? Maybe he recalled this on leaving the Abbey, when he and Dorothy were halted in their carriage by a great press of people, whose white faces were pressed up against the windows. The marooned couple were only rescued by a detachment of mounted police after several frightening minutes. No sooner was Henry inside the house in Richmond Terrace, than he staggered to his wife's painting room 'and laid himself down on the sofa, looking very pale and suffering'. And there he remained while Dorothy greeted their guests alone.[40]

Several hours later, the married couple, with Dr Parke and Sali, left Richmond Terrace in an open carriage, bound for Waterloo Station and a honeymoon in the New Forest. They had been lent Melchett Court, a large country house near Romsey, formerly the seat of the 2nd Lord Ashburton, whose family owned Baring's bank. His widow, Louisa, Lady Ashburton – the house's present owner – was a patron of many female artists, one of whom (Harriet Hosmer, an American) was her lover – a fact unknown to Dorothy, whose paintings (and possibly her person) had also aroused Louisa's interest.[41] Though feeling woozy after shots of morphine, Stanley managed to write in his diary on arriving in Hampshire: 'I was too weak to experience anything save a calm delight at the fact that I was married, & that now I shall have a chance to rest.' But the following morning he was visited by Dolly and felt 'rapture & wonder that she was my own from this time forth'. He then committed to the pages of his diary his greatest hope for the future: 'During my long bachelorhood I have often wished that I had but one tiny child to love.'[42] Dorothy echoed this in her diary on the same day, admitting to 'a longing which amounts to anxiety ... the intense hope that our union may produce a child – That his love will find me fruitful.'[43]

In the full satisfaction of being Mrs Henry M. Stanley, Dorothy's first letter written from Melchett was to the supplanted Mrs Sheldon. In it, she reassured her that Stanley was on a milk and arrowroot diet and that 'the inflammation of the stomach seems to have passed'. She described for May the glories of a honeymoon at Melchett: with the old master paintings, the tapestries, and 'the gardens like Eden', and said that the beautiful dressing gown Mrs Sheldon had sent was 'such a comfort to him'. If Mrs Sheldon was upset not to hear from Stanley himself, she gave no indication of it, and soon Dorothy was writing again thanking her for sending so many 'fragrant gifts'.[44] Inevitably, Dorothy did not want May Sheldon to continue her close friendship with her husband, and would soon use her alleged fear of journalists as a reason to see a lot less of her.[45] Upset by the possibility of a rift, Stanley warned his old friend against ever admitting to Dorothy that she was still working as a journalist – though he conceded that this was 'an amusing request', given his own years as a newspaperman.

Reviews of his recently published *In Darkest Africa* began to appear in the week of his wedding, and most were favourable. Even the patrician *Spectator* pronounced: 'The writing is always clear and rises into passages of high literary merit ... it leaves a fresh impression of the task accomplished: the grandeur of that heroic march, with its permanent hunger, its attacks of horrible disease, its seeming endlessness.' The equally demanding *Athenaeum* and the *Edinburgh Review* also praised the book, with only minor cavils, and unquestioningly accepted Stanley's account of the disaster that had overtaken the Rear Column. The shortcomings of Emin Pasha were also taken on trust.[46] The *Saturday Review*'s critic thought Stanley wrong to have appointed the inexperienced Barttelot to a post requiring him to deal with the wily Tippu Tip. Yet all else in this review was praise.

In no other expedition of Mr Stanley's has his strength better appeared. The mere struggle, three times repeated, through forest and famine was a great thing ... But greatest of all was the manner in which, despite his own health, despite the Pasha's vacillation, despite the treachery of the Egyptians ... he brought safely out from one of the least accessible spots in the whole world, by routes almost unknown, the mob of recalcitrant refugees who were committed to his care.

At this very time the negotiators of the latest Anglo-German Agreement were finalizing the boundaries of the new protectorates of Uganda and Zanzibar and adding to Uganda the land to the west of Lake Victoria that, without Stanley's agitation, would have been placed in the German sphere. In deference to his influence, the *Saturday Review* declared that 'it has been Mr Stanley's good fortune and good deed ... to give English statesmen reason to insist, that no other nation shall enter into the fruit of these English labours. And for this he deserves the perpetual thanks of all good Englishmen.'[47]

In the *Whitehall Review*'s notice, Stanley was described as 'the great harbinger of trade'. This reviewer sensed (as did many thinking people at the time) that a moment in history had arrived comparable with the white settlement of America.

It is almost too vast to imagine what it really means, and what those millions of miles of African field and flood and forest are destined to become. But the work has begun in earnest. It will not be long until the steamer shall plough the lake, and railways scour the plain; not long ere savagery will have ceased, and a truer type of humanity have regenerated the old ... The book must always live ... a history which, hundreds of years hence, will tell of the babyhood of Africa.[48]

The *Leeds Mercury* summed up: 'The voice of criticism becomes dumb in the presence of the simple record of the work he has accomplished.' Each week brought more reviews.

For Dorothy, to walk in Melchett's beautiful gardens with a husband who was history's harbinger, and a literary lion to boot, was a heady experience: 'I didn't think it was given to people to be so happy.'[49] Evie Myers came to stay and thought the newlyweds were 'so strange together!! & odd and happy ... Mr Stanley is so wonderfully charming, so boyish and so loving'.[50] As for Stanley himself, he told his friend Alexander Bruce rather stiltedly: 'I shall always regard this stay at Melchett as the most exquisitely enjoyable of any portion of my life ... A beautiful home life could not fail to impress one, who like myself, had no idea of what lay within the portals of domestic felicity.'[51]

As a long-standing bachelor, he really *did* have no idea about domestic relationships, having spent his time exactly as he chose, passing the greater part of it working. When he and Dorothy began to have their first quarrels a couple of months later, they would be about Dolly's refusal to leave him alone for an hour or two every day. 'She will not understand how essential a little quietness is to me.' He needed it psychologically, and to write the numerous lectures that he would be delivering in America that autumn. 'It really is very hard with Dolly's determination to monopolize my time.'[52] Dorothy shocked him by weeping when she could not persuade him to her point of view. 'It struck me that if married life was to be a conflict of this nature, between marital duty, and that which one owes to the public, there will be little happiness in future. The utter hopelessness of compatibility between her ideas and mine, [was] revealed to me so suddenly that I was speechless for a time ...'[53]

Another bone of contention was that Dorothy loved to be the focus of public attention when walking in cities and visiting art galleries – whereas Stanley hated being stared at and craved anonymity. 'I do not consider it wifely to procure these pleasures at the cost of making me feel like a monkey in a cage. I detest these staring crowds, & would prefer my African fever and privations to enduring them ... I get no pleasure in cities in consequence.'[54] One biographer has used the first of these sentences (without quoting the second and third) to argue that Stanley was repelled by his wife's sexual pleasures, which made him feel like a monkey in a cage![55] In fact, as Stanley's health improved, it would be physical attraction that made them more tolerant of one another's foibles.

Dolly wrote later that year, while Stanley was away for a few days: 'I miss you very, very much ... I long for your dear face and your dear voice and all that goes to make up my Bula Matari ... I am very impatiently looking forward to next Wednesday when I shall have you to hug ....'[56] 'How thankful I am to be your wife ... At will I can see your lips and put my forefinger just under the lower lip and look into your eyes and I can hear your laugh when it bursts forth.'[57] Not that she ever learned to resist interrupting him when he was working.

Often, darling, when I just look in on you – it is because I love you so – I want only to look at your dear face and just to stroke the back of your neck ... If you were in the next room [now], do you think it would be possible to resist going in to you and giving you just one kiss?

Dorothy made a joke of her interruptions, calling herself Xantippe, after the shrewish first wife of Socrates, who had spoiled the philosopher's peace of mind.[58]

Stanley certainly loved Dorothy, though she often vexed him: 'Dorothy, sweet Dorothy, how I love that name – Angel of my soul, my thoughts are with you ... I love you loyally & truly and do not care for any person in comparison with my own.'[59] 'My darling wife, I quite realise the depth & truth of your love and I respond to it with heart & soul. To me you are more beautiful & precious each day.'[60]

That Dorothy's possessiveness was going to stop Stanley using his unique abilities to open up Uganda for Mackinnon was even apparent at Melchett, when he refused, in deference to her wishes, to accept any formal connection with the Imperial British East Africa Company.[61] At this early stage, it was not yet a source of unhappiness to him that he might never be able, because of his marriage, to return to Africa. For the present, Henry was preoccupied with his forthcoming American tour, which he owed to Major Pond as compensation for the lecture series abandoned in 1886.

Before leaving for America in the autumn, Stanley and Dolly continued their honeymoon in Belgium, France, Italy and Switzerland, where they met up briefly with Sir Richard and Lady Burton. The elderly traveller and scholar was engaged in writing what he described as 'an anthropology of men and women', which Stanley predicted would be 'cursed with cynicism'. He advised Burton to be charitable about people in his memoirs. 'I don't give a fig for charity,' exploded

Sir Richard. 'If I write at all, I must write truthfully of all I know.' There the discussion stopped, without Stanley pointing out that seeing a little virtue in people could be as truthful as seeing none at all.[62] Already he was writing in a small notebook about incidents from his early life and worrying about how truthful he could bear to be. 'Will you read some more to me of the pocket book,' begged Dorothy, early in 1891. 'That history will be your greatest literary work.'[63]

Still in Switzerland, Stanley, Dorothy and Sali walked along the Engandin Valley onto the magnificent Forno glacier accompanied by the Revd J. E. C. Welldon, the headmaster of Harrow, and Oscar Browning, then teaching undergraduates as a fellow of King's College, Cambridge. Welldon was one of those late Victorian 'muscular Christian' public school heads, who sought, in his own words, to inspire boys 'with faith in the divinely ordered mission of their country' and the desire to 'carry into the world the great principles of truth and religion'. Stanley felt at home with this late Victorian talk of mission, and its Livingstonian coupling of moral virtue with the right to power. As 'citizens of the greatest Empire under heaven', headmaster Welldon told his boys, they owed it to themselves to become 'bright examples of personal morality'.[64] Unknown to Stanley and to the virtuous Welldon, Oscar Browning, who was walking with them, had been clandestinely dismissed as an Eton housemaster for molesting the boys in his charge. This was the sort of detail that would have amused the cynical Richard Burton, had he observed the little party wending its way along the glacier.

The Stanleys returned to England via France and Belgium, where King Leopold welcomed them warmly at the Chalet Royal, Ostend, making a considerable fuss of Dorothy.[65] The king feared that Stanley was more likely, from now on, to work for Mackinnon, than to agree to take charge of pet projects of his own, such as extending the Congo Free State's boundaries to the Nile. But Sir William did not fancy his chances of employing Stanley. Dorothy still seemed dead against it. So, on her return from Belgium, Mackinnon wrote begging her to bring Henry to stay with him.

I have a great deal to tell him about East Africa. I do wish he could have given himself to the work there. I am sure he would have kept us out of many mistakes & our progress would have been threefold or tenfold ... I count so much on his cooperation and advice. The work is a great one & it needs men like Stanley to carry it on.[66]

But there was nothing the shipping magnate could do when Dorothy refused to come to Scotland. Shortly before leaving for his American tour, Stanley wrote to his friend of his 'deep unwavering love' for her, and added: 'Having fulfilled all my engagements, I might think European life too dreary to be endured.'[67]

Three days before Henry was due to leave on his American tour, Major Barttelot's edited diaries and letters were published in book form by his family, and it seemed that Stanley's entire reputation might be too badly damaged to make him useful to anyone.

TWENTY-NINE

Was the Emin Pasha Expedition Piratical?

Two sentences written by Stanley – one in his best-seller *In Darkest Africa*, and one in a private letter inadvertently published in the *Standard* – so enraged the families of Major Barttelot and James Jameson that they published a memoir of each man consisting of diary extracts connected by a commentary full of bitter criticism of Stanley. They also flung themselves into a frenzy of letter-writing to the press. The sentence in Henry's book that so distressed them was: 'My conclusion was that the officers at Yambuya had manifestly been indifferent to the letter of instruction [which Stanley had handed to Barttelot before leaving with the Advance Column], and had forgotten their promises.'[1] And the sentence in the letter published in the *Standard* was that the Rear Column had been 'wrecked by the irresolution of its officers, their neglect of their promises and their indifference to their written orders'.[2] To their relations, this was the equivalent of saying that the dead men had behaved dishonourably.

On finishing his chapter on the Rear Column in *In Darkest Africa*, Stanley had been convinced that he had bent over backwards to be fair. Barttelot had committed shocking crimes such as flogging a man to death, despite fierce remonstrations by his officers and men, and Jameson had made a payment that had led to a young girl being killed and eaten by cannibals. Yet instead of mentioning such horrors, Stanley had written of the major as being 'a generous, frank, and chivalrous English officer'; and had praised the Irish whisky heir for 'his alacrity, capacity, and willingness to work'.[3] Nor did he make an issue of the crime that had upset him most of all, the collective failure of the officers at Yambuya to pay any attention to the diet of the Wangwana and to stop them poisoning themselves by not properly preparing their manioc tubers. His silence on this matter had not been due to generosity alone. He had known that to admit that they had thrown away 150 lives needlessly would have led the public to ask how such callous men had ever been selected to serve under him. So, rather than let them off entirely, Stanley had chosen to pillory them for lesser shortcomings that were not entirely their fault – such as their failure to march. In the course of fewer than twenty pages of his immense two-volume book, Stanley had sown seeds that now threatened to destroy him.

The Barttelot and Jameson families were able to show, with little difficulty, that Stanley had been unreasonable to expect their kinsmen to march out of Yambuya before Tippu Tip had produced his carriers. Since Stanley and his 389 men had sustained very heavy losses in the Ituri Forest on their way to Lake Albert, carrying fewer loads than the Rear Column had been expected to transport, what chance would these inexperienced travellers have had when trying to follow their leader across such deadly terrain? Stanley countered by pointing out that Barttelot should have known, when Tippu Tip broke his first promise to bring men by a given date, that it was most unlikely he would help them at all, and that he and his officers and his 270 men should therefore have shifted for themselves as soon as possible. Many great journeys had been performed with fewer men than they had, including Stanley's Livingstone search mission. Barttelot and his officers had been given 'instructions' that, claimed Stanley, had not had the status of military orders, and could have been treated flexibly in the light of changed circumstances.[4]

Barttelot recorded that on the day Stanley left him at Yambuya forty-eight of his men were sick.[5] His family would make much of the fact that Stanley had taken the fittest men with his Advance Column. According to Stanley, some sick men had indeed been left behind in order to have a period of rest in which to regain their strength – and if they had been fed properly they would have recovered. After all, no whites starved at Yambuya. The moment it had become apparent to Barttelot that more men were falling sick than were recovering, he ought, argued Stanley, to have marched at once in order to save the majority. But instead the major had shuttled back and forth a humiliating six times to plead with Tippu Tip at Stanley Falls.[6] Indeed, there was much sense in what Stanley said. But the question about whether he ought to have split his expedition in the first place, and should ever have left a large part of it in the hands of a young man without experience of Africa, were in the end more damaging than arguments about whether Barttelot should have marched or stayed.

It should be understood that it was not Stanley's book, or his letter, but the publication of *The Life of Edmund Musgrave Barttelot* (edited by his brother Walter) that sent sky-high the public reputation of the whole expedition and its members. The appearance of Jameson's diary soon afterwards merely compounded the damage. Claims made by Walter Barttelot in his introduction that Stanley had abandoned the Rear Column to the tender mercies of a notorious slave trader, whose followers had made it impossible for the officers at Yambuya to buy food from local villagers, were difficult to refute. Articles soon appeared in the press in which it was suggested that Stanley, by placing unstable men like Barttelot and Jameson in command of the Rear Column, 'had caused all these calamities'. Stanley declared that he was being found guilty by association, rather than by actual involvement. But though this was true, it did not help him.

The EPRE committee managed to divert some public attention away from Barttelot's and Jameson's crimes to Tippu Tip as the sole architect of the Rear Column's misfortunes.[7] This was sensible, since if mud was flung at the dead men, some was sure to stick to Stanley. Yet quotations from Barttelot's and Jameson's diaries (taken from their memoirs) soon appeared in the press, making it very plain that John Henry, a mission-educated African, had been flogged to death in very brutal circumstances, and that Burgari Mohammad, whose original crime was nothing worse than stealing some meat, had been shot in even more disturbing circumstances.[8] Worse than that, the diaries proved that Jameson had indeed purchased a child for the price of six handkerchiefs. He claimed she had been stabbed too quickly for him to save her, but most journalists condemned him for failing to make 'the slightest effort to save the child's life after he discovered his mistake'. The girl – it was now established – had only been offered to him because of his eager questions about cannibalism, which had led a chief at Riba Riba to tell him, if he wanted to find out if people were really eaten: 'Give to me a piece of cloth and see.' Having handed over the handkerchiefs, Jameson ought to have been ready to act instantaneously.[9]

In Bonny's opinion, Barttelot had become insane by May 1888, and Troup, though he disliked Stanley for vetoing publication of his book, held Barttelot responsible for all the Rear Column's crimes.[10] But Herbert Ward – who was smarting because Stanley had publicly accused him of mislaying his personal boxes – damaged Henry by claiming that he had observed nothing in Barttelot's behaviour 'derogatory to his position as an officer'.[11] However, Edward Glave, who had served on the Congo with Stanley in the early 1880s and was a friend of Ward, had been told by him, in a private conversation, that he thought Barttelot's treatment of the Wangwana had been 'harsh and inhuman' and that the major had been 'insane'. Glave earned Stanley's lifelong gratitude by swearing an affidavit revealing what Ward really thought. This was published in *The Times* on 15 November 1890, and Ward never issued a contradiction.[12]

Having failed to gain support from his son's colleagues, Barttelot's father declared that Stanley had broken his contract with Tippu and had never expected the Rear Column to leave camp. Instead, its members had been cynically left to rot. Yet this was contradicted by the major's stated belief that he would be leaving the camp soon after the *Stanley* steamship returned to Yambuya. And Stanley himself had written to Mackinnon at this time (June 1887) predicting that Tippu Tip would definitely produce 'a fair number of men' for Barttelot.[13] A day earlier he had noted in his diary: 'I have always regarded Tippu as more high-minded than the average Arab.'[14]

The reason why Stanley has been said to have 'known' that Tippu would break his contract and arrive too late, if at all, was because (as Stanley well knew) there was not enough gunpowder at Yambuya to honour his agreement to provide each of the promised carriers with a personal supply.[15] But since Barttelot had told Tippu Tip, very clearly, on 17 June that the promised gunpowder would be arriving on the *Stanley* from Leopoldville within weeks, why would Tippu have minded a short wait? After all, he was having to collect carriers from 'all the villages around', and would not be able to bring them to Yambuya any earlier than the *Stanley*'s arrival.[16] So what would he lose by waiting until then? Stanley could not reasonably have been expected to send powder and ammunition to Tippu at Stanley Falls before he had produced the carriers. So if Barttelot was right, and Tippu really thought that Stanley had broken faith with him by leaving his powder for the second steamer trip, the slave trader's logic was seriously at fault.[17] Eventually, when Tippu brought 400 carriers almost a year late, Barttelot had no difficulty paying him in gunpowder and honouring the contract. In Barttelot's own words, he paid Tippu: 'An advance in cloth and powder; this I gave him to the value of £836' – a very substantial sum.[18] At no point in Barttelot's negotiations did Tippu Tip mention having been short-changed on gunpowder.[19] That he might later have lied about this seems not to have occurred to Stanley's critics. Sergeant Bonny's description of that cruel and deceitful man, who had brought so much suffering to so wide a region, should act as a corrective. 'His eyes are restless & turn often. When talking he often shifts about on his seat ... Very polite in manner towards you, if you were a trouble to him, he would cut your throat, as he has many thousands before.'[20]

But Stanley could not repair his former reputation, even though he demonstrated in the press that Barttelot had destroyed the Rear Column by neglecting the health of his men, and by alienating his officers. The more convincing the case he made against Barttelot, the more he was blamed for employing him. Stanley also made a serious mistake in suggesting in New York that Barttelot had been killed rather than murdered, since this seemed to imply that the man who had shot him had thought the British officer's relationship with his wife and other African women had been improper. In fact the most that Stanley had said was that Barttelot had kicked the woman to the ground and had threatened her with his revolver, thus provoking Sanga, the husband to shoot him. The public's desire not to believe that British gentlemen could behave as Barttelot and Jameson had done was very powerful. Only if they could be excused could the slur on the nation be lifted. Yet when Bonny began speaking to journalists in November 1890, it became clear that Barttelot had been guilty of many acts of violence in addition to 'judicial' killings and fatal floggings. After Bonny's statements, there was no hope that the officers could be exonerated.[21] It would be believed that the 'American' Stanley had unnecessarily dragged the British nation through the mud.

The whole expedition became tainted by its association with the misdeeds of those two men – though, mercifully for Stanley, their possession of sex slaves at Yambuya had not emerged. Dr Parke blamed the public scandal on the major's father, Sir William Barttelot, Bart. 'He played the fool by publishing his book ... I will certainly speak up for Stanley.'[22] Colonel Grant also felt that Stanley had got the better of his adversaries, 'and quite right too ... they [the Barttelots] look upon natives as only fit to be kicked and shot'.[23]

411

The public row about the Rear Column went far beyond attempts to find out who was most to blame for the loss of life. For a time, it led many people to condemn exploration per se. Because of the scandal, articles appeared for the first time in newspapers and periodicals questioning whether it was possible, in present circumstances, to mount *any* African expeditions that would be conducted in a humane fashion. The best article on this theme appeared in the *Forum* in February 1891, and was entitled: 'Was the Emin Pasha Expedition Piratical?' The writer began with a genuine tribute:

The expedition for the rescue of Emin Pasha must always remain, so far as Mr Stanley is concerned, one of the greatest feats of courage and endurance in the annals of adventure ... Mr Stanley crossed Africa on foot at the head of a column of unwilling, uncivilized followers, for whom he had to supply all the necessary food and clothing and arms and ammunition and health ... Whether in the presence of pestilence, or famine, or savage enemies, he had to maintain his *sang froid* many a time within what seemed a hair's breadth of ruin.

Then the author described Stanley's predicament when he arrived near Lake Albert, and the local tribes refused to negotiate or give him passage, but instead attacked him, despite his efforts to make peace. Facing death and disaster, what else could he have done but kill some of them to stop the mass coming close enough to overwhelm his column with their vastly superior numbers? 'There was no other mode of self-preservation,' conceded the article's author. Indeed all exploring expeditions had to employ 'soldiers' to protect the vital trade goods needed to purchase food, and to defend the porters carrying the bulky equivalent of money. And if carriers or soldiers deserted in significant numbers, with their loads or their rifles, as had happened to Stanley, the whole expedition was placed in mortal danger. 'He had to flog or hang his own men to maintain discipline,' agreed the *Forum*'s journalist. 'He had to shoot ... in order to protect himself against treachery and to supply himself with provisions.'

And then the author put his finger on the central, insoluble problem.

From whom did he get authority to begin the series of military operations that ended in depositing Emin Pasha at Zanzibar? Under whose orders did he enlist troops and exercise among Africans the power of a general in the field? ... Neither the British nor the Egyptian government would pay to send Stanley to do what the British public wanted – rescue Emin Pasha. But a committee and the loose loan of Stanley by the King of the Belgians could not confer authority ... Every lawful military enterprise has a government behind it, to which its officers are accountable, to which they are obliged to make careful reports ... No judicial machinery now exists for the investigation of the charges which Mr Stanley brings against his officers of the rear-guard.

The support of a philanthropic committee was not nearly good enough, argued the article's author. Lacking government sanction and authority, the expedition had indeed been piratical.[24]

The Aborigines' Protection Society felt that the expedition had actually been mounted 'with the approval of Her Majesty's ministers, and that half its expenses were provided under instructions tantamount to commands from our Foreign Office to the Egyptian authorities'. In the Society's eyes, this made the British government as guilty as Stanley. When Henry heard that it had been proposed, at a meeting of the Aborigines' Protection Society in January 1891, that the Society should initiate criminal proceedings against him under the Slave Trading Acts or under acts relating to murder or manslaughter, he told the Society's secretary that if members were to raise the money he would begin libel proceedings against the Barttelots and certain newspapers. 'That is the best way to get at the truth,' he declared.[25] The Society backed off. And when their secretary, H. R. Fox Bourne, reviewed Dr Parke's book, he stated:

The Society is not condemning Mr Stanley or his subordinates so much, but the mounting of an expedition with aims and methods which almost necessitated the cruelties and slaughters that were incident to it ... It seems better to remain in arm-chairs and pass resolutions than wantonly to embark on perilous enterprises which can only be carried out by means that degrade Englishmen ...

The Society's members were also shocked that many of Stanley's Wangwana on this expedition had been slaves – though he had never intended this, having trusted the firm of Smith, Mackenzie & Co. to recruit free men.[26]

Another brickbat flung at Stanley and his humanitarian backers was the claim that, when men like Mackinnon were involved in African business enterprises, their philanthropic aims merely masked their greed. The idea that profits could be guaranteed to anyone running an African chartered company in the late nineteenth century began early, and was mistaken from the start. Areas lacking gold, diamonds or rubber – and that was most of Africa – were never going to create instant fortunes for anyone. But this did not stop critics of imperialism condemning Stanley for confusing civilization with 'the extension of a shoddy commercialism' under the barrels of 'the Martini-Henry rifle and the Gatling gun'. Such critics seemed unaware that men like Stanley and Mackinnon sincerely believed that unless the slave traders were driven out by European traders and settlers, the bloodshed would go on indefinitely.[27]

Sadly, the Rear Column debacle cast a shadow over Stanley's relations with Sir William. In the EPRE committee's report, regret was expressed that 'Mr Stanley should have been obliged, at a most important stage in the expedition, to separate himself from a considerable portion of his force, and most valuable part of his relief stores'. It was also stated that if Barttelot had possessed 'Mr Stanley's experience, resources, and influence ... the plan [of splitting the expedition in two] would have been the best that could have been adopted' – the implication being that because Barttelot had possessed no such qualities, the plan had not been the best possible. Barttelot's right to have stayed at Yambuya was also upheld, on account of Stanley's warnings to him about the importance of the stores.[28] But worst of all, in Stanley's eyes, was the committee's failure to own up to the crimes of the officers of the Rear Column. In response to Barttelot's book, he himself had gone public in naming the officers' offences. So, according to Stanley, Mackinnon had, by failing to support his expedition leader's version of events in his report, published 'a condemnation of those who had lived, and a defence of those who died'.[29]

Perhaps the worst harm done to Stanley personally by the Rear Column scandal was the way in which it reminded newspaper editors of all the old charges of brutality made against him in the years following his attack on Bumbireh. In 1878 the editor of the *Pall Mall Gazette* had written: 'Exploration under these conditions is in fact exploration plus buccaneering, and ... the cause of civilization is not a gainer thereby but a loser.'[30] Once again, as in 1878, Stanley was held up as 'the dark shadow to throw up the brightness of Livingstone's fame'. The stage was now set, a few years hence, for the Congo 'red rubber' slaughter to complete the destruction of Stanley's reputation with yet more guilt by association. Stanley – the man who had done his utmost to make fair treaties with the chiefs on the Congo – was about to be launched on history's tide as a prototype for Kurtz in *Heart of Darkness*, and a prime begetter of the new imperialism.

THIRTY

Africa or a Child

Gertrude Tennant had made it clear to Stanley, when he asked for her daughter's hand, that she would expect Dolly to go on living at Richmond Terrace with her. Stanley had raised no difficulties and agreed to move in too. After a lifetime of hotel rooms and service flats, he felt he had little to lose, and did not renew the lease on his Kensington flat.[1]

Gertrude was an entertaining but manipulative woman, who charmed her son-in-law but subjected Dolly to some ferocious emotional blackmail.[2] A journalist on the Chicago *Daily News* amusingly deduced what might have been said when Henry asked Gertrude to consent to his marrying Dolly: 'She is yours, and so am I!'[3] Being a greenhorn on the subject of maternal affection, Stanley mistook Gertrude's possessiveness for disinterested love. So he allowed Gertrude to come to America with Dolly and himself, and even let her bring her loquacious cousin, Charles Hamilton Aidé, a sixty-four-year-old playwright and novelist, described by Henry James as a 'foolish, faded, fribble [*sic*]'.[4]

A large party came on Stanley's American tour, with Jephson and Sali included, as well as Major Pond, Henry's lecture agent, and Pond's wife and her sister. Before Stanley returned to England from Africa, Pond had written anguished letters to Mrs Sheldon, also a client, about how to secure her heroic friend for a replacement tour.[5] The impresario need not have worried. When, at last, he screwed up his courage and presented himself at Stanley's flat, the explorer welcomed him warmly. The hard-bitten agent's eyes filled with tears to see the change in him. 'There was Stanley: not the Stanley of three and a half years ago. His hair was now white. We grasped each other by the hand, and it was some time before Stanley said: "It's all right, major. I am glad to see you."' The lectures were not mentioned, and Pond had almost resigned himself to the idea that Stanley might never have the strength to give them, when a few days later he received a telegram: ON 10 OCTOBER I TAKE A DEGREE AT CAMBRIDGE. THEN I OWE YOU EIGHTY-NINE LECTURES.[6] A special Pullman car, named 'Henry M. Stanley' was obtained by Pond for the party. It contained a kitchen, a resident chef, a dining car, a dormitory, a drawing room with piano, three state-bedrooms and, rather stingily, one bathroom. Starting on 7 November 1890 in New York, Stanley gave 110 talks, earning a total of £12,000 – about £400,000 in today's money. Pond noticed that Henry was happiest in the company of children and journalists, from whom he expected no special treatment.[7] Though submitting to Pond's extraordinarily arduous schedule, he found a mere seven days' rest per month – all spent travelling – terribly wearing.

The most disconcerting part of the tour for Stanley was his arrival with his affluent wife at New Orleans, where he had disembarked three decades earlier literally without a cent. On 29 March he wrote in his diary: 'Drove to ... St Charles Hotel. Took walk in afternoon with Dolly to Tchoupitoulas St then to Levee. Gazed across the full river ...'[8] James Speake's grocery store, where he had worked, was in Tchoupitoulas Street. Three and a half months before his arrival with Dolly in New Orleans, a piece had appeared in the best-known local paper, the *Daily Picayune*, linking, for the first time, the rather vaguely described Mr Henry Stanley of New Orleans (long claimed by the explorer as his adoptive father) with an actual and identifiable Henry Stanley, who had lived and worked in the city as a cotton broker. The *Picayune*'s journalist had taken, as his basis for John Rowland's adoption, the account printed in John Hotten's book and had named, as his adopter, Henry Hope Stanley, the only Henry Stanley listed as a cotton broker in the trade directories for the late 1850s and early 1860s. Faced with this actual man and his family, Stanley would never confirm, verbally or in print, that Henry Hope was indeed *his* Henry Stanley. He knew from the *Daily Picayune* that Henry Hope was dead, but had to assume that some of his relatives would still be alive.[9] So he refused to give interviews in New Orleans, or to talk to anyone whom he had known thirty years earlier. Such people would have been able to recall that he had still been calling himself Rowlands, or Rollins, until the day he actually left New Orleans.[10]

Shortly after the special Pullman car steamed out of New Orleans in March 1891, an old acquaintance gave an interview to another local paper, the *Daily States*, providing information proving beyond doubt that she had known John Rowlands in the 1860s. She said she had recently called at the St Charles Hotel, and had been left waiting for two hours without being permitted to see Mr Stanley.[11] It must have distressed Henry to feel compelled to hide in his room and humiliate this woman. But he could not endure the possibility that his invented adoption – which was currently being presented as a fact in several new biographies – might be exposed as a lie. His right to use the very name he now shared with his wife seemed to depend upon his ability to protect the thirty-year-old fiction. This visit to New Orleans convinced him that, to make possible the autobiography he wanted to write, he would need to return and do enough research to find a suitable Stanley family to claim as his adopters. Ideally, there should be no living family members around to challenge his 'recollections'.

Dolly and Henry returned to England on 23 April 1891, and immediately found themselves seriously at loggerheads over whether he should return to Africa. In early March 1891, Alexander Bruce – Agnes Livingstone's husband and one of Mackinnon's directors – had told Stanley that he would shortly be recommending the Board of the Imperial British East Africa Company to offer him the job of Chief Administrator, if he now felt ready to accept the post.[12] Stanley replied confidently that he was ready: 'I can keep the whole of East Africa in order from Uganda to the sea.' His experience on the Congo, he went on, made him the ideal man for the job. All that was needed was that the directors tell him his duties without delay.[13] When Mackinnon heard that Stanley would after all work for him, he was delighted and wrote to Bruce about 'the extreme desirability of having him [Stanley] for East Africa'.[14]

On 27 April, Bruce told Stanley: 'I have heard from Mackinnon, who says if you can go to East Africa, he is prepared to give you a perfectly free hand on the lines laid down in your letter to me.'[15] This, then, was the great moment for which Stanley had waited. Against all odds, the offer he had rejected in the previous October had been repeated at a more propitious time. But when he tried to persuade Dorothy, he found her as opposed as she had been six months earlier. Everyone in the family was aware of how heartbroken she felt. Yet not everyone thought her right to try to force her husband to refuse. Frederick Myers told his wife, Evie, that though he 'deeply sympathized with Dolly ... There would not really have been happiness for Stanley in simply being fattened up in RT [Richmond Terrace]. Let him have a few more years of work & duty & fame!'[16] But now that the crisis had come, Dolly was determined not to give in. On 12 June, she asked Stanley what answer he had given Sir William, and told him that the company's managing director, George Mackenzie, had come, uninvited, to Richmond Terrace in his absence, asking where he was: 'They all make me shiver [George Mackenzie and Sir William Mackinnon]; they are like the harpies described in Virgil, who wheel about over the sea and claw the unhappy sailor to his doom ... but never mind I <u>have</u> you – you are mine.'[17]

Just at this time, King Leopold declared, with lamentable timing, that *he* wanted Stanley to go back to Africa. Henry feared that because of the annual retainer paid to him he might have to serve eighteen months on the Congo to escape Leopold's clutches before being able to work for Mackinnon, as he wished to do. Dorothy thought the Congo a worse threat even than East Africa. 'Africa <u>haunts</u> me,' she lamented:

it is so easy for others to advise and spur you on ... Can I say 'go' when 20 days away from you seems intolerably long? ... Sometimes I think that you have too much unused energy in you yet – that Africa might appease your spirit – Oh God knows, I cannot say – it seems so terrible to say any word like 'go', when I shall want to unsay it tomorrow.[18]

In America, Dolly had come to the conclusion that, though Henry loved her, he was still utterly 'self-sufficient' and that she was 'not necessary to him'. So despite her initial success in thwarting Mackinnon, she believed she would remain vulnerable unless she could conceive.

Oh if only the sweet solution of a child might come – then he would stay and feel the tie, but without a child I am the incomplete wife for him. He would not want anything if he had a child. That would completely & fully satisfy him ... He longs, longs for a child ....[But if he returned to Africa] how remote, how lessened our chances of a child [would be]...[19]

Only a week after returning to England, Stanley began two months of lecturing in Britain – which he had been coerced into by a lecture agent with whom he was in dispute. Dorothy could see looming, at the end of this tour, an Australian lecture series, which was already organized and threatened to keep them apart for six months. If Stanley decided to leave for Africa after that, how would they ever produce the child they both longed for? At thirty-six, she might not have many years of fertility left.[20] Because she missed Henry, and wanted to be impregnated, Dolly could not 'resist rushing off to him for a day or so every week' during his tour. 'In this way I joined him at Hull ... Sheffield & Bradford.' Meanwhile the London season had started, and soon after a grand Foreign Office party, Dorothy felt herself on the verge of a breakdown. 'After so much travelling I needed complete rest,' she wrote in her diary.[21] She was also coping with the terror that if she could not become pregnant, Stanley would inevitably return to Africa.

During the first week of May she had a minor gynaecological operation, and was told that it had gone successfully.[22] Later in May, she again consulted her gynaecologist, Dr William Littleton Webber, who advised her to stay for the whole of June in a clinic at Kissingen, Bavaria, where, through a regime of relaxation, gentle exercise, and avoidance of anxiety, she would make it more likely that her 'Great Expectation and deep desire' (as she called it) would come to pass. It was already planned that Stanley should join her in Switzerland in July. She wrote telling him about her plan, and how the doctor believed their efforts to have a child would be crowned with success. From Glasgow, where he was lecturing, Henry wrote sensibly urging her not to pin all her hopes for future happiness on this one objective: 'I quite realise the depth & truth of your love and I respond to it with heart & soul ... But we are not always able to govern ourselves, or the circumstances which surround us. We can only strive & hope, and love on, even if every effort is thwarted.'[23] At intervals while she was at Kissingen, Stanley wrote imploring her to abide by Webber's advice and above all to stop worrying. Yet this was difficult, since the separation was alarming her lest he soon stop missing her. 'Oh, my dearest,' he replied, 'there is no fear, no shadow of a possibility of lessening of love ... It is hard to be separated ... but we must abide by the physician's advice.'[24]

Henry was torn in opposing directions by his desire to go back to Africa, and his longing for a child. If he accepted Mackinnon's offer, it might mean he would never get Dorothy pregnant. He therefore hoped to manage it in Switzerland, where she would be joining him for three weeks after leaving Kissingen. Stanley arrived on 9 July at the mountain village of Mürren with its spectacular views across the valley to the rock faces of the snow-covered Eiger and Jungfrau. Although he was delighted to be with Dolly again, Africa had not left his thoughts. Indeed, he had just been staying with Mackinnon in Scotland discussing his return there.[25] Perhaps after he impregnated Dorothy, she would not mind him going to Africa for a year, say. A lot would depend upon their lovemaking during this brief holiday. The resort was at a higher altitude than he liked, and almost at once he caught a chill, which was not a good start for a man with health problems. But the Kissingen rest cure appeared to have done wonders for his wife. He wrote happily in his diary that 'the real honeymoon, so long deferred through illness & lecture tours, has come'.[26] In the day they walked amidst majestic scenery, and in the evening went early to bed.

After a few days, they were joined by Dolly's sister, Evie, and her eldest son, nine-year-old Leo, with whom Stanley enjoyed snowballing and whom he taught how to throw spears.[27] Evie was intrigued by Stanley, viewing him with a critical and supercilious eye. 'He is quaint and so strange ... such a mixture of force & weakness, consistency and inconsistency, manliness & childishness ... He has been reading "The Tragic Muse"... Oh, such high flown trash ... and can't read Henry James's clever story, calls it words!' When Evie defended James, 'there was a look of disgust on his [Stanley's] face, "Oh! that is your narrow Cambridge want of sentiment & feeling."' 'He won't even listen,' complained Evie; 'perhaps this doggedness makes him achieve things.'[28] In fact Stanley often read intellectually challenging books, and had recently enjoyed a life of Macaulay, and had written to Dolly a withering criticism of Sir Alfred Lyall's 'colourless' *Warren Hastings*.[29] Fred Myers, Evie's intellectual husband, admired Henry, and hoped Leo would 'learn much from him ... & get a notion of a hero'.[30] However, it surprised Fred when Stanley advised Evie against sending Leo to a tough boarding school. 'The happy days of childhood are flying fast,' warned Henry, '& the holidays are so brief & few, and home pictures are so dear when we grow up.'[31]

A reporter – Aubrey Stanhope of the *New York Herald* – appeared one day in Mürren, and came to the Grand Hotel des Alpes, asking for Mr and Mrs Stanley. Once summoned to the couple's sitting room, he announced that he was investigating rumours that the Stanleys had been living apart. Henry refused to discuss his private life, but wrote out a statement denying that there had ever been a separation. He ended: 'Our life is one of ever increasing, pure & unalloyed happiness.' Dolly penned a statement attacking 'this shameful fabrication'.[32] This example of how hard it was for them to escape attention was not the couple's only misfortune in Switzerland.

An abscess swelled up in Dolly's mouth, distorting her whole face, and becoming so painful that she had to be given morphine injections.[33] Then, on an ill-starred morning, a light-hearted Stanley chased after his recently recovered wife, and 'affected to wrestle' with her.[34] Evie was watching them 'frolicking' when, to her dismay, Stanley 'slipped & fell heavily, rolling backwards with Dolly on him – he groaning and crying out ... Our terror was lest his spine was injured.' While Dolly cradled her husband's head in her lap, Evie and Leo ran for help.[35] Dr Hugh Playfair of King's College, London, who happened to be holidaying in Mürren, appeared with Evie several hours later and diagnosed a break in the left fibula just above the dislocated ankle. Later that day, when Henry had been carried back to the hotel, Playfair and another English doctor reset the leg and strapped it to a board.[36] Stanley wrote sadly to his friend Alexander Bruce: 'I might have avoided the accident had I remembered I was "stern faced, sombre tempered Stanley"... but in a moment of true joy & innocent delight, I fell and broke my leg and ruptured the ligaments of the ankle. The moral of this is do not give way to friskiness.'[37]

Dolly was mortified to have fallen across Stanley's leg, causing the break. It seemed absurd that a man who had not broken as much as a finger in all his years in Africa should have been injured by a tumble in a quiet Alpine meadow. Fearing that the accident would be thought comical and undignified, Dolly wrote to May Sheldon – confident that she would sell her improved version of the story to plenty of newspapers – telling her that Stanley had swung round and slipped when teaching Leo how to throw spears 'like a native'. This invention would appear in many newspapers, and even in several biographies.[38]

For Henry and Dorothy, the incident did more than spoil their holiday. It made it even harder for him to accept Mackinnon's offer, since he could not guarantee a return to full mobility. It also set back his and Dolly's hopes of starting a baby. With his leg encased in plaster, lovemaking – though not impossible – was hampered for weeks, and Henry could not expect to be mobile much before his departure for Australia. Dolly now persuaded him that whatever he might decide to do about Africa in 1892, 'we should go together to Australia ... those four months may give us our Heart's Desire – and I shall be with you. That is the great, the principle [*sic*] thing'.[39]

But if no child was conceived, and Stanley still yearned for Africa, what then?

THIRTY-ONE

An End to 'Noble Objects'

During Stanley's Antipodean tour, his ship was steaming towards Wellington, New Zealand, when he chanced to meet his old friend William Webb of Newstead Abbey in the smoking room. Webb was travelling with two of his still unmarried daughters, Geraldine and Ethel – the first of whom Stanley had once hoped might be interested in him. He had not seen any of the Webbs since the mid-1880s, and though he knew that Emilia had died in 1889, he had not realized until now that the family had also lost a daughter through illness and their eldest son by his own hand. Years ago Henry had thought the Webbs 'one of the happiest [families] in a land full of happy hours'. Meeting them at this low point was a salutary reminder of the vulnerability of everyone and the shortness of life.[1] At Henry's age, he could expect few second chances. If he returned to Africa it would have to be soon. If not, what else might he do while getting older, with no child to love?

He was still keen to write his autobiography. But a chance meeting in Australia with the widow and children of David Owen, one of his first cousins, was a straw in the wind telling him just how hard it was going to be to be honest about his life. Because he had been pursued by journalists during this tour, he felt unable to entertain his relatives openly, or even to admit who they were. He felt ashamed of himself, but still could not greet them properly, or even share his memories of working on their family's farm. 'Poor cousins,' wrote Stanley in his diary. 'I stretch my hands to you all the same, and were we anywhere beyond reach of newspapers my heart would go out to you with all affection.'[2]

In Australia, Dolly confessed to Henry her keen ambition for him to become a Liberal-Unionist MP. Dolly's principal motive was transparent. 'At the back of my mind was the haunting fear of his returning to the Congo. I thought that, once in Parliament, he would be safely anchored.' (In the preceding October, King Leopold had mentioned that he might have 'a big task' for Henry in Africa after he returned from Australia. And although Stanley had not taken this very seriously, Dorothy had been acutely worried.) Knowing that he hated dining out and was very reluctant to join her circle, she also hoped that once in the Commons he would meet influential men and develop a social life of his own.[3] Though non-committal, Henry himself was not entirely discouraging. At this moment, his prospects struck him as unpromising. His accident the previous summer had stopped him clinching a firm agreement with Mackinnon involving a date for his return to Africa, and since then the tycoon had not renewed the offer. So on 25 April 1892, a week after returning to England, Dorothy felt safe to ask Alexander Bruce to name some parliamentary seats that 'Stanley could fight with some chance of winning'.[4]

For many people whose spouses (of either sex) are determined to have their way, and then nag at them in order to achieve it, the temptation to give in for a quiet life can be overwhelming. Stanley certainly decided at an early stage to offer no active opposition.[5] His lifelong insecurity was partly responsible. After all, Dorothy was the first woman with whom he had had a lasting relationship, and the thought of going against her wishes, on a matter that was very important to her, alarmed him. Though sometimes exasperated by Dolly, his love for her continued. 'My darling, I kiss your hands, your lips, your hair – & wish you Heaven's blessings in abundance,'[6] he wrote at this time. Even so, he refused to take active steps to begin a political career. Knowing this, Dorothy took charge of the now urgent task of reclaiming her husband's British nationality. It frightened her that he might have been abroad too long in the last decade to qualify for naturalization; so, leaving nothing to chance, she went to plead with Mr Henry Matthews, the home secretary. She had – as she put it – 'dressed very becomingly', and was soon rewarded with encouraging words.[7] Dolly rapidly established that Stanley had spent five years and twenty weeks in Britain during the last twenty years, which was deemed sufficient by Mr Matthews. Everything went through at breakneck speed, and Henry took the oath of allegiance on 20 May, receiving his certificate of readmission on the last day of the month.[8] As a British citizen, he could now become a parliamentary candidate.

One day in early June, Dolly called at Liberal Unionist headquarters and learned that the sitting MP for North Lambeth, Sir Charles Fraser, had just resigned. Though time was short, she managed to get Stanley adopted as the Liberal Unionist candidate several weeks before polling day. Since the area was a rough one, despite being close to Westminster, Dolly should have warned Henry to expect some ferocious heckling from the supporters of the Radical candidate, Alderman Francis Coldwells. But she did not, and though Stanley emphasized in his printed address to the electors that his 'strongest sympathies were with the working classes',[9] the hostility at his first big public meeting came as a great shock. The barracking was so loud that he was reduced to silence and could only glare at his tormentors. Dolly burst into tears, rose to her feet and then sank back into her seat. Her distress briefly calmed the shouters, but after she cried out, 'When all of you are dead, the name of Stanley will live,' derisive laughter filled the hall.[10] Nevertheless, Dolly spoke at several meetings after this.[11] Stanley eventually lost the election by the narrowest of margins – 130 votes – not a bad result for a man who had refused to canvass. Thomas Guthrie, a young Liberal Unionist, returned to Richmond Terrace with Stanley in a hansom cab after hearing the result declared, and said later that Stanley had not cared at all.[12]

For someone of Stanley's temperament, politics could only be uncongenial. Indispensable to all politicians is the ability to brush off insults and not take them personally, so that yesterday's enemy can become tomorrow's friend, and no falling out need be final. For a man of Stanley's sensitivities, tactical friendships, and all forms of dissembling, were impossible. Being used to exercise command rather than negotiate alliances, he lacked the easy manner and clubbable smiles with which politicians mask naked ambition. Yet though Dorothy was intelligent, her need to stop her husband returning to Africa, and her own passion for politics, drove her to urge him to stand a second time, against all common sense. During the period of their first courtship, Dorothy had admitted that she found politics 'dangerously fascinating', and had said 'if I were a man I would throw myself into the arena'.[13] Perhaps her father's less than dazzling period as an MP accounted for her longing to associate herself with a more successful career. Whatever the cause – and though Stanley made it very clear that he did not want to stand again at the next election – she put him under such immense pressure that he finally conceded. Several times during the brief 1892 campaign it had enraged Dolly that Henry had done so little to win the electors' hearts.[14] Yet to ask strangers to like and vote for him was more than he could ever do. Rejection would only be tolerable if he could tell himself he had not really tried. Though he never explained this to Dorothy, he agreed to stand again only on certain conditions. He would never visit 'house to house', and would only speak at formal meetings. 'Never will I degrade myself by asking a man for his vote.'[15]

If the next general election had been called swiftly, Henry's obligation to contest the seat would not have weighed on him so heavily. But an election would not be called until 1895. Worse than that – with the life of the Liberal ministry depending on the fragile co-operation of the divided Irish nationalists – a dissolution seemed imminent many times, obliging Stanley to make speeches in readiness, time and again. 'If I am defeated,' he told Dorothy, 'I hope it will be an overwhelming majority that will forever prove to you my incapacity as a candidate.' Even before a second campaign was in sight, Stanley was complaining to her about 'the cesspool of slander & calumny' surrounding the House of Commons like 'a moat'. He dreaded being heckled in the street, and wrote reproachfully: 'I wonder that you have cared to put anyone you profess to respect at such a disadvantage ... I have still a large capacity for the quieter enjoyments, but it seems that until I am past enjoying anything, my life is to be wasted in struggle.'[16]

The 1892 election had come at a difficult time in the Stanleys' marriage. They possessed dissimilar temperaments and had very different interests and needs. So to keep Henry hanging about in London was sure to cause disharmony. His main desire – failing a return to Africa – was to have plenty of time to himself and 'to avoid nonsensical society duties'.[17] 'Just because a person sends a polite invitation to dinner, or tea, or to a reception, must one,' he groaned, 'cut out that period of existence from this short life?'[18] When not relaxing and walking, he told Dolly, they should be able to read, think or work, whenever they wished. To make his point, he divided humanity into bees and butterflies – he being a bee that liked to pass time purposefully, rather than frittering it as a social butterfly. 'I might stand it [London society] for a week, perhaps a month, but the utter waste of life would soon begin to present itself as ... an accusing phantom of lost days & weeks.'[19]

Dorothy countered reasonably enough that entertaining friends was an essential part of 'home life [which] you have never experienced ... I maintain that to shut yourself up – a recluse ... will be bad for you morally and mentally.' Dolly enjoyed the company of intellectuals and reformers like Herbert Spencer, William Lecky, Thomas Huxley, William Gladstone and John Morley, 'who can hardly be called butterflies'. 'I want to know the best, to learn from them.' So why should he prefer 'dark sepulchral retirement', she demanded.[20] If Henry and Dolly had been spending as much time in the country as in London, he would have felt happier. His desire to be quiet and solitary led Dorothy to tell him that his commander's 'life of solitude and action' had never obliged him 'to "trim" with – or make allowances for people'. 'Family life,' she insisted, 'is different.'[21]

When they had rows, Dolly tended to shout and lose control whereas Stanley sank into himself, presenting a façade so cold that his wife became ever shriller. Because of his many childhood rejections, Henry found it hard to endure criticism, especially when several people were present. Yet when Dolly lost her temper she could 'scold him like a schoolboy', whoever might hear.[22] It also upset him that she often interrupted him at dinner parties and spoke without thinking.[23] 'Dolly opens her rosebud and out pours her thoughts & views & opinions, while I must be silent ... My dear, let us hope ... that these jars may be only temporary.'[24]

As 1892 progressed, Stanley found himself tied into a maddening political process, forcing him to be pleasant to numerous people he would otherwise have avoided. Nor had the longed-for child been conceived, either in Australia or in England, and with every passing month a pregnancy seemed less likely. In letters to one another, Dorothy and Stanley called this hoped-for child 'the General'. 'Possibly, God in his mercy will send the General,' Dolly had written shortly before Henry broke his leg.[25] Then Uganda burst into the news again, late in 1892, thoroughly unsettling Henry.

In July a year earlier, Sir William Mackinnon had received a devastating report from Uganda, written by an unknown army officer whom the company had sent out in 1890. Although Captain Frederick Lugard had thwarted the Germans in Uganda, and his tiny force had crushed a coup mounted by supporters of French missionaries, the young officer had insisted that unless Mackinnon financed a garrison strong enough to keep out the dangerous Kabarega, and the King of Ankole, Uganda would be lost. Already facing vast additional expenditure, Mackinnon suffered another blow: Lord Salisbury, the prime minister, who had promised government funding for the East African railway, changed his mind. Stanley wrote sadly: 'Africa contains sufficient germs of good to resist the oppression [of the slave trade] ... but it cannot be done without the railway.'[26]

The Ugandan crisis peaked in October 1892, when Stanley joined forces with the recently returned Captain Lugard in a 'Save Uganda' campaign got up by Mackinnon.[27] Lugard and Stanley spoke in numerous cities, claiming that a great human disaster would follow if the government (now led by Mr Gladstone) decided not to tide over the Imperial British East Africa Company and help finance the railway. Their prophecy of a bloodbath if the company were to leave Uganda attracted such wide coverage in the press that Gladstone and his cabinet were forced to relive the nightmare of being held responsible for Gordon's death. They remembered all too clearly Bishop Hannington's grisly murder in Uganda, and the torture and execution of many Christian converts. What if it were true, as Lugard claimed, that the bankruptcy of Mackinnon's company would lead the banished Muslims to return? Would they then massacre the missionaries and their supporters, as Lugard was predicting?[28] It must have been galling for Stanley when Captain Lugard – who had killed twenty times more Africans than Stanley had shot on Bumbireh – was hailed everywhere as an English knight errant: the chivalrous rescuer of British missionaries from a tyrannical African despot. But, like the general public, Stanley was also won over by Lugard's haggard good looks and crumpled khaki jacket.[29]

Within weeks, rapturous support for Lugard in the press brought Gladstone's cabinet to the point of collapse, enabling the imperialist Rosebery to bring the prime minister and his Chancellor of the Exchequer, Sir William Harcourt, to their knees over Uganda. Gladstone had no alternative but to extend a financial lifeline to Mackinnon and to accept that Uganda would become a British colony. This was the only way he could win for his administration sufficient time to achieve Home Rule for Ireland. From now on it would be Britain's policy, even under a Liberal government, to take over Uganda, secure the Nile sources, recapture the Sudan, keep out the French and Germans, and rule Egypt permanently. Stanley was proud to reflect that without his 1876 appeal for missionaries to go to Buganda, and without his long partnership with Mackinnon, African colonial history would have been very different. Few people can claim that events they have set in train have helped transform a great political party and changed their nation's intentions towards a whole continent, but from 1892 the workhouse boy could do just that, as could the self-made shipping tycoon. But Lord Rosebery's victory within Gladstone's cabinet brought an agonizing decision for Stanley personally.

In December 1892, Sir William surprised and moved Henry by offering him the Chief Administrator's post one last time, having hinted in late November that he might do so. At first Stanley had kept this possibility from Dorothy, but when the offer came, he had no choice but to discuss it with her. Having learned nothing from his unhappiness during the recent election, she insisted that he refuse Sir William's offer, on the preposterous grounds that because the Liberal cabinet was split on Uganda, a general election might be imminent. It would therefore be dishonourable, she told him, to let down the North Lambeth Unionists. Furthermore, he had given *her* his word that he would stand again. Most reluctantly, Stanley wrote letters of refusal to his honorary father, Sir William Mackinnon and to his confidant, Alexander Bruce, telling them, with a brusqueness that could not hide his raw emotion: 'I cannot go to East Africa, for the reason that I feel myself pledged to N. Lambeth.' To Bruce he added a more truthful postscript: 'I am looking for a defeat, and if it will only be crushing enough, it will relieve me from Mrs Stanley's pressure and desire to get me into Parliament.'[30] If the election could only come quickly enough, he might still be able to return to Africa – or so he thought. But Gladstone soldiered on, against all odds, until 1894, and after that Lord Rosebery clung to power for fifteen more precarious months. Writing to Alexander Bruce, Dorothy acknowledged that 'Stanley longs for work' and she promised 'not to be an obstacle', but when she wrote about what was 'owed' to the North Lambeth Liberal Unionist supporters, it became obvious that she would never let her husband go.[31]

Though Stanley permitted Dorothy to deny him his very last chance to redeem himself in Africa after all the mud-slinging over the Rear Column, he felt bitterly angry with her. There would now be no crowning final chapter to his African career. On Christmas Eve – the day after he had written his refusals to Bruce and Mackinnon – he felt desperate enough to leave England over the holiday season, for Pau, a small town in the foothills of the Pyrenees on the French side, taking his valet to look after him. W. J. Hawkes had been with him since June 1891, and was intelligent and undemanding.[32] In London, Dolly felt 'blank &

melancholy', and deeply embarrassed to have to explain the sudden departure of her husband just before Christmas.[33] 'People seem to think it odd my not being with you. I have to say airily that I am soon going to join you. I wonder whether you feel it odd to leave your Dolly!'[34] Stanley wrote to her very briefly on the 27th, saying he was glad to have come away, and ended much more formally than usual: 'Yours affectionately, Henry M. Stanley.'[35] On 3 January, alarmed by his anger, Dolly wrote to Bruce claiming, disingenuously: 'if he [Stanley] decided he ought to go ... I would not say a word to dissuade him.'[36]

On 30 December 1892, Stanley wrote with almost saintly forbearance: 'I forget & forgive ... I hope that this coming year will unite us closer and bring us the General – the long looked for – upon whose soft lips, you and I, please God, may re-plight our vows, and re-pledge our love.'[37] Now that he had no career – other than an unwanted parliamentary candidacy – all Henry's hopes for future happiness hung upon the birth of a son or daughter. Still unable to believe his friend would throw away such a sublime opportunity, Bruce wrote wishing him a Happy New Year, and urging him one last time to choose between being an MP and becoming Britain's East African proconsul. In reality, the moment of decision had passed. In the same letter Bruce confessed that Mackinnon's health was failing.[38]

In Pau, Stanley relished having time to himself. 'The absolute peace is delicious ... I have banished London & its worries from my mind ... I am deep in books & papers and these give me quite a sufficient interest.'[39] On 3 January, after almost two weeks away, Stanley wrote a deeply felt letter to Dolly. He described doing something that would have been quite impossible in London – partly because of the pressure of social events, and partly because he was always recognized in public places. Quite simply he had sat on a bench in a park and listened to an outdoor concert. Around him everyone was totally absorbed; 'they had forgotten their businesses ... their souls were whirling about in the air, dancing to the measures, while their grosser selves stood passive ... and I was one of these, dearest; and I looked into my heart for you and cried, Why? Why? Oh, why?' Also in this letter, he described how desperate he felt when she talked at him incessantly and organized his time. He explained that all his needs could 'not be gratified ... even by you'. But this, he added, need not be a disaster. 'What is to be done? We must bear & forebear ... I must try to make you happy, provided it is not asked at the cost of my unhappiness.'[40]

A week later he wrote venting his deep irritation with the pointless 'struggle' of an election. But instead of letting him withdraw his candidature, Dolly wrote back full of election plans: 'This-afternoon I have 75 ladies to tea. We are bound to win.'[41] Stanley replied sadly en route home from Biarritz: 'As for your political arrangements, make them as you please. I shall be ready to assist any decent work ... but no silly personal canvassing ... I am not well at all.'[42]

No sooner was he back in London than it dawned on Henry how misguided he had been to give in to Dorothy. The great philanthropist's health continued to decline, and a repeat of his offer was already impossible. On 22 June 1893, Sir William died. He had been killed, Stanley believed, by 'depression of spirits' caused by the way in which successive governments had used his company to hold back the Germans, free of charge to the British tax-payer. Yet as Stanley stood by his friend's coffin in the Burlington Hotel, in the tycoon's spacious suite, where they had often sat and planned, he must have known that his own refusal to go out to Africa and push on the company's work had also contributed to Sir William's final collapse.[43] 'The New Year has just begun,' he had written to Mackinnon from Pau. 'If I could pray for anything ... my first thought would be of you. Friends are few, but you I would wish to cling to while I have life.' A few days later, he had told his honorary father: 'Your time will come yet, and the full measure of your work will be yet known and trumpeted ...'[44] His memory of these words must have sounded very hollowly to him now.

At this time of disappointment and marital disharmony, the now-widowed May Sheldon announced that she intended to become an African explorer. This must have suggested to Stanley that if he had only remained single and then married this courageous woman, she would have rejoiced to go out with him to Africa as wife of the Administrator General.[45] 'Africa,' wrote May, thinking of Stanley, Stairs and Nelson, 'is a most fascinating wild mistress. She gets a tenacious hold on most persons; bewitching, magnetic, irresistible ... and once experienced is never lulled into forgetfulness.'[46] Stanley could only have agreed.

William Stairs had gone out to Africa in 1891, and in June 1892 had succumbed to haematuric fever, after securing Katanga for King Leopold. In December 1892, Robert Nelson died of dysentery, while working for Mackinnon's company in the Kikuyu District of East Africa. Early deaths seemed to be awaiting all Stanley's friends and associates. After Mackinnon's demise, Alexander Bruce died of influenza in November 1893.[47] Two months earlier, Dr Parke had died of a brain tumour. Stanley learned, when it was too late, that Parke had been ill and poor for years. After the funeral, Jephson wrote his old boss a stinging letter, asking him why he had not shown more interest in the lives of his officers. Jephson then disclosed that he himself had a shadow on a lung, and was suffering from heart disease. Shocked, Stanley asked him why he and Parke had not confided in him. After all, in consecutive years, he had invited both to stay with him in Switzerland, and had written introductions to their books about Africa. Yet Jephson brushed this aside, insisting that one only tells a friend one's troubles 'if one senses their sympathy'.[48] With his marriage under strain at the time, Stanley was hurt deeply by Jephson's criticisms.

At this depressing time, he kept in touch with several men who had served him on the Congo in the early 1880s. One of them, Edward Glave, would give a sharp focus to his interest in Africa, and even console him for his own inability to return there. Glave became of special

Edward J. Glave

interest to Stanley because he had turned out to be a practical idealist with a Livingstonian determination to expose the slave trade and other evil-doing in the interior. In the late 1880s, when King Leopold was dismissing all his non-Belgian officers, Glave – along with other enterprising 'foreign' station chiefs, like Anthony Swinburne and Roger Casement – had joined Henry Sanford's ivory company. He served until Leopold squeezed out all international competition, prior to creating state monopolies in the early 1890s.[49]

In 1890, Glave had visited the United States for several months to lecture about the Congo, and in December had met up with Stanley, then on his own extended American tour. That was when Glave had done secretarial work for Henry and had helped him by swearing that Ward's favourable remarks about Barttelot had not reflected his true opinions.[50] In May 1891 Stanley had helped Glave raise funds to explore Alaska, and a year later wrote an introduction to his book, *Six Years of Adventure in Congoland*. Then, in November 1892, just when Stanley's own hopes of returning to the 'Dark Continent' had been dashed, Glave electrified him by announcing that he meant to return to Africa for 'a big & noble object'.

His admiration became warmer still when the young man explained that he had been inspired by a piece that Stanley had recently written for *Harper's Magazine*, entitled 'Slavery and the Slave Trade in Africa'.[51] In it, Henry had named a new generation of brutal slavers – Karema, Kibruga, Kilonga-Longa, Kibongo and Tippu's Tip's son, Sefu, and nephews Rashid and Nasur-bin-Suliman – who were extending their operations beyond Tippu's furthest limits, importing ever more gunpowder. Believing that similar press exposés offered the only way to bring about European intervention, Glave was delighted when, with Stanley's help, he persuaded the editor of America's *Century Magazine* to pay him £1,200 to travel across Africa to discover more facts about the slave trade and publish them to the world.[52] Well aware that this exceedingly dangerous mission was one that David Livingstone would have loved to attempt, Henry entertained Glave at Richmond Terrace and gave him practical advice. Glave's plan was to repeat the first third of Livingstone's final journey, travelling via the Rovuma to the southern end of Lake Nyasa, and thence to Lake Bangweolu where the doctor had died, and thereafter northwards through Manyema to the Lualaba and the Upper Congo, and so, eventually, to the Pool and the Atlantic.[53] Even without the task of exposing the slave traders, his journey would have been an epic of exploration.

Glave sailed from the port of London on 25 June 1893, and Stanley said a solemn farewell to him in his cabin. Both men knew there was a distinct possibility that they would never meet again. A few days earlier Glave had written promising to do his 'very utmost to deserve your [Stanley's] approval'.[54] Facing his own mundane and unwanted electoral battle, Stanley was struck by this brave young man's mission as a shining example of the self-sacrificing heights to which individual human beings could sometimes rise when a great cause beckoned. He received his first letter from his protégé in the late summer of 1894. Writing from near Lake Nyasa, Glave praised the British authorities in Nyasaland – which had become a protectorate in 1891 – for destroying the slavers' strongholds and cutting off slave dhows on the lake with their two steamships. But with only three officers, 200 Sikhs and a native levy of a similar size, the British (led by Stanley's former friend Harry Johnston) were struggling to stop gunpowder coming in from the port of Kilwa in Arab-Swahili caravans.[55]

On 26 November, Glave wrote the last letter Stanley would receive from him. By now, he was on the western shore of Lake Tanganyika. He had just visited Lake Bangweulu where he had managed 'to discover the actual tree under which the heart of Dr Livingstone was buried' – a feat that many travellers had unsuccessfully attempted in the twenty-one years since Susi, Chuma and their companions had buried their master's heart and carried away with them the rest of his body. Ahead of Glave lay the towns of Kabambare, Kasongo, Riba-Riba and, further downstream on the Congo, Stanley Falls, Equator and Lukolela, where he had once been station chief. At most of these places he would see sights, and hear accounts of atrocities, that would lead him to write a fearsome denunciation of the Belgians and the brutal way in which they were exploiting their vast colony and its inhabitants. These accounts would not be published until 1897, and in the meantime Glave succumbed to fever at Matadi on 12 May 1895, tragically close to the sea. Lawson Forfeitt, a missionary who was with Glave when he died, told Stanley that he had been conscious to within an hour of his death; and he had showed Forfeitt a letter from Stanley, which he had always carried with him.

Glave left clear instructions to send his papers and photographic plates to *Century Magazine*.[56] (The immense international row that Glave's damning revelations about Belgian brutality would cause will be dealt with later.) In May 1895, his only article yet published in *Century Magazine* was one about finding Livingstone's tree; a photograph of the young man standing beside it appeared next to the text. His finding of the exact spot where Livingstone died became, in Stanley's mind, another bond between them. In the October issue, the magazine's editor wrote of the dead man as being 'cast in a mould of gentleness and heroism, of generosity and justice and unselfishness'.[57]

Ten years earlier, a disillusioned Stanley had written revealingly to the charismatic Harry Johnston, 'It is about time I stopped in this search for the perfect man.'[58] In Edward Glave, he had finally found perfection, he believed. From a working-class family, Glave came very close to duplicating Stanley's own rise to distinction through dedication alone.[59] Glave had even seemed to possess the goodness that Stanley had attributed to Livingstone. Because he himself had been driven by a consuming need to succeed, Henry had been drawn to the modest Glave, with his indifference to fame and riches. When Edward Glave died, Henry was campaigning in North Lambeth and hating it, and the news of his friend's fate crushed him.

With no child of his own blood in prospect, Glave had become an honorary son to Stanley. Unlike Jephson and Stairs (his favourites for a while), Glave had never disappointed. Henry's misery over his loss emerges most powerfully in a letter to Glave's brother-in-law, William J. Davy, who had served on the Congo during Stanley's years as Chief Agent, and had come with Stanley to say goodbye to Glave when his ship had sailed in 1893:

My dear Friend,

I am so terribly upset by your sad news, that I can scarcely trust myself to write ... [about] one who had become very dear to me and whom I admired more than I can tell you – he was in every respect so loveable ... I feel it all so deeply that I have at present no interest in the future whatever. My ambitions depended so much on him indirectly, and he too was so interested in my doings, that I feel suddenly I have become quite alone ... You remember on board ... how he made you all go out of his cabin while he said goodbye to me alone ... I can't think of it all without crying ... It is so dreadful to think of him having none of his own people with him at the last, and that he should be lying out there so far away ... Do not think me selfish if I ask you to write ... the slightest smallest detail will be of wonderful interest to me as you will easily understand ... One day I should hope to see you all again – I could not bear it just at present ... I must tell you candidly that I had more respect, admiration & love for him than for any other man I have ever met ... He was, as I said before, my ideal ...'[60]

435

Certainly Stanley had never been so much affected by a death. Though the general election campaign was at its height, he insisted that Dolly stop electioneering and write a letter of condolence to enclose with his to Glave's mother.[61] In grieving for his friend, Stanley was also grieving for the many young men whose deaths he had witnessed during the past two decades and been too hard-pressed, or too traumatized, to mourn at the time.

In the 1890s there was a further softening in his character and his more spiritual side appeared. He loved to escape from London for days at a time and stay on the coast to walk and find peace. Eighteen months earlier, he had spent a solitary week at Cromer, walking on the endless Norfolk sands, which reminded him of Africa. With the 'deep, solemn, continuous' sound of the waves in his ears, came 'a rapturous upswing of joy' to his 'very finger tips'. He found himself scooping up round pebbles from 'the glorious floor of sand' and then amazed himself 'by bursting into song' on the deserted beach. 'Fancy – years and years ago I think I last sang ... but something of my real old self was in me still – such is civilized man – he enters a groove and exit is there none until solitariness discovers that the boy lay hidden under a thick kernel of civilized custom.'[62] The 'groove' Stanley had 'entered' was British politics. If Edward Glave had only survived, he would have become a public figure, directing the eyes of the world to Africa's suffering. With such an ally, Stanley could have joined the battle that had long obsessed him. Glave had been as determined as he was to separate the slavers from essential supplies, such as arms and gunpowder. If his young protégé had lived, Henry might even have been inspired to attack the Congo Free State – 'a noble object' indeed.

Two months after Glave's death, Henry was elected to represent North Lambeth, and his undesired victory seemed to spell *finis* to all other hopes.[63] At the moment of victory by 405 votes, Stanley was swung up onto the shoulders of his supporters and carried to a table to cries of 'Speech! Speech!'. But when put down, he merely said 'with a steady look: "Gentlemen, I thank you, and now good-night!"' In a homebound carriage with Dorothy, he did not speak at all.[64] The next day, he wrote his wife a deeply ironic letter: 'I beg you will kindly accept this expression of my esteem for the personal service you have done me & the patriotic zeal you have so conspicuously displayed on behalf of the country. With the warmest grateful sentiments, I beg to remain yours most faithfully ...'[65] There would be no other thanks for her work, ever. By the year's end, he would be suffering a prolonged attack of gastritis that by mid-1896 would leave him looking fifteen years older than his fifty-five years. And life as a Member of Parliament turned out to be every bit as bad as he had expected. Since the ventilation system of the chamber did not work, a fresh-air lover like Stanley suffered more than most. 'I have had a frontal headache for quite ten days now and the sap seems quite gone out of me ... When 500 people have sat in it for 10 hours, air is worse than that of a swamp.'[66]

It distressed him very much that, thanks to Parliament, he might never have the time or health to get to grips with his autobiography. If he died before making progress, he told Dolly: 'how little after all you would know of me – how still less the world outside ... The inner existence, the ME – what does anyone know of ...? I am the best evidence for myself ... Up to the moment of death we should strive to leave behind us something ...' And all the time he was wasting his life in the House or making fatuous speeches. 'I can never make up for this lost time. But I will stop, or I must rage.'[67]

The press did not respond kindly to Stanley's maiden speech. His subject was foreign policy and East Africa.

Mr Henry M.Stanley burst upon an astonished house on Wednesday. No fewer than three times did the famous African explorer intervene in debate. He made not one but three maiden speeches ... There is generally a certain movement of surprise when this small man, with snow-white hair, snow-white moustache, and an expression of supreme Oriental tranquillity, is pointed out as the world famed traveller ... Whether Mr Stanley will be as successful as a legislator, as he has been in so many other walks of life, is open to question.[68]

A journalist friend summarized the reasons why, in his opinion, the explorer would never make any impression on the House: 'He has little sympathy with parliamentary manners and ways of thought, and has entered on the new world too late to fall in with them.'[69] This prophecy would be fulfilled – mainly because of Stanley's continuing lack of interest.

Some time in 1894, Henry had pleaded with Dorothy to agree to adopt a child. She had refused. But by the autumn of 1895 he had at last persuaded her how very deeply he longed to adopt, and thus brought about a change of heart.[70] Without the hope of one day raising a child, Stanley's life would have felt bleak indeed. Then towards the end of the year, a son of one of his first cousins died, leaving a widow, who was too poor to support her six-month-old son – at least this was the story that Henry would later tell close friends. Dorothy supplied confirmatory details for her closest confidantes, telling them that the boy's father had died in an accident and that his mother had needed to work in order to support herself – hence Henry's providential offer to adopt and the widow's acceptance. However, despite what Stanley and his wife told their friends, it is almost certain that the boy was really the illegitimate grandson of Stanley's half-sister Emma. So why did Henry hide the truth? Mainly to spare the boy the stigma of illegitimacy as he grew up. Even Dorothy seems to have been told the cousin version by him. It appears that Stanley concealed the child's birth details from her because fearing that if he had admitted the real reason for adopting, she might have rejected this particular child. So instead he had justified an adoption by telling her that the boy's lawfully married father had recently died leaving no money. Henry had also known that his wife would find it more palatable to adopt the great-nephew of a cousin than the great-grandson of his (Stanley's) mother, whom Dorothy had always thought a monster for abandoning him[71] [see this note for full evidence of the boy's identity].

Stanley was in bed, suffering from severe gastritis, on the day the thirteen-month-old boy was first brought to his house. 'One day in July,' wrote Dorothy, 'I was told that there was a baby with a lady downstairs – and sure enough there was this little relative – a wee delicate featured beautiful little boy with a finely shaped head, and eyes beaming with intelligence – grey eyes and soft brown curly hair ... Well! I just carried him up to Stanley, who was too weak to sit up; and I sat the boy down beside him. They looked at each other and then Stanley said, "We will keep him forever – he is ours."[72]

Given Stanley's resentment of Wales and his Welsh family for the unhappiness he had endured as a boy, it might be thought that the adoption of the child of a close Welsh relative had only been the fortuitous result of an unwanted pregnancy. But though in one sense it was, Stanley's attitude to his family had never simply been characterized by hurt and anger. Always there had been an ache of sympathy for their poverty and lack of privilege. The way he had taken his mother and his half-sister Emma to London in 1868, and to Paris and London in 1869, had been extraordinarily forgiving. He had also paid for them to stay in good hotels, and bought them many new clothes.[73] But

perhaps the most touching fact about his love for his undeserving family lies in his admiration for a book that has all the wish-fulfilling
appeal of a typical best-seller, but a lot more besides. Dolly could have
learned much about Henry if she had only agreed to look at 'that best
of romances ... which I have never been able to persuade you to read'.
This was Lew Wallace's epic of ancient Rome, *Ben Hur* – the story of
a man who had been unjustly sent to the galleys and then adopted by
a senator whose life he had saved in a sea battle. After becoming the
greatest charioteer in the Roman Empire, Ben Hur tried to find his
mother and sister – also victims of injustice. Eventually, he found them
in a valley where lepers were forced to live in isolation. Ignoring the
stigma and the danger, he had the courage to bring them to his home.
The parallels with Stanley's life – invented and real – were remarkable.
Stanley had been unjustly 'sentenced' to confinement in a workhouse.
He had worked in ships, and claimed to have been adopted, before
becoming an empire's greatest explorer. He too, when famous, had
risked going to see his mother and sister, whose 'disease' was not lep-
rosy but social inferiority.[74] When Stanley had lectured in Wales in
1891, he had been touched at Caernarvon when people called on God
to help his work: 'I need prayers,' he told Dolly, 'and their blessings
were precious.'[75] His interest in his Welsh family became much greater
during the 1890s.

In November 1893, he had sent his trusted valet, W. J. Hawkes, to
try to find out more about his immediate family, including the state of
health of Robert Jones junior, his forty-four-year-old half-brother,
who had been bedridden for a decade. Without divulging who he was,
Hawkes visited the Cross Foxes pub at Bodelwyddan, where Stanley
had once been turned away by his mother. She had died seven years
previously, but Hawkes found Stanley's aged stepfather, Robert Jones,
and his half-brother, Robert Jones junior, and Robert junior's wife,
Catherine (née Parry), and their daughter, Catherine Elizabeth, who
was nineteen and very pretty.

Hawkes saw for himself that Stanley's brother, Robert, was blind,
bedridden and unable to turn in bed, or even feed himself. For many
years he had suffered from acute rheumatism of the joints and inflammation of the heart. He was in pain all the time, and wept when
Hawkes talked to him. Pleas for financial help had regularly been sent
to Henry by his half-brother and by his sister-in-law, Catherine Jones,
and he invariably responded with money – although on one occasion

he sent a water bed. Hawkes brought back a photograph of Catherine Elizabeth, his master's niece, and Stanley was moved on noting a strong resemblance to his younger self in this girl's face. Also at the Cross Foxes had been James W. Jones, Stanley's youngest half-brother, to whom he had sent gifts of clothes when he was a boy.

The poverty and ill-health of his closest relatives caused Stanley considerable distress when he heard of it from Hawkes.[76] But unlike the lepers in *Ben Hur*, the Jones family would not be invited to Richmond Terrace; nor would Stanley go to Wales to visit them. Childhood memories still caused him shame and distress. But while his inability to accept his past did not bode well for his autobiography, it never tempted him to sever all ties with his relations. Against this background it can easily be seen why – when the opportunity had unexpectedly presented itself – he had eagerly adopted a child from within his own family.

Right from the baby's first day with him, while he was still too ill to get up, Stanley's greatest pleasure was to have the year-old child placed beside him on the bed. 'Ah, it is worthwhile now to get well,' he told Dolly.[77] The child was baptized with water from Lake Albert in Cadoxton Church, near the Tennants' country house in south Wales. Stanley and Dorothy said they had decided on the name Denzil, because she would have been called it, had she been a boy. (Dolly was descended from Oliver Cromwell, one of whose close friends was Denzil Holles.) Stanley would privately have relished this name since Den suggested *Den*bigh and *zil* is Liz spelled backwards. Stanley's mother had been a Liz and the adopted child's mother had also been called Elizabeth.[78] From now on, Stanley's happiness became almost entirely bound up with giving his son the love he himself had never known. Even his sidelined autobiography caused him fewer pangs of conscience.

Nine months before the adoption of Denzil, Stanley had travelled to New Orleans to try to work out what to do about his own fictitious 'adoption'. He returned to the city incognito, as Mr S. M. Henry. Knowing, from several press articles, that the presence of surviving Stanley relatives in New Orleans made it unsafe for him to claim to have been adopted by Henry Hope Stanley, he decided to search in the city's cemeteries for a family of Stanleys who had lived in New Orleans at the right time and were now dead. He needed a Mrs Stanley who had died in 1859 or 1860 to support his fiction of 'his mother's' early death. Between 14 and 18 October, he walked for miles in several large burial grounds. He found the grave of a Mary Ann Stanley in Metairie Cemetery, but he made no comment in his notebook to show that he realized he had stumbled upon his 'father's' first wife, even though the words 'Wife of Henry Stanley, a native of Cheshire, England' were carved into the stone.[79] It is hard to resist the conclusion that Stanley did not know that H. H. Stanley came from Cheshire, or had once been married to a first wife. In any case, her death in 1846 had been over a decade too early to be of any use. He found the gravestones of a number of other Stanleys and noted down their dates of death. It seems he did not go near the shared grave of Henry Hope Stanley and his second wife, Frances, which was in another part of the cemetery in which Mary Ann lay buried.

Despite all his efforts, Henry failed to find a safely defunct Stanley family with roughly the right dates. Given his precarious health, there is something unbearably poignant about this world-famous man peering at the graves of total strangers for hour after hour, all because he could not endure the thought of admitting that his adoption had never happened. The hurt went so deep that he still needed to pretend that he had been cherished by an adoptive family, and dreaded being ridiculed should he fail to furnish 'proofs' to support his story. But one graveyard visit that October was inspired by a genuine desire to pay his respects. This was to the tomb of James Speake, the storekeeper who had done so much for him, and beside whose dead body he had watched the whole night through, before his burial.[80]

While walking through the city for the very last time, and visiting the places he remembered, Stanley crossed Orange Street on his way to St Thomas Street, where he had lived in a boarding house in 1859 and 1860, and naturally he did not pause, en route, to look at Henry Hope Stanley's house, although it was then only twenty-five yards away. On this sentimental journey through familiar streets, he had no desire to search out houses where he had never lived. His final aim on this trip was to return to Baltimore via Hagerstown, to visit the village where he had been nursed back to health in 1862. In New York, he dined with Edward King, his oldest friend, who had known him in Spain before he had found Livingstone. King would die in March the following year, so the few hours the two men spent together, and which King (in his own words) 'immeasurably enjoyed', would be their last.[81] It would also be Stanley's final visit to the country that had been the springboard for his career.

On returning to London, Henry effectively abandoned his autobiography. In a section of uncompleted manuscript, he wrote: 'To lie is considered mean, and it is no doubt a habit to be avoided by every self-respecting person. But the best of men & women are sometimes compelled to resort to lying to avoid a worse offence. On certain occasions I have had to lie ... to defend myself against inquisitiveness & stop impertinence.'[82] He would have needed to publish some epic lies to sustain the story of his adoption; and though he did invent a fictitious Mr Stanley (significantly different from Henry Hope), he could not have relished the prospect of exposing his invention to a readership inevitably including people who had known him in 1859. For this reason – and to avoid writing truthfully about his Welsh relatives – he stopped work, blaming his failure to finish on his duties as an MP. His polished manuscript ended in 1862 – though he had also written draft accounts of the Livingstone meeting and of his great Congo journey, and the Emin Pasha expedition. The typescripts made, after his death, by Dolly and her hired professional author, George Merriam, replaced Stanley's earlier manuscripts (many of which no longer exist).

Stanley failed to write the book that could have been his most enduring work, but at least, when he returned from America, it was to his little son. In the person of Denzil, he told Dolly, 'the secret object of my inward thoughts is realized ... as though it were a pre-natal vision embodied in actual existence'.[83]

THIRTY-TWO

Stanley, Leopold and the Atrocities

From the mid-1890s, tragic developments on the Congo cast a long shadow over some of Stanley's greatest achievements – especially his years of pioneering. All his prodigious labours seemed merely to have ended with the creation of a colony in which atrocities were used to boost rubber production as a matter of deliberate policy. Clearly, the nature of his response to these atrocities is important for his moral reputation. In the early 1890s he, like Sir William Mackinnon, Sir John Kirk, Baroness Burdett-Coutts and many humanitarians, continued to believe in Leopold's desire to help civilize Africa using humane methods. Of course, Stanley and the rest of them knew that the king wanted to make money from the Congo, but this seemed perfectly natural, given the monarch's staggering annual losses. In October 1890, Leopold told Stanley that unless he could raise £50,000 more per annum by taxation, he could not continue to find the £170,000 required each year to pay for the state's administration. As Henry understood it, the future of the colony was at stake. The only tax Leopold was permitted to levy under the Berlin decrees was an export duty, on ivory and palm oil, then producing about a tenth of the cost of the State. Since the king's expenses were rising every year, and he would soon be paying for a war against the Arabs, Stanley was willing to stick his neck out and argue the need for Leopold to impose an additional tax.[1]

Leopold did not mention to Stanley his decrees of October 1891 and May 1892, by which he made it illegal for natives to hunt elephants or harvest wild rubber, unless they handed over these commodities to the State's officers for a small fixed sum per kilo.[2] Nor was Stanley informed of the decree of 30 October 1892, by which 'vacant' lands (that is, those not lived on or farmed by Africans) were to be divided into three zones, one of which, the *Domaine Privé*, was a vast territory that included the valleys of the Aruwimi and the Uele – all of which would be reserved entirely for the State.[3] In 1892, although the Dunlop Tyre Company was by now trading in Europe and America, rubber sales were still only achieving one-thirtieth of the tonnage recorded at the century's end, so it was not yet apparent that rubber would save the finances of the Congo Free State. Apart from the king's debts, there was another reason why Henry did not speak in public against Leopold's new policies. By the time he heard about 'vacant lands' late in 1892, the king's *force publique* had attacked the Arab-Swahili in the east of Leopold's vast country and the war Stanley had been urging for years had started.

It took almost a year of fighting for the State to defeat the slave traders and their African allies in the Aruwimi valley, on the Lomani and the Upper Congo. Recalling the carnage inflicted by these same slave traders in the 1880s, Stanley was delighted by Leopold's success-ful campaign.[4] It would be several years before Henry discovered that Captain Francis Dhanis (Leopold's most brilliant commander) had fought in alliance with 10,000 cannibals of the Batetela tribe, and that scores of their captives had been eaten on the field of battle.[5] Inevitably, this brutal campaign did not bring security or prosperity to the 'liberated' areas. News from this anarchic and deeply traumatized region only reached the outside world in 1896 and 1897. But before these terrible revelations reached him, Stanley was outraged by an act of Belgian injustice against an individual who happened to be a British subject. The beginning of the end of Stanley's long relationship with Leopold was at hand.

Stanley had met the trader and former lay missionary Charles Stokes in Cairo, and had corresponded with him in 1889 about his intention of arming Mwanga in order to restore him to the Bugandan throne.[6] Though Stanley disliked the idea of selling guns in Africa full stop, he considered that selling arms to Africans was not as heinous as supplying them to Arabs. So he was horrified when he heard in August 1895 that Stokes had been arrested and summarily hanged by a Bel-gian officer, Captain H. J. Lothaire. The Briton's alleged crime was importing guns into the Congo from German East Africa. When the relevant papers were sent to Stanley by Charles Liebrechts, the Free State's Secretary General of the Interior, he saw that, though Stokes had been 'foolish, rash, and even wicked ... Lothaire's conduct had been utterly indefensible'. Stokes had not smuggled 'two or three hundred breech loaders with some thousands of cartridges' into the Congo, but only obsolete muzzle loaders; and he had neither resisted arrest, nor withheld his property from Lothaire. Stanley considered that the worst that should have been done to him was the imposition of a heavy fine and a prison sentence.[7] When Stanley met the king at the Grosvenor Hotel, in London, in January 1896, he was taken aback to find him totally unapologetic.[8] The Stokes affair obliged Henry to see that the king could be callously indifferent to an individual case of injustice, even when he knew all the facts. Stanley would not forget this.

In April 1895, Henry had been visited at Richmond Terrace by William Hoffman, his former valet, and by the Dutch trader and consul at Leopoldville, Antoine Greshoff, shortly before they both returned to the Congo. In the past few years, the Dutchman, whom Stanley considered a friend, had written a stream of letters warning him never to go back to the Congo – even if Leopold asked him to. The Belgian officers, he said, were as brutal as the Arabs. Furthermore, the State's officials were deliberately destroying free trade on the river. Stanley suspected that Greshoff hated the Belgians because they had wrecked his business, but he still found his letters disconcerting.[9] With William Hoffman's departure, Stanley realized that he would now have a chance to test Greshoff's accusations. William had earned his former master's admiration by going out to the Congo to work as an interpreter for the State in November 1891, after serving for a year in Mombassa with Mackinnon's company.[10] In June 1892, Hoffman had joined an expedition to the Nile watershed, and had then served on the River Congo itself until 1894.[11] He returned to the Congo Free State again in April 1895 as a lieutenant, and would soon be stationed in the troubled eastern 'Zone Arabe'.

But in November 1895, before Stanley had received any significant information from Hoffman, an American missionary from Equator Station, J. B. Murphy, told a Reuter's correspondent that, in his area, Africans were having their hands cut off if they failed to collect large amounts of rubber.[12] Corroboration of these claims came from a source Stanley had to take seriously. Two years earlier he had himself recommended two Britons, Captain Philip H. B. Salusbury and Sergeant Graham, for service with the State's *force publique*. Although

Graham was killed and eaten by cannibals a year later,[13] in September 1896, Salusbury and another Englishman, Alfred Parminter – both of whom had worked for Sanford's company – published articles in the British press alleging that there had been many recent atrocities in the Congo, some gratuitous and some inspired by a desire to force the Congolese to collect more ivory and rubber. Officers of the State were poorly paid, claimed Salusbury, and received a 25 per cent commission on ivory and 12 per cent on rubber.[14]

Faced with these revelations, Leopold asked Stanley to write to *The Times*, suggesting that the atrocities had been isolated incidents.[15] Stanley's letter – published in the paper on 16 September – was a disappointment to Leopold. Henry obligingly stated that the recent atrocities had been committed by a tiny proportion of the total number of officers in the *force publique* (as indeed they had been), but he made it very clear that truly horrifying crimes really had been committed by Belgians, or by Africans under their orders. Stanley repeated unchallenged the claims that a Lieutenant Hansen had ordered a woman's breasts to be cut off, that a Lieutenant Jansen had flogged a woman with 200 lashes, and that a Lieutenant Bunsen had caused a girl to be dismembered. He also repeated Parminter's statement that he had seen a Lieutenant Blochteur praise a native sergeant who had just brought him a collection of severed ears. The fact that Stanley named names, as Parminter had done, showed that he was entirely convinced that these particular crimes had happened and had no intention of whitewashing anyone. He also repeated a ghastly account of Bangala soldiers cutting off a girl's feet when under the command of a Lieutenant de Keyser.

Stanley reproved Parminter for failing to name the worst officer of all, whom he had accused of giving two women several hundred lashes each, and then ordering his men to cut off their breasts and leave them to die. 'When and where was such a revolting crime committed? Was the District Governor informed of it, and if so, what did he do about it?' Stanley stated his conviction that if the authorities were told about such cases, they would act decisively against the evil-doers. He applauded the publication of allegations of brutality, since 'it could not fail to act as a deterrent on evil doing, as there is no station so distant as to be beyond the moral effect of a newspaper'.[16]

A few days later Stanley backtracked somewhat, suggesting in a letter to the *Saturday Review* that some of the atrocities might have been invented in trading stations, as a result of anti-Belgian sentiment.[17] But in reality, he was desperately upset by what Parminter and Salusbury had revealed, and the day after his letter appeared in *The Times* he wrote to William Hoffman, enclosing Parminter's most recent revelations and asking his old valet if *he* could name the Belgian officer who had ordered a woman's breasts to be cut off. 'Are the Belgian officers as cruel as reported? Do they allow their soldiers to riot, murder and mutilate? Is it a common report? ... I may have to speak about these Congo matters in Parliament – of course nothing but the absolute truth will do.'[18] William's reply was written in December and arrived three months after that. It was not reassuring. He explained how the Batetela warlord, Gongo Lutete, who had served under Dhanis in the war against the Arabs, had been accused of plotting against the Belgians and had been tried by four young officers and shot before Dhanis could save him. This deplorably foolish act had led to a Batetela mutiny, which was spreading dangerously. William reported that in recent fighting against the mutinous Batetela cannibals, sixteen Belgians had died and 200 government black soldiers. No mercy had been shown to women and children, who had been 'cut up and eaten' by the mutineers, who had also 'hung up [captives] by their feet along the roadside ...[with] all the chair humaine [human flesh] cut off'. Government blacks were also eating their enemies.

Recently, between Leopoldville and Kasongo on the Upper Congo, eight whites had been sentenced for sickening crimes: one had 'tossed a girl into the river with hands and feet bound'. This murderer had received a five-year sentence and a fine of 5,000 francs. But lighter sentences had been given to men guilty of similarly bestial crimes. Although these eight criminals had been whites, others crimes were being carried out by Africans with the knowledge of whites, or without it. William said that in the current fighting against the Batetela, 'many cruel acts were often committed without the white man knowing anything about them'. This terrible picture was one that Stanley had to believe.[19] It comforted him that Hoffman was in the lawless 'Zone Arabe', which was still experiencing the aftermath of war. And even there, atrocities were being detected and punished (albeit inadequately). These crimes, Henry prayed, were the work of very few Belgians and their ill-disciplined black troops. For surely, if such barbarities were truly widespread, there would have been an outcry from many of the 400 missionaries on the Congo. George Grenfell, the

Baptist missionary and friend of Stanley, had told him nothing.[20]

However, Stanley did not wait for further information from the missionaries but wrote firmly to Leopold: 'I would suggest to your Majesty that something should be done to prevent this continuous supply of Congo sensations ... people fed as they are with stories of atrocities will be apt to believe that some of them must be true and that the state ought to be suppressed in consequence.' He warned the king that there was a real danger that Britain might join France in open hostility to the Congo Free State. More atrocities would lead to demands for international action.[21] Stanley's tone shook the king, who replied that he had 'given new orders to suppress all irregularities ... and the state inspector has been charged to proceed to all places alleged to have been the scene of such'.[22] Leopold wrote to his Secretary of State for the Congo, Baron Edmond van Eetvelde: 'If there are abuses in the Congo, we must stop them. If they are perpetuated they will bring about the collapse of the State.' Leopold set up a 'Commission for the Protection of the Natives', made up of three Catholic and three Protestant missionaries who were to inform the Governor-General of any cases of brutality that came to their notice. Whether Leopold meant this commission to succeed is open to question. The individual missionaries were hundreds of miles apart. In any case, it was the systematic use of forced labour for rubber collection that needed to be changed, and that was left in place.[23]

On 6 April 1897, the first of two devastating extracts from Edward Glave's diary was published in *Century Magazine*. Here, at last, was a source that Stanley accepted as gospel truth. In the first diary extract, Glave stated that in 1895 the State had been using Baluba and Manyema soldiers, without white officers, against local tribes on the Upper Congo around Kabambare, Kasongo and Nyangwe. In consequence there had been many massacres of innocent people. The released slaves of the Arab-Swahili, not long after returning as free men to their villages, had been 'shipped south to be soldiers, workers, &c., on the State stations'; 'what were peaceful families have been broken up'. Glave had seen 'in stations in charge of white men ... strings of poor emaciated old women, some of them mere skeletons, working from six in the morning till noon, and from half-past two till six ...'. These innocent 'prisoners of war' had been brought in by black government soldiers to be forced labourers.[24] Five months later, far worse revelations from Glave's diaries would be published, with graphic descriptions of hangings and floggings. 'I conscientiously believe that a man who receives 100 blows is often killed and has his spirit broken for life.' Then this grave indictment:

The State has not suppressed slavery, but established a monopoly by driving out the Arab and Wangwana competitors. The State soldiers are constantly stealing, and sometimes the natives are so persecuted that they resent this by killing and eating their tormentors. Recently the State post on the Lomani lost two men, killed and eaten by the natives. Arabs were sent to punish the natives; many women and children were taken, and twenty-one heads were brought to the Falls, and have been used by Captain Rom as a decoration round a flower-bed in front of his house ... [Rebellion] is the natural outcome of the harsh, cruel policy of the State in wringing rubber from these people without paying for it. The revolution will extend ... Does the King of the Belgians know about this? If not, he ought to.[25]

For Stanley, even the milder April instalment of his dear friend's diaries had been enough to galvanize him into urging further action from Leopold. On 23 April 1897, Henry had travelled to Brussels to tell the king he ought to permit an international 'High Tribunal' to visit the Congo in order to establish what was really happening there. If the atrocities were isolated events, the tribunal would merely confirm this. The king was outraged by the suggestion. There were plenty of other countries that ought to admit tribunals to their colonies before he did. Britain should admit one to Matabeleland (Rhodesia) where Cecil Rhodes and two British regiments – for whose services the diamond king was paying the Colonial Office – were attempting to crush the Matabele (Ndebele). And why not send a tribunal to Ireland to investigate the grievances of the Fenians? Another one could look at what the Americans were doing in the Philippines. As a parting shot, the king reminded Stanley that Britain had been the last of the powers to recognize the Congo Free State and had always been prejudiced against it.[26]

From 3 to 7 September, Stanley went to Belgium to see the Congo Exhibition at Tervuren, just outside Brussels. To generate a more sympathetic interest in the Congo among his fellow countrymen, Leopold had paid for 267 African men, women and children to be brought from the Lower Congo to be living exhibits. They were installed in three specially built 'villages' in the park, one beside a lake, mimicking river frontage. Stanley arrived incognito and took a tram to Tervuren like any member of the public. He went unrecognized through the site, although Dorothy's portrait of him was prominently on show. At first

Stanley had no desire to see Leopold again, but then, on 6 September, the day before he was due to leave, he sent a note asking for an audience. Although the king was in Brussels and received this letter on the day it was written, he did not reply until the 8th, saying disingenuously that he was sorry not to have had an opportunity to meet him.[27] This brush-off meant that the two men never met again.

But even though he was disillusioned with Leopold, Stanley (like many high-profile people with Congo links) went on believing, to the century's end, that the king was doing what he could to prevent more atrocities. George Grenfell, the Baptist missionary with almost twenty years' experience of the Congo, wrote as late as 1904: 'I cannot believe His Majesty is careless of the people so long as the rubber comes in, or I would have to join his accusers.'[28] Even Edmund Morel, the mastermind behind the campaign to expose the atrocities, had doubted until 1900 that Leopold's officials could be systematically using forced labour, beatings and mutilations to compel Africans to collect rubber for nothing. After all, out of those 400 missionaries, only a handful had professed any knowledge of deliberate brutality.

For us today, after the facts have appeared in print many times, it is easy enough to accept that a man known for years as Europe's most philanthropic monarch had in fact employed 'legalized robbery enforced by violence' to make himself unbelievably rich.[29] But for King Leopold's contemporaries – especially men like Stanley, who had worked for him – the pill of having been utterly deceived was too bitter to swallow whole. If the report that Roger Casement, Britain's consul on the Congo, prepared for his government about the atrocities had been published earlier, Stanley would have had no option but to accept his conclusions. He had liked Casement when he had met him in April 1887, working for Sanford's company.[30] But by February 1904 – the month of Casement's publication – Stanley only had two and a half months to live, and was too ill to read. Before that, he had seen the problems on the Congo as being due less to the king's greed and inhumanity than to a criminally incompetent Congo Free State government.

It is highly significant that Roger Casement – who would do so much to expose Leopold – admired Stanley, and had written to him in June 1890 from the Congo, telling him that he (Casement) had been 'proud to be serving under your [Stanley's] orders in the founding of the Free State'.[31] With phrases such as 'moral malaria ... and deep layers of filth', Stanley hinted at corruption without making specific accusations against the State's senior officials. 'An erring and ignorant policy' combined with 'unqualified officers ... cumbersome administration, neglect at every station ... and waste in every office' had produced, he said, a disgraceful situation. Henry was sure that if Leopold had ever sent him back to deal with what he called 'that Augean stables', it would surely have killed him.[32]

Stanley visited Africa one final time during the last decade of his life. But though this was a flying visit to witness the opening of the railway line linking Mafeking with Bulawayo, it faced him again with the complexities of what 'civilizing' a vast and complex continent really involved. Before leaving, he wrote for an American magazine some thoughts on this subject: 'Africa is practically explored, and the intelligence of its inhabitants demonstrated ... What we want now is to develop the country, not so much for the white man, but for the natives themselves.'[33] Stanley neither liked nor trusted Cecil Rhodes, the arch-imperialist. When he met the diamond king in January 1895, Rhodes was then prime minister of the Cape government, the virtual owner of Kimberley, as well as the mighty joint stock company, Gold Fields of South Africa. Yet Stanley was unimpressed. 'Rhodes's self-control is not so perfect that he is not liable to the defect of vanity. He is now under the influence of his latest success and I fear it may lead him to undertake something that may lead to a disastrous collapse.'[34] How right he was, with the disastrous Jameson Raid only a year away. Stanley had never been inspired to go to Africa by the thought of making a personal fortune – and had never profited except by his books. Livingstone, rather than Rhodes, had been his model.

Stanley believed in colonialism, despite his disdain for Rhodes's model. Henry's personal experience had convinced him that British officials would not behave like the young Belgians he had sent home in the early 1880s. Men like Glave, Swinburne, Saulez, Grant Elliot and Davy had got on well with Africans and had learned their languages. Interestingly enough, Joseph Conrad himself – despite his scathing indictment of imperialism in *Heart of Darkness*, and his contempt for Belgian officers – admired the British Empire builders of the 1890s, and even compared them with creative artists. In *A Personal Record*, he wrote of that 'interior world' where novelists, like frontiersmen, were drawn to 'imagined adventures where there are no policemen, no laws, no pressure of circumstance, or dread opinion to keep them within bounds'. In *The Rescuer*, the imperial administrator is seen as 'one of those unknown guides of civilization, who, on the advancing edge of progress, are ... like great artists, a mystery to the masses, appreciated only by the influential few'.[35] In *Heart of Darkness* itself, Marlow is made to say that British colonies were 'good to see at any time, because one knows that real work is done in there'. And Marlow was speaking for his Polish-born creator, who had written that 'liberty ... can only be found under the English flag all over the world'.[36] Certainly the benefits of British colonial administration seemed very real to Stanley while travelling south from Bulawayo on the newly opened railway, through peaceful British Bechuanaland (Botswana) where David Livingstone had once worked as a missionary.

But whatever his personal views, there can be no denying that Stanley was one of the unwitting begetters of the historical process that led to terrible exploitation and crimes against humanity on the Congo. This is deeply ironic, since he had spent nine months trying to persuade the British government to take over the Congo before going ahead with Leopold as his second choice. He had dismissed Belgian officers for cruelty, and criticized Leopold's attempts to keep out foreigners and restrict trade. Stanley would therefore have been amazed to read, in the past couple of decades, ill-informed condemnation of his pioneering work by respectable academics. 'The purpose behind Stanley's work in the Congo for Leopold II,' wrote Richard Brantlinger in a well-known book, *Rule of Darkness: British Literature and Imperialism 1830–1914* (1988), 'was not far removed from the Eldorado Exploring Expedition in Heart of Darkness: "to tear treasure out of the land was their desire, with no more moral purpose at the back of it than there is in burglars breaking into a safe".'[37]

Elsewhere Stanley has been listed as the prototype for Joseph Conrad's diabolical Mr Kurtz – a claim resting on the mistaken assumption that Conrad had spent his six months on the Congo between 1879 and 1884 – rather than in 1890, five years after Stanley had ceased to be the king's Chief Agent in Africa.[38] *Heart of Darkness* was not published till 1899 and its inspiration lay in the bloody events of the late 1890s. It was Conrad's reading of Glave's articles, especially his description of Captain Rom, that seems to have inspired him to create the evil Kurtz. What an irony that the young man, whom Stanley had admired more than any other, should have provided a great novelist with the ammunition to create a monster who was later compared with Stanley, his hero.

THIRTY-THREE

'Before it is Too Late'

When I was your age – how I scorned valetudinarians. I was coming down the Congo then with energy enough to satisfy a score of such as I am now. Emaciated it is true – but every nerve like steel wire & a strong healthy heart that renewed life through & through with every beat. Heavens, what a change.

Stanley to his wife 1890s [1]

By the late 1890s, Africa was ceasing to be the overwhelming preoccupation for Stanley that it had been in earlier years. While briefly in southern Africa in 1897, he had felt homesick for England and especially for Denzil – though his dog (another Randy) and his grey parrot also merited enquiries in his letters home. But Denzil was his new focus – 'our own cherub', he called him – and he urged Dolly to 'let him be the apple of your eye, as he is to me'. Though Henry's relations with his wife had been damaged by her determination to force him into politics, he assured her that his love was still strong. 'Look well into your own heart, try & recall when once it was full of tenderest [sic] love, and trust that in mine is something very like what yours was then.' [2]

From his mid-fifties Henry looked an old man, thanks to the terrible punishment his body had taken in Africa. Apart from himself, only Mounteney Jephson and William Hoffman survived of all the Europeans who had travelled in the party that had found Emin Pasha. And Jephson – a handsome young man ten years earlier – was almost unrecognisable by 1900, shocking both Dolly and Stanley by his 'dreadfully altered appearance'. [3] Henry himself was gravely ill for two months in 1896, and two years later suffered another dangerous attack of gastritis, which began while he was holidaying in the Pyre-

453

nees. He was rapidly moved to Biarritz, where doctors were on hand. After each slight improvement, Dolly dreaded the onset of another attack, with the shivering 'so violent that the bed he lay on would shake, and the glasses on the table vibrate and ring' – the pain being so sharp that he would cry out. 'I knew by the sound of his voice, when he called me in the middle of the night, that the pain had come; sometimes it left quite suddenly, and we looked at each other, I, pale with fear, lest it should return.'[4] He was seriously ill from August to October, and though Denzil, and Dolly's nephews, Harold and Leo Myers, were playing every day on Biarritz beach, Henry could not join them. Instead he lay in his room in a comatose, morphine-induced state for the entire holiday.[5]

Earlier that year, Stanley had taken three-year-old Denzil to Lowestoft for a brief break from London. 'Baby is ever delightful,' he wrote home to Dolly. 'The sound of his voice just thrills me, it is so birdlike & sweet. He tells me lots of things which make me smile ... His eyes are brilliant & they have quite an arch expression.'[6] Nothing gave Henry greater pleasure than to be a loving parent to this little boy who, like himself, had been born illegitimate. The idea of being for Denzil what no man had ever been willing to be for him when he had been abandoned lay at the heart of his great love for his adopted son. In May 1899, Stanley took Denzil, now aged four, to Seaford on the Sussex coast, with his nurse, Mrs Ballianis – 'Balley'. As usual, Dolly had chosen to stay in London. 'Nurse and I take long walks with baby who is quite a pedestrian able to make his four miles a day ... He is perpetually chatting & dancing up and down to the smallest trifle.' Stanley would occasionally speak of Denzil as 'baby' until he was six – perhaps prolonging his delight on first adopting him. At Seaford he took photographs of his son, preserved his drawings, and delighted in all his quaint sayings. That same year, the little boy caused much amusement on being lifted up by the returning Arctic explorer, Dr Nansen, and insisting that the hero should: 'Look at my new boots.' Henry told his friend and agent, Major Pond, that 'every morning I take him [Denzil] a ride by train to some distant part of the States – Chicago to San Francisco, or to New Orleans and he delights in playing the conductor's part – and calling out "Salt Lake City!", "Sacramento!" or Atlanta!"'[7]

Stanley kept an eye on his son's toys, and when a friend gave six-year-old Denzil a gun he was told very pointedly that at the moment 'a new monkey called Mr Puff' was monopolizing the boy's attention.[8] The South African war was in progress, and Henry reproved Denzil for saying he hated the Boers. The boy responded: 'If they are not wicked people, why do we fight them?'[9] – a very sharp reply for a six-year-old, and a tricky question for Stanley, who, though pro-government in public, privately held different views. In fact, only a year after the war ended, Stanley welcomed to his home the Boers' two most brilliant generals, Louis Botha and Koos de la Rey.[10] Stanley also held out a hand of friendship to another man who had suffered a great ordeal. This was Captain Alfred Dreyfus, the victim of anti-Semitism and injustice within the French army. Henry and Dolly wrote expressing their sympathy and admiration for his courage, and saying that when he came to England they would be honoured if he would stay with them.[11]

While Stanley spent much of his time with Denzil, Dolly painted portraits, and attended social events, which held no appeal for her husband. One such had been the society wedding of her cousin, Margot Tennant, to Herbert Asquith, the gifted young heir apparent to the Liberal party.[12] Because Henry loathed dressing up in uncomfortable clothes, and having to make small talk, he tried to avoid such occasions. Once he wrote revealingly to Dr Parke: 'I am alone again, and free for a while from feminine supervision. It is grand to be able to draw a free breath once in a while. When Mrs Dolly comes to my door and says, "Bula Matari! I want to speak to you", I have to drop the cigar & the book and ... pretend that I am glad to have been relieved from the tedium of loneliness. Ah, marriage is a great institution!'[13]

In the summer of 1894, Dolly and Henry had visited Switzerland and the Italian lakes, and in December the same year they stayed in Monte Carlo, Cannes and Mentone. This was to satisfy Stanley's love of clear skies and sunshine. In letters to friends, Dolly made it clear that she herself could be 'as happy at home in dear foggy, muddy London – where lamps & firelight are compensation for sunshine'.[14] In fact Dorothy's love of London, and Stanley's desire to be in the country, once mutually conceded, provided them with the time they needed to be apart from one another. If compelled to be more than two or three weeks away from the capital, Dorothy would complain of feeling 'homesick'.[15]

In November 1898, Stanley longed for the next general election to be announced so his period of being an MP would be at an end. The stale air in the House of Commons, the interminable hours, the endless debates about matters that did not interest him, and the numerous speeches by men he thought foolishly self-satisfied exasperated him. Nor were the speakers he admired – such as Sir Charles Dilke and Arthur Balfour – on their feet often enough to give him much pleasure. It was a very hot summer when he was first elected, and quite often Stanley returned home in the early hours feeling as if he 'had undergone a long march'. 'We are herded in the lobbies like so many sheep in a fold; and among my wonders has been that such a number of eminent men could consent voluntarily to such servitude.'[16] Then there was the expense of postage and secretarial help – by 1900, he had paid out £4,600 in the years since his first candidature. It made him wonder why he had not resisted Dolly and had not instead chosen to be 'a writer on a daily newspaper', rather than 'a dumb dog' with less influence than a political journalist.

'To live at all I must have the open air,' he wrote in his diary after being ill. A house in the country 'with a few acres attached' now became his most cherished ambition. 'It is imperative to possess one before it is too late,' he added, anxiously.[17] In November 1898, he visited about twenty houses in the Home Counties, and the following month another thirty. Then, on 16 December, he was shown Furze Hill, a large Victorian mansion at Pirbright, Surrey, built in the Tudor half-timbered style. Dolly claimed she liked it – perhaps because it was only forty minutes from London by rail. Although let to a champion revolver shot, the fifty-six-acre grounds were overrun by rabbits, and the house itself was in poor repair. Nevertheless, Stanley liked the view, and was pleased with the mix of woodland and pasture. Although the house had too many small rooms, he was happy to contemplate refashioning the interior and adding a new wing.

By 1 January, he had agreed a price of £10,000, and a date, in the summer, for taking possession.[18] Work on the house and grounds started in June, but this did not stop Henry staying there for days at a time from September onwards, occasionally with Dolly, but more often with Denzil and his nurse. Stanley installed an electric lighting plant, bought a small fire engine, and excavated the lake to a larger size. This was the very first house he considered to be his home. Furze Hill was also intended to be where Denzil would spend most of his school holidays. No detail was too insignificant to merit Stanley's attention. As well as monitoring the building work, he planned walks, threw bridges across streams, planted trees, and built a little farm to his own designs. Dorothy was struck by how happy he was as the house and grounds took shape. If she resented him calling his house 'the Bride', she did not show it.[19]

In April 1900, Sir Alfred Lyall came to stay – perhaps making Dolly feel less upstaged – and a little later Mark Twain (whom Henry had first met in 1867) spent a few days there as their guest. Just before these visits the boat house had been finished and the carriage drive surfaced. In May, with the decorators close to completing their task, Dolly was urged to come and see it all.[20] Henry relished the fact that Furze Hill was entirely his creation, and that Dolly was on *his* turf for a change whenever she came.[21]

By now (1899) Henry was Sir Henry, and Dolly was Lady Stanley. Though Stanley had been a British subject since 1892, Lord Salisbury, the prime minister, in his letter offering Stanley the Grand Cross of the Bath, referred to his change of nationality as if it had only just been resolved.[22] Yet Salisbury had known ever since 1892, when Stanley had first contested a parliamentary seat, that he was British. The truth was that only now – after almost a decade had elapsed – did Salisbury feel that the Rear Column scandals were remote enough to make rewarding Stanley uncontroversial. As well as keeping many letters of congratulation, Henry kept some insulting notes too, among them a scrap of paper from 'one with you in Africa' – very likely a man he had sacked while working as the king's Chief Agent in the 1880s – suggesting that his knighthood was the undeserved reward meted out to 'the Yankee Adventurer' for 'years of lying, toadying & petty humbug and fraud'.[23]

Stanley himself had long stopped hoping that he might receive official recognition. He was not being falsely modest when he told Sir Arthur Sullivan, the composer, that he had expected nothing.[24] Writing about her husband's knighthood in the *Autobiography*, Dorothy did not, as she might have done, complain that the greatest explorer of the age had received the same reward as was doled out routinely to senior civil servants and military officers. It showed the modest side of Stanley's nature that he also seemed satisfied. The first person 'he thought of when he read Lord Salisbury's letter, was his old grandfather, in the Welsh cottage, who used to call him his "Man of Men"'.[25] In the same year, Major-General Kitchener was created Baron Kitchener and given £30,000 by parliament for destroying the Mahdist forces at Omdurman (killing about 11,000 and wounding 16,000 in a storm of mechanized slaughter) before re-taking Khartoum. Kitchener had used machine guns, and improvised dum-dum bullets, as well as the latest field artillery.[26] Stanley's 'massacre' of the islanders of Bumbireh pales into insignificance compared with this act of military overkill.

In the year he was knighted, Stanley paid his last visit to Wales. His mother, Elizabeth Jones, his half-bother, Robert, and his half-sister, Emma, were all dead, and Robert Jones, his stepfather, would be gone by the end of the year. During his visit, he was taken in a closed carriage to Ffynnon Beuno, his aunt Mary Owen's former farmhouse and inn at Tremeirchion. He was surprised to find that Fynnon Beuno was no longer a public house, but this did not stop him asking permission to visit the dairy, where he helped himself to a drink from a large earthenware jug of buttermilk, as he had done in boyhood.[27] His aunt had died many years ago, and all his cousins, including his favourite, John Owen, were now dead. Nevertheless, at the Cross Foxes, Bodel-wyddan, his twenty-five-year-old niece, Catherine Elizabeth Jones (his recently deceased half-brother Robert's daughter) was still in residence. Because Denzil was a blood member of his original Welsh family, Stanley's curiosity about his own origins had become more intense of late. His adopted son enabled him to reconnect with his past in a way that nobody else had ever made possible. His new interest in his family caused him, in 1898, to send William Hoffman to take photographs for him in St Asaph, Bodelwyddan, and Tremeirchion (Fynnon Beuno).[28]

When William visited Furze Hill, he found that his master had called the lake Stanley Pool and the pinewoods the Aruwimi Forest. '"Come down to Stanley Pool, William," he would say to me, half-sadly, half-humorously, when I went down to Pirbright.'[29] In 1901, William lost his savings in a phonograph company that failed, and began working for a bakery that rarely allowed him enough time off to stay overnight at Furze Hill. Occasionally Stanley sent him money. On one of Hoffman's visits to Pirbright, the butler took him into the library to meet Stanley, only to be confronted by an empty room. At length, a voice boomed out hollowly: 'Find me!' Stanley had concealed himself behind a hidden panel, as he did in his games with Denzil.[30]

Stanley felt that through his long service on the Congo, William had redeemed himself for his thefts and lies during the Emin Pasha

Expedition, and though Dorothy disliked him, Stanley remained loyal to the former boot boy. Out of gratitude, Hoffman did whatever he could to be of service, such as warning his old master, after Bonny's death, that the hospital sergeant's diaries would probably be published, exposing Stanley, Hoffman said, to 'the malicious spite he seems to have had against you'. Stanley was touched when Hoffman offered to state in public that he did not know of anything he (Stanley) had 'done unbecoming ... as the commander of us all'.[31] Forewarned, Stanley bought the diaries from Bonny's estate, and found that they would have revealed the keeping of sex slaves by the Rear Column's officers.

Two upsetting deaths took place in 1901, that of his niece Catherine Jones, at the tragically early age of twenty-seven, and then, nine months later, that of Frederick Myers, Stanley's brother-in-law – his death posing for Stanley a problem about his own religious beliefs. This was because Fred was the author of a classic book, *Human Personality and its Survival of Bodily Death*, and a founder of the Society for Psychical Research.

In 1892, when hearing Fred lecture at Toynbee Hall in the East End, Stanley had been utterly unconvinced by his claims that mediums made contact with the dead.[32] When writing about the immortality of the soul in February 1903, Henry was perceptibly less sceptical: 'We are all inclined to believe in it, but most of us, I fancy, secretly suspend judgment.'[33] William James, the founding father of psychology, wrote an account of Fred's serene and fearless death, which would have been read by Dolly and Stanley. The deathbed scene, wrote James, 'was in the grand style and something decidedly exceptional'. Myers had died in Rome, and Stanley's presence at his funeral marked his final trip abroad.[34] In the 1890s, possibly after William Mackinnon's death, Henry wrote of the 'ever-living essence' which he believed survived death.

Many years passed before I could get rid of that awful feeling which kept me as though spell-bound, or as though my soul had fled into the void of the universe searching for its lost mate. I am not so free of it yet, that I can be indifferent to the bereavement and satisfied with my knowledge – or accept my loss as though it were natural.[35]

Stanley brought his daily diary to a close at the end of 1901.[36] After that, his visits to London grew increasingly rare, and he turned down numerous invitations to dinners and meetings. In 1902 he was elected to membership of the Athenaeum Club, having been blackballed when his name had been put up nine years earlier.[37]

His last journey to London for a national event was his attendance at Edward VII's coronation in Westminster Abbey on 9 August 1902. He had complained a great deal about going, realizing that Dolly would make him stay on in the capital for four or five days, but the day itself impressed him, less for his proximity to 'the most honoured sons and daughters of the British Empire' than for 'the beauty of the music that filled aisle and nave ... and soared up to the heights'. The moment he thought 'supremest [sic] of all was when the Westminster boys added their boyish voices, crying out: "Vivat, Vivat, Vivat, Regina, and Vivat, Vivat, Vivat King Edward the 7th" with clear, sharp insistence':.'Then I really felt I was glad I was there without reserve.'[38] Youth had never lost its power to move him.

Early in 1900, Mark Twain had introduced Stanley to a Swedish doctor called Kellgren who, by massaging his stomach during a bout of gastritis, managed to release the gases and accelerate his recovery. Kellgren insisted that, provided he always underwent massage, the milk and water diets, which had always left him so weak in the past, would be unnecessary.[39] But though his gastritis had become more manageable, in March 1903 Henry complained of bouts of giddiness. When walking with Dolly near St James's Park, he swayed and almost fell.

The final works that he managed to supervise at Furze Hill were the fitting out of a billiard room for the enjoyment of his guests (he himself had never learned to play), and the installation of a new marble mantelpiece in the drawing-room, decorated with sculptured cupids – a tribute to his love of babies.[40] After Furze Hill's completion, Dolly had just eleven days to see how happy his country house had made her husband. Perhaps during this precious time, she wondered why she had forced him into politics and delayed this moment for so long. Almost ten years earlier, he had written: 'If I could only persuade you to let me resign my candidacy, I should be so rejoiced. I am weak even to fragility.'[41]

Dorothy came down from London on 2 April 1903. On the 13th he suffered a stroke in the night, with paralysis lasting for three minutes. Dorothy sent for Sir Victor Horsley, one of Britain's leading neurosurgeons, who said that no harm had been done and recommended massage and more nourishment. Four nights later, Stanley wakened his wife with a cry. A blood vessel had burst in the right side of his brain, paralysing the whole of his left side, giving him double vision and impairing his speech, but leaving his mind agonizingly clear. Horsley returned, and in due course his assistant, Dr Henry Curtis, arrived with two nurses and stayed in the house, along with the local doctor, Dr Templeton. In the *Autobiography*, Dorothy wrote of Stanley, by superhuman determination, shaving himself the very next morning. In letters to friends there was no such pretence. 'He is utterly helpless,' she told one.

He cannot sit up or turn in bed. I have two nurses and a doctor in the house ... The paralysis may pass ... He is very emotional by reason of this weakness, & at certain allusions to 'work' for example, or any subject which awakens a sad train of thought, he breaks into an agony of tears, which I can hardly bear ... It is all such anguish ... I am anxious to keep the word Paralysis from the papers. No one knows but our immediate friends.

Looking back, it agonized her to recall: 'he had showed me with such pride the new billiard room ... all the drawing room hung with silk – exquisite tapestries in the hall – all done secretly to surprise mother & me'.[42]

At this terrible time, Henry Wellcome, the American pharmaceutical tycoon, offered himself as a rock for Dorothy to lean on in all practical matters – one of which looked set to be making the arrangements for his funeral. Stanley had met Wellcome through Mrs Sheldon in 1884, and perhaps because of Stanley's fondness for May, and the rumours about her close relationship with Wellcome, the two men had never become intimate friends.[43] Nevertheless, Wellcome idolized Stanley, and thirteen years earlier, at a rowdy and hostile meeting of the Aborigines' Protection Society, had defended him most trenchantly from allegations of brutal acts committed during the Emin Pasha Relief Expedition.[44] Now, at another moment of need, the tycoon was ever ready to help and sympathize. 'My beloved husband – My dear Stanley has been very ill,' Dolly wrote to him on 29 April, and then sent regular progress reports every few days. On 4 May, Stanley was too tired to sit in a chair and had to return to bed. On the 13th he managed to move his arm in the night, and by the 22nd was able to sit in a chair in the garden for an hour or two. An attack of malaria then caused a setback; but by the end of May he could manage slight movements of his arm and his leg on his paralysed side. Dolly was pitched between hope and despair as signs of recovery were succeeded by setbacks and *vice versa*. In early June his 'good' leg swelled up, indicating that his heart had been affected, but his eyes steadily improved and he was soon able to read to himself. Whenever he was able to spend several hours in the open air, he slept better.

In late June Jephson came to see his old commanding officer, and though he was the more mobile of the two, he too looked doomed.[45] For a time, in the early 1890s, he had been a Queen's Messenger carrying important diplomatic despatches all over Europe, but when he was found unconscious on a train, he had had no choice but to resign. In 1891, he had fallen in love with a Californian girl, Anna Head, whose rich father had thought him a penniless adventurer, and had vetoed any engagement. Stanley had written to Mr Head unsuccessfully urging him to reconsider. But Addison Head died at the end of 1902, and now the mortally sick Jephson was planning his marriage.[46] Stanley had cared more for Jephson than for any other officer on the Emin Pasha expedition and it distressed him to see him in a state as parlous as his own. Someone else whose visits Henry encouraged was William Hoffman. When William first came, his master's face was drawn and stiff and he could neither speak intelligibly nor see properly. But when his old valet returned a few weeks later, Henry greeted him from his wheelchair in the garden: 'One day you will find that the miracle has happened and I am walking once more.' For William, who had walked across the African continent with Stanley, it was heartbreaking to see him unable to take a single step.[47]

Henry's heart condition now threatened to stop any further improvement. But after 'all the known remedies, Digitalis, and keeping up both feet', as well as electric treatment, and massage, Stanley was able to be taken out in a pony trap. In September, he even managed to stand unsupported for a few moments. Months ago, in May, eight-year-old Denzil and Dolly's mother had returned to London – the boy for his school lessons – so Dolly was now left in the country with her husband for several months. It was a difficult time, she told George Bernard Shaw, whom she had known since the mid-1890s. 'I want to see hansom cabs, omnibuses, and "extra specials" running, and handsome policemen, and the jostling multitude. I only put up with trees.'[48]

At last, at the end of October, Henry was well enough to return to London, where Dolly had arranged for him to be seen by Professor James Risien Russell, another distinguished neurologist. The sick man's treatment was not changed. Wellcome called on Henry, at Richmond Terrace, every few days, and Dolly took him out in a carriage each afternoon. Until his bedtime at seven, he would sit in the morning room, reading and smoking. His serene acceptance disturbed Dolly. 'At times,' she confessed, 'I have wanted him to accept less calmly ... I have really at moments resented his submission.' By now Dolly had come to love Denzil and found him 'indescribably charming and sympathetic' at this harrowing time.[49] Against all the odds, by February 1904, Stanley could walk slowly, dragging his left leg, with a stick in his right hand. Dorothy summoned a photographer to take pictures of him, and with a shaky hand he signed a few for friends. He sits very stiffly and sadly in his chair, looking like a man of eighty, but with a stern and determined expression, as if making a great effort to resemble the old public Stanley.[50]

Henry asked to return to Furze Hill for Easter, and even managed to walk part of the way along the station platform. But though he expressed pleasure to be back in his country home, in mid-April he became gravely ill with pleurisy and Dorothy took him back to London on the 27th in an 'ambulance-carriage'. On 1 May 1904 she wrote despairingly to Henry Wellcome: 'My darling husband may no longer be spared to me. His heart is rapidly failing. He is just conscious.' She asked Wellcome to write to Jephson for her. On 3 May, Denzil came into Stanley's room and kissed his hand, which woke him. As Henry touched the boy's cheek, Denzil said: 'Father, are you happy?' 'Always when I see you, dear,' he replied. It was this late relationship with a fatherless boy, rather than his undoubted greatness as an explorer, that brought him, in his declining years, the most intense happiness he had ever known.

From the evening of Friday the 5th Henry drifted in and out of consciousness, only uttering occasional words. Once, in a moment of clarity, he cried out: 'I want to be free! I want to go into the woods.' He also spoke brokenly of 'his men' and 'circumnavigation'. On the 7th Dorothy wrote to Henry Wellcome: 'My darling is sinking, slowly and painlessly. His clear mind wanders at times, and his eyes look far away. The Great Change cannot be far off now.' William Hoffman came to Richmond Terrace, Whitehall, on the 9th, but Dorothy told him Stanley was too ill to see him and that he should come back the following day. At four o' clock on the morning of the 10th, Stanley opened his eyes as nearby Big Ben was striking. 'How strange,' he murmured, 'so that is time.' He died two hours later, soon after the great clock had struck six.[51]

AFTERWORD

'How can I ever make anyone understand what he really was?'
Mounteney Jephson May 1904

On the day Stanley died, Henry Wellcome approached the Dean of Westminster, the Very Reverend Armitage Robinson, to acquaint him with the great explorer's wish to be buried in the Abbey, close to Dr Livingstone's grave. The dean's decision was made public three days later: 'It is officially announced that only the first half of the funeral of the late Sir Henry Morton Stanley will take place in Westminster Abbey.'¹ Although members of Stanley's family were never told Dean Robinson's reasons for denying him burial in the Abbey, the dean was more forthcoming with the king's private secretary: 'One of our highest geographical authorities lays stress on the violence and even cruelty, which marked some of his [Stanley's] explorations, and contrasts this with the peaceful successes of other explorers. This chiefly weighed with me in giving my decision to restrict the honour done to him to what I may call <u>second</u> honours, i.e. burial refusal but the first part of the funeral service granted.'²

Dorothy strongly suspected that the dean had been got at by Sir Clements Markham, the former secretary of the RGS, who had loathed Henry ever since he had made a fool of him on his return from finding Livingstone.³ The current Secretary of the RGS, Sir John Keltie, had no such reservations, and agreed at once to be a pall-bearer. The king showed his disapproval of Robinson's decision by sending the Duke of Abercorn, his Special Envoy to various European courts, to be a pall-bearer. Sir Harry Johnston also gladly accepted an invitation. He had seen Stanley negotiate with the Congolese, and concurred with Jephson's statement that he 'never saw him do a cruel or wanton thing'.[4] Livingstone's daughter, Agnes, felt the greatest indignation. 'Your dear Stanley,' she told Dorothy, 'was so associated with my father and my husband [Alexander Bruce] that I seem to have lost them again by his passing from us ... I shall do my utmost to protect my dear friend's memory.'[5]

'When we married,' Dolly told Henry Wellcome, 'he wanted nothing from the world.'[6] And this was true. Stanley's desire to avoid being recognized in public, and to have no contact either with London society or with the establishment, was entirely genuine. Yet Dorothy had longed for him to be respected, more than he had wanted it for himself; so it hurt her deeply that, after his long-delayed knighthood, he had received this posthumous snub. Eight-year-old Denzil, who followed his father's coffin on foot from Richmond Terrace to the Abbey, never forgot his mother's anguish. It amazed him that his loving father could be considered cruel by anyone important. The problem, as Mounteney Jephson pointed out, was Henry's public image. 'The side of him generally known to the public was that of a hard, unsympathetic, self-contained and apparently self-seeking man; the other side – that which his intimate friends saw and loved – was absolutely simple and affectionate.'[7]

That Stanley should have presented a tough and indifferent outer shell to the world was hardly surprising, given his treatment in childhood. But Dorothy was ideally placed, when she assembled the *Autobiography*, to show the vulnerable private man whom 'his intimate friends' knew. Yet she did not understand that Stanley's best defence was the truth. Far from emphasizing the wrongs done him in childhood, she gave the press an incorrect date of birth solely in order to direct historians away from documents that would have proved him illegitimate.[8] When newspapers stated that his parents had been unmarried, she sent denials to the editors.[9] By the time she brought to Pirbright from Dartmoor the huge monolith that would mark her husband's grave, she had decided that the correct date should at least appear on this stone, but she also chose to cut into the granite (nature's hardest rock) the words *Bula Matari* – a symbolic error as unfortunate as her choice of stone.

This marked the beginning of a long and misguided process by which she, and then Denzil, sought to protect Henry's memory, not by being more open, but by strengthening his defences – in her case with lies, and in Denzil's by denying historians precisely those personal papers, such as Stanley's letters to Katie Gough Roberts and to Dolly herself, that would have enabled them to present the man not as an unfeeling martinet, but as a man who had longed all his life to experience the love denied him in childhood. That the supposed 'Breaker of Rocks' had been long-suffering enough to allow Dorothy – who had never loved him as she had loved Sir Alfred Lyall – to force him into politics, shows how inappropriate his African nickname had long since become.

Sadly, the concealments and omissions made by Dorothy, and later by Denzil, played a significant role in delaying Stanley's rehabilitation. It is a truism that no man is a hero to his valet, and Dorothy would have done well to publish the fact that W. J. Hawkes – Stanley's valet from 1891 to 1897 – had begged to be allowed to follow his master's body on foot to its final resting place, 'if Lady Stanley will allow'.[10] Whether Hawkes ever received a ticket for the funeral is unknown, but poor William Hoffman definitely did not. 'It nearly broke my heart not to have a ticket,' he told Dorothy. So instead, the man who had walked through the Ituri Forest with Stanley recalled: '[I] stood at Richmond Terrace Gate to see my dear good master's coffin ... and it gave me such pain that I fainted.'[11] This anecdote, if used, would have spoken volumes about the affection Stanley inspired in servants.

Dorothy also omitted to mention that Henry's only bequests in his will (other than those to her, to Denzil, and to Jephson) were to William Hoffman, the former shoe black, and to his mother's favourite son, James William Jones, who worked on a railway station. But Dorothy found no place at all in the *Autobiography* for Stanley's humbler friends – not even for Edward Glave, whom Stanley had idolized. She granted only a single sentence to Anthony Swinburne, who had kept de Brazza out of Stanley Pool, and had first worked for Stanley as a teenager. Mrs Sheldon was excluded entirely, as was her fellow American Edward King, though both had been intimate friends, as well as exceptional people. Nor did Dorothy remark upon the numerous letters of recommendation Henry wrote on behalf of colleagues who had fallen on hard times.[12] Henry's hatred of the needless slaughter of wild animals was also left out – though this too would have shown his gentler side. He had felt strongly enough to beg Sir Francis de Winton to ignore Leopold's orders and stop shooting elephants on the Congo. 'Do not murder any more, for sheer pity ... Let the ground of the Association [the Congo] be sacred to the elephants.'[13]

The decisions made by Denzil, and his adopted son, Richard, about the custody of his papers also did much to prevent Stanley's appearing in a favourable light. It was Denzil who decided that the Stanley family archive ought never to be owned by a British institution. This was because on the fiftieth anniversary of his father's death, there had been no official commemoration anywhere in Britain – whereas, in the same year, Denzil and Richard were welcomed warmly at the Congo Museum by the Belgian government's Minister of the Colonies, who eulogized Stanley before an audience of a thousand people.[14] Denzil vowed several years later to sell his house and all his father's papers to the Belgian state.[15] After his sudden death, it was left to Richard to carry out his wishes and sell more than half the papers to Belgium. That was in 1982 – and after Richard's death, his widow and her sons sold the rest in 2000. Because access to these papers was denied to historians from 1982 until 2002, Denzil's preference for Belgium above Britain as the final destination for his father's papers denied to both Frank McLynn and John Bierman many documents that would have ensured that they wrote more sympathetic biographies.

Stanley had fallen out badly with Leopold, so if he had ever been able to travel in time and stand outside the neo-classical 'Stanley Pavilion' beside the lake that flanks the king's chateau-like Congo Museum, and be told that his papers were within, his thoughts would have been unprintable. Nor would he have been comforted to hear that his archive had been flown to Brussels in a Belgian air force jet, almost as if bearing away from morally superior Britain the corpse of his reputation. But there the archive rests, close to a museum containing scores of beautiful African artefacts, as well as Stanley's self-designed tropical hat and the Stars and Stripes he took to his meeting with Livingstone. Nearby is a room called 'The Gallery of Remembrance', which is not dedicated to the millions of Africans who perished during the 1890s and early 1900s, but to the 1,508 Belgians, who died in the Congo during Leopold's reign.

So where does this leave Stanley, and his papers and other possessions? I fear it leaves them as part of the history of Belgium's most unprincipled king's efforts to steal the resources, the labour, and indeed the lives of his 'subjects' in Africa's largest country. Given Stanley's very different hopes and aims, and his feelings for the Congolese, it would have amazed him that this should be his permanent memorial.

Yet the facts of Stanley's life, and the truth about his personality, can (and I believe *will*) rescue his posthumous reputation. In 1878, after his greatest journey, Mark Twain declared: 'Stanley is almost the only man alive today whose name and work will be familiar one hundred years hence.' Twain, like most of his male contemporaries in America, valued above all other human virtues courage, physical endurance, and the goal of increasing man's knowledge of the planet, at whatever personal cost. And this feeling spanned continents. Anton Chekhov, the master of understated artistry, saw Stanley's 'stubborn invincible striving towards a certain goal, no matter what privations, dangers and temptations for personal happiness are entailed ... [as] personifying the highest moral strength ... One Stanley is worth a hundred good books.' [16] Stanley had gone back to Africa again and again, apparently indifferent to the increased risk of death on each return. His courage, and his unparalleled geographical feats, had certainly not grown less remarkable as the years had passed. But technological and medical progress made the nature of his achievement harder to appreciate for succeeding generations. Today, outside the field of sport, such qualities are not so highly regarded in a world in which sexual equality has made many purely masculine pursuits seem chauvinistic, or simply masochistic. The fact that African explorers could not avoid terrible sickness and privation is largely forgotten.

By another of the many ironies that constantly afflicted Stanley, the press – which had made him famous after he found Livingstone – destroyed him after the Barttelot and Jameson families had taken exception to his restrained criticism of their relatives. Because Stanley was seen as an American criticizing British officers, it scarcely registered in editors' minds that he himself had been innocent of the appalling acts perpetrated by members of his notorious Rear Column. *He* had not bought a young girl and sketched her being killed and eaten, nor had he flogged men to death, and starved them when copious preserved food was in store. Yet because of the Rear Column scandals, from late 1890 onwards Stanley's very name seemed to summon up images of cannibalism, brutality and moral disintegration. Then from the mid-nineties this damage had been compounded by the increasingly stomach-turning revelations emanating from the Congo.

Ask a dozen people who was the greatest land explorer in the greatest age of exploration since the voyages of the Portuguese and Spanish navigators, and maybe one (but more likely none) will name Stanley – and not just on account of his undeserved 'conquistador' stereotype. Because of the power of the numerous visual depictions of his meeting with Livingstone under the folds of the Stars and Stripes, he is often thought of as an American journalist, rather than as an explorer. 'Dr Livingstone, I presume?' has been remembered, but not his wretched Welsh childhood and the workhouse, not the suffering, not the working class companions, his Civil War fighting, his gold rush failures, Turkish fiasco, enlightened reporting of the Indian wars, triumph in Abyssinia – virtually none of the elements that made Stanley such a unique British hero, though of course he is not acknowledged as such. He had packed more into his life before he set out to find Livingstone, aged twenty-nine, than many adventurers could claim to have experienced in their entire lives.

Still in his early thirties, between 1874 and 1877 Stanley circumnavigated Lake Victoria in a small boat crewed by only eleven men, proving that it was a single body of water and not several, which made Speke's northern outlet almost certain to be the primary source of the Nile. His circumnavigation of Lake Tanganyika established that the only outflow from the lake flowed into the Lualaba to the west. By making regular observations for latitude and longitude at noon on clear days, using a sextant and a chronometer, he made the first reliable maps of the two largest northern lakes, and the river system of the central African watershed. He also mapped the course of the Congo, joining a series of dots that recorded each of the positions obtained by his regular midday observations. He took boiling-point readings to establish heights above sea level and used a theodolite to estimate the height of distant hills. By following the Lualaba north and then west, he proved that it had no connection with the Nile, or the Niger, and was therefore the Congo, and he mapped its entire course to the Atlantic from Nyangwe. Despite his problems with hostile tribes, with rapids, and with lack of food, he managed to take nineteen observations between 4 February and 2 March 1877, during which time he delineated the entire top of the river's majestic hoop-like curve. His original map of the Congo was sold as Lot 38 at Christie's Africa Sale on 24 September 2002 for £78,000, almost four times its minimum estimate of £20,000. This unique map was bought by an American private collector. It should surely have been bought for the British nation.[17]

In 1876 Stanley had stated that he thought the Kagera River was 'the true parent of the Victoria Nile', which is exactly what has just been claimed in 2006 by the members of a New Zealand and British expedition.[18] In 1889 Stanley established that Lake Edward fed the Semliki river, which flowed on into Lake Albert – proving that this lake was a secondary source of the Nile, and no rival to Lake Victoria (or to the Kagera that fed it). Also in 1889, Stanley established the role of the rain-making Ruwenzori mountains in feeding the Nile. Stanley was not inferior to Livingstone in scientific observation, and made no mistakes as serious as the elder man's miscalculations at Lake Bangweulu; nor did he leave the Congo at a vital point, as Livingstone had done for almost 300 miles east of Victoria Falls when mapping the Zambezi. That one omission had wrecked Livingstone's subsequent Zambesi Expedition.

To have been a great leader of African exploring expeditions in the anarchic last three decades of the nineteenth century required very unusual personal qualities – characteristics, in fact, that sensible, well-balanced modern men and women, leading safe lives, tend to find alarming: such as being inspired, fearless, obsessed, able to frighten, able to suffer, but also able to command love and obedience. Such men tended to be haunted by their longing to solve mysteries, by their dedication to a cause, or by the belief that God had sent them, or by their need to earn love and respect through the strength of their will. They are an extinct species, and all the more remarkable for that.

After Freud linked human behaviour with unconscious desires and unmasked the self-deception inherent in Victorian 'will-power', the well-informed came to mistrust other nineteenth-century virtues like 'duty' and 'sense of mission'. 'I was not sent into the world to be happy ... I was sent for a special work,' wrote Stanley, and believed it.[19] What was wrong with those explorers, we ask, knowingly, these days. And even if we acquit them of being the masochistic victims of their own thwarted impulses, books with men of action as their protagonists remain out of favour with sophisticated people. Failure to understand the mindset of a lost era has done much to limit our appreciation of Homeric lives like Stanley's. Disapproval of the adventurous hero began with the birth of English seriousness in the eighteenth century, and despite the subsequent popularity of Scott and Stevenson (and their less talented B-movie successors), the adventurer would never appeal to intellectuals of later generations. Only a blighted, self-doubting fictional specimen, like Conrad's eponymous Lord Jim, stood any chance. But Stanley was blighted too, very like Jim, by his inability to live up to his ideals. More modern still, Stanley failed to deny himself the fame he both craved and detested. For Stanley, adventure was not a secret failing, like reading pulp fiction in bed (which he sometimes did), but a Nietzschean confrontation that was the breath of life to him, a breaking away from the daily self he knew and could not endure, into a persona in which he could escape past humiliations, and stretch the boundaries of the human condition in denial of his own mortality.

A few days after Frank Pocock's and Kalulu's canoes had hurtled into a foaming maelstrom of rocks and white water, drowning them both, Stanley was himself close to death, by starvation rather than drowning.

This poor body of mine has suffered terribly [he wrote], it has been degraded, pained, wearied & sickened, and has well nigh sunk under the task imposed on it; but this was but a small portion of myself. For my real self lay darkly encased, & was ever too haughty & soaring for such miserable environments as the body that encumbered it daily.[20]

Indeed, there was an unearthly quality about the man, which people noticed. Major James Pond, his lecture agent, was one of them. When the explorer returned from his pioneering on the Congo in the mid-1880s, Pond was surprised, on first meeting Stanley, to find him small, reticent and surprisingly gentle. Yet the man's pale and extraordinarily penetrating blue-grey eyes fascinated him. They had lunch at the Café Royal and afterwards, when they had parted at the end of a short walk, the hard-bitten agent, who represented ex-presidents and kings, found himself hurrying after his guest as if impelled by an unseen force. 'I cannot tell why it was but I could not help following him. He had produced a most remarkable impression on me. I kept saying to myself: "That is Stanley! Stanley the wonderful explorer! What a life he has had!"'[21]

In a photographic exhibition in London, in August 2005, there was a photograph of a broken statue of Henry Stanley, lying on the rotting deck of the *AIA* , one of his own steamers launched on the Upper Congo in November 1882. The man and the little ship have lain together since the 1970s in a public works lot in Kinshasa. Both are popular with photographers, since the fallen figure of Stanley in his solar topee (regulation wear for imperial officials) speaks eloquently of the absurdity of white supremacist ideas and the fate that had always awaited them. I doubt whether Stanley would have been surprised by the fall of his effigy, or by the fact that the government of Zambia is trying to get Zimbabwe to hand over to them the statue of a man, whom 'the Zambians have a great deal of affection for'. It is not Stanley, of course, but the much-photographed one of striding Dr Livingstone that overlooks Victoria Falls.[22]

The fact that the Livingstone problem seems likely to cloud Stanley's reputation for many years to come is another of those great ironies afflicting him. In 1872, Henry had thought it made a better newspaper story to have found a wise and pious old man in the heart of Africa than to have rescued one obsessed with past insults and injuries. Through what he wrote about him, Stanley made the public forget about the deaths and disasters of the Zambezi Expedition, and enabled them to acclaim a British saint. Yet having made the man an icon of goodness, he would never escape from being adversely compared with the mythic figure he had created. 'Well may he call his lecture "Through the Dark Continent",' wrote the editor of *The Anti-Slavery Reporter* in November 1878. 'It will be dark for him. He will stand in everlasting contrast to Livingstone, and act as a dark shadow to throw up the brightness of Livingstone's fame.'

Although it is now (as I write) over three decades since I revealed, in my 1973 biography, that Livingstone's neglected wife became an alcoholic and his eldest son changed his name and left the country, and that he failed spectacularly to be a humane and popular leader of Europeans, the doctor's saintly image marches on. He made a number of serious geographical errors (one of which cost him his life), and he converted only a single African, who lapsed. Then, during his last journey, he failed so comprehensively to discipline his African followers that their crimes would include rape, murder and even slave-dealing. As a consequence, he would be forced to depend on Arab-Swahili slave traders to protect him. Long ago he had fallen out with almost all his colleagues, and even blamed sick and dying missionaries for letting him down. Yet he is still saintly Dr Livingstone to most people. This seems to be his immutable stereotype, just as brash and brutal Stanley seems to be his. Of course, Livingstone had been genuinely godly too, as well as self-sacrificing, brave, enlightened, idealistic, uninterested in money and in fame, a lover of Africans and Africa, and a genius at writing about the continent. Great flaws and great virtues – and was that so utterly different from Stanley's personality?

Yet Livingstone's fame had been due not so much to what he had done, as to what he had come to represent in *moral* terms. By praising a man who was said to have died on his knees in Africa while saving the heathen, the British public could feel pride without any nagging guilt over their country's wealth and power. Through him they could enjoy again the sense of moral superiority they had known when Britain had led the fight against the Atlantic slave trade (having once been its leading participant). Yes, *he* had made people feel good about themselves, and *he* had been British. So what had Stanley (the Welshman, turned American, turned Englishman) come to represent? The hard man of African travel, the 'conquistador', who had taken huge expeditions to Africa because he liked to travel that way, and was somehow responsible for Emin Pasha's shortcomings, and the deaths on the Congo during the 1890s (though he had left in 1884). Who was going to feel good about admiring *him*?

The Victorians were hooked on needing to feel virtuous and, in our own way, we are too. With the benefit of hindsight, we know that colonialism had some disastrous consequences: the millions who died in Leopold's Congo, the badly drawn borders causing future conflicts, the German massacre of the Hereros, the Italian genocide in Libya, and British crimes committed while suppressing the Kenyan Mau Mau insurrection. So we virtuously condemn those who did not see these things coming many decades before they actually came to pass. And yet we forget that between the late 1880s and 1910, the various colonial administrations brought to an end large-scale enslavement of Africans; and subsequently, in British and French territories at least, maintained over much of the continent relatively incorrupt government under the rule of law.[23] We also fail to ask ourselves what would have happened if the Arab-Swahili had remained unopposed throughout Africa. Darfur provides a clue.

Men like Mackinnon and Stanley believed in the moral worth of the new industrial society, having seen for themselves the outlawing of child labour, the advent of compulsory state education, and the way in which an increase in national wealth had brought prosperity to far more people than had once seemed possible. They had not seen European nations fight two bloody world wars, nor dreamed of anything so terrible as the gas chambers, or the dropping of the atom bomb, nor suspected that technological advances might one day threaten the planet. So Stanley never felt as if European society was morally suspect, or that explorers were culturally arrogant first movers in an exploitative colonial process designed to destroy African customs. He believed he was bringing numerous advantages to the Africans. So European intervention in Africa seemed wholly desirable.

If he were alive today he would be horrified to learn about Europe's failure to intervene to prevent the genocide in Rwanda. It would have amazed him that the UN has not been given enough troops to end fighting in eastern Congo, which to date has cost 3,000,000 lives. Nor would he have understood why the Sudanese government is not confronted over events in Darfur. He himself had done better in changing something similar. Six of his despatches (including those relaying Livingstone's accounts of the massacre of runaway slaves at Nyangwe) appeared in the press shortly before the House of Commons debated the report of the Select Committee on the East African slave trade, and his journalism played an important part in persuading the British government to opt for total abolition of the seaborne East African trade. Few people alive today can feel as secure as he once did about having made a direct contribution to saving the lives of hundreds of thousands of human beings. The Victorians sent the Royal Navy to end the slave trade on both sides of Africa, and kept up their effort for decades, regardless of the deaths of sailors and the expense. It seems unlikely that, a century hence, present day efforts to help Africa will be thought superior to that sixty-year undertaking.

Today, a vivid and uniquely adventurous life like Stanley's challenges our ability to be just and objective, both about his story, and about the vices and virtues of his contemporaries' world view. His absence of racism was all the more remarkable for his having lived in the Deep South – as were the many affectionate things he wrote about Africans seventy-five years before state troopers forcibly ended segregation in Little Rock's schools. In the 1950s children in America and Europe (and I was one of them) watched Cowboys and Indians fighting each other in film after film of a kind that would rightly be thought outrageous if shown to children today. But in that decade, people were still being hanged for murder in Britain, homosexuals were being persecuted and delinquents were being 'birched'. And of course, Stanley's opinions should be judged against the values of the far more violent world of the Victorian workhouse and the American Civil War, a whole century earlier.

When Henry described his work on the Congo as 'a sacred task',[24] he was not being hypocritical. His hopes for Africa undoubtedly turned out to be far too optimistic. But without his optimism and his belief in his mission, he would not have risked his life in Africa for all the years he did, and would never have recorded his greatest achievements. One of his officers wrote in 1889, on seeing his leader return to camp 'ragged and cadaverous': 'I never felt so forcibly as now, how much this man was suffering ... He might very well have been living in luxury ... housed in some sumptuous mansion ... I had never before so fully believed in Stanley's unswerving sense of duty.'[25] A friend who had known him on the Congo told Dorothy that if only Henry could have been killed in Africa, the government would have sent a punitive expedition to avenge 'the great Stanley', and he would have been buried in Westminster Abbey beside Livingstone.[26] But this is to speculate. Facts, too, can change reputations, and there are more than enough in the mighty family archive in Brussels to make sure that, one day, Henry Morton Stanley will no longer be a scapegoat for the post-colonial guilt of successive generations.

ACKNOWLEDGEMENTS

In September 2002, the late Maurits Wynants invited me to Brussels to begin my work in the Stanley Archive at the Musée Royal de l'Afrique Centrale while the collection was still being catalogued. I therefore remember him with particular gratitude. But my greatest debt is to Peter Daerden, formerly of the Musée Royal, who while cataloguing the immense archive and compiling the inventory promptly responded to my numerous requests and lines of inquiry when I was in Brussels. Later, he sent to London scores of e-mails, notes and many photocopies, not only of requested documents but of letters and diary entries he felt I should see. My book has benefited immensely from his input. In Wales, the local historian Bob Owen, author of articles about Stanley's origins, answered my queries, undertook investigations on my behalf, and taught me much about Denbigh in Stanley's time. Dr Iain Smith of the University of Warwick, whose account of the Emin Pasha Expedition (1972) is still the best, lent me his books on the subject and photocopies of articles in rare periodicals and newspapers. Iain Maciver, Head of Manuscripts at the National Library of Scotland, answered many questions, sent photocopies from the library's Livingstone and Stanley collections, and made suggestions for further research in other collections in his care. I owe an equal debt to Alicia Clarke, Director of the Sanford Museum, Florida, who drew my attention not merely to the many Stanley letters at the museum but to letters written to Henry Sanford by Stanley's employees on the Congo, several of whom became friends. Richard Sawyer, the rare books/manuscripts dealer, and his client Russell Train permitted me to see Mr Train's large and varied Africana collection before it was donated to the Smithsonian Library. This collection contains the correspondence of Captain R. H. Nelson, and other unpublished Emin Pasha papers. Margaret Stewart, a granddaughter of Katie Gough Roberts (the first woman to whom Stanley proposed), let me see copies of the dozen unpublished letters written by Stanley to her grandmother. Lady Stanley failed to buy these from Katie when she obtained the rest. These letters were sold at Christie's, London, in 1992. Nathaniel C. Hughes, author of the excellent *Sir Henry Morton Stanley, Confederate*, answered my queries about Stanley's time in America, as did Lisa Singleton of Tulane University, New Orleans. John Pinfold, librarian at Rhodes House, Oxford, sent me copies of the Pocock papers and letters from John Kirk, Horace Waller and others.

Tracey Jean Boisseau, author of a biography of May Sheldon, identified Mrs Sheldon for me in several group photographs and corresponded with me on the subject of Stanley's relations with her. Jane Stanley (widow of H. M. Stanley's adopted grandson) clarified various matters for me, and sent me a photograph of Dorothy's first portrait of Stanley. Haidee Jackson, Curator of Newstead Abbey, arranged for an unknown portrait of Emilia Webb (an early confidante of Stanley) to be photographed. Kevin Matthias, County Archivist of Denbighshire, and Dyfed Roberts searched out details of Stanley's Welsh family, as did Paul F. Mason, Archivist at the Flintshire Record Office. Guy Tillim sent me his evocative photograph of Stanley's fallen statue in Kinshasa. Professor Simon Keynes gave me access to the late Quentin Keynes's unique African collection before its sale at Christie's in April 2004. Dr Michael Brooks (a member of the family of Henry Hope Stanley, who allegedly adopted H. M. Stanley) gave me new factual information.

My warm thanks to Julian Loose of Faber & Faber for commissioning the book, and to Henry Volans, also of Faber, for his perceptive commentary, which has helped me give *Stanley* its present shape. My thanks also to the production team at Faber and to Alex Lazarou and Wendy Toole. Jon Jackson, formerly of Gillon Aitken Associates, made useful comments on the whole text. Once again my wife, Joyce, was sympathetic when my research threatened to overwhelm me, and generously forgave me for devoting so much time to the task.

All the following helped me: Sarah Strong, Archivist, Royal Geographical Society; Pauline Hubner, RGS Picture Department; Professor Gustaaf Janssens, Archivist at the Royal Palace, Brussels; Pierre Dandoy, Diplomatic and African Archive, Brussels; Mathilde Leduc, Musée Royal de l'Afrique Centrale; Professor Anthony M. Gibbs, Macquarie University, Sydney; Sally Harrower, new Head of Manuscripts, National Library of Scotland; Karen Carruthers, David Livingstone Centre, Blantyre; Rachel M. Rowe, Smuts Librarian in South Asian & Commonwealth Studies, Cambridge University; Lona Jones, Assistant Librarian, National Library of Wales, Aberystwyth; Andrew Dulley and Sarah Phillips, Archivists, West Glamorgan Archive Service; Julie Snelling, Assistant Archivist, the Royal Archives, Windsor; the staff of the Manuscripts Room, British Library; Sue Mills, Archivist, Regent's Park College, Oxford; Marcelle Graham, Librarian, and Diana Madden, Manuscripts Librarian, the Brenthurst Library, Johannesburg; Dr Tony Trowles, Librarian, Westminster Abbey; Cliff Davies, Archivist, Wadham College, Oxford; Adam C. Greene, Assistant Archivist, Trinity College, Cambridge; Christine Mason, Bodleian Library, Oxford; the staff of the Wellcome Medical Library; Robert W. Mills, Librarian, Royal College of Physicians in Ireland; Mary O'Doherty, Librarian/Archivist, Royal College of Surgeons in Ireland; Christine Holgate, Northallerton Library; Bruce Tabb, Assistant Professor, Special Collections Librarian, University of Oregon; Margaret Acton, Librarian, Centre for the Study of Christianity in the Non-Western World, Edinburgh University; J. E. Griffiths, Crewe; Carol Leadenham, Hoover Institution Library, Stanford University; Denison J. Beach, Library Assistant, Houghton Library, Harvard University; Jason D. Stratman, Library Assistant, Missouri Historical Society; Janie C. Morris, Research Librarian, Duke University, North Carolina; staff of the Louisiana Division, New Orleans Public Library; Dr C. M. Rider, Archivist, Inner Temple, London; Guy Holborn, Librarian, Lincoln's Inn Library, London.

SOURCES

MANUSCRIPT COLLECTIONS CONSULTED

Musée Royal de l'Afrique Centrale, Tervuren, Brussels

The most important collection of Stanley's papers in the world. Exploration diaries, notebooks, maps, early manuscript drafts of his autobiography, private correspondence to and from his wife, letters from his Welsh family, and from friends including David Livingstone, Edward S. King, E. J. Glave, May Sheldon, Alice Pike, Lewis Noe, Alexander Bruce, Sir William Mackinnon, Edward Marston; correspondence with British and Belgian ministers, with Leopold II, James Gordon Bennett Jr, Edwin Arnold, and with members of his major expeditions, including the diary of William Bonny; also correspondence with his valet, William Hoffman, and his private notes on the EPRE. Dorothy Stanley's diaries and correspondence with friends and family. The Luwel papers contain one of only two extant original treaties that Stanley signed with Congolese chiefs. Scrapbooks, press cuttings, photographs. Inventory has 426 pp.

National Library of Scotland, Edinburgh

Stanley's letters to David Livingstone, to Agnes Livingstone (Bruce), to Alexander L. Bruce, to J. A. Grant, Sir John Kirk, and copies of letters to J. B. Pond. Also Edward Glave to Stanley in 1890, enclosing a statement in Swahili by Saleh bin Osman (trans by Glave). Other letters relating to the EPRE.

Mackinnon Papers, School of Oriental and African Studies, London

Stanley's letters to Sir William Mackinnon, important in the colonial history of East Africa and the Congo. Dorothy Stanley's letters to Mackinnon. Complete papers of the EPRE Committee, including letters from Stanley, from expedition members, committee members, politicians, etc.

SOURCES

Sanford Museum, Sanford, Florida

The papers of 'General' Henry Shelton Sanford, including 48 letters from Stanley, from Leopold II's secretary, Count Borchgrave, from Sir William Mackinnon, and from friends of Stanley who served under him on the Congo: A. B. Swinburne, H. P. Bailey, E. J. Glave, who later worked for Sanford's ivory company. The collection is a key source for the early history of the Congo Free State.

British Library, London

Various Add Mss letters including Stanley to J. Bolton, the cartographer, to H. W. Bates, E. M. Parker, T. H. S. Escott, H. Bey, etc., etc. Dorothy Stanley's letters to George Bernard Shaw. RP photocopies of numerous Stanley letters, also microfilm of Stanley's exploration diaries and notebooks (originals in Brussels), and of some correspondence. Livingstone's letters to his daughter Agnes.

Royal Geographical Society, London

Letters of Stanley and Dorothy to H. W. Bates, J. S. Keltie, and to Henry Wellcome, including letters concerning Stanley's final illness, funeral and the purchase of letters from Mrs Bradshaw (Katie Gough Roberts). Letters from William Hoffman to H. Wellcome, from Stanley to May Sheldon. Photographs, press cuttings.

Trinity College, Cambridge

The papers of F. W. H. Myers (brother-in-law of Stanley) and his wife Eveleen (née Tennant), including many letters from Stanley and Dorothy to them both. Also letters from Stanley to their children.

Rhodes House, Oxford

The diaries of Edward and Frank Pocock. A 17-page letter about Stanley from Horace Waller to David Livingstone, and other correspondence about Kirk and Stanley; also correspondence of the Anti-Slavery Society.

Wellcome Library, Euston Road, London

Papers of Henry S. Wellcome, friend of Stanley and Dorothy, with letters from them both, also from William Hoffman, Mounteney Jephson, and papers concerning May Sheldon. Drafts of Hoffman's book. Newspaper cuttings about Dorothy Tennant/Stanley.

Cambridge University Library

An important book-length t/s 'Portrait of Stanley' by Gerald Sanger, a close friend of Denzil Stanley, who had shown to Sanger his father's correspondence with Alice Pike, and with Dorothy Tennant before she married Stanley. Also long verbatim quotations from Dorothy's diaries up to the date of her marriage.

Diplomatic Archive and Africa Archive, Ministry of Foreign Affairs, Brussels

Nine alleged copies, in a secretarial hand, of treaties with Congolese chiefs purporting to be verbatim transcripts of vanished originals signed by Stanley. One original treaty bears Stanley's signature and is dated Vivi 13.06.1880.

Archives du Palais Royal, Brussels

Correspondence of King Leopold II, including Stanley's to the king, many of which are quoted in part by Stanley in his Congo Diaries (CD).

Archives Générales du Royaume, Brussels

Correspondence between King Leopold and Stanley 1886. Eetvelde Papers. Papers relevant to EPRE.

Russell E. Train Collection, Smithsonian Institution Libraries, Washington DC

The unpublished papers of Captain R. H. Nelson, one of Stanley's EPRE officers, including letters from Stanley and to Nelson from Jephson and Stairs. Nelson's letters to his family. Mrs J. S. Jameson's hand transcription of her late husband's papers and Major Barttelot's which he had boxed up after the major's murder. Early letters from Dorothy Tennant to her friend Mary Millais, and several important letters written by Stanley to Edward Levy-Lawson (owner *Daily Telegraph*).

West Glamorgan Archive Service, Swansea

The Tennant family's papers: letters to and from Dorothy Tennant/Stanley, and her brother Charles Coombe Tennant and her sister-in-law, Winifred. Papers relating to Stanley's marriage and funeral, and to his mother's illiteracy.

Robert Owen Private Collection, Denbigh

Correspondence between Denzil Stanley and editor of *Denbighshire Free Press* (1954); photocopies of Owen 'Morien' Morgan's notes of an interview with Stanley's mother; census info about Stanley's uncle, Thomas Parry, and his wife. Letters from Katie Gough Roberts's father, Thomas, to his solicitor. Local postcard collection, including one showing only existing photographic image of Stanley's mother and stepfather.

Quentin Keynes Collection, sold Christie's, London, 2004

Letters from Stanley to friends and to Agnes Livingstone, also his famous letter 'To any gentleman ... at Emboma' 4.08.1877. Several Livingstone letters.

SOURCES

National Library of Wales, Aberystwyth

32 letters from Dorothy Stanley to members of the Hills-Johnes family.

David Livingstone Centre, Blantyre, Scotland

Originals of Livingstone's last diaries, field notebooks, etc.

Baptist Missionary Society Archives, Regent's Park College, Oxford

Stanley's letters to various Baptist missionaries including W. H. Bentley, T. J. Comber, Lawson Forfeitt, and their letters to the secretary of their society.

University of Oregon, Eugene, Oregon

Stanley's letters to Lieutenant L. Van de Velde in Van de Velde papers.

National Archives and Record Administration, Washington, DC

Stanley's Civil War Enlisted Branch File, CSR Card, Muster Records, Adjutant-General's office records.

Denbighshire Record Office

St Hilary's Church register recording Stanley's baptismal entry. Memorial Scroll written by Stanley in 1866 to commemorate his grandfather, Moses Parry.

Flintshire County Record Office

St Asaph Union Workhouse records, including Stanley's admission and discharge entries. Census and parish records, two Stanley letters. Lucy M. Jones's notes on H.M. Stanley and family.

Brenthurst Library, Johannesburg; Houghton Library, Harvard University; Duke University, South Carolina; Pierpont Morgan Library, New York; Royal College of Physicians of Ireland Library, Dublin; Royal College of Surgeons in Ireland, Dublin

All have a few letters from Stanley and in several cases from Dorothy, and the Brenthurst Library also has a long letter from Livingstone to James Gordon Bennett Jr.

Nottingham University, Special Collections

A large collection of letters from A. J. M. Jephson to his relative, Lady Middleton, describing his time with Stanley in America in 1890–91 and subsequent relations.

BIBLIOGRAPHY

1 Stanley's publications

How I Found Livingstone in Central Africa (1872)
My Kalulu, Prince, King and Slave (1873)
Coomassie and Magdala (1874)
Through the Dark Continent, 2 vols (1878)
The Congo and the Founding of its Free State (1885)
My African Travels (1886)
In Darkest Africa, 2 vols (1890)
My Dark Companions and their Strange Stories (1893)
My Early Travels and Adventures in America and Asia, 2 vols (1895)
Through South Africa (1898)

2 Other publications (see notes for most articles in learned journals and periodicals referred to in the text)

Anstey, Roger T. *Britain and the Congo in the Nineteenth Century* (1962)
Anstruther, Ian *I Presume: Stanley's Triumph and Disaster* (1956)
Arnold, Julian B. *Giants in Dressing Gowns* (1942)
Ascherson, Neal *The King Incorporated* (1963)
Axelson, S. *Culture Confrontation in the Lower Congo* (1970)
Bailey, H. (Bula N'Zau) *Travel and Adventures in the Congo Free State* (1894)
Baker, Samuel White *The Albert Nyanza* 2 vols (1874)
Barttelot, W. G. *The Life of Edmund Musgrave Barttelot* (1890)
Beachey, R. 'The Arms Trade in East Africa in the late 19th century', *Journal of African History* iii no 3 (1962)
— *The Slave Trade of Eastern Africa* (1976)
Bennett, Norman R. *Arab versus European: Diplomacy and War in Nineteenth Century East Central Africa* (1986)
— *A History of the Arab State of Zanzibar* (1978)
— *Mirambo of Tanzania* (1971)
— ed *Stanley's Despatches to the New York Herald 1871–1877* (1970)

Bentley, W. H. *Pioneering on the Congo* 2 vols (1900)

Bierman, John *Dark Safari: The Life behind the Legend of Henry Morton Stanley* (1990)

Birmingham, D. and Martin, P. M. eds *History of Central Africa* vol 2 (1983)

Blashford-Snell, John *In the Steps of Stanley* (1975)

Boisseau, Tracey J. *White Queen: May Sheldon and the Origins of American Feminist Identity* (2004)

Bontinck, François *Aux Origines de l'État Indépendent du Congo* (1966)

Britten, Emma Hardinge *The Electric Physician* (1875)

Brode, H. *Tippu Tip* (1906)

Burrows, Guy *The Curse of Central Africa* (1903, withdrawn after court case)

—*The Land of the Pygmies* (1898)

Burton, Richard F. *The Lake Regions of Central Africa* 2 vols (1860)

Cairns, H. A. C. *Prelude to Imperialism: British Reactions to Central African Society 1840–1890* (1965)

Cameron, Verney L. *Across Africa* 2 vols (1877)

Casada, James A. *Dr Livingstone and Sir Henry Morton Stanley* (1976)

Casati, Gaetano *Ten Years in Equatoria and the Return with Emin Pasha* 2 vols (1891)

Ceulemans, Père *La Question Arabe et le Congo 1883–1892* (1959)

Chadwick, O. *Mackenzie's Grave* (1959)

Chaillé-Long, C. *Central Africa* (1876)

Chavannes, P. de *Avec Brazza: Souvenirs de la Mission de l'Ouest Africain* (1935)

Collins, Robert O. *King Leopold, England and the Upper Nile* (1968)

Cookey, S. J. S. *Britain and the Congo Question 1885–1913* (1968)

Coquilhat, Camille *Sur le Haut-Congo* (1888)

Cornet, R. J. *La Bataille du rail* (1953)

Coupland, Reginald *The Exploitation of East Africa 1856–1890* (1939)

Crowe, S. E. *The Berlin West Africa Conference 1884–85* (1942)

Darby, Phillip *Three Faces of Imperialism: British and American Approaches to Asia and Africa 1870–1970* (1987)

Decle, Lionel *Three Years in Savage Africa* (1898)

Doyle, Arthur Conan *The Crime of the Congo* (1909)

Durand, H. M. *The Life of Sir Alfred Comyn Lyall* (1913)

Emerson, Barbara *Leopold II of the Belgians: King of Colonialism* (1979)

Farwell, Byron *The Man who Presumed* (1957)

Farwell, Byron *Queen Victoria's Little Wars* (1973)

Forbath, Peter *The River Congo* (1978)

Forrest, D. W. *Francis Galton: The Life and Work of a Victorian Genius* (1974)

Foskett, Reginald *The Zambezi Doctors: David Livingstone's Letters to John Kirk 1858–1872* (1964)

Fox-Bourne, W. R. *Civilisation in Congoland: A Story of international Wrongdoing* (1903)

— *The Other Side of the Emin Pasha Relief Expedition* (1891)

Fraser, A. Z. *Livingstone and Newstead* (1913)

Fry, Joseph A. *Henry S. Sanford: Diplomacy and Business in Nineteenth Century America* (1982)

Galbraith, J. S. *Mackinnon and East Africa 1878–1895* (1972)

Gann, L. H. and Duignan, P. *Burden of Empire: An Appraisal of Colonialism in Africa* (1968)

Gann, L. H. and Duignan, P. *The Rulers of Belgian Africa 1884–1914* (1979)

Gathorne-Hardy, Jonathan *The Public School Phenomenon* (1977)

Gauld, Alan *Founders of Psychical Research* (1968)

Gifford, P. and Louis, W. R *Britain and Germany in Africa* (1971); see chapter by Stengers, Jean 'King Leopold and Anglo-French Rivalry 1882–84'

Glave, E. J. *Six Years of Adventure in Congoland* (1893)

Grant, James *A Walk Across Africa* (1864)

Gray, Sir John 'Early Treaties in Uganda 1881–91, *Uganda Journal* xii no 1 (1950)

Green, Jeffrey P. *Dictionary of National Biography* (2005), article on William Hoffman

Green, Martin *Dreams of Adventure, Deeds of Empire* (1980)

Guthrie, Thomas A. *A Long Retrospect* (1936)

Hall, Richard *Stanley: An Adventurer Explored* (1974)

Harker, G. *The Life of George Grenfell, Congo Missionary and Explorer* (1909)

Harman, Nicholas *Bwana Stokesi and his African Conquests* (1986)

Harms, Robert W. *River of Wealth, River of Sorrow: The Cenral Zaire Basin in the Era of the Slave and Ivory Trade 1500–1891* (1981)

Harrison, J. W. *The Story of the Life of Mackay of Uganda* (1898)

Hart, James A. *A History of the Missouri Globe-Democrat* (1961)

Helly, Dorothy O. *Livingstone's Legacy: Horace Waller and Victorian Mythmaking* (1987)

Hinde, Samuel L. *The Fall of the Congo Arabs* (1897)

Hird, Frank *H. M. Stanley: The Authorised Life* (1935)

Hochschild, Adam *King Leopold's Ghost: A Story of Greed, Terror and Heroism in Colonial Africa* (1998)

Hoffmann, W. *With Stanley in Africa* (1938)

Hotten, John C. *The Finding of Dr Livingstone by H. M. Stanley* (1872)

Hughes, Nathaniel C., Jr. *Sir Henry Morton Stanley, Confederate* (2000)

Inglis, Brian *Roger Casement* (1973)

Jackson, Frederick *Early Days in East Africa* (1930)

Jackson, Peggy *Meteor out of Africa* (1962)

James, Robert Rhodes *Henry Wellcome* (1994)

James, William *Correspondence of William James* vols iii & iv 1885–1896 (1994)

Jameson, James S. *The Story of the Rear Column of the Emin Pasha Relief Expedition* (1890)

Jeal, Tim *Livingstone* (1973)

Jephson, A. J. Mounteney *Emin Pasha and the Rebellion at the Equator* (1890)

Jephson, Maurice Denham *An Anglo-Irish Miscellany: some records of the Jephsons of Mallow* (1964)

Johnston, Harry H. *The River Congo* (1884)

— *The Story of my Life* (1923)

Jones, Emir W. *Sir Henry M. Stanley: The Enigma* (1989)

Jones, Lucy M. *H. M. Stanley and Wales* (1972)

Jones, Roger *The Rescue of Emin Pasha* (1972)

Junker, W. *Travels in Africa 1882–86* 3 vols (1887–88)

Kerfyser E. *Henry M. Stanley* (1890)

Keltie, J. S. *The Partition of Africa* (1895)

Lagergren, D. *Mission and State in the Congo* (1970)

Levy, George *To Die in Chicago: Confederate Prisoners at Camp Douglas 1862–65* (1994)

Liebowitz, D. & Pearson C. *The Last Expedition: Stanley's Mad Journey through the Congo* (2005)

Liebrechts, Charles *Congo: Suite à mes souvenirs de l'Afrique* (1920)

Livingstone, D. *Missionary Travels and Researches in South Africa* (1857)

— *The Last Journals of David Livingstone in Central Africa* ed Waller, H. (1874)

Livingstone's Private Journals 1851–53 ed Schapera, I. (1960)

Livingstone, David and Charles *Narrative of an Expedition to the Zambezi* (1866)

Lloyd, Christopher *The Navy and the Slave Trade* (1949)

Longford, Elizabeth *Victoria RI* (1964)

Louis, W. R. *Ruanda-Urundi 1884–1919* (1963)

Louis, W. R. & Stengers, J. E. D. *Morel's History of the Congo Reform Movement* (1968)

Lovejoy, Paul *Transformations in Slavery* (1983)

Lucy, Henry *Sixty Years in the Wilderness* (1909)

Lugard, Frederick *The Rise of Our East African Empire* 2 vols (1893)

Luwel, M. *Stanley* (1959)

Luwel, M. *Sir Francis de Winton: Administrator-General of the Congo 1884–1886* (1964)

— *H. M. Stanley, H. H. Johnston et le Congo* (1978)

Lyons, J. B. *Surgeon-Major Parke's African Journey 1887–1889* (1994)

Macdonald, E. A. *The Story of Stanley:The Hero of Africa* (1891)

MacGregor, R. *The Rob Roy on the Jordan* (1869)

MacLaren, Roy ed *African Exploits: The Diaries of William Stairs 1887–1892* (1998)

McLynn, Frank *Stanley:The Making of an African Explorer* (1989)

— *Stanley: Sorcerer's Apprentice* (1991)

Manning, Patrick *Slavery and African Life* (1990)

Markham, Clements *Private History of the Royal Geographical Society* (n.d.)

Marston, Edward *How Stanley Wrote 'In Darkest Africa'* (1890)

— *After Work* (1904)

Maurice, Albert *H. M. Stanley: Unpublished Letters* (1957)

Middleton, Dorothy *Baker of the Nile* (1949)

— *Victorian Lady Travellers* (1965)

— ed *The Diaries of A. J. Mounteney Jephson* (1969)

Moir, F. L. M. *After Livingstone* (1923)

Moorhead, Alan *The White Nile* (1864)

Morel, E. D. *Great Britain and the Congo: The Pillage of the Congo Basin* (1909)

Morris, H. F. *A History of the Ankole* (1962)

Newman, James L. *Imperial Footprints: Henry Morton Stanley's African Journeys* (2004)

Niccoll, D. J. *Stanley's Exploits, or Civilizing Africa* (1891)

Oliver, Roland *The Missionary Factor in East Africa* (1965)

— *Sir Harry Johnston and the Scramble for Africa* (1957)

— ed *Six Unpublished Letters of H. M. Stanley* (1957)

Oliver, Roland & Atmore, Anthony *Africa Since 1800* (1981)

Pakenham, Thomas *The Scramble for Africa* (1991)

Parke, T. H. *My Personal Experiences in Equatorial Africa* (1891)

— *Guide to Health in Africa* (1893)

Patience, K. *Zanzibar, Slavery and the Royal Navy* (2000)

Peiris, William *Edwin Arnold* (1970)

Perham, Margery *Lugard:The Years of Adventure 1858–98* (1956)

— ed *The Diaries of Lord Lugard* vols 1 & 2 (1959)

Peschuel-Loesche, M. *Kongoland* (1886)

Peters, Carl *New Light on Dark Africa* (1891)

Pond, J. B. *Eccentricities of Genius* (1901)

Puleston, Fred *African Drums* (1930)

Reddall, Henry F. *Henry M. Stanley: A Record* (1890)

Robinson, R., Gallagher, J. & Denny, A. *Africa and the Victorians* (1961)

Roeykens, P. A. *Les débuts de l'oeuvre africaine de Leopold II 1876–1879* (1955)

— *La periode initiale de l'oeuvre africaine de Leopold II1875–83* (1957)

Rowlands, Cadwalader (pseud for John C. Hotten) *H. M. Stanley: The Story of his Life* (1872)

Schweitzer, G. *Emin Pasha: His Life and Work* 2 vols (1898)

Schynse, A. W. *Travers l'Afrique avec Stanley et Emin Pasha* (1890)

Segal, Ronald *Islam's Black Slaves* (2000)

Seitz, Don C. *The James Gordon Bennetts* (1928)

Severin, Timothy *The African Adventure* (1973)

Sherriff, Abdul *Slaves, Spices and Ivory in Zanzibar* (1987)

Simpson, Donald *Dark Companions* (1975)

Slade, Ruth M. *English-speaking Missions in the Congo Independent State 1878–1908* (1959)

— *King Leopold's Congo* (1962)

Smith, Iain R. *The Emin Pasha Relief Expedition 1886–1890* (1972)

Smith, Ronald *Stanley in Africa* (1890)

Speke, John Hanning *Journal of the Discovery of the Source of the Nile* (1863)

Stanhope, Aubrey *On the Track of the Great* (1914)

Stanley, Dorothy ed *The Autobiography of Sir Henry Morton Stanley* (1909)

Stanley, Richard & Neame, Alan eds *The Exploration Diaries of H. M. Stanley* (1961)

Starkie, Enid *Flaubert* (1967)

Stevens, Thomas *Scouting for Stanley in East Africa* (1890)

Stuhlmann, Franz ed *Die Tagebücher von Dr Emin Pascha* 5 vols (1917–27)

Surtees, V. *The Ludovisi Goddess: a life of Louisa, Lady Ashburton* (1984)

Swann, A. J. *Fighting the Slave Hunters in Central Africa* (1910)

Symons, A. J. A. *H. M. Stanley* (1933)

Thomson, Joseph *Through Masailand* (1885)

Thys, A. *Au Congo et Kasai* (1888)

Tip, Tippu *The Autobiography of Tippu Tip* translated by Whitely, W. H. (1966)

Troup, J. Rose *With Stanley's Rear Column* (1890)

Vansina, Jan *The Tio Kingdom of the Middle Congo 1880–1892* (1973)

Wack, Henry W. *The Story of the Congo Free State* (1905)

Wallis, J. P. R. *The Zambezi Expedition of David Livingstone 1858–63* (1956)

Ward, Herbert *A Voice from the Congo* (1910)

— *Five Years with the Congo Cannibals* (1891)

— *My Life with Stanley's Rear-Guard* (1890)

Ward, Sarita *A Valiant Gentleman* (1928)

Wassermann, Jacob *Bula Matari* (1932)

Weeks, John H. *Among Congo Cannibals* (1913)

— *Among the Primitive Bakongo* (1914)

Werner, J. R. A. *A Visit to Stanley's Rear Guard* (1889)

West, Richard *Brazza of the Congo* (1972)

White, James P. *The Sanford Exploring Expedition* (1967)

Wilkins, W. H. *The Romance of Isabel Lady Burton* 2 vols (1897)

Wolseley, Garnet *The Story of a Soldier's Life* 2 vols (1903)

Yule, H. & Hyndman, H. M. *Mr Henry Morton Stanley and the Royal Geographical Society: being the Record of a Protest* (1878)

NOTES

ABBREVIATIONS IN THE NOTES

All manuscript entries without identification by me are from the Stanley Archive in the Musée Royal de l'Afrique Centrale at Tervuren, Brussels. Occasionally, for purposes of clarity, I have distinguished a Stanley Archive document with the letters 'Ter' (for Tervuren).

S	Henry Morton Stanley
DS	Dorothy Stanley/Tennant
SD	Stanley's Diaries I identify by date and only occasionally by extra description. His diaries, journals and field notebooks start in 1866. They sometimes lapse entirely between expeditions (when they are most detailed). He kept a daily diary from his marriage on 12 Jul 1890 until 19 Dec 1901, three and a half years before his death. His diaries occupy 13 pp of the inventory of the Stanley Papers in the Musée Royal de l'Afrique Centrale.
CD	Stanley's Congo Diaries. He devoted four specific volumes to his work on the Congo and his subsequent relations with Leopold II of Belgium and his Ministers.
DD	Dorothy Stanley's private diaries
Lii	King Leopold II of Belgium

APR	Archives du Palais Royal
BL	British Library
CFFS	*The Congo and the Founding of its Free State* (1885)
DL	David Livingstone
EPRE	Emin Pasha Relief Expedition
HIFL	*How I Found Livingstone in Central Africa* (1872)
IDA	*In Darkest Africa*, 2 vols (1890)
KGR	Katie Gough Roberts
LLJ	Livingstone, D. *The Last Journals of David Livingstone in Central Africa* ed Waller, H. (1874)

MP	Mackinnon Papers, SOAS
MS	May Sheldon
RGS	Royal Geographical Society
S&N	Stanley, Richard & Neame, Alan eds *The Exploration Diaries of H. M. Stanley* (1961)
TDC	*Through the Dark Continent*, 2 vols (1878)
UL	Maurice, Albert *H. M. Stanley: Unpublished Letters* (1957)

Anstruther	Anstruther, I. *I Presume: Stanley's Triumph and Disaster* (1956)
Ascherson	Ascherson, Neal *The King Incorporated* (1963)
Auto	Stanley, Dorothy ed *The Autobiography of Sir Henry Morton Stanley* (1909)
Bartt	Barttelot, W. G. *The Life of Edmund Musgrave Barttelot* (1890)
Bennett	Bennett, Norman R. ed *Stanley's Despatches to the New York Herald 1871–1877* (1970)
Bierman	Bierman, John *Dark Safari: The Life behind the Legend of Henry Morton Stanley* (1990)
Bonny	William Bonny's diaries at Tervuren
Bontinck	Bontinck, François *Aux Origines de l'État Indépendant du Congo* (1966)
Emerson	Emerson, B. *Leopold II of the Belgians: King of Colonialism* (1979)
Hall	Hall, Richard *Stanley: An Adventurer Explored* (1974)
Hotten	Rowlands, Cadwalader (pseud for John C. Hotten) *H. M. Stanley: The Story of his Life* (1872)
Hughes	Hughes, Nathaniel C., Jr. *Sir Henry Morton Stanley, Confederate* (2000)
Jeal	Jeal, Tim *Livingstone* (1973)
Jephson	Middleton, Dorothy ed *The Diaries of A. J. Mounteney Jephson* (1969)
McLynn i	McLynn, Frank *Stanley:The Making of an African Explorer* (1989)
McLynn ii	McLynn, Frank *Stanley: Sorcerer's Apprentice* (1991)
Newman	James, L. *Imperial Footprints: Henry Morton Stanley's African Journeys* (2004)
Parke	Lyons, J. B. *Surgeon-Major Parke's African Journey 1887–89* (1994)
Smith	Smith, Iain R. *The Emin Pasha Relief Expedition 1886–1890* (1972)
Stairs	Roy Maclaren ed *African Exploits: The Diaries of William Stairs 1887–1892* (1997)
Stengers	Chapter by Jean Stengers, 'King Leopold and Anglo-French Rivary 1882–84' in Gifford, P & Louis, W. R. eds *France and Britain in Africa* (1971)

INTRODUCTION

1 Quoted H. A. C. Cairns *Prelude to Imperialism*, 1965, 3.
2 S to Any gentleman 4 Aug 1877, Quentin Keynes Collection sold Christie's 7.04.2004.
3 This t/s is now in the Cambridge University Library and was previously in the

Royal Commonwealth Society Library in London. *Portrait of Stanley*: Gerald Sanger RCS. Mss 4c99s Cambridge University Library.

4   Frank McLynn *Stanley: The Making of an African Explorer*, 1989, (McLynn i) 14, 29–30; Frank McLynn *Stanley: The Sorcerer's Apprentice*, 1991, (McLynn ii) 334; McLynn i 329–30; John Bierman *Dark Safari*, 1990, 239.

5   McLynn ii 395.

6   Bierman 357.

7   *The Henry M. Stanley Archives: Inventory,* Brussels 2004, Royal Museum of Central Africa compiled by Peter Daerden and Maurits Wynants.

8   *HIFL* p 10.

9   S to E. Marston 10 Jul 93.

10   Stanley's Congo Diaries (CD) 28 Oct 1881.

11   H. M. Stanley *The Congo and the Founding of its Free State*, 1886, 2 vols, i 248 *(CFFS)*.

12   CD 19 Nov 1881.

13   Richard Stanley and Alan Neame eds *The Exploration Diaries of H. M. Stanley*, 1961, *(S & N)* p. 199 18.07.1877 for quote about 'fighting 32 battles on land and water'. In fact by December 1877 Stanley reckoned he had only 32 men able to offer effective resistance with firearms (hardly a number capable of terrorizing whole districts). Chapter 14 of this book for details, esp. 195–202, also notes 10 p. 514 and 37 p. 515.

14   Richard West *Brazza of the Congo*, 1972, 84, 121.

15   Gordon to Burton 19 Oct 1877 in Wilkins, *Romance of Isabel Lady Burton* vol ii p 661; Richard Burton *The Lake Regions of Central Africa*, 1860, 328ff.

16   Tim Jeal *Livingstone*, 1973, 241, O. Chadwick *Mackenzie's Grave*, 1959, 49.

17   Jeal 341; *Times* 17.11.1877, quoting *Cape Argus*; D. Stanley ed *The Autobiography of Sir Henry Morton Stanley*, 1909, 295 *(Auto)*; Stanley's Diaries 25.02.1874 (SD).

18   *Times* 17.11.1877, quoting interview in *Cape Argus*; *Auto* 295; travellers beating Africans in H. A. C. Cairns *Prelude to Imperialism*, 1965, 42ff; *S&N* 193–5.

19   CD 15.10.1880.

20   Ronald Segal *Islam's Black Slaves*, 2000, 56, 154–5, 160–2, 164, 166–74, 176; Paul Lovejoy *Transformations in Slavery*, 1983, 137.

21   H. Waller ed *The Last Journals of David Livingstone in Central Africa*, 1874, vol i 62–3 (LLJ)

22   Livingstone to Lord Clarendon 20 Aug 1866 FO 84/1265.

23   *Livingstone's Private Journals 1851–53*, 1960,, ed I. Schapera 210.

24   S&N 148 1.01.1877; S to Strauch 27 Jan 84; H. Waller ed *The Last Journals of David Livingstone in Central Africa*, 1874, 2 vols, ii 135; CFFS ii 144–5, CD 27.11.1883.

25   Daniel Liebowitz and Charles Pearson *The Last Expedition: Stanley's Mad Journey through the Congo*, 2005, 337.

26   SD Notebook 1877, end pages.

ONE: Dreams of Love and Freedom

1 Funeral register, Denbigh: Moses Parry, Castle, 22 Jun 1846 R. J. Roberts, Rector. In *Auto* his age is incorrectly given as 84.

2 Evan Pierce MD to Denbighshire Free Press 9 Feb 1889; Bill Wynn Wood-house *Hel Achau* 15 1985 Spring 35–44.

3 Memorial scroll to Moses Parry 1866 Denbighshire Local Authority.

4 *Auto* 7; DS to Lady Hills Johnes 7 Jun 99 Dolaucothi L 9605.

5 *Auto* 7; handwritten notes in DS's copy of *Auto*, sold Christie's 2002. Report from the Commissioners in Ed in Wales 1847 vol xxvii Part ii North Wales p 31; *Auto* 8–9.

6 Cadwalader Rowlands (pseud for John C. Hotten) *H. M. Stanley: The Story of his Life*, 1872, 37 (Hotten).

7 In S to Katie Gough Roberts (KGR) 22.03.1865, he blamed his uncle Thomas Parry and his wife for 'cutting me adrift', implying that his uncle Moses Parry had not. In fact both were to blame. Thomas did not marry until 1851 (1851 Census, information Bob Owen).

8 *South Wales Daily News* 14 May 1904 Interview with Richard Price; *Auto* 10.

9 *Auto* 12.

10 Emyr W. Jones *Sir Henry M. Stanley: The Enigma*, 1989, 29.

11 *Auto* 11; small black leather ledger.

12 *Auto* 11.

13 S Early Journal 1841–79, 1841–57 in Swahili. The invented beating of Francis in *Auto* resembles Chapter 13 in Dickens's *Nicholas Nickleby*, as was first noted by Richard Hall in 1974. Another model may have been the frontiersman Daniel Boone, who knocked down *his* teacher before leaving school. Roderick Random – hero of a novel S possessed in later years – also trounced his schoolmaster. But probable plagiarism does not diminish the reality of the anguish that led to the fantasy in the first place.

14 *Auto* 12.

15 See note 5, Report from the Commissioners; W. Wynne Woodhouse 'Elizabeth Parry of Denbigh, an Extraordinary Woman ...' *Hel Achau*, Spring 1885, 42.

16 S to KGR 10 Sept 1869.

17 Efficiency award Hall 107, PRO NM12/16140, Reports Relating to the Education of Pauper Children Vol xlviii p 631 1856; xlv p207 1857. Mr Jelinger Symons QC, the inspector whom Stanley had liked as a boy, declared that in the past he had been 'very gloomy' about St Asaph Union, but by the mid-1850s the workhouse school was very well conducted.

18 *Auto* 24–5.

19 Hotten 43.

20 *Auto* 14–15.

21 *South Wales Daily News* 14 May 1904 (*SWDN*).

22 Hotten 42, 48, 51.

23 S to KGR 15.05.1869.

24 *Auto* 29.

25 Richard Hall *Stanley: An Adventurer Explored*, 1974, 100 (Hall); Lewis Noe

will be shown photo of Elizabeth Parry by S see note 43 Chapter 3; photograph of Cross Foxes, published in *Illustrated Africa* 25.09.1897 621 photographer D. Hughes St Asaph; Bob Owen collection postcard of same picture. In neither the magazine picture, nor the post card, were the small figures standing in front of the Cross Foxes public house identified as Robert and Elizabeth Jones, circa 1875.

26 *Auto* 20.

27 Census 1851.

28 Owen 'Morien' Morgan's notes of an interview with Elizabeth Parry 1886, Cardiff Public Library (Morien's notes); *SWDN* 14 May 04.

29 David Davies to S 14 May n.y.

30 Discharge book 13 May 1856.

31 *Auto* 37–8.

32 Information about children Wynne Woodhouse *Hel Achau* Spring 1985. John Rowlands had good reason for feeling he was the most hard done by of all Elizabeth Parry's children. His mother and her son Robert (born 1848), and her daughter Elizabeth (born 1850, and died in infancy), would be inmates at the workhouse between Dec 1850 and Apr 1851, a mere five months. Emma (born in 1843) was boarded out in Denbigh for several years, but in Jun 1851, soon after her mother was discharged, she was placed in the workhouse with John, and would be left there for five years. John would be an inmate for nine years. This shared experience made him feel closer to Emma than to his other half-siblings.

33 St Hilary's Church, Denbigh, register of baptisms 19 Feb 1841; Evan Pierce letter to *Denbighshire Free Press* 9 Feb 1889.

34 Morien's notes.

35 Hall 101.

36 Sources on James Horne are Emyr Wynn Jones *National Library of Wales Journal* 1993 vol 28 'Stanley: The Mystery of the Three Fathers' 127–51; also Bob Owen *Hel Achau* No 15 1985 'Stanley's Father, I Presume' esp 23–7. Among locals believing that Horne was S's father was a Dr John Lloyd Roberts, who worked in a Denbigh medical practice, where the senior partner, Dr Evan Pierce, had attended Elizabeth Parry at Stanley's birth. Pierce lived in Vale Street, a few houses away from James Horne. Dr Lloyd Roberts became Medical Officer at St Asaph Workhouse, in succession to the MO of Stanley's day. He was married to the daughter of John Parry Jones, who had acted as Horne's solicitor while he lived, and had then acted for Horne's widow. The Lloyd Roberts family was also closely connected to Thomas Evans, who had shared an office in Vale Street with James Horne in the early 1840s, when Horne is alleged to have seduced Elizabeth Parry, then working as a maid in the same street. Dr Lloyd Roberts told his daughter Ruth that James Horne was definitely S's father, and Ruth told the historian Emyr Wynne Jones the same. Her cousin, Rennel Mason – a former Professor of Geography at Oxford – informed her in a letter that his cousin, Frank Evans (grandson of Thomas Evans, who had shared Horne's office), had told him that 'Horne was the unacknowledged father of Henry Morton Stanley', and ended, 'I accepted it as a

fact.' Evidence exists to show that Horne was estranged from his wife for many years before his death in 1848. Elizabeth Parry named two of her sons James – the first died as a child, and her final son she also called James – perhaps in memory of James Horne. Elizabeth's second child, her daughter Emma, was born in April 1843, and the man named as her father in her baptismal entry was John Evans, a tenant farmer, late of Llanrhaeadr, near Denbigh, where James Horne had connections – his wife being the daughter of the lord of the manor. John Rowlands, junior, also lived in this same village during his final decade and was buried there. This Llanrhaeadr link has led one local historian (Bob Owen) to claim that Horne had been the father not only of Elizabeth's first child but perhaps of her second as well. Knowing both Rowlands and Evans personally, it has been argued that Horne, to protect his reputation, paid them to admit to the paternity of John and Emma, respectively. John Rowlands, junior, never saw his supposed son, and there is no evidence that John Evans ever took the slightest interest in Emma. But these men's admissions of paternity would certainly shift interest away from Horne, who was Coroner for the Borough, Town Clerk and an alderman, as well as owning a thriving solicitor's practice.

37 Griffiths family of Garn, Henllan. Mr J. E. Griffiths of Betley, near Crewe, closest living descendant has no paintings.

38 Family 'Necrology' document by S, Moses Owen born 1837 died 1864 aged 27; *Auto* 41.

39 *Auto* 51; 47.

40 *Auto* 48.

41 *Auto* 49; small black ledger notebook.

42 *Auto* 48.

43 Hotten 51–2.

44 *Auto* 30.

45 *Auto* 45–6.

46 S to KGR 01.07.1869.

47 John Rowlands to Thomas Morris early Jun 1858, obtained by DS after publication of *Auto*.

48 *Auto* 55–8.

49 *Auto* 58; re streets in Liverpool – John Parkinson, who lived with Morris family was at 26, Rosommon St in 1858–9 in Gore's Liverpool Directory; by 1861, census has them all living at 22, Sherriff St.

50 *Auto* 58–64.

51 Ian Anstruther *I Presume: Stanley's Triumph and Disaster*, 1956, 18; Lloyd's records have Harding not Hardinge as in *Auto*; *Auto* 67, 70–1.

52 *Auto* 72–3; 68 and note in DS's personal copy of *Auto*, see Christie's Catalogue Africa Sale Sep 2002.

TWO: In the Name of the Father

1 *Auto* 137.

2 Unpaginated notes for *Auto* 95.

3 *Auto* 86–9.

4 *Auto* 91–3.

5 *Auto* 90.

6 *Auto* 97–101; 105.

7 *Auto* 105–6 and 112–13 By chance, claimed S, Mrs Stanley's brother-in-law, Captain Stanley, was in town on a visit from Havana where he lived. It was he, said S, who arranged the funeral in *Auto*, having told young Rowlands to push off since his presence was no longer required.

8 *Auto* 113–21 In the original m/s of *Auto*, after the words, supposedly spoken by Mr Stanley, 'You are to bear my name Henry Stanley', Stanley added 'and in remembrance of my wife, your middle name shall be what hers was before I married her'. The second Mrs Henry Hope Stanley's maiden name was Miller, rather than Morton, and the first Mrs Stanley's maiden name was Foster. Wisely, Stanley's widow cut out this sentence as offering too many hostages to fortune.

9 *Auto* 90.

10 *Auto* 142–61.

11 *Auto* 119.

12 Bierman 27–8, and Newman 5 take the same line about John's relations with Mr Stanley, but Newman perceptively adds that Rowlands probably 'simply appropriated' the name. The idea of Rowlands appropriating the name, rather than being given it, is also to be found in a letter sent by him to Thomas Gee, a prominent citizen of Denbigh in 1872.

13 Morien's notes; *Western Mail* 12 May 1889.

14 Hotten 63; *SWDN* 14.05.1904, quoting S to Thomas Gee, editor of *Baner Cymru.*

15 E. Kerfyser *Henry M. Stanley*, 1890; E. A. Macdonald *The Story of Stanley,* 1891; Ronald Smith *Stanley in Africa,* 1890.

16 Such as A. A. Schenk (formerly Greg Waring) to S 13.04.1891. Schenck had worked for Speake with S in 1859. From November 1872 to April 1873, Stanley was in America lecturing about Livingstone. There is no evidence that S ever got in touch with any member of Henry Hope Stanley's family. Indeed, the lack of any letters from any family member argues strongly against any relationship.

17 New Orleans City Directories 1859–61.

18 *Auto* 101, 121.

19 Draft of *Auto*, quoted F. McLynn i 38.

20 McLynn vol i 37.

21 S's New Orleans Notebook 18.10.1895. S visited the grave at Odd Fellows Rest to find that Speake's remains had been moved to Girod Street Cemetery.

22 DS's annotated t/s of *Auto* 161.

23 In the notebook containing Stanley's earliest accounts of his time in New Orleans, some of the most important pages are missing. The passage that preceded the one about 'father's death' has been torn out and, still more surprisingly, someone has torn out half of the highly memorable page in which John Rowlands meets and asks the man who he claims would one day adopt him: 'Do you want a boy?' In the torn manuscript page, Rowlands met 'a gentleman of middle

age, seated in front of *his store* reading the morning newspaper. I took him by his sober dark clothes and tall hat to be the proprietor of *the store* [my emphases].' In Stanley's later manuscript of the *Auto*, the italicized words read 'of No. 3 store' and 'of the building'. In other words, in the first Stanley draft the gentleman owned the store, and in the second he owned the building, rather than the store. It seems clear that when Stanley wrote this very first draft of the *Auto*, he was toying with the idea of airbrushing James Speake out of his story and making Mr Stanley his employer *and* his adoptive father. But at that time, he had not yet invented a story to explain when and where he had got to know Mr Stanley. As stated above, too many people still alive in New Orleans in the 1890s (when Stanley wrote the final version of his early life in that city) would have known about Speake's kindness to John for it to have been safe for Stanley to have omitted the shopkeeper's important role. This problem inspired him to come up with the solution presented in the published book – namely that Mr Stanley, the owner of the building, introduced him to Mr Speake, the humble storekeeper.

24 Meller and Mellor in McLynn and Bierman; but Miller in local New Orleans press obituaries.

25 1860 Census. Strange, too, was the failure to mention Joanne, who had been adopted by Mr Stanley's first wife, Mary Ann (née Foster), who had died in 1846 (New Orleans Notebook 1895). Strangest of all was his claim that Mr Stanley had visited the 'Infant Asylum' in the Faubourg St Mary and 'had made no choice, from over-fastidiousness', and had therefore remained childless (*Auto* 120). In fact, in 1842, Mr Stanley and his first wife visited a private infirmary on South Rampart Street and as a result adopted their daughter, Joanna, whose mother had just died in the infirmary. Mistaken about H. H. Stanley's children, the great explorer would also be incorrect in stating that his supposed benefactor's brother lived in Cuba. I have traced a direct descendant of Henry Hope Stanley's half-brother and heir, James Howard Brooks. Dr Michael Brooks does not believe that Henry Hope's brother, John Stanley, ever lived in Havana. He visited America from time to time, but lived in England with his wife and her daughter by an earlier marriage (Dr Michael Brooks to Tim Jeal 22.01.2003). The real reason for Henry Hope Stanley's fictitious visit to Havana and his fictitious death there would seem to have been the knowledge that no one would ever, given the state of Cuban records, be able in later years to find any proof that he had *not* died there.

26 Hall, McLynn, Newman.

27 H. M. Stanley's last three substantial biographers have incorrectly explained the reason he chose to lie about Mr and Mrs Stanley's dates of death as being, first, his way of avenging rejection by the man he had hoped would treat him as a son; second, as being an attempt to cover up the supposed fact that their loving relationship had ended as a result of a quarrel; and third, to save himself from the pain of admitting to himself that he had given his love to a man who had rejected him in the end (Bierman 28; McLynn 38; Hall 121).

28 New Orleans City Directories 1859–61.

29 Catherine B. Dillon 'From Wharf Waif to Knighthood' *Roosevelt Review* Jun 1944; *Daily Picayune* 28.12.1890.

30 In a New Orleans census taken on 1 Jun 1860, he is listed as J. Rollings at a house in St Thomas street. He had to have left for Cypress Bends by early Jul in order to be there by 22 Aug when he was named in the census taken then (giving a few weeks in which to be adopted and then sent packing!). No census records exist to show John ever stayed at H. H. Stanley's country estate in Tangipahoa Parish north of the city.

31 *Roosevelt Review* Jun 1944.

32 A. A. Schenk to S 13.04.1891.

33 *Auto* 93.

34 Census 1860 New Orleans 1 Jun 4th Ward.

35 Nathaniel Cheairs Hughes Jr. *Sir Henry Morton Stanley: Confederate*, 2000, 140 (Hughes), quoting CSR 26.07.1861 W. H. Stanley.

36 The 'William' had gone by the time S was at Camp Douglas see note 20 chapter 3.

37 *Auto* 124.

38 New Orleans *Daily States* 16.04.1891.

THREE: A Terrible Freedom

1 *Auto* 151–8.

2 *Daily States* 16.04.1891.

3 A. Schumacher to S 17.07.1892 and to DS same date.

4 *Auto* 84.

5 *Auto* 107–11.

6 A. A. Schenck to HMS 13.04.1891; F. McLynn vol i 36.

7 Hotten 51–2.

8 *Auto* 162–5, information re Dr Goree etc. Hughes 89.

9 *Auto* 92, 102–3.

10 *Auto* 165–6; Hughes 89; Hall and Bierman name Margaret Goree.

11 Nathaniel Cheairs Hughes Jr. in *Sir Henry Morton Stanley: Confederate*, 2000, subjects Stanley's account of his service in the Civil War to exhaustive cross-checking and finds it largely reliable.

12 *Auto* 172, 176–7.

13 *Auto* 187–9.

14 *Auto* 200.

15 Statistics about Shiloh, see Hughes; *Auto* 203; James Slate to S 28.03.1891; *Auto* 168.

16 George Levy *To Die in Chicago: Confederate Prisoners at Camp Douglas 1862–65*, 1994, 4.

17 *Auto* 211.

18 *Auto* 212–13.

19 Levy 50–1.

20 Enlisted Branch File 3739 – c (EB) 1885, RG 94: Records of the Adjutant-General's Office, NA, USA; also CSR Card No: 46045291 confirming that H. Stanley joined the Irish Brigade, 1st Illinois Light Artillery Battery L. Colonel J. A. Mulligan, had commanded the 23rd Illinois Volunteer Infantry earlier in the war. His volunteer force had also been known as the 'Irish Brigade'. It had been forced to surrender by the Confederates at Lexington, Missouri. Then,

Mulligan was exchanged for an imprisoned Union officer, and was appointed to command Camp Douglas. A major preoccupation during his first six months there was raising a new brigade. He had completed it by Jun 1862 when he left the camp, as did Private H. Stanley, whose service card states that his artillery regiment was part of the Irish Brigade.

21 Records of the Adjutant General's office.
22 Ibid. pages headed Musters; Hughes 149 note.
23 Small black leather ledger notebook: section headed 'Soldiers at Shiloh'; *Auto* 78.
24 *Auto* 167–8.
25 *Auto* 214–15; S's American Notebook 1895.
26 Hotten p 104; Morien's notes Cardiff Public Library.
27 S to DS 18.11.1893, Ter.
28 *Auto* 219.
29 S to DS 18.11.1893, Ter.
30 S to KGR 22.03.1869.
31 *Auto* 219; S Australian notebook 24.11.1891; *Auto* 220.
32 S to KGR 22.03.1869.
33 *Auto* 220; Hall 133–4; McLynn vol i 45; J. C. Smith to Wellcome 3 Nov 1907, RGS, interview with Lewis Noe.
34 Thomas Nisbet to HMS 10.05.1890 (Nisbet gives wrong date – should have been 1863).
35 *Auto* 220; Hall 134; A. A. Schenck to S 13.04.1891.
36 National Archives, USA, Old Military & Civil Records Correspondence between Rebecca A. Livingston and Ella Lonn, also Navy Dept., Bureau of Historical Research 12.02.1940.
37 Frank Hird *H. M. Stanley: The Authorized Life*, 1935, 44; *Auto* 220; HMS to KGR 22.03.1869.
38 Smith to Wellcome 27.10.1907 RGS; Bennett 241; SD Turkish journey Jul 1866.
39 McLynn – vol i 54, 65 – claims relationship was homosexual.
40 Norman R. Bennett ed *Stanley's Despatches to the New York Herald 1871–2*, 1970, 406.
41 Photo in Arab garb Christie's catalogue Sep 2002, Plate 7; Bennett 432; Noe to ed of The NY *Sun* 16.08.1872.
42 *Sun* 16.08.1872; L. Stegman to S 20.04.1865, 30.11.1886.
43 J. C. Smith to Wellcome 3.11.1907 RGS.

FOUR: An Accident-prone Apprenticeship

1 J. C. Smith interviews with L. Noe 23.10 and 2.11.1907, RGS; W. H. Cook t/s sent to DS 05.05.1910; McLynn i 49 note 6 quoting Richard Hall article; also James A. Hart *A History of the Missouri Globe-Democrat*, 1961, 97 etc.
2 T/s by W. H. Cook for DS; E. R. Sheak to H. H. Cook brother of WHC May 1910.
3 Sheak; t/s for DS.
4 Bennett 432.

5 Cook t/s to DS; Cook to DS 31.5.1910.
6 Bennett 408.
7 SD 1866; Bennett 413.
8 Hall 142; Bennett 410.
9 *Levant Herald* 17 Oct 1866.
10 Bennett 413–14.
11 Bennett 442; Bennett 409.
12 Receipt dated 28.11.1866; SD 25.10.1866. His bitterness over this probably explains his claim that he had only signed the receipt because he had been threatened by S. Lewis's hatred would continue because, even six years later, he still had not been paid his share of the Turkish Government's $1,200 compensation. He had still received nothing as late as 1886. S never forgave the discreditable things Noe told the newspapers about him in 1872, and never pressed Cook to pay him. (Copy of letter from Noe to Cook 24.10.1872, enclosed letter from Cook to DS 12.04.1910; Major James Pond to Noe 6.12.1886.)

FIVE: War Correspondent

1 Bennett 442.
2 Christie's Catalogue Sep 2002 p 20 no 7, S in naval US uniform. References to naval uniform photographs: card dated 18 Feb 1889 stating that S's cousin Henry Parry had naval photo Box 5 ref 15/16 RGS; Hotten 70; *Shrewsbury Chronicle* 2 April 1886 mentions J. Laing taking picture of S at 38 Castle St. A photo of him in uniform was published by Edwin Balch in *Geographical Review* vol v Jan–Jun, 1918.
3 Bennett 442.
4 Reproduced in Hall 148. In Christie's catalogue: S's entry in Denbigh Bowling Green's visitors' book is in the form of a card on which he copied his earlier words during a later visit to Denbigh.
5 Hall 147.
6 Morien's notes 4.
7 Letters to KGR for details about Catherine Parry, 3, 15 May 1869; Census 1871 for Catherine's age; S describes her unflatteringly, but this was after the twenty-five-year-old Henry had been 'cast off' by the teenager. She later married his half-brother, Robert Jones, who was eighteen in 1866 and therefore much closer to his cousin in age. RGS 16/4 for dates of letters to Noe.
8 S to Noe 25.12.1866 Bodelwyddan Village, nr St Asaph.
9 *SWDN* 12.05.1904 by 'Morien'.
10 Typed page SD 16–23.10.1868 shows that Emma and Mrs Jones stayed at the Castle & Falcon Hotel, London, 18–22.10.1868, and that on 23 Oct Stanley left for Alexandria. The reference in Hotten (p 105) about S visiting Denbigh just after his return from Abyssinia is incorrect. Mrs Jones confused 1868 with 1869, when he *did* come to Denbigh. All previous biographers have suggested that Stanley had waited to tell his mother he had been adopted until October 1868, after his return from Abyssinia. This is very unlikely. Elizabeth made a point of telling Morien that she had learned about the new name while

her son had been at the Cross Foxes, and in October 1868 she met him in a London hotel.

11 *S WDN* 12.05.1904 by 'Morien'.

12 This lie was first told in Dec 1866 and committed to writing 22.03.1869, S to KGR.

13 Jephson to Lady Middleton 14.12.1890 Mi4F2 Nottingham University Special Colls.

14 Hotten 75.

15 G. T. Miller to Ed *Denbighshire Free Press* 21.05.1904.

16 Bierman 44–5.

17 SD 2.01.1868.

18 Bennett 415, Lewis Noe to Ed of New York *Sun* 16.08.1872.

19 Bennett 51.

20 Viz *Times* 17 Dec 1866.

21 Report for *NYHerald* 28.08.1872; Jeal 338 for DL's movements, also *Times* index; Finley Anderson to S 3.01.1867; Hall 148.

22 SD 27 Mar–1Apr 1867.

23 *Bulletin of the Missouri Hist Soc (BMHS)* vol xvii no 3 April 1961.

24 My *Early Travels in America and Asia* 2 vols, 1895, i 13, 129 (ET).

25 BMHS 277–8.

26 Hall 153.

27 *ET* i 240, 282.

28 *ET* i 155–6.

29 *Auto* 221–2; Annie Ward to S 1.07.67, 14.08.67; S to DS re Annie being married and there being a rival 8.01.1886; Bennett xvii, 451–2; RGS 16/23 Box 5 press cutting; Omaha press cutting, inventory 5356, Ter; W. Fayel to S 11.09.1874.

30 W. P. Webb quoting F. J. Turner *The Frontier and the 400 Year Boom*, 1956 88.

31 *ET* i xv–xvi.

32 Fayel to S 19.08.1872.

33 *Chicago Republican* to S 12.12.1867; *BMHS* 269; *Auto* 227.

34 Don C Seitz *The James Gordon Bennetts*, 1928, 220, 222–3.

35 *Auto* 228.

36 SD 28.01.1868.

37 SD 3,10 Mar 1868; Hall 162.

38 SD Mar various and 8 Jul 1868.

39 *Herald* 3.06.1868, McLynn i 69; SD 28.06.1868.

SIX: How are we to be Married?

1 R. Foskett ed *The Zambesi Doctors*, 1964, 19; *Times* 22 Nov, 10 Dec 1867.

2 *Auto* 230ff.

3 Ibid.

4 BL Add Ms 37448–37471, 37461–37463.

5 S to HBey 14.09.1868 BL Add ms 37463 f 407.

6 Ibid. f 410.

7 SD 13.09.1868; RGS 16/23, Box 5.
8 Ambellas to S 14.06.1869.
9 McLynn, i 75, argues that S (the repressed homosexual) engineered situations in which women were sure to reject him. But Bierman (70) suggests that S was keener on Virginia than she and her family were on him.
10 *Auto* 237–8.
11 *Times* 8.10.1868.
12 Even if Noe's claim – that S had been obsessed with finding Livingstone since 1866 – is ignored, it still seems implausible that Gordon Bennett dreamed up the Livingstone story, given his remarks to S in Dec 1867 about Americans not being interested in Africa. I believe S told Anderson about his desire to 'find' Livingstone in Jan 1867, or in London exactly a year later, before leaving for Abyssinia. (SD 4.01.1868). Otherwise, knowing all Bennett's prejudices, Anderson would hardly have picked an expensive African story solely on the unsupported evidence of a single letter in *The Times*. There are other reasons for ruling out Bennett as the originator of the Livingstone search. John Hotten, the London publisher, whose life of Stanley was published in 1872, and who interviewed Stanley's relations in that year, was sure that S had had the Livingstone idea. What Hotten wrote on the subject has not been quoted by previous biographers: 'Among other articles left by Mr Stanley with his mother ... was a kind of pocket cash-book ... [now missing TJ]' which, said Hotten, pre-dated S's commission to find Livingstone, and contained a page of calculations of 'Expenses re Livingstone Expedition'. Hotten also mentioned 'a friend who carried on a correspondence with Mr Stanley for several years, who states that he [Stanley] "often said it was the height of his ambition to find Dr Livingstone"' (Hotten 150–1). Gordon Bennett's biographer attributes the originating role to Colonel Anderson, offering no facts to support the assertion (Seitz 303). All the actual evidence suggests that credit for the famous journalistic event should be S's alone.
13 SD 15–17.10.68.
14 F. Anderson to S 20.10.68.
15 T/s version of SD Oct 1868.
16 S Appointment Diary 17–22.10.1868; Mary E. Grimsley to Winifred Coombe Tennant 17.08.1935 and attached note in Winifred's hand saying that Mrs G wrote S's mother's letters for her since she and her daughter were illiterate. Tennant papers, West Glamorgan Archives.
17 SD 17.11.1868.
18 Ibid. Nov 23 (S notes that he writes to F. R. Webb).
19 SD 02.1869 (hears from Webb); F. R. Webb to S 26.12.1868.
20 SD 7.01.1869.
21 Ibid. New Year's Day 1869; SD 9.02.1869.
22 Ibid. 16, 23 Feb 1869.
23 RGS Box 4 13/1–2, Morien is wrong about the date being autumn 1868. In SD 3.03.1869, S says he had met her 'some years ago'.
24 SD 3.03.1869.
25 18.01.1870 Death cert.

26 Morien descript RGS as above; Information Guy Holborn, Lincoln's Inn; Dr Clare Rider Inner Temple.
27 Information Cliff Davies, Librarian, Wadham College, Oxford.
28 St Hilary's Church Baptismal Registers Nov 19 1847; Jan 25 1849; Jan 2 1852; Mar 28 1856; Jun 20 1859, information from Bob Owen, Denbigh; T.G. Roberts to Messrs Longueville Sons Solicitors 28 Sept 1868, Bob Owen Private Collection.
29 T.G. Roberts to S late Apr 1869, photocopies of letters formerly owned by Margaret H. Stewart, Bath; SD 3.03.1869.
30 S to T.G. Roberts 12.04.1869 Bath.
31 S to K.G. Roberts 22.03.1869 Bath.
32 S to K.G. Roberts n.d. but 1869, from Spain.
33 S to KGR 1869, photocopies M. H. Stewart, Bath.
34 T.G. Roberts to S n.d. but April 1869, Bath.
35 S to T.G. Roberts 4.05.1869, Bath.
36 Description of events in Valencia *Scribner's Monthly*, 5, 1872, Edward King 'An Expedition with Stanley'; S to King 31.10.1876 Houghton Library, Harvard.
37 SD 1.09.1869 'King and I went to Valencia ...'; *Dictionary of American Biog* Edward Smith King 1848–96.
38 S to KGR 3.05.1869.
39 Morien letters 19 and 24 Aug 1904 RGS 13 1–2; McLynn i 96.
40 S to KGR 15.05.1869.
41 Ibid. 3.05.1869.
42 Ibid. 27.06.1869 Ter; Ibid. 13.07.1869, Bath; 1.07.1869, Bath.
43 Ibid. 27.06.1869.
44 Ibid. 27.06.1869.
45 Ibid. 3.05.1869 and 27.06.1869.
46 Levien to S 10.06.1869.
47 S to Bennett 17.01.1871; SD 28.10; HIFL xviii ff; S to KGR 3.04.1870.
48 S to Bennett 17.01.1871. Yet though penny-pinching and monumentally inconsiderate, Bennett wanted Stanley to succeed (Levien to S 29.11.1869). There is no evidence that Bennett had had another journalist in mind and had chosen Stanley because his preferred candidate was unavailable (Randolph Keim see Hall 381).
49 S to KGR 12.1869.
50 Info Katie's granddaughter, Margaret H. Stewart.
51 S to KGR 8.11.1869, Bath.
52 Ibid. 3.04.1870.
53 Ibid. 7.10.1869.
54 Information about KGR: Miss M. H. Stewart, Bath, and Bob Owen.
55 *Scribner's Monthly* 5, 1872, 105–12.
56 Balch to S 28 Mar, 6 Apr 1869.
57 Balch to S 21.05.1869.
58 *Times* 20.04.1869.
59 Balch to S 10.06.1869.
60 S to Bennett 17.01.1871.

SEVEN: The Long-imagined Quest

1 Henry M. Stanley *How I Found Livingstone in Central Africa*, 1872, 2 (*HIFL*).
2 S to Bennett Jan 17 1871; S to Bennett May 18 1872; Webb to S Jul 16 1871, Ter.
3 S to NYH 4.07.1871, Bennett 4.
4 S to Bennett 17.01.1871; Richard Francis Burton *The Lake Regions of Central Africa*, S's copy contains copious notes of finances and equipment in S's hand, Christie's Lot 16 26–27: The Africa Sale 24 Sep 2002.
5 Account Book (fair copy) Abyssinia – Jun 1879; Item in *Times* quoting NYH 12.08.1872; at end of 1871 in small diary S accurately recorded the drafts for $3,750 and $1,250 but added a fictitious $3,000 draft to make the total $8,000 rather than the $5,000 requested from Bennett in S to Bennett 17.01.1871.
6 DL had £500 RGS, £500 Govt, £1,000 from James Young, Jeal 289–90. McLynn 106 has $8,000 just for S's trade goods, Bierman 83 puts total cost at $20,000; MacLynn i 109 underlines Bennett's 'huge financial outlay'.
7 *HIFL* 68; S to Bennett 17.01.1871; McLynn vol i p 108 gives total as 192, Newman 40 gives total of 192. In his diary (SD 21, 25 Feb 1871) S states his second caravan or column contained 12 *pagazi* – in *HIFL* their number was given as 24. In the diary his third caravan had 11 *pagazi* in it – in *HIFL* 22. S's exaggeration of costs and numbers would give the erroneous impression that even on this, his maiden journey, he had entered Africa at the head of a small army.
8 Christie's Lot 16 as above n 5. It also helped S that Consul Webb doubled as the Zanzibar agent of a Boston and Salem trading company, John Bertram & Co., and introduced him to his dragoman, Johari bin Saif, who taught him about local overcharging for trade goods (SD 11.01.1871; Bennett 5; *HIFL* 22–5).
9 *HIFL* 21.
10 Christie's Africa Sale Lot 15 25.
11 SD 9.01.1871; *HIFL* 12.
12 *HIFL* 14 ff.
13 S to Gordon Bennett 17.01.1871; SD 28.05.1872; Jeal 262–5.
14 Foskett, DL to Kirk 26.06.1871 and 28.02.1872, 153, 156; Intro 23–4 Foskett; PRGSL 414 as below.
15 Kirk to Pres of RGS 25.09.1871 PRGSL vol xvi 1871–2 415.
16 SD 31.12.1871 £553.11.3.
17 *HIFL* 27; SD 21.11.1870.
18 *HIFL* 351–2
19 *HIFL* 28.
20 *HIFL* 10.
21 Quoted Bierman 82.
22 S to Shepherd 14.07.1872; DL to Murchison 3.3.72 PRGSL 434; Sir Reginald Coupland *East Africa and its Invaders*, 1956, 325.
23 Kirk to Earl Granville 18.02.1871, quoted *HIFL* 697; see also S to Ed of *Times* 13.11.1872.

24 Bennett 13 Despatch 4.07.1871, gives 1 Apr as date of departure, *HIFL* 70 gives 21 Mar; SD 1 Apr 'really got started', implying he had left town earlier, and then halted before starting again.
25 Bennett 13.
26 SD 11.10.1870.
27 *HIFL* 70.
28 *HIFL* 72.
29 Bennett 14–15.

EIGHT: 'I Cannot Die!'

1 DL to Agnes Livingstone 5 Feb 1871, BM Ad Ms 50184.
2 Jeal 288; Lord John Russell to DL 28.03.1865 FO 84/1249.
3 PRGSL vol xvi 1871–2, 414.
4 Foskett 109.
5 Dorothy Helly *Livingstone's Legacy: Horace Waller and Victorian Mythmaking* 1987, 172–81.
6 *HIFL* 73.
7 Bennett 16; HIFL p 262, quoted Cairns p 26.
8 Bennett 40.
9 *HIFL* 126–9; Bennett 17; Webb to S 25.09.1871.
10 Bennett 19.
11 SD 20.04.1871.
12 SD 22, 27 Dec 1871.
13 *HIFL* 66–7.
14 SD 6–8 Apr 1871.
15 *HIFL* 145.
16 Ibid. 157.
17 T. Griffiths-Jones 'W. L. Farquhar's Grave' Tanganyika Notes & Records No 5 1948, 28–33 (*TNR*).
18 *HIFL* 160.
19 Jeal 232.
20 Bennett 19.
21 SD 4.06.1871.
22 Bennett 20.
23 Ibid. 20–1.
24 *HIFL* 264.
25 SD 20 Jun, 18 May 1871.
26 Bennett 22.
27 N. R. Bennett *Mirambo of Tanzania*, 1971, 22 ff; R. W. Beachey *The Slave Trade of Eastern Africa*, 1976, 186; Roland Oliver and Anthony Atmore *Africa Since 1800*, 1981, 67ff.
28 Bennett 8.
29 Ibid. 45; *HIFL* 279; SD 23.08.1871.
30 SD 28.07.1871; *HIFL* 268.
31 *Auto* 257; *HIFL* 275.
32 Bennet 45–7; *HIFL* 282ff.

33 *HIFL* 303; number given as 54 in *HIFL* 313; SD 22.08.1871.
34 SD 23, 24 Aug 1871.
35 SD 7.09.1871.
36 SD 13.09.1871.
37 *HIFL* 309.
38 *HIFL* 411.
39 *LLJ* ii 135, 154.
40 Ibid. 146–7.
41 Ibid. 154.
42 *HIFL* 313.
43 SD 20.09.1871.
44 *HIFL* 321.
45 *HIFL* 325–7.
46 Bennett 51.
47 *HIFL* 403–4.
48 *HIFL* 405.
49 DL to Thomas Maclear and Mr Mann 17 Nov 1871 PRGSL vol xvii 1872–3 p 69–73.
50 Ibid.
51 *Auto* 261–2.
52 Bennet 89; *HIFL* 409–10.
53 *HIFL* 410–12; SD 3 Nov substituted for 10th; Bennett 89; Jeal 336.

NINE: Canonizing Dr Livingstone

1 *HIFL* 411.
2 *Auto* 264.
3 *HIFL* 411.
4 Small original SD starting October 1870, 3 Nov redated 10 Nov, 11 and 12 Nov are missing.
5 DL to Sir Thomas Maclear and Mr Mann 17.11.1871 PRGSL xvii 1872–3, 72; DL to Bennett Nov 1871 HIFL 616 ff; DL to Agnes L 18 Nov 1871 BL; DL to Earl Granville 18 Dec 1871 LFDL p 297; DL to W. Black 19 Nov and Capt White 15 Nov 1871 both NLS.
6 In this neat and flawless journal, starting on the day of the meeting, Stanley wrote: 'The diary entry of this date has already been published in *How I Found Livingstone*. Copy that first and proceed to next page.'
7 Small SD 3.11.1871.
8 Quoted Jeal 389.
9 See Jeal Appendix B 389; Mrs J. Stanley conversation with author 16.02.04.
10 The Date of the Livingstone Stanley Meeting: I. C. Cunningham in Appendix 6 of the National Library of Scotland's publication *David Livingstone: A Catalogue of Documents* (Edinburgh 1985) attempted to examine all the evidence and establish a reliable date for the meeting. The problem is that DL lost count of the days of the month long before they met, and S briefly thought he had lost count too. (Attacks of fever could last several weeks and be accompanied by lapses into unconsciousness.) According to DL's journal (NLS

David Livingstone a Catalogue of Documents 273 no 11), he discovered, because of the arrival of the Muslim month of Ramadhan on 14.02.1871, that his diary entries were 21 days ahead of the actual date. DL had initially believed that S had reached Ujiji on 16 Nov, so the change meant that S had arrived on 27 Oct, if DL was right about the 21 days, and if the Arabs in Ujiji could be relied upon to have started their Ramadhan fasting on the correct date. (S had brought with him a Nautical Almanac for 1871, which contained the information that Ramadhan began on the 14th that year.)

Cunningham plumps for 27.10.1871 as the correct date, and in doing so is much influenced not only by Livingstone, but by François Bontinck's argument put forward in 'La date de la Rencontre Stanley – Livingstone' (*Africa, Rivista trimestrale di studi documentazione dell'Istituto Italo-Africano*, xxiv 3.09.1979, 225–45). However, Bontinck was ignorant of much of DL's evidence, and relied heavily on S's despatch to the *New York Herald* dated by the explorer 10.11.1871, in which he stated that, having reflected on the matter, he thought he had arrived at Ujiji on 3.11.1872, rather than the 10th. In *HIFL* 274–5, S stated that he had recovered from a prolonged bout of fever and delirium on the real date of 14 Jul 1871, and on coming round had been told that the date was in fact 21 Jul. S claimed that he had there and then altered his diary to the new date, thus ensuring that he would think the famous meeting happened a week later than it did. So when S wrote in *HIFL* that the meeting took place on 10 Nov, Bontinck concluded (since S really thought 3 November was the correct date, according to his almost contemporary 10 Nov despatch to the *NYH*) that the explorer had mistakenly added rather than subtracted a week. (By subtracting a week from 3 November he would indeed have arrived at 27 Oct, the date Bontinck proclaimed to be correct.) But S's date of 3 Nov for the meeting is clearly itself the result of a subtraction – being a week earlier than S's diary date for the meeting of 10 Nov, given in his most reliable and earliest diary notebook. To confuse matters further, the claims advanced about dates in S's despatch, supposedly of 10 Nov, must be considered suspect. He and DL did not discuss their muddle over dates until 14 Nov (the start of Ramadhan).

In *HIFL*, S claimed he altered his diary, changing 14 Jul into 21 Jul. In fact, no such alteration was made by him in his notebook diary. (He related on 14 Jul that he recovered his senses on that day, and remained convalescent in bed till the 25th, when he got up.) So what are we to make of this fact, and the fact that he retained the 10 Nov date, both in *HIFL*, and in the fair copy diary that he wrote up after completing his book? It seems to me that when DL expounded his views about the true date to S after Ramadan started, the younger man, who hero-worshipped DL, felt briefly uncertain of his own ideas about the date. Because DL continued to believe that the meeting had taken place two weeks earlier than 10 Nov, Stanley seems to have defensively concocted the story of being misinformed by Shaw about the date after coming round from delirium in mid-Jul. He used this fiction about Shaw to *seem* to move his date closer to DL's, but when it came to fixing the date permanently, both in *HIFL* and his copy diary, he reverted to his original notebook diary date, presumably because he believed that it was right. For instance, the date he gives for his final departure from Ujiji with DL is the same in his notebook diary (27 December), in *HIFL* 566, and in his fair copy diary. In all three, the meeting is stated to have occurred on 10 Nov. It could be argued that S stuck to his original date because he hated being wrong, but it could also be argued that he stuck to it because he knew it was right, and that he had only ever pretended otherwise out of deference to DL.

As to whether DL's calculations were right, I do not believe it is possible to be sure. DL's confusion about the date on which he arrived at Ujiji, and S's confusion springing from it (Cunningham note 4 p 40), should alert one to the strong possibility that the 21-day discrepancy is by no means a proven quantity. DL in his field diary 39 said that he reached Ujiji on 23 Oct, whereas S gained the impression, presumably from DL, that he had arrived on 16 October (S to *NYH* 10 Nov Bennett p 59). S in this same despatch said that the meeting took place 18 days later. Yet on 11 Nov in S's large copy diary he says that he reached Ujiji 14 (corrected from 10) days after DL had reached it.

It is only safe to say that S either met DL on a day in late October, or during the first half of November 1871. I incline more towards S's chosen date of 10 November, than to DL's late October date. That is because S's natural inclination, as Livingstone's honorary son, would have been to support the older man's date.

11 *HIFL* 560–1.
12 Bennett 96.
13 SD 11.11.1871.
14 *HIFL* 418.
15 Bennett 99.
16 Ibid. 95–6.
17 Ibid. 95.
18 *HIFL* 234.
19 *HIFL* 432; SD 16.11.1871.
20 SD 4.03.1872; SD 5.01.1870.
21 SD 11.11.1871; *HIFL* 424.
22 Bennett 95.
23 *HIFL* 416.
24 Bennett 96.
25 Ibid. 97.
26 SD 16.11.1871.
27 SD 28.11.1871.
28 DL to Agnes L 23.8.72 BL.
29 SD 8.01.1872.
30 DL to Agnes L 12.12.1871.
31 SD 14.11.1871.
32 Feb 1872 Brenthurst Library, 9 April 1872 Ter; Nov 1871 *HIFL* 616.
33 SD 5.01.1872.
34 LLJ ii 93.
35 *HIFL* 430.
36 *Times* 20.01.1863.

37 SD 6, 9 Jan 1872.
38 SD 21.02.1872.
39 SD 3.03.1872.
40 SD 28.11.1871.
41 SD 14.2.1872.
42 'A Memorial to Livingstone' Lecture 21.04.1894.
43 SD 4.03.1872.
44 SD 12.11.1871.
45 SD 28.02.1872 .
46 SD 22.11.1871.
47 SD 17.01.1872.
48 DL to Agnes L Feb 1872 BL.
49 DL to Agnes L 1.7.72 BL.
50 SD 27.01.1872.
51 SD 15.02.1871.
52 SD 5.03.1872.
53 Ibid.
54 SD 24.02.1872.
55 SD 7.03.1872.
56 SD 24.02.1872.
57 SD 6.03.1872.
58 SD 13.11.1871.
59 SD 14.11.1871; quoted Hird 94.
60 SD13.03.1872.
61 SD 14.03.1872.
62 Ibid.
63 S to DL 15.03.1871 NLS; quoted McLynn186-7.
64 DL to John L Dec 1872 Quentin Keynes; DL to Bates 20.2.72 NLS.
65 S to DL 20.03.1872 NLS.
66 S to Bennett 18.05.1872.
67 DL to Bennett Feb 1872 Brenthurst Library; DL to Bennett Nov 1871 *HIFL* 619.
68 Ibid.
69 SD 13.03.1872.

TEN: 'Fame is Useless to Me'

1 SD 10.07.1872.
2 *HIFL* 629; S to TGough Roberts 4 May 1869, Bath.
3 *HIFL* 661.
4 Hall 212.
5 SD 7.5.1872.
6 *Daily Tel* 25.07.1872.
7 SD 31.07.1872.
8 Livingstone's letters written pre Stanley's arrival show that he was already angry with Kirk, viz DL to Kirk 30.10.1871 *HIFL* 704-7, 710-13.
9 DL to Kirk 30 Oct in *HIFL* 704-6; Kirk to Granville 9.05.1872 *HIFL* 708-9; 'A friend of Stanley' to *Times* 13.11.1872.

10 That is, DL to Waller 2–3 Nov 1871 Rhodes House; DL to Sir Roderick Murchison 13.03.1872 PRGSL Vol xvi 1871–2 434.

11 *HIFL* 675.

12 Edward King to S 14 Sept and 18 Oct 1872.

13 SD 29.07.1872.

14 S to *Times* 12.11.1872.

15 Hotten 156–7. Hotten's reputation for scurrility and dishonesty, which had been enhanced by his recent pirating of books by Mark Twain, lent weight to Stanley's denunciations. Hotten had also published books about prostitution and aphrodisiacs. He modestly disclaimed authorship of *Henry M. Stanley: The Story of his Life,* attributing it to Cadwalader Rowlands, by deliberate implication a close relative of Stanley. This was actually a pseudonym for Hotten himself.

16 Long autobiographical letter from S to DS 18.11.1893.

17 SD 1.08.1872.

18 S to DS 18.11.1893.

19 SD 11.08.1872.

20 Deeds of Castle Arms courtesy Bob Owen.

21 SD 8.08.1872.

22 SD 1.08.1872.

23 SD 2.08.1872; Lord Granville to S 2.08.1872.

24 Bierman 128.

25 Anstruther 143.

26 PRGS xvi 241 Meeting 13.05.1872.

27 Rawlinson to S 6.08.1872.

28 Waller had read in the *Daily News* (2 Aug) a description of the Paris banquet, in which Stanley was quoted as saying that he 'had a mission from Dr Livingstone to describe Dr Kirk as a traitor'. (Waller to S 5.08.1872 Rhodes House). After a long and acrimonious meeting with S at the Langham, Waller wrote an obsessive 18-page letter to DL attacking the journalist and excusing Kirk, his relation by marriage. Waller to DL 12.08.1872 Rhodes House, Oxford.

29 Quoted Bierman 129.

30 *Auto* 289.

31 King to S 14.09.1872.

32 SD 16.08.1872.

33 McLynn i 215; *Enigma* 25, 116.

34 SD 11.08.1872.

35 J. B. Browne to ed *Times* 22.08.1872; *Daily News* J. C. Parkinson 19 Aug 72.

36 Anstruther 154 attr to *DTel* 27 Aug.

37 D. W. Forrest *Francis Galton* 1974, 118–19; Markham to Stanley 5 and 12 Sept 1872; Forrest 119–20.

38 Marston to S 28.09.1872.

39 *Enigma* 116.

40 Anstrutruther 161.

41 *HIFL* 398–9.

42 Ibid. 9–10.

43 A typical example: James Greenwood *The Wild Man at Home, or Pictures of Life in Savage Lands,* 1871, Chapters: Savage Pastime, Savage Storytellers, Savage Adornment, Abominable Chinook Customs etc.; even in 1896 R. Baden-Powell, *The Downfall of Prempeh*, is full of examples.
44 Quoted McLynn i 222.
45 S to Rawlinson 2.09.1872.
46 See A. Z. Fraser *Livingstone and Newstead*, 1913, 193–202 for reaction of Webb family to S.
47 Agnes L to S 3.08.1872.
48 Morien to Wellcome 24.08.1904 RGS Box 4 13/1–2.
49 SD 7.08.1872.
50 King to S 18.10.1872.
51 SD 21 Sep, 1 Oct 1872.
52 *Auto* 288.
53 S to Markham 5.10.1872 RGS; Markham to S 8.10.1872. Lieutenant W. J. Grandy R. N. would fail to get any further up the Congo than the first cataracts.
54 Quoted Hall 225.
55 Cameron to S 25.10.1872.
56 S to Edward Levy 13.08.1876, Bennett 465.

ELEVEN: A Destiny Resumed

1 Bierman 137; Seitz 299–300.
2 NYH 4.12.1872.
3 Anstruther 174.
4 Noe NY*Sun* 16, 29 Aug 1872.
5 SD 1.01.1873.
6 F. Anderson to S 22.09.1873.
7 Louis J. Jennings ed *New York Times* to S 9.01.1873.
8 S to Marston 28.08.1873.
9 *My Kalulu*, 1873.
10 Hall 233.
11 A. Z. Fraser 200–1.
12 Kalulu to S n.d.
13 Hall 234.
14 H. M. Stanley *Comassie and Magdala*, 1874, 167, 230–1.
15 S employed Swinburne as his secretary on the Congo in 1879.
16 Christ's Hospital Archives.
17 London Street Directories. Census etc.
18 Fanny Swinburne to S 27.12.1873.
19 A. B. Swinburne to S 4.01.1874.
20 Christie's catalogue Sep 2002 Swinburne pictures in album; Swinburne to S 4.01.1874.
21 Helly 113.
22 S to Agnes L 18.03.1874 Quentin Keynes Collection.
23 Helly 108–11.
24 S to Agnes L 28.01.1878 RP 4900 BL.

25 SD 25.02.1874. Ink very dark as in re-written diaries, and no hesitancies or corrections; the sentiment is very late imperial and 1890s.
26 *Auto* 295, and SD 25.02.1874.
27 DL to S n.d. 1873 Lake Bangweulu; Emilia Webb to S 1.04.1874.
28 Jeal 370.
29 PRGSL 445 vol xviii 1873–4.
30 Agnes L to S 17.04.1874.
31 Jeal 376–7.
32 *NYH* 7.4.1874.
33 E. Arnold to S n.d. but Mar/Apr 1874.
34 Hird 129–30; *Auto* 298.

TWELVE: Love and the Longest Journey

1 *TDC* i 2.
2 SD 13.05.1874.
3 SD 16.05.1874.
4 SD 17.05.1874.
5 SD 13.06.1874.
6 SD 8 and 11 Jul 1874.
7 Marriage Pledge 12.07.1874.
8 SD 17.07.1874.
9 SD 18.07.1874.
10 *TDC* i 5.
11 Ibid.
12 Bennett 483; House of Commons 1871 xiii (ii) Report from the Select Committee on the Slave Trade (East Africa). The Committee had concluded in its report that the trade could only be ended by a new treaty with the Sultan of Zanzibar and increased naval patrols, but in the wake of the debate the government went further. By the time Sir Bartle Frere left Britain, in early November 1872, to negotiate with the Sultan, the British government had instructed him to achieve the 'complete suppression of this cruel & destructive traffic'. The government authorized Dr Kirk, who took over from Frere, to tell Sultan Barghash that his refusal to sign would be met by the immediate blockade of his island by the Royal Navy. Barghash capitulated and the treaty conceding the end of the seaborne trade was signed on 5 Jun 1873 (R. W. Beachey *The Slave Trade of Eastern Africa* 109, 112–13). The toughening of attitude in British ruling circles had coincided with the three months Stanley spent in Britain championing 'saintly' Dr Livingstone and his anti-slavery aims.
13 Paul E. Lovejoy *Transformations in Slavery*, 1983, 224–5.
14 *TDC* i facing 37.
15 S to AP 14.08.1875.
16 *TDC* i 47.
17 Hall 31–2.
18 *NYH* 26.07.1874.
19 *TDC* i 83.
20 S to AP 4.03.1875; S to F. Lafontaine 21.05.1875; S & N 46.

21 *S & N* 25; Muster List naming 227 is No *6993* Tervuren register. So to reach his claimed total of 356, might he have recruited 128 more followers in Bagamoyo within the space of four days (he left for the interior on the 17th)? Not according to his despatch to the *New York Herald*, dated 12 Dec. Although devoting two paragraphs to his time in Bagamoyo, no mention is made of recruiting porters – a topic he had been obsessed with at Bagamoyo before the Livingstone expedition (S to NYH 12.12.1874, Bennett 189). One difficulty in trying to calculate his numbers is that his statement that there were 36 women and 10 boys at the outset seems to have been about double their true number, since he later asserted that only four women died, and in mid-journey gives the number of survivors as 16 – and in a list named 14 as having returned safely to Zanzibar at journey's end (TDC i 82; TDC ii 193, picture facing ii 480, ii 513 list).

22 AP to S 13.10.1874.

23 AP to S 28 Oct, 4, 5, 13 Nov, 4 Dec.

24 AP to S 2.12.1874.

25 *TDC* i 81–2.

26 Ibid.

27 *TDC* i 82, *TDC* ii 193, pic facing ii 480, ii 513 list.

28 *TDC* ii 510 lists 33 deaths since start of Exped to 31.01.1875. On 16 Jan he would claim to have only 230 people left out of an original 347 – a horrifying loss of 117 in the three months since starting. However, a close reading of the diary suggests he had by then suffered only 26 men lost through death, disease or desertion (S & N 25). Between 16 Jan and the end of the month, S lists a further 27 deaths and desertions in his diary, yet on 31 Jan he suggests, also in his diary, that he only has 173 men left, implying a loss of 57 men since 16 Jan. So what is going on? I believe that on 31 Jan he really *did* have between 170 and 180 men in his party. This true figure can be arrived at by assuming that he started with 228 (as stated in his diary), then lost about 50, principally through death, but also through desertion, by 31 Jan (*TDC* ii 510 lists 33 deaths since start of exped to 31 Jan) and so S had 178 with him on that day (174 if not counting the Europeans). Given his usual skill at keeping men alive and preventing desertions – for S to have lost even 50 men (about 20 per cent of his 228 starters in two and a half months) shows what a hellish journey this was from the beginning. The hugely exaggerated loss of 117 had been entered in his diary simply in order to make the inflated 356 (his published starting figure) seem credible. Once again S had been pushed into lies by Bennett's desire to appear an unstinting Maecenas, and by his own workhouse boy's desire to seem the best equipped and most glorious of all explorers.

29 *TDC* i 100–1.

30 Ibid. 108.

31 SD 12.01.75.

32 *TDC* i 112.

33 Norman R. Bennett ed *Stanley's Despatches to the New York Herald 1871–2, 1874–7*, 1970, 458 (Bennett 458).

34 SD 16.01.75; S to H. J. Pocock 4.03.75 Bennett 208.

35 *Auto* 301; Bennett 197.
36 SD 23.01.1875.
37 S to E. King 19.05.75, Bennett 456.
38 SD 23.01.75.
39 SD 24–5.01.1875; Bennett 202.
40 Bennett 458.
41 *S & N* 55.
42 *TDC* i 136–42.
43 Ibid. 142.
44 *S & N* 63.
45 166 given as figure in SD 28 Feb S & N 60; but 10 oarsmen taken from this.
46 Ibid.
47 *TDC* i 136–7.
48 *S & N* 63.
49 S to J. R. Robinson 11.11.1874 BL RP1100.
50 S to AP 4.03.1875.

THIRTEEN: The Island of Death

1 Which S would assume, at first, to be a major feeder of the lake – until he found the more important Kagera River (Bennett 206 note 17).
2 Bennett 214.
3 Ibid. 217; *TDC* i p 180.
4 *NYH* 29.07.1875, Bennett 248.
5 Opening pages of 'Uganda Diary' 1875–6.
6 *S & N* 70; Bennett 220.
7 Bierman 176.
6 Bennett 46–7; ibid. 225ff S to *NYH* 14.04.1875; *S & N* 71–2.
9 Drafts of *DT* and *NYH* letters 1.06.1876.
10 Preface to 'Uganda Diary' 1875–6.
11 *S & N* 70.
12 Ibid.
13 *TDC* i 198.
14 McLynn i 258 quoting: Chaille-Long *Central Africa*, 1876, 310; Alan Moorehead *The White Nile*, 1964 ed, 140.
15 *TDC* i 202–3 re 10.04.1875; *TDC* i 202, 405.
16 *NYH* 14.04.1875.
17 *TDC* i 322, 448; *TDC* ii 166.
18 Quoted Bierman 178; Bellefonds Journal 13.04.1875, Bennett 233.
19 Bennett 242.
20 Ibid. 243.
21 Ibid. 243–4.
22 SD 28.04.1875.
23 *TDC* i 230–1.
24 Small Australian notebook 1891–2.
25 SD 28.04.1875.
26 Bennett 246.

27 Ibid. 242ff.

28 S to AP 15.05.1875; S to King 19.05.1875, Bennett 258.

29 *Auto* 316; in SD 22.07.1875 (S & N 88) he mentions that it was rumoured on the neighbouring island of Iroba that he had killed 14 men on Bumbireh; but he also quoted an island rumour that he had been killed on Bumbireh.

29 Bennett 248.

30 S to *NYH* 29.11.1875.

31 PRGS 3.06.1878, 387ff.

32 Bennett 228–9.

33 Ibid. 240; S & N 78.

34 Bennett 157 and note 6.

35 F. Pocock to parents 15.05.1875 Bennett 469.

36 *TDC* i 246; Bennett 253.

37 *S & N* 82; Bennett 255.

38 *S & N* 83–5.

39 *TDC* i 277–8.

40 *TDC* ii 274.

41 *S & N* 91–2.

42 Ibid. 92.

43 Bennett 257.

44 *TDC* i 285.

45 *S & N* 92–3.

46 F. Pocock Diaries A and D Aug 3 (error for 4) 1877 Rhodes House, Oxford.

47 Pocock Diary A 3–4 Aug; confirms 33 were thought killed; *S & N* 95.

48 Bennett 260.

49 *S & N* 96–7.

50 Gordon to S 20.04.1875.

51 S to Edward Levy 15.08.1875.

52 *S & N* 99.

53 Bennett 274.

54 S to AP 2.06.1876.

55 *S & N* 117–18.

56 S to AP 2.06.1876.

57 Ibid.

58 *S & N* 120.

59 *TDC* ii 9–10.

60 S to AP 2.06.1876.

61 PRGS 3.06.1878, 391ff.

62 *S & N* 123–4.

63 S to AP 14.08.1876.

64 S to E Levy-Lawson 13.08.1876 Bennett 463ff.

65 41 in *TDC* ii 65 is exaggeration for desertions alone; see *S & N* 130–1; Bennett 315–16.

66 *TDC* ii p 62ff.

67 *S & N* 130.

68 *TDC* ii 78.

69 *TDC* ii 79–83.

70 *TDC* ii 85.

71 Bennett 323.

72 *TDC* ii 92.

73 *Auto* 319.

74 N. R. Bennett *Mirambo of Tanzania*, 1971, 146.

75 Ruth Slade *King Leopold's Congo*, 1962, 88.

76 *TDC* ii p 95–6.

77 *S & N* 132–3.

78 Clements Markham *Private History of the RGS* n.d. 401–2 RGS.

79 *TDC* ii 96–7.

80 *TDC* ii 117, 96.

81 Jeal 298.

82 Kirk to Rawlinson 15.01.1872 PRGS xvi 227.

83 *TDC* ii 120.

84 *TDC* ii 118; Bennett 322.

85 Bennett 324–7.

86 Ibid. 335.

87 *S & N* 146. Report on Livingstone Congo Expedition 28 Jan 75 by W. J.
    Grandy RN, PRGS Vol xix 104ff. In December 1874, in London, Lieutenant
    W. J. Grandy, RN, having failed to progress up the Congo far beyond Boma,
    told the members of the RGS that his expedition had been destroyed by his
    inability to hire reliable porters. In his opinion, a caravan of 500 men with
    guns would be essential for a successful journey up the Congo.

88 S made out that Tippu Tip brought 400 *TDC* ii 130; but his diary figure (*S & N*
    139 20 Nov) giving a total of 458 for both parties is probably right – the count
    being made at a river crossing. Subtract S's 146 and one gets 312 for TT. In Ben-
    nett 322 he lists the male contingent as 210 (140 with guns and 70 with spears).

89 S to King 31.10.1876 Bennett 459 ff .

FOURTEEN: 'The Great Struggle with this Mystery'

1 *TDC* ii 130–1.

2 Ibid. 132–3, 138.

3 Ibid. 138–9.

4 *S & N* 136–7.

5 *S & N* 139.

6 *TDC* ii 145 and footnote; *S & N* 138–9; Pocock in Hall 69.

7 *S& N* 139.

8 *S & N* 141.

9 *S & N* 139–40 .

10 See Bennett 377, 385–6 for large exaggerations – all S's self-proclaimed 32
    battles on the Congo (except one bloodless brush on 9 Mar) took place
    between 24 Nov 1876 and 14 Feb 1877 *S & N* 140–164. The 'fight of fights'
    and penultimate 'battle' (no 31) was on 14 Feb and Stanley massively exag-
    gerated the number of combatants in TDC and in *S & N* 164 – for actual
    numbers see this book pp 201–2 and note 37 p. 515 quoting Frank Pockock's

figures. See this book 192 for Stanley's small number of competent marksmen. There is no supporting evidence in his original diaries to support his claim (made in a single throwaway note S&N 199) to have captured $50,000 worth of ivory or to have destroyed 28 towns. These assertions are fantasy like the 32 battles. After being attacked, he set fire to some huts in three villages during this period of constant danger. On many occasions he tried to make peace, see S & N 18 Dec, 1–2 Jan and 7 Feb, Mar 1–2. On 26 Nov he wrote: 'I gave strictest orders that no native should be molested unless he was near camp at night.' S & N 141.

11 *S & N* 142–4.
12 *S & N* 143; *TDC* ii 170, 176–7; *S & N* 137.
13 J. S. Jameson *The Story of the Rear Column of the Emin Pasha Relief Expedition*, 1890, 300; McLynn i 304 quoting *The Autobiography of Tippu Tip*; *TDC* ii 189.
14 Bennett 380.
15 *TDC* ii 197–8.
16 *S & N* 31 Dec 146 (= 109 men out of 143); *TDC* ii 124, 188, 311.
17 *S & N* 146.
18 Ibid. 147.
19 Cannibalism; evidence of Livingstone, Jeal 327, J. H. Weeks, the missionary (see books in bibliog); McLynn i note 3 388. Also see notes 29 and 38 below; also see p. 194 of this book.
20 *S & N* 148 1.01.1877.
21 *Auto* 327.
22 McLynn i 315; S to NYH 24.11.1877.
23 H. M. Stanley *The Congo and the Founding of Its Free State*, 1885, ii 120.
24 *S & N* 130.
25 Bennett 387.
26 *TDC* ii 247–8; *S & N* 150–1.
27 *S & N* 157.
28 *TDC* ii 241.
29 Ibid. 274.
30 *S & N* 163.
31 *TDC* ii 226; *S & N* 160, 156 and *TDC* ii 254.
32 *S & N* 159–60.
33 *S & N* 160–1.
34 *TDC* ii 288.
35 Ibid. 291; *S & N* 163.
36 Ibid. 163.
37 D. F. Pocock Diary 14–15 Feb Rhodes House; *TDC* ii 298–301; S & N 164–5; Original SD 14.02.1877 has 54 but this is written over 27, itself a large exaggeration.
38 W. Holman Bentley *Pioneering on the Congo*, 1900, 64, quoted by McLynn i 319.
39 *S & N* 166.
40 *CFFS* i 5–7. This had been achieved in 1816 by the Englishman Captain James K.

Tuckey, RN, when he led a party of 56 men, 18 of whom died of fever during their upriver push from Banana on the sea to the Nsongo Yellala falls, 172 miles up the Congo. Ahead of Tuckey had lain 155 miles of cataracts, which had forced him to travel on overland. Of his land party of 30, 14 died in this phase, including Tuckey himself, after whose death the whole expedition was withdrawn.

41 Bennett 387–8.

42 Boma letter mentions 115 souls; p 99 *S & N*, 17 Jul, gives deaths on the river at 13; 143 people had been alive at Nyangwe so 14 had died between there and the Pool; p 174 *S & N*, 29 Mar, gives canoe numbers.

43 *TDC* i 51–2.

44 S to King 2.10.1877 .

45 When S addressed the Wangwana, he did so paternalistically, speaking of himself as their father. In one sense, he had reconstituted in Africa a sort of workhouse family. Replacing Kalulu, he now had new young favourites, such as the teenager Billali, who was a brilliant hunter. There was Majwara, the boy who had been with DL when he died, and who now acted as S's and Pocock's tent boy, and in addition spied for his master, reporting on thefts of supplies. And lastly there was Kadu, one of Mutesa's pages, who would be with S in Britain for several years. *TDC* ii 159; *S & N* 30; *TDC* ii 379; *TDC* ii 166.

46 Bennett 362.

47 *TDC* ii 360, 369.

48 Bennett 479, 482.

49 *TDC* ii 336.

50 *S & N* 173; *TDC* ii 338.

51 SD 3.04.1877; *S & N* 174.

52 *S & N* 174–5.

53 Ibid. 176–7.

54 Ibid. 179.

55 Ibid. 180; *TDC* ii 348–9.

56 *S & N* 181–2.

57 Ibid. 183–4; *TDC* ii 361 .

58 *TDC* ii 368; *S & N* 185 .

59 *TDC* ii 375.

60 Ibid. 378–83.

61 Ibid.

62 *S & N* 189.

63 Ibid. 189; *TDC* ii 397.

64 *S & N* 192.

65 Ibid. 192, 195.

66 *TDC* ii 405.

67 *S & N* 193–5.

68 Ibid. 196–7.

69 Ibid.

70 SD after 10.05.1877 unpublished.

71 *S & N* 199.

72 Ibid. 200; *TDC* ii 431–2.

73 *S & N* 201; *TDC* ii 433.

74 Bennett 388–9.

75 Ibid. 390.

76 *S & N* 202.

77 I have quoted from the version bought in the 1970s by Quentin Keynes (whose executors sold it at Christie's on 7.04.2004), which strikes me, from crossings-out and hesitancies, as being the first written. The date is 4 Aug – changed later to 6th, possibly not by Stanley. There is another English version at the Sociedade de Geografia de Lisboa, which is different in many minor details and starts Banza N'Sanga, is dated 5 Aug and does not include the phrase 'To any gentleman who speaks English at Emboma'. A version slightly different from both was printed in *TDC* ii 447–9, so it would seem that at some stage Stanley had kept a copy for himself – though none exists in his archive at the present date.

78 *TDC* ii 461; Bennett 340–1.

79 *TDC* ii 462.

80 SD 9.08.1877; Hall 21.

81 *TDC* ii 470–1. SD on 27 Sept has 114 men women and two infants.

82 Bennett 346.

83 S to Edward Levy-Lawson 17.08.1877 Russell Train Coll.

84 Papers of C. R. Blandy record £1,533.13.6 despatched from Madeira, first tranche 26 Oct 77 to S at Cape, Russell Train Coll.

85 Jeal 230; these members of the Kololo tribe (one fewer than the 115 people S had brought to Kabinda) were abandoned by DL without resources at Tete on the Zambesi in April 1856. It would be four years (the summer of 1860, two years after DL had returned to the Zambesi) before he would finally find time to take the Kololo back to central Africa.

86 S to Levy-Lawson 16.09.1877; *Geographical Magazine*, and *PMG* 28.12.1875.

87 *TDC* ii 470; *Auto* 536.

88 S to Levy-Lawson 16.09.18 77 Russell Train Coll.

89 SD13.08.1877.

90 *Bulletin Missouri Historical Society*, April 1962, 265–6 'On The Trail of a New H. M. Stanley Letter' by Douglas Wheeler; SD 20–26.08.1877.

91 S to Levy-Lawson 16.09.1877 Russell Train Coll.

92 S to King 2.10.1877.

93 Eight AP letters are at Tervuren.

94 AP to S 4.12.1874.

95 Marston to S 25 Sep, 11 Oct 1877; V. Ambella to S 10.10.1877.

96 *S & N* 25; *TDC* ii 514–15; in S's *My Dark Companions and their Strange Stories*, 1893, in Bunyoro five Ugandans had been with S, but none were included in *TDC* lists of dead or returned. Details about Baruti, Kassim, Katembo and Kadu in this book; *TDC* ii 124; *TDC* ii 515.

97 *TDC* ii 513, 477, 480.

98 Ibid. 482–3.

99 Bennett 457; also see *My Dark Companions*.

100 Preface to Uganda Diary 1875–6.

FIFTEEN: 'I Hate Evil and Love Good'

1 AP to S 17.11.77.
2 *Daily News* 14.12.1877.
3 Quoted Bierman 213 from Edward Marston *After Work*, 1904, 226.
4 *Saturday Review* 16.02.1877; *Pall Mall Gazette* 11.02.1877.
5 Marston to S 11.10.1877. Indeed the perception that he was an American was all but universal. Edwin Arnold shared it, as did Serpa Pinto, the Portuguese explorer, from whom Stanley had begged that personal favour of mailing a letter to his 'pequena' in New York. Pinto had pronounced Stanley a 'true Yankee', and had written to friends quoting 'his many Americanisms' (Douglas L. Wheeler *Bulletin Missouri Historical Society*, April 1962, 265). On this particular return to Britain, S made no clandestine visits to north Wales, unwilling to risk a repeat of the controversy about his nationality that had distressed him in 1872.
6 Arnold to S 29.1. 1877; Marston to S 11.10.1877.
7 H. Yule to ed of *Anti -Slavery Reporter* 14.02.1878.
8 RGSP xxi 1876–7, 62–3.
9 CD 15.10.1880 .
10 Bennett 458.
11 Quoted in *Times* 17.11.1877.
12 Gordon to Burton 19.10.1877, quoted McLynn ii 14.
13 Baker to Edwin Arnold 20.01.1878.
14 *Anti-Slavery Reporter* 1.04.1873; Dorothy Middleton *Baker of the Nile*, 1949, 191.
15 Middleton, *Baker* ... 163; Cairns 206.
16 Margery Perham *Lugard: The Years of Adventure 1858–1898*, i, 1956, 198, 238, 303, 350.
17 Ibid. 197.
18 CD 15.10.1880; Rotberg 270, 274.
19 CD ibid.
20 S to Strauch 8.08.1883.
21 *Saturday Review* 16.02.1878.
22 *Geographical Magazine* March 1878, 53.
23 *Saturday Review* 16.02.1878.
24 *Edinburgh Review* Francis Galton 'Stanley's Discoveries and the Future of Africa' cxlv ii 1878, 167, 171.
25 CD as n 9.
26 Sir Rutherford Alcock to S 31.01.1878; *Standard* 9 Feb; Yule to *PMG* 25.01.1878.
27 *Saturday Review* 16.02.1878.
28 'My First Fight with Savages' *Home Journal* Jan 1898.
29 Ibid.
30 J. Farler to A. Buzacott 28.12.1877 Rhodes House Mss Brit Emp; S & N 199 has ref to 133 tusks and 32 battles, and destroying 28 large towns, quoted later by detractors, but this was a typical Stanley exaggeration verging on downright lying.

31 Hall 245.

32 Kirk to MacKinnon 13.12.1877 FO 84/1514; S to Kirk 1.12.1877 copy Ter.

33 Quoted McLynn ii 4.

34 Hall 245–6; Bierman 223.

35 Scorn for Shaw throughout HIFL; S to H.H. Johnston 15.04.1883 *Academie Royale des Sciences Coloniale* iii-1957-2 349.

36 Bennett 317 ff; S to NYH Nyangwe 28.10.1876; Pocock to brother 20.07.1876 Bennett 477ff.

37 J. Kirk to Derby 1 May 1878 FO 84/1514).

38 Elizabeth Longford *Victoria RI* 527 quoting the Queen's diary 26.06.1878.

39 Jeal 22 etc; Cairns 193.

40 Quoted Jeal 186, also 105.

41 SD 13.08.1877, Bennett 341–6.

42 Bennett 371–2; also *Times* 17.11.1877.

43 SD 1877 notebook, end pages 26 Jun 1878.

44 Neal Ascherson *The King Incorporated*, 1963, 46.

45 *Times* 11.01.1876.

46 Ascherson 90.

47 Quoted Pakenham 21.

48 Emerson 77.

49 Ascherson 95.

50 APR Fonds Congo 100/1 Leopold to Solvyns 17 Nov 1877.

51 Lii to Solvyns 17.11.1877 quoted Ascherson 104, and a little differently Emerson 85.

52 *CFFS* i 21.

53 Bontinck 28 Sanford to US Secretary of State 21.01.1878 .

54 *CFFS* i 21.

55 S's Appointment diary 1878.

56 Longford 527; APR Fonds 10/2 Beaconsfield to Lii 29.10.1878; Emerson 88.

SIXTEEN: A Colony for a King

1 S to JS Keltie 17.09.1884 RGS 2/1/7.

2 *Manchester Courier* 26.11.1878 .

3 Samuel Tibbins to My dear Phillips, Edinburgh University Library LOA 239 f28.

4 *TDC* i 61–2.

5 Hird 202–3; CD 14.08.1879.

6 Greindl to S 5.10.1878. The inference intended to be drawn from a book title such as *Stanley: Sorcerer's Apprentice* (volume ii of McLynn's biography) is that Stanley fell under the influence of a man versed in the dark arts, and then learned how to practise them himself. '1877 marked the meridian point,' wrote McLynn, 'when the influence of the saintly Livingstone started to wane and that of the evil genius of King Leopold II began to appear,' ushering in the part of Stanley's life when thanks to the king, he faced his own 'dark interior' (McLynn vol i 329–30). In reality, the influence of Livingstone did not diminish after Stanley signed his contract with Leopold.

7 *UL* 149.

8 Ascherson 98.

9 CD 13.10.1878.

10 Solvyns to S 6.06.1878 quoted CD.

11 CD 4.01.1879.

12 Emerson 86.

13 Ibid. 84; Bennett *Mirambo of Tanzania* 113 ff.

14 S to Sanford 10, 19 Oct, 16 Nov 1878 Sanford Museum.

15 CD 5.11.1878 and 9.12.1878. Rumour of £4,000 advance salary, see Bontinck 49, quoting G. S. Mackenzie to Sanford 16.07.1881.

16 Greindl to S 25.11.1878.

17 CD 9–10 Dec 1879.

18 Emerson 89–90; Ascherson 116–17.

19 *UL* 21, 51–2.

20 Sanford to S 4.08.1879.

21 CD 14.08.1879 (S had stayed with the king in Jun and Dec 1878 and Jan 1879).

22 S to Strauch 8.01.1880.

23 S to Sanford 27.02.1879 Sanford Museum.

24 CD 9.02.1879.

25 *UL* 36.

26 *CFFS* i 23; S to Strauch 30.07.1879.

27 CD 18–27 Mar 1879; S to Strauch 20.08.1879.

28 CD 3–5 Oct 1879.

29 Swinburne to S 25.11.1884.

30 Swinburne to S 15 Nov, 29 Dec 1877 .

31 CD 8.03.1879.

32 S to Strauch 20 Aug, 3 Dec 1879, Jan 8, Mar 15, Sep 20 1880.

33 S to Strauch 20.08.1879.

34 *CFFS* i 80, 96.

35 CD Aug 27–29 1879.

36 *CFFS* i 33–8, 473, 475, 495, ii 48, 195–7; see Hochschild 71; Bierman 239 .

37 S to Strauch 14.10.1879; CD 28.09.1879.

38 S to Strauch 8.07.1879.

39 *CFFS* i 142.

40 CD 1–3 Dec 1879; *CFFS* i 148.

41 Ibid. 148–51.

42 S to Strauch 6 Feb, 17 May 1880.

43 CD 1.01.1881.

44 S to Strauch 25.10.1880; S to Kirkbright 22.05.1880; S to Strauch n.d. Nov 1880.

45 CD 19.06.1880; S to Sparhawk 24.11.1880.

46 S to Strauch 26.03.1880.

47 CD 1880–83 many refs to Stanley's 'favourites'. By 1883 Dualla would be receiving the same pay as many Europeans.

48 S to Strauch 6.07.1881.

49 Explanatory Intro to CD.
50 S to Strauch 25.10.1880; *CFFS* i 225.
51 CD 9.11.1880 and 27.0.1881; 9.03.1880.
52 Richard West *Brazza of the Congo*, 1972, 102–3; CD 7.11.1880.
53 CD 3.01.1881 and 9.11.1880.
54 CD 27.02.1881.
55 CD whole of May 1881; 1.06.1881; *CFFS* i 273–5 .
56 CD 5.06.1881.
57 CD 15.01.1882, quoting Strauch to S 31.10.1881.
58 CD 25.03.1882, quoting Strauch letter, original 25.11.82 destroyed, not listed at Tervuren.
59 S to Strauch 25.03.1882; published minus most contentious matters *UL* 106 ff.
60 Treaty signed with Chief Kimpallamballa at Ntamo (Kintamba 31.12.1881).
61 CD 25.03.1882; 1.01.1882.
62 UL 137–8.
63 CD 27–28 Jul 1881; *CFFS* i 292–3; *UL* 68, 72.
64 CD 31.07.1881.
65 CD 31 Jul–13 Aug 1881.
66 *UL* 84; S to Strauch n.d. Nov 1881.
67 *CFFS* i 350–1.
68 Ibid. 348; *UL* 86; Bentley to Baynes 2.08.1882 Bapt Missy Society Archive, Regent's Park Coll, Oxford.
69 *UL* 87.
70 Treaty dated 31.12.1881 and 1.01.1882 Kintamba, Ntamo Witnesses Makoko, Ngamberengy, Dualla, Kmiyara, Kimpallamballa, Henry. M. Stanley occupation granted to 'Henry M. Stanley or his representative', Luwel Papers, Ter.
71 *UL* 87–8; CD 7, 8 Nov 1881.
72 T. J. Comber to Baynes 4.07.1882 and 5.10.18 82 Regent's Park Coll, Oxford.
73 CD 6, 23 Feb 1881.
74 CD 28.10.1881; S to Strauch 20.09.1880.
75 *UL* 59–60.
76 CD 16 Mar, 6 Jul 1881; *CFFS* ii 257.
77 *CFFS* i 394-40; *UL* 142.
78 *CFFS* i 444.

SEVENTEEN: A Banquet in Paris

1 CD 30.09.1882.
2 *UL* 152.
3 Strauch to S 27.03.1882; model convention 1883.
4 S to Strauch 29.12.1881 Ter; Strauch to S 27.03.1882.
5 CD Jan 1890 p 88.
6 S to Strauch 8.01.1880.
7 T. J. Comber to brother 7.08.1882 Regent's Park Coll, Oxford; Comber to Baynes 5.09.1882; Swinburne to Stanley 1.01.1883; *UL* 158 .

8 Britons appointed 1882–3: Captain J. Grant Elliott, Captain Seymour Saulez, Mr E. J. Glave, Mr D. H. G. Keys, Major Parminter, Major Francis Vetch, Mr E. Massey Shaw, Mr Spenser Burns, Mr John Rose Troup, Dr Ralph Leslie and Engineer Binnie. Carte de Visite Album sold Christie's, Sep 2002.

9 Jean Stengers 156 n 105.

10 CD 1–4 Oct 1882; Bentley to Baynes 12.08.82; Regent's Park Coll; S to Strauch 25.03.1882; Lii to Stanley 31.12.1881; S to Strauch 10.04.1882.

11 *UL* 134; CD 1–4 Oct 1882.

12 *UL* 161; S to Strauch 8.07.1879.

13 *UL* 161–2.

14 *UL* 160; Strauch to S 30.04.83; S to Mackinnon 10.05.1884 MP 55 SOAS.

15 CD 12.10.1882.

16 CD 12, 19 Oct 1882.

17 *Brazza* 121–2.

18 *UL* 153–5; *Times* 20, 21 Oct 1882; Pakenham 159–60.

19 *Brazza* 123; *UL* 155.

20 CD 19.10.1882; Bierman 236.

21 CD 19–21 Oct 1882.

EIGHTEEN: After the Slave Raids

1 CD 3.01.1881.

2 CD 1.01.1881.

3 King to S early Nov 1882.

4 May Sheldon (MS) letters to S in 1884 .

5 Henry F. Reddall *Henry M Stanley: A Record*, 1890, 21.

6 Dorothy Middleton *Victorian Lady Travellers*, 1965, Chap iv.

7 Anonymous note dated 6.10.1882 from Amsterdam.

8 CD 12.11.1882.

9 MS to S 6.30 p.m 13.11.1882.

10 King to S 27.11.1882.

11 *CFFS* i 469.

12 S to Lii 22.03.1883.

13 S to Strauch 21.03.1883.

14 *CFFS* i 486.

15 S to Strauch 21.03.1883 Reel 3; S to Lii 31.03.1883.

16 S to Strauch 7.05.1883.

17 S to H. H. Johnstone 15.04.1883 *Academie Royale des Sciences Coloniale* iii-1957-2 349.

18 S to Lii 6.04.1883 .

19 CD 1.01.1883; S to Johnston 9.07.1883.

20 H. H. Johnston *The River Congo*,1884, 46, 291f; CD 24.04.1883.

21 S to Johnston 23.07.1883.

22 Johnston to S 13.02.1885.

23 S to Johnston 15.02.1885.

24 S to Strauch 8.07.1883.

25 S to Lii 11.08.1883; S to Strauch 12.07.1883.

26 CD 16.07.1883.

27 CD 29, 5, 13 Jul 1883.

28 Edward Glave *Six Years of Adventure in Congoland*, 1893, 16.

29 CD 24.07.1883.

30 Glave 38–9, 42–3, 69, 109; CD 24 Jul, 15 Sept etc 1883.

31 *CFFS* ii, 119, 89. This was possible because all along the river his great journey had passed into oral history and legend. People would even date events before or after the time 'when Stanley passed our village a long time ago' (Glave 44). The name Bula Matari had also travelled upstream and was as well known as Tandley, Tandelay and Standley (S to Johnston 9.07.18 83).

32 S to Johnston 9.07.1883 .

33 CD 22.11.1883.

34 *CFFS* ii 138–40.

35 CD 27.11.1883.

36 S to S 27 Jan 84.

37 *CFFS* ii 144–5; CD 27.11.1883.

38 S to Strauch 27.01.1884.

39 *CFFS* ii 186.

40 Swinburne's success was in sharp contrast to the situation Henry found at Kimpoko, where the Belgian station chief, Louis Amelot, had killed a chief and six of his headmen, after quarrelling with them about a rotting hippopotamus carcase. Meanwhile, at Equator, lieutenants Vangele and Coquilhat had shot Chief Ikenge and five men (S to Lii ? Aug 1883; S to Strauch 27.07.1883; S to Strauch 27.01.1884).

41 S to Strauch 8.07.1883.

42 S to Lii 23.04.1884; *CFFS* ii 18.

43 Gordon to S 6.01.1884.

44 CD 27.02.1884; Lii to S 7.01.1884.

45 Lii to S 7.01.1884; CD 27.02.1884.

46 Lii to S 28.03.1884 .

47 M. Luwel *Sir Francis de Winton*, 1964, 46, 77.

48 S to Strauch 11.05.1884.

49 Ibid.; Jun n.d. 1884; *Brazza*, 130–1; P de Chavannes *Avec Brazza*, 1935, 182–3; M. Luwel *Sir Francis de Winton* 167–9 .

50 Ibid. 167.

51 Lalaing to S 10.09.1884.

52 *CFFS* ii facing 257.

53 S to Lii 23.04.1884.

NINETEEN: Who Stole the Congo?

General note: Most of the key documents in the early history of the Congo Free State were destroyed on Leopold II's orders in the opening years of the twentieth century.

1 *Times* 25.11.1883.

2 Lii to S 30.09.1883.

3 P. Gifford and W. R. Louis eds *France and Britain in Africa*, 1971, in chap by Jean Stengers 'King Leopold and Anglo French Rivalry 1882–4' (Stengers) 158–60; Emerson 107.

4 CD S to Lii 16.01.1886; Jules Ferry to de Brazza 25.04.1884 quoted in n 114 Stengers 158.

5 Ibid. Jules Ferry to Leopold 25.04.1884.

6 Hall 268.

7 Bierman 239; Bierman also accused Stanley of being flippant about 'the people he had duped', when describing them as 'An imposing family! And to think that I am under an obligation to love and defend the whole lot to the death!' (*UL* 164). In fact this phrase referred to the chiefs who had become his blood brothers. Hochshild 71–2 quotes 450 chiefs and treats *CFFS* as a reliable source proving gross exploitation.

8 S to Strauch 8.07.1879.

9 Despite Lii's destruction of key documents, a copy of this letter from Strauch to S has survived in the archives of the Department of Foreign Affairs, which from the date of S's response to it (see next note) can be dated mid-Jun 1879, *UL* 22–3.

10 S to Strauch 8.07.1879.

11 CD 15.01.1882 quoting Strauch to S 31.10.1881.

12 *UL* 161, Lii to Strauch 16.10.1882.

13 Identification of treaty makers: Strauch to Valcke 1.02.1884; Strauch to S 4.01.1883 mentioning Harou's instructions; Strauch to S 1.02.1884 mentioning instructions to Hansenns; S to Elliott 7.01.84 (Stengers 141 and note 37; Diplomatic Blue Book Africa No 5, 1884, c-4023 Papers Presented to both Houses of Parliament quoting treaties and signatories). Sovereignty was demanded by Leopold as a vital ingredient in treaties from 1882, and the earliest agreements of this sort were made by Valcke in October that year at Inkissi, and by Parfoury at Isangila in November, when S was away in Europe. Most of these sovereignty treaties were obtained by Valcke, Orban, Vangele, Harou, Hansenns and Elliot, who all received their orders directly from the king, without any reference to S. All the other 'exclusive', or monopolistic, treaties that are known about were made on dates in the second half of 1882 when S was either hundreds of miles away on the upper Congo, or in Europe or on his way there. (Known monopolistic treaties such as Isangila, Manyanga, Ngombi, Leopoldville, Ndandanga, Msuata and Lufuntchu were all made in the second half of 1882 when S was in Europe. S's own non-monopolistic treaties at Isangila and Manyanga had been signed over two years earlier.) The treaty agreed between Lutete, chief of Ngombi, and the Belgian officer, Lieutenant Valcke, on 20.10.1882 is typical of all monopolistic agreements: 'The chiefs cede absolutely' the land specified in the treaty, and 'none other than the agents of the aforesaid Comité is authorised to come and trade within the limits of the territory of the said Chiefs' (Blue Book: Africa 5 1884, 1–7; Stengers 130).

14 Bontinck 378–9, S to Mrs Sanford 31.10.1895.

15 S to Lii 11.08.1883; S to Strauch 12.07.1883. Given the efforts Stanley had made to convince Strauch and Leopold that the ownership of the land should

remain in the hands of the chiefs, he was later appalled by the claim made by 'Colonel' George Washington Williams, the black American preacher and author, that he (S) had used tricks involving galvanic batteries and cigar lighters to persuade chiefs to part with their land and give it to King Leopold. Article: 'The Difficulty of Avoiding a Law Court', t/s by S early 1890s; Hochschild, 109–10, quotes Williams's 'Open Letter' to the US President, appearing to accept that Williams was stating facts.

16 Wack, Henry W. *The Story of the Congo Free State*, 1905, gives text of forgeries that he considered true 487–91; in the Mininstry of Foreign Affairs Archives, Brussels, nine copies of alleged Stanley treaties are kept but the originals have disappeared; significantly, six of these alleged copies (written by secretaries) are dated 1884, during S's last months on the Congo, when he feared that the French might take all his stations by force. Prof G. Janssens, Archivist of the Palais Royal, Brussels, has confirmed that there are no original Stanley treaties in his archive.

17 S to Strauch 14.10.1879; CD 28.09.1879.

18 Vivi Treaty 13.06.1880 Foreign Affairs Archive, Brussels.

19 CD quotes S to Strauch 25.03.1882.

20 S Treaty at Ntamo 31.12.1881, Luwel papers, Tervuren; confirmed in S to Strauch 14.01.1882 UL 98ff.

21 Strauch to S 30.04.1883.

22 S to Lii 23.4.1884.

23 Stengers 130 n 19, 128 n 13; altered treaties in H. W. Wack *The Story of the Congo Free State* 488–9, 487–8.

24 Mistakenly he wrote 8 Jan.

25 *CFFS* ii 205; Blue Book Africa no 5 1884 c-4023.

26 CD 19.08.1884.

27 Bierman p 239; see note 7 above.

28 *CFFS* ii 197–204.

29 Lalaing to S 10.09.1884; see also Borchgrave to S 2, 23 Feb, 16 Mar 1885.

30 Hochschild 71–2.

31 Original copy *CFFS*.

32 Memo by T. V. Lister and P. Anderson 2 and 3 Mar 1884 FO 84/1809.

33 S to Harold Frederic 24.07.1885.

34 Bontinck 276.

35 *Times* 28.03.1883.

36 W. H. Holman to Baynes 2.08.1882 Regents Park Coll.

37 *CFFS* ii 22–3.

38 Ibid. 123.

39 *CFFS* i 394.

TWENTY: A Pawn in Great Power Politics

1 New York *Sun* 7.08.1885.

2 *Manchester Guardian* 22.10.1884; *Saturday Review* 25.10.1884.

3 *Saturday Review* 25.10.1884.

4 CD Sep n.d. 1882.

5 CD 24.08.1884.
6 Lalaing to S 4, 10 Sep, 12 Oct 1884.
7 Bontinck 135; Emerson 103–4.
8 Stengers n 128 and n 130; Hochschild 78–9; Vivi Treaty in former Historic Colonial Collection in Foreign Affairs Library, now called Diplomatic Archive and Africa Archive, Brussels.
9 Emerson 104; *CFFS* vol ii 383.
10 Stengers 163.
11 Ascherson 132.
12 Stengers 192; CD 12.10.1884.
13 Borchgrave to S 10.11.1884.
14 Wack 22–30; general books: S. E. Crowe, *The Berlin West Africa Conference 1884–5*, 1942; Emerson; Stengers; R. T. Anstey, *Britain and the Congo in the Nineteenth Century*, 1962.
15 CD 30.11.1884; Stengers n 128 and n 130.
16 S to Sanford 3.01.1885 Sanford Museum; CD 1.01.1885.
17 CD 4.12.1884.
18 S to de Winton 26.11.1885 Luwel *De Winton* 134–5.
19 Borchgrave to S 23.02.1885.
20 S to Sanford 14.03.1885 Sanford Museum.
21 T/s 237 vol ii of *CFFS*.
22 3739/c Adjt General's Office E. B. Rec'd May 14 1885; Navy Records from Old Military and Civil Records, National Archives and Records Administration, Washington DC.
23 *Scottish Geographical Soc Mag* Jan-March 1884, 42.
24 Bruce to S 20.08.1885; S to Bruce 24.03.1885.
25 Bruce to S 3.06.1885.
26 Pakenham 342–3.
27 *Scottish Geog Soc Mag* 44.
28 Anstey 67–70.
29 Report of General Meeting of Committee ... 17 Nov 1879 MP; Anstey 170.
30 S to Mackinnon 16 Sept 85 MP 55.
31 CD n.d. but early Jul quoting Borchgrave to S 28.06.1885.
32 Lii to S 29.07.1885.

TWENTY-ONE: 'A Kind of Innocence'

1 May Sheldon (MS) to S 27 Mar, 1 Aug 1884.
2 MS to S 1.08.1884.
3 S to Mackinnon 26.08.1884 from Paris Mackinnon Papers, MP; King to S 5.09.1884.
4 MS to S 24.08.1884.
5 These photographs are referred to in Tracey J. Boisseau's biography of May Sheldon *White Queen: May Sheldon and the Origins of American Feminist Identity,* 2004.
6 MS to S 24.08.1884.
7 Robert Rhodes James *Henry Wellcome*, 137.

8 MS to S 25.10.1884.
9 Hall 274, quoting Lii to Strauch 7.08.1884.
10 Henry F. Reddall *Henry M Stanley*, 1890, 21; M. Shuey *Southwest Review* xxv 1940, 378ff.
11 S to Wellcome 16.07.1886 RGS.
12 S to Bruce 26.05.1885 NLS.
13 S to Bruce 30.12.1884 NLS; McLynn ii 118.
14 S to MS 17.06.1885 RGS.
15 MS to S 18.06.1885.
16 S to MS 25.06.1885 RGS.
17 Arnold to S 19.06.1885.
18 Charles Tennant born 1796 m Gertrude Collier 1847, Dolly born 1854 Isle of Wight.
19 Dorothy's Diary (DD) xv 11.03.1888.
20 Artists' registers, Dorothy taught in Paris by Jean Jacques Henner.
21 William Peiris *Edwin Arnold*, 1970.
22 GTrevelyan to DS 6.08.1884.
23 DD Jan 1885.
24 Julian B. Arnold *Giants in Dressing Gowns*, 1942, 79.
25 DD 24–5 Jun, 18 Jul 1885. Unsent letter to A. Carnegie, attached to 1883 DD.
26 1891 Census.
27 Enid Starkie *Flaubert* 1967, 72, 85, 86–9, 91–2, 102–3; letter quoted Julian Barnes *Flaubert's Parrot* 71.
28 DS to S 1.07.1885.
29 DD 20.07.1885.
30 Ibid.
31 S to Bruce 18, 27 Jul, 15 Aug 1885 NLS.
32 Ibid. 15 Aug 1885, 3 Sep 1886 NLS.
33 DS to S 4.08.1885.
34 DS to S 2.09.1885.
35 S to DS 6.09.1885.
36 DS to S 2.10.1885.
37 DD 23.11.1885.
38 CD Dec 1885; Anstey 192, 196–7; Emerson 146–7.
39 S to Lii 16.01.1886 quoted in CD.
40 Borchgrave to S 19.01.1886.
41 S to Mackinnon 29.12,1885, 14.01.1886.
42 DD 6.01.1886.
43 Ibid. 7.01.1886.
44 S to DS 8.01.1886.
45 DS to S 9.01.1886.
46 DD 10.01.1886.
47 S to DS 22.02.1886, DS to S 23.02.1886; S to Dear Sir 29.03.1886 RP1691 BL.
48 DD 12–13 Feb 1886.

49 S to MS 26.03.1886 RGS.
50 S to Hoffman 26.03.1886; S to DS 19.10.1885.
51 3 Apr 1886.
52 DS to S 28.04.1886.
53 S to DS 2.05.1886; DD 7.01.1886.
54 DD 21.07.1886.
55 S to DS 16.08.1986.
56 S to DS 7.05.1890.
57 DD 23.01.1887.
58 S to Sanford 15.07.1885, Sanford Museum.
59 S to Sanford 20.08.1886, Sanford Museum.
60 J. B. Pond to S plus contract 25.08.1886.
61 S to Sanford 9.09.1886 Sanford Museum.
62 CD 12.09.1886.
63 S to Mackinnon 23.09.1886 MP 55.

TWENTY-TWO: Why Rescue Emin Pasha?

1 CD 27.07.1884.
2 *Times* 29.10.1886.
3 *Scotsman* 6.11.1886.
4 During his journey of 1874–77, S had corresponded with Gordon, and a year later had asked the then Governor of Equatoria not to claim any Bugandan territory for the Egyptian Khedive's government, but instead to establish friendly relations with King Mutesa for the sake of the missionaries, who had gone out in response to S's newspaper appeal. Gordon had written promising to respect Mutesa's territory, adding: 'I have sent a first rate man up there, Emin Effendi, & in every way am disposed to help the mission' (Gordon to S 15.03.1878). S did not give Emin another thought for eight years, until reading his letters in the press in late Oct 1886.
5 In fact Emin's move south, which took place in Jul, brought about the collapse of his power in northern Equatoria, and had been premature. Unknown to him, the Mahdi had died a month earlier, and his followers were already returning to their homes.
6 Iain R. Smith *The Emin Pasha Relief Expedition 1886–90*, 1972, 28–9.
7 Smith 32, quoting Mackay to Emin 2.06.1886.
8 Anstey Chaps 9 and 10.
9 CD 28.01.1886.
10 Smith 43–4, quoting Memo of Wolseley 2.10.1886.
11 *Scotsman* 25.11.1886 and Smith 45.
12 Emin to Felkin 7 and 22 Jul 1886, pub Times 9.12.1886.
13 Smith 59; Salisbury to Hutton 26.11.1886 .
14 Baring to Iddesleigh 23.11.1886 FO 84/1770; Smith 60; govt involvement is underlined by meetings and letters between Mackinnon and J. F. Hutton with members of the govt, and later between S and Sir Percy Anderson of the Africa Department at the FO. MP has many references, and CD 5.01.1887.
15 Original telegram, received 11.12.1886.

16 *Scotsman* 28.12.1886; J. B. Pond *Eccentricities of Genius*, 1901, 268–9.

17 S to Bruce 7.01.1887 NLS.

18 Kirk to Mackinnon 31.08.1885 MP 93 and Kirk to Mackinnon 6.11.1886 MP 94.

19 Smith 52–3; Kirk to Mackinnon 30.10.1886 MP 94.

20 Quoted J. S. Galbraith *Mackinnon and East Africa 1878–95*, 1972, 114.

21 Galbraith 117; Mackinnon to S 5.04.1889 MP.

22 Report of EPRE Committee (confidential).

23 S to Lii 27.12.1886 quoted CD.

24 CD 11.03.1886; SD 29–30 1886.

25 SD 1.01.1887; IDA i 40.

26 Gen Redvers Buller to S 27.12.1886 EPRE Committee Report; Stairs 22; small EPRE notebook.

27 SD 13.01.1887; EPRE Report H. W. Bates of RGS recommended 12.01.1887.

28 SD 14.01.1887; IDA i 43; Jephson Diary 1–5.

29 H. M. Stanley, *In Darkest Africa* 2 vols, 1890, i 40–1 (*IDA*); SD.03.1887.

30 SD 10.01.1887; IDA i 42, 80.

31 IDA i 81–2; Bonny Diary 26.05.1887.

32 DNB William Hoffman article by Jeffrey Philip Green gives d.o.b. as 1867; 'boots' rather than apprentice bag-maker RP 2435 ii Batch 2 BL Hoffman Court Martial by Stanley's officers. Claim that MS recommended him, and that he was hired for his knowledge of German is in W. Hoffmann *With Stanley in Africa*, 1938, 1–2; letter from Mr Hoffman senior to S 6.01.1887.

33 IDA i 41; SD 7.01.1887; Roy Maclaren ed *African Exploits: The Diaries of William Stairs 1887–1892*, 1997, 23 (Stairs).

34 J. B. Lyons ed *Surgeon-Major Parke's African Journey 1887–89*, 1954, 11 (Parke); SD 7.03.1887.

35 SD 28.01.87.

36 IDA i 68.

37 J. S Jameson *The Story of the Rear Column of the Emin Pasha Relief Expedition*, 1890, 4, 7 (Jameson); SD 23 Feb; IDA i 63; W. H. Whitely trans *Autobiography of Tippu Tip*, 1958, 123 (*TTAuto*) ; N. R. Bennett *Arab versus European: Diplomacy & War in Nineteenth Century East Central Africa*, 1986, 224–6; Tanganyika Notes and Records (TNR) No 18 Dec 1944, 13.

38 TTAuto 123; IDA i 64; TNR No 18 Dec 1944, 13.

39 Herbert Ward *A Voice from the Congo*, 1910, 163.

40 Dorothy Middleton ed *The Diaries of A. J. Mounteney Jephson*, 1969, 74 25 Feb (*Jephson*); IDA i 72–3.

41 IDA i 37.

42 IDA i 93.

43 Herbert Ward *Five Years with the Congo Cannibals*, 1891, 33.

44 Jephson 390.

45 Barttelot, W. G. *The Life of Edmond Musgrave Barttelot*, 1890, 60 (Bartt).

46 IDA i 84.

47 Jameson 18.

48 SD 5.04.1887.

49 SD 20.04.1887; Parke 34; SLD 14 Apr, 25 Jun18 87; William Bonny's Diary 22.04.1887.
50 Jameson 31, 33.
51 Lot 192/1 Purple Album, Christie's Africa Sale Sep 2002.
52 A. B. Swinburne to Sanford 17.11.1886 Sanford Museum.
53 SD 20.03.1887.
54 Borchgrave to S 7.01.1887.
55 SD 20.03.1887; Swinburne to Sanford 29.09.1887 Sanford Museum; SD 1.05.1887.
56 SD 20 Mar, 1 Apr 1887.
57 SD 18–19 Jan 1887.

TWENTY-THREE: A Fateful Decision

1 Bentley to S 5.04.1887; S to Bentley 5,18, 21 Apr 1887 Regents Park Coll; *IDA* i 92.
2 Jephson 96; *IDA* i 99.
3 SD 11.05.1887.
4 Bartt 90–1 5.05.1887.
5 Ibid. 118.
6 SD 20.05.1887.
7 Parke 42, 20; also Jameson 20.05.1887.
8 Bonny 20 Mar, 2 Apr 1887.
9 Ibid. 26 May, 29 Nov, 10 Dec 1887.
10 SD 20.05.1887, 29.07.1890.
11 Small EPRE notebook.
12 Nelson to his father 15.06.1887, Russell Train Coll; Stairs to Bartt 12.06.1888, copied by Stanley.
13 SD 20.05.1887.
14 Parke 41; Bartt 93; SD 20.05.1887.
15 Quoted Roger Jones *The Rescue of Emin Pasha*, 1972, 117.
16 Jameson 59.
17 Ibid. 65.
18 Parke 44–5.
19 Bonny 27.03.1888.
20 Jephson 110.
21 SD 22.06.1887.
22 S Instructions to Bartt, printed Bartt 134 date 24 Jun 1887.
23 Jameson 75.
24 Bartt 117; *IDA* i 131.
25 Bartt 112, 116–17.
26 Rose Troup *With Stanley's Rearguard*, 1890, 114–16.
27 *IDA* i 134; T. H. Parke in *My Personal Experiences in Equatorial Africa*, 1891, 72, records no such words spoken by Bartt and affirms he had intended coming after them.
28 SD 27.06.1887.
29 SD 28.06.1887.

TWENTY-FOUR: The Enigma of Emin Pasha

1 *IDA* i 136.
2 Jephson 386.
3 Parke 51.
4 *IDA* i 137–8; Jephson 113.
5 Jephson 113, 118–19.
6 Ibid. 121.
7 Newman 246; *IDA* i 163.
8 *IDA* i 152, 162, 171.
9 Jephson 13.
10 Parke 54–6.
11 *IDA* i 182–4.
12 SD 29.08.1887.
13 SD 12.09.1887.
14 Parke 56.
15 SD 21.08.1887.
16 SD 14.09.1887.
17 Stairs 113–14; Parke 63.
18 IDA i 198 ff; Parke 59.
19 Bartt 179 ff.
20 *IDA* i 198.
21 *IDA* i 201–4; SD 21–22 Sept 1887; Parke 62; Jephson 145.
22 SD 3, 6 Oct 1887; IDA i 210.
23 Jephson 159; Parke 65; Parke *My Personal Experiences* 129–30.
24 SD 15.10.1887.
25 S to Nelson 24.10.1887 RP 860 BL; *IDA* i 215.
26 Jephson 166–7.
27 *IDA* i 224–6.
28 RP 860 as n 25; SD 21.10.1887.
29 Parke 73.
30 Smith 132; Newman 253.
31 S to Nelson 17.11.1887 Russell Train Coll.
32 *IDA* i 230.
33 SD 19–23 Nov 1887.
34 *IDA* i 255.
35 Stairs 134.
36 S to Grant 8.09.1888 NLS.
37 Jephson 201–4, 207 .
38 Stairs 146.
39 *IDA* i 307.
40 *IDA* i 310, 313.
41 *IDA* i 311.
42 Jephson 213.
43 *IDA* i 314–15.
44 Jephson 214.

45 Ibid. 215.
46 *IDA* i 310.
47 *IDA* i 328ff.
48 Letter quoted in Bartt 184–92.
49 Hoffman 62–3.
50 Parke 85–7.
51 Jephson 232; S to Nelson 31.03.1888 Russell Train Coll; Stairs 169.
52 IDΛ i 357.
53 Hoffman 65 cited Smith 139.
54 Jephson 251.
55 Hoffman 66.
56 IDA i 374.
57 Emin Diary 29.04.1888 (Franz Stuhlmann ed *Die Tagebücher von Dr Emin Pascha* 5 vols, 1917–27, esp vol iv; SD 29.04.1888.
58 G. Schweitzer *Emin Pasha: His Life and Work*, 2 vols, 1898, i 270–1.
59 G. Casati *Ten Years in Equatoria and the Return with Emin Pasha*, 1891, ii p 159, cited Jones 221.
60 IDA i 240.
61 Emin Diary 2.05.1888. This point is very well made by Smith 155.
62 *IDA* i 376 ff.
63 SD 30.04.1888.
64 SD 1.05.1888.
65 S to Mackinnon 3.09.1888 MP 55; *IDA* i 380–1.
66 Schweitzer i pp 272–3 quoting Emin's diary 1 May.
67 S to Mackinnon 3.09.1888 MP 55.
68 Schweitzer i 276; Emin Diary 3.05.1888.
69 Emin Diary 6.05.1888.
70 Hoffman 72–3, 81.
71 S to Euan Smith 19.12.1889 Africa 4, 1890, C5906 p 9.

TWENTY-FIVE: 'Evil Hangs over this Forest...'

1 *IDA* i 489; Smith 196; Jones 254.
2 Smith 199. Stanley knew that Bonny had brought 130 Zanzibaris from Bolobo to Yambuya, where they had joined 131 men already there, most of whom had been Zanzibaris. Bartt 148, 117.
3 *IDA* i 476–7, 493–4; *IDA* ii 2.
4 *IDA* i 493.
5 Bonny 14.08.1888.
6 Smith 202.
7 *IDA* i p 483.
8 *IDA* i 439.
9 SD 24.08.1888.
10 Bonny 14.10.1888.
11 SD18 Aug 88.
12 Bonny 18.08.1888.
13 Ibid. 10.02.1889.

14 Ibid. 26.08.1888.

15 Troup 145.

16 Bonny 3.10.1888.

17 Ibid. 23.08.1888; Jameson 207.

18 Bartt 229.

19 Jameson 165, 204, 207.

20 SD Oct 1890.

21 Bonny 23.08.1888; t/s speech or preface by S concerning the Rear Column 12, 10; Bonny 21.04.1888.

22 SD Oct 1890; Bartt 123.

23 SD Oct 1890.

24 S to Mackinnon 3.09.1888.

25 *Standard* 19.09.1888.

26 Report of the Committee to the Subscribers of the Emin Pasha Relief Fund 68–97, 103,109, 123, etc.

27 Mrs Ethel Jameson's transcription of husband's and Barttelot's papers p 86, Russell Train Coll.

28 Bonny 7–27 Mar 1888.

29 Ibid. 2 Apr, 23 May 1888.

30 At end of Jan–Jun notebook 1889.

31 Ward *My Life with Stanley's Rear-Guard*, 1890, 162.

32 Stairs to Bartt 12.06.1888, copied in Stanley's hand into his diary; SD 28.09.1888.

33 SD 28.09.1888. Notes made the following year but n.d.

34 Parke 19.07.1888, 99, 107–8, 113–14.

35 Bonny 29.09.1888.

36 Stairs 185.

37 Fred Puleston *African Drums*, 1930, 241.

38 Smith 204; *IDA* ii 12–15.

39 *IDA* i 126.

40 Note under heading 'officers' BL RP 2435 i Box 6.

41 SD 8.01.1889 commenting on Jameson's entry for 17.08.1887; SD Oct 1890; *IDA* I 489, 495.

42 *IDA* i 498; Bonny 15.09.1888; *IDA* ii 16 .

43 Bonny 4, 14 Sep, 8 Dec 1888.

44 *IDA* ii 48–9.

45 Bonny 6, 8, 11 Dec 1888.

46 *IDA* ii 59–63.

47 Bonny 15.12.1888.

48 Parke 118.

49 Hoffman 100.

50 Quoted from Parke *My Personal Experiences* McLynn ii 259.

TWENTY-SIX: Keeping Emin Pasha's Secret

1 S to Jephson 17.01.1889; IDA ii 114.

2 *IDA* ii 109.

3 *IDA* ii 111–14.

4 *IDA* ii 126.

5 Emin Diary 1.12.1888 iv 192, cited Smith 242.

6 Smith 254.

7 S to Emin 17.01.1889; *IDA* ii 118–19.

8 S to Jephson 18.01.1889; *IDA* ii 117–18.

9 Emin Diary 14.01.1889 iv 202; Smith 241.

10 Jephson Report for S 7.02.1889, *IDA* 126–7.

11 *IDA* ii 133.

12 Emin to S 13.02.1889; *IDA* ii 135.

13 *IDA* ii 137, 144.

14 Jephson 350.

15 SD 6 May, 6 Mar 1889.

16 *IDA* ii 161–2.

17 *IDA* ii 180ff; Smith 255; Jephson 341–3; SD 5.04.1889.

18 Jephson 342, 354.

19 *IDA* ii 187, 192; Africa 4, 1890, Report to Euan Smith gives the local native contingent as 400 rather than 550 as in *IDA*.

20 Jephson 346–7.

21 Ibid. 347–9; Parke 147; Report to EPRE Comm: Proceedings of a Court of Enquiry 2.05.1889; Parke 160.

22 Jephson 332; SD 24.07.1890.

23 Jephson 352.

24 Bennett 475.

25 *IDA* ii 233, 238–9.

26 *IDA* ii 257, 247.

27 He also investigated a stretch of water to the north-east, and found that it was the small lake (Lake George), which he had discovered in January 1876, when trying to reach Lake Albert.

28 When S had met DL, the older man had told him that there might be substance in Ptolemy's claim, made in the second century AD, that the western branch of the Nile was fed by the Mountains of the Moon, and this, astonishingly, S had now proved to be true – though nowhere near the position that DL had imagined these mountains to occupy (*HIFL* 455ff).

29 Jephson 382; *IDA* ii 349.

30 *IDA* ii 337–41.

31 Pakenham 314.

32 SD 13–15 Jun 1889; S to Mackinnon 31.08.1889 MP 55.

33 S to Bruce 15.10.1889 NLS.

34 S to Revd Addison Allen 19.02.1903.

35 Parke 164; Jephson 397.

36 Ibid. 399.

37 S to Mackinnon 31.08.1889 MP55; Pakenham 345–6.

38 SD 31.08.1889.

39 Vol i Schweitzer xli-xliii.

40 S to Mackinnon 18.08.1889 MP 55.

41 Mackay to S 29.09.1889; Jephson 39.

42 Mackay to S 5.01.1890.

43 *IDA* ii 393.

44 S to C. B. Euan Smith 28.12.1889, being S's report on EPRE Africa 4, 1890, 14–16; SD 12.09.1889; S to Mackinnon 28, 29 Dec 1889 MP 55.

45 Jephson 402–4.

46 *IDA* ii 403.

47 Jephson 407–9.

48 Emin Diary 10.11.1889 iv 417.

49 Ibid. 18 Nov 89.

50 Thomas Stevens *Scouting for Stanley in East Africa*,1890, 235–68.

51 Appointment size diary 1894 but filled with notes on EPRE.

52 S to Mackinnon 25.03.1890 MP 55.

53 Hoffman's letters to S n.d. but May 1890, 17 Feb, 14 May, 7, 8 Oct 1891; Hoffman's father to S 1.03.1890.

54 *IDA* ii 411.

55 *IDA* ii 416–17; Parke 167.

56 Mss of *IDA* ii 515–23.

57 Notes on Emin Pasha n.d. but 1890.

58 Parke 169.

59 Mss *IDA* ii 520–1 ; Stairs 298 n.

60 Schweitzer ii 92–4.

61 Ibid. 12–17.

62 Stairs to S 9.5.1890.

63 S to Mackinnon 31.08.1889, 19.01.1890 MP 55; Mss *IDA* ii 522; S to Mackinnon 15.03.1890 MP 55.

64 Schweitzer ii 23; Jones 392–4; Pakenham 444.

65 *Auto* 411–12.

66 Smith 212.

67 SD en route to Aden, quoted Newman 298.

68 Jephson 383.

69 Schweitzer i 309; J. S. Galbraith *Mackinnon and East Africa 1878–1895*, 1972; Roger Anstey *Britain and the Congo in the 19th Century*, 1962, 215, 223.

70 Hird 271, and footnote; *IDA* ii 426, 461.

71 Jephson 207.

72 The expedition started out by ship from Zanzibar on 24.02.1887 with 708 expedition members, 623 of whom were Wangwana. When S left Mackay's mission, his own original followers had dwindled to 215, a figure that, according to Jephson, would fall to 210 by the time they reached Bagamoyo. S's claim in his report to Colonel Euan Smith to have returned 225 Wangwana must be an exaggeration since his diary – always more accurate than other sources – contains the figure of 215 for his entire following on 12 Sep, the day he left Mackay's. (There were 233 expedition members present at Fort Bodo on 22.12.1888, and in his book he would give a figure of 230 for 10.04.1889.) All of which makes it look very likely that Jephson's figure of

210, for all S's men who made it back to Zanzibar alive is very nearly correct. To this figure should be added two Europeans and seven Sudanese who had returned home via the Congo, bringing the total to 219 survivors.

73 S to Mackinnon 3.09.1888 MP 55; S to Mackinnon 15.03.1890 MP 55.
74 Ter Inventory no 4805, list dated 7.11.1889.
75 A list in Jephson's hand inserted in SD gives a larger number of 311 on 4 Dec at Bagamoyo.
76 *IDA* ii 431.
77 S to Strauch 27.01.1884.
78 Africa 4 S to Euan Smith as note 44 above.

TWENTY-SEVEN: The Shape of Things to Come...

1 SD 511; McLynn ii 315; Parke 107.
2 S to MS 6 Feb, 11 Mar 1890 RGS.
3 S to Wellcome 29.07.1891, Wellcome Medical Library.
4 Mackinnon to S 5.04.1889; *Auto* 446.
5 S to Mackinnon 19.01.1890 MP 55.
6 S to Mackinnon 4.02.1890 MP 55; Sir John Gray *Early Treaties in Uganda*, 1881–1891, *Uganda Journal*, xii, no 1 (1950).
7 E. Marston *How Stanley Wrote 'In Darkest Africa'*, 1890, 19.
8 S to Mackinnon 4 Feb 90 MP 55; Early Treaties in Uganda Sir John Gray see Smith 266.
9 Mackinnon to S 12.05.1890; Mackinnon sent Stanley's map to Salisbury on 14.05.1890, Gray *Early Treaties in Uganda* 25.
10 DL to FO 15.10.59, ZJ (2) 332–7; Palmerston to Russell FO 63/871; Russell to DL 17.4.60 copy National Archives of Zimbabwe.
11 Mackinnon to S 16.06.1890.
12 Jephson 401.
13 McLynn ii 313–14.
14 S to the Executive Committee of the Stanley & African Exhibition 17.05.1890 Grant Papers NLS.
15 Hird 272; Marston *How Stanley* ... 16, 21.
16 CD early Sep 1882.
17 CD 20–26 Apr 1890.
18 Emerson 155, 234–5.
19 CD 20–26 Apr 1890.
20 Ibid. 117ff.

TWENTY-EIGHT: Dorothy's Other Love

1 *Auto* 419; Hird 278; Hall 335 ff.
2 Hird 278; S to Mackinnon 25.02.1890 MP 55.
3 S to Fred Myers 3.06.1899 Myers Papers Trin Coll, Cambridge; Hall 335.
4 Queen Victoria's Journal 1872, p 272.
5 Quoted Sanger 280–1.
6 DS to S 26.04.1890.

7 DS to S 28.04.1890.
8 S to DS 3.05.1890.
9 DS to S 4.05.1890.
10 S to DS 4.05.1890.
11 DS to S 6.05.1890.
12 S to DS 7.05.1890.
13 S to DS 8.05.1890.
14 DS to S 9.05.1890.
15 DS to S 13.05.1890.
16 DS to S 15.05.1890.
17 Mackinnon to DS 4.08.1887 MP 55; DS to Mackinnon 21.12.1888 MP 55.
18 Mackinnon to DS 3.05.1889.
19 DS to Mackinnon 4.05.1890 MP 55.
20 DS to Mackinnon 15, 18 May 1890 MP 55.
21 DD 11 Mar, 2 May, 8, 24, 25 Dec 1888.
22 DD 27 Nov, 27 Dec 1888; 19, 23 Jan, 11, 16 Feb 1889 .
23 DD 26.04.1888; Mackinnon to DS 3.05.1889; DD 15.05.1889.
24 DD 15.05.1889; DD 17 May, 14 Jun, 28 Jul 1889.
25 DS to Alfred Lyall (AL) 5 Sept 1889; DD 13.09.1889.
26 Draft DS to Lyall n.d. but Sep 1889.
27 Draft DS to Lyall draft n.d. but late 1889.
28 DD 17 Feb, 19 Mar, 6 Apr; DS to S 26.04.1890.
29 DD 23.01.1887.
30 DS to S Sunday late May 1890.
31 Ibid.
32 DS to S 20.05.1890; S to DS 21.05.1890.
33 Myers to S 16.05.1890 Sanger 261ff.
34 DS to S 17.06.1890; DS to S 19.06.1890 .
35 S to Mackinnon 23.07.1890 MP 55.
36 Stairs to S 1.07.1890.
37 S to DS 11.12.1890.
38 DS to Gertrude Tennant [12] Jul 1890.
39 Parke 181.
40 DD 12.07.1890.
41 Details about Lady Ashburton in 'Essay in Women's Writing' vol x no ii, 2003, 'Laocooning in Rome: Harriet Hosmer and Romantic Friendship'; see also Virginia Surtees *The Ludovisi Goddess: a Life of Louisa, Lady Ashburton*, 1984.
42 SD 12–13 Jul 1890.
43 DD 12, 29 Jul 1890.
44 DS to MS 15 Jul, Aug 1890 RGS.
45 DS to MS 27.09.1890.
46 *Edinburgh Review, Athenaeum* both 5.07.1890.
47 *Saturday Review* 5.07.1890.
48 *Whitehall Review* 5.07.1890.
49 DS to Mackinnon 20.07.1890 MP 55.
50 E. Myers to F. Myers 3, 10 Aug 1890 Trin Coll, Cambridge.

51 S to Bruce 1.08.1890 NLS.
52 SD 22.08.1890.
53 SD 4.09.1890.
54 SD 9.09.1890.
55 McLynn vol ii 334.
56 DS to S 9.12.1890.
57 DS to S 22.02.1891.
58 DS to S 25.02.1891.
59 S to DS 9.05.1891.
60 S to DS May [late] n.d. 1890.
61 S to DS 6.05.1891; S to Mackinnon 6.08.1890 MP 55.
62 SD 18.08.1890.
63 DS to S 22.02.1891.
64 Jonathan Gathorne-Hardy *The Public School Phenomenon*, 1977, 212.
65 DS to Mackinnon 9.10.1890 MP55.
66 Mackinnon to DS 3.10.1890.
67 S to Mackinnon 12.10.1890 MP55.

TWENTY-NINE: Was the Emin Pasha Expedition Piratical?

1 *IDA* i 480.
2 S to Mackinnon 5.08.1889 printed in the *Standard* 25.11.1889.
3 Mss of Speech given on US tour n.d. RP 1691 BL; *IDA* i 472.
4 *IDA* i 480–1, 487.
5 Barrt 117.
6 *IDA* i 489.
7 Report of the EPRE Committee, 1891, 99.
8 *Graphic* 22.11.1890; *Daily Chronicle* 22.11.1890.
9 *Graphic* 22 Nov; Jameson to Mackinnon EPRE report to committee 117–22.
10 Bonny 2.05.1888; J. Rose Troup *With Stanley's Rear Column*, 1890, 145 .
11 Ward to S 22.06.1890; *Times* 12.11.1890.
12 *Times* 15.11.1890, Glave to S 15.03.1891, 12.11.1890 NLS.
13 Cited Newman 242.
14 SD 22.06.1887.
15 McLynn ii 183.
16 SD 22.06.1887.
17 Bartt 108.
18 Ibid. 245.
19 Jameson 302; Bartt 239–41.
20 Bonny 1.05.1887.
21 *Times* 8 and 10 Nov 1890.
22 Parke to J. Knott 13 Nov 90 Royal College of Surgeons of Ireland.
23 Quoted McLynn ii 350.
24 E. L. Godkin *Forum* vol x 1890–1 633 ff.
25 *Weekly Witness*, Montreal 14.01.1891.
26 *Aborigines' Protection Society Transactions* 190–6 No iii vol iv 89–99, 163,
    249–50.

27 By agreeing to use the West Coast route, Mackinnon had denied himself the chance to get S to do what would have been most useful to him commercially: to establish trading posts for his company between Mombassa and Lake Victoria. In 1890, Leopold was lucky to be bailed out by the Belgian government after a decade of losses on the Congo, but Mackinnon knew *he* could not expect the same largesse from any British cabinet. (Accusations in *Universal Review* 331; 'Stanley's Exploits of Civilizing Africa' by D. J. Nicoll 1891.)

28 EPRE Committee Report 95–7.

29 S to Mackinnon 6.06.1891 MP 55.

30 *Pall Mall Gazette* 11.02.1878.

THIRTY: Africa or a Child

1 Gertrude Tennant to MS n.d. RGS; SD 14.12.1892.

2 Gertrude Tennant to DS 12.09.1890.

3 Quoted Bierman 341.

4 Henry James to William James 9.12.1890 *Correspondence of William James* vol 3 1885–1896, 1994.

5 Pond to MS 16 Nov, 14 Mar 1890 RGS.

6 J. B. Pond *Eccentricities of Genius*, 1901, Pond 270–2.

7 SD 11.0.1891; Pond 279.

8 SD Mar 1891.

9 *Daily Picayune* Mrs Nichol sister of 2nd Mrs H. H. Stanley was still alive and living just north of the city, Bierman 28.

10 Old New Orleans acquaintances not permitted to see Stanley, see my note 25 chapter 2, cutting at Tervuren.

11 *Daily States* 16.04.1891.

12 Bruce to S 10.03.1891.

13 S to Bruce 26.03.1891.

14 Mackinnon to Bruce 22.05.1891.

15 Bruce to S 27.04.1891.

16 Frederic Myers to Eveleen Myers 6.05.1891 Trin Coll, Cambridge.

17 DS to S 12.06.1891.

18 DS to S 6.05.1891.

19 DD 8.04.1891.

20 DD 8.04.1891.

21 DD 13.06.1891.

22 S to DS 9.05.1891.

23 DD 13.06.1891; S to DS 29.05.1891.

24 S to DS 10.06.1891; S to DS 26.06.1891.

25 DS to Mackinnon 28.05.1891.

26 SD Jul 1891, 111.

27 E to F. Myers 11, 12 Jul 1891 Trin Coll, Cambridge.

28 E to F. Myers 15 Jul 1891 Trin Coll.

29 S to DS 24, 29 May 1891.

30 F to E. Myers 27.12.1893 Trin Coll.

31 S to E. Myers 12.12.1894 Trin Coll.

32 E to F. Myers 24.07.1891 Trin Coll; Aubrey Stanhope *On the Track of the Great*, 1914, 152–4.
33 E to F. Myers 24.07.1891 Trin Coll.
34 SD Jul 1891, 111.
35 E to F. Myers Jul n.d. 1891 Trin Coll.
36 SD 111–12 .
37 S to Bruce 19.08.1891 NLS.
38 McLynn ii 340; Newman 318.
39 DS to S 6.05.1891.

THIRTY-ONE: An End to 'Noble Objects'

1 SD 22.01.1892.
2 Quoted Newman 319. The grandson of S's first cousin Edward Owen would become Australia's Lord Chief Justice and as Sir Owen Dixon be awarded the O.M., Lucy Jones's notes in Flintshire Archives.
3 DS writing in *Auto* 439, 'big task' SD 2–4 Oct 1891 .
4 DS to Bruce 25.04.1892 NLS.
5 SD 20.06.1892.
6 S to DS 16–17 Jun 1891.
7 DD 2.05.1892.
8 Letters from DS to Henry Matthews all May 1892, 6084 register; Hird 295.
9 Election Address 21.06.1892.
10 *Boston Daily Globe* 25.06.1892.
11 *Hobart Mercury* 25.08.1892.
12 Thomas A. Guthrie *A Long Retrospect*, 1936, Chapter 7.
13 DS to S 2.10.1885.
14 DS to S n.d. but Dec-Jan 1892-3.
15 *Auto* 439.
16 S to DS 10.01.1893.
17 S to DS 21.02.1891.
18 S to DS 25–27 Feb 1891.
19 Ibid.
20 DS to S 1.03.1891.
21 DS to S n.d. Dec 1892/Jan 93 .
22 SD 12.10.1890.
23 S to DS 8.12.1891.
24 S to DS 3.01.1893.
25 DS to S 6.05.1891.
26 S to C. P. Huntington 1.02.1891 MP 55.
27 SD Oct 8, 24, 26 1892.
28 McLynn ii 366; Newman 320; Pakenham 430 .
29 S to Mackinnon 8.10.1892 MP 55.
30 S to Bruce 23.12.1892 NLS; S to Mackinnon 23.12.1892 MP 55.
31 DS to Bruce 21.12.1892 NLS.
32 DS to Mackinnon 4.08.1892 MP 55.
33 DD Christmas Day 1892.

34 DS to S 30.12.1892.
35 MS to DS 27.12.1892.
36 DS to Bruce 3.01.1893 NLS.
37 S to DS 30.12.1892.
38 Bruce to S 2.01.1893.
39 S to DS 29.12.1892.
40 S to DS 3.01.1893.
41 S to DS 10.01.1893; DS to S 13.01.1893.
42 S to DS 15.01.1892.
43 SD 22.06.1893.
44 S to Mackinnon 3 Jan, 11 Feb 1892 MP 55.
45 Henry Wellcome papers WA/HSW/CO/ Ind/A6–8, Wellcome Medical Library.
46 Quoted in biography by Emma Hardinge Britten *The Electric Physician*, 1875.
47 S to Agnes Livingstone (Mrs Bruce) 27.11.1873.
48 S to DS 12.10.1893; Jephson to S 8.10.1893.
49 Correspondence Glave to Sanford and vice versa Sanford Museum, Florida; Emerson 152–5.
50 E. J. Glave *Times* 12.11.1890; Glave to S 15.03.91 Pond Collection, copy NLS.
51 *Harper's Magazine* Mar 1893, 613 ff; see too *Times* 16.03.1893.
52 Glave to S 19.11.1892; 5.05.1893.
53 S to Bruce 31.05.1893 NLS.
54 Glave to S 25.06.1893.
55 Glave to S 2.05.1894.
56 Glave to S 26.11.1894; L. Forfeitt to S 24.05.1895.
57 *Century Magazine* vol 50 no 1 May 1895; Ibid. vol 50 no 6 1895.
58 S to H. H. Johnstone 15.02.1885 National Archives of Zimbabwe.
59 1881 British Census; additional info Christine Holgate Northallerton Library.
60 S to My Dear Friend (W. J. Davy) late Jun 1895.
61 DS to Mrs Glave n.d. but Jun 1895.
62 S to DS 18.10.1893.
63 S to DS 30.08.1895.
64 *Auto* 466–7.
65 S to DS 20.07.1895.
66 S to DS 30.08.1895.
67 S to DS 25.11.1893.
68 Press cutting. n.d. but 22.08.1895, Ter.
69 Henry Lucy *Sixty Years in the Wilderness*, 1909, 228.
70 SD 13.07.1896, 348.
71 For S's and DS's statements that the child was the grandson of a cousin see S to Mrs Bruce 2.10.1896 NLS, and DS to Lady Hills Johnes 11.02.1896 National Library of Wales; in DS to S n.d. but early 1903, DS shows she believed that the boy's father had died in 1895 or early 1896. The case for Denzil Stanley being the grandson of Stanley's half-sister, Emma, rests largely on the word of Lucy M. Jones, the former matron of H.M. Stanley Hospital,

St Asaph, author of *H.M. Stanley and Wales* (1972), a booklet which added greatly to public knowledge of Stanley's Welsh family. It was published to coincide with an exhibition at St Asaph Cathedral for which the Stanley family provided original material. Her revelation about Denzil's identity is not in her booklet. However, she got to know Mrs Denzil Stanley at this time and perhaps learned from her about Denzil's origins. There is a compelling note in the dependable Miss Jones's hand in the Flintshire Archives: 'Denzil's mother, Elizabeth Ann, was a daughter of Stanley's sister, Emma. I met Denzil's brother, the late David Bartlett [actually David Henry Bartley] on several occasions...' So perhaps David H. Bartley told Miss Jones about Denzil's parentage. Elizabeth Ann Hughes was indeed the daughter of Stanley's half-sister Emma (see my note 36 of Chap One for the possibility that she was his whole sister. Emma married Llewelyn Hughes in 1872). According to Stanley's diary (SD 15.09.1896) Denzil was born on 2 Jun 1895, at which time Elizabeth Ann Hughes was 22 and unmarried (I could find no earlier marriage certificate). She married David Bartley in 1901. Bob Owen, the local historian, thinks it significant that though David Bartley was a poorly paid tailor, in 1904 after Stanley's death he and Elizabeth were able to open a grocer's shop, acquire a substantial house and later buy a row of terraced houses and employ a housekeeper and maid – information from a 1942 obituary cutting for Elizabeth Ann Bartley in Flintshire Archives. The Bartleys were not beneficiaries in Stanley's will, so a gift seems to have been managed in some other way. Stanley or Dorothy obliterated all references to Denzil's identity in SD 12, 13 Jul 1896. The truth was a well-kept family secret since Gwyn Bartley, D.H.Bartley's solicitor son, was unaware of it when I spoke to him. I am much indebted to Bob Owen for his help and ideas on this subject.

72 DS to Lady Hills Johnes 11.02.1897 Dolaucothi ms L 9604 National Library of Wales.

73 Bills for gifts at Tervuren: B. & M. Clack Ladies General Underclothing 1868 or 1869; Bill for Lady's Dressing Case made out to 'Henry Morlake Sydney' by S. Fisher 188, Strand 18.03.1869.

74 S to DS 22.06.1891.

75 *Auto* 431.

76 Illness described in letter from Robert Jones's medical attendant to S 29.03.1892. Letters to S from his family requesting cash: Robert jnr 20 Jun 91, 2 Apr, 11 Oct, 29 Nov 1892; Catherine Jones n.d. 1895? S to DS long letter, quoting Hawkes about condition of his relatives at Cross Foxes 18.11.1893.

77 *Auto* 483.

78 SD13 Jul 1896, 348–9. Lucy M.Jones (see note 71 above) remarked on the Den of *Den*zil representing Denbigh and Bob Own recognized that *zil* is Liz backwards: the name of Denzil's mother.

79 Small American notebook 1895.

80 SD 18.10.1895.

81 E. King to S 12.11.1895.

82 Quoted Newman 323 .

83 S to DS 21.12.1896.

THIRTY-TWO: Stanley, Leopold and the Atrocities

1 CD Lii to S 22 Oct, 17 Nov 1890.
2 Emerson 153, 235.
3 Ibid. 154; Ascherson 197.
4 S to DS 17.11.1893.
5 Slade 108ff; Pakenham 435–49.
6 Stokes to S 21.11.1889.
7 CD 1, 2 Sep 1895.
8 SD 13.01.1896.
9 SD 6, 28 Apr 1895; Greshoff to S 10.12.1890, 20.08.1891, 14.06.1892, 27.02.1893, 8.09.1894; Greshoff to DS 20.08.1891.
10 Hoffman to S 10.10.1891.
11 S to Hoffman 14.11.1894.
12 Times 18.11.1889.
13 Salusbury to S 16, 27 Jun, 4 Jul 1894; Hoffman to DS 22.07.1895.
14 Statistics in United Services Magazine Sep 1896 vol xiii.
15 Drafty reply by S to United Services Mag article.
16 Times 16.09.1896.
17 Saturday Review 19.09.1896.
18 S to Hoffman 17.09.1896.
19 Hoffman to S 20.12.1896.
20 G. Grenfell to Baynes 3.12.1895 Regents Park Coll, Oxford.
21 CD S to Lii 16.09.1896.
22 CD 20.09.1896, 174.
23 Emerson 237–8.
24 E. J. Glave Century Magazine vol 53 6.04.97 903ff.
25 Century Mag vol 54 703 ff.
26 CD 23.04.1897, 176.
27 CD 6–8 Sept 97; SD 3–8 Sep 1897; S to DS 5.09.1897; Lii to S 8.09.1897.
28 Ascherson 247.
29 Pakenham 591.
30 SD 15.04.1887.
31 R. Casement to S 28.06.1890.
32 Small black notebook n.d. approx 1895.
33 Illustrated Africa no 82 Oct 1895.
34 CD S to Lii 9.03.1893.
35 John A. McLure Kipling and Conrad: The Colonial Fiction 89–90, quoted Brantlinger 273.
36 Gerard Jean-Aubry Joseph Conrad: Life and Letters, 1927, i 288, quoted Hochschild 146.
37 Brantlinger 181.
38 Ian Watt Conrad in the Nineteenth Century quoted by Brantlinger 267.

THIRTY-THREE: 'Before it is Too Late'

1 S to DS n.d. but early 1890s.
2 S to DS 9, 13, 25 Oct 1897.
3 DS to H. Wellcome 22.06.1903 RGS.
4 *Auto* 383–4.
5 *Auto* 485; Silvia Myers to F. Myers 13, 15 Sep 1898 Trin Coll.
6 S to DS 24.02.1898.
7 S to Pond 25.11.1899 RP 1594 BL.
8 S to Wellcome 4.09.1901, quoted McLynn ii 383.
9 S to Pond 25.11.1899 BL.
10 DS to Lady Hills Johnes ? Nov 1902 Dolaucothi L 9611 National Library of Wales.
11 DS to A. Dreyfus 22.10.1899.
12 DS to Mary Millais 12 May 1894 Russell Train Collection.
13 S to T. H. Parke 20.02.1891 Royal College of Physicians of Ireland Library.
14 DS to Lady Hills Johnes 30.12.1894 National Library of Wales.
15 DS to George Bernard Shaw 27.08.1903 Ad Ms 70951 BL.
16 *Auto* 473–6.
17 SD Nov 1898; Jul 1900, 449–50.
18 SD Dec 1898, Jan 1899, 431–2.
19 *Auto* 507–8.
20 SD 11, 14.04.1900, 448; S to DS 23.01.1900; S to DS 30.06.1900.
21 S to DS 21.07.1901.
22 Lord Salisbury to S 19.05.1899.
23 Anonymous note 10.06.1899.
24 S to Sir A. Sullivan 4.06.1899 Pierpont Morgan Library.
25 DS to Lady Hills Johnes 7.06.1899 Dolaucothi L 9605.
26 Pakenham 542, 546.
27 Lucy M. Jones *H. M. Stanley and Wales*, 1972, 26.
28 Hoffman to S 3, 13 March; 6.05.1898.
29 W. Hoffman *With Stanley in Africa*, 1938, 263.
30 Ibid.
31 Hoffman to S 1.06.1900.
32 SD 13.11.1892.
33 Alan Gauld *Founders of Psychical Research*, 1968, 236–7; S to Addison Allen 19.02.1903 copy Tervuren.
34 William to Henry James 17.01.1901 *Correspondence of William James* vol 4 (1897–1910) 1994.
35 Undated autobiographical t/s pp 21–2.
36 SD 19.12.1901.
37 SD 11.02.1893.
38 S to Mr Clapp 15.09.1902 copy made by DS.
39 SD Jan to Mar 1900, 444–7.
40 *Auto* 513–14.
41 S to DS 29.11.1893.

42 DS to Lady Hills Johnes 28.04.1903; DS to Wellcome 29.04.1903.
43 Robert Rhodes James, *Henry Wellcome*, 1994, 133–8.
44 *Morning Post* 13.12.1890.
45 DS to Wellcome 4, 13, 22, 31 May, 5, 7, 18, 22 Jun 1903 RGS.
46 Jephson's letters to Lady Middleton 14.01.1897 – 15 Sept 1903, Nottingham University; Jephson 418–19.
47 Hoffman *With Stanley* 265–7.
48 DS to GBS 27 Aug 1903 Ad Ms 50514 BL.
49 DS to Lady Hills Johnes 7.10.1903 Dolocauthi L 9613; John Cunningham Geikie 27.11.1903 West Glamorgan Archives.
50 DS to Geikie 2.02.1904 photo attached.
51 M/s about S's last hours in DS's hand in Wellcome Funeral File 11 1–3 in RGS; *Auto* 514–15; DS to Wellcome 1, 7.05.1904; Hoffman 267.

AFTERWORD

1 Dean Armitage Robinson press release 13.05.1904 Wellcome Funeral File 11 1–3 RGS.
2 Quoted McLynn ii 388.
3 DS to Wellcome n.d. RGS 3–5.
4 H. H. Johnston to S 24.05.1883.
5 Mrs Bruce to DS 11.05.1904.
6 DS to H. Wellcome n.d. May 1904 RGS.
7 *Scribner's Magazine* Sept 1904.
8 Date of birth correctly stated by *South Wales Daily News* 16 May, also by *Western Mail* 12 May 04 as 28 Jan 1841 rather than 10 Jun 1840, originally given out by DS.
9 *Pall Mall Gazette* 19.01.1910 DS letter 29.10.1909.
10 W. J. Hawkes to Abbey tickets secretary 13.05.1904.
11 Hoffman to DS n.d. 6228 in register.
12 See S's letters to Pincoffs, Saulez, Revd George Williams.
13 S to de Winton 10.09.1884 quoted Marcel Luwel *Sir Francis de Winton: Administrator-General of the Congo 1884–1886*, 1964, 73.
14 Denzil Stanley to Ed *Denbighshire Free Press* 20.05.1954 Bob Owen Collection.
15 See M. Luwel *Les Papiers Stanley de Pirbight à Tervuren* (n.d. but approx 1983) for Denzil's hopes for selling to Belgium his father's house and papers.
16 Mark Twain's *Notebooks and Journals* ii 304, quoted McLynn ii 24; from Chekhov's obituary of Nikolai Przhevalsky quoted in Rosamund Bartlett's *Chekhov: Scenes from a Life*, 2004, 163.
17 BIMMCC Newsletter No 21.01.2005 'Cartographic entries in Stanley's sketch books' Peter Daerden 11ff; Stanley made his first scientific observations on 19 Nov 1874; on his Livingstone Search he had used the far less accurate method of dead reckoning.
18 Bennett 274.
19 *Auto* xvii.
20 SD after 10.05.1877.
21 J. B. Pond *The Eccentricities of Genius*, 1901, 263–4.

22 Guy Tillim photo was published *Independent* 30.07.2005; earlier version in 1989 in Lorenzo Ricciardi's *African Rainbow*; also photographed by Saski Kolff. For Zambia/Zimbabwe dispute *Daily Telegraph* 1.08.2004. It is another of those endless ironies that the man, who tried so hard to look after the interests of the Congolese, should have become a photographic icon, symbolizing the end of white oppression. S's statue by the Belgian sculptor Arthur Dupagne had been promised to Denzil by the Minister of the Colonies in 1954 at the Brussels celebrations for the fiftieth anniversary of S's death. Denzil's son, Richard, was photographed beside it in 1957, three years before the Congo's independence. The latest picture, by the South African photographer Guy Tillim, drives home the point about the transience and vanity of white rule by including, for good measure, a boy urinating against the steamship's bow. Strangely, the steamship has a story to tell that is also germane to S's present fate. In 1927, the president of the colonial museum in Ostend arranged for the steamer to be transported back to Belgium and preserved as a historic vessel. The people of Ostend never showed much interest in the *AIA*, so she was moved to Leopold's Congo Museum at Tervuren. But even here the ship was unwanted, and in 1956 she was returned to the Congo. (Internet site article: *Congo River Shipping at the end of the 19th & Beginning of 20th Century* pandora.be/urbiehome/Con.) [W1] That anyone might wish to bring S's statue back to Europe, as the *AIA* had once been brought back, seems a vain hope for the friendless Welsh–American workhouse boy.

23 Patrick Manning *Slavery and African Life*, 1990, 140–144, 160; Lovejoy 224–5.

24 CD 28.10.1881.

25 T. H. Parke *My Personal Experiences...* 335.

26 A. Gresshoff to DS 20.08.1891.

INDEX